THE ATLAS OF

ECONOMIC COMPLEXITY

MAPPING PATHS TO PROSPERITY

| Ricardo Hausmann | César A. Hidalgo | Sebastián Bustos | Michele Coscia | Alexander Simoes | Muhammed A. Yıldırım |

THE ATLAS OF ECONOMIC COMPLEXITY
MAPPING PATHS TO PROSPERITY

AUTHORS:

Ricardo Hausmann | *César A. Hidalgo* | *Sebastián Bustos*
Michele Coscia | *Alexander Simoes* | *Muhammed A. Yıldırım*

ACKNOWLEDGMENTS

The research on which this Atlas is based began around 2006 with the idea of the product space. In the original paper published in Science in 2007, we collaborated with Albert-Laszlo Barabasi and Bailey Klinger. The view of economic development of countries as a process of discovering which products a country can master, a process we called self-discovery, came from joint work with Dani Rodrik and later also with Jason Hwang. We explored different implications of the basic approach in papers with Dany Bahar, Bailey Klinger, Robert Lawrence, Francisco Rodriguez, Dani Rodrik, Charles Sabel, Rodrigo Wagner and Andrés Zahler. Throughout, we received significant feedback and advice from Lant Pritchett, Andrés Velasco and Adrian Wood. We would also like to thank Sarah Chung and Juan Jimenez for their contributions to the 2011 edition of The Atlas.

We want to thank the dedicated team that runs Harvard's Center for International Development (CID) for helping bring The Atlas to life: Marcela Escobari, Jennifer Gala, Andrea Carranza, Melissa Siegel, Victoria Whitney, Adriana Hoyos, Erinn Wattie and Anne Morriss. We are also indebted to the NeCSys team at the MIT Media Lab and to Sandy Sener. We thank the leadership at Harvard Kennedy School and the MIT Media Lab who were early enthusiasts of our work. The editorial design of this book was produced by Draft Diseño (www.draft.cl). We would like to especially acknowledge the contributions of Francisca Barros and Draft Diseño team.

MIT Press books may be purchased at special quantity discounts for business or sales promotional use. For information, please email special_sales@mitpress.mit.edu or write to Special Sales Department, The MIT Press, 55 Hayward Street, Cambridge, MA 02142.

This book was printed and bound in Malaysia.

Library of Congress Cataloging-in-Publication Data.

The atlas of economic complexity: mapping paths to prosperity / edited by Ricardo Hausmann and César A. Hidalgo.
  p. cm
Includes bibliographical references.
ISBN 978-0-262-52542-8 (pbk. : alk. paper)
1. Technological innovation—Economic aspects. 2. Industrial management—Economic aspects. 3. Economic development. 4. Gross domestic product. I. Hausmann, Ricardo. II. Hidalgo, César A. (Professor)
HC79.T4A85   2013
330.1—dc23
2013010258

10 9 8 7 6 5 4 3 2 1

Center for International Development
at Harvard University

HARVARD Kennedy School
JOHN F. KENNEDY SCHOOL OF GOVERNMENT

Macro Connections
MIT Media Lab

MIT

THE ATLAS OF
ECONOMIC COMPLEXITY

MAPPING PATHS TO PROSPERITY

| Ricardo Hausmann | César A. Hidalgo | Sebastián Bustos |
| Michele Coscia | Alexander Simoes | Muhammed A. Yıldırım |

The MIT Press, Cambridge, Massachusetts, London, England

We thank the many individuals who, early on, understood the potential impact of research on economic growth, and shared our team's vision. The generosity of these supporters made this work feasible and now makes it available to individuals, organizations and governments throughout the world.

THE AUTHORS WANT TO ACKNOWLEDGE THE GENEROUS SUPPORT OF:

| Alejandro Santo Domingo | Standard Bank | Anonymous Donor |

FOREWORD TO
THE UPDATED EDITION

It has been two years since we published the first edition of *The Atlas of Economic Complexity*. "The Atlas", as we have come to refer to it, has helped extend the availability of tools and methods that can be used to study the productive structure of countries and its evolution.

Many things have happened since the first edition of The Atlas was released at CID's Global Empowerment Meeting, on October 27, 2011. The new edition has sharpened the theory and empirical evidence of how knowhow affects income and growth and how knowhow itself grows over time. In this edition, we also update our numbers to 2010, thus adding two more years of data and extending our projections. We also undertook a major overhaul of the data. Sebastián Bustos and Muhammed Yildirim went back to the original sources and created a new dataset that significantly improves on the one used for the first edition. They developed a new technique to clean the data, reducing inconsistencies and the problems caused by misreporting. The new dataset provides a more accurate estimate of the complexity of each country and each product. With this improved dataset, our results are even stronger.

The online sister site of this publication, The Atlas online (http://atlas.cid.harvard.edu) has been significantly enhanced with the use of an updated dataset which now covers up to 2011; the addition of bilateral trade data; and the inclusion of trade information classified according to the Harmonized System, a recently developed data set which goes back to 1995, as well as the more traditional Standardized International Trade Classification (SITC-4) dating back to 1962. The Atlas online now also includes multilingual support, country profiles, bulk data downloads, and a large number of design features, including dynamic text for the Tree Map visualizations and an improved design of the Product Space visualizations.

The Atlas online was originally launched as The Observatory and was developed by Alex Simoes with the assistance of Crystal Noel. The Atlas online is currently managed by Romain Vuillemot at the Center for International Development at Harvard University.

All in all, the new versions of The Atlas and its website provide a more accurate picture of each country's economy, what products are in its "adjacent possible" and its future growth potential. ●

PREFACE

Over the past two centuries, mankind has accomplished what used to be unthinkable. When we look back at our long list of achievements, it is easy to focus on the most audacious of them, such as our conquest of the skies and the moon. Our lives, however, have been made easier and more prosperous by a large number of more modest, yet crucially important feats. Think of electric bulbs, telephones, cars, personal computers, antibiotics, TVs, refrigerators, watches and water heaters. Think of the many innovations that benefit us despite our limited awareness of them, such as advances in port management, electric power distribution, agrochemicals and water purification. This progress was possible because we got smarter. During the past two centuries, there has been an explosion of 'productive knowledge', by which we mean, the knowledge that goes into making the products we make. This expansion was not, however, an individual phenomenon. It was a collective phenomenon. As individuals we are not much more capable than our ancestors, but as societies we have developed the ability to make all that we have mentioned – and much, much more.

A modern society can amass large amounts of productive knowledge because it distributes bits and pieces of knowledge among its many members. But to make use of it, this knowledge has to be put back together through organizations and markets. Thus, individual specialization begets diversity at the national and global level. Our most prosperous modern societies are wiser, not because their citizens are individually brilliant, but because these societies hold a diversity of knowhow and because they are able to recombine it to create a larger variety of smarter and better products.

The social accumulation of productive knowledge has not been a universal phenomenon. It has taken place in some parts of the world, but not in others. Where it has happened, it has underpinned an incredible increase in living standards. Where it has not, living standards resemble those of centuries past. The enormous income gaps between rich and poor nations are an expression of the vast differences in productive knowledge amassed by different nations. These differences are expressed in the diversity and sophistication of the things that each of them makes, which we explore in detail in this Atlas.

Just as nations differ in the amount of productive knowledge they hold, so do products. The amount of knowledge that is required to make a product can vary enormously from one good to the next. Most modern products require more knowledge than what a single person can hold. Nobody in this world, not even the savviest geek or the most knowledgeable entrepreneur knows how to make a computer from scratch. We all have to rely on others who know about battery technology, liquid crystals, microprocessor design, software development, metallurgy, milling, lean manufacturing and human resource management, among many other skills. That is why the average worker in a rich country works in a firm that is much larger and more connected than firms in poor countries. For a society to operate at a high level of total productive knowledge, individuals must know different things. Diversity of productive knowledge,

however, is not enough. In order to put knowledge into productive use, societies need to reassemble these distributed bits through teams, organizations and markets.

Accumulating productive knowledge is difficult. For the most part, it is not available in books or on the Internet. It is embedded in brains and human networks. It is tacit and hard to transmit and acquire. It comes from years of experience more than from years of schooling. Productive knowledge, therefore, cannot be learned easily like a song or a poem. It requires structural changes. Just like learning a language requires changes in the structure of the brain, developing a new industry requires changes in the patterns of interaction inside an organization or society.

Expanding the amount of productive knowledge available in a country involves enlarging the set of activities that the country is able to do. This process, however, is tricky. Industries cannot exist if the requisite productive knowledge is absent, yet accumulating bits of productive knowledge will make little sense in places where the industries that require it are not present. This "chicken and egg" problem slows down the accumulation of productive knowledge. It also creates important path dependencies. It is easier for countries to move into industries that mostly reuse what they already know, since these industries require adding modest amounts of productive knowledge. By gradually adding new knowledge to what they already know, countries can economize on the chicken and egg problem. That is why we find empirically that countries move from the products that they already create to others that are "close by" in terms of the productive knowledge that they require.

The Atlas of Economic Complexity attempts to measure the amount of productive knowledge that each country holds. Our measure of productive knowledge can account for the enormous income differences between the nations of the world and has the capacity to predict the rate at which countries will grow. In fact, it is much more predictive than other well-known development indicators, such as those that attempt to measure competitiveness, governance, education and financial depth.

A central contribution of this Atlas is the creation of a map that captures the similarity of products in terms of their knowledge requirements. This map depicts a network of products, and shows paths through which productive knowledge is more easily accumulated. We call this map the product space. Using data on what each country exports, we are able to place where each country's production is located in the product space, illustrating their current productive capabilities and identifying products that lie nearby.

Ultimately, this Atlas views economic development as a social learning process, but one that is rife with pitfalls and dangers. Countries accumulate productive knowledge by developing the capacity to make a larger variety of products of increasing complexity. This process involves trial and error. It is a risky journey in search of the possible. Entrepreneurs, investors and policymakers play a fundamental role in this economic exploration.

By providing rankings, we wish to clarify the scope of the achievable, as revealed by the experience of others. By tracking progress, we offer feedback regarding current trends. By providing maps, we do not pretend to tell potential product space explorers where to go, but to pinpoint what is out there and what routes may be shorter or more secure. We hope this will empower these explorers with valuable information that will encourage them to take on the challenge and thus speed up the process of economic development.●

RICARDO HAUSMANN

Director, Center for International Development at Harvard University,
Professor of the Practice of Economic Development, Harvard Kennedy School,
George Cowan Professor, Santa Fe Institute.

CÉSAR A. HIDALGO

ABC Career Development Professor, MIT Media Lab,
Massachusetts Institute of Technology (MIT),
Faculty Associate, Center for International Development at Harvard University.

CONTENTS

PART 1 | WHAT, WHY AND HOW?

PART 2 | COMPLEXITY RANKINGS

PART 3 | COUNTRY PAGES

PART I WHAT, WHY AND HOW?

SECTION I
What Do We Mean by *Economic Complexity*?

One way of describing the economic world is to say that the things we make require machines, raw materials and labor. Another way is to emphasize that products are made with knowledge. Consider toothpaste. Is toothpaste just some paste in a tube? Or do the paste and the tube allow us to access knowledge about the properties of sodium fluoride on teeth and about how to achieve its synthesis? The true value of a tube of toothpaste, in other words, is that it manifests knowledge about the chemicals that kill the germs that cause bad breath, cavities and gum disease.

When we think of products in these terms, markets take on a different meaning. Markets allow us to access the vast amounts of knowledge that are scattered among the people of the world. Toothpaste represents knowledge about the chemicals that prevent tooth decay, just like cars embody our knowledge of mechanical engineering, metallurgy, electronics and design. Next time you bite into an apple, consider that thousands of years of plant domestication has been combined with knowledge about logistics, refrigeration, pest control, food safety and the preservation of fresh produce to bring you that piece of fruit. Products are vehicles for knowledge, and the process of embedding knowledge in products requires people who possess a working understanding of that knowledge. Most of us have no idea how toothpaste works, let alone how to make it, because we can rely on the few people who know how to create this molecular cocktail, and who, together with their colleagues at the toothpaste factory, can create a product that we use every day.

We owe to Adam Smith the idea that the division of labor is the secret of the wealth of nations. In a modern reinterpretation of this idea, the reason why the division of labor is powerful is that it allows us to access a quantity of knowledge that none of us would be able to hold individually. We rely on dentists, plumbers, lawyers, meteorologists and car mechanics to sustain our standard of living, because few of us know how to fill cavities, repair leaks, write contracts, predict the weather or fix our cars. Markets and organizations allow the knowledge that is held by few to reach many. In other words, they make us collectively wiser.

The amount of knowledge embedded in a society, however, does not depend mainly on *how much knowledge* each individual holds. It depends, more fundamentally on *the diversity of knowledge* across individuals and on their ability to combine this knowledge, and make use of it, through complex webs of interaction. A hunter-gatherer in the Arctic must know a lot of things to survive. Without the knowledge held by each member of an Inuit community, most people unfamiliar with the Arctic would die. While the knowledge held by each individual, or within each family, is essential for survival and wellbeing, the total amount of knowledge embedded in a hunter-gatherer society is not very different from that which is embedded in each one of its members. The secret of modern societies is not that each person holds much more productive knowledge than those in a more traditional society. The secret to modernity is that we collectively use large volumes of knowledge, while each one of us holds only a few bits of it. Society functions because its members form webs that allow them to specialize and share their knowledge with others.

▶

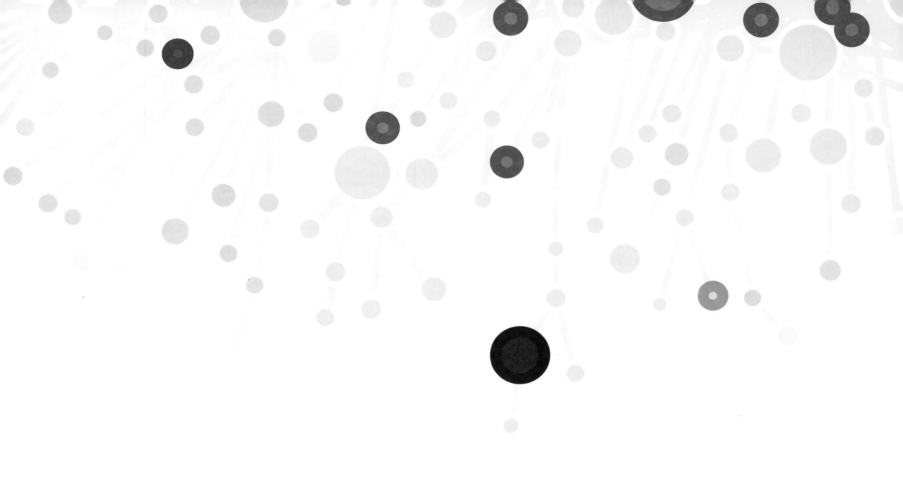

We can distinguish between two kinds of knowledge: explicit and tacit. Explicit knowledge can be transferred easily by reading a text or listening to a conversation. Yesterday's sports results, tomorrow's weather forecast or the size of the moon can all be learned quickly by looking them up in a newspaper or on the web. And yet, if all knowledge had this characteristic, the world would be very different. Countries would catch up very quickly to frontier technologies, and the income differences across the world would be much smaller than those we see today. The problem is that crucial parts of knowledge are tacit and therefore hard to embed in people. Learning how to fix dental problems, speak a foreign language, or run a farm requires a costly and time-consuming effort. As a consequence, it does not make sense for all of us to spend our lives learning how to do everything. Because it is hard to transfer, tacit knowledge is what constrains the process of growth and development. Ultimately, differences in prosperity are related to the amount of tacit knowledge that societies hold and to their ability to combine and share this knowledge.

Because embedding tacit knowledge is a long and costly process, we specialize. This is why people are trained for specific occupations and why organizations become good at specific functions. To fix cavities you must be able to identify them, remove the decayed material and fill the hole. To play baseball, you must know how to catch, field and bat, but you do not need to know how to give financial advice or fix cavities. On the other hand, to perform the function of baseball player, knowing how to catch a ball is not enough (you must also be able to field and bat). In other words, in allocating productive knowledge to individuals, it is important that the chunks each person gets be internally coherent so that he or she can perform a certain function. We refer to these modularized chunks of embedded knowledge as **capabilities.** Some of these capabilities have been modularized at the level of individuals, while others have been grouped into organizations and even into networks of organizations.

For example, consider what has happened with undergraduate degrees, which in the United States require four years of study. This norm has remained constant for the last four centuries. During the same period, however, knowledge has expanded enormously. The university system did not respond to the increase in knowledge by lengthening the time it takes to get a college degree. Instead, it increased the diversity of degrees. What used to be a degree in philosophy was split into natural and moral philosophy, the former later splitting into physics, chemistry and biology and later into other disciplines such as ecology, earth sciences and genetics. The Bureau of Labor Statistics' Standard Occupation Classification for 2010 lists 840 different occupations, including 78 in healthcare, 16 in engineering, 35 kinds of scientists – in coarse categories such as economists, physicists and chemists, five types of artists, and eight kinds of designers. We all certainly can imagine an even more nuanced classification in our respective fields. For instance, we could

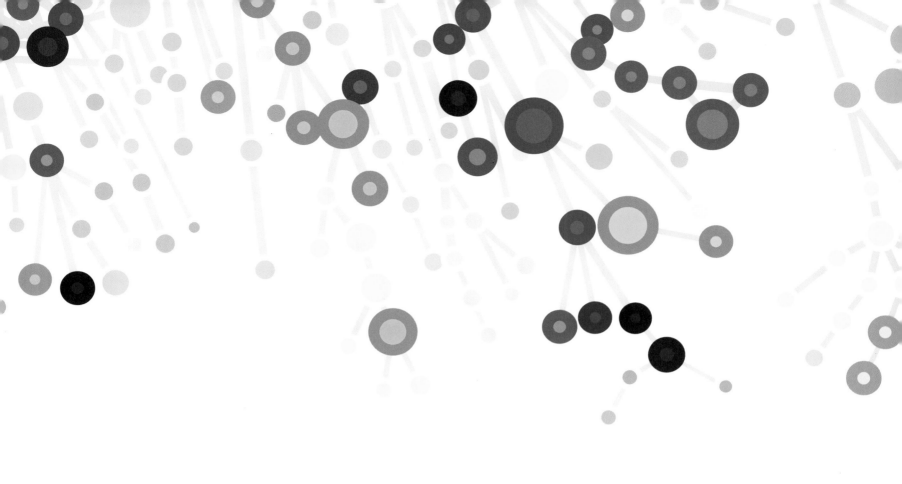

distinguish between economists that specialize in labor, trade, finance, development, industrial organization, macro and econometrics, among others. If we did this further dis-aggregation for all occupations, we would easily go into the tens of thousands. The only way that society can hold all of the knowledge we have is by distributing coherent pieces of it among individuals. This is how the world adapts to expanding knowledge.

Specialization allows societies to store more knowledge, but the question becomes how to put the different chunks of specialized knowledge to use. Most products that are used today require more knowledge than can be mastered by any individual. Hence, those products require that individuals with different capabilities interact with each other. We call the amount of knowledge held by one person a *personbyte*. How can you make a product that requires the input of 100 different people, or 100 *personbytes*? Obviously, it cannot be made by a micro-entrepreneur working alone. It has to be made either by an organization with at least 100 individuals (each with a different personbyte), or by a network of organizations that can aggregate these 100 personbytes of knowledge.

Consider how a shirt is made and sold. It first needs to be designed, and then fabric must be procured, cut and sewn. It needs to be packed, branded, marketed and distributed. In a firm that manufactures shirts, different people will hold expertise in each of these knowledge chunks – the shirt business requires all of them. Moreover, you need to finance

the operation, hire the relevant people, coordinate all the activities and negotiate everybody's buy-in, which in itself requires different kinds of knowhow. To make shirts, you can import the fabric and, by doing so, access the knowledge about looms and threading that is embedded in a piece of cloth. Yet some of the knowledge required cannot be accessed through shipped inputs. The people with the relevant knowledge must be near the place where shirts are made.

This does not begin to list all that is required to make and sell a shirt. To operate efficiently, firms rely on a large set of complementary systems, networks and markets. Raw materials need to be shipped in and the final product shipped out using transportation companies, ports, roads, airplanes or airports. Workers need to get to work and back home using some kind of urban transportation system. Machines need to be powered by electricity and processes need access to water and water treatment facilities. To be able to operate, the plant manager needs all of these services to be locally available, but she does not need to organize them herself. Other organizations are responsible for organizing and aggregating the personbytes required to generate power, provide clean water, and run a transportation system. The relevant capabilities to perform all of these functions reside in organizations that are able to package the relevant knowledge into transferable bundles. These are bundles of knowhow that are more efficiently organized separately and transferred as intermediate inputs or services. We can think

▶

of these bundles as organizational capabilities the manufacturer needs. In fact, just as knowhow is modularized in people in the form of individual capabilities, larger amounts of knowhow are modularized in organizations, and networks of organizations.

Ultimately, to make the products that have been invented in the past 200 years, many personbytes have to be put together. These different personbytes have to reside in different people. To utilize the diversity of knowledge in a complex society, many people have to come together in many ways. They form teams we call firms and organizations and these are in turn connected through markets and other forms of interaction. The amount of productive knowledge that a society uses is reflected in the variety of firms it has, in the variety of occupations these firms require and in the extent of interactions between firms. **Economic complexity** is a measure of how intricate this network of interactions is and hence of how much productive knowledge a society mobilizes. Economic complexity, therefore, is expressed in the composition of a country's productive output and reflects the structures that emerge to hold and combine knowledge.

Knowledge can only be accumulated, transferred and preserved if it is embedded in networks of individuals and organizations that put this knowledge into productive use. Knowledge that is not used is not transferred, and will disappear once the individuals and organization that have it retire or die.

Said differently, countries do not make all the products and services they use and need. They make the ones they can, using the knowledge embedded in their own people and organizations. Some goods, like medical imaging devices or jet engines, require large amounts of knowledge and are the results of very large networks of people and organizations. By contrast, wood logs or coffee beans require much less knowledge and the networks required to support these operations do not need to be as large. Complex economies are those that can weave vast quantities of relevant knowledge together, across large networks of people, to generate a diverse mix of knowledge-intensive products. Simpler economies, in contrast, have a narrower base of productive knowledge and as a result they produce fewer and simpler products, requiring smaller webs of interaction. Because individuals are limited in what they know, the only way societies can expand their knowledge base is by facilitating the interaction of individuals with different knowledge sets in increasingly complex webs of organizations and markets. Increased economic complexity is necessary for a society to be able to hold and use a larger amount of productive knowledge. Because of this, we can measure complexity by looking at the mix of products that countries are able to make. ●

SECTION 2
How Do We Measure *Economic Complexity?*

As we have argued, productive knowledge is the key to prosperity. Larger amounts of productive knowledge require increasingly complex webs of human interaction, which we call economic complexity. In this Section we develop measures of the amount of productive knowledge held by different societies. How can we go about doing this, given that there are no direct ways to look at a country and know how much knowledge is embedded in it? Our approach is based on the following trick: we can look at what countries make, and from this, we can begin to infer what a country knows.

We can observe how many different kinds of products a country is able to make. We call this the **diversity** of a country (Figure 2.1). We can also observe the number of countries that are able to make a product. We call this the **ubiquity** of a product (Figure 2.1). We assume that countries are only able to make the products for which they have the requisite knowledge. From this simple claim, it is possible to extract a few implications that can be used to construct a measure of economic complexity.

The game of Scrabble is a useful analogy. In Scrabble, players use tiles containing single letters to make words. For instance, a player can use the tiles **A, C** and **R** to construct the words **CAR** or **ARC.** In this analogy, words are like products and letters are like capabilities, or modules of embedded knowledge. We assume that each player has plenty of copies of the letters that they do have. This means that if a country has a certain module of knowledge, it can use that knowledge in many different settings. Our challenge is to measure the number of different letters the players have by looking at two things: first, the number of words that each player can write; second, the number of players who can write a particular word.

Players who have more letters should be able to make more words. We can expect the diversity of words (products)

that players (countries) can make to be strongly related to the number of letters (capabilities) that they have. Hence, diversity is a first measure of how much knowledge a country has.

Let us look now at words. The number of players who can make a word is indicative of how many letters the word has. Longer words will tend to be less common, since they can only be put together by players who have all the requisite letters. Similarly, more complex products will be less common because only the countries that have all the requisite knowledge will be able to make them. Products that require little knowledge should be more ubiquitous and vice versa.

The diversity of a country's exports is a crude approximation of the variety of capabilities available in the country, just as the ubiquity of a product is a crude approximation of the variety of capabilities required by a product. Consider medical imaging devices. These machines are made in few places, and the countries that are able to make them, such as the United States or Germany, also export a large number of other products. From this we can infer that medical imaging devices are complex because few countries make them and those that do tend to be diverse. Now consider the case of raw diamonds. These products are extracted in very few places, making their ubiquity quite low. But is this a reflection of the high knowledge-intensity of raw diamonds? Not at all! If raw diamonds were complex, then the countries that extract diamonds should also be able to make many other things because they would have the many capabilities required by diamonds. We see though that Sierra Leone and Botswana principally export diamonds. This indicates that, unlike medical imaging devices, something other than large volumes of knowledge makes diamonds rare. Both of these measures are affected by the existence of rare capabilities, which, using the Scrabble analogy, would be represented by letters like Q and X. So, here we have used the diversity of the countries making a product (say, diamonds) to nuance the first impression given by the (low) ubiquity of the product.

FIGURE 2.1:

▶ Graphical representation of diversity and ubiquity.

DIVERSITY ($k_{c,0}$):
Diversity is related to the number of products that a country exports. This is equal to the number of links that this country has in the network that relates countries to the products that they export. In this example, the diversity of the Netherlands is 5, that of Argentina is 3, and that of Ghana is 1.

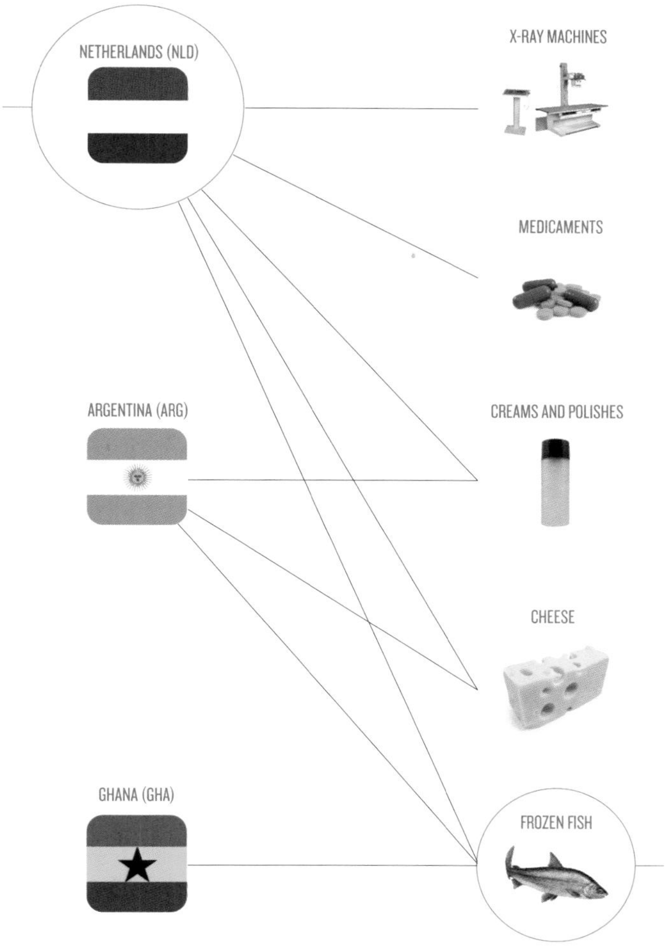

NETHERLANDS (NLD)

X-RAY MACHINES

MEDICAMENTS

ARGENTINA (ARG)

CREAMS AND POLISHES

CHEESE

GHANA (GHA)

FROZEN FISH

UBIQUITY ($k_{p,0}$):
Ubiquity is related to the number of countries that export a product. This is equal to the number of links that this product has in this network. In this example, the ubiquity of cheese is 2, that of fish is 3 and that of medicaments is 1.

By the same token, we can improve the first impression about the complexity of a country that is given by its diversity, by also looking at the ubiquity of the products that it makes. Consider a country that chooses to concentrate in a few very complex products. It does so, not because it has few letters, but because it prefers to use them in very long words. Hence, the diversity of the country may give the wrong impression about the availability of capabilities. But if we look at the ubiquity of the products that the country makes, we would see that it specializes in low ubiquity products. We can look further into how diversified the countries that make those products are, and we will find that highly diversified countries make them. The information about how many capabilities the country has is contained not only in the number of products that it makes, but also in the ubiquity of those products and in the diversity of the other countries that make them.

Consider the case of Switzerland and Egypt. The population of Egypt is 11 times larger than that of Switzerland. At purchasing power prices their GDPs are similar since Switzerland is about 8 times richer than Egypt in per capita terms. Under the classification we use in this Atlas, they both export a similar number of different products, about 180. How can products tell us about the conspicuous differences in the level of development that exist between these two countries? Egypt exports products that are on average exported by 28 other countries (placing Egypt in the 60th percentile of countries in terms of the average ubiquity of its products), while Switzerland exports products that are exported on average by only 19 other countries, putting it in the 5th percentile. Moreover, the products that Switzerland exports are exported by highly diversified countries, while those that Egypt exports are exported by poorly diversified countries. Our mathematical approach exploits these second, third and higher order differences to create measures that approximate the amount of productive knowledge held in each of these countries. Because of these differences, Switzerland is ranked way above Egypt in productive knowledge (Switzerland is ranked 3rd, and Egypt is ranked 67th out of 128 countries in year 2010). Ultimately, what countries make reveals what they know.

This example illustrates that we can improve the estimate of the productive knowledge of a country that we infer from its diversity by looking at the ubiquity of the products that it makes. We can refine it further by looking at the diversity of the countries that make those products and at the ubiquity of the products that those countries make. Similarly, we can improve the estimate of the productive

▶

FIGURE 2.2:

▶ Map of the World colored according to ECI Ranking.

knowledge a product requires that we infer from its ubiquity by looking at the diversity of the countries that make it, as we did with diamonds and Botswana. We can refine it further by looking at the ubiquity of the other products that diamond exporters make and at the diversity of the countries that make those other products. We can do this an infinite number of times using mathematics. This process converges after a few iterations and represents our quantitative measures of complexity. For countries, we refer to this as the **Economic Complexity Index** (ECI). The corresponding measure for products gives us the **Product Complexity Index.** Technical Box 2.2 presents the mathematical definition of these two quantities and Ranking 1 in Part 2 lists countries sorted by their ECI. Figure 2.2 shows a map of the world colored according to a country's ECI ranking. Information Box 2.1 lists the most and least complex products.

This Atlas relies on international trade data. We made this choice because it is the only dataset available that has a rich and detailed cross-country information linking countries to the products that they produce using a standardized classification. This data offers great advantages, but does have limitations. First, it includes data on exports, not production. Countries may be able to make things that they do not export, although the fact that they are unable to sell those products abroad may be indicative of low productivity or quality, and hence knowledge deficiencies. Countries may also export things they do not make but only re-export. To circumvent this issue we require that countries export a *"fair share"* of the products we associate with them (see Technical Box 2.1). A second limitation is that this dataset includes only goods and not services, because the latter do not go through customs offices, which are the source of the statistical records. This is an important drawback, as services are a rising share of international trade. Unfortunately, the statistical efforts of most countries have not kept up with this reality and it is difficult to capture international flows of services in a reliable way. We explored a very coarse dataset of services and found it did not add to the precision with which we can measure economic complexity (see Technical Box 3.3). Finally, the data does not include information on non-tradable activities, such as construction, electricity distribution and restaurants. These activities are not exported because producers and consumers need to meet in the same place. They are an important part of the economic eco-system, but at present there are no global datasets that capture this information. Our current research is focused on finding implementable solutions to these limitations. ●

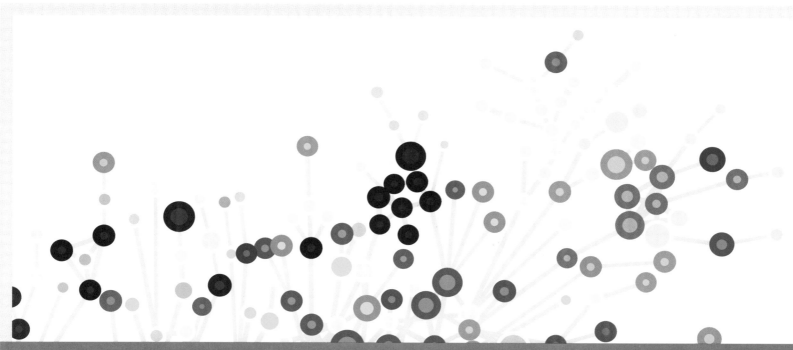

INFORMATION BOX 2.1: THE WORLD'S MOST AND LEAST COMPLEX PRODUCTS

Table 2.1.1 and Table 2.1.2 show respectively the products that rank highest and lowest in the complexity scale. The difference between the world's most and less complex products is stark. The most complex products are sophisticated chemicals and machinery that tend to emerge from organizations where a large number of high skilled individuals participate. The world's least complex products, on the other hand, are raw minerals or simple agricultural products. The economic complexity of a country is connected intimately to the complexity of the products that it exports. Ultimately, countries can only increase their score in the Economic Complexity Index by becoming competitive in an increasing number of complex industries.

TABLE 2.1.1: TOP 5 PRODUCTS BY COMPLEXITY

Product Code (SITC4)	Product Name	Product Community		Product Complexity Index
7367	Other machine tools for working metal or metal carbide	Machinery		2.08
8744	Instrument & appliances for physical or chemical analysis	Chemicals & Health		2.02
7742	Appliances based on the use of X-rays or radiation	Chemicals & Health		1.96
8821	Chemical products and flashlight materials for use in photography	Chemicals & Health		1.91
7373	Welding, brazing, cutting, etc. machines and appliances, parts, N.E.S.	Machinery		1.86

TABLE 2.1.2: BOTTOM 5 PRODUCTS BY COMPLEXITY

Product Code (SITC4)	Product Name	Product Community		Product Complexity Index
2631	Raw cotton, excluding linters, not carded or combed	Cotton, rice, soy beans and others		-2.51
2876	Tin ores and concentrates	Mining		-2.57
2320	Natural rubber latex; natural rubber and gums	Tropical tree-crops and flowers		-2.63
2225	Sesame seeds	Cotton, rice, soy beans and others		-2.99
0721	Cocoa beans, raw, roasted	Tropical tree-crops and flowers		-3.10

▶

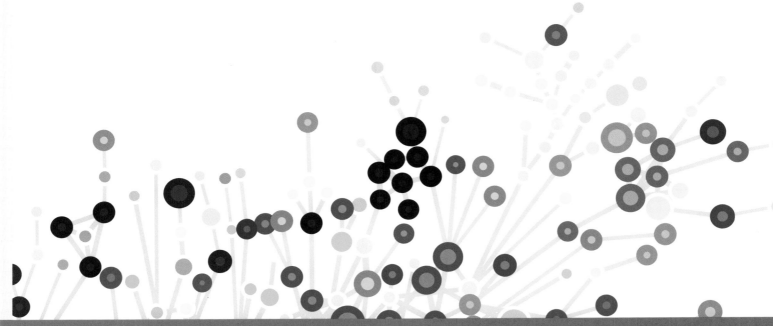

TECHNICAL BOX 2.1: MEASURING ECONOMIC COMPLEXITY:

Consider M_{cp}, as a matrix in which rows represent different countries and columns represents different products. An element of the matrix is equal to I if country c produces product p, and 0 otherwise. We can measure diversity and ubiquity simply by summing over the rows or columns of that matrix. Formally, we define:

$$Diversity = k_{c,0} = \sum_p M_{cp} \qquad (1)$$

$$Ubiquity = k_{p,0} = \sum_c M_{cp} \qquad (2)$$

To generate a more accurate measure of the number of capabilities available in a country, or required by a product, we need to correct the information that diversity and ubiquity carry by using each one to correct the other. For countries, this requires us to calculate the average ubiquity of the products that it exports, the average diversity of the countries that make those products and so forth. For products, this requires us to calculate the average diversity of the countries that make them and the average ubiquity of the other products that these countries make. This can be expressed by the recursion:

$$k_{c,N} = \frac{1}{k_{c,0}} \sum_p M_{cp} \cdot k_{p,N-1} \qquad (3)$$

$$k_{p,N} = \frac{1}{k_{p,0}} \sum_c M_{cp} \cdot k_{c,N-1} \qquad (4)$$

We then insert (4) into (3) to obtain

$$k_{c,N} = \frac{1}{k_{c,0}} \sum_p M_{cp} \frac{1}{k_{p,0}} \sum_{c'} M_{c'p} \cdot k_{c',N-2} \qquad (5)$$

$$k_{c,N} = \sum_{c'} k_{c',N-2} \sum \frac{M_{cp} M_{c'p}}{k_{c,0} k_{p,0}} \qquad (6)$$

and rewrite this equation as:

$$k_{c,N} = \sum_{c'} \widetilde{M}_{cc'} k_{c',N-2} \qquad (7)$$

where

$$\widetilde{M}_{cc'} = \sum_p \frac{M_{cp} M_{c'p}}{k_{c,0} k_{p,0}} \qquad (8)$$

We note that (7) is satisfied when $k_{c,N} = k_{c,N-2} = 1$. This corresponds to the eigenvector of $\widetilde{M}_{cc'}$ which is associated with the largest eigenvalue. Since this eigenvector is a vector of ones, it is not informative. We look, instead, for the eigenvector associated with the second largest eigenvalue. This is the eigenvector that captures the largest amount of variance in the system and is our measure of economic complexity. Hence, we define the Economic Complexity Index (ECI) as:

$$ECI = \frac{\vec{K} - <\vec{K}>}{\text{stdev}(\vec{K})} \qquad (9)$$

where < > represents an average, and stdev stands for the standard deviation and

$$\qquad (10)$$

$$\vec{K} = Eigenvector\ of\ \widetilde{M}_{cc'}\ associated\ with\ second\ largest\ eigenvalue.$$

Analogously, we define a Product Complexity Index (PCI). Because of the symmetry of the problem, this can be done simply by exchanging the index of countries (c) with that for products (p) in the definitions above. Hence, we define PCI as:

$$PCI = \frac{\vec{Q} - <\vec{Q}>}{\text{stdev}(\vec{Q})} \qquad (11)$$

where

$$\qquad (12)$$

$$\vec{Q} = Eigenvector\ of\ \widetilde{M}_{pp'}\ associated\ with\ second\ largest\ eigenvalue.$$

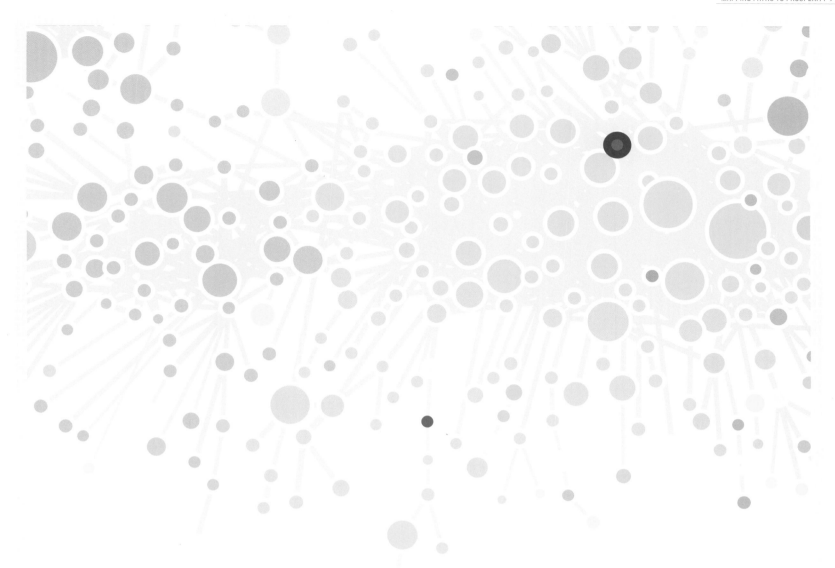

TECHNICAL BOX 2.2: WHO MAKES WHAT?

When associating countries to products it is important to take into account the size of the export volume of countries and the world trade in each product. This is because, even for the same product, we expect the volume of exports of a large country like China, to be larger than the volume of exports of a small country like Uruguay. By the same token, we expect the export volume of products that represent a large fraction of world trade, such as cars or footwear, to represent a larger share of a country's exports than products that account for a small fraction of world trade, like cotton seed oil or potato flour.

To make countries and products comparable we use Balassa's definition of Revealed Comparative Advantage or RCA. Balassa's definition says that a country has Revealed Comparative Advantage in a product if it exports more than its *"fair share"*, that is, a share that is equal to the share of total world trade that the product represents. For example, in 2010, with exports of $42 billion, soybeans represented 0.35% of world trade. Of this total, Brazil exported nearly $11 billion, and since Brazil's total exports for that year were $140 billion, soybeans accounted for 7.8% of Brazil's exports. This represents around 22 times Brazil's *"fair share"* of soybean exports (7.8% divided by 0.35%), so we can say that Brazil has a high revealed comparative advantage in soybeans.

Formally, if X_{cp} represents the exports of product p by country c, we can express the Revealed Comparative Advantage that country c has in product p as:

$$RCA_{cp} = \frac{X_{cp}}{\sum_c X_{cp}} \bigg/ \frac{\sum_p X_{cp}}{\sum_{c,p} X_{cp}} \qquad (1)$$

We use this measure to construct a matrix that connects each country to the products that it makes. The entries in the matrix are 1 if country c exports product p with Revealed Comparative Advantage larger than 1, and 0 otherwise. Formally we define this as the M_{cp} matrix, where

$$M_{cp} = \begin{cases} 1 & if\ RCA_{cp} \geq 1; \\ 0 & otherwise. \end{cases} \qquad (2)$$

M_{cp} is the matrix summarizing which country makes what, and is used to construct the product space and our measures of economic complexity for countries and products. In our research we have played around with cutoff values other than 1 to construct the M_{cp} matrix and found that our results are robust to these changes.

Going forward, we moderate changes in export values induced by fluctuations in commodity prices by using a modified definition of RCA in which the denominator is averaged over the previous three years.

SECTION 3
Why Is *Economic Complexity* Important?

Economic complexity reflects the amount of knowledge that is embedded in the productive structure of an economy. Seen this way, it is no coincidence that there is a strong correlation between our measures of economic complexity and the income per capita that countries are able to generate. Figure 3.1 illustrates the relationship between the Economic Complexity Index (ECI) and income per capita for the 128 countries studied in this Atlas. In this graph, we separate countries according to their intensity in natural resource exports. We color in red those countries for which natural resource exports, such as minerals, gas and oil, represent at least 10% of GDP. For the 75 countries with a limited relative presence of natural-resource exports (in blue), economic complexity accounts for 78 percent of the variance in income per capita. But as the Figure 3.1 illustrates, countries with a large presence of natural resources can be relatively rich without being complex. It is easy to see why. But if we take into account the income that is generated from extractive activities, which has more to do with geology than know-how, economic complexity can explain about 78 percent of the variation in income across all 128 countries. Figure 3.2 shows the tight relationship between economic complexity and income per capita that emerges after we take into account a country's natural resource income. The more complex your economy, the more likely you are to have a higher level of income.

Economic complexity, therefore, is related to a country's level of prosperity. As such, it is just a correlation of things we care about. The relationship between income and complexity, however, goes deeper than this. To see this, note that this relationship is tight but not perfect. As we said before, ECI accounts for 78 percent of the variance, not 100 percent. Countries are not on the red line of Figure 3.2. Some countries are above this line and others are below. Are these gaps just a mistake of the theory or do they contain information about where countries are going? Take, for example, the case of India. Given how much it knows, we would have expected India to be richer. Well, maybe India should be richer. If so, India's recent rapid growth would be caused by the fact that the country already possesses the knowledge to be richer than it is and is, therefore, moving to "where it belongs" in the regression line. Take by contrast the case of Greece. Our approach would say that Greece is too rich for the little knowledge it has. Well, maybe Greece cannot sustain its recent level of income, which has been propped up artificially through massive borrowing that has proven unsustainable: the country is now rapidly moving to "where it belongs", but in the case of Greece it is in the opposite direction of that of India. **Countries whose economic complexity is greater than what we would expect, given their current level of income, tend to grow faster than those that are "too rich" for their current level of economic complexity.** Figure 3.3 shows the relationship between the gaps between of ECI and income in 2000 and growth in the decade 2000-2010. The relationship is strong and statistically significant: the gaps between a country's income and its complexity do tend to be closed in the future through differential growth. **In this sense, economic complexity is not just a symptom or an expression of prosperity: it is a driver.**

▶

FIGURE 3.1:

▶ Shows the relationship between income per capita and the Economic Complexity Index (ECI) for countries where natural resource exports are larger than 10% of GDP (red) and for those where natural resource exports are lower than 10% of GDP (blue). For the latter group of countries, the Economic Complexity Index accounts for 78% of the variance, a variable commonly known as R^2. Countries in which the levels of natural resource exports is relatively high tend to be significantly richer than what would be expected given the complexity of their economies, yet the ECI still correlates strongly with income for that group.

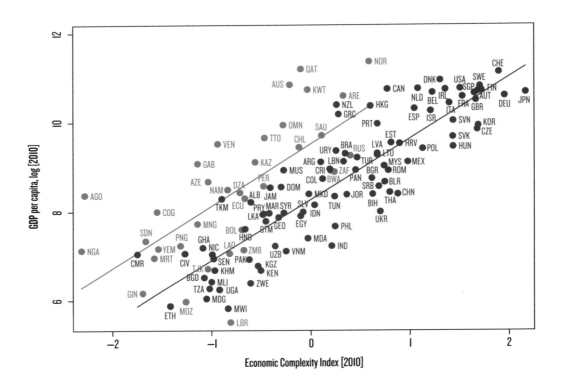

FIGURE 3.2:

▶ Shows the relationship between economic complexity and income per capita obtained after controlling for each country's natural resource exports. After including this control, through the inclusion of the log of natural resource exports per capita, economic complexity and natural resources explain 78% of the variance in per capita income across countries.

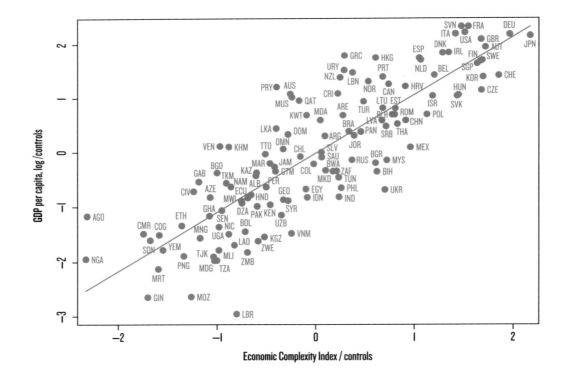

FIGURE 3.3:

▶ Shows the relationship between the annualized GDP per capita growth for the period between 2000 and 2010 and the Economic Complexity Index for 2000, after taking into account the initial level of income and the increase in natural resource exports during that period (in constant dollars as a share of initial GDP).

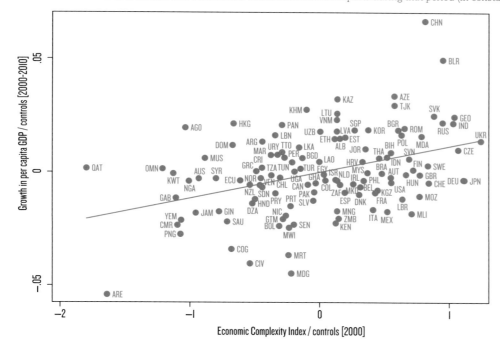

Technical Box 3.1 shows the statistical evidence that supports our claim that economic complexity precedes and hence drives long run levels of income and consequently growth. The analysis uses a country's initial level of economic complexity to predict growth over the subsequent decade, after controlling for initial income and the rise in natural resource exports over the decade.

The ability of the ECI to predict future economic growth suggests that countries tend to move towards an income level that is compatible with their overall level of productive knowledge. On average, their income tends to reflect their embedded knowledge. But when it does not, as the cases of India and Greece illustrate, it gets corrected over time through accelerated or diminished growth.

Over time economic complexity evolves: countries expand their productive capabilities and begin to make more and more complex products. This process will be studied at greater length in Section 5, but for now consider that making a product that is new to a country requires the addition of all missing capabilities. Adding a product for which a country needs many new capabilities often proves difficult because it requires solving a complicated "chicken and egg" problem. An industry may not exist because the productive capabilities it requires may not be present. But there will be scant incentives to develop the productive capabilities required by industries that do not exist. Furthermore, developing those capabilities will be difficult because there is nobody in the country from which to learn the requisite know-how. Because of this problem, countries tend to preferentially develop products for which most of the requisite productive capabilities are already present, leaving fewer

"chicken and egg" problems to be solved. We say that these products are "nearby" in terms of productive capabilities.

What differs between countries is the abundance of products that they do not yet make but that are near their current endowment of capabilities. Countries with an abundance of such nearby products will find it easier to deal with the chicken and egg problem of coordinating the acquisition of missing capabilities with the development of the industries that demand them. This should allow them to find an easier path towards capability acquisition, product diversification and development. Countries with few nearby products will find it hard to acquire more capabilities and hence to increase their economic complexity.

In Section 5 we will show how we measure the abundance of products that are near a country's current set of productive capabilities. We call it the **Complexity Outlook Index** (COI). This variable **is based on the distance between the products that a country is currently making and those that it is not, weighted by the complexity of the products it is not making.** Being near a complex product is worth more than being near a simple product, and being near is worth more than being far.

We show the Complexity Outlook Index plotted against the Economic Complexity Index in Figure 3.4. The graph shows an inverted U shape. Countries with low ECI (those with few capabilities) find most products very "far" and opportunities very limited. This is reflected in a low COI. Countries with a high ECI are highly diversified: they already make most of the existing products, and hence have few options to move into other existing complex products. Hence, they also exhibit a low COI. These countries can

FIGURE 3.4:

▶ Shows the relationship between the Economic Complexity Index for 2010 and the Complexity Outlook Index for 2010.

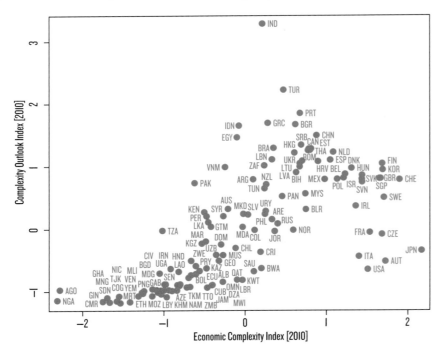

only diversify by pushing out the technological frontier, inventing products that are new to the world. Countries with intermediate ECI are in a sweet spot in which they are very near many products for which they already have many of the requisite capabilities. They face relatively smaller "chicken and egg" problems and should be able to rapidly diversify. In fact, as we show in Section 5, the Complexity Outlook Index (COI) predicts remarkably well the changes in the Economic Complexity Index, meaning that it predicts the speed at which countries acquire productive capabilities.

If the Complexity Outlook Index affects the acquisition of productive capabilities, its initial value should predict subsequent growth, even after controlling for the initial level of productive capabilities, as measured by ECI. In other words, countries not only grow based on the mismatch between their capabilities and their current income, but also according to how easy it is for them to acquire more productive capabilities as captured by the COI. As we show in Technical Box 3.1, COI is by itself a strong predictor of future growth and together with the Economic Complexity Index, initial income and the growth in natural resource exports they can explain 50 percent of the variance in 10-year growth rates for a sample of over 100 countries over three decades. As we shall see in Section 4, this is a much higher percentage than many of the variables used in the voluminous growth literature are able to achieve.

It is important to note what the Economic Complexity variables are not about: they are not about export-oriented growth, openness, export diversification or country size. They are, instead, about productive knowledge and the ease

with which it can be acquired. Although we calculate the ECI and COI using export data, the channel through which they contribute to future growth is not limited to their impact on the growth of exports. Clearly, countries whose exports grow faster, all other things being equal, will necessarily experience higher GDP growth. This is simply because exports are a component of GDP. However, as Technical Box 3.2 shows, the contribution of ECI and COI to future economic growth remains strong after accounting for the growth in the *quantity* of exports.

The economic complexity of a country is also not about openness to trade: the impact of ECI and COI on growth is essentially unaffected if we account for differences in openness measured as the ratio of exports to GDP. And the ECI is not a measure of export diversification. Controlling for standard measures of export concentration, such as the Herfindahl-Hirschman Index, does not affect our results. In fact, neither openness nor export concentration are statistically significant determinants of growth after controlling for the ECI and COI (see Technical Box 3.2).

Finally, the ECI and COI are not about a country's size. The ability of the Complexity variables to predict growth is unaffected when we take into account a country's size, as measured by its population, while the population itself is not statistically significant (see Technical Box 3.2).

In short, economic complexity matters because it helps explain differences in the level of income of countries, and more importantly, because it predicts future economic growth. Economic Complexity might not be simple to accomplish, but the countries that do achieve it tend to reap important rewards. ●

TECHNICAL BOX 3.1: THE GROWTH EQUATION

To analyze the impact of the Economic Complexity Index (ECI) and Complexity Outlook Index (COI) on future economic growth we estimate two regressions where the dependent variable is the annualized growth rate of GDP per capita for the periods 1978-1988, 1988-1998 and 1998-2008 (We excluded Liberia for our 1988 sample and Zimbabwe for 1998 sample because they were extreme outliers). In the first of these equations we do not include ECI nor COI and use only two control variables: the logarithm of the initial level of GDP per capita in each period and the increase in natural resource exports in constant dollars as a share of initial GDP. The first variable captures the idea that, other things equal, poorer countries should grow faster than rich countries and catch up. This is known in the economic literature as convergence. The second control variable captures the effect on growth caused by increases in income that come from natural resource exports, which complexity does not explain. In addition, we include a dummy variable for each decade, capturing any common factor affecting all countries during that period, such as a global boom or a widespread financial crisis. Taken together, these variables account for 29 percent of the variance in countries' growth rates. This is shown in the first column of Table 3.1.1.

In addition to initial income and the growth in natural-resource exports, the second regression includes the effect of the value of the Economic Complexity Index (ECI) at the beginning of the period. The second column of Table 3.1.1 shows that ECI is strongly associated with future economic growth. The variable is highly significant both economically and statistically. Its inclusion increases the explanatory power of the equation in column 1 by 66 percent. A 1-standard deviation increase in ECI is estimated to accelerate annual growth by 1.9 percent.

In column 3 we introduce the Complexity Outlook Index (COI) and the two control variables of column 1. It also shows that COI is highly significant, both economically and statistically, raising the explanatory power of the equation by 52 percent relative to column 1. A 1-standard deviation improvement in COI is associated with a 1.2 percent increase in growth of GDP per capita.

In column 4 we introduce both ECI and COI into our growth equation. Both variables remain highly significant and the equation as a whole explains half of the variance of 10-year growth over three decades in our sample of over 100 countries. The difference between columns 4 and 1 indicates that the ECI and COI jointly increase the regression's R^2 in 21 percentage points or 72 percent of the R^2 of equation 1.

We use the equation in column 4 of Table 3.1.1 to forecast the growth in GDP per capita and present the results in Part 2, Ranking 3. To predict average annualized growth between 2010 and 2020 we make two assumptions. First, we assume a worldwide common growth term for the decade, which we take to be the same as that observed in the 2000-2010 period. Changing this assumption would affect the growth rate of all countries by a similar amount but would not change the rankings. Second, we assume that there will be no change in the real value of natural resource exports per capita as a share of initial GDP. This implies that natural resource exports in real terms in the next decade will remain at the record-high levels achieved in 2010. This assumption may underestimate the effect on countries whose volumes of natural resource extraction will increase significantly and over-estimate the growth in countries that will see their natural-resource export volumes declines. A higher or lower constant dollar price of natural resource exports would respectively improve or reduce the projected growth performance of countries by an amount proportional to their natural resource intensity.

TABLE 3.1.1

VARIABLES	Annualized growth in GDP pc (by decade)			
	(1978-1988, 1988-1998, 1998-2008)			
	(1)	(2)	(3)	(4)
Initial Income per capita, log	-0.001	-0.011***	-0.006***	-0.011***
	(0.001)	(0.001)	(0.001)	(0.001)
Increase in net natural resource exports .	0.059***	0.065***	0.065***	0.067***
- in constant dollars (as a share of initial GDP)	(0.012)	(0.009)	(0.010)	(0.009)
Initial Economic Complexity Index		0.019***		0.014***
		(0.002)		(0.002)
Initial Complexity Outlook Index			0.012***	0.007***
			(0.002)	(0.002)
Constant	0.023***	0.097***	0.058***	0.095***
	(0.007)	(0.010)	(0.009)	(0.010)
Observations	301	301	301	301
Adjusted R^2	0.291	0.472	0.436	0.498
Year FE	Yes	Yes	Yes	Yes

Standard errors clustered by country are shown in parentheses. *** p<0.01, ** p<0.05, * p<0.1

▶

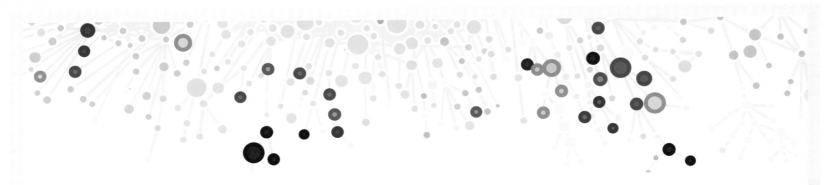

TECHNICAL BOX 3.2: ECONOMIC COMPLEXITY IS DIFFERENT FROM COUNTRY SIZE, OPENNESS, EXPORT SUCCESS OR PRODUCT CONCENTRATION

This box explores the robustness of the impact of the complexity variables, Economic Complexity Index and Complexity Outlook Index, on growth. While the ECI and COI are constructed using export data, their relationship with future growth is not driven by the growth in the volume of exports or by their concentration. To show this, we start with our basic growth equation, which we replicate as column I in Table 3.2.I. Column 2 adds to this equation the increase in the real value of the exports of goods and services in the decade in question as a fraction of initial GDP. Exports are a component of GDP, and therefore, we expect them to contribute to growth. Nevertheless, after including the increase in exports, the effect of ECI

and COI on growth remains strong and significant, indicating that the effect of economic complexity goes beyond its impact on export growth. Column 3 introduces exports as a share of GDP. We use this as a measure of openness. Column 4 includes the Herfindahl-Hirschman index as a measure of export concentration. Column 5 includes the log of initial population as a measure of size. This is equivalent to introducing total GDP, given that we are already controlling for GDP per capita. The contribution to growth of the variables introduced in columns 3, 4 and 5 are estimated to be very close to zero, are not statistically significant and do not affect the ability of the ECI and COI to predict future economic growth.

TABLE 3.2.I

VARIABLES	Annualized growth in GDP pc (by decade)				
	(1978-1988. 1988-1998. 1998-2008)				
	(1)	(2)	(3)	(4)	(5)
Initial income per capita. log	-0.011***	-0.010***	-0.011***	-0.010***	-0.011***
	(0.001)	(0.001)	(0.001)	(0.001)	(0.001)
Increase in net natural resource exports	0.067***	0.025**	0.067***	0.068***	0.067***
- in constant dollars (as a share of initial GDP)	(0.009)	(0.010)	(0.010)	(0.009)	(0.009)
Initial Economic Complexity Index	0.014***	0.011***	0.014***	0.012***	0.014***
	(0.002)	(0.002)	(0.002)	(0.002)	(0.002)
Initial Complexity Outlook Index	0.007***	0.005***	0.006***	0.006***	0.007***
	(0.002)	(0.001)	(0.001)	(0.002)	(0.002)
Increase in exports (goods and services)		0.039***			
- in constant dollars (as a share of initial GDP)		(0.006)			
Exports to GDP			0.011		
			(0.007)		
Initial Exports Concentration (Herfindahl)				-0.012	
				(0.008)	
Initial Population. log					0
					(0.001)
Constant	0.095***	0.076***	0.096***	0.094***	0.104***
	(0.010)	(0.010)	(0.010)	(0.010)	(0.021)
Observations	301	289	300	301	301
R^2	0.5	0.65	0.5	0.5	0.5
Year FE	Yes	Yes	Yes	Yes	Yes

Standard errors clustered by country are shown in parentheses. *** $p<0.01$, ** $p<0.05$, * $p<0.1$

TECHNICAL BOX 3.3: WHAT ABOUT SERVICES?

The measures, ranking and figures in this Atlas are all based on trade data, which only contains information on tradable goods. Economies, however, produce not only goods, but also services, such as tourism, finance and consulting. The lack of service data can bias our results if the complexity of a country's service structure carries different information than can be inferred from its trade in goods. Yet, we can expect service data to provide little additional information in a world where countries that have complex goods structures also have complex service structures.

Unfortunately, highly disaggregated data on services is not available, since services are not controlled at borders through customs agents in the way goods are. Hence, because of data constraints, we are limited to exploring the role of services at a more aggregate level. We used the service data from the World Bank based on IMF Balance of Payments dataset, which classifies exports of services in 12 different categories. These categories are very broad. For instance, the transportation services category encompasses all different types of transformation such as sea, rail, air and land transportation as well as bulk, containerized and refrigerated services. Business services puts together

accounting, engineering, legal and management consulting in the same category. Nevertheless, this dataset is the most diverse that we have found, so we decided to use it to see whether our results are affected by the absence of this data.

Figure 3.3.1 shows the comparison of ECIs calculated using only goods to the ECI calculated with goods and services, combined. Overall, we see an almost perfect correlation, meaning that the inclusion of services does not change our basic story. Another way of calculating ECI would be to use just the services data. We checked whether all these three indices, namely ECI calculated with goods (ECIg), ECI calculated with goods and services (ECIgs) and ECI calculated only using the data from services (ECIs), are predictive of growth. Table 3.3.1 shows that ECIg and ECIgs are both good predictors of growth, whereas ECIs does not predict growth. When put together, ECIg beats ECIgs in terms of its correlation with future growth. This may be due to the fact that the services data is very coarse and does not capture well the very large differences in complexity of the different services it groups under the same heading. Hence, for now, we think that the services data is not disaggregate enough to be included in our economic complexity calculations.

FIGURE 3.3.1:

▶ Relationship between ECI calculated with goods and ECI calculated with goods and services.

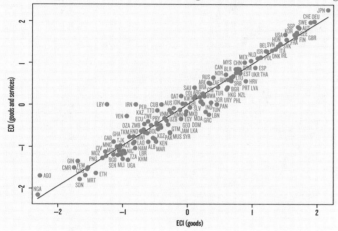

TABLE 3.3.1

| VARIABLES | Annualized growth in GDPpc (by decade) | | | | | |
| | (1988-1998, 1998-2008) | | | | | |
	(1)	(2)	(3)	(4)	(5)	(6)
Initial income per capita, log	-0.002***	-0.011***	-0.010***	-0.002***	-0.011***	-0.011***
	(0.001)	(0.001)	(0.001)	(0.001)	(0.002)	(0.001)
Increase in natural resource exports - in constant dollars (as a share of initial GDP)	0.055***	0.062***	0.062***	0.055***	0.062***	0.062***
	(0.013)	(0.009)	(0.010)	(0.013)	(0.009)	(0.009)
Initial Economic Complexity Index (using goods)		0.016***			0.019***	0.016***
		(0.002)			(0.007)	(0.002)
Initial Economic Complexity Index (using goods and services)			0.015***		-0.003	
			(0.002)		(0.007)	
Initial Economic Complexity Index (using services)				-0.001		-0.001
				(0.001)		(0.001)
Constant	0.046***	0.110***	0.109***	0.046***	0.110***	0.111***
	(0.007)	(0.012)	(0.012)	(0.007)	(0.012)	(0.012)
Observations	218	218	218	218	218	218
Adjusted R²	0.307	0.460	0.446	0.308	0.461	0.462
Year FE	Yes	Yes	Yes	Yes	Yes	Yes

Standard errors clustered by country are shown in parentheses. *** p<0.01, ** p<0.05, * p<0.1

SECTION 4

How Is *Complexity* Different
from Other Approaches?

We are certainly not the first to look for correlates or causal factors of income and growth. One strand of the literature has looked at the salience of institutions in determining growth, whereas others have looked at human capital or broader measures of competitiveness. Clearly, more complex economies tend to have better institutions, more educated workers and more competitive environments, so these approaches are not completely at odds with each other or with ours. In fact, the strength of institutions, quality of education, competitiveness, financial depth and economic complexity all emphasize different aspects of the same intricate reality. It is not clear, however, that these different approaches have the same ability to capture factors that are verifiably important for growth and development. In this section, we compare each of these measures with our Complexity Indices and gauge their marginal contribution to income and economic growth.

MEASURES OF GOVERNANCE AND INSTITUTIONAL QUALITY

Some of the most respected measures of institutional quality are the six Worldwide Governance Indicators (WGIs), which the World Bank has published biennially since 1996. These indicators are used, for example, as eligibility criteria by the Millennium Challenge Corporation (MCC) to select the countries they choose to support. These criteria are based on the presumption of a causal connection between governance, on the one hand, and potential for growth and poverty reduction, on the other.

To the extent that governance is important to allow individuals and organizations to cooperate, share knowledge and make more complex products, it should be reflected in the kind of industries that a country can support. Therefore, the Economic Complexity variables indirectly capture information about the quality of governance in a country. Which indicator captures information that is more relevant for growth is an empirical question.

Here we compare the contribution to the predictibality of future economic growth accounted for by the WGIs and the Economic Complexity variables, ECI and COI using a technique described in Technical Box 4.1. Briefly, our technique involves removing the variables of interest, either one by one or in groups, from an estimation equation that initially includes all of the variables. This allows us to determine how much of the predictive power can be attributed singularly to each variable. The attributions are measured as the amount of variance that is accounted uniquely by the variable of interest. Since the WGIs are available only since 1996, we perform this exercise using the 1996-2008 period as a whole and as two consecutive 6-year periods. We also compare with each individual WGI and with the six of them together.

Figure 4.1 shows that the Economic Complexity variables account for 18.3 percent of the variance in economic growth during the 1996-2008 period, while the six WGIs combined account only for 3 percent. For the estimation using the two six-year periods, we find that ECI accounts for 10.9% of the variance in growth, whereas the six WGIs combined account for 2.2%.

We conclude that as far as future economic growth is concerned, **the Economic Complexity and Complexity Outlook**

▶

FIGURE 4.1:

▶ Contribution to the variance of economic growth from complexity variables (ECI and COI) and from the measures of governance and institutional quality.

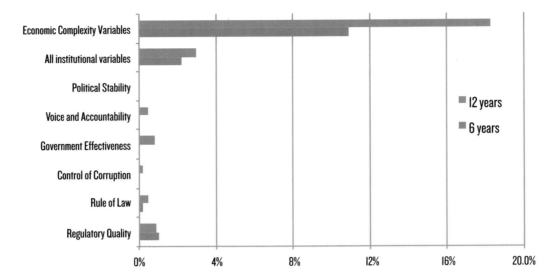

Indices capture significantly more growth-relevant information than the 6 World Governance Indicators, either individually or combined. This does not mean that governance is not important for the economy. It suggests that the aspects of governance important for growth are weakly reflected in the WGIs and appear to be more strongly reflected in measures of economic complexity.

EDUCATION-BASED MEASURES OF HUMAN CAPITAL
Another strand of the growth and development literature has looked at the impact of human capital on economic growth. The idea that human capital is important for income and growth is not unrelated to our focus on the productive knowledge that exists in a society. The human capital literature, however, has placed its attention on the *amount* of knowledge the *average* citizen has, and has measured this in years of formal education. Our approach emphasizes the *variety* of productive knowledge that *different* individuals have, including their tacit knowledge, and emphasizes the interactions that enable productive knowledge to be used in networks of individuals and firms.

The standard variables used as a proxy for human capital are the number of years of formal schooling attained by those currently of working age, as well as the school enrollment rates of the young population (Barro and Lee, 2010). Since these indicators do not take into account the quality of the education received by pupils, they have been subject to criticism resulting in new measures of educational quality. These measures use test scores from standardized international exams, such as the OECD Programme for International Student Assessment (PISA) or the Trend in International

Mathematics and Science Study (TIMSS). Hanuschek and Woessmann (2008) collected data for all the countries that participated in either program and used this information to generate a measure of the average cognitive ability of students for a cross-section of countries around the year 2000.

The information about productive knowhow captured by the economic complexity variables, and the information reflected in education-based measures of human capital are not just two sides of the same coin. Analytically, education indicators try to measure how much of the *same* knowledge individuals have, whether knowledge is measured as years of study of the national curriculum or as the skills mastered by students according to standardized international tests. In contrast, the Economic Complexity variables try to capture the total amount of productive knowledge that is embedded in a society as a whole and is related to the diversity of knowledge that its individuals have. Clearly, for a complex economy to exist, its members must be able to read, write and manipulate symbols, such as numbers or mathematical functions. This is what is taught in schools. Yet, the converse is not true: the skills acquired in school may be a poor proxy for the productive knowledge of a society.

What a society can produce, however, often has little relationship to what people learn in school. For example, if a country were to achieve the goal of having every pupil complete a good secondary education and if this was the extent of its productive knowledge, no one would know how to make a pair of shoes, a metal knife, a roll of paper or a patterned piece of cotton fabric. The skills that are required to make these products are acquired mostly on the job. That is why job advertisements often request years of particular

FIGURE 4.2:

▶ Relationship between Years of Schooling and the Economic Complexity Index (ECI) for the year 2000.

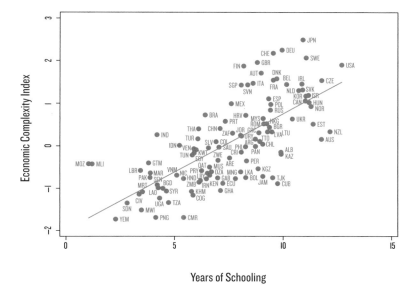

FIGURE 4.3:

▶ Relationship between Cognitive Ability and the Economic Complexity Index (ECI) for the year 2000.

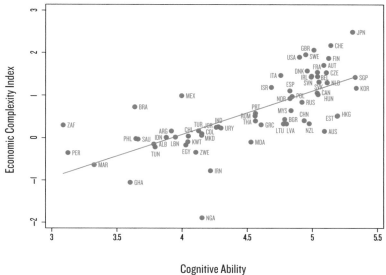

experience, not just years of schooling. In fact, what a country produces determines the kinds of skills its citizens can acquire through on-the-job experience. The education-based human capital approach overlooks this important fact by assuming implicitly that what workers formally study is what affects what a society is able to do.

Figure 4.2 shows the relationship between our measure of economic complexity and years of schooling for the year 2000. It is clear that there is positive relationship between the two (R^2=50%). Countries like India and Uganda, or Mongolia and Mexico, have very similar levels of average formal education. Yet, they differ dramatically in economic complexity. India is much more complex than Uganda, and Mexico is much more complex than Mongolia.

Figure 4.3 shows that the relationship between cognitive ability and economic complexity is also positive. Here we find that Brazil and Ghana are two countries with similar levels of cognitive ability, but very different levels of economic complexity. Brazil is two standard deviations more complex than Ghana. The same is true for Colombia and Nigeria. Their measured cognitive abilities are the same, but Colombia is nearly 1.5 standard deviations more complex than Nigeria.

For illustration purposes, consider the case of Ghana and Thailand. Both countries had similar levels of schooling in 1970, but Ghana expanded education more vigorously than Thailand in the subsequent 40 years (Figure 4.4). However, Ghana's economic complexity and income stagnated as it remained an exporter of cocoa, aluminum, fish and forest products. By contrast, between 1970 and 1985 Thailand underwent a massive increase in economic complexity, equivalent to a change of one standard deviation in the Economic

Complexity Index (Figure 4.5). This caused a sustained economic boom in Thailand after 1985. As a consequence, the level of income per capita between Ghana and Thailand has since diverged dramatically (Figure 4.6). Ghana's population may have gone through more schooling than Thailand's, but Thailand has more productive knowledge.

Next, we measure how well these indicators account for the current level of income of countries and to predict future economic growth, using the same technique that we employed to compare Economic Complexity variables, ECI and COI, with the World Governance Indicators (see Technical Box 4.1). We begin by looking at the level of income per capita. While data on years of schooling and school enrollment is available for several years, the data on educational quality exists only for a cross-section of countries around the year 2000. We use the data for this year to estimate equations where the dependent variable is the level of income per capita and the independent variables are the years of schooling of the labor force, the Hanushek and Woessmann measure of cognitive ability, and the ECI. We do not use school enrollment as this variable affects future human capital but not the human capital invested in creating today's income. The results, presented in Figure 4.7, indicate that the Economic Complexity Index explains 17 percent of the variance, after controlling for the education variables, while years of schooling and cognitive ability together account for only 4 percent of the variance that is not explained by the complexity variables. This shows that the ECI contains more information relevant to the generation of income than the educational variables.

We also look at how well human capital and complexity explain future growth. To do this we follow a methodology

▶

FIGURE 4.4:

▶ Years of schooling of Thailand and Ghana as a function of time.

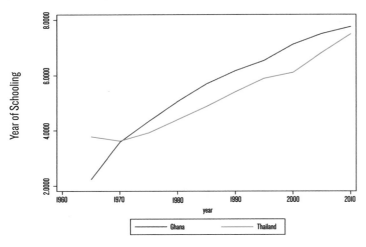

FIGURE 4.5:

▶ Economic Complexity Index (ECI) of Thailand and Ghana as a function of time.

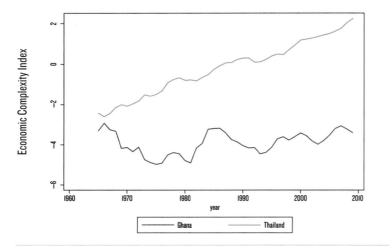

FIGURE 4.6:

▶ Evolution of the GDP per capita of Thailand and Ghana as a function of time.

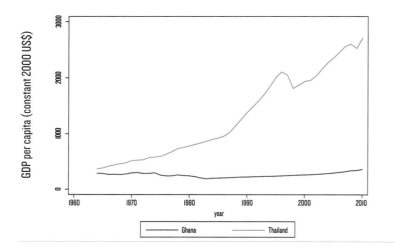

similar to that used for the analysis of governance on growth (see Technical Box 4.2). In this case, we include data on school enrollment at the secondary and tertiary levels as these would affect the years of schooling of the labor force going forward. We do not include cognitive ability as this variable exists only for a single year.

Figure 4.8 shows that economic complexity accounts for 15 percent of the variance in economic growth rates unexplained by education for the three decades between 1978 and 2008. All education variables, on the other hand, when combined account only for 3 percent of the variance not explained by economic complexity.

These results show that the Economic Complexity Index contains information that is more directly related to a country's level of income and its future rate of growth than the standard variables used to measure human capital.

MEASURES OF COMPETITIVENESS

Let us now turn to measures of competitiveness. The most respected source of these measures is the World Economic Forum's Global Competitiveness Index (GCI). The GCI has been published since 1979. Over the course of more than 30 years, the coverage of the GCI has been expanded and improved methodologically, going through two major revisions in 2001 and 2006. In 1995, the Global Competitiveness Report (GCR) ranked less than 50 countries, but over the years this number has increased and now it ranks over 130 countries. The claim of the GCR is that the GCI captures the fundamental variables that drive growth in the medium term:

"We define competitiveness as the set of institutions, policies, and factors that determine the level of productivity of a country. Because the rates of return are the fundamental drivers of the growth rates of the economy, a more competitive economy is one that is likely to grow faster in the medium to long run."

(GLOBAL COMPETITIVENESS REPORT 2010 CHAPTER I.I, PAGE 4)

FIGURE 4.7:

▶ Contribution to the variance of income from the Economic Complexity Index (ECI) and measures of human capital from Hanuschek and Woessmann (2008).

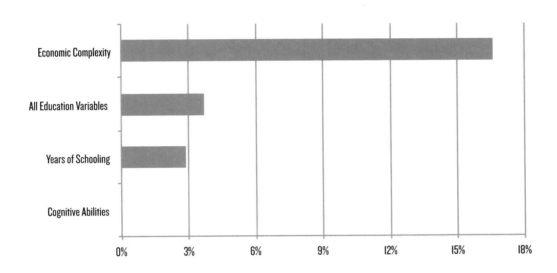

FIGURE 4.8:

▶ Contribution to the variance of economic growth from the Economic Complexity Index (ECI) and measures of human capital from Barro and Lee (2010).

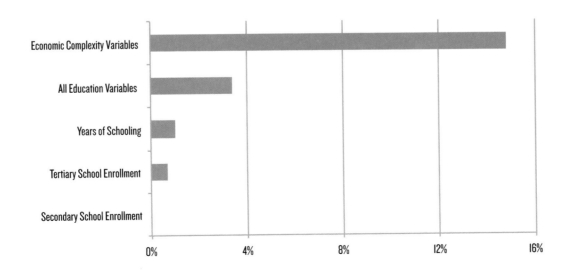

FIGURE 4.9:

▶ Contribution to the variance of economic growth from the Economic Complexity Index (ECI) and measures of competitiveness.

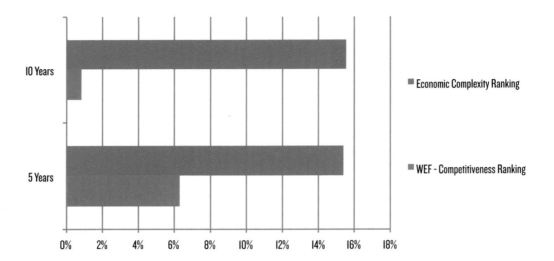

The GCR develops over 150 measures of elements that it considers important for competitiveness and then averages them. The ECI looks, instead, at the actual industries that a country can support. Both should capture information that is relevant to an economy's ability to grow. Next, we compare the two rankings to establish which captures more growth-relevant informations.

Since we only have data for the GCI rankings, and not the underlying values of the index, we do the analysis using the rankings of the Economic Complexity Index. This allows for a fairer comparison. We compare using 5- and 10-year panels starting in 1979. What we find is surprising: with 10-year panels, the complexity variables explain 15 percent more of the variance unexplained by the GCI, while the GCI explains only 1 percent of the variance not explained by the ECI. This means that **the GCI rankings are less informative about growth prospects than the complexity indicators** (see Technical Box 4.3 and Figure 4.9).

MEASURES OF FINANCIAL DEPTH

There is a broad literature discussing the links between finance and growth. How much the financial sector lends relative to the size of the economy is referred to as the 'depth' of the financial system, and there are varying interpretations of the role this plays in growth. Some have found a positive effect (King and Levine, 1993; Beck, Levine and Loayza, 2000; Demirgüç-Kunt and Levine, 2001; Levine, 2005; Aghion, Howitt, and Mayer-Foulkes, 2005), while others have found inconclusive (Easterly, 2005; Trew, 2006) or even negative links (Arcand, Berkes and Panizza, 2012).

The typical argument in favor of a connection between

finance and growth is the following: when a financial system is able to discriminate between good and bad investments, more people will be willing to trust the system with their savings. Entrepreneurs with good projects but little capital will be more able to implement their ideas, which would in turn lead to higher growth. Development of the financial sector has been seen as critical to overall development strategies in recent decades, and has received priority attention from the World Bank, the International Monetary Fund and other development agencies.

Here we contrast how strongly standard financial depth indicators and complexity indicators correlate with subsequent growth. For measures of financial depth we use the two most frequently used financial variables in this area, the ratio to GDP of domestic credit provided by the banking system, either in total or restricted to the private sector. We use both measures because, as argued by Barro and Sala-i-Martin (2004), financing greater government consumption may not contribute to growth as much as other forms of private spending.

To study the relative importance of complexity indicators and financial depth indicators on growth, we apply the same method we have been using throughout this chapter. Figure 4.10 and Technical Box 4.4 present our results. For the three decades starting in 1978, the economic complexity variables can account for 21.5 percent of the variance in 10-year growth rates that is unexplained by the financial development variables, the initial level of development, and the growth in natural resource income. This represents an increase of more than 74 percent in future growth predictability

FIGURE 4.10:

▶ Contribution to the variance of economic growth from the Economic Complexity variables (ECI and COI) and measures of financial depth.

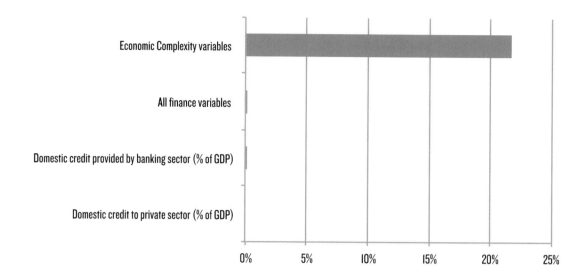

relative to the equation that excludes the complexity variables. By contrast, after controlling for the complexity indicators, the level of development and the growth in natural resource exports, the measures of financial depth are not statistically or economically significant and contribute essentially nothing to the predictability of future growth, whether taken individually or jointly. We conclude that complexity indicators hold more growth-relevant information relative to measures of financial depth. A view including financial measures does not offer more statistically significant insights than complexity taken on its own.

EXPORT SOPHISTICATION MEASURES
In 2007 Hausmann, Hwang and Rodrik (HHR) developed a measure of product and country sophistication using export data and showed that it was correlated with future growth: countries converged to the income level of their competitors in export markets. The HHR paper, by using export data and by using information on other countries to characterize a given country, inspired our approach. However the variables HHR developed are different. To measure complexity of a product, which they called PRODY, they calculate average wealth of the countries that export this product. PRODY is the weighted average of the GDP per capita of the countries that export the product, where the weights are given by the Revealed Comparative Advantage (RCA, see Technical Box 2.2) of the country in that product. They then calculate the export sophistication of a country, which they call EXPY. This variable can be interpreted as a measure of how rich a country's competitors are, meaning how rich, on average, is a synthetic combination of countries that export the same

basket of goods that a particular country exports. This is calculated as the weighted average of the PRODYs where the weights are the shares of each product in the country's export basket (see Technical Box 4.5).

The major difference between our approach and HHR is that EXPY uses information about the GDP per capita of countries that export the same products as a particular country, while ECI and COI do not use GDP per capita information. Instead, ECI and COI exploit the network of connections between a country, the products that it makes, the other countries that make them, the products that they make, etc. This is a cleaner measure, as we do not use information on GDP per capita of other countries to explain either the GDP per capita or the growth rate of a given country. But does it perform better in explaining growth?

We compared EXPY with ECI in predicting growth (see Technical Box 4.5) and conclude that, while EXPY does correlate with future growth, it explains a smaller fraction of the variance of growth, and when put together with ECI, the contribution of EXPY becomes statistically insignificant, while the effect of ECI remains fundamentally unaffected.

Overall, we are able to conclude that the Economic Complexity variables contain more information regarding the income and growth potential of countries than other commonly used indicators. Considered alongside measures of governance, human capital, competitiveness or even country and product sophistication, Economic Complexity measures are best able to predict future growth. ●

TECHNICAL BOX 4.1: GOVERNANCE AND COMPLEXITY

We compare the contribution to economic growth of the Worldwide Governance Indicators (WGIs) and economic complexity by estimating a growth regression where all of the WGIs and the Economic Complexity variables are used as explanatory variables. As controls we include the logarithm of per capita income, the increase in natural resource exports during the period and the initial share of GDP represented by natural resource exports. The contribution of each variable is estimated by taking the difference between the R^2 obtained for the regression using all variables and that obtained for

TABLE 4.1.1

| VARIABLES | Annualized growth in GDP pc | | | | | | | | |
| | 1996-2002, 2002-2008 | | | | | | | | |
	(1)	(2)	(3)	(4)	(5)	(6)	(7)	(8)	(9)
Initial income per capita, log	-0.00268***	-0.00158***	-0.00267***	-0.00270***	-0.00270***	-0.00264***	-0.00270***	-0.00266***	-0.00236***
	(0.000)	(0.000)	(0.000)	(0.000)	(0.000)	(0.000)	(0.000)	(0.000)	(0.000)
Net natural resource exports as a share of GDP	0.01618***	0.01139***	0.01616***	0.01624***	0.01598***	0.01624***	0.01633***	0.01623***	0.01568***
	(0.003)	(0.004)	(0.003)	(0.003)	(0.003)	(0.003)	(0.003)	(0.003)	(0.003)
Increase in net natural resource exports	0.00119	-0.00239	0.00114	0.00128	0.00119	0.00126	0.00125	0.00133	0.00095
- in constant dollars (as a share of initial GDP)	(0.004)	(0.004)	(0.004)	(0.004)	(0.003)	(0.003)	(0.003)	(0.003)	(0.003)
Initial Economic Complexity Index	0.00262***		0.00271***	0.00258***	0.00271***	0.00264***	0.00266***	0.00259***	0.00274***
	(0.001)		(0.001)	(0.001)	(0.001)	(0.001)	(0.001)	(0.001)	(0.001)
Initial Complexity Outlook Index	0.00076***		0.00075***	0.00076***	0.00067**	0.00078***	0.00074***	0.00075***	0.00069**
	(0.000)		(0.000)	(0.000)	(0.000)	(0.000)	(0.000)	(0.000)	(0.000)
Initial Control of Corruption	-0.00004	-0.00121		-0.00020	-0.00012	0.00014	-0.00004	-0.00006	
	(0.001)	(0.001)		(0.001)	(0.001)	(0.001)	(0.001)	(0.001)	
Initial Government Effectiveness	-0.00040	0.00096	-0.00069		-0.00026	-0.00022	-0.00044	-0.00040	
	(0.001)	(0.001)	(0.001)		(0.001)	(0.001)	(0.001)	(0.001)	
Initial Political Stability	0.00102**	0.00097**	0.00090*	0.00100**		0.00111**	0.00102**	0.00098**	
	(0.000)	(0.000)	(0.000)	(0.000)		(0.000)	(0.000)	(0.000)	
Initial Rule of Law	0.00061	0.00142	0.00083	0.00048	0.00126		0.00056	0.00055	
	(0.001)	(0.001)	(0.001)	(0.001)	(0.001)		(0.001)	(0.001)	
Initial Regulatory Quality	-0.00017	-0.00114	-0.00012	-0.00021	-0.00024	-0.00009		-0.00032	
	(0.001)	(0.001)	(0.001)	(0.001)	(0.001)	(0.001)		(0.001)	
Initial Voice and Accountability	-0.00028	0.00023	-0.00027	-0.00028	-0.00012	-0.00025	-0.00034		
	(0.001)	(0.001)	(0.001)	(0.001)	(0.001)	(0.001)	(0.001)		
Constant	0.02505***	0.01706***	0.02503***	0.02516***	0.02517***	0.02473***	0.02521***	0.02491***	0.02252***
	(0.003)	(0.003)	(0.003)	(0.003)	(0.003)	(0.003)	(0.003)	(0.003)	(0.003)
Observations	243	243	244	243	243	243	243	243	248
R^2	0.568	0.459	0.566	0.568	0.558	0.568	0.568	0.568	0.546
R^2 difference		10,9%	0,2%	0,0%	1,0%	0,0%	0,0%	0,0%	2,2%
Year FE	Yes	Yes	Yes	Yes	Yes	Yes	Yes	Yes	Yes

Robust standard errors in parentheses *** $p<0.01$, ** $p<0.05$, * $p<0.1$

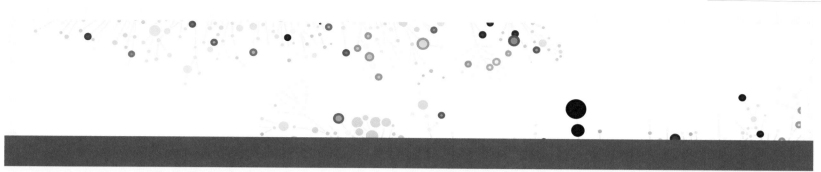

the regression where the variable was removed.

Table 4.1.1 shows the results of this procedure using two consecutive six-year periods. Table 4.1.2 shows the same procedure using one twelve-year period (1996-2008). Figure 4.1 of the main text, illustrates the differences in R² between the regression using all variables and those where individual variables were removed.

TABLE 4.1.2

VARIABLES	Annualized growth in GDP pc (12 years)								
	1996-2008								
	(1)	(2)	(3)	(4)	(5)	(6)	(7)	(8)	(9)
Initial income per capita, log	-0.00223***	-0.00160***	-0.00221***	-0.00231***	-0.00225***	-0.00216***	-0.00221***	-0.00218***	-0.00212***
	(0.000)	(0.000)	(0.000)	(0.000)	(0.000)	(0.000)	(0.000)	(0.000)	(0.000)
Net natural resource exports as a share of GDP	0.00807***	0.00647***	0.00802***	0.00811***	0.00780***	0.00810***	0.00799***	0.00798***	0.00783***
	(0.001)	(0.002)	(0.001)	(0.001)	(0.001)	(0.001)	(0.001)	(0.001)	(0.001)
Increase in net natural resource exports	0.00438***	0.00366*	0.00427***	0.00457***	0.00433***	0.00439***	0.00435***	0.00460***	0.00448***
- in constant dollars (as a share of initial GDP)	(0.001)	(0.002)	(0.001)	(0.001)	(0.001)	(0.001)	(0.001)	(0.001)	(0.001)
Initial Economic Complexity Index	0.00237***		0.00243***	0.00223***	0.00247***	0.00241***	0.00234***	0.00227***	0.00235***
	(0.000)		(0.000)	(0.000)	(0.000)	(0.000)	(0.000)	(0.000)	(0.000)
Initial Complexity Outlook Index	0.00066**		0.00062**	0.00069***	0.00058**	0.00069***	0.00067***	0.00065**	0.00065***
	(0.000)		(0.000)	(0.000)	(0.000)	(0.000)	(0.000)	(0.000)	(0.000)
Initial Control of Corruption	0.00030	-0.00074		-0.00009	0.00024	0.00046	0.00030	0.00008	
	(0.001)	(0.001)		(0.001)	(0.001)	(0.001)	(0.001)	(0.001)	
Initial Government Effectiveness	-0.00091	0.00007	-0.00091		-0.00077	-0.00075	-0.00090	-0.00073	
	(0.001)	(0.001)	(0.001)		(0.001)	(0.001)	(0.001)	(0.001)	
Initial Political Stability	0.00072**	0.00074	0.00060	0.00066*		0.00082**	0.00071**	0.00060*	
	(0.000)	(0.000)	(0.000)	(0.000)		(0.000)	(0.000)	(0.000)	
Initial Rule of Law	0.00064	0.00199**	0.00093	0.00038	0.00102		0.00067	0.00049	
	(0.001)	(0.001)	(0.001)	(0.001)	(0.001)		(0.001)	(0.001)	
Initial Regulatory Quality	0.00010	-0.00085	0.00012	0.00002	0.00002	0.00019		-0.00022	
	(0.001)	(0.001)	(0.001)	(0.001)	(0.001)	(0.001)		(0.001)	
Initial Voice and Accountability	-0.00070	-0.00016	-0.00064	-0.00061	-0.00056	-0.00065	-0.00067		
	(0.000)	(0.001)	(0.000)	(0.000)	(0.000)	(0.000)	(0.000)		
Constant	0.02068***	0.01605***	0.02055***	0.02123***	0.02073***	0.02019***	0.02057***	0.02034***	0.01969***
	(0.002)	(0.003)	(0.002)	(0.002)	(0.002)	(0.002)	(0.002)	(0.002)	(0.002)
Observations	119	119	120	119	119	119	119	119	122
R²	0.618	0.435	0.613	0.613	0.609	0.616	0.618	0.610	0.588
R² difference		18,3%	0,5%	0,5%	0,9%	0,2%	0,0%	0,8%	3,0%

Robust standard errors in parentheses *** p<0.01, ** p<0.05, * p<0.1

►

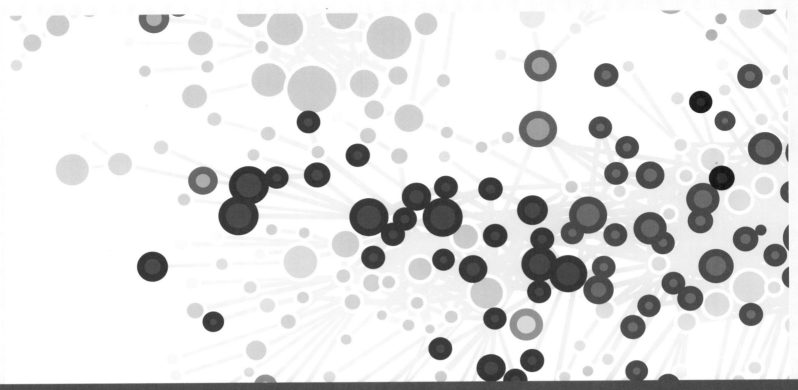

TECHNICAL BOX 4.2: EDUCATION, COGNITIVE ABILITY AND ECONOMIC COMPLEXITY

We compare the contribution to income of education, cognitive ability and economic complexity by regressing income against years of schooling, cognitive ability and the Economic Complexity Index. The contribution to income of each variable is estimated by taking the difference between the R^2 obtained for the regression using all variables and that obtained for a regression where the variable in question was removed.

Table 4.2.1 shows the results of this procedure for the year 2000, when cognitive ability data is available. Figure 4.7 in the main text summarizes the results.

We compare the contribution to growth of education and economic complexity variables by regressing growth against years of schooling secondary school enrollment, tertiary school enrollment, the Economic Complexity Index and the Complexity Outlook Index. As additional controls we include the change in natural resource exports during the period, the logarithm of per capita income and year fixed effects. The contribution of each variable to growth is estimated by taking the difference between the R^2 obtained for a regression using all variables and one obtained for a regression where the variable in question was removed.

Table 4.2.2 shows the results of this procedure for ten year panels starting in 1978, 1988 and 1998. Figure 4.8 in the main text summarize the results.

TABLE 4.2.1

VARIABLES	Income per capita, log – Year 2000				
	(1)	(2)	(3)	(4)	(5)
Economic Complexity Index	1.013***		1.085***	1.024***	1.245***
	(0.182)		(0.194)	(0.143)	(0.114)
Years of schooling	0.148*	0.209**		0.151**	
	(0.081)	(0.086)		(0.073)	
Cognitive ability	0.027	0.876***	0.287		
	(0.279)	(0.290)	(0.275)		
Constant	6.585***	2.884***	6.645***	6.675***	7.844***
	(1.043)	(0.997)	(1.114)	(0.606)	(0.167)
Observations	60	60	60	60	60
R^2	0.598	0.432	0.569	0.598	0.561
Difference in R^2		0.17	0.03	0.00	0.04

Robust standard errors in parentheses *** p<0.01, ** p<0.05, * p<0.1

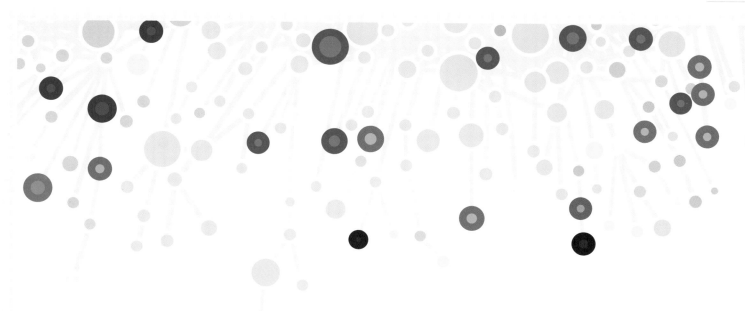

TABLE 4.2.2

VARIABLES	Annualized growth in GDP pc (by decade)					
	(1978-1988, 1988-1998, 1998-2008)					
	(1)	(2)	(3)	(4)	(5)	(6)
Initial Income per capita, log	-0.012***	-0.006***	-0.011***	-0.012***	-0.012***	-0.010***
	(0.002)	(0.001)	(0.001)	(0.002)	(0.002)	(0.001)
Increase in natural resource exports	0.068***	0.048*	0.068***	0.069***	0.068***	0.075***
- in constant dollars (as a share of initial GDP)	(0.025)	(0.027)	(0.026)	(0.025)	(0.025)	(0.026)
Initial Economic Complexity Index	0.011***		0.012***	0.011***	0.011***	0.013***
	(0.002)		(0.002)	(0.002)	(0.002)	(0.002)
Initial Complexity Outlook Index	0.006***		0.007***	0.006***	0.006***	0.007***
	(0.002)		(0.002)	(0.002)	(0.002)	(0.002)
Years of schooling (standardized)	0.008*	0.013***		0.009***	0.004	
	(0.004)	(0.004)		(0.002)	(0.003)	
Secondary school enrollment (standardized)	0.001	0.002	0.005***		0.003	
	(0.003)	(0.003)	(0.002)		(0.003)	
Tertiary school enrollment (standardized)	-0.004*	-0.004*	-0.001	-0.004**		
	(0.002)	(0.002)	(0.001)	(0.002)		
Constant	0.117***	0.074***	0.111***	0.118***	0.119***	0.105***
	(0.013)	(0.012)	(0.012)	(0.013)	(0.013)	(0.011)
Observations	275	275	275	275	275	275
R^2	0.412	0.264	0.402	0.412	0.405	0.378
Year FE	Yes	Yes	Yes	Yes	Yes	Yes
Difference in R^2		0.15	0.01	0.00	0.01	0.03

Robust standard errors in parentheses *** p<0.01, ** p<0.05, * p<0.1

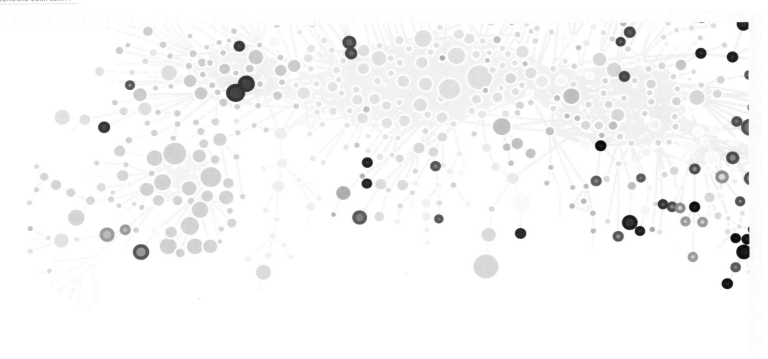

TECHNICAL BOX 4.3: GLOBAL COMPETITIVENESS INDEX AND GROWTH

Here we compare the contribution of the Global Competitiveness Index (GCI) and the ECI to economic growth. We use the ranking of countries in the GCI and the ranking of countries in ECI to predict growth using 5 and 10 year panels. As controls, we use the increase in natural resource exports during the period as well as the logarithm of the initial GDP per capita and year fixed effects. We estimate the contribution of the GCI and ECI to growth by taking the difference between the R^2 obtained for the equation in which they were both included and that in which one or the other is missing.

Table 4.3.1 shows that eliminating the rank of the ECI from the regression results in a much larger loss of explanatory power than removing the rank of GCI. This is true for both 5 and 10 year panels. Figure 4.9 on the main text illustrates these results.

TABLE 4.3.1

	Annualized growth in GDP pc (by decade)					
	5 year panels			10 year panels		
VARIABLES	(1)	(2)	(3)	(4)	(5)	(6)
Ranking of GCI	-0.00054**	-0.00032		-0.00025	-0.00005	
	(0.000)	(0.000)		(0.000)	(0.000)	
Ranking of ECI	-0.00064***		-0.00052***	-0.00057***		-0.00052***
	(0.000)		(0.000)	0		(0.000)
Initial income per capita, logs	-0.01562***	-0.00490***	-0.01152***	-0.01388***	-0.00463**	-0.01183***
	(0.004)	(0.002)	(0.003)	(0.004)	(0.002)	(0.003)
Increase in natural resource exports	0.03144	-0.03117	0.01553	0.07837*	0.02263	0.07271*
- in constant dollars (as a share of initial GDP)	(0.058)	(0.058)	(0.059)	(0.042)	(0.040)	(0.039)
Constant	0.19376***	0.07390***	0.13923***	0.17354***	0.06911***	0.14689***
	(0.046)	(0.017)	(0.033)	(0.041)	(0.023)	(0.030)
Observations	101	101	101	81	81	81
Adjusted R^2	0.223	0.069	0.160	0.243	0.088	0.235
Year FE	Yes	Yes	Yes	Yes	Yes	Yes
Difference in R^2		0,154	0,063		0,155	0,008

Robust standard errors in parentheses *** $p<0.01$, ** $p<0.05$, * $p<0.1$

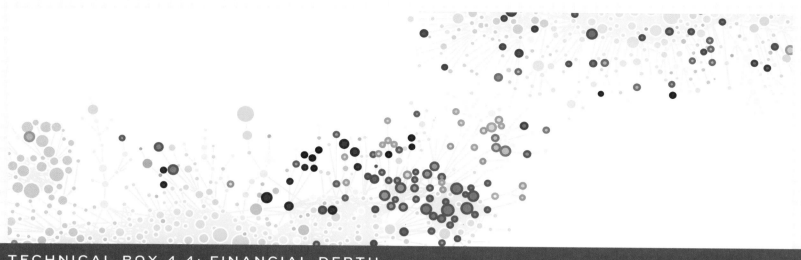

TECHNICAL BOX 4.4: FINANCIAL DEPTH

In this Technical Box we explore the impact of financial development on growth after accounting for complexity indicators and vice versa. We use data for the three 10-year periods since 1978. We measure financial depth through two variables. First, we consider the ratio to GDP of total domestic credit provided by the banking system. Second, we consider the ratio to GDP of credit to the private sector provided by the banking system. We measure these variables at the start of each 10-year period. We also control for the initial level of GDP per capita and the growth of the value of natural resource exports during the period. Table 4.4.1 shows our results. The first column includes all the variables under consideration. In this regression the complexity variables remain highly significant, both economically and statistically, while the financial variables have essentially no relationship with growth. The overall R^2 of the equation is 0.504. To estimate the marginal contribution of financial depth variables after controlling for complexity variables, we compare column 1 with columns 2, 3 and 4, which sequentially eliminate one, the other, and then both financial variables. In all these equations, the R^2 as well as the coefficients on the complexity variables are essentially unaffected, while estimated coefficients on the remaining financial variables are essentially zero. To estimate the marginal impact of the complexity variables we compare column 1 with column 5, which excludes both complexity variables. Here the R^2 declines from 0.504 to 0.215 – a 74 percent decline – while the coefficients on the financial variables remain essentially equal to zero.

We conclude that the complexity indicators are much more strongly informative of subsequent growth than the financial depth indicators, whether considered individually or in group.

TABLE 4.4.1

VARIABLES	Annualized growth in GDP pc (by decade)				
	(1978-1988, 1988-1998, 1998-2008)				
	(1)	(2)	(3)	(4)	(5)
Initial income per capita, log	-0.01053***	-0.00166	-0.01043***	-0.01026***	-0.01066***
	(0.002)	(0.002)	(0.002)	(0.002)	(0.002)
Increase in natural resource exports - in constant dollars (as a share of initial GDP)	0.07468***	0.06949***	0.07474***	0.07555***	0.07612***
	(0.009)	(0.010)	(0.009)	(0.009)	(0.009)
Initial Economic Complexity Index	0.01607***		0.01611***	0.01572***	0.01504***
	(0.002)		(0.002)	(0.002)	(0.002)
Initial Complexity Outlook Index	0.00650***		0.00652***	0.00661***	0.00665***
	(0.002)		(0.002)	(0.002)	(0.002)
Domestic credit to private sector (% of GDP)	0.00002	0.00010		-0.00005	
	(0.000)	(0.000)		(0.000)	
Domestic credit provided by banking sector (% of GDP)	-0.00006	-0.00001	-0.00005		
	(0.000)	(0.000)	(0.000)		
Constant	0.11082***	0.03633**	0.11019***	0.10780***	0.10874***
	(0.014)	(0.014)	(0.013)	(0.013)	(0.012)
Observations	277	277	277	277	277
Adjusted R^2	0.504	0.287	0.505	0.503	0.503
Year FE	Yes	Yes	Yes	Yes	Yes
R^2 difference		0,217	0	0,001	0,001

Standard errors clustered by country are shown in parentheses. *** p<0.01, ** p<0.05, * p<0.1

▶

TECHNICAL BOX 4.5: EXPY AND ECI

In an influential paper, Hausmann, Hwang and Rodrik (HHR) showed that what a country exports – and not just how much a country exports – affects its income level. To characterize the degree of sophistication of a product, HHR calculated the average wealth of the countries that make that product and called it PRODY. To characterize the degree of sophistication of a country's exports, they calculated the average income of a country's competitors and called it EXPY. More precisely, product sophistication, *PRODY*, was obtained by taking a weighted average of the per-capita GDPs of the countries exporting the product. The weights are given by the revealed comparative advantage of each country in that product to distinguish between the successful and unsuccessful exporters of the product. Formally, *PRODY* of a product *p* is defined as:

$$\widehat{PRODY}_{\tilde{c}p} = \sum_{c \neq \tilde{c}} \frac{X_{cp}/\sum_p X_{cp}}{\sum_{c' \neq \tilde{c}} X_{c'p}/\sum_p X_{c'p}} GDPpc_c$$

where X_{cp} is the export of country c of product p. Here we do not include the country of interest in the calculation of the PRODY of its exports in order to avoid circularity. From this product level variable, HHR calculate a country-level measure EXPY, using a weighted average of the *PRODY's* of a country's exports where the weights are the export shares of the country in the product:

$$EXPY_{\tilde{c}} = \sum_p \frac{X_{\tilde{c}p}}{\sum_{p'} X_{\tilde{c}p'}} \widehat{PRODY}_{\tilde{c}p}$$

HHR showed that these variables predict GDP growth of countries. Figure 4.5.I shows that ECI and EXPY are strongly correlated, but they differ especially for countries with low ECI and GDPpc. When we compare ECI to EXPY in terms of their power to the predict future, both variables are individually predictive of growth (see Table 4.5.I columns 2 and 3, respectively). However, ECI is more powerful in explaining the variance of growth. When both EXPY and ECI are put together (column 4), EXPY becomes statistically insignificant while ECI remains essentially unaffected. This exercise shows that ECI is more informative of future growth than EXPY.

FIGURE 4.5.I:

▶ Relation between ECI and EXPY for year 2010 (R² =50%)

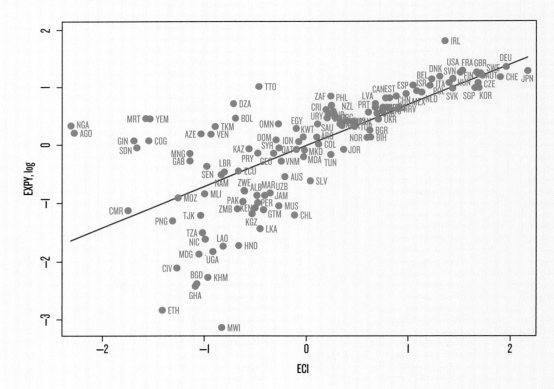

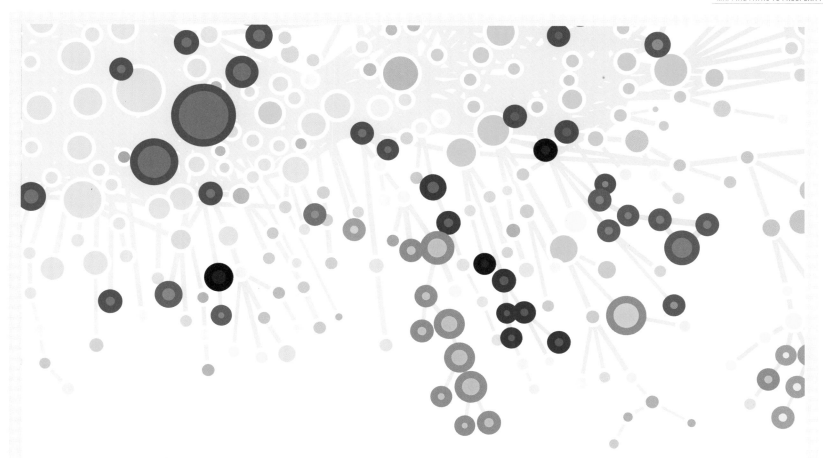

TABLE 4.5.1

| VARIABLES | Real GDP growth per capita by decade | | | |
	(1978-1988, 1988-1998, 1998-2008)			
	(1)	(2)	(3)	(4)
Initial income per capita, log	-0.001	-0.011***	-0.007***	-0.011***
	(0.001)	(0.001)	(0.001)	(0.001)
Increase in natural resource exports - in constant dollars (as a share of initial GDP)	0.059***	0.065***	0.056***	0.064***
	(0.012)	(0.009)	(0.012)	(0.009)
Initial Economic Complexity Index		0.019***		0.017***
		(0.002)		(0.002)
Initial EXPY, log			0.011***	0.002
			(0.002)	(0.002)
Constant	0.023***	0.097***	0.068***	0.100***
	(0.007)	(0.010)	(0.011)	(0.011)
Observations	301	301	301	301
R^2	0.291	0.472	0.367	0.474
Year FE	Yes	Yes	Yes	Yes

Standard errors clustered by country are shown in parentheses. *** $p<0.01$, ** $p<0.05$, * $p<0.1$

SECTION 5
How Does *Economic Complexity* Evolve?

Economic complexity seems to matter: it affects a country's level of income per capita and drives its future growth. It also provides a view of a country that is distinct from the information captured by measures of governance, human capital, competitiveness, financial depth and export sophistication. But how does complexity evolve? How do societies increase the amount of productive knowledge they have? How do they become more complex? What limits the speed of this process? And why does it happen in some places but not in others?

In our interpretation, the complexity of a country's economy is a reflection of the amount of productive knowledge it contains. This knowledge is costly to acquire and transfer, and is modularized into chunks we call capabilities. Capabilities are difficult to accumulate because doing so encounters a complicated chicken and egg problem. On the one hand, countries cannot create products that require capabilities they do not have. On the other hand, there are scant incentives to accumulate capabilities in places where the industries that demand them do not exist. This is particularly true when the missing capabilities required by a potential new industry are numerous. In this case, supplying any single missing capability will not be enough to launch the new industry. Using the Scrabble analogy, if the goal is to write a word for which you lack several letters, getting one of the many missing letters will not allow you to write the word.

Consider the following example. A country that does not export fresh produce probably does not have a cold-storage logistics chain, an expedited green lane at the customs service, or a globally recognized food safety certification system. All these things are needed to export produce. An investor planning to invest in cold-chain logistics would worry about how its clients would certify their produce and whether their shipments could go through customs inspection without undue delay. If these essential processes are not in place, demand for a cold-storage logistics chain would be nil, making the investment unwise.

It follows then that new capabilities will be more easily accumulated if they can be combined with others that already exist. This reduces the need to coordinate the accumulation of several new capabilities simultaneously. In our example, if the country already had a certification mechanism and a green lane at the customs service, it would be easier to convince an investor to develop a cold chain, by arguing that with the addition of this new capability, the fresh produce export industry would take off, and his services would be demanded.

For this reason, countries are more likely to move into products that can make use of capabilities that the country already has. These capabilities are available, however, because they are being used by some other industry. This implies that a country will diversify by moving from the industries that already exist to others that require a similar set of capabilities. Arguably, it is easier to move from shirts to blouses than it is to move from shirts to jet engines. This is because, in terms of embedded knowledge, shirts are more similar to blouses than they are to jet engines. A testable implication of this logic is that countries will move into products that are similar, in terms of the capabilities they require, to the ones they already make.

▶

FIGURE 5.1:

▶ The product space.

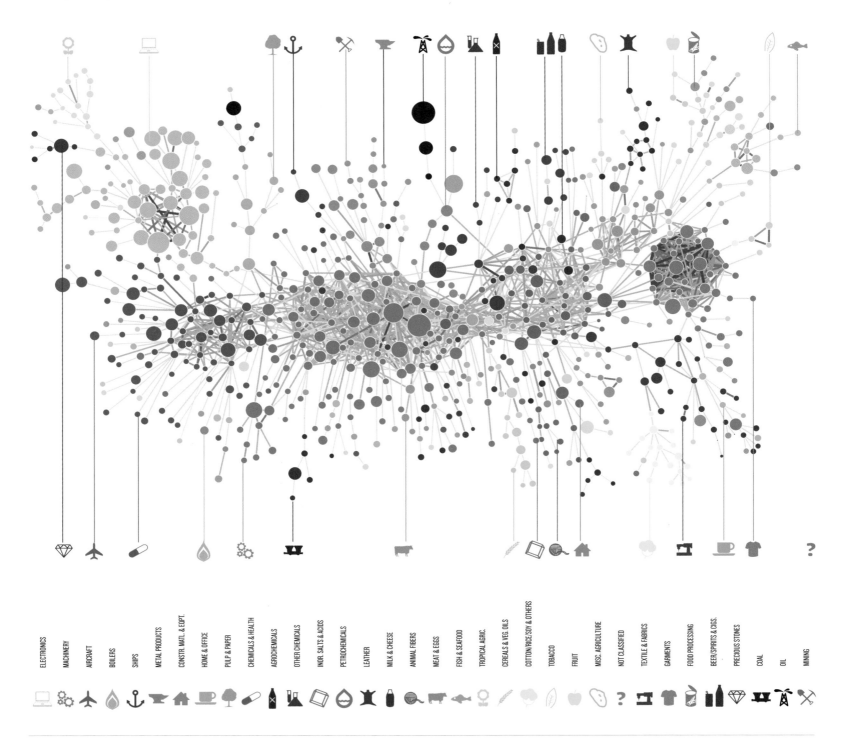

ELECTRONICS · MACHINERY · AIRCRAFT · BOILERS · SHIPS · METAL PRODUCTS · CONSTR. MATL. & EQPT. · HOME & OFFICE · PULP & PAPER · CHEMICALS & HEALTH · AGROCHEMICALS · OTHER CHEMICALS · INOR. SALTS & ACIDS · PETROCHEMICALS · LEATHER · MILK & CHEESE · ANIMAL FIBERS · MEAT & EGGS · FISH & SEAFOOD · TROPICAL AGRIC. · CEREALS & VEG. OILS · COTTON/RICE/SOY & OTHERS · TOBACCO · FRUIT · MISC. AGRICULTURE · NOT CLASSIFIED · TEXTILE & FABRICS · GARMENTS · FOOD PROCESSING · BEER/SPIRITS & CIGS. · PRECIOUS STONES · COAL · OIL · MINING

Measuring the similarity in the capability requirements of different products is not simple. In order to identify the precise technical and institutional requirements of each product, we would have to collect a mindboggling volume of information. Instead, we measure similarity using a simple trick. If shirts require knowledge that is similar to that required by blouses, but different from that required by jet engines, then the probability that a country exporting shirts will also export blouses will be higher than the probability that it will also export jet engines. So the probability that a pair of products is co-exported carries information about how similar these products are. We use this idea to measure the proximity between all pairs of products in our dataset (see Technical Box 5.1 on Measuring Proximity). The collection of all proximities is a network connecting pairs of products that are significantly likely to be co-exported by many countries. This network is what we call the **product space.** We use the product space to study the productive structure of countries.

We care about the structure of the product space because it affects how easily countries can increase their complexity. A tightly connected product space implies that neighboring

FIGURE 5.2:

▶ The product space revisited. The same as Figure 5.1 but with node sizes proportional to the Product Complexity Index (PCI).

products differ in few of their requisite capabilities. Countries would find it easier to add products to their basket by accumulating the few missing capabilities. They can repeat this process many times as they add more products and capabilities to their basket. Conversely, a sparsely connected product space tells us that neighboring product have less in common, implying that they use different capabilities. Adding a neighboring product would require the simultaneous acquisition of several missing capabilities, implying a more challenging "chicken and egg" problem, and making the growth of complexity more difficult.

Once again, a metaphor may help to clarify these ideas. Imagine that the product space is a forest, where every product is a tree. Trees that require similar capabilities are near each other, while distant trees require very different capabilities. If countries are a collection of firms that make different products, we can think of firms as monkeys that live on trees, meaning that they exploit certain products because they have the requisite capabilities. Countries differ in the number and location of the monkeys they have in this common forest. The development process, which implies essentially increasing product diversity and complexity, is akin to monkeys populating the forest, occupying more

trees, and moving especially into the more complex products or fruitier trees.

Monkeys would prefer to make short jumps to nearby trees because this would minimize the chicken and egg problem of having to accumulate several missing capabilities at once. Furthermore, if trees are densely packed together, it will be relatively easy for monkeys to move from tree to tree and cover a large area in several hops. But if trees are far apart, monkeys may be stuck in their current trees, since the next potential trees are too many capabilities away to solve the "chicken and egg" problem. If the product space is heterogeneous, there may be some patches of highly related products, where adding capabilities and expanding into new products would be easier, and other patches of more loosely connected products that make the process of capability accumulation and diversification harder.

What is the shape of the product space we live in? Is it a world in which the forest is dense or sparse? Figure 5.1 shows a visualization of the product space constructed using international trade data for the years 2006-2008. Here, nodes represent products and their size is proportional to total world trade in that good. Links connect products with a high probability of being co-exported (see Technical Box 5.2).

▶

FIGURE 5.3:

▶ Community characteristics. Average complexity of the products in each community as a function of the community's connectedness. Bubble size is proportional to the community's participation in world trade.

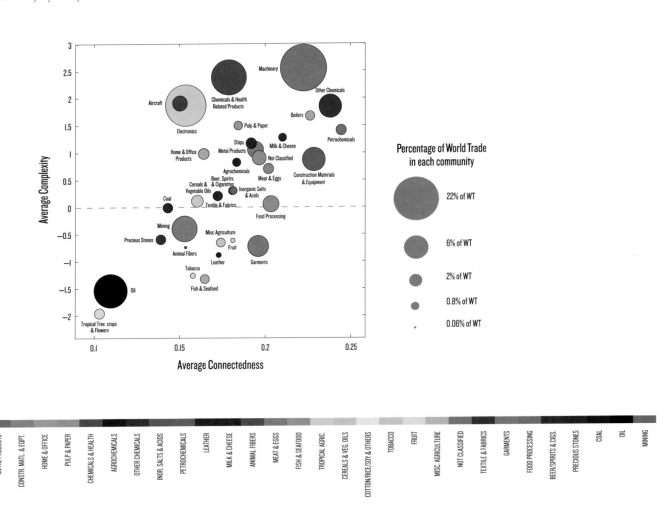

The visualization reveals that the product space is highly heterogeneous. Some sections of it are composed of densely connected groups of products whereas others tend to be more peripheral and sparse.

The product space shows that many goods group naturally into highly connected communities. This suggests that products in these communities use a similar set of capabilities. We can identify communities because the products that belong to them are more closely connected to each other than to products outside of the community. Here, we use network science algorithms to discover the communities of products that are hidden in the data (see Technical Box 5.3 for a discussion of the method). We use these communities to make the discussion of products more tractable. The nearly 800 products in the SITC4 classification were grouped into 34 communities, which we identify by color in our visualization of the product space (Figure 5.1). The names, complexity, market size and other characteristics of the communities appear in Table 5.1.

Figure 5.2 shows a visualization of the product space that is similar to Figure 5.1, but where the size of the nodes is proportional to the complexity of products they represent,

as estimated by the Product Complexity Index (PCI). It shows that communities tend to have similar levels of complexity. Products in the Machinery, Electronics and Chemical communities tend to be much more complex than those in the Garments cluster or in peripheral communities such as Oil or Tropical Agriculture.

Figure 5.3 shows some of the network characteristics of these communities. Connectedness is a measure of how centrally located a community is in the product space. It is the average proximity of a community's products to all other products, where proximity is the measure of distance between two products used to construct the product space. The figure shows the average connectedness of the products in each community and their average complexity estimated by the PCI. The figure reveals a positive relationship between how centrally located the communities are in the product space and how complex their products are. Poorly connected communities such as petroleum, cotton, rice and soybeans tend to be low in complexity. Machinery, by contrast, is very complex and that part of the product space is highly connected. Communities of products such as garments, textiles and food processing are, on the

TABLE 5.1:

CHARACTERISTICS OF PRODUCT COMMUNITIES

Community Name	Average PCI	Number of Products	World Trade	World Share	Top 3 Countries by Export Volume	Top 3 Countries by Number of Products (RCA>1)
Machinery	2.54	125	4.4T	20.29%	DEU, USA, JPN	DEU, ITA, AUT
Electronics	2.25	52	3.6T	16.71%	CHN, HKG, USA	CHN, HKG, MYS
Oil	-2.08	4	2.3T	10.49%	SAU, RUS, NOR	EGY, KAZ, DZA
Chemicals & Health	2.52	64	1.6T	7.47%	USA, DEU, BEL	USA, BEL, DEU
Other Chemicals	1.67	24	1.2T	5.49%	DEU, USA, FRA	DEU, ITA, ESP
Construction Materials & Equipment	0.77	44	1.1T	5.23%	CHN, DEU, ITA	CZE, POL, SVN
Mining	-0.59	48	1.1T	5.01%	AUS, USA, CHL	CAN, AUS, KAZ
Garments	-0.43	42	1.1T	4.63%	CHN, HKG, ITA	CHN, VNM, TUN
Food Processing	-0.07	26	603B	2.74%	DEU, ITA, USA	SRB, ESP, BEL
Metal Products	0.76	17	496B	2.26%	JPN, DEU, KOR	ZAF, UKR, SVK
Aircraft	1.48	10	440B	2.00%	FRA, DEU, GBR	CAN, GBR, FRA
Not Classified	0.93	36	426B	1.94%	USA, CHN, DEU	CHN, FRA, GBR
Cereals & Vegetable Oils	-0.34	21	295B	1.34%	USA, BRA, ARG	PRY, MDA, ARG
Home & Office	1.16	23	250B	1.14%	CHN, CHE, USA	CHN, PAN, PRT
Meat & Eggs	0.64	23	242B	1.10%	USA, BRA, DEU	FRA, BEL, POL
Ships	0.83	8	232B	1.05%	KOR, CHN, JPN	ROU, POL, HRV
Petrochemicals	1.22	5	220B	1.00%	DEU, USA, BEL	PRT, BEL, FRA
Boilers	1.56	14	193B	0.88%	CHN, DEU, JPN	CHN, TUR, KOR
Fish & Seafood	-1.23	11	191B	0.87%	CHN, NOR, THA	CHL, NAM, SYC
Textile & Fabrics	0.18	32	189B	0.86%	CHN, ITA, HKG	CHN, TUR, IND
Tropical Agriculture	-1.95	16	190B	0.86%	IDN, NLD, MYS	IDN, CIV, CRI
Coal	0.21	6	183B	0.83%	AUS, IDN, RUS	CZE, COL, RUS
Misc Agriculture	-0.79	22	170B	0.78%	BRA, DEU, FRA	ESP, TZA, NIC
Precious Stones	0.02	4	170B	0.77%	IND, ISR, BEL	GBR, LBN, LKA
Pulp & Paper	1.77	11	148B	0.67%	USA, CAN, SWE	SWE, FIN, CAN
Agrochemicals	0.40	13	141B	0.64%	DEU, USA, CAN	BEL, JOR, DEU
Milk & Cheese	1.14	7	134B	0.61%	DEU, FRA, NLD	NLD, BLR, LTU
Beer, Spirits & Cigarettes	0.07	6	124B	0.57%	GBR, NLD, DEU	JAM, BEL, NLD
Inorganic Salts & Acids	-0.22	10	117B	0.53%	USA, CHN, DEU	ISR, JOR, USA
Cotton, Rice, Soy & Others	-2.25	18	96B	0.44%	USA, IND, THA	TZA, MOZ, GRC
Tobacco	-1.46	6	64B	0.29%	DEU, NLD, BRA	PHL, GRC, SEN
Leather	-0.85	14	53B	0.24%	ITA, USA, HKG	ALB, SOM, ESP
Fruit	-0.58	4	45B	0.21%	ESP, USA, CHL	NLD, LBN, LTU
Animal Fibers	-0.85	7	12B	0.06%	AUS, CHN, ITA	URY, NZL, ZAF

▶

FIGURE 5.4:

▶   Complexity Outlook as a function of the Economic Complexity Index and GDP per capita.

FIGURE 5.4a:

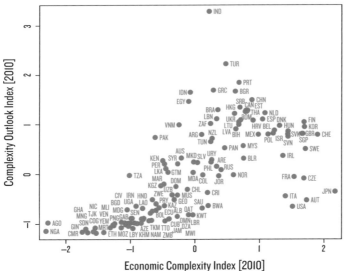

FIGURE 5.4b:

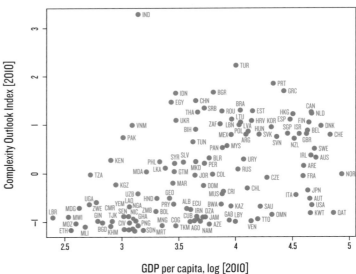

other hand, in an intermediate position, being connected to many products but not very sophisticated. Electronics and Health-Related Chemicals are very complex but not as connected as machinery. This suggests they use specific capabilities relevant within their communities but not outside of them.

We have shown in previous research (Hausmann and Klinger, 2006, 2007 and Hidalgo et al 2007) that the probability that a country will make a new product is strongly related to how close that product is to other products the country already makes. So the location of a country in the product space captures information regarding both the productive knowledge that it possesses and the capacity to expand that knowledge by moving into other nearby products. The ability of countries to diversify and to move into more complex products is crucially dependent on their initial location in the product space.

The product space gives us a glimpse of the embedded knowledge countries have by highlighting the productive capabilities they posses and the opportunities these imply. We can evaluate a country's overall position in the product space by calculating how far it is to alternative products and how complex these products are. We call this measure the **Complexity Outlook Index** and it can be thought of as the value of the option to move into more and to more complex products, given how far they are from a country's current position in the product space (see Technical Box 5.4).

Figure 5.4a compares Complexity Outlook with the Economic Complexity Index. Countries with low levels of complexity tend to have few opportunities available. This is because the products they make tend to have few neighbors. Complex economies tend to have few remaining

opportunities because they already occupy a large portion of the better part of the product space. Countries with an intermediate level of complexity, on the other hand, differ greatly in their Complexity Outlook. Some countries, like Saudi Arabia, Jamaica and Chile, are located in sparse parts of the product space that imply few easy diversification opportunities. Others, like India, Greece, Turkey, Brazil and Indonesia are located in parts of the product space where opportunities are plentiful. Figure 5.4b plots the Complexity Outlook Index against the income per capita of countries. It shows that countries with similar incomes face dramatically different opportunities.

Does the position of a country in the product space affect how fast its complexity will increase? Said differently, does the Complexity Outlook Index (COI) predict how the Economic Complexity Index (ECI) will evolve? Technical Box 5.5 answers this question in the affirmative. It shows that for both 5- and 10-year horizons, COI has a very strong impact on the growth of ECI. The estimated effects are large and consistent at both horizons.

Finally, we illustrate how countries move through the product space by looking at Ghana, Poland, Thailand and Turkey (Figure 5.5). Here, highlighted nodes are used to indicate the products that each of these countries was exporting with comparative advantage at each point in time. In all cases we see that new industries –new black squares– tend to lie close to the industries already present in these countries. The productive transformation undergone by Poland, Thailand and Turkey, however, look striking compared to that of Ghana. Thailand and Turkey, in particular, moved from mostly agricultural societies to manufacturing powerhouses during the 1975-2010 period. Poland, also moved into the center of

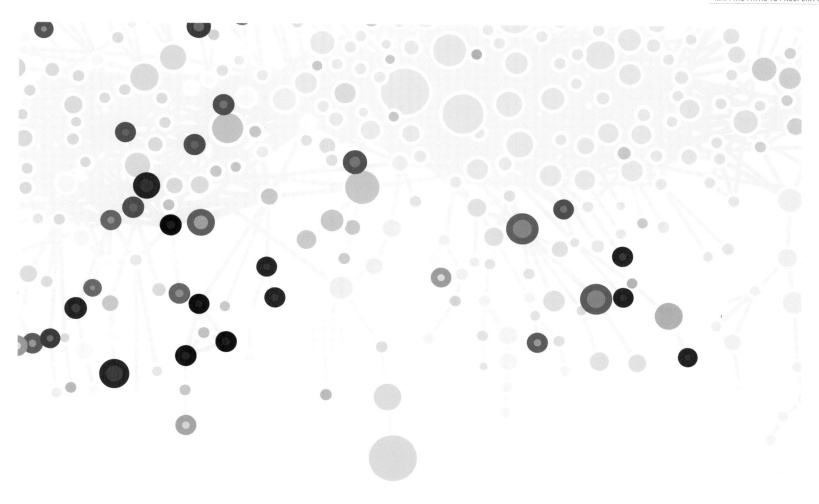

the product space during the last two decades, becoming a manufacturer of most products in both the Home and Office and the Processed Foods community and significantly increasing its participation in the production of machinery. These transformations imply an increase in embedded knowledge that is reflected in our Economic Complexity Index. Ultimately, it is these transformations that underpinned the impressive growth performance of these countries.

We started this section asking several questions: How does complexity evolve? And how do societies increase the total amount of productive knowledge embedded in them? Here we have shown that countries expand their productive knowledge by moving into nearby goods. This increases the likelihood that the effort to accumulate any additional capability will be successful, as the complementary capabilities needed to make a new product are more likely to be present in the production of the nearby goods.

What limits the speed of this process? Since capabilities are useful only when combined with others, the accumulation of capabilities is slowed down by the chicken and egg problem. New products may require capabilities that do not exist precisely because the other products that use them are not present. Moreover, since capabilities are chunks of tacit knowledge, accumulating them is difficult even when there is demand for them, because the country does not have any exemplars to copy.

Most importantly, we must ask why this process of development occurs in some places but not in others. There are many possible explanations, but our approach adds a new answer to the mix by showing that a country's position in the product space determines its opportunities to expand its productive knowledge and increase its level of economic complexity. But since the product space is highly heterogeneous, it confronts countries with radically different opportunities. Ultimately, development is the expansion of the total amount of productive knowledge that is embedded in a society , but the process by which this knowledge is accumulated has a structure that, thanks to the product space, we are only now starting to understand. •

►

FIGURE 5.5:

▶ The evolution of Ghana, Poland, Thailand and Turkey in the product space: 1975, 1990 and 2010. Highlighted nodes indicate the products in which these countries had RCA>1.

1975

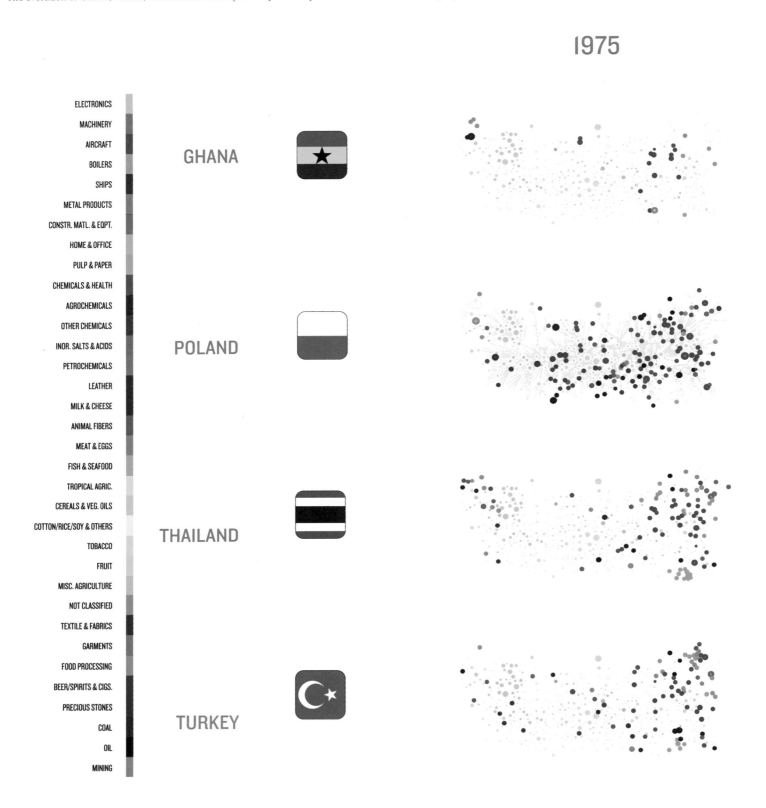

1990   2010

TECHNICAL BOX 5.1: MEASURING PROXIMITY

Making products requires chunks of embedded knowledge, which we call capabilities. The capabilities needed to produce one good may or may not be useful in the production of other goods. Since we do not observe capabilities directly, we create a measure that infers the similarity between the capabilities required by a pair of goods by looking at the probability that they are co-exported. To quantify this similarity we assume that if two goods share most of the requisite capabilities, the countries that export one will also export the other. By the same token, goods that do not share many capabilities are less likely to be co-exported.

Our measure is based on the conditional probability that a country that exports product p will also export product p' (Figure 5.1.1). Since conditional probabilities are not symmetric we take the minimum of the probability of exporting product p, given p' and the reverse, to make the measure symmetric

and more stringent. For instance, suppose that, 17 countries export wine, 24 export grapes and 11 export both, all with RCA>1. Then, the proximity between wine and grapes is 11/24=0.46. Note that we divide by 24 instead of 17 to reduce the likelihood that the relationship is spurious. Formally, for a pair of goods p and p' we define proximity as:

$$\varphi_{p,p'} = \frac{\sum_c M_{cp} M_{cp'}}{\max{(k_{p,0} k_{p',0})}}$$

Where $M_{cp} = 1$ if country c exports product p with RCA>1 and 0 otherwise. $k_{p,0}$ is the ubiquity of product p.

FIGURE 5.1.1:

▶ An illustration of the method used to calculate proximity.

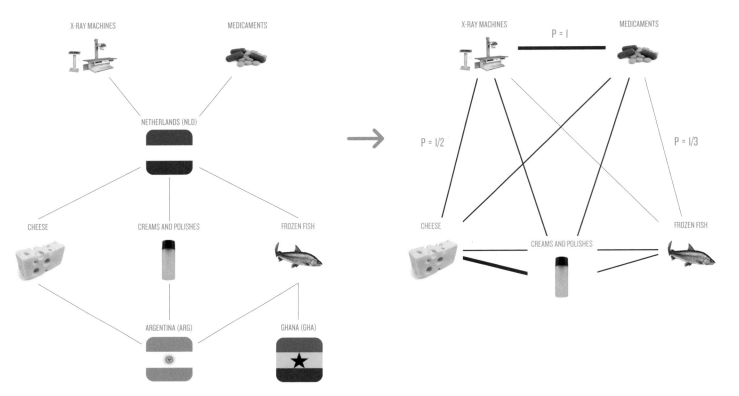

TECHNICAL BOX 5.2: VISUALIZING THE PRODUCT SPACE

To visualize the product space we use some simple design criteria. First, we want the visualization of the product space to be a connected network. By this, we mean avoiding islands of isolated products. The second criterion is that we want the network visualization to be relatively sparse. Trying to visualize too many links can create unnecessary visual complexity where the most relevant connections will be occluded. This is achieved by creating a visualization in which the average number of links per node is not larger than 5 and results in a representation that can summarize the structure of the product space using the strongest 1% of the links.

To make sure the visualization of the product space is connected, we calculate the maximum spanning tree (MST) of the proximity matrix. MST is the set of links that connects all the nodes in the network using a minimum number of connections and the maximum possible sum of proximities. We calculated the MST using Kruskal's algorithm. Basically the algorithm sorts the values of the proximity matrix in descending order and then includes links in the MST if and

only if they connect an isolated product. By definition, the MST includes all products, but the number of links is the minimum possible.

The second step is to add the strongest connections that were not selected for the MST. In this visualization we included the first 1,006 connections satisfying our criterion. By definition a spanning tree for 774 nodes contains 773 edges. With the additional 1,006 connections we end up with 1,779 edges and an average degree of nearly 4.6.

After selecting the links using the above mentioned criteria we build a visualization using a force-directed layout algorithm. In this algorithm nodes repel each other, just like electric charges, while edges act as spring trying to bring connected nodes together. This helps to create a visualization in which densely connected sets of nodes are put together while nodes that are not connected are pushed apart.

Finally, we manually clean up the layout to minimize edge crossings and provide the most clearly representation possible.

TECHNICAL BOX 5.3: IDENTIFYING PRODUCT COMMUNITIES

In network science, groups of highly interconnected nodes are known as communities. In the product space, communities represent groups of products that are likely to require many of the same capabilities.

We assign products to communities using the algorithm introduced by Rosvall and Bergstrom (2008). This algorithm finds communities using a two step process. First, it explores the network using a collection of random walkers. The intuition behind this first step is that nodes belonging to the same community are more likely to lie close by in the sequence of nodes visited by a random walker. For instance, take photographic film, photographic chemicals and silicones. These are three products that are interconnected and belong to a densely connected region of the product space. Hence, the random walker is much more likely to go through the sequences {silicones, photographic chemicals, photographic film} or {photographic film, silicones, photographic chemicals} than {photographic film, grapes, blouses}. The emergence of these sequences indicates that photographic film, photographic chemicals and silicones, probably belong to the same community. After several iterations of random walks have been recorded, the algorithm compresses these sequences by looking for ways to rename nodes so as to minimize the amount of space required to store the relevant information about these sequences. For instance, if silicones, photographic films, and photographic chemicals are grouped into a community called photographic materials this would allow compressing the sequence by replacing each time it appears by a reference to that community. The algorithm looks for a compression that preserves as much information as possible. This avoids the trivial solution in which all products are assigned to the same community.

The communities determined through this algorithm were manually named and merged into 34 communities (see Table 5.1 for details).

We compare the ability of these communities to summarize the structure of the product space by introducing a measure of *community quality*. This is the ratio between the average proximity of the links within a community, and those connecting products from that community to products in other communities.

To get a sense of the community quality we compare our assignment of products into communities with a baseline null model and three popular categorizations. The baseline null model is given by an ensemble of communities of the same size, where nodes have been assigned to each community at random. In this case the average strength of the links within communities is equal to the average strength of links between communities, and the community quality is 1. The three categorizations we use as comparators are: the first digit of the Standard International Trade Classification, the categories introduced by Leamer (1984) -based on factor intensities- and the technology categories introduced by Lall (2000). All three classifications produce values of the community quality between 1.3 and 1.4, indicating that links within communities tend to be, on average, 30% to 40% stronger than those between communities. The communities we propose here have a community quality value of 1.94, indicating that the links between nodes in the same community are, on average, 94% stronger than those connecting nodes between communities (Figure 5.3.1). The difference in community quality of our proposed community system and that of the three alternative categorizations is highly statistically significant with a p-value<1×10^{-30}.

FIGURE 5.3.1:

▶ Community quality. The figure compares the ability of the different classification schemes to capture the structure of the product space.

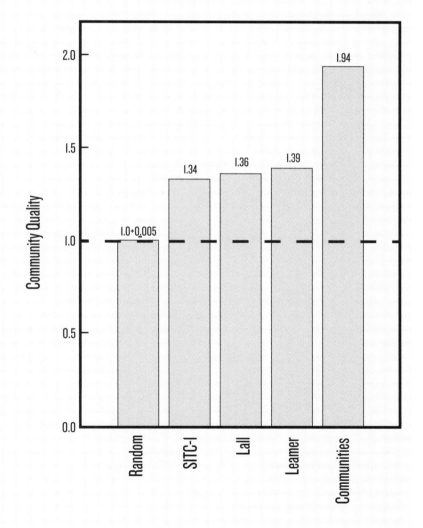

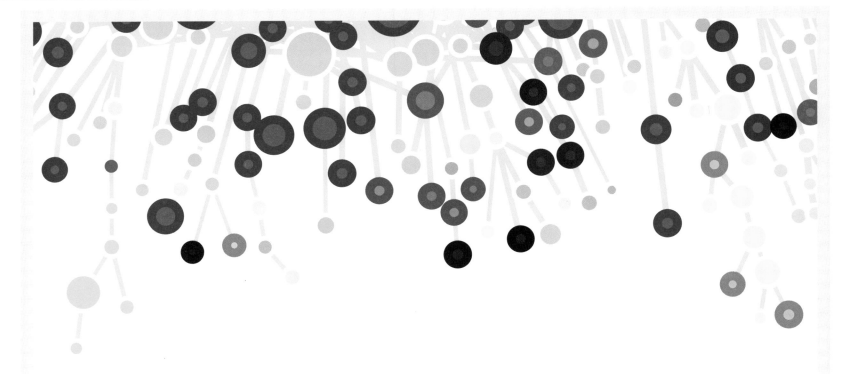

TECHNICAL BOX 5.4: UNDERSTANDING THE POSITION OF COUNTRIES IN THE PRODUCT SPACE: DISTANCE, COMPLEXITY OUTLOOK AND COMPLEXITY OUTLOOK GAIN

The product space is based on a measure of the similarity of the knowledge set required by products. In this box we develop measures related to the position of countries in the product space. One first measure attempts to capture how far away a product is from a country's knowledge set, as expressed by its current export basket. This is a measure that relates a country c to a product p that it is not currently exporting in its fair share (see Technical Box 2.2). We call this measure distance and calculate it based on the proportion of knowledge relevant to the product that the country does not have. The knowledge that it does have is captured by the proximity between the products that it is currently making and the particular product of interest p. The knowledge that it does not have can be inferred from the proximity between the products that it is currently not making and the product of interest p. Distance is, therefore, the sum of the proximities between a particular good p and all the products that country c is currently not exporting normalized by the sum of proximities between all products and product p. If country c exports most of the goods connected to product p, then the distance will be short, close to 0. But, if country c only exports a small proportion of the products that are related to product p then the distance will be large (close to I). Formally,

$$d_{c,p} = \frac{\sum_c \left(1 - M_{cp\prime}\right)\varphi_{p,p\prime}}{\sum_{p\prime} \varphi_{p,p\prime}}$$

Distance gives us an idea of how far each product is relative to a country's current mix of exports. Yet, it would be useful to have a holistic measure of the opportunities implied by a country's position in the product space. We can develop this measure by calculating how close a country is to the products it is currently not effectively making. Here, since more complex products are as-

sociated with higher incomes, it is useful to weigh products by their complexity. Some countries may be located near few, poorly connected and relatively simple products, while others may have a rich unexploited nearby neighborhood of highly connected or complex products. This means that countries differ not just in what they make, but also in where their opportunities lie. We can think of this as the value of the option to move into other products.

Hence, to quantify the "Complexity Outlook" of a country's unexploited prospects we sum the "closeness", i.e. I minus the distance, to the products that the country is not currently making weighted by the level of complexity of these products. We can write this mathematically as:

$$complexity\ outlook_c = \sum_{p\prime} \left(1 - d_{c,p}\right)\left(1 - M_{cp\prime}\right)PCI_{p\prime}$$

Where PCI is the Product Complexity Index of product $p\prime$. The term $1 - M_{cp\prime}$ makes sure that we count only the products that the country is not currently producing. Higher Complexity Outlook implies being in the vicinity of more products and/or of products that are more complex.

We can use Complexity Outlook to calculate the potential benefit to a country if it were to move to a particular new product. We call this the "Complexity Outlook Gain" that country c would obtain from making product p. This is calculated as the change in Complexity Outlook that would come as a consequence of developing product p. Opportunity gain quantifies the contribution of a new product in terms of opening the doors to more, and more complex products. Formally, we can write the opportunity gain as:

$$complexity\ outlook\ gain_{c,p} = \left[\sum_{p\prime} \frac{\varphi_{p,p\prime}}{\sum_{p\prime\prime} \varphi_{p\prime\prime,p\prime}}\left(1 - M_{cp\prime}\right)PCI_{p\prime}\right] - \left(1 - d_{c,p}\right)PCI_p$$

TECHNICAL BOX 5.5: HOW DOES COMPLEXITY EVOLVE?

The Complexity Outlook Index (COI) measures the position of a country in the product space. A country with a higher COI is closer to more complex products that it is not currently making than a country with a lower COI. A country with a higher COI should have an easier time solving the "chicken and egg" problems associated with coordinating the development of new industries and the accumulation of their requisite capabilities. Industries that are closer to a country's current capabilities should have fewer coordination failures to resolve and hence, provide an easier path to the accumulation of capabilities.

This box explores the effects of the Complexity Outlook Index on the future ECI in 5- and 10-year periods, controlling for the initial value of ECI. Table 5.5.1 shows that for the period 1978-2008, COI is a very strong predictor of future ECI at both horizons.

We can calculate the implied long-run effect of COI on ECI, by assuming that they have a long term relationship of the form:

$$\widehat{ECI_t} = \alpha COI_0 + \gamma \qquad (1)$$

where α represents the long-run effect. We assume that in any period, ECI covers a fraction β of the distance between its initial value and its long-term value:

$$ECI_t - ECI_0 = \beta\left(\widehat{ECI_t} - ECI_0\right) + \delta \qquad (2)$$

Substituting (2) into (1) we get:

$$ECI_t = \beta(\alpha COI_0) + (1 - \beta)ECI_0 + \varepsilon \qquad (3)$$

From this equation we can estimate both the long-term effect of COI on ECI (α) and the speed of adjustment β. The two panels expressed in columns 1 and 2 give an estimate of α of about 0.91 ~ 0.95 and a speed of adjustment β of 8.5 percent in 5 years and 14.3 percent in 10 years, consistent with exponential decay.

We conclude that the Complexity Outlook Index does affect the evolution of the Economic Complexity Index.

TABLE 5.5.1

VARIABLES	Economic Complexity Index (1978-2008)	
	5-Year Periods	10-Year Periods
	(1)	(2)
Initial Economic Complexity Index	0.915***	0.857***
	(0.017)	(0.036)
Initial Complexity Outlook Index	0.078***	0.136***
	(0.017)	(0.034)
Constant	-0.016	-0.064**
	(0.035)	(0.030)
Observations	637	313
R²	0.926	0.892
Year FE	Yes	Yes
Speed of adjustment, α	0.085	0.143
Long run effect, β	0.918	0.951

Standard errors clustered by country are shown in parentheses. *** p<0.01, ** p<0.05, * p<0.1

SECTION 6
How Can This Atlas Be Used?

This Atlas is meant to help countries find paths to prosperity. It does so, first, by developing a framework that clarifies what economic development requires, namely, the accumulation of productive knowledge and its use in both *more* and *more complex* industries. Second, The Atlas allows the user to identify development paths that make it easier to coordinate the accumulation of new productive capabilities with the development of the new industries that need them.

The Atlas does this by measuring several elements of the puzzle. It assesses the current state of productive knowledge in any given country, through the Economic Complexity Index. It measures how steep the way forward is, as captured by the Complexity Outlook Index. It describes where the country is in the product space, clarifying the diversification options a country faces. The Atlas describes the neighborhood each country finds itself in by pointing out which products are in the "adjacent possible", how complex they are and how their development would unlock further opportunities. The country pages included in this Atlas provide a concise look at all these aspects and the Observatory of Economic Complexity permits a deeper exploration online.

This Atlas is, one may say, one more publication that calls attention to an interpretation of the world that, according to the authors, is an important contribution to achieving some commonly shared goal. Other exemplars include freedom, human development, solvency, business environment, competitiveness, governance, educational quality, and many others.

Indexes generally do three things. They benchmark performance vis-à-vis the best achievers, provide intermediate targets on a path towards a longer-term goal, and offer a guide to action.

As a benchmark, the critical question is whether the index is able to adequately represent the information that it wants to capture. In this respect, in the Economic Complexity Index (ECI), countries improve by increasing the number and complexity of the products they successfully export. In the Complexity Outlook Index they improve by developing activities that are in parts of the product space that are more connected and that have more complex products. These indicators are based on real data and not on opinion surveys or *de jure* provisions that may not be important in practice. They have the limitations of the dataset they use: international trade data at a certain level of disaggregation that do not include tradable services or other activities that are not exported.

As an appropriate intermediate target on a path towards a longer-term goal, the question is whether improvements

▶

in the indicator can be expected to lead to the ultimate goal. If the goal is to accelerate the pace of economic development, as captured by the growth in GDP per capita, then the Economic Complexity Index and the Complexity Outlook Index do a much better job than the World Economic Forum's Global Competitiveness Index or the World Bank's Governance, Financial Development or Education Indicators. The empirical evidence presented in this Atlas suggests that focusing on improving the complexity indicators is a more reliable way to achieve the ultimate goal of faster economic development.

As a guide to action, the question is whether countries can derive recommendations that can offer a clear plan of action to improve the intermediate target. In this respect, indexes differ greatly. At one extreme, the World Bank's Doing Business Index is based on the statutory requirements to perform certain functions. Countries can pretty much figure out which statutory changes will improve their performance on the intermediate target. If a country streamlines the procedure to register a business, it will perform better on the index at the next calculation. Whether this change will actually have any significant economic effect depends on the strength of the connection between the index and the ultimate goal.

On other questions though, such as improving educational quality, the mapping is not so clear. It is hard to know precisely which changes in current practice would be reflected in better performance. Should schools reduce class size, improve teacher training, increase nutritional assistance or implement standardized exams? Should a country trying to improve rule of law direct its resources to deploying more policemen in the streets, to revamp the judicial system, or to revise their gun laws?

It is important to understand the characteristics of the complexity indexes as guides to action. In the Economic Complexity Index (ECI), countries improve by increasing the number and complexity of the products they successfully export. In the Complexity Outlook Index they do better if they move closer to parts of the product space that are denser and that have more complex products. If they do so, they will find it easier to achieve subsequent increases in complexity and growth.

But how can countries achieve these changes? As a guide to action, the complexity indexes define the intermediate goals but not the actions that lead to them.

What a country needs to do to increase its complexity is highly specific to its context. The "adjacent possible" of each country is different and the missing productive capabilities that limit movement to any new industry in the product space will also be country-specific. In some instances, the provision of better seeds could cause an agricultural revolution; improved infrastructure could open up new possibilities for light manufacturing; clarifying property rights and human subject regulations may allow for participation in pharmaceutical research; changing the responsiveness of training institutions to the needs of new sectors may unleash their growth. The list goes on. Whether improvements in any of these areas will trigger the desired outcomes in a particular country depends on the presence of the other complementary capabilities that are required for those industries to grow. Countries differ greatly in this dimension. The plan of action must, therefore, reflect this specificity.

The policy message for most countries is clear: create an environment where a greater diversity of productive activities can thrive, paying particular attention to activities that are relatively more complex or that open up more opportunities. Countries are more likely to succeed in this agenda if they understand the trade-offs between focusing on products that are close to their current set of productive capabilities vs. focusing on those that may be a bit further away but that offer opportunities for higher complexity or for subsequent diversification and growth. Nearby products facilitate the identification and provision of missing capabilities, a task that becomes increasingly difficult as the target industry is further away. We therefore accompany our indexes with maps that help chart the opportunities and rewards available for each country. These are maps that are specific to each country and do not represent one-size-fits-all development advice.

These maps can also be used by firms that are searching for a new location or that are looking to diversify into other products. These maps carry information about the productive capabilities that are present in a given country and the degree to which these capabilities are relevant to support other industries.

A map does not tell people where to go, but it does help them determine their destination relative to their current location, and chart their journey towards it. A map empowers by describing opportunities that would not be obvious in the absence of it. If the secret to development is the accumulation of productive knowledge, at a societal rather than individual level, then the process necessarily requires the involvement of many explorers, not just a few planners. This is why the maps we provide in this Atlas are intended for everyone to use. ●

SECTION 7
Which Countries Are Included in This Atlas?

FIGURE 7.1:

▶ Schematic of the procedure used to determine the countries that were included in The Atlas.

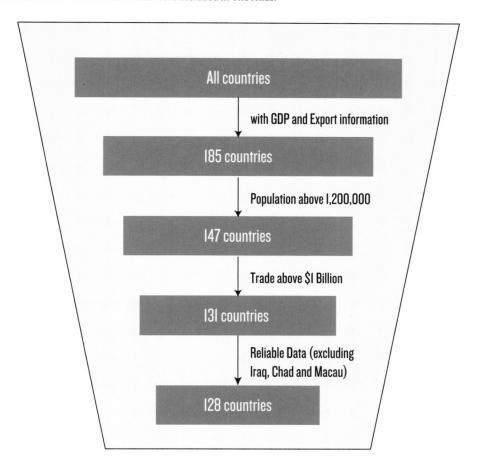

this Atlas includes data for 128 countries. These account for 99% of world trade, 97% of the world's total GDP and 95% of the world's population. To generate this list we used a variety of criteria. First, we limit ourselves only to the set of countries for which there is product-level trade data available in the UN COMTRADE and income data available for 2010. Second, we only use data on countries with a population above 1,200,000. Third, we only consider countries that exported at least 1 billion dollars per year, on average, between 2006 and 2010. Finally, we remove from this sample Iraq, Macau and Chad, three countries with severe data quality issues (Figure 7.1).

Countries are highly heterogeneous. When it comes to the size of their population, territory, income and economy, countries differ by orders of magnitude. When it comes to land, Russia is 1,000 times larger than Kuwait. In terms of population, China is more than 600 times more populous than Slovenia. And as for Gross Domestic Product, that of the United States is more than 1,300 times larger than Namibia's. All of these are countries that made it into this Atlas, illustrating the large cross section of the world captured in this book.

Products also differ enormously in terms of their world market size. Depending on the year, crude oil represents five to ten percent of world trade while goat skins represent less than one part in one hundred thousand of total world trade. To make countries and products comparable we control for the size of the country and of the product by calculating their Revealed Comparative Advantage (see Technical Box 2.2). This means that large and small countries and products with big and small markets count the same as far as our method is concerned. Moreover, the data of each country affects the calculations of all others so including data that is noisy or unreliable greatly affects the integrity of our calculations. Countries that are too small in terms of their export base, such as Tuvalu or Vanuatu, or with data that is highly unreliable or not adequately classified, do not provide us with a sufficiently broad sample to infer their structure. ●

PART 2

COMPLEXITY RANKINGS

In this part we present five different rankings. These rankings sort countries according to:

RANKING 1: Economic Complexity Index (ECI).	RANKING 2: Complexity Outlook Index (COI).	RANKING 3: Expected Growth in Per Capita GDP to 2020.	RANKING 4: Expected GDP Growth to 2020.	RANKING 5: Change in Economic Complexity (1964-2010).

Each of these five rankings captures a different aspect of the world economy. This is well illustrated by the fact very different countries top the rankings for complexity (Japan), ease to increase complexity and growth (India) and past increases in complexity (Mauritius). The heterogeneity of this group shows the wide range of dimensions that are captured by these five different rankings (Table I). Next, we comment each one of them briefly, and invite readers to explore them by themselves.

TABLE I

▶ Correlations between the five different rankings. The low correlations between the rankings indicate that these tend to capture different dimensions of the world economy.

	R2: Complexity Outlook	R3: Per capita Growth Potential	R4: Total Growth	R5: Change in Complexity
R1: Economic Complexity	0.74	0.42	-0.05	0.32
R2: Complexity Outlook		0.65	0.24	0.44
R3: Per capita Growth Potential			0.75	0.53
R4: Total Growth				0.43

RANKING 1:

Economic Complexity Index

RANKING 1 shows the Economic Complexity ranking. Here countries are sorted based on the amount of productive knowledge that is implied in their export structures *(see Part 1, Section 2: How do we measure economic complexity?)*. The countries in the top ten of this ranking are Japan, Germany, Switzerland, Austria, Sweden, South Korea, Finland, Czech Republic, the UK and Singapore. Immediately after the top 10 we have France and the US. Of the top 20 countries, 11 are in Western Europe, 3 are in East Asia, and surprisingly 4 are in Eastern Europe. Israel closes the list of the top 20. Mexico is the most complex Latin American country, ranked at 24, way ahead of Brazil, Argentina and Chile, ranked 46, 60 and 68, respectively. High-ranking countries possess productive structures that are able to hold vast amounts of productive knowledge, and manufacture and export a large number of sophisticated goods. Of the bottom 16 countries, 12 are from Sub-Saharan Africa. Mongolia, Libya, Papua New Guinea and Yemen are the least complex countries outside of Sub-Saharan Africa. *Figure 1* illustrates the relative levels of economic complexity of countries in Ranking 1 by plotting ECI as a function of a country's current level of GDP per capita. In *Map 1*, countries are color coded according to their position in ranking 1.

Interestingly among the least complex countries in Western Europe are Portugal (35) and Greece (49), two countries whose high income cannot be explained by either their complexity or their natural resource wealth. We do not think that this is unrelated to their present difficulties: their current income has been propped up by massive capital inflows and, as these decline to more sustainable levels, internal weaknesses come to the fore. The ECI, however, illustrates clearly how these mismatches can be identified from the data.

BY REGION:

By region, the most complex economies in Eastern Europe and Central Asia are the Czech Republic, Hungary and Slovenia, while the worst performing ones are Tajikistan, Turkmenistan and Azerbaijan. In Latin America and the Caribbean the best performer is Mexico (ranked 24). Brazil ranks third (46 in the worldwide scale) followed by Uruguay (51). Panama ranks high at 43, but this is probably due to the misclassification of ships and electronics re-exports as if they were locally produced. The worst performers are Ecuador (92), Bolivia (94), Venezuela (103) and Nicaragua (106). In East Asia and the Pacific, the best performers are Japan (1), Korea (6) and Singapore (10) followed by China (26), Thailand (28), Malaysia (32) and Hong Kong (40). The worst performers are Lao (98), Mongolia (115) and Papua New Guinea (119). In South Asia, the best performing country is India (55) followed by Sri Lanka (80) and Pakistan (90). The list is closed by Bangladesh (112).

In the Middle East and North Africa, the best performers are Israel (20), Jordan (45), Lebanon (47), United Arab Emirates (48) and Tunisia (53). The worst performers are Algeria (95), Iran (96), Libya (116) and Yemen (121), where the overwhelming presence of oil indicates a narrow base of productive knowledge.

Finally, In Sub-Saharan Africa the most complex economies are South Africa (54), Botswana (56), Mauritius (72) and Kenya (85). The worst performers are Sudan (124), Guinea (125), Cameroon (126), Angola (127) and Nigeria (128). We note that many African countries are not in the ranking because they did not satisfy our data filtering criteria (see Part 1, Section 7: Which countries are in the Atlas?). ●

RANKING I. ECONOMIC COMPLEXITY INDEX

RANK ECI (2010)	REGIONAL ECI RANKING	COUNTRY NAME	ISO CODE	ECI 2010	RANK INCOME 2010 [USD]	INCOME 2010 [USD]	REGION
1	1/16	Japan	JPN	2.17	14	43,063	East Asia and Pacific
2	1/16	Germany	DEU	1.96	17	39,852	Western Europe
3	2/16	Switzerland	CHE	1.90	3	67,644	Western Europe
4	3/16	Austria	AUT	1.73	12	44,885	Western Europe
5	4/16	Sweden	SWE	1.71	6	49,257	Western Europe
6	2/16	Korea. Rep.	KOR	1.69	30	20,540	East Asia and Pacific
7	5/16	Finland	FIN	1.69	13	44,091	Western Europe
8	1/27	Czech Republic	CZE	1.68	31	18,789	Eastern Europe and Central Asia
9	6/16	United Kingdom	GBR	1.67	20	36,186	Western Europe
10	3/16	Singapore	SGP	1.65	16	41,987	East Asia and Pacific
11	7/16	France	FRA	1.53	19	39,170	Western Europe
12	1/2	United States	USA	1.51	7	46,702	North America
13	2/27	Hungary	HUN	1.44	38	12,863	Eastern Europe and Central Asia
14	3/27	Slovenia	SVN	1.44	27	22,898	Eastern Europe and Central Asia
15	4/27	Slovak Republic	SVK	1.43	33	16,036	Eastern Europe and Central Asia
16	8/16	Italy	ITA	1.40	21	33,788	Western Europe
17	9/16	Ireland	IRL	1.36	10	45,873	Western Europe
18	10/16	Denmark	DNK	1.31	4	56,278	Western Europe
19	11/16	Belgium	BEL	1.23	15	42,833	Western Europe
20	1/16	Israel	ISR	1.21	25	28,522	Middle East and North Africa
21	5/27	Poland	POL	1.13	40	12,303	Eastern Europe and Central Asia
22	12/16	Netherlands	NLD	1.08	8	46,597	Western Europe
23	13/16	Spain	ESP	1.05	24	30,026	Western Europe
24	1/21	Mexico	MEX	0.98	49	9,133	Latin America and the Caribbean
25	6/27	Croatia	HRV	0.90	36	13,774	Eastern Europe and Central Asia
26	4/16	China	CHN	0.88	74	4,433	East Asia and Pacific
27	7/27	Estonia	EST	0.81	35	14,045	Eastern Europe and Central Asia
28	5/16	Thailand	THA	0.80	70	4,614	East Asia and Pacific
29	8/27	Romania	ROU	0.78	57	7,539	Eastern Europe and Central Asia
30	2/2	Canada	CAN	0.78	9	46,212	North America
31	9/27	Belarus	BLR	0.75	63	5,819	Eastern Europe and Central Asia
32	6/16	Malaysia	MYS	0.74	53	8,373	East Asia and Pacific
33	10/27	Ukraine	UKR	0.70	83	2,974	Eastern Europe and Central Asia
34	11/27	Serbia	SRB	0.69	66	5,273	Eastern Europe and Central Asia
35	14/16	Portugal	PRT	0.68	28	21,358	Western Europe
36	12/27	Latvia	LVA	0.67	44	10,723	Eastern Europe and Central Asia
37	13/27	Lithuania	LTU	0.67	42	11,046	Eastern Europe and Central Asia
38	14/27	Bosnia and Herzegovina	BIH	0.63	75	4,427	Eastern Europe and Central Asia
39	15/27	Bulgaria	BGR	0.62	60	6,335	Eastern Europe and Central Asia
40	7/16	Hong Kong SAR. China	HKG	0.61	23	31,758	East Asia and Pacific
41	15/16	Norway	NOR	0.59	1	85,443	Western Europe
42	16/27	Turkey	TUR	0.47	46	10,050	Eastern Europe and Central Asia
43	2/21	Panama	PAN	0.45	55	7,614	Latin America and the Caribbean

RANKING I. ECONOMIC COMPLEXITY INDEX

RANK ECI (2010)	REGIONAL ECI RANKING	COUNTRY NAME	ISO CODE	ECI 2010	RANK INCOME 2010 [USD]	INCOME 2010 [USD]	REGION
44	17/27	Russian Federation	RUS	0.40	45	10,481	Eastern Europe and Central Asia
45	2/16	Jordan	JOR	0.36	76	4,370	Middle East and North Africa
46	3/21	Brazil	BRA	0.35	43	10,993	Latin America and the Caribbean
47	3/16	Lebanon	LBN	0.33	48	9,227	Middle East and North Africa
48	4/16	United Arab Emirates	ARE	0.33	18	39,625	Middle East and North Africa
49	16/16	Greece	GRC	0.28	26	26,433	Western Europe
50	8/16	New Zealand	NZL	0.26	22	32,620	East Asia and Pacific
51	4/21	Uruguay	URY	0.25	41	11,742	Latin America and the Caribbean
52	9/16	Philippines	PHL	0.24	94	2,140	East Asia and Pacific
53	5/16	Tunisia	TUN	0.24	78	4,194	Middle East and North Africa
54	1/26	South Africa	ZAF	0.24	59	7,272	Sub-Saharan Africa
55	1/4	India	IND	0.21	101	1,375	South Asia
56	2/26	Botswana	BWA	0.20	58	7,427	Sub-Saharan Africa
57	5/21	Costa Rica	CRI	0.19	54	7,774	Latin America and the Caribbean
58	6/21	Colombia	COL	0.12	61	6,238	Latin America and the Caribbean
59	6/16	Saudi Arabia	SAU	0.11	32	16,423	Middle East and North Africa
60	7/21	Argentina	ARG	0.10	50	9,124	Latin America and the Caribbean
61	8/21	El Salvador	SLV	0.04	82	3,460	Latin America and the Caribbean
62	18/27	Macedonia, FYR	MKD	-0.02	73	4,434	Eastern Europe and Central Asia
63	19/27	Moldova	MDA	-0.03	97	1,632	Eastern Europe and Central Asia
64	7/16	Kuwait	KWT	-0.03	11	45,437	Middle East and North Africa
65	10/16	Indonesia	IDN	-0.08	85	2,952	East Asia and Pacific
66	8/16	Qatar	QAT	-0.10	2	72,398	Middle East and North Africa
67	9/16	Egypt, Arab Rep.	EGY	-0.10	90	2,698	Middle East and North Africa
68	9/21	Chile	CHL	-0.12	39	12,640	Latin America and the Caribbean
69	11/16	Australia	AUS	-0.21	5	50,746	East Asia and Pacific
70	12/16	Vietnam	VNM	-0.25	106	1,224	East Asia and Pacific
71	10/16	Syrian Arab Republic	SYR	-0.27	86	2,893	Middle East and North Africa
72	3/26	Mauritius	MUS	-0.27	56	7,584	Sub-Saharan Africa
73	11/16	Oman	OMN	-0.28	29	20,791	Middle East and North Africa
74	10/21	Dominican Republic	DOM	-0.30	67	5,195	Latin America and the Caribbean
75	20/27	Georgia	GEO	-0.32	91	2,614	Eastern Europe and Central Asia
76	21/27	Uzbekistan	UZB	-0.36	100	1,377	Eastern Europe and Central Asia
77	11/21	Cuba	CUB	-0.40	64	5,397	Latin America and the Caribbean
78	12/21	Jamaica	JAM	-0.41	68	5,133	Latin America and the Caribbean
79	13/21	Guatemala	GTM	-0.42	87	2,873	Latin America and the Caribbean
80	2/4	Sri Lanka	LKA	-0.45	92	2,400	South Asia
81	14/21	Trinidad and Tobago	TTO	-0.47	34	15,614	Latin America and the Caribbean
82	15/21	Peru	PER	-0.48	65	5,292	Latin America and the Caribbean
83	16/21	Paraguay	PRY	-0.48	88	2,840	Latin America and the Caribbean
84	12/16	Morocco	MAR	-0.48	89	2,795	Middle East and North Africa
85	4/26	Kenya	KEN	-0.50	117	795	Sub-Saharan Africa
86	22/27	Kyrgyz Republic	KGZ	-0.53	114	880	Eastern Europe and Central Asia

RANKING I. ECONOMIC COMPLEXITY INDEX

RANK ECI (2010)	REGIONAL ECI RANKING	COUNTRY NAME	ISO CODE	ECI 2010	RANK INCOME 2010 [USD]	INCOME 2010 [USD]	REGION
87	23/27	Kazakhstan	KAZ	-0.56	51	9,070	Eastern Europe and Central Asia
88	24/27	Albania	ALB	-0.61	81	3,701	Eastern Europe and Central Asia
89	5/26	Zimbabwe	ZWE	-0.61	120	595	Sub-Saharan Africa
90	3/4	Pakistan	PAK	-0.62	113	1,019	South Asia
91	17/21	Honduras	HND	-0.66	95	2,019	Latin America and the Caribbean
92	18/21	Ecuador	ECU	-0.67	79	4,008	Latin America and the Caribbean
93	6/26	Zambia	ZMB	-0.68	104	1,253	Sub-Saharan Africa
94	19/21	Bolivia	BOL	-0.70	96	1,979	Latin America and the Caribbean
95	13/16	Algeria	DZA	-0.71	71	4,567	Middle East and North Africa
96	14/16	Iran, Islamic Rep.	IRN	-0.80	72	4,526	Middle East and North Africa
97	7/26	Liberia	LBR	-0.81	128	247	Sub-Saharan Africa
98	13/16	Lao PDR	LAO	-0.82	108	1,158	East Asia and Pacific
99	8/26	Malawi	MWI	-0.83	127	339	Sub-Saharan Africa
100	9/26	Namibia	NAM	-0.84	69	4,876	Sub-Saharan Africa
101	25/27	Turkmenistan	TKM	-0.90	80	3,967	Eastern Europe and Central Asia
102	10/26	Uganda	UGA	-0.92	122	515	Sub-Saharan Africa
103	20/21	Venezuela, RB	VEN	-0.94	37	13,658	Latin America and the Caribbean
104	14/16	Cambodia	KHM	-0.96	116	795	East Asia and Pacific
105	11/26	Senegal	SEN	-0.98	112	1,034	Sub-Saharan Africa
106	21/21	Nicaragua	NIC	-0.99	110	1,139	Latin America and the Caribbean
107	12/26	Mali	MLI	-1.00	119	613	Sub-Saharan Africa
108	13/26	Tanzania	TZA	-1.02	121	527	Sub-Saharan Africa
109	26/27	Azerbaijan	AZE	-1.03	62	5,843	Eastern Europe and Central Asia
110	27/27	Tajikistan	TJK	-1.04	115	820	Eastern Europe and Central Asia
111	14/26	Madagascar	MDG	-1.05	124	421	Sub-Saharan Africa
112	4/4	Bangladesh	BGD	-1.07	118	675	South Asia
113	15/26	Ghana	GHA	-1.09	102	1,319	Sub-Saharan Africa
114	16/26	Gabon	GAB	-1.14	52	8,768	Sub-Saharan Africa
115	15/16	Mongolia	MNG	-1.14	93	2,250	East Asia and Pacific
116	15/16	Libya	LBY	-1.24	47	9,957	Middle East and North Africa
117	17/26	Mozambique	MOZ	-1.26	125	394	Sub-Saharan Africa
118	18/26	Côte d'Ivoire	CIV	-1.27	107	1,161	Sub-Saharan Africa
119	16/16	Papua New Guinea	PNG	-1.31	99	1,382	East Asia and Pacific
120	19/26	Ethiopia	ETH	-1.41	126	358	Sub-Saharan Africa
121	16/16	Yemen, Rep.	YEM	-1.53	103	1,291	Middle East and North Africa
122	20/26	Congo, Rep.	COG	-1.55	84	2,970	Sub-Saharan Africa
123	21/26	Mauritania	MRT	-1.58	111	1,045	Sub-Saharan Africa
124	22/26	Sudan	SDN	-1.66	98	1,538	Sub-Saharan Africa
125	23/26	Guinea	GIN	-1.69	123	474	Sub-Saharan Africa
126	24/26	Cameroon	CMR	-1.75	109	1,147	Sub-Saharan Africa
127	25/26	Angola	AGO	-2.28	77	4,322	Sub-Saharan Africa
128	26/26	Nigeria	NGA	-2.31	105	1,242	Sub-Saharan Africa

MAP I:

▶ Countries are color coded according to their ranking in Economic Complexity Index.

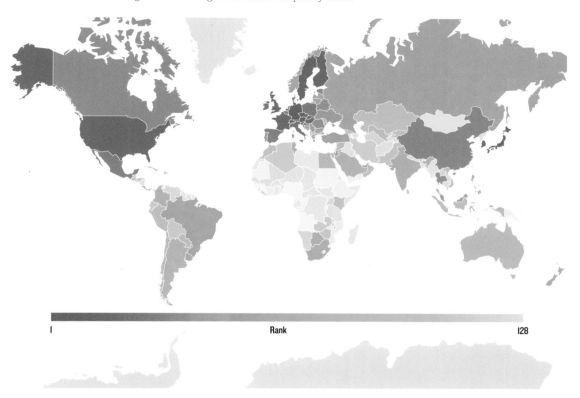

FIGURE I:

▶ Illustrates the relative levels of economic complexity of countries in Ranking 1 by plotting ECI as a function of a country's current level of GDP per capita.

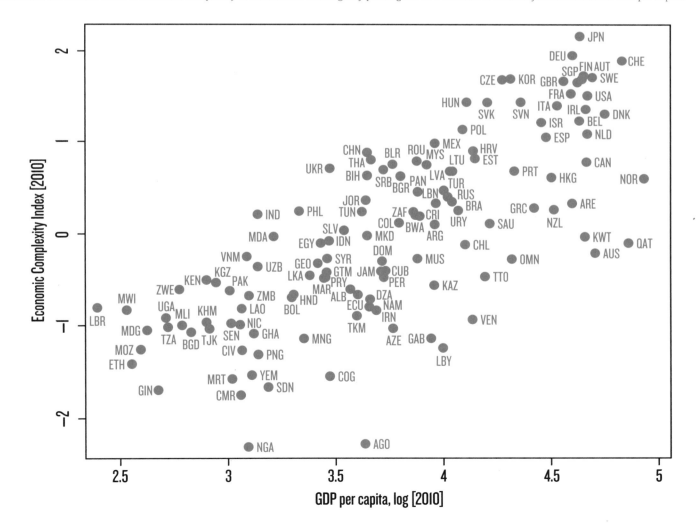

RANKING 2:
Complexity Outlook Index

RANKING 2 sorts countries according to their Complexity Outlook Index as of 2010 *(see Part 1, Section 5: How does Economic Complexity Evolve?)*. This index captures how well countries are positioned in the product space by quantifying how close the products that they make are to the products that they do not make, weighted by how complex those products are. Countries that are closer to more complex products will have an easier time sorting out the chicken and egg problems that slow down the accumulation of productive capabilities. In Technical Box 5.5 we showed that the Complexity Outlook Index strongly affects the growth of the Economic Complexity Index over time.

The countries that top the list are India, Turkey, Portugal, Greece, Bulgaria, Indonesia and China. In general, these countries have experienced remarkable changes in their productive structure and are well positioned to move into more and more complex products. In the year 2000, the top countries were India, China, Indonesia, Turkey, Bulgaria, Poland, Spain and Thailand, countries that in general experienced rapid transformation in the 2000-2010 decade.

We noted in Part I, Section 3 that Portugal and Greece are countries whose current level of income is well above that which would be expected given their relatively low complexity. Together with Spain, these are countries that experienced a capital inflows boom that followed the adoption of the Euro and which led to a stronger real exchange rate and less dynamic exports. With the end of the capital inflows booms, these countries were left in dire circumstances. Here we note that these countries are well positioned to increase their complexity, making their recovery potentially easier.

The bottom of the list is occupied by Germany and Yemen. Germany's position is due to the fact that the country already makes most of the most complex products, so it can only increase its complexity by inventing products that do not yet exist. For the case of Yemen, the problem is caused by the fact that they have so few capabilities that alternative products are many capabilities away. The Complexity Outlook Index is not a simple function of a country's GDP per capita, as illustrated in *Figure 2*. Countries with similar levels of income per capita may exhibit very different COIs. Rich countries with low COIs are typically either highly diversified into most complex products (e.g., Germany, Austria and the US), or are rich in natural resources and hence placed very peripherally in the product space. *Map 2* depicts the worldwide distribution of the countries according to their COI.

BY REGION:

By region, 6 out of the top 10 countries are in Europe. In Western Europe, less developed countries like Portugal (3) and Greece (4) lead the list, whereas highly diversified countries such as Austria (78) and Germany (128) are the laggards. In Eastern Europe and Central Asia, the leaders are Turkey (2), Bulgaria (5), Serbia (9) and Estonia (11); whereas the laggards are Tajikistan (109), Turkmenistan (112) and Azerbaijan (116).

In South Asia, India is the regional and global leader (1), while Bangladesh is the laggard (113) with Pakistan (40) and Sri Lanka (57) in between, as they were in the ECI. In East Asia and the Pacific the leaders are Indonesia (6), China (7) and Thailand (13), while Mongolia (117), Papua New Guinea (118) and Cambodia (120) have the lowest COI.

In the Middle East and North Africa, Egypt (8), Lebanon (17) and Israel (31) lead the COI rankings, while the laggards are Iran (94), Algeria (102), Libya (111) and Yemen (127).

In Latin America the leaders are Brazil (10), Mexico (36) and Argentina (37), while the laggards are Jamaica (99), Trinidad and Tobago (103) and Venezuela (107).

In Sub-Saharan Africa, South Africa (23), Kenya (50) and Tanzania (63) have the greatest potential to increase their economic complexity, while the laggards are Cameroon (124), Ethiopia (125) and Sudan (126). ●

RANKING 2. COMPLEXITY OUTLOOK INDEX

RANK COI (2010)	REGIONAL COI RANKING	COUNTRY NAME	ISO CODE	COI (2010)	COI (2000)	RANK COI (2000)	ΔCOI (00 - 10)	RANK ΔCOI (00 - 10)	ΔECI (00 - 10)	RANK ΔECI (00 - 10)	REGION
1	1/4	India	IND	3.29	2.61	1	0.68	12	-0.05	74	South Asia
2	1/27	Turkey	TUR	2.22	1.79	4	0.43	16	0.30	22	Eastern Europe and Central Asia
3	1/16	Portugal	PRT	1.85	1.15	19	0.69	11	0.10	52	Western Europe
4	2/16	Greece	GRC	1.69	1.52	9	0.17	39	-0.03	72	Western Europe
5	2/27	Bulgaria	BGR	1.67	1.77	5	-0.10	81	0.18	36	Eastern Europe and Central Asia
6	1/16	Indonesia	IDN	1.65	1.85	3	-0.20	93	-0.09	85	East Asia and Pacific
7	2/16	China	CHN	1.49	2.38	2	-0.88	119	0.47	6	East Asia and Pacific
8	1/16	Egypt, Arab Rep.	EGY	1.46	0.16	54	1.30	1	0.06	57	Middle East and North Africa
9	3/27	Serbia	SRB	1.34							Eastern Europe and Central Asia
10	1/21	Brazil	BRA	1.29	1.46	10	-0.17	86	-0.38	110	Latin America and the Caribbean
11	4/27	Estonia	EST	1.28	0.84	32	0.44	15	0.30	24	Eastern Europe and Central Asia
12	5/27	Romania	ROU	1.28	1.05	26	0.23	33	0.27	27	Eastern Europe and Central Asia
13	3/16	Thailand	THA	1.26	1.54	8	-0.28	99	0.40	12	East Asia and Pacific
14	1/2	Canada	CAN	1.25	1.38	12	-0.12	84	-0.28	99	North America
15	3/16	Netherlands	NLD	1.23	1.40	11	-0.17	87	-0.21	93	Western Europe
16	4/16	Hong Kong SAR, China	HKG	1.21	1.20	16	0.01	67	0.08	54	East Asia and Pacific
17	2/16	Lebanon	LBN	1.11	0.39	46	0.72	10	0.31	20	Middle East and North Africa
18	4/16	Spain	ESP	1.10	1.62	7	-0.51	112	-0.06	78	Western Europe
19	6/27	Ukraine	UKR	1.09	1.18	17	-0.09	80	0.07	55	Eastern Europe and Central Asia
20	7/27	Croatia	HRV	1.08	1.14	20	-0.06	76	0.18	37	Eastern Europe and Central Asia
21	8/27	Lithuania	LTU	1.05	0.79	33	0.25	30	0.34	14	Eastern Europe and Central Asia
22	5/16	Finland	FIN	1.04	1.02	27	0.03	63	-0.18	91	Western Europe
23	1/26	South Africa	ZAF	1.01	1.26	14	-0.25	97	-0.06	80	Sub-Saharan Africa
24	9/27	Latvia	LVA	0.99	0.27	49	0.73	9	0.34	15	Eastern Europe and Central Asia
25	5/16	Vietnam	VNM	0.99	0.15	55	0.84	5	0.44	9	East Asia and Pacific
26	6/16	Denmark	DNK	0.97	1.17	18	-0.20	91	-0.27	96	Western Europe
27	6/16	Korea, Rep.	KOR	0.95	1.09	23	-0.15	85	0.52	4	East Asia and Pacific
28	10/27	Bosnia and Herzegovina	BIH	0.90	0.71	37	0.20	34	0.27	26	Eastern Europe and Central Asia
29	7/16	Belgium	BEL	0.88	1.25	15	-0.38	106	-0.21	92	Western Europe
30	11/27	Hungary	HUN	0.86	1.28	13	-0.42	107	0.42	10	Eastern Europe and Central Asia
31	3/16	Israel	ISR	0.82	1.05	25	-0.23	96	0.02	62	Middle East and North Africa
32	8/16	United Kingdom	GBR	0.81	0.64	39	0.17	38	-0.29	102	Western Europe
33	7/16	Singapore	SGP	0.81	0.66	38	0.15	41	0.23	30	East Asia and Pacific
34	12/27	Poland	POL	0.80	1.69	6	-0.89	120	0.16	41	Eastern Europe and Central Asia
35	13/27	Slovak Republic	SVK	0.80	1.12	21	-0.33	102	0.12	47	Eastern Europe and Central Asia
36	2/21	Mexico	MEX	0.79	0.99	28	-0.19	90	-0.01	68	Latin America and the Caribbean
37	3/21	Argentina	ARG	0.79	0.91	31	-0.11	82	-0.06	79	Latin America and the Caribbean
38	9/16	Switzerland	CHE	0.79	0.77	34	0.02	64	-0.27	98	Western Europe
39	14/27	Slovenia	SVN	0.75	1.09	24	-0.34	104	0.01	66	Eastern Europe and Central Asia
40	2/4	Pakistan	PAK	0.74	-0.41	70	1.15	3	0.13	46	South Asia
41	8/16	New Zealand	NZL	0.71	0.64	40	0.07	53	-0.08	83	East Asia and Pacific
42	4/16	Tunisia	TUN	0.65	-0.30	68	0.95	4	0.45	8	Middle East and North Africa
43	9/16	Malaysia	MYS	0.57	0.27	50	0.30	28	0.10	51	East Asia and Pacific

RANKING 2. COMPLEXITY OUTLOOK INDEX

RANK COI (2010)	REGIONAL COI RANKING	COUNTRY NAME	ISO CODE	COI (2010)	COI (2000)	RANK COI (2000)	ΔCOI (00 - 10)	RANK ΔCOI (00 - 10)	ΔECI (00 - 10)	RANK ΔECI (00 - 10)	REGION
44	4/21	Panama	PAN	0.53	0.07	57	0.45	13	0.46	7	Latin America and the Caribbean
45	10/16	Sweden	SWE	0.51	0.97	30	-0.46	109	-0.36	106	Western Europe
46	11/16	Ireland	IRL	0.37	0.49	45	-0.12	83	-0.09	86	Western Europe
47	10/16	Australia	AUS	0.32	0.99	29	-0.66	117	-0.37	109	East Asia and Pacific
48	15/27	Belarus	BLR	0.32	0.50	44	-0.18	88	0.06	58	Eastern Europe and Central Asia
49	5/21	Uruguay	URY	0.29	0.35	47	-0.06	75	0.02	63	Latin America and the Caribbean
50	2/26	Kenya	KEN	0.27	-0.51	72	0.79	6	0.19	34	Sub-Saharan Africa
51	16/27	Macedonia, FYR	MKD	0.24	0.08	56	0.17	40	-0.08	84	Eastern Europe and Central Asia
52	11/16	Philippines	PHL	0.24	-0.15	66	0.39	20	0.26	28	East Asia and Pacific
53	6/21	El Salvador	SLV	0.23	-0.13	63	0.36	22	0.08	53	Latin America and the Caribbean
54	5/16	Syrian Arab Republic	SYR	0.21	-1.02	101	1.23	2	0.80	1	Middle East and North Africa
55	7/21	Peru	PER	0.21	-0.10	62	0.30	27	-0.12	87	Latin America and the Caribbean
56	6/16	United Arab Emirates	ARE	0.16	-0.57	75	0.73	8	0.61	3	Middle East and North Africa
57	3/4	Sri Lanka	LKA	0.11	-0.24	67	0.35	23	0.16	40	South Asia
58	17/27	Russian Federation	RUS	0.09	0.74	35	-0.65	114	-0.44	115	Eastern Europe and Central Asia
59	8/21	Guatemala	GTM	0.04	-0.03	59	0.07	54	-0.02	70	Latin America and the Caribbean
60	18/27	Moldova	MDA	0.04	-0.14	64	0.17	36	0.07	56	Eastern Europe and Central Asia
61	12/16	Norway	NOR	-0.02	0.26	51	-0.27	98	-0.33	105	Western Europe
62	9/21	Colombia	COL	-0.02	0.21	53	-0.23	95	0.02	65	Latin America and the Caribbean
63	3/26	Tanzania	TZA	-0.02	-0.78	88	0.76	7	0.32	18	Sub-Saharan Africa
64	7/16	Jordan	JOR	-0.03	0.30	48	-0.33	103	0.12	48	Middle East and North Africa
65	13/16	France	FRA	-0.05	1.10	22	-1.15	122	-0.01	69	Western Europe
66	19/27	Czech Republic	CZE	-0.08	0.57	43	-0.66	116	0.15	44	Eastern Europe and Central Asia
67	8/16	Morocco	MAR	-0.20	-0.53	74	0.34	25	0.16	43	Middle East and North Africa
68	20/27	Kyrgyz Republic	KGZ	-0.23	-0.58	76	0.35	24	0.01	67	Eastern Europe and Central Asia
69	10/21	Dominican Republic	DOM	-0.25	-0.65	80	0.40	18	0.26	29	Latin America and the Caribbean
70	11/21	Chile	CHL	-0.30	-0.09	61	-0.22	94	-0.16	90	Latin America and the Caribbean
71	12/16	Japan	JPN	-0.35	0.58	42	-0.92	121	-0.32	104	East Asia and Pacific
72	12/21	Costa Rica	CRI	-0.37	-0.34	69	-0.03	73	0.34	17	Latin America and the Caribbean
73	21/27	Uzbekistan	UZB	-0.41	-0.71	84	0.29	29	0.30	23	Eastern Europe and Central Asia
74	4/26	Mauritius	MUS	-0.42	-0.86	91	0.44	14	0.34	16	Sub-Saharan Africa
75	14/16	Italy	ITA	-0.44	0.72	36	-1.16	124	-0.07	81	Western Europe
76	22/27	Georgia	GEO	-0.51	0.25	52	-0.76	118	-0.79	123	Eastern Europe and Central Asia
77	13/21	Honduras	HND	-0.51	-0.83	89	0.32	26	0.16	42	Latin America and the Caribbean
78	15/16	Austria	AUT	-0.52	0.64	41	-1.15	123	0.02	64	Western Europe
79	5/26	Zimbabwe	ZWE	-0.59	0.04	58	-0.63	113	-0.27	97	Sub-Saharan Africa
80	14/21	Paraguay	PRY	-0.63	-0.64	79	0.02	65	0.11	50	Latin America and the Caribbean
81	6/26	Botswana	BWA	-0.63							Sub-Saharan Africa
82	7/26	Uganda	UGA	-0.64	-1.06	108	0.43	17	0.32	19	Sub-Saharan Africa
83	2/2	United States	USA	-0.65	-0.14	65	-0.51	111	-0.39	113	North America
84	23/27	Kazakhstan	KAZ	-0.67	-0.48	71	-0.19	89	-0.37	107	Eastern Europe and Central Asia
85	9/16	Saudi Arabia	SAU	-0.68	-0.78	86	0.10	48	0.14	45	Middle East and North Africa
86	13/16	Lao PDR	LAO	-0.68	-1.08	110	0.40	19	0.17	38	East Asia and Pacific

RANKING 2. COMPLEXITY OUTLOOK INDEX

RANK COI (2010)	REGIONAL COI RANKING	COUNTRY NAME	ISO CODE	COI (2010)	COI (2000)	RANK COI (2000)	ΔCOI (00 - 10)	RANK ΔCOI (00 - 10)	ΔECI (00 - 10)	RANK ΔECI (00 - 10)	REGION
87	8/26	Madagascar	MDG	-0.71	-0.95	95	0.24	31	0.22	31	Sub-Saharan Africa
88	24/27	Albania	ALB	-0.72	-0.07	60	-0.65	115	-0.46	116	Eastern Europe and Central Asia
89	15/21	Ecuador	ECU	-0.74	-0.78	87	0.04	60	0.22	32	Latin America and the Caribbean
90	16/21	Bolivia	BOL	-0.78	-0.76	85	-0.02	69	0.05	60	Latin America and the Caribbean
91	10/16	Qatar	QAT	-0.81	-1.05	107	0.24	32	0.40	11	Middle East and North Africa
92	11/16	Kuwait	KWT	-0.81	-0.96	96	0.14	42	0.06	59	Middle East and North Africa
93	12/16	Oman	OMN	-0.85	-1.02	102	0.17	35	0.29	25	Middle East and North Africa
94	13/16	Iran, Islamic Rep.	IRN	-0.88	-0.86	90	-0.03	72	-0.02	71	Middle East and North Africa
95	9/26	Senegal	SEN	-0.88	-0.97	98	0.09	51	-0.05	75	Sub-Saharan Africa
96	17/21	Nicaragua	NIC	-0.88	-0.68	83	-0.20	92	-0.22	94	Latin America and the Caribbean
97	10/26	Malawi	MWI	-0.89	-1.26	124	0.36	21	0.68	2	Sub-Saharan Africa
98	18/21	Cuba	CUB	-0.89	-1.06	109	0.17	37	0.48	5	Latin America and the Caribbean
99	19/21	Jamaica	JAM	-0.90	-0.93	93	0.03	62	0.31	21	Latin America and the Caribbean
100	11/26	Liberia	LBR	-0.91	-0.98	100	0.07	55	-0.23	95	Sub-Saharan Africa
101	12/26	Zambia	ZMB	-0.93	-0.98	99	0.05	58	0.18	35	Sub-Saharan Africa
102	14/16	Algeria	DZA	-0.93	-1.03	105	0.10	46	-0.06	77	Middle East and North Africa
103	20/21	Trinidad and Tobago	TTO	-0.94	-0.58	77	-0.36	105	-0.57	120	Latin America and the Caribbean
104	13/26	Gabon	GAB	-0.96	-1.04	106	0.08	52	-0.38	111	Sub-Saharan Africa
105	14/26	Angola	AGO	-0.97	-1.10	112	0.13	44	-0.54	118	Sub-Saharan Africa
106	15/26	Ghana	GHA	-0.97	-0.97	97	-0.01	68	-0.03	73	Sub-Saharan Africa
107	21/21	Venezuela, RB	VEN	-0.98	-0.65	81	-0.32	101	-0.87	125	Latin America and the Caribbean
108	16/26	Mali	MLI	-0.98	-0.68	82	-0.30	100	-0.57	119	Sub-Saharan Africa
109	25/27	Tajikistan	TJK	-0.98	-0.92	92	-0.07	77	-0.28	100	Eastern Europe and Central Asia
110	17/26	Namibia	NAM	-0.98							Sub-Saharan Africa
111	15/16	Libya	LBY	-0.99	-1.03	104	0.05	59	-0.60	121	Middle East and North Africa
112	26/27	Turkmenistan	TKM	-0.99	-1.11	114	0.12	45	0.16	39	Eastern Europe and Central Asia
113	4/4	Bangladesh	BGD	-1.01	-1.11	115	0.10	49	-0.07	82	South Asia
114	18/26	CÙte d'Ivoire	CIV	-1.02	-0.93	94	-0.09	79	-0.13	88	Sub-Saharan Africa
115	19/26	Mozambique	MOZ	-1.03	-0.53	73	-0.51	110	-0.84	124	Sub-Saharan Africa
116	27/27	Azerbaijan	AZE	-1.04	-0.62	78	-0.43	108	-0.67	122	Eastern Europe and Central Asia
117	14/16	Mongolia	MNG	-1.07	-1.03	103	-0.05	74	-0.37	108	East Asia and Pacific
118	15/16	Papua New Guinea	PNG	-1.07	-1.21	121	0.13	43	0.38	13	East Asia and Pacific
119	20/26	Congo, Rep.	COG	-1.08	-1.10	113	0.03	61	-0.38	112	Sub-Saharan Africa
120	16/16	Cambodia	KHM	-1.09	-1.15	118	0.07	56	0.11	49	East Asia and Pacific
121	21/26	Guinea	GIN	-1.10	-1.20	120	0.10	47	0.04	61	Sub-Saharan Africa
122	22/26	Nigeria	NGA	-1.14	-1.23	123	0.09	50	-0.42	114	Sub-Saharan Africa
123	23/26	Mauritania	MRT	-1.15	-1.13	116	-0.02	71	-0.49	117	Sub-Saharan Africa
124	24/26	Cameroon	CMR	-1.16	-1.21	122	0.05	57	-0.06	76	Sub-Saharan Africa
125	25/26	Ethiopia	ETH	-1.17	-1.10	111	-0.07	78	-0.14	89	Sub-Saharan Africa
126	26/26	Sudan	SDN	-1.17	-1.15	117	-0.02	70	-0.31	103	Sub-Saharan Africa
127	16/16	Yemen, Rep.	YEM	-1.18	-1.20	119	0.01	66	0.20	33	Middle East and North Africa
128	16/16	Germany	DEU	-3.87	-2.64	125	-1.23	125	-0.29	101	Western Europe

MAP 2:

▶ Countries are color coded according to their ranking in Complexity Outlook Index.

FIGURE 2:

▶ Complexity Outlook Index with respect to GDP per capita in 2010.

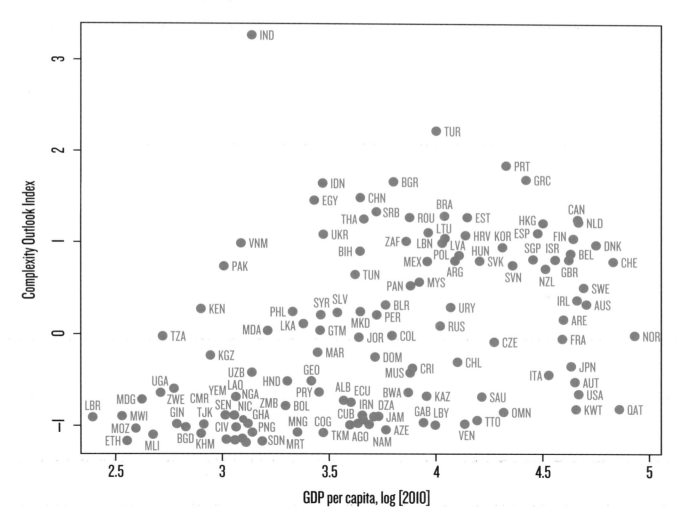

RANKING 3:

Expected Growth in Per Capita GDP to 2020

RANKING 3 sorts countries according to their expected annual per capita growth rate. To calculate the expected growth rate for this ranking, we use the growth equation developed in Technical Box 3.1 and consider four factors as explanatory variables: the level of income; the Economic Complexity Index (ECI) for 2010; the Complexity Outlook Index (COI) for 2010; and the expected growth in the value of natural resource exports per capita. The projection requires an assumption about the future value of natural resource exports. For convenience, we will assume this value remains constant in real terms. Although commodity prices in 2010 were unusually high and are therefore likely to fall in future, extraction rates may increase over time, so we believe that assuming a constant value in real terms over time is reasonable. To the extent that prices or quantities extracted deviate from this assumption, growth will deviate from our expectations accordingly. For instance, our ranking will tend to underestimate growth for countries where natural resource production grows faster than population, and will tend to overestimate growth for countries where natural resource production falls behind population growth.

India, China, Ukraine, Thailand, Vietnam, Serbia, Bulgaria, Bosnia-Herzegovina and Liberia are at the top of this ranking. In general, these are countries that rank very high in their ECI and COI, relative to their low GDP per capita. For example, the ranking of India in its ECI and COI is 46 and 100 positions above its ranking in GDP per capita. The equivalent numbers for China are 48 and 57. Serbia, Bosnia-Herzegovina and Liberia are countries whose income collapsed because of civil war, and they should be well positioned to go back to levels of income they were able to sustain two decades ago.

The countries at the bottom of the list are all oil exporters, including Gabon, Kuwait, Venezuela, Libya, Qatar and Angola. These countries rank in ECI and COI some 70 positions below their ranking in GDP per capita. The developed countries whose growth is expected to be lowest are Norway and Aus-

tralia, two natural resource exporters that exhibit low complexity and are poorly positioned in the product space.

This ranking shows that the two regions of the world where the potential of per capita growth is higher are East Asia and Eastern Europe *(Map 3)*. Per capita growth potential as a function of GDP per capita is illustrated in *Figure 3*.

BY REGION:

By region, the top performers in East Asia and the Pacific are China (2), Thailand (4), Vietnam (5), Indonesia (10) and Philippines (15) while very poor performance is expected in Papua New Guinea (97), New Zealand (100), Mongolia (104) and Australia (122). In South Asia, India is the regional leader (1), while Bangladesh is the laggard (61).

In the Middle East and North Africa, the expected leaders in GDP per capita growth are Egypt (12), Tunisia (28) and Jordan (41), while the laggards are Kuwait (124), Libya (126) and Qatar (127), three oil exporters that are dragged down by their low complexity and by our assumption that oil exports per real terms will remain at 2010 levels.

In Eastern Europe and Central Asia, the leaders in GDP per capita growth are expected to be Ukraine (3), Serbia (6), Bulgaria (7), and Bosnia and Herzegovina (8). The laggards would be Turkmenistan (110), Kazakhstan (114) and Azerbaijan (117), three low-complexity oil exporters. To the extent that these latter countries will carry out their planned oil expansion, their growth performance will be better than we project.

In Latin America the leaders are Mexico (20), El Salvador (42), Panama (46), Brazil (48) and Guatemala (60), while the laggards are expected to be Cuba (102), Chile (103), Trinidad and Tobago (121) and Venezuela (125), four exporters of natural resources.

In Sub-Saharan Africa, the growth leaders are expected to be Liberia (9), Kenya (13), Malawi (22), Zimbabwe (24), Tanzania (26) and Uganda (34), while the laggards are expected to be Nigeria (119), Gabon (123) and Angola (128). ●

RANKING 3. EXPECTED GROWTH IN PER CAPITA GDP TO 2020

RANK EXP. GROWTH IN GDP P/C	REGIONAL RANKING EXP. GROWTH IN GDP P/C	COUNTRY NAME	ISO CODE	EXPECTED GROWTH IN GDP P/C 2010-2020	GROWTH IN GDP P/C 2000-2010	RANK INCOME 2010 [USD]	INCOME 2010 [USD]	RANK EXPY	EXPY	RANK INCOME 2020	EXPECTED INCOME 2020 [USD]	REGION
1	1/4	India	IND	5.8%	5.8%	101	1,375	99	1,454	94	2,406	South Asia
2	1/16	China	CHN	4.2%	9.8%	74	4,433	71	4,621	65	6,710	East Asia and Pacific
3	1/27	Ukraine	UKR	4.2%	5.0%	83	2,974	83	3,098	78	4,470	Eastern Europe and Central Asia
4	2/16	Thailand	THA	3.9%	3.4%	70	4,614	70	4,795	64	6,782	East Asia and Pacific
5	3/16	Vietnam	VNM	3.8%	6.1%	106	1,224	105	1,270	100	1,771	East Asia and Pacific
6	2/27	Serbia	SRB	3.7%	3.8%	66	5,273	64	5,467	62	7,575	Eastern Europe and Central Asia
7	3/27	Bulgaria	BGR	3.6%	4.9%	60	6,335	60	6,563	55	9,031	Eastern Europe and Central Asia
8	4/27	Bosnia and Herzegovina	BIH	3.5%	3.9%	75	4,427	73	4,583	66	6,249	Eastern Europe and Central Asia
9	1/26	Liberia	LBR	3.5%	3.4%	128	247	128	256	128	348	Sub-Saharan Africa
10	4/16	Indonesia	IDN	3.5%	4.0%	85	2,952	84	3,054	81	4,154	East Asia and Pacific
11	5/27	Hungary	HUN	3.4%	2.2%	38	12,863	38	13,304	35	18,021	Eastern Europe and Central Asia
12	1/16	Egypt, Arab Rep.	EGY	3.4%	3.0%	90	2,698	90	2,791	84	3,776	Middle East and North Africa
13	2/26	Kenya	KEN	3.4%	1.4%	117	795	116	822	115	1,111	Sub-Saharan Africa
14	6/27	Romania	ROU	3.4%	4.8%	57	7,539	56	7,795	51	10,525	Eastern Europe and Central Asia
15	5/16	Philippines	PHL	3.3%	2.8%	94	2,140	94	2,212	92	2,972	East Asia and Pacific
16	6/16	Korea, Rep.	KOR	3.3%	3.6%	30	20,540	29	21,224	28	28,499	East Asia and Pacific
17	2/4	Pakistan	PAK	3.3%	2.7%	113	1,019	111	1,052	105	1,408	South Asia
18	7/27	Turkey	TUR	3.3%	2.5%	46	10,050	46	10,379	42	13,868	Eastern Europe and Central Asia
19	8/27	Slovak Republic	SVK	3.1%	4.7%	33	16,036	32	16,541	31	21,865	Eastern Europe and Central Asia
20	1/21	Mexico	MEX	3.1%	0.5%	49	9,133	49	9,419	46	12,436	Latin America and the Caribbean
21	9/27	Moldova	MDA	3.1%	5.4%	97	1,632	97	1,683	98	2,219	Eastern Europe and Central Asia
22	3/26	Malawi	MWI	3.1%	1.8%	127	339	127	350	126	461	Sub-Saharan Africa
23	10/27	Poland	POL	3.0%	4.0%	40	12,303	40	12,675	37	16,574	Eastern Europe and Central Asia
24	4/26	Zimbabwe	ZWE	3.0%	-5.0%	120	595	120	613	119	801	Sub-Saharan Africa
25	11/27	Belarus	BLR	3.0%	8.0%	63	5,819	62	5,993	61	7,817	Eastern Europe and Central Asia
26	5/26	Tanzania	TZA	3.0%	4.1%	121	527	121	542	121	705	Sub-Saharan Africa
27	12/27	Kyrgyz Republic	KGZ	2.9%	2.9%	114	880	114	906	113	1,175	Eastern Europe and Central Asia
28	2/16	Tunisia	TUN	2.9%	3.4%	78	4,194	77	4,314	72	5,567	Middle East and North Africa
29	13/27	Croatia	HRV	2.8%	2.7%	36	13,774	36	14,155	34	18,098	Eastern Europe and Central Asia
30	14/27	Estonia	EST	2.8%	3.7%	35	14,045	35	14,433	33	18,448	Eastern Europe and Central Asia
31	7/16	Malaysia	MYS	2.8%	2.6%	53	8,373	53	8,604	50	10,995	East Asia and Pacific
32	15/27	Czech Republic	CZE	2.7%	3.1%	31	18,789	31	19,304	30	24,621	Eastern Europe and Central Asia
33	16/27	Slovenia	SVN	2.7%	2.4%	27	22,898	27	23,525	27	30,003	Eastern Europe and Central Asia
34	6/26	Uganda	UGA	2.7%	4.0%	122	515	122	529	122	673	Sub-Saharan Africa
35	7/26	Madagascar	MDG	2.7%	-0.4%	124	421	124	432	123	550	Sub-Saharan Africa
36	17/27	Lithuania	LTU	2.7%	5.0%	42	11,046	42	11,342	39	14,393	Eastern Europe and Central Asia
37	18/27	Latvia	LVA	2.7%	4.3%	44	10,723	44	11,011	40	13,970	Eastern Europe and Central Asia
38	1/16	United Kingdom	GBR	2.6%	1.1%	20	36,186	20	37,126	16	46,767	Western Europe
39	19/27	Uzbekistan	UZB	2.6%	5.4%	100	1,377	100	1,412	99	1,775	Eastern Europe and Central Asia
40	2/16	Finland	FIN	2.6%	1.4%	13	44,091	12	45,222	6	56,799	Western Europe
41	3/16	Jordan	JOR	2.6%	3.9%	76	4,370	76	4,482	71	5,623	Middle East and North Africa
42	2/21	El Salvador	SLV	2.5%	1.5%	82	3,460	82	3,548	79	4,445	Latin America and the Caribbean
43	8/26	South Africa	ZAF	2.5%	2.2%	59	7,272	59	7,455	53	9,326	Sub-Saharan Africa

RANKING 3. EXPECTED GROWTH IN PER CAPITA GDP TO 2020

RANK EXP. GROWTH IN GDP P/C	REGIONAL RANKING EXP. GROWTH IN GDP P/C	COUNTRY NAME	ISO CODE	EXPECTED GROWTH IN GDP P/C 2010-2020	GROWTH IN GDP P/C 2000-2010	RANK INCOME 2010 [USD]	INCOME 2010 [USD]	RANK EXPY	EXPY	RANK INCOME 2020	EXPECTED INCOME 2020 [USD]	REGION
44	3/16	Portugal	PRT	2.5%	0.2%	28	21,358	28	21,892	29	27,336	Western Europe
45	4/16	Lebanon	LBN	2.5%	3.9%	48	9,227	48	9,453	48	11,756	Middle East and North Africa
46	3/21	Panama	PAN	2.4%	4.5%	55	7,614	55	7,800	52	9,694	Latin America and the Caribbean
47	8/16	Singapore	SGP	2.4%	3.2%	16	41,987	16	43,002	10	53,322	East Asia and Pacific
48	4/21	Brazil	BRA	2.4%	2.5%	43	10,993	43	11,257	41	13,943	Latin America and the Caribbean
49	9/16	Japan	JPN	2.3%	0.7%	14	43,063	14	44,070	8	54,260	East Asia and Pacific
50	5/16	Syrian Arab Republic	SYR	2.3%	2.4%	86	2,893	86	2,959	86	3,630	Middle East and North Africa
51	9/26	Mozambique	MOZ	2.3%	5.1%	125	394	125	403	125	494	Sub-Saharan Africa
52	6/16	Israel	ISR	2.2%	1.1%	25	28,522	25	29,161	24	35,592	Middle East and North Africa
53	4/16	Switzerland	CHE	2.2%	0.8%	3	67,644	3	69,152	1	84,323	Western Europe
54	10/26	Mali	MLI	2.2%	2.5%	119	613	119	627	120	762	Sub-Saharan Africa
55	20/27	Macedonia, FYR	MKD	2.2%	2.2%	73	4,434	75	4,532	74	5,512	Eastern Europe and Central Asia
56	3/4	Sri Lanka	LKA	2.2%	4.4%	92	2,400	92	2,452	91	2,979	South Asia
57	5/16	Spain	ESP	2.2%	0.7%	24	30,026	24	30,672	22	37,146	Western Europe
58	6/16	Sweden	SWE	2.1%	1.6%	6	49,257	6	50,303	5	60,772	Western Europe
59	11/26	Ethiopia	ETH	2.1%	5.9%	126	358	126	365	127	440	Sub-Saharan Africa
60	5/21	Guatemala	GTM	2.0%	0.8%	87	2,873	87	2,930	87	3,499	Latin America and the Caribbean
61	4/4	Bangladesh	BGD	2.0%	4.4%	118	675	118	688	118	821	South Asia
62	10/16	Lao PDR	LAO	2.0%	5.5%	108	1,158	107	1,181	106	1,406	East Asia and Pacific
63	6/21	Argentina	ARG	1.9%	3.4%	50	9,124	50	9,301	49	11,064	Latin America and the Caribbean
64	12/26	Zambia	ZMB	1.9%	3.1%	104	1,253	104	1,277	102	1,513	Sub-Saharan Africa
65	11/16	Cambodia	KHM	1.9%	6.6%	116	795	117	810	117	960	East Asia and Pacific
66	7/16	Belgium	BEL	1.9%	0.8%	15	42,833	15	43,633	14	51,542	Western Europe
67	21/27	Georgia	GEO	1.9%	6.2%	91	2,614	91	2,663	90	3,145	Eastern Europe and Central Asia
68	7/21	Colombia	COL	1.9%	2.5%	61	6,238	61	6,353	63	7,493	Latin America and the Caribbean
69	22/27	Tajikistan	TJK	1.8%	7.2%	115	820	115	835	116	984	Eastern Europe and Central Asia
70	8/16	Netherlands	NLD	1.8%	0.9%	8	46,597	7	47,439	7	55,738	Western Europe
71	7/16	Morocco	MAR	1.8%	3.8%	89	2,795	89	2,845	88	3,335	Middle East and North Africa
72	9/16	France	FRA	1.8%	0.4%	19	39,170	17	39,862	17	46,667	Western Europe
73	23/27	Russian Federation	RUS	1.7%	5.1%	45	10,481	45	10,664	45	12,460	Eastern Europe and Central Asia
74	10/16	Denmark	DNK	1.7%	0.2%	4	56,278	4	57,259	3	66,892	Western Europe
75	13/26	Senegal	SEN	1.7%	1.3%	112	1,034	113	1,052	110	1,228	Sub-Saharan Africa
76	8/21	Honduras	HND	1.7%	2.0%	95	2,019	95	2,053	95	2,386	Latin America and the Caribbean
77	11/16	Ireland	IRL	1.6%	0.7%	10	45,873	10	46,625	9	53,974	Western Europe
78	12/16	Greece	GRC	1.6%	1.8%	26	26,433	26	26,864	26	31,075	Western Europe
79	9/21	Nicaragua	NIC	1.6%	1.6%	110	1,139	109	1,157	108	1,336	Latin America and the Caribbean
80	13/16	Austria	AUT	1.6%	1.1%	12	44,885	11	45,595	12	52,513	Western Europe
81	12/16	Hong Kong SAR, China	HKG	1.6%	3.4%	23	31,758	23	32,255	23	37,096	East Asia and Pacific
82	10/21	Uruguay	URY	1.6%	2.8%	41	11,742	41	11,924	43	13,700	Latin America and the Caribbean
83	14/16	Italy	ITA	1.5%	-0.2%	21	33,788	21	34,293	21	39,191	Western Europe
84	11/21	Paraguay	PRY	1.5%	2.0%	88	2,840	88	2,882	89	3,293	Latin America and the Caribbean
85	12/21	Costa Rica	CRI	1.5%	2.5%	54	7,774	54	7,889	56	9,008	Latin America and the Caribbean
86	13/21	Bolivia	BOL	1.5%	2.0%	96	1,979	96	2,008	97	2,293	Latin America and the Caribbean

RANKING 3. EXPECTED GROWTH IN PER CAPITA GDP TO 2020

RANK EXP. GROWTH IN GDP P/C	REGIONAL RANKING EXP. GROWTH IN GDP P/C	COUNTRY NAME	ISO CODE	EXPECTED GROWTH IN GDP P/C 2010-2020	GROWTH IN GDP P/C 2000-2010	RANK INCOME 2010 [USD]	INCOME 2010 [USD]	RANK EXPY	EXPY	RANK INCOME 2020	EXPECTED INCOME 2020 [USD]	REGION
87	14/26	Guinea	GIN	1.5%	4.0%	123	474	123	481	124	548	Sub-Saharan Africa
88	1/2	Canada	CAN	1.4%	0.8%	9	46,212	9	46,868	11	53,202	North America
89	15/26	Botswana	BWA	1.4%	3.0%	58	7,427	58	7,529	58	8,514	Sub-Saharan Africa
90	14/21	Peru	PER	1.4%	4.4%	65	5,292	66	5,365	67	6,063	Latin America and the Caribbean
91	15/21	Dominican Republic	DOM	1.3%	3.8%	67	5,195	67	5,265	68	5,931	Latin America and the Caribbean
92	16/26	Ghana	GHA	1.3%	3.3%	102	1,319	102	1,336	104	1,495	Sub-Saharan Africa
93	2/2	United States	USA	1.2%	0.6%	7	46,702	8	47,242	13	52,400	North America
94	17/26	Côte d'Ivoire	CIV	1.1%	-0.7%	107	1,161	108	1,174	109	1,299	Sub-Saharan Africa
95	24/27	Albania	ALB	1.0%	4.8%	81	3,701	81	3,737	83	4,078	Eastern Europe and Central Asia
96	18/26	Mauritius	MUS	0.9%	3.0%	56	7,584	57	7,648	59	8,255	Sub-Saharan Africa
97	13/16	Papua New Guinea	PNG	0.8%	1.3%	99	1,382	101	1,394	103	1,503	East Asia and Pacific
98	16/21	Ecuador	ECU	0.8%	3.0%	79	4,008	79	4,040	80	4,338	Latin America and the Caribbean
99	17/21	Jamaica	JAM	0.8%	0.4%	68	5,133	68	5,173	73	5,543	Latin America and the Caribbean
100	14/16	New Zealand	NZL	0.7%	1.1%	22	32,620	22	32,863	25	35,130	East Asia and Pacific
101	19/26	Mauritania	MRT	0.7%	2.2%	111	1,045	112	1,052	114	1,124	Sub-Saharan Africa
102	18/21	Cuba	CUB	0.7%	5.0%	64	5,397	65	5,436	69	5,803	Latin America and the Caribbean
103	19/21	Chile	CHL	0.6%	2.8%	39	12,640	39	12,714	44	13,403	Latin America and the Caribbean
104	15/16	Mongolia	MNG	0.6%	5.1%	93	2,250	93	2,262	96	2,377	East Asia and Pacific
105	8/16	Yemen, Rep.	YEM	0.5%	1.1%	103	1,291	103	1,298	107	1,362	Middle East and North Africa
106	9/16	Algeria	DZA	0.5%	2.2%	71	4,567	72	4,588	76	4,783	Middle East and North Africa
107	20/26	Cameroon	CMR	0.4%	1.1%	109	1,147	110	1,152	111	1,193	Sub-Saharan Africa
108	10/16	Iran, Islamic Rep.	IRN	0.4%	3.7%	72	4,526	74	4,544	77	4,706	Middle East and North Africa
109	11/16	Saudi Arabia	SAU	0.4%	0.1%	32	16,423	33	16,484	36	17,040	Middle East and North Africa
110	25/27	Turkmenistan	TKM	0.3%	12.3%	80	3,967	80	3,980	82	4,100	Eastern Europe and Central Asia
111	12/16	United Arab Emirates	ARE	0.3%	-4.8%	18	39,625	19	39,730	19	40,690	Middle East and North Africa
112	21/26	Namibia	NAM	0.2%	3.1%	69	4,876	69	4,885	75	4,971	Sub-Saharan Africa
113	22/26	Sudan	SDN	0.2%	3.8%	98	1,538	98	1,541	101	1,568	Sub-Saharan Africa
114	26/27	Kazakhstan	KAZ	0.1%	7.3%	51	9,070	51	9,079	54	9,163	Eastern Europe and Central Asia
115	15/16	Germany	DEU	-0.2%	1.0%	17	39,852	18	39,786	20	39,205	Western Europe
116	23/26	Congo, Rep.	COG	-0.3%	2.0%	84	2,970	85	2,961	93	2,883	Sub-Saharan Africa
117	27/27	Azerbaijan	AZE	-0.3%	13.6%	62	5,843	63	5,825	70	5,667	Eastern Europe and Central Asia
118	16/16	Norway	NOR	-0.3%	0.6%	1	85,443	1	85,173	2	82,782	Western Europe
119	24/26	Nigeria	NGA	-0.4%	3.8%	105	1,242	106	1,237	112	1,189	Sub-Saharan Africa
120	13/16	Oman	OMN	-0.5%	2.6%	29	20,791	30	20,683	32	19,742	Middle East and North Africa
121	20/21	Trinidad and Tobago	TTO	-0.5%	5.2%	34	15,614	34	15,532	38	14,812	Latin America and the Caribbean
122	16/16	Australia	AUS	-0.6%	1.5%	5	50,746	5	50,430	15	47,670	East Asia and Pacific
123	25/26	Gabon	GAB	-0.8%	0.3%	52	8,768	52	8,695	60	8,063	Sub-Saharan Africa
124	14/16	Kuwait	KWT	-1.0%	1.7%	11	45,437	13	44,980	18	41,073	Middle East and North Africa
125	21/21	Venezuela, RB	VEN	-1.0%	1.4%	37	13,658	37	13,515	47	12,297	Latin America and the Caribbean
126	15/16	Libya	LBY	-1.1%	2.2%	47	9,957	47	9,845	57	8,889	Middle East and North Africa
127	16/16	Qatar	QAT	-1.6%	0.7%	2	72,398	2	71,243	4	61,647	Middle East and North Africa
128	26/26	Angola	AGO	-1.6%	7.6%	77	4,322	78	4,252	85	3,670	Sub-Saharan Africa

MAP 3:

▶ Countries are color coded according to their ranking in Expected Growth in Per Capita GDP to 2020.

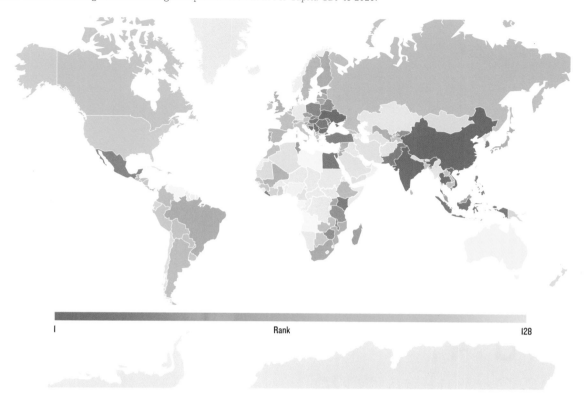

FIGURE 3:

▶ Expected annual GDP per capita growth with respect to GDP per capita in 2010.

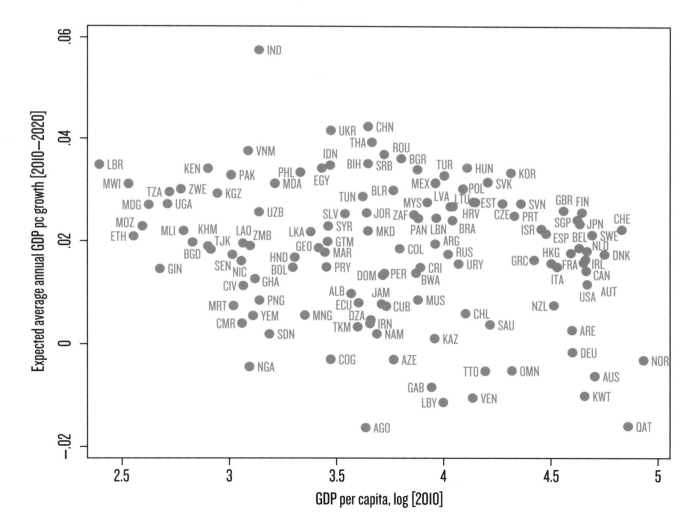

RANKING 4:
Expected GDP Growth to 2020

RANKING 4 shows the ranking for total GDP growth. To calculate this ranking we add the projected rate of population growth estimated by the United Nations to the expected growth in GDP per capita of Ranking 3.

The top country in this ranking is India, driven to that position because of its high growth in GDP per capita we expect from Ranking 3. The remaining 9 countries in the top 10 are all in Sub-Saharan Africa, buoyed by their high projected population growth. This can be seen by the difference in their rankings in total GDP growth and in GDP growth per capita (in parenthesis). In order from 2nd to 10th they are Malawi (22), Tanzania (26), Liberia (9), Kenya (13), Uganda (34), Madagascar (35), Zimbabwe (24), Mali (54) and Zambia (64). *Map* 4 shows the geographic pattern of total GDP growth. It shows the concentration of growth in East Africa, India, Pakistan, China and other East Asian countries, Mexico, Turkey and Egypt. *Figure* 4 plots total GDP growth as a function of GDP per capita.

BY REGION:

By region, in East Asia and the Pacific the expected leaders in GDP growth are Philippines (13), Vietnam (14) and China (15), while the laggard is Australia (123). In South Asia the best performing country is expected to be India (1), while Sri Lanka is the laggard (64). In Eastern Europe and Central Asia the top performers are Turkey (20), Kyrgyz Republic (25) and Uzbekistan (32). The worst performers in this region are Kazakhstan (116) and Azerbaijan (120).

In Latin America the fastest growing countries are expected to be Guatemala (17), Mexico (24) and Panama (29) while very poor performance is expected in Cuba (122), Venezuela (125) and Trinidad and Tobago (127). Egypt (11), Jordan (21) and Syria (27) are expected to lead GDP growth in the Middle East and North Africa, while the laggards are Qatar (121) and Libya (126).

While countries in Sub-Saharan Africa are in 9 of the 10 top spots for total GDP growth, the worst performers in the region, namely Mauritius (110), Gabon (118) and Angola (119), are among the worst in the world. While Gabon and Angola are affected by their reliance on oil, Mauritius is impacted by its high level of income relative to its ECI and COI and by its low expected population growth.

GDP growth in Western Europe is expected to be lead by The United Kingdom (47), followed by Finland (65). At the bottom of the list we expect to find Norway (124) and Germany (128). ●

RANKING 4. EXPECTED GDP GROWTH TO 2020

RANK EXPECTED GDP GROWTH	REGIONAL RANK EXPECTED GDP GROWTH	COUNTRY NAME	ISO CODE	EXPECTED GDP GROWTH 2010-2020	GDP GROWTH 2000-2010	RANK INCOME 2010 [USD]	INCOME 2010 [USD]	EXPECTED POPULATION GROWTH	REGION
1	1/4	India	IND	7.0%	7.4%	101	1,375	1.3%	South Asia
2	1/26	Malawi	MWI	6.4%	4.7%	127	339	3.3%	Sub-Saharan Africa
3	2/26	Tanzania	TZA	6.1%	7.0%	121	527	3.1%	Sub-Saharan Africa
4	3/26	Liberia	LBR	6.1%	7.0%	128	247	2.6%	Sub-Saharan Africa
5	4/26	Kenya	KEN	6.0%	4.1%	117	795	2.6%	Sub-Saharan Africa
6	5/26	Uganda	UGA	5.8%	7.4%	122	515	3.1%	Sub-Saharan Africa
7	6/26	Madagascar	MDG	5.5%	2.6%	124	421	2.8%	Sub-Saharan Africa
8	7/26	Zimbabwe	ZWE	5.2%	-4.9%	120	595	2.1%	Sub-Saharan Africa
9	8/26	Mali	MLI	5.1%	5.7%	119	613	2.9%	Sub-Saharan Africa
10	9/26	Zambia	ZMB	5.1%	5.6%	104	1,253	3.2%	Sub-Saharan Africa
11	1/16	Egypt, Arab Rep.	EGY	5.0%	4.8%	90	2,698	1.6%	Middle East and North Africa
12	2/4	Pakistan	PAK	5.0%	4.6%	113	1,019	1.7%	South Asia
13	1/16	Philippines	PHL	5.0%	4.8%	94	2,140	1.6%	East Asia and Pacific
14	2/16	Vietnam	VNM	4.7%	7.3%	106	1,224	0.9%	East Asia and Pacific
15	3/16	China	CHN	4.6%	10.5%	74	4,433	0.3%	East Asia and Pacific
16	10/26	Mozambique	MOZ	4.5%	7.8%	125	394	2.2%	Sub-Saharan Africa
17	1/21	Guatemala	GTM	4.5%	3.3%	87	2,873	2.5%	Latin America and the Caribbean
18	4/16	Indonesia	IDN	4.4%	5.2%	85	2,952	0.9%	East Asia and Pacific
19	5/16	Thailand	THA	4.3%	4.3%	70	4,614	0.4%	East Asia and Pacific
20	1/27	Turkey	TUR	4.3%	3.9%	46	10,050	1.0%	Eastern Europe and Central Asia
21	2/16	Jordan	JOR	4.3%	6.3%	76	4,370	1.8%	Middle East and North Africa
22	11/26	Senegal	SEN	4.3%	4.1%	112	1,034	2.6%	Sub-Saharan Africa
23	6/16	Malaysia	MYS	4.3%	4.6%	53	8,373	1.5%	East Asia and Pacific
24	2/21	Mexico	MEX	4.2%	1.8%	49	9,133	1.1%	Latin America and the Caribbean
25	2/27	Kyrgyz Republic	KGZ	4.1%	4.0%	114	880	1.2%	Eastern Europe and Central Asia
26	12/26	Ethiopia	ETH	4.1%	8.4%	126	358	2.0%	Sub-Saharan Africa
27	3/16	Syrian Arab Republic	SYR	4.0%	4.9%	86	2,893	1.7%	Middle East and North Africa
28	13/26	Guinea	GIN	3.9%	5.8%	123	474	2.5%	Sub-Saharan Africa
29	3/21	Panama	PAN	3.8%	6.3%	55	7,614	1.4%	Latin America and the Caribbean
30	4/16	Tunisia	TUN	3.8%	4.4%	78	4,194	0.9%	Middle East and North Africa
31	5/16	Israel	ISR	3.8%	3.1%	25	28,522	1.6%	Middle East and North Africa
32	3/27	Uzbekistan	UZB	3.7%	6.9%	100	1,377	1.2%	Eastern Europe and Central Asia
33	7/16	Korea, Rep.	KOR	3.7%	4.2%	30	20,540	0.3%	East Asia and Pacific
34	4/27	Ukraine	UKR	3.6%	4.3%	83	2,974	-0.5%	Eastern Europe and Central Asia
35	4/21	Honduras	HND	3.6%	4.1%	95	2,019	1.9%	Latin America and the Caribbean
36	5/27	Serbia	SRB	3.5%	3.7%	66	5,273	-0.1%	Eastern Europe and Central Asia
37	6/16	Yemen, Rep.	YEM	3.5%	4.3%	103	1,291	3.0%	Middle East and North Africa
38	14/26	Ghana	GHA	3.5%	5.8%	102	1,319	2.2%	Sub-Saharan Africa
39	8/16	Singapore	SGP	3.4%	5.6%	16	41,987	1.0%	East Asia and Pacific
40	15/26	Côte d'Ivoire	CIV	3.3%	1.1%	107	1,161	2.2%	Sub-Saharan Africa
41	6/27	Tajikistan	TJK	3.3%	8.3%	115	820	1.5%	Eastern Europe and Central Asia
42	7/27	Slovak Republic	SVK	3.3%	4.8%	33	16,036	0.2%	Eastern Europe and Central Asia
43	8/27	Hungary	HUN	3.3%	2.0%	38	12,863	-0.2%	Eastern Europe and Central Asia

RANKING 4. EXPECTED GDP GROWTH TO 2020

RANK EXPECTED GDP GROWTH	REGIONAL RANK EXPECTED GDP GROWTH	COUNTRY NAME	ISO CODE	EXPECTED GDP GROWTH 2010-2020	GDP GROWTH 2000-2010	RANK INCOME 2010 [USD]	INCOME 2010 [USD]	EXPECTED POPULATION GROWTH	REGION
44	9/16	Lao PDR	LAO	3.2%	7.1%	108	1,158	1.3%	East Asia and Pacific
45	9/27	Bosnia and Herzegovina	BIH	3.2%	4.1%	75	4,427	-0.3%	Eastern Europe and Central Asia
46	5/21	El Salvador	SLV	3.2%	1.9%	82	3,460	0.7%	Latin America and the Caribbean
47	1/16	United Kingdom	GBR	3.2%	1.7%	20	36,186	0.6%	Western Europe
48	6/21	Brazil	BRA	3.2%	3.6%	43	10,993	0.8%	Latin America and the Caribbean
49	3/4	Bangladesh	BGD	3.2%	5.8%	118	675	1.2%	South Asia
50	10/27	Romania	ROU	3.1%	4.3%	57	7,539	-0.2%	Eastern Europe and Central Asia
51	7/21	Paraguay	PRY	3.1%	4.0%	88	2,840	1.6%	Latin America and the Caribbean
52	7/16	Lebanon	LBN	3.1%	5.1%	48	9,227	0.7%	Middle East and North Africa
53	10/16	Cambodia	KHM	3.1%	8.0%	116	795	1.2%	East Asia and Pacific
54	8/21	Colombia	COL	3.1%	4.1%	61	6,238	1.2%	Latin America and the Caribbean
55	11/27	Poland	POL	3.1%	3.9%	40	12,303	0.0%	Eastern Europe and Central Asia
56	9/21	Bolivia	BOL	3.0%	3.8%	96	1,979	1.6%	Latin America and the Caribbean
57	16/26	South Africa	ZAF	3.0%	3.5%	59	7,272	0.5%	Sub-Saharan Africa
58	12/27	Czech Republic	CZE	3.0%	3.4%	31	18,789	0.2%	Eastern Europe and Central Asia
59	11/16	Papua New Guinea	PNG	3.0%	3.8%	99	1,382	2.1%	East Asia and Pacific
60	10/21	Nicaragua	NIC	2.9%	2.9%	110	1,139	1.3%	Latin America and the Caribbean
61	13/27	Bulgaria	BGR	2.9%	4.1%	60	6,335	-0.7%	Eastern Europe and Central Asia
62	17/26	Mauritania	MRT	2.9%	5.0%	111	1,045	2.2%	Sub-Saharan Africa
63	14/27	Slovenia	SVN	2.9%	2.7%	27	22,898	0.2%	Eastern Europe and Central Asia
64	4/4	Sri Lanka	LKA	2.9%	5.2%	92	2,400	0.7%	South Asia
65	2/16	Finland	FIN	2.9%	1.8%	13	44,091	0.3%	Western Europe
66	11/21	Argentina	ARG	2.8%	4.3%	50	9,124	0.8%	Latin America and the Caribbean
67	12/21	Costa Rica	CRI	2.7%	4.3%	54	7,774	1.2%	Latin America and the Caribbean
68	8/16	Morocco	MAR	2.7%	4.9%	89	2,795	0.9%	Middle East and North Africa
69	3/16	Ireland	IRL	2.7%	2.4%	10	45,873	1.1%	Western Europe
70	4/16	Spain	ESP	2.7%	2.1%	24	30,026	0.5%	Western Europe
71	5/16	Sweden	SWE	2.7%	2.1%	6	49,257	0.6%	Western Europe
72	15/27	Estonia	EST	2.7%	3.5%	35	14,045	-0.1%	Eastern Europe and Central Asia
73	16/27	Belarus	BLR	2.7%	7.4%	63	5,819	-0.3%	Eastern Europe and Central Asia
74	6/16	Switzerland	CHE	2.6%	1.7%	3	67,644	0.4%	Western Europe
75	12/16	Hong Kong SAR, China	HKG	2.6%	4.0%	23	31,758	1.0%	East Asia and Pacific
76	17/27	Croatia	HRV	2.6%	2.7%	36	13,774	-0.2%	Eastern Europe and Central Asia
77	18/26	Sudan	SDN	2.5%	6.3%	98	1,538	2.3%	Sub-Saharan Africa
78	18/27	Moldova	MDA	2.5%	5.1%	97	1,632	-0.6%	Eastern Europe and Central Asia
79	19/26	Cameroon	CMR	2.5%	3.3%	109	1,147	2.1%	Sub-Saharan Africa
80	13/21	Dominican Republic	DOM	2.5%	5.3%	67	5,195	1.1%	Latin America and the Caribbean
81	14/21	Peru	PER	2.5%	5.7%	65	5,292	1.1%	Latin America and the Caribbean
82	7/16	Portugal	PRT	2.4%	0.6%	28	21,358	0.0%	Western Europe
83	9/16	Saudi Arabia	SAU	2.4%	3.3%	32	16,423	2.0%	Middle East and North Africa
84	20/26	Botswana	BWA	2.3%	4.1%	58	7,427	0.9%	Sub-Saharan Africa
85	1/2	Canada	CAN	2.3%	1.9%	9	46,212	0.9%	North America
86	19/27	Latvia	LVA	2.3%	3.7%	44	10,723	-0.4%	Eastern Europe and Central Asia

RANKING 4. EXPECTED GDP GROWTH TO 2020

RANK EXPECTED GDP GROWTH	REGIONAL RANK EXPECTED GDP GROWTH	COUNTRY NAME	ISO CODE	EXPECTED GDP GROWTH 2010-2020	GDP GROWTH 2000-2010	RANK INCOME 2010 [USD]	INCOME 2010 [USD]	EXPECTED POPULATION GROWTH	REGION
87	10/16	United Arab Emirates	ARE	2.3%	4.3%	18	39,625	2.0%	Middle East and North Africa
88	20/27	Lithuania	LTU	2.3%	4.4%	42	11,046	-0.4%	Eastern Europe and Central Asia
89	21/27	Macedonia, FYR	MKD	2.3%	2.5%	73	4,434	0.1%	Eastern Europe and Central Asia
90	8/16	France	FRA	2.2%	1.1%	19	39,170	0.5%	Western Europe
91	13/16	Japan	JPN	2.2%	0.7%	14	43,063	-0.1%	East Asia and Pacific
92	9/16	Belgium	BEL	2.1%	1.4%	15	42,833	0.3%	Western Europe
93	21/26	Nigeria	NGA	2.1%	6.4%	105	1,242	2.6%	Sub-Saharan Africa
94	10/16	Denmark	DNK	2.1%	0.6%	4	56,278	0.3%	Western Europe
95	11/16	Netherlands	NLD	2.1%	1.4%	8	46,597	0.3%	Western Europe
96	15/21	Ecuador	ECU	2.0%	4.6%	79	4,008	1.2%	Latin America and the Caribbean
97	14/16	Mongolia	MNG	2.0%	6.5%	93	2,250	1.5%	East Asia and Pacific
98	2/2	United States	USA	2.0%	1.6%	7	46,702	0.8%	North America
99	16/21	Uruguay	URY	1.9%	3.0%	41	11,742	0.4%	Latin America and the Caribbean
100	22/26	Congo, Rep.	COG	1.9%	4.6%	84	2,970	2.2%	Sub-Saharan Africa
101	12/16	Greece	GRC	1.8%	2.1%	26	26,433	0.2%	Western Europe
102	23/26	Namibia	NAM	1.8%	4.6%	69	4,876	1.6%	Sub-Saharan Africa
103	15/16	New Zealand	NZL	1.7%	2.3%	22	32,620	1.0%	East Asia and Pacific
104	13/16	Austria	AUT	1.7%	1.5%	12	44,885	0.1%	Western Europe
105	11/16	Algeria	DZA	1.7%	3.7%	71	4,567	1.3%	Middle East and North Africa
106	14/16	Italy	ITA	1.6%	0.4%	21	33,788	0.1%	Western Europe
107	22/27	Russian Federation	RUS	1.6%	4.8%	45	10,481	-0.1%	Eastern Europe and Central Asia
108	23/27	Turkmenistan	TKM	1.5%	13.6%	80	3,967	1.2%	Eastern Europe and Central Asia
109	17/21	Chile	CHL	1.4%	3.9%	39	12,640	0.8%	Latin America and the Caribbean
110	24/26	Mauritius	MUS	1.3%	3.8%	56	7,584	0.5%	Sub-Saharan Africa
111	12/16	Iran, Islamic Rep.	IRN	1.3%	5.3%	72	4,526	0.9%	Middle East and North Africa
112	24/27	Albania	ALB	1.3%	5.2%	81	3,701	0.3%	Eastern Europe and Central Asia
113	25/27	Georgia	GEO	1.2%	6.2%	91	2,614	-0.6%	Eastern Europe and Central Asia
114	13/16	Oman	OMN	1.2%	4.7%	29	20,791	1.7%	Middle East and North Africa
115	14/16	Kuwait	KWT	1.2%	5.3%	11	45,437	2.2%	Middle East and North Africa
116	26/27	Kazakhstan	KAZ	1.1%	8.3%	51	9,070	1.0%	Eastern Europe and Central Asia
117	18/21	Jamaica	JAM	1.1%	0.8%	68	5,133	0.3%	Latin America and the Caribbean
118	25/26	Gabon	GAB	1.1%	2.3%	52	8,768	1.9%	Sub-Saharan Africa
119	26/26	Angola	AGO	1.0%	11.1%	77	4,322	2.6%	Sub-Saharan Africa
120	27/27	Azerbaijan	AZE	0.8%	14.9%	62	5,843	1.1%	Eastern Europe and Central Asia
121	15/16	Qatar	QAT	0.7%	12.4%	2	72,398	2.3%	Middle East and North Africa
122	19/21	Cuba	CUB	0.7%	5.2%	64	5,397	-0.1%	Latin America and the Caribbean
123	16/16	Australia	AUS	0.6%	3.1%	5	50,746	1.3%	East Asia and Pacific
124	15/16	Norway	NOR	0.4%	1.5%	1	85,443	0.7%	Western Europe
125	20/21	Venezuela, RB	VEN	0.4%	3.1%	37	13,658	1.4%	Latin America and the Caribbean
126	16/16	Libya	LBY	0.0%	4.3%	47	9,957	1.1%	Middle East and North Africa
127	21/21	Trinidad and Tobago	TTO	-0.3%	5.6%	34	15,614	0.2%	Latin America and the Caribbean
128	16/16	Germany	DEU	-0.3%	0.9%	17	39,852	-0.2%	Western Europe

MAP 4:

▶ Countries are color coded according to their ranking in Expected GDP Growth to 2020.

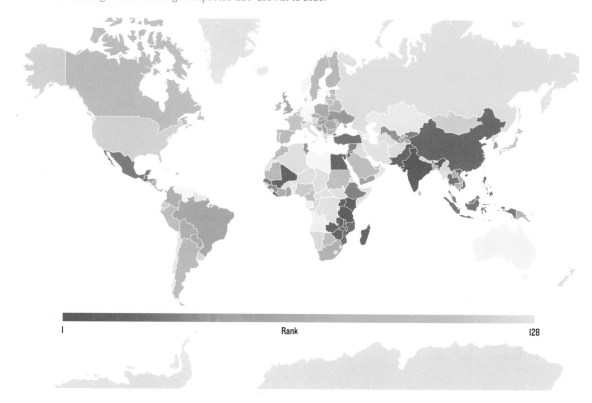

FIGURE 4:

▶ Plots expected total GDP growth between 2010 and 2020 as a function of GDP per capita.

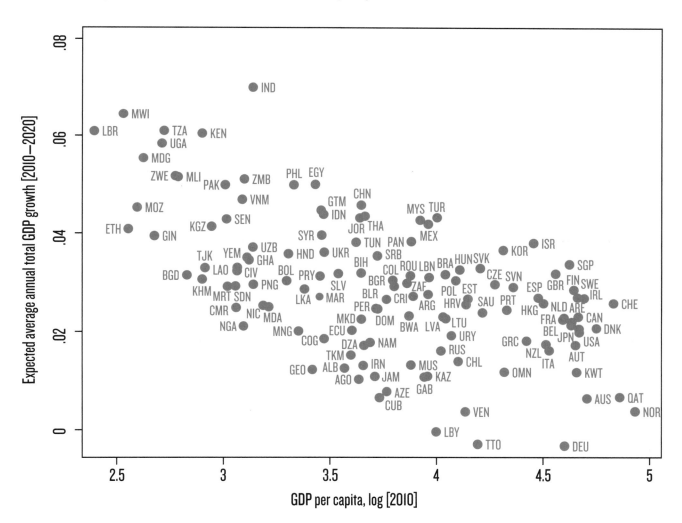

RANKING 5:

Change in Economic Complexity (1964-2010)

FIGURE 5.1:

▶ Evolution of the ranking of countries based on ECI between 1964 and 2008.

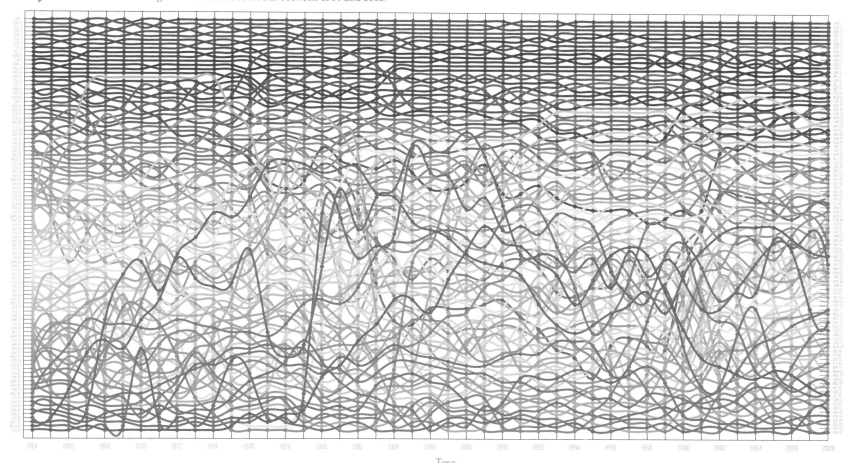

Time

RANKING 5 looks at changes in economic complexity. Here countries are ranked according to the change in ECI experienced between 1964 and 2010. Because of data availability, this ranking is limited to 101 countries. The countries that improved the most during this period are Mauritius, Thailand, Brazil, Malaysia, Singapore, Turkey, Dominican Republic, Philippines, Indonesia and South Korea. All of these countries dramatically transformed their economies during this forty-six year period *(see Part 1, Section 5: How does economic complexity evolve?)*. These transformations can be seen in detail in their respective country pages. *Figure* 5 shows the change in ECI observed between 2000 and 2010 as a function of a country's current level of income. *Map* 5 illustrates the spatial distribution of these changes. *Figure* 5.1 provides a visual representation of the change in ECI rankings. Here, each line represents a country, and the vertical position of the line indicates the position on the ranking for a given year. Lines were assigned a color using a perfect gradient according to their ranking in the initial year (1964). This helps identify movements in the ranking of economic complexity during the observed period.

BY REGION:

By region, in East Asia and the Pacific the countries that changed their economic complexity the most were Thailand (2), Malaysia (4), Singapore (5) and Philippines (8). China occupies the 18th position in this ranking. The relatively low position of China in this ranking reflects the fact that China's transformation built on an initial productive structure that was more sophisticated than that of many of its regional neighbors. After all, the country was able to develop the atomic bomb by 1964. The laggards of this region are Australia (86), Hong Kong (91) and Mongolia (93). In South Asia the best performing country was India (23), while Pakistan (83) is the laggard.

In Eastern Europe and Central Asia the top performers were Turkey (6) and Hungary (20). The lack of historical data for the region is substantial, however, since many of the countries in the region used to be part of the Soviet Union and were not in the international trade statistics of the day.

In Latin America the countries that experienced the largest change in economic complexity were Brazil (3), Dominican Republic (7) and Mexico (11). The laggards were Nicaragua (82), Panama (85) and Venezuela (97). In the Middle East and North Africa, Saudi Arabia (12), Tunisia (14) and Israel (16) increased their ECI the most, while the laggards were Oman (98), Kuwait (99), which used to be the most complex economy of the region in 1964, and Libya (100).

Finally, in Western Europe the changes in ECI between 1964 and 2010 is led by that of Spain (19), Ireland (25) and Finland (28) and the laggards of the region were United Kingdom (77), Belgium (81) and Norway (94). We note that Western Europe is a region in which all countries have always had positive ECI values, which limits the range of potential positive changes. ●

RANKING 5. CHANGE IN ECONOMIC COMPLEXITY (1964-2010)

RANKING △ ECI (64-10)	REGIONAL RANK △ ECI (64-10)	COUNTRY NAME	ISO CODE	1970	1980	1990	2000	2010	△ ECI (64-10)	△ ECI (00-10)	RANK △ ECI (00-10)	REGIONAL RANK △ ECI (00-10)	REGION
1	1/22	Mauritius	MUS	-0.94	0.15	-0.25	-0.61	-0.27	1.52	0.34	16	23/24	Sub-Saharan Africa
2	1/16	Thailand	THA	-0.68	-0.17	0.18	0.40	0.80	1.45	0.40	12	13/16	East Asia and Pacific
3	1/21	Brazil	BRA	-0.81	0.16	0.42	0.73	0.35	1.38	-0.38	110	3/21	Latin America and the Caribbean
4	2/16	Malaysia	MYS	-0.54	-0.29	0.25	0.65	0.74	1.12	0.10	51	7/16	East Asia and Pacific
5	3/16	Singapore	SGP	0.01	0.40	0.99	1.42	1.65	1.06	0.23	30	10/16	East Asia and Pacific
6	1/6	Turkey	TUR	-0.52	-0.30	0.22	0.17	0.47	1.02	0.30	22	23/26	Eastern Europe and Central Asia
7	2/21	Dominican Republic	DOM	-0.82	-0.20	-0.35	-0.55	-0.30	0.85	0.26	29	17/21	Latin America and the Caribbean
8	4/16	Philippines	PHL	-0.49	-0.35	-0.08	-0.02	0.24	0.82	0.26	28	11/16	East Asia and Pacific
9	5/16	Indonesia	IDN	-1.26	-1.19	-0.32	0.01	-0.08	0.79	-0.09	85	4/16	East Asia and Pacific
10	6/16	Korea, Rep.	KOR	0.73	0.82	0.89	1.17	1.69	0.76	0.52	4	16/16	East Asia and Pacific
11	3/21	Mexico	MEX	0.33	0.82	0.76	0.99	0.98	0.75	-0.01	68	9/21	Latin America and the Caribbean
12	1/15	Saudi Arabia	SAU	0.25	0.43	0.28	-0.03	0.11	0.75	0.14	45	8/16	Middle East and North Africa
13	2/22	Uganda	UGA	-1.45	-2.12	-1.42	-1.24	-0.92	0.67	0.32	19	21/24	Sub-Saharan Africa
14	2/15	Tunisia	TUN	-0.07	-0.14	0.03	-0.22	0.24	0.55	0.45	8	14/16	Middle East and North Africa
15	3/22	Kenya	KEN	-0.62	-0.52	-0.68	-0.69	-0.50	0.52	0.19	34	19/24	Sub-Saharan Africa
16	3/15	Israel	ISR	0.36	1.02	1.04	1.19	1.21	0.48	0.02	62	4/16	Middle East and North Africa
17	4/22	South Africa	ZAF	-0.15	0.05	-0.24	0.30	0.24	0.47	-0.06	80	13/24	Sub-Saharan Africa
18	7/16	China	CHN	0.48	0.28	0.38	0.41	0.88	0.43	0.47	6	15/16	East Asia and Pacific
19	1/16	Spain	ESP	0.96	0.91	1.29	1.11	1.05	0.40	-0.06	78	12/16	Western Europe
20	2/6	Hungary	HUN	1.06	0.71	0.81	1.02	1.44	0.39	0.42	10	26/26	Eastern Europe and Central Asia
21	3/6	Romania	ROU	0.89	0.59	0.53	0.52	0.78	0.38	0.27	27	19/26	Eastern Europe and Central Asia
22	8/16	Japan	JPN	1.82	1.91	2.33	2.49	2.17	0.35	-0.32	104	3/16	East Asia and Pacific
23	1/3	India	IND	0.08	0.13	0.39	0.26	0.21	0.32	-0.05	74	2/4	South Asia
24	4/21	Ecuador	ECU	-1.28	-0.86	-0.84	-0.89	-0.67	0.30	0.22	32	16/21	Latin America and the Caribbean
25	2/16	Ireland	IRL	0.97	1.08	1.38	1.45	1.36	0.28	-0.09	86	10/16	Western Europe
26	5/21	Paraguay	PRY	-0.65	-0.93	-0.82	-0.58	-0.48	0.28	0.11	50	14/21	Latin America and the Caribbean
27	5/22	Tanzania	TZA	-1.31	-0.84	-1.04	-1.34	-1.02	0.27	0.32	18	22/24	Sub-Saharan Africa
28	3/16	Finland	FIN	1.57	1.36	1.88	1.87	1.69	0.25	-0.18	91	9/16	Western Europe
29	2/3	Sri Lanka	LKA	-1.18	-0.60	-0.47	-0.61	-0.45	0.24	0.16	40	4/4	South Asia
30	6/22	Gabon	GAB	-1.15	-1.51	-1.07	-0.76	-1.14	0.23	-0.38	111	7/24	Sub-Saharan Africa
31	7/22	Ghana	GHA	-1.76	-1.77	-1.38	-1.06	-1.09	0.19	-0.03	73	16/24	Sub-Saharan Africa
32	4/15	Lebanon	LBN	0.50	0.42	0.21	0.02	0.33	0.18	0.31	20	12/16	Middle East and North Africa
33	6/21	Colombia	COL	-0.27	-0.27	-0.18	0.10	0.12	0.13	0.02	65	10/21	Latin America and the Caribbean
34	7/21	Argentina	ARG	-0.12	-0.05	0.22	0.16	0.10	0.12	-0.06	79	7/21	Latin America and the Caribbean
35	4/6	Poland	POL	0.84	0.96	0.70	0.97	1.13	0.12	0.16	41	15/26	Eastern Europe and Central Asia
36	8/21	Peru	PER	-0.60	-0.07	-0.09	-0.36	-0.48	0.11	-0.12	87	6/21	Latin America and the Caribbean
37	4/16	Greece	GRC	0.27	0.21	0.20	0.31	0.28	0.09	-0.03	72	13/16	Western Europe
38	5/15	Jordan	JOR	0.33	0.62	0.38	0.25	0.36	0.08	0.12	48	7/16	Middle East and North Africa
39	9/21	Trinidad and Tobago	TTO	0.25	0.06	0.43	0.11	-0.47	0.08	-0.57	120	2/21	Latin America and the Caribbean
40	6/15	Egypt, Arab Rep.	EGY	-0.18	-0.44	-0.26	-0.17	-0.10	0.04	0.06	57	6/16	Middle East and North Africa
41	10/21	Jamaica	JAM	-0.52	-0.53	-0.37	-0.72	-0.41	0.04	0.31	21	18/21	Latin America and the Caribbean
42	8/22	Mozambique	MOZ	-0.90	-0.55	-0.20	-0.42	-1.26	0.03	-0.84	124	1/24	Sub-Saharan Africa
43	9/16	Lao PDR	LAO	-0.84	-0.34	-0.84	-0.99	-0.82	0.02	0.17	38	9/16	East Asia and Pacific

RANKING 5. CHANGE IN ECONOMIC COMPLEXITY (1964-2010)

RANKING Δ ECI (64-10)	REGIONAL RANK Δ ECI (64-10)	COUNTRY NAME	ISO CODE	1970	1980	1990	2000	2010	Δ ECI (64-10)	Δ ECI (00-10)	RANK Δ ECI (00-10)	REGIONAL RANK Δ ECI (00-10)	REGION
44	11/21	Costa Rica	CRI	0.52	0.09	0.00	-0.15	0.19	0.02	0.34	17	19/21	Latin America and the Caribbean
45	10/16	Vietnam	VNM	0.19	-0.08	-0.76	-0.69	-0.25	0.02	0.44	9	14/16	East Asia and Pacific
46	12/21	Uruguay	URY	0.09	0.20	0.24	0.23	0.25	0.00	0.02	63	11/21	Latin America and the Caribbean
47	9/22	Senegal	SEN	-0.81	-0.49	-0.86	-0.92	-0.98	-0.01	-0.05	75	15/24	Sub-Saharan Africa
48	7/15	Syrian Arab Republic	SYR	-0.32	-0.25	-0.55	-1.07	-0.27	-0.03	0.80	1	16/16	Middle East and North Africa
49	13/21	Chile	CHL	-0.04	-0.07	-0.26	0.04	-0.12	-0.09	-0.16	90	5/21	Latin America and the Caribbean
50	14/21	Bolivia	BOL	-0.84	-0.93	-0.61	-0.75	-0.70	-0.09	0.05	60	12/21	Latin America and the Caribbean
51	11/16	New Zealand	NZL	0.03	0.24	0.38	0.34	0.26	-0.10	-0.08	83	5/16	East Asia and Pacific
52	5/16	Denmark	DNK	1.36	1.21	1.65	1.57	1.31	-0.12	-0.27	96	6/16	Western Europe
53	12/16	Cambodia	KHM	-1.12	1.00	-0.52	-1.07	-0.96	-0.14	0.11	49	8/16	East Asia and Pacific
54	10/22	Sudan	SDN	-1.55	-1.28	-0.90	-1.35	-1.66	-0.14	-0.31	103	8/24	Sub-Saharan Africa
55	13/16	Papua New Guinea	PNG	-1.38	-2.01	-1.42	-1.69	-1.31	-0.15	0.38	13	12/16	East Asia and Pacific
56	8/15	Yemen, Rep.	YEM	-1.39	0.06	-1.05	-1.73	-1.53	-0.16	0.20	33	10/16	Middle East and North Africa
57	11/22	Zambia	ZMB	-0.95	-0.47	-0.98	-0.86	-0.68	-0.16	0.18	35	18/24	Sub-Saharan Africa
58	12/22	Madagascar	MDG	-1.05	-1.27	0.19	-1.27	-1.05	-0.16	0.22	31	20/24	Sub-Saharan Africa
59	15/21	Honduras	HND	0.01	-0.43	-0.34	-0.82	-0.66	-0.16	0.16	42	15/21	Latin America and the Caribbean
60	16/21	Cuba	CUB	-0.25	-1.05	-0.83	-0.89	-0.40	-0.17	0.48	5	21/21	Latin America and the Caribbean
61	6/16	Switzerland	CHE	1.85	2.01	2.23	2.17	1.90	-0.19	-0.27	98	5/16	Western Europe
62	13/22	Mali	MLI	-0.87	-1.08	-0.61	-0.43	-1.00	-0.20	-0.57	119	2/24	Sub-Saharan Africa
63	17/21	Guatemala	GTM	0.14	0.09	-0.01	-0.40	-0.42	-0.20	-0.02	70	8/21	Latin America and the Caribbean
64	7/16	Austria	AUT	1.85	1.58	1.91	1.71	1.73	-0.21	0.02	64	15/16	Western Europe
65	8/16	Sweden	SWE	1.84	1.88	2.16	2.06	1.71	-0.21	-0.36	106	1/16	Western Europe
66	9/16	France	FRA	1.68	1.42	1.63	1.54	1.53	-0.22	-0.01	69	14/16	Western Europe
67	10/16	Germany	DEU	2.09	1.97	2.24	2.25	1.96	-0.23	-0.29	101	4/16	Western Europe
68	14/22	Côte d'Ivoire	CIV	-1.40	-1.91	-1.28	-1.14	-1.27	-0.24	-0.13	88	12/24	Sub-Saharan Africa
69	15/22	Liberia	LBR	-0.57	-1.51	-1.28	-0.58	-0.81	-0.25	-0.23	95	10/24	Sub-Saharan Africa
70	1/2	Canada	CAN	1.01	1.67	0.78	1.06	0.78	-0.27	-0.28	99	2/2	North America
71	11/16	Italy	ITA	1.70	1.43	1.75	1.47	1.40	-0.27	-0.07	81	11/16	Western Europe
72	2/2	United States	USA	1.65	2.03	1.62	1.89	1.51	-0.28	-0.39	113	1/2	North America
73	16/22	Ethiopia	ETH	-1.23	-1.06	-0.96	-1.27	-1.41	-0.28	-0.14	89	11/24	Sub-Saharan Africa
74	5/6	Bulgaria	BGR	0.72	0.51	0.56	0.44	0.62	-0.29	0.18	36	18/26	Eastern Europe and Central Asia
75	12/16	Netherlands	NLD	1.27	1.04	1.37	1.30	1.08	-0.29	-0.21	93	7/16	Western Europe
76	13/16	Portugal	PRT	0.84	0.81	0.72	0.58	0.68	-0.30	0.10	52	16/16	Western Europe
77	14/16	United Kingdom	GBR	1.89	1.75	1.91	1.96	1.67	-0.31	-0.29	102	3/16	Western Europe
78	6/6	Albania	ALB	-0.06	0.22	-0.06	-0.15	-0.61	-0.31	-0.46	116	3/26	Eastern Europe and Central Asia
79	9/15	Morocco	MAR	-0.20	-0.22	-0.34	-0.64	-0.48	-0.32	0.16	43	9/16	Middle East and North Africa
80	18/21	El Salvador	SLV	0.58	0.17	0.45	-0.05	0.04	-0.32	0.08	53	13/21	Latin America and the Caribbean
81	15/16	Belgium	BEL	1.47	1.31	1.50	1.44	1.23	-0.34	-0.21	92	8/16	Western Europe
82	19/21	Nicaragua	NIC	0.10	-0.31	-0.41	-0.77	-0.99	-0.36	-0.22	94	4/21	Latin America and the Caribbean
83	3/3	Pakistan	PAK	-0.25	-0.29	-0.41	-0.75	-0.62	-0.39	0.13	46	3/4	South Asia
84	10/15	Iran, Islamic Rep.	IRN	-0.14	-0.72	-1.08	-0.78	-0.80	-0.41	-0.02	71	3/16	Middle East and North Africa
85	20/21	Panama	PAN	0.75	0.30	0.14	-0.01	0.45	-0.42	0.46	7	20/21	Latin America and the Caribbean
86	14/16	Australia	AUS	-0.04	-0.05	-0.02	0.16	-0.21	-0.50	-0.37	109	1/16	East Asia and Pacific

RANKING 5. CHANGE IN ECONOMIC COMPLEXITY (1964-2010)

RANKING Δ ECI (64-10)	REGIONAL RANK Δ ECI (64-10)	COUNTRY NAME	ISO CODE	1970	1980	1990	2000	2010	Δ ECI (64-10)	Δ ECI (00-10)	RANK Δ ECI (00-10)	REGIONAL RANK Δ ECI (00-10)	REGION
87	11/15	Algeria	DZA	-0.21	0.17	-0.64	-0.66	-0.71	-0.51	-0.06	77	2/16	Middle East and North Africa
88	17/22	Congo, Rep.	COG	-1.09	-1.73	-1.36	-1.16	-1.55	-0.53	-0.38	112	6/24	Sub-Saharan Africa
89	12/15	Qatar	QAT	0.91	0.51	0.19	-0.50	-0.10	-0.58	0.40	11	13/16	Middle East and North Africa
90	18/22	Cameroon	CMR	-1.34	-1.78	-1.81	-1.69	-1.75	-0.68	-0.06	76	14/24	Sub-Saharan Africa
91	15/16	Hong Kong SAR, China	HKG	1.29	0.79	0.80	0.52	0.61	-0.68	0.08	54	6/16	East Asia and Pacific
92	19/22	Guinea	GIN	-1.31	-2.34	-1.78	-1.74	-1.69	-0.71	0.04	61	17/24	Sub-Saharan Africa
93	16/16	Mongolia	MNG	-0.57	-0.36	-0.40	-0.77	-1.14	-0.73	-0.37	108	2/16	East Asia and Pacific
94	16/16	Norway	NOR	1.33	1.26	1.05	0.93	0.59	-0.89	-0.33	105	2/16	Western Europe
95	20/22	Nigeria	NGA	-1.89	-1.61	-1.76	-1.89	-2.31	-0.97	-0.42	114	5/24	Sub-Saharan Africa
96	21/22	Angola	AGO	-1.53	-0.80	-1.87	-1.74	-2.28	-0.99	-0.54	118	3/24	Sub-Saharan Africa
97	21/21	Venezuela, RB	VEN	-0.56	0.09	0.08	-0.07	-0.94	-1.00	-0.87	125	1/21	Latin America and the Caribbean
98	13/15	Oman	OMN	0.40	1.08	-0.33	-0.57	-0.28	-1.11	0.29	25	11/16	Middle East and North Africa
99	14/15	Kuwait	KWT	1.18	0.86	-0.53	-0.09	-0.03	-1.23	0.06	59	5/16	Middle East and North Africa
100	15/15	Libya	LBY	0.69	-0.09	-0.65	-0.64	-1.24	-1.29	-0.60	121	1/16	Middle East and North Africa
101	22/22	Mauritania	MRT	-0.08	-0.94	-1.49	-1.08	-1.58	-2.31	-0.49	117	4/24	Sub-Saharan Africa
		Malawi	MWI	-0.86	-0.92	-1.34	-1.52	-0.83		0.68	2	24/24	Sub-Saharan Africa
		United Arab Emirates	ARE	0.60	0.47	-0.20	-0.28	0.33		0.61	3	15/16	Middle East and North Africa
		Lithuania	LTU				0.33	0.67		0.34	14	25/26	Eastern Europe and Central Asia
		Latvia	LVA				0.33	0.67		0.34	15	24/26	Eastern Europe and Central Asia
		Uzbekistan	UZB				-0.66	-0.36		0.30	23	22/26	Eastern Europe and Central Asia
		Estonia	EST				0.51	0.81		0.30	24	21/26	Eastern Europe and Central Asia
		Bosnia and Herzegovina	BIH				0.36	0.63		0.27	26	20/26	Eastern Europe and Central Asia
		Croatia	HRV				0.72	0.90		0.18	37	17/26	Eastern Europe and Central Asia
		Turkmenistan	TKM				-1.06	-0.90		0.16	39	16/26	Eastern Europe and Central Asia
		Czech Republic	CZE				1.53	1.68		0.15	44	14/26	Eastern Europe and Central Asia
		Slovak Republic	SVK				1.31	1.43		0.12	47	13/26	Eastern Europe and Central Asia
		Ukraine	UKR				0.63	0.70		0.07	55	12/26	Eastern Europe and Central Asia
		Moldova	MDA				-0.10	-0.03		0.07	56	11/26	Eastern Europe and Central Asia
		Belarus	BLR				0.69	0.75		0.06	58	10/26	Eastern Europe and Central Asia
		Slovenia	SVN				1.43	1.44		0.01	66	9/26	Eastern Europe and Central Asia
		Kyrgyz Republic	KGZ				-0.54	-0.53		0.01	67	8/26	Eastern Europe and Central Asia
		Bangladesh	BGD		-0.80	-0.61	-1.00	-1.07		-0.07	82	1/4	South Asia
		Macedonia, FYR	MKD				0.06	-0.02		-0.08	84	7/26	Eastern Europe and Central Asia
		Zimbabwe	ZWE	1.29	-0.39	-0.49	-0.34	-0.61		-0.27	97	9/24	Sub-Saharan Africa
		Tajikistan	TJK				-0.75	-1.04		-0.28	100	6/26	Eastern Europe and Central Asia
		Kazakhstan	KAZ				-0.20	-0.56		-0.37	107	5/26	Eastern Europe and Central Asia
		Russian Federation	RUS				0.84	0.40		-0.44	115	4/26	Eastern Europe and Central Asia
		Azerbaijan	AZE				-0.36	-1.03		-0.67	122	2/26	Eastern Europe and Central Asia
		Georgia	GEO				0.46	-0.32		-0.79	123	1/26	Eastern Europe and Central Asia
		Botswana	BWA					0.20					Sub-Saharan Africa
		Namibia	NAM					-0.84					Sub-Saharan Africa
		Serbia	SRB					0.69					Eastern Europe and Central Asia

MAP 5:

▶ Countries are color coded according to their ranking in Change in Economic Complexity (1964-2010).

FIGURE 5:

▶ Provides a visual representation of the change in ECI rankings.

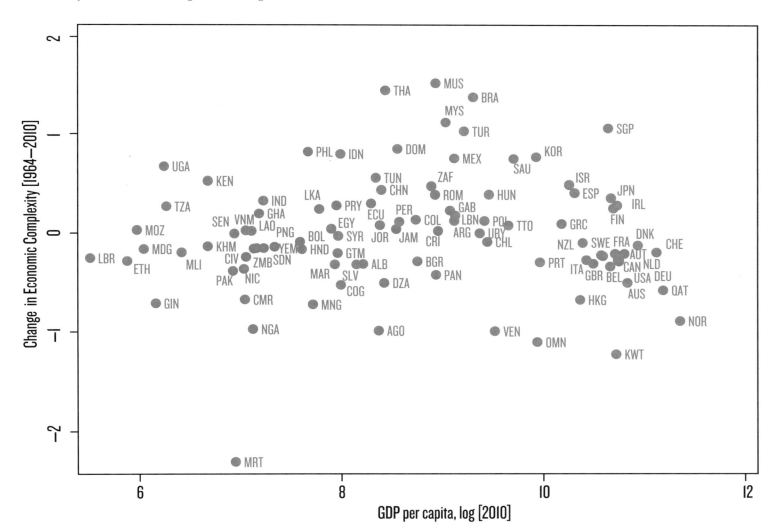

PART 3 | COUNTRY PAGES

HOW TO READ THE COUNTRY PAGES

I. IDENTITY:
Here we identify the country using its name and flag.

2. MAIN INDICATORS:
This section shows the Economic Complexity Index (ECI) and Complexity Outlook Index (COI) for the year 2010 and the expected average annualized growth for the 2011-2020 period. The first number shows the value of the indicator. Numbers in parenthesis show the global ranking among 128 countries.

5. THE PRODUCT SPACE:
This section shows the position of a country in the product space. The product space is the network summarizing global similarities in the productive knowhow required by products (see Part I, Section 5). Nodes represent products and are colored according to communities shown in the color legend that can be found at the top right of the next page. Node size is proportional to global trade in that product and links connect products that tend to be exported by the same countries (see Technical Box 5.1). The footprint of a country on the product space is indicated using full colors and the products that are not made by the country are indicated by transparent colors. These are the goods that the country exports with RCA>1 (see Part I, Section 2).

6. EXPORT OPPORTUNITY SPECTRUM:
These two figures summarize the position of a country in the product space. Here, bubbles represent a community of products and their size is proportional to global trade in that product community. The fraction of each bubble that is shown in white represents the fraction of all goods in that community for which the country has an RCA>1. In both charts, the horizontal axis shows "distance" (see Technical Box 5.4) between the country's current productive structure to each one of the product communities. The vertical axis on the top figure shows the "complexity outlook gain" which quantifies the contribution of a new product in terms of opening up the doors to more and more complex products if the country were to move into that community (see Technical Box 5.3). The vertical axis in the bottom figure shows the average complexity of the products in that community that the country is not currently making. The dashed grey line in the bottom figure indicates the country's Economic Complexity Index (ECI). For both the distance and opportunity gain measures, only the products that are more complex than the country's complexity level are considered. Natural resource based communities are not shown (mining, precious stones, coal and oil). Communities for which countries export all products are also not shown.

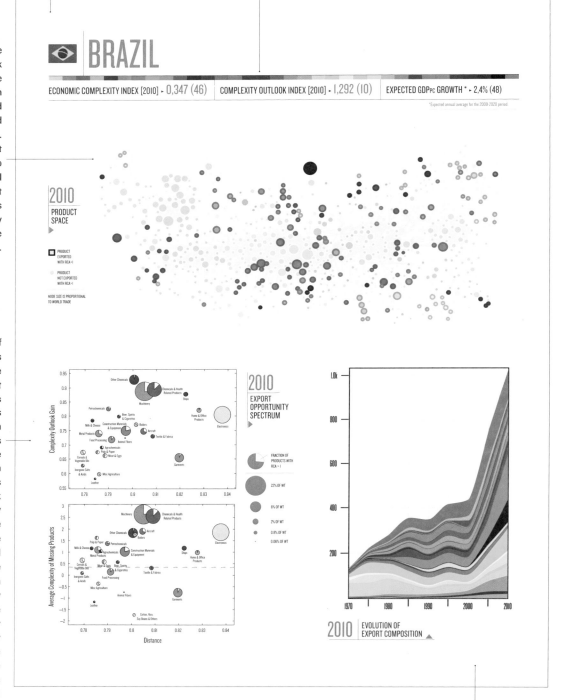

BRAZIL

ECONOMIC COMPLEXITY INDEX [2010] - 0,347 (46)   COMPLEXITY OUTLOOK INDEX [2010] - 1,292 (10)   EXPECTED GDPᴘᴄ GROWTH * - 2,4% (48)

*Expected annual average for the 2009-2020 period.

2010 PRODUCT SPACE

PRODUCT EXPORTED WITH RCA>1
PRODUCT NOT EXPORTED WITH RCA>1
NODE SIZE IS PROPORTIONAL TO WORLD TRADE

2010 EXPORT OPPORTUNITY SPECTRUM

FRACTION OF PRODUCTS WITH RCA >1

22% OF WT
6% OF WT
2% OF WT
0.3% OF WT
0.06% OF WT

2010 | EVOLUTION OF EXPORT COMPOSITION

7. EVOLUTION OF EXPORT COMPOSITION:
This section shows the evolution of the country's exports per capita in constant 2010 US Dollars between 1962 and 2010. Colors indicate product communities. These are indicated in the top right corner of the next page (see point 4 on the opposite side).

3. TRADITIONAL INDICATORS:

This section shows a small set of indicators that can be used to put the country in context. For each indicator, the first number shows its value and the numbers in parenthesis show the country's corresponding global.

4. PRODUCT COMMUNITIES:

This legend shows the colors used to indicate the community to which each product belongs. These are the colors used to identify product communities in the Product Space, Export Opportunity Spectrum, Evolution of Export Composition and Export Treemap sections of the country page.

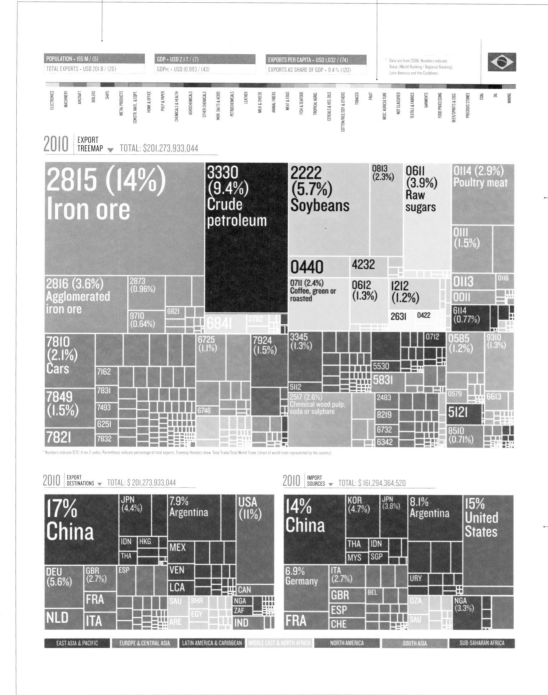

8. EXPORT TREEMAPS:

Here we show a treemap summarizing the composition of a country's total exports for the year 2010. The total area represents 100% of the country's exports, whereas the smaller areas represent the share of each product. Products are grouped in communities and colored accordingly. The first number shows the SITC4 rev2 code for the product. Numbers in paranthesis show the share of trade represented by that good. Name of products with large export shares are shown for 2010. For a full list of products please refer to the table on pages 360-365.

9. EXPORT DESTINATIONS AND IMPORT SOURCES:

This section shows treemaps summarizing the composition of a country's export destinations and import sources for 2010. Countries are colored according to their regional classification provided by the World Bank.

More interactive visualizations

can be found at:

http://atlas.cid.harvard.edu

ALBANIA

ECONOMIC COMPLEXITY INDEX [2010] ► -0.605 (88) | COMPLEXITY OUTLOOK INDEX [2010] ► -0.719 (88) | EXPECTED GDPᴘᴄ GROWTH * ► 1.0% (95)

*Expected annual average for the 2010-2020 period.

2010
PRODUCT SPACE ►

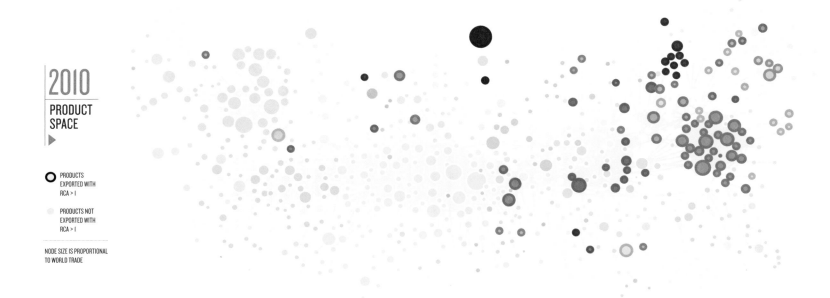

○ PRODUCTS EXPORTED WITH RCA > 1

○ PRODUCTS NOT EXPORTED WITH RCA > 1

NODE SIZE IS PROPORTIONAL TO WORLD TRADE

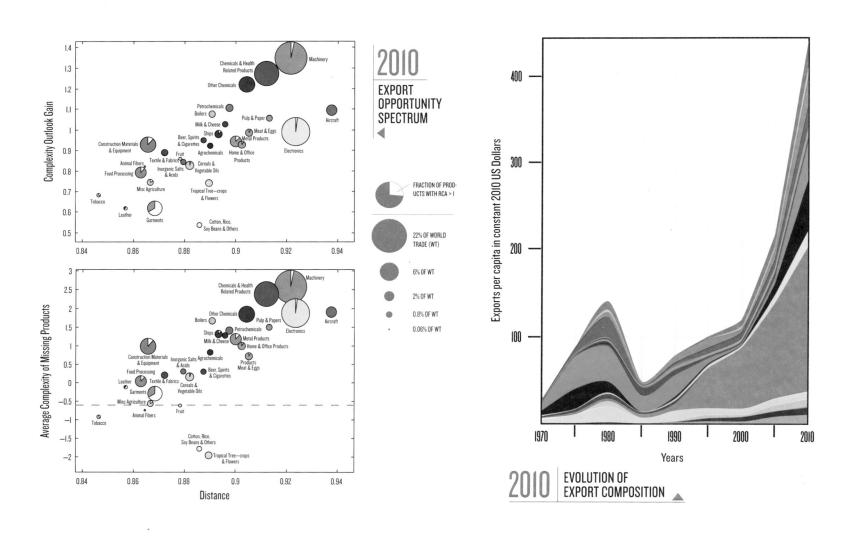

2010
EXPORT OPPORTUNITY SPECTRUM ◄

FRACTION OF PRODUCTS WITH RCA > 1

22% OF WORLD TRADE (WT)

6% OF WT

2% OF WT

0.8% OF WT

0.06% OF WT

2010 | EVOLUTION OF EXPORT COMPOSITION ▲

POPULATION ▸ 3.2 M / (114)	GDP ▸ USD 12 B / (108)	EXPORTS PER CAPITA ▸ USD 444 / (95)	* Data are from 2010. Numbers indicate:
TOTAL EXPORTS ▸ USD 1.4 B / (118)	GDPᴘᴄ ▸ USD 3701 / (81)	EXPORTS AS SHARE OF GDP ▸ 12 % / (114)	Value (World Ranking among 128 countries) Region: Eastern Europe and Central Asia

ELECTRONICS · MACHINERY · AIRCRAFT · BOILERS · SHIPS · METAL PRODUCTS · CONSTR. MATL. & EQPT. · HOME & OFFICE · PULP & PAPER · CHEMICALS & HEALTH · AGROCHEMICALS · OTHER CHEMICALS · INOR. SALTS & ACIDS · PETROCHEMICALS · LEATHER · MILK & CHEESE · ANIMAL FIBERS · MEAT & EGGS · FISH & SEAFOOD · TROPICAL AGRIC. · CEREALS & VEG. OILS · COTTON/RICE/SOY & OTHERS · TOBACCO · FRUIT · MISC. AGRICULTURE · NOT CLASSIFIED · TEXTILE & FABRICS · GARMENTS · FOOD PROCESSING · BEER/SPIRITS & CIGS. · PRECIOUS STONES · COAL · OIL · MINING

2010 | EXPORT TREEMAP ▾ TOTAL: $ 1,422,153,483

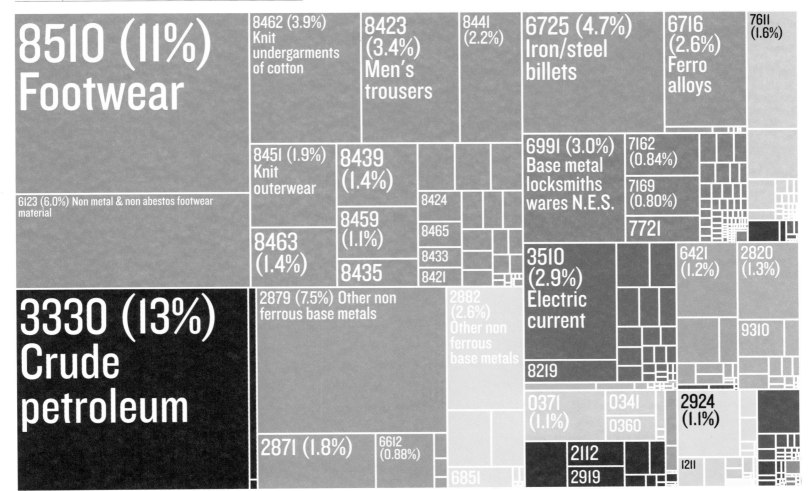

* Numbers indicate SITC-4 Rev 2 codes which can be found in the Appendix. Percentages next to the product codes indicate proportion of the product in the exports of the country. Treemap headers show the total trade of the country.

2010 | EXPORT DESTINATIONS ▾ TOTAL: $ 1,422,153,483

2010 | IMPORT SOURCES ▾ TOTAL: $ 4,178,967,927

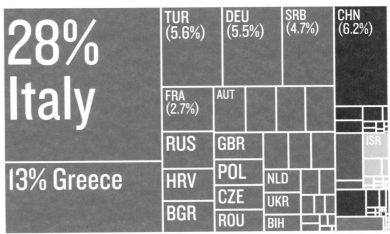

EAST ASIA & PACIFIC · EUROPE & CENTRAL ASIA · LATIN AMERICA & CARIBBEAN · MIDDLE EAST & NORTH AFRICA · NORTH AMERICA · SOUTH ASIA · SUB-SAHARAN AFRICA

ALGERIA

| ECONOMIC COMPLEXITY INDEX [2010] ▸ -0.715 (95) | COMPLEXITY OUTLOOK INDEX [2010] ▸ -0.931 (102) | EXPECTED GDPᴘᴄ GROWTH * ▸ 0.5% (106) |

*Expected annual average for the 2010-2020 period.

2010 PRODUCT SPACE ▶

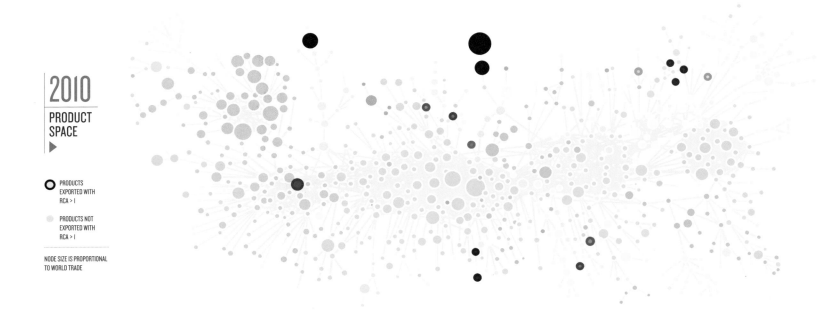

○ PRODUCTS EXPORTED WITH RCA > I

○ PRODUCTS NOT EXPORTED WITH RCA > I

NODE SIZE IS PROPORTIONAL TO WORLD TRADE

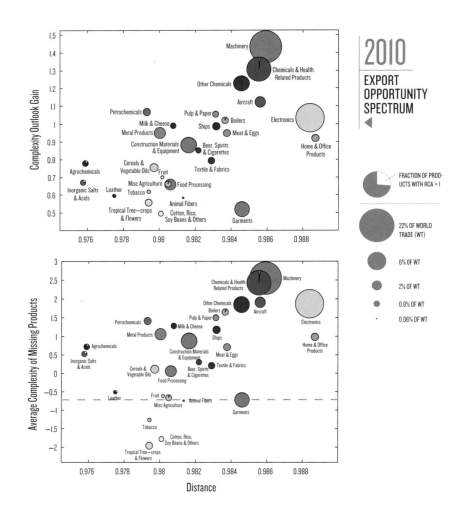

2010 EXPORT OPPORTUNITY SPECTRUM ◀

◔ FRACTION OF PRODUCTS WITH RCA > I

● 22% OF WORLD TRADE (WT)

● 6% OF WT

● 2% OF WT

● 0.8% OF WT

· 0.06% OF WT

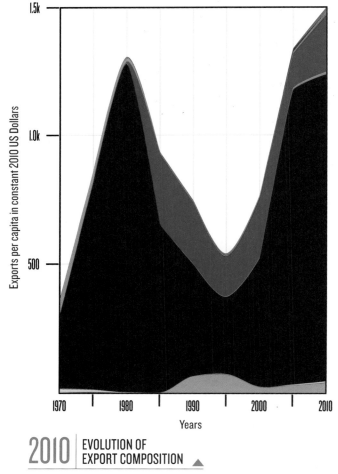

2010 | EVOLUTION OF EXPORT COMPOSITION ▲

| POPULATION ▸ 35 M (32) | GDP ▸ USD 162 B (48) | EXPORTS PER CAPITA ▸ USD 1,500 (61) |
| TOTAL EXPORTS ▸ USD 53 B (48) | GDPᴘᴄ ▸ USD 4,567 (71) | EXPORTS AS SHARE OF GDP ▸ 33 % (45) |

* Data are from 2010. Numbers indicate:
Value (World Ranking among 128 countries)
Region: Middle East and North Africa.

ELECTRONICS · MACHINERY · AIRCRAFT · BOILERS · SHIPS · METAL PRODUCTS · CONSTR. MATL. & EQPT. · HOME & OFFICE · PULP & PAPER · CHEMICALS & HEALTH · AGROCHEMICALS · OTHER CHEMICALS · INGR. SALTS & ACIDS · PETROCHEMICALS · LEATHER · MILK & CHEESE · ANIMAL FIBERS · MEAT & EGGS · FISH & SEAFOOD · TROPICAL AGRIC. · CEREALS & VEG. OILS · COTTON·RICE·SOY & OTHERS · TOBACCO · FRUIT · MISC. AGRICULTURE · NOT CLASSIFIED · TEXTILE & FABRICS · GARMENTS · FOOD PROCESSING · BEER/SPIRITS & CIGS. · PRECIOUS STONES · COAL · OIL · MINING

2010 | EXPORT TREEMAP ▾ TOTAL: $ $53,192,493,590

3330 (44%) Crude petroleum

3414 (20%) Petroleum gases

3413 (15%) liquified hydrocarbons

3345 (15%) Lubricating petroleum oils

9310 (2.5%) Unclassified transactions

7810 (0.81%)

* Numbers indicate SITC-4 Rev 2 codes which can be found in the Appendix. Percentages next to the product codes indicate proportion of the product in the exports of the country. Treemap headers show the total trade of the country.

2010 | EXPORT DESTINATIONS ▾ TOTAL: $ 53,192,493,590

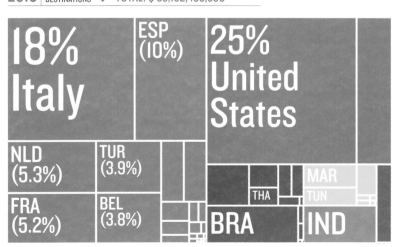

18% Italy
ESP (10%)
25% United States
NLD (5.3%)
TUR (3.9%)
FRA (5.2%)
BEL (3.8%)
THA
MAR
TUN
BRA
IND

2010 | IMPORT SOURCES ▾ TOTAL: $ 38,561,599,090

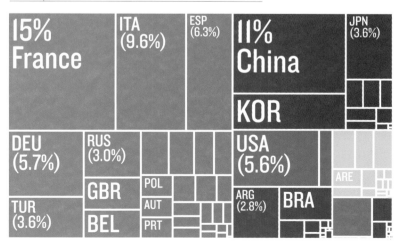

15% France
ITA (9.6%)
ESP (6.3%)
11% China
JPN (3.6%)
KOR
DEU (5.7%)
RUS (3.0%)
USA (5.6%)
ARE
GBR
POL
TUR (3.6%)
BEL
AUT
PRT
ARG (2.8%)
BRA

EAST ASIA & PACIFIC · EUROPE & CENTRAL ASIA · LATIN AMERICA & CARIBBEAN · MIDDLE EAST & NORTH AFRICA · NORTH AMERICA · SOUTH ASIA · SUB-SAHARAN AFRICA

ANGOLA

ECONOMIC COMPLEXITY INDEX [2010] ▸ -2.279 (127) | **COMPLEXITY OUTLOOK INDEX [2010]** ▸ -0.972 (105) | **EXPECTED GDP$_{PC}$ GROWTH** * ▸ -1.6% (128)

*Expected annual average for the 2010-2020 period.

2010
PRODUCT SPACE ▶

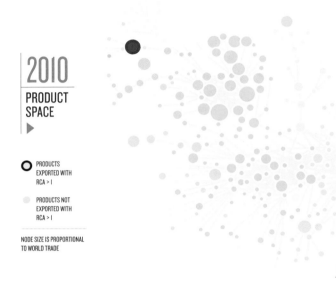

○ PRODUCTS EXPORTED WITH RCA > 1

○ PRODUCTS NOT EXPORTED WITH RCA > 1

NODE SIZE IS PROPORTIONAL TO WORLD TRADE

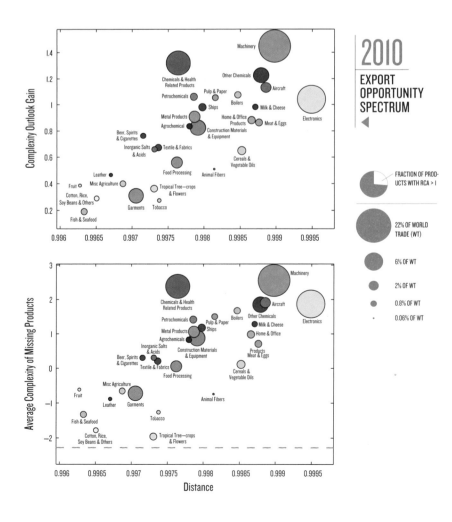

2010
EXPORT OPPORTUNITY SPECTRUM ◀

◔ FRACTION OF PRODUCTS WITH RCA > 1

● 22% OF WORLD TRADE (WT)

● 6% OF WT

● 2% OF WT

● 0.8% OF WT

· 0.06% OF WT

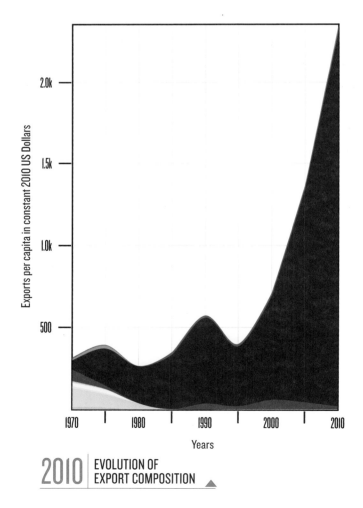

2010 | EVOLUTION OF EXPORT COMPOSITION ▲

POPULATION ▸ 19 M / (52)	GDP ▸ USD 82 B / (61)	EXPORTS PER CAPITA ▸ USD 2,359 / (50)	* Data are from 2010. Numbers indicate:
TOTAL EXPORTS ▸ USD 45 B / (51)	GDPᴘᴄ ▸ USD 4,322 / (77)	EXPORTS AS SHARE OF GDP ▸ 55 % (17)	Value (World Ranking among 128 countries) Region: Sub-Saharan Africa.

ELECTRONICS · MACHINERY · AIRCRAFT · BOILERS · SHIPS · METAL PRODUCTS · CONSTR. MATL. & EQPT. · HOME & OFFICE · PULP & PAPER · CHEMICALS & HEALTH · AGROCHEMICALS · OTHER CHEMICALS · INOR. SALTS & ACIDS · PETROCHEMICALS · LEATHER · MILK & CHEESE · ANIMAL FIBERS · MEAT & EGGS · FISH & SEAFOOD · TROPICAL AGRIC. · CEREALS & VEG. OILS · COTTON/RICE/SOY & OTHERS · TOBACCO · FRUIT · MISC. AGRICULTURE · NOT CLASSIFIED · TEXTILE & FABRICS · GARMENTS · FOOD PROCESSING · BEER/SPIRITS & CIGS. · PRECIOUS STONES · COAL · OIL · MINING

2010 | EXPORT TREEMAP ▾ — TOTAL: $ 45,010,895,709

3330 (97%) Crude petroleum

* Numbers indicate SITC-4 Rev 2 codes which can be found in the Appendix. Percentages next to the product codes indicate proportion of the product in the exports of the country. Treemap headers show the total trade of the country.

2010 | EXPORT DESTINATIONS ▾ — TOTAL: $ 45,010,895,709

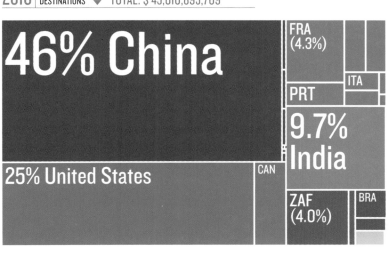

2010 | IMPORT SOURCES ▾ — TOTAL: $ 14,064,483,534

EAST ASIA & PACIFIC · EUROPE & CENTRAL ASIA · LATIN AMERICA & CARIBBEAN · MIDDLE EAST & NORTH AFRICA · NORTH AMERICA · SOUTH ASIA · SUB-SAHARAN AFRICA

ARGENTINA

ECONOMIC COMPLEXITY INDEX [2010] ► 0.101 (60) COMPLEXITY OUTLOOK INDEX [2010] ► 0.793 (37) EXPECTED GDPᴘᴄ GROWTH * ► 1.9% (63)

*Expected annual average for the 2010-2020 period.

2010 PRODUCT SPACE ►

○ PRODUCTS EXPORTED WITH RCA > 1

○ PRODUCTS NOT EXPORTED WITH RCA > 1

NODE SIZE IS PROPORTIONAL TO WORLD TRADE

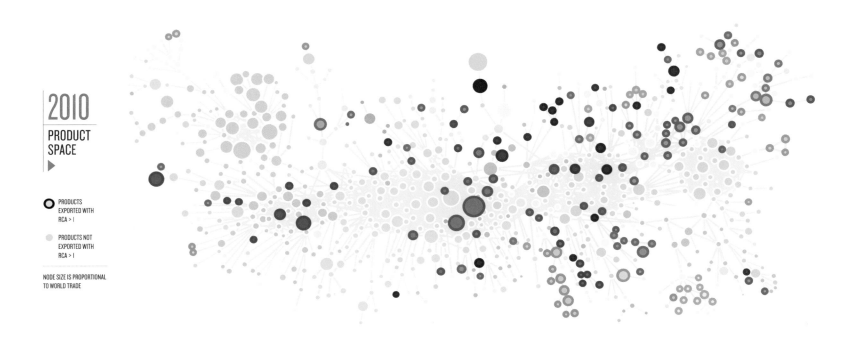

2010 EXPORT OPPORTUNITY SPECTRUM ◄

◔ FRACTION OF PRODUCTS WITH RCA > 1

22% OF WORLD TRADE (WT)

6% OF WT

2% OF WT

0.8% OF WT

0.06% OF WT

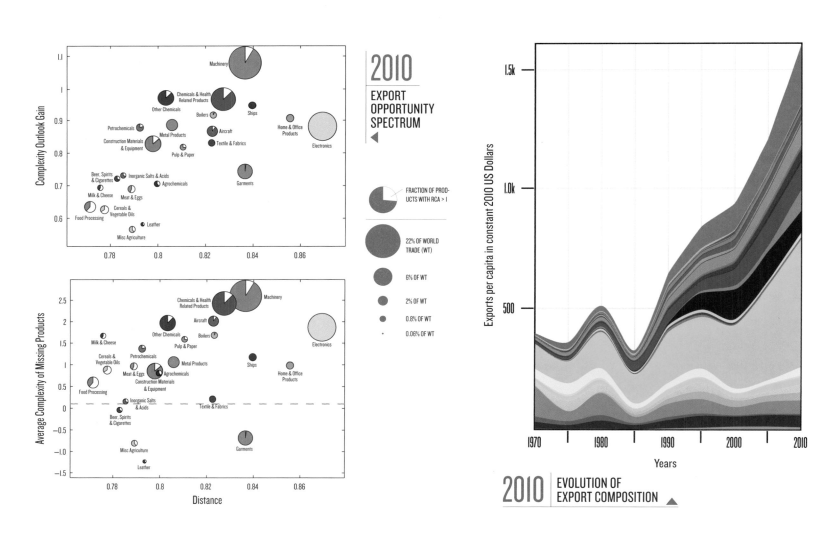

2010 EVOLUTION OF EXPORT COMPOSITION ▲

POPULATION ▸ 40 M / (30)	GDP ▸ USD 369 B / (27)	EXPORTS PER CAPITA ▸ USD 1,611 / (59)	* Data are from 2010. Numbers indicate:
TOTAL EXPORTS ▸ USD 65 B / (39)	GDPpc ▸ USD 9,124 / (50)	EXPORTS AS SHARE OF GDP ▸ 18 % / (89)	Value (World Ranking among 128 countries) Region: Latin America and the Caribbean.

ELECTRONICS | MACHINERY | AIRCRAFT | BOILERS | SHIPS | METAL PRODUCTS | CONSTR. MATL. & EQPT. | HOME & OFFICE | PULP & PAPER | CHEMICALS & HEALTH | AGROCHEMICALS | OTHER CHEMICALS | INOR. SALTS & ACIDS | PETROCHEMICALS | LEATHER | MILK & CHEESE | ANIMAL FIBERS | MEAT & EGGS | FISH & SEAFOOD | TROPICAL AGRIC. | CEREALS & VEG. OILS | COTTON·RICE/SOY & OTHERS | TOBACCO | FRUIT | MISC. AGRICULTURE | NOT CLASSIFIED | TEXTILE & FABRICS | GARMENTS | FOOD PROCESSING | BEER/SPIRITS & CIGS. | PRECIOUS STONES | COAL | OIL | MINING

2010 EXPORT TREEMAP ▾ TOTAL: $ 65,108,843,688

0813 (13%) Oilcake

2222 (8.1%) Soybeans

7810 (5.6%) Cars

0440 (4.7%) Unmilled maize

4232 (4.6%) Soya bean oil

0412 (1.4%)

4236

0811
0422
0482
0488
0571
1212
0611

7821 (3.4%) Trucks & vans
6251
7849 (1.5%)
7132

7239 (0.99%)
7924 (0.90%)
6841
0111 (1.5%)
0616 0149
0116
1121 (1.1%)
0579

9710 (3.0%) Gold, non monetary

2871 (1.7%) Copper

2890

3330 (3.8%) Crude petroleum

3413 (1.3%)

3345 (3.0%) Lubricating petroleum oils

5112
5416
5417 (1.0%)

0360 (0.94%)
0344
6114 (1.5%)

0585 0980
0545 8931
0914 0565
0546

0224 (0.64%)

5989 (1.9%)

5913

* Numbers indicate SITC-4 Rev 2 codes which can be found in the Appendix. Percentages next to the product codes indicate proportion of the product in the exports of the country. Treemap headers show the total trade of the country.

2010 EXPORT DESTINATIONS ▾ TOTAL: $ 65,108,843,688

20% Brazil

6.9% Chile
COL | PER
MEX | VEN

ESP (3.3%) | NLD (2.9%) | CHE
DEU | ITA | GBR
RUS

9.5% China
MYS | JPN
USA (5.7%)
ZAF
DZA | IND
EGY

2010 IMPORT SOURCES ▾ TOTAL: $47,620,954,236

34% Brazil

14% China

MEX (3.4%)
JPN (2.1%)
KOR

DEU (6.0%)
ITA
ESP (1.9%) | CHE
NLD
GBR | RUS

11% United States

| EAST ASIA & PACIFIC | EUROPE & CENTRAL ASIA | LATIN AMERICA & CARIBBEAN | MIDDLE EAST & NORTH AFRICA | NORTH AMERICA | SOUTH ASIA | SUB-SAHARAN AFRICA |

AUSTRALIA

ECONOMIC COMPLEXITY INDEX [2010] ▶ -0.211 (69)	COMPLEXITY OUTLOOK INDEX [2010] ▶ 0.324 (47)	EXPECTED GDP PC GROWTH * ▶ -0.6% (122)

*Expected annual average for the 2010-2020 period.

2010 PRODUCT SPACE ▶

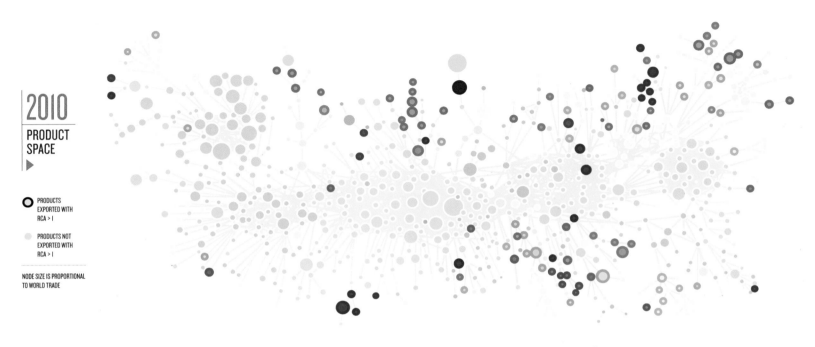

○ PRODUCTS EXPORTED WITH RCA > 1

○ PRODUCTS NOT EXPORTED WITH RCA > 1

NODE SIZE IS PROPORTIONAL TO WORLD TRADE

2010 EXPORT OPPORTUNITY SPECTRUM ◀

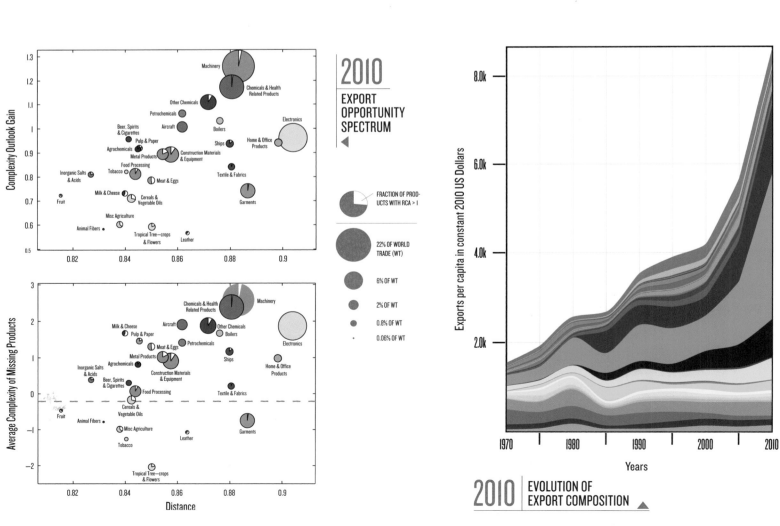

FRACTION OF PRODUCTS WITH RCA > 1

22% OF WORLD TRADE (WT)

6% OF WT

2% OF WT

0.8% OF WT

0.06% OF WT

2010 EVOLUTION OF EXPORT COMPOSITION ▲

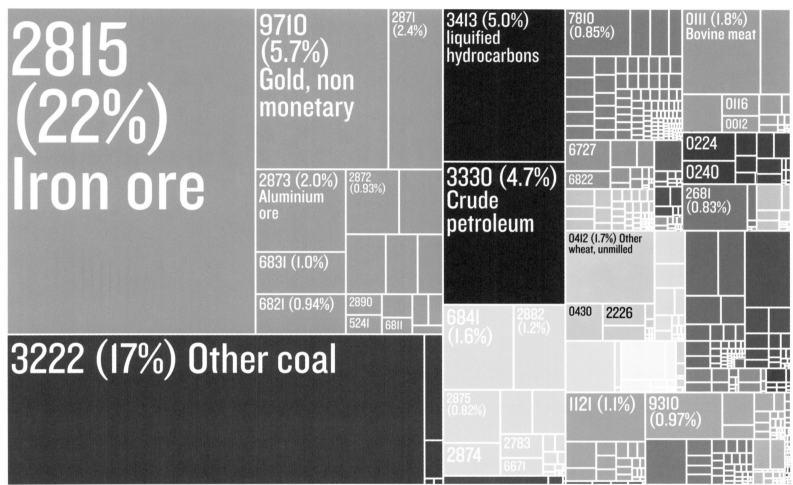

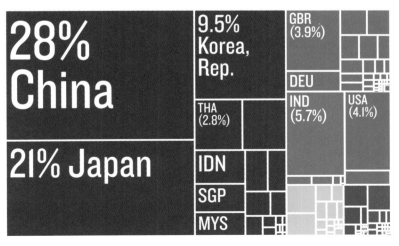

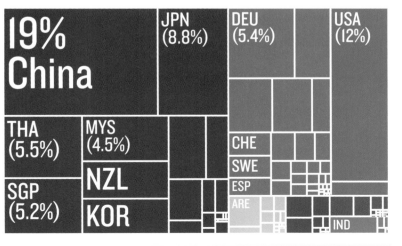

AUSTRIA

ECONOMIC COMPLEXITY INDEX [2010] ▸ 1.725 (4) | **COMPLEXITY OUTLOOK INDEX [2010]** ▸ -0.517 (78) | **EXPECTED GDPᴘᴄ GROWTH** * ▸ 1.6% (80)

*Expected annual average for the 2010-2020 period.

2010
PRODUCT SPACE ▶

○ PRODUCTS EXPORTED WITH RCA > 1

○ PRODUCTS NOT EXPORTED WITH RCA > 1

NODE SIZE IS PROPORTIONAL TO WORLD TRADE

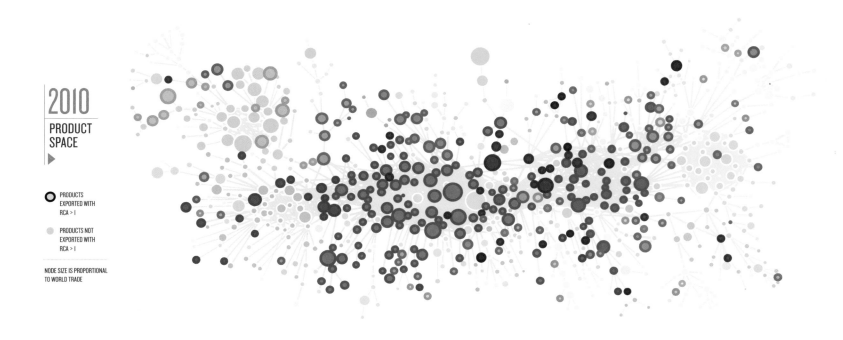

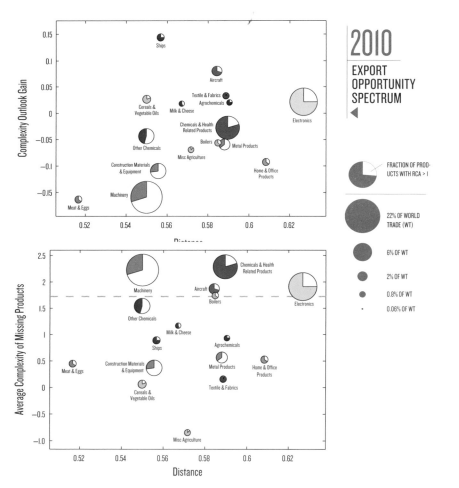

2010
EXPORT OPPORTUNITY SPECTRUM ◀

◔ FRACTION OF PRODUCTS WITH RCA > 1

● 22% OF WORLD TRADE (WT)

● 6% OF WT

● 2% OF WT

• 0.8% OF WT

· 0.06% OF WT

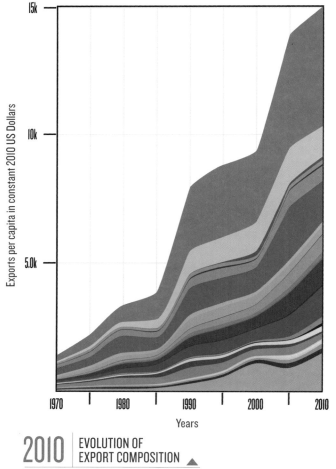

2010 EVOLUTION OF EXPORT COMPOSITION ▲

POPULATION ▸ 8.4 M / (77)
TOTAL EXPORTS ▸ USD 127 B / (28)

GDP ▸ USD 377 B / (26)
GDPᴘᴄ ▸ USD 44,885 / (12)

EXPORTS PER CAPITA ▸ USD 15,077 / (10)
EXPORTS AS SHARE OF GDP ▸ 34 % (43)

* Data are from 2010. Numbers indicate:
Value (World Ranking among 128 countries)
Region: Western Europe.

ELECTRONICS | MACHINERY | AIRCRAFT | BOILERS | SHIPS | METAL PRODUCTS | CONSTR. MATL. & EQPT. | HOME & OFFICE | PULP & PAPER | CHEMICALS & HEALTH | AGROCHEMICALS | OTHER CHEMICALS | INOR. SALTS & ACIDS | PETROCHEMICALS | LEATHER | MILK & CHEESE | ANIMAL FIBERS | MEAT & EGGS | FISH & SEAFOOD | TROPICAL AGRIC. | CEREALS & VEG. OILS | COTTON, RICE/SOY & OTHERS | TOBACCO | FRUIT | MISC. AGRICULTURE | NOT CLASSIFIED | TEXTILE & FABRICS | GARMENTS | FOOD PROCESSING | BEER, SPIRITS & CIGS. | PRECIOUS STONES | COAL | OIL | MINING

2010 | EXPORT TREEMAP ▼ TOTAL: $ 126,493,546,498

7132 (3.0%) Motor vehicle engines
7849 (2.8%) Other vehicle parts
7810 (2.2%) Cars
7284 (1.6%)
7764 (1.4%)
7763 (0.78%)
7712

7721 (1.3%)
6954
7783
7493
7224
6418
6760
7452
8947
7611
7768
7781

6991 (1.1%)
7212
6731
7281
7188
7499
8743
6782
7413

7821 (1.1%)

6749 (1.2%)
6746
6744
7711
6745
6724

5416 (1.8%) Glycosides & vaccines
5415
8720
5156
8996
5831
5832
6658
2820
5833
8972
5823
8928
6999

3345 (1.0%)

5417 (3.3%) Medicaments
8939 (0.91%)
0819
5542
5139
5413

9310 (7.2%) Unclassified transactions

6842 (1.2%)
3510 (0.73%)
6911 (0.70%)
7731 (0.65%)
6415 (0.88%)
6412

2482 (1.2%)
6416
6924
8211
6652
8842
6953

1110 (1.5%)
8931
6421
2882
6841

0113
0111

* Numbers indicate SITC-4 Rev 2 codes which can be found in the Appendix. Percentages next to the product codes indicate proportion of the product in the exports of the country. Treemap headers show the total trade of the country.

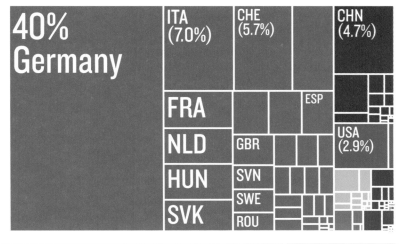

2010 | EXPORT DESTINATIONS ▼ TOTAL: $ 126,493,546,498

32% Germany
ITA (7.9%)
CHE (5.6%)
FRA (4.0%)
CZE (2.9%)
GBR (2.7%)
RUS
ESP
BEL
SVN
NLD
SVK
SWE
CHN (3.1%)
KOR
SGP
USA (5.0%)

2010 | IMPORT SOURCES ▼ TOTAL: $ 130,325,258,338

40% Germany
ITA (7.0%)
CHE (5.7%)
FRA
NLD
HUN
SVK
GBR
SVN
SWE
ROU
CHN (4.7%)
ESP
USA (2.9%)

EAST ASIA & PACIFIC | EUROPE & CENTRAL ASIA | LATIN AMERICA & CARIBBEAN | MIDDLE EAST & NORTH AFRICA | NORTH AMERICA | SOUTH ASIA | SUB-SAHARAN AFRICA

AZERBAIJAN

ECONOMIC COMPLEXITY INDEX [2010] ▸ -1.032 (109) | COMPLEXITY OUTLOOK INDEX [2010] ▸ -1.042 (116) | EXPECTED GDPᴘᴄ GROWTH * ▸ -0.3% (117)

*Expected annual average for the 2010-2020 period.

2010 PRODUCT SPACE ▶

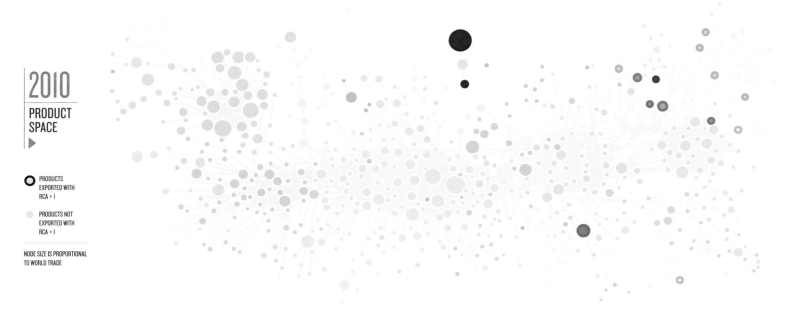

○ PRODUCTS EXPORTED WITH RCA > 1

○ PRODUCTS NOT EXPORTED WITH RCA > 1

NODE SIZE IS PROPORTIONAL TO WORLD TRADE

2010 EXPORT OPPORTUNITY SPECTRUM ◀

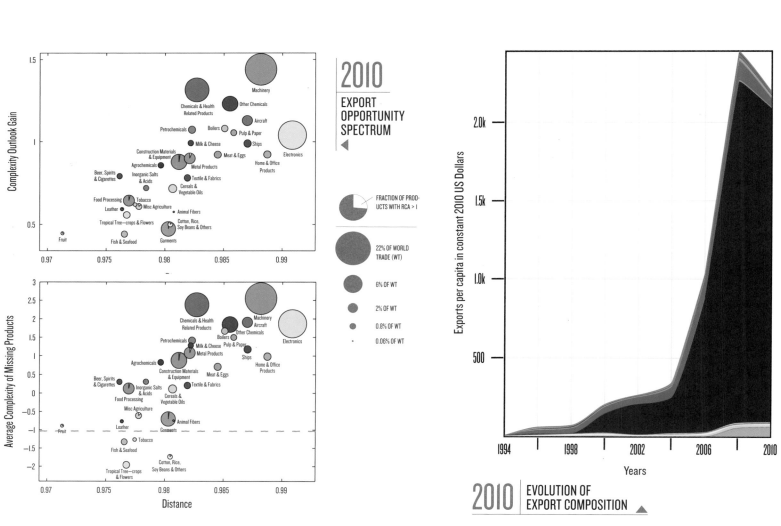

FRACTION OF PRODUCTS WITH RCA > 1

22% OF WORLD TRADE (WT)

6% OF WT

2% OF WT

0.8% OF WT

0.06% OF WT

2010 | EVOLUTION OF EXPORT COMPOSITION ▲

POPULATION ▸ 9.1 M / (76)	GDP ▸ USD 53 B / (70)	EXPORTS PER CAPITA ▸ USD 2,214 / (51)	* Data are from 2010. Numbers indicate:
TOTAL EXPORTS ▸ USD 20 B / (64)	GDPPC ▸ USD 5,843 / (62)	EXPORTS AS SHARE OF GDP ▸ 38 % (37)	Value (World Ranking among 128 countries) Region: Eastern Europe and Central Asia.

ELECTRONICS · MACHINERY · AIRCRAFT · BOILERS · SHIPS · METAL PRODUCTS · CONSTR. MATL. & EQPT. · HOME & OFFICE · PULP & PAPER · CHEMICALS & HEALTH · AGROCHEMICALS · OTHER CHEMICALS · INOR. SALTS & ACIDS · PETROCHEMICALS · LEATHER · MILK & CHEESE · ANIMAL FIBERS · MEAT & EGGS · FISH & SEAFOOD · TROPICAL AGRIC. · CEREALS & VEG. OILS · COTTON/RICE/SOY & OTHERS · TOBACCO · FRUIT · MISC. AGRICULTURE · NOT CLASSIFIED · TEXTILE & FABRICS · GARMENTS · FOOD PROCESSING · BEER/SPIRITS & CIGS. · PRECIOUS STONES · COAL · OIL · MINING

2010 EXPORT TREEMAP ▾ TOTAL: $ 20,047,358,264

3330 (89%) Crude petroleum

9310 (2.9%)

3345 (2.4%)

5831

* Numbers indicate SITC-4 Rev 2 codes which can be found in the Appendix. Percentages next to the product codes indicate proportion of the product in the exports of the country. Treemap headers show the total trade of the country.

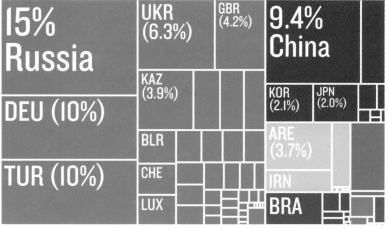

2010 EXPORT DESTINATIONS ▾ TOTAL: $ 20,047,358,264

32% Italy
7.5% France
CZE (5.4%)
9.2% United States
UKR (4.3%)
CHE (4.2%)
TUR (4.0%)
CAN
IDN (4.1%)
GEO
ESP
PRT
DEU (7.8%)
HRV
RUS
IND

2010 IMPORT SOURCES ▾ TOTAL: $ 6,805,697,148

15% Russia
UKR (6.3%)
GBR (4.2%)
9.4% China
KAZ (3.9%)
KOR (2.1%)
JPN (2.0%)
DEU (10%)
BLR
ARE (3.7%)
TUR (10%)
CHE
IRN
LUX
BRA

EAST ASIA & PACIFIC · EUROPE & CENTRAL ASIA · LATIN AMERICA & CARIBBEAN · MIDDLE EAST & NORTH AFRICA · NORTH AMERICA · SOUTH ASIA · SUB-SAHARAN AFRICA

BANGLADESH

ECONOMIC COMPLEXITY INDEX [2010] ▸ -1.073 (112) | COMPLEXITY OUTLOOK INDEX [2010] ▸ -1.014 (113) | EXPECTED GDPᴘᴄ GROWTH * ▸ 2.0% (61)

*Expected annual average for the 2010-2020 period.

2010 PRODUCT SPACE ▶

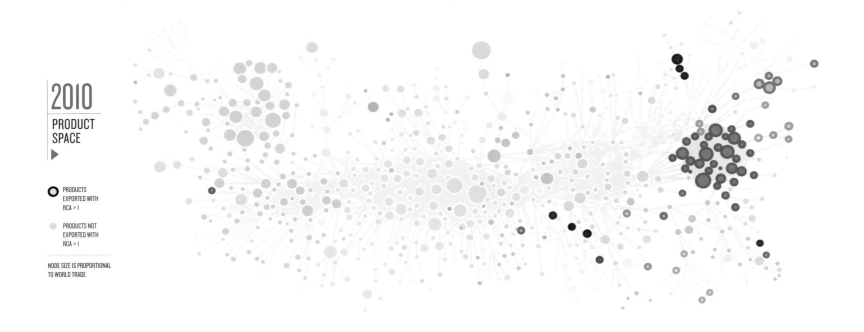

- ⬤ PRODUCTS EXPORTED WITH RCA > 1
- ⬤ PRODUCTS NOT EXPORTED WITH RCA > 1

NODE SIZE IS PROPORTIONAL TO WORLD TRADE

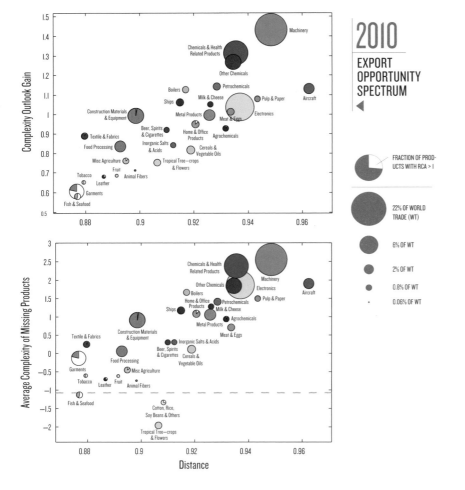

2010 EXPORT OPPORTUNITY SPECTRUM ◀

⬤ FRACTION OF PRODUCTS WITH RCA > 1

- ⬤ 22% OF WORLD TRADE (WT)
- ⬤ 6% OF WT
- ⬤ 2% OF WT
- ⬤ 0.8% OF WT
- · 0.06% OF WT

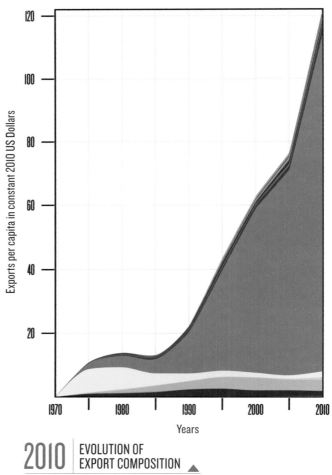

2010 EVOLUTION OF EXPORT COMPOSITION ▲

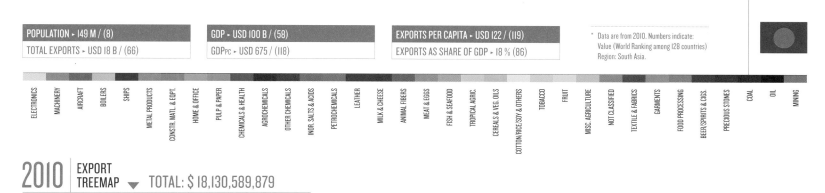

* Data are from 2010. Numbers indicate: Value (World Ranking among 128 countries) Region: South Asia.

POPULATION ▸ 149 M / (8)	GDP ▸ USD 100 B / (58)	EXPORTS PER CAPITA ▸ USD 122 / (119)
TOTAL EXPORTS ▸ USD 18 B / (66)	GDPᴘᴄ ▸ USD 675 / (118)	EXPORTS AS SHARE OF GDP ▸ 18 % (86)

2010 | EXPORT TREEMAP ▾ TOTAL: $ 18,130,589,879

8462 (21%) Knit undergarments of cotton

8451 (15%) Knit outerwear

8423 (14%) Men's trousers

8459 (7.4%) Other knit outerwear

8441 (6.4%) Men's undershirts

6584 (2.4%) Linens & furnishings

8429 (2.0%)

8435 (1.8%)

8510 (1.4%)

8452 (1.1%)

8434

8463 (1.0%)

8433

8431

8439 (9.5%) Other women's outerwear

0360 (2.3%) Crustaceans & molluscs

6114 (1.0%)

2640 (1.0%)

1212

7852

*Numbers indicate SITC-4 Rev 2 codes which can be found in the Appendix. Percentages next to the product codes indicate proportion of the product in the exports of the country. Treemap headers show the total trade of the country.

2010 | EXPORT DESTINATIONS ▾ TOTAL: $ 18,130,589,879

15% Germany

ESP (4.6%)

TUR (4.2%)

22% United States

GBR (9.0%)

POL

CAN

IND

FRA (7.4%)

DNK

CHE

IRL

AUT

NOR

CHN

2010 | IMPORT SOURCES ▾ TOTAL: $ 24,117,528,248

28% China

KOR (6.2%)

MYS (5.2%)

12% India

IDN (4.2%)

JPN (4.0%)

THA (3.7%)

PAK

SGP (6.9%)

HKG

CAN

USA

BRA (2.2%)

ARG

| EAST ASIA & PACIFIC | EUROPE & CENTRAL ASIA | LATIN AMERICA & CARIBBEAN | MIDDLE EAST & NORTH AFRICA | NORTH AMERICA | SOUTH ASIA | SUB-SAHARAN AFRICA |

BELARUS

ECONOMIC COMPLEXITY INDEX [2010] ► 0.749 (31) | COMPLEXITY OUTLOOK INDEX [2010] ► 0.317 (48) | EXPECTED GDPᴘᴄ GROWTH * ► 3.0% (25)

*Expected annual average for the 2010-2020 period.

2010 PRODUCT SPACE ▶

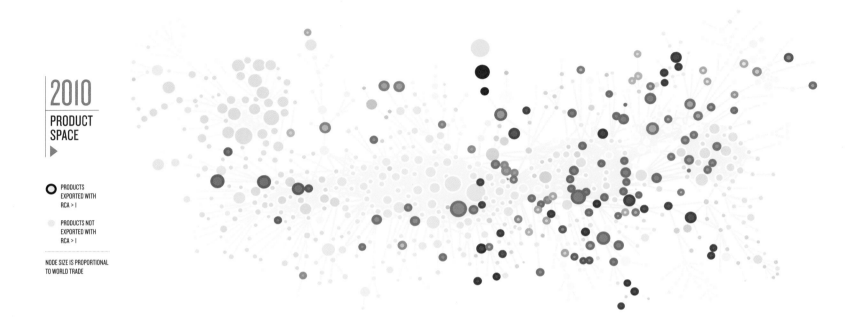

○ PRODUCTS EXPORTED WITH RCA > 1

○ PRODUCTS NOT EXPORTED WITH RCA > 1

NODE SIZE IS PROPORTIONAL TO WORLD TRADE

2010 EXPORT OPPORTUNITY SPECTRUM ◀

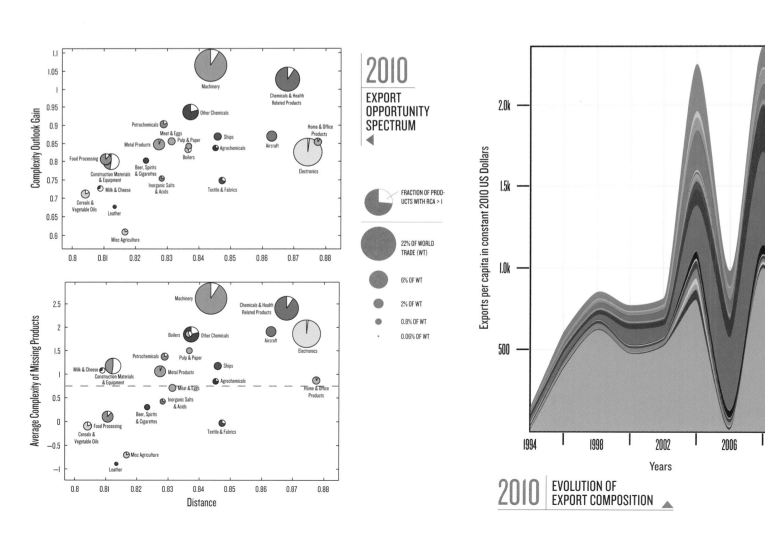

FRACTION OF PRODUCTS WITH RCA > 1

22% OF WORLD TRADE (WT)

6% OF WT

2% OF WT

0.8% OF WT

0.06% OF WT

2010 EVOLUTION OF EXPORT COMPOSITION ▲

ELECTRONICS · MACHINERY · AIRCRAFT · BOILERS · SHIPS · METAL PRODUCTS · CONSTR. MATL. & EQPT. · HOME & OFFICE · PULP & PAPER · CHEMICALS & HEALTH · AGROCHEMICALS · OTHER CHEMICALS · INOR. SALTS & ACIDS · PETROCHEMICALS · LEATHER · MILK & CHEESE · ANIMAL FIBERS · MEAT & EGGS · FISH & SEAFOOD · TROPICAL AGRIC. · CEREALS & VEG. OILS · COTTON/RICE/SOY & OTHERS · TOBACCO · FRUIT · MISC. AGRICULTURE · NOT CLASSIFIED · TEXTILE & FABRICS · GARMENTS · FOOD PROCESSING · BEER/SPIRITS & CIGS. · PRECIOUS STONES · COAL · OIL · MINING

2010 | EXPORT TREEMAP ▾ TOTAL: $ 8,929,749,681

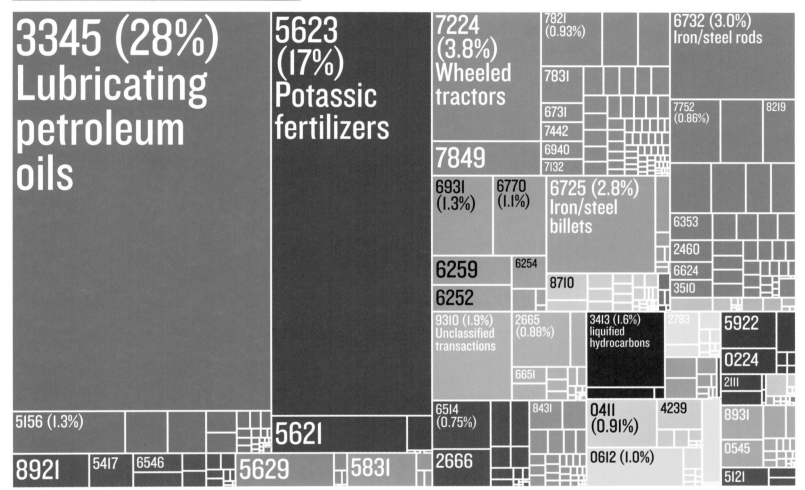

* Numbers indicate SITC-4 Rev 2 codes which can be found in the Appendix. Percentages next to the product codes indicate proportion of the product in the exports of the country. Treemap headers show the total trade of the country.

2010 | EXPORT DESTINATIONS ▾ TOTAL: $ 8,929,749,681

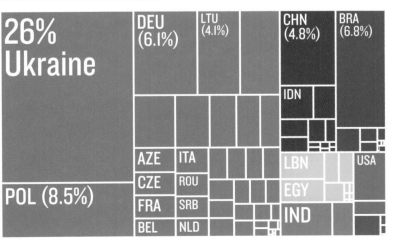

2010 | IMPORT SOURCES ▾ TOTAL: $ 30,389,084,418

EAST ASIA & PACIFIC | EUROPE & CENTRAL ASIA | LATIN AMERICA & CARIBBEAN | MIDDLE EAST & NORTH AFRICA | NORTH AMERICA | SOUTH ASIA | SUB-SAHARAN AFRICA

BELGIUM

ECONOMIC COMPLEXITY INDEX [2010] ▸ 1.228 (19) | **COMPLEXITY OUTLOOK INDEX [2010]** ▸ 0.879 (29) | **EXPECTED GDPᴘᴄ GROWTH** * ▸ 1.9% (66)

*Expected annual average for the 2010-2020 period.

2010 PRODUCT SPACE ▶

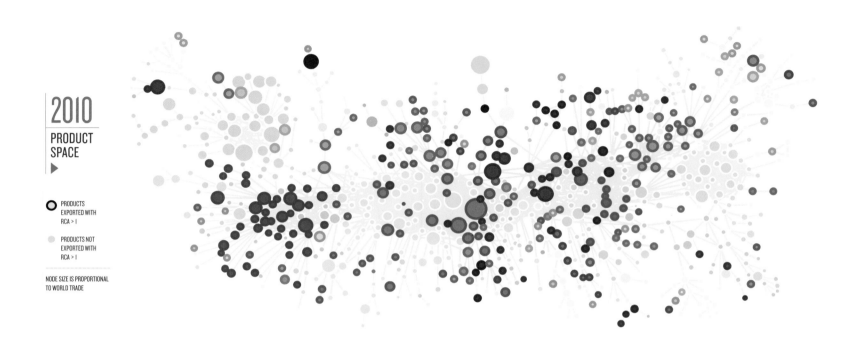

○ PRODUCTS EXPORTED WITH RCA > 1

● PRODUCTS NOT EXPORTED WITH RCA > 1

NODE SIZE IS PROPORTIONAL TO WORLD TRADE

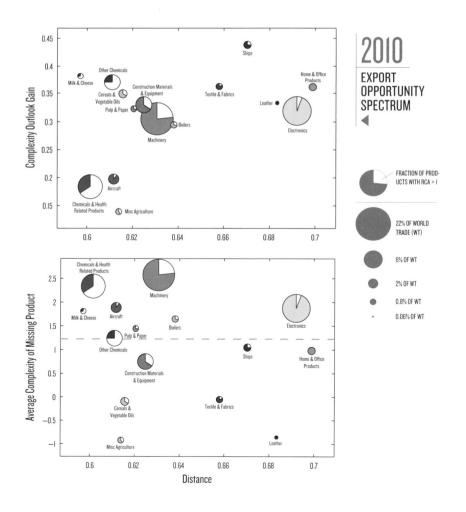

2010 EXPORT OPPORTUNITY SPECTRUM ◀

◖ FRACTION OF PRODUCTS WITH RCA > 1

22% OF WORLD TRADE (WT)

6% OF WT

2% OF WT

0.8% OF WT

· 0.06% OF WT

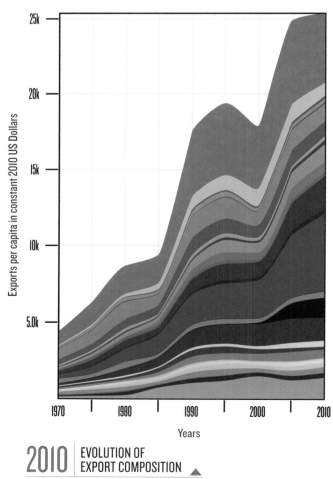

2010 EVOLUTION OF EXPORT COMPOSITION ▲

POPULATION ► 11 M / (66)
TOTAL EXPORTS ► USD 276 B / (13)

GDP ► USD 467 B / (21)
GDPᴘᴄ ► USD 42,833 / (15)

EXPORTS PER CAPITA ► USD 25,361 / (5)
EXPORTS AS SHARE OF GDP ► 59 % (13)

* Data are from 2010. Numbers indicate:
  Value (World Ranking among 128 countries)
  Region: Western Europe.

ELECTRONICS · MACHINERY · AIRCRAFT · BOILERS · SHIPS · METAL PRODUCTS · CONSTR. MATL. & EQPT. · HOME & OFFICE · PULP & PAPER · CHEMICALS & HEALTH · AGROCHEMICALS · OTHER CHEMICALS · INOR. SALTS & ACIDS · PETROCHEMICALS · LEATHER · MILK & CHEESE · ANIMAL FIBERS · MEAT & EGGS · FISH & SEAFOOD · TROPICAL AGRIC. · CEREALS & VEG. OILS · COTTON/RICE/SOY & OTHERS · TOBACCO · FRUIT · MISC. AGRICULTURE · NOT CLASSIFIED · TEXTILE & FABRICS · GARMENTS · FOOD PROCESSING · BEER/SPIRITS & CIGS. · PRECIOUS STONES · COAL · OIL · MINING

2010 | EXPORT TREEMAP ▼ | TOTAL: $ 276,331,474,529

* Numbers indicate SITC-4 Rev 2 codes which can be found in the Appendix. Percentages next to the product codes indicate proportion of the product in the exports of the country. Treemap headers show the total trade of the country.

2010 | EXPORT DESTINATIONS ▼ | TOTAL: $ 276,331,474,529

16% France
15% Germany
NLD (13%)
8.6% United Kingdom
ITA (5.7%)
CHN (2.6%)
ISR
POL · DNK
RUS · AUT
CZE
TUR · GRC

2010 | IMPORT SOURCES ▼ | TOTAL: $ 350,501,544,547

19% Netherlands
11% France
GBR (5.4%)
CHN (4.0%)
SGP
JPN
IRL (5.2%)
RUS (2.1%)
USA (5.5%)
17% Germany
ITA (3.1%)
LUX
CHE
ESP
AUT

EAST ASIA & PACIFIC | EUROPE & CENTRAL ASIA | LATIN AMERICA & CARIBBEAN | MIDDLE EAST & NORTH AFRICA | NORTH AMERICA | SOUTH ASIA | SUB-SAHARAN AFRICA

BOLIVIA

ECONOMIC COMPLEXITY INDEX [2010] ▸ -0.696 (94) | COMPLEXITY OUTLOOK INDEX [2010] ▸ -0.779 (90) | EXPECTED GDPᴘᴄ GROWTH * ▸ 1.5% (86)

*Expected annual average for the 2010-2020 period.

2010 PRODUCT SPACE ▶

○ PRODUCTS EXPORTED WITH RCA > 1

● PRODUCTS NOT EXPORTED WITH RCA > 1

NODE SIZE IS PROPORTIONAL TO WORLD TRADE

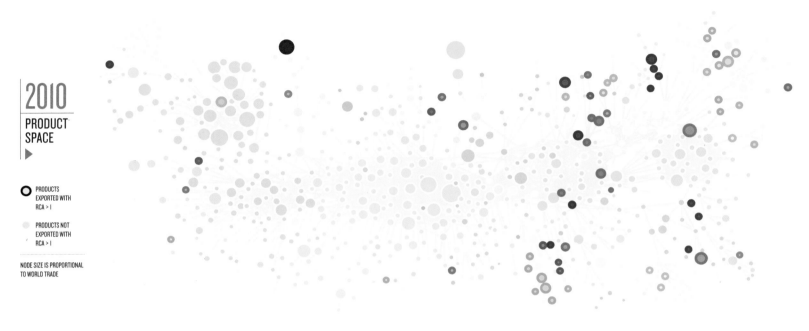

2010 EXPORT OPPORTUNITY SPECTRUM ◀

FRACTION OF PRODUCTS WITH RCA > 1

22% OF WORLD TRADE (WT)

6% OF WT

2% OF WT

0.8% OF WT

0.06% OF WT

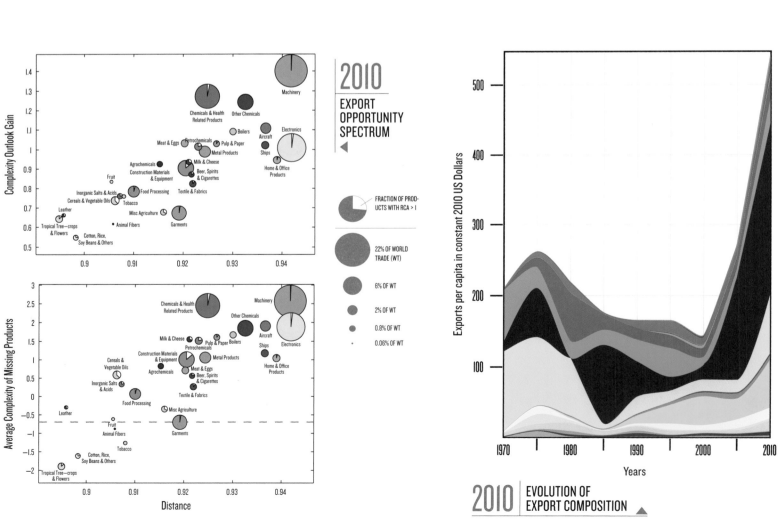

2010 EVOLUTION OF EXPORT COMPOSITION ▲

POPULATION ▸ 9.9 M / (72)	GDP ▸ USD 20 B / (96)	EXPORTS PER CAPITA ▸ USD 546 / (88)	* Data are from 2010. Numbers indicate:
TOTAL EXPORTS ▸ USD 5.4 B / (90)	GDPᴘᴄ ▸ USD 1,979 / (96)	EXPORTS AS SHARE OF GDP ▸ 28 % (57)	Value (World Ranking among 128 countries) Region: Latin America and the Caribbean.

ELECTRONICS · MACHINERY · AIRCRAFT · BOILERS · SHIPS · METAL PRODUCTS · CONSTR. MATL. & EQPT. · HOME & OFFICE · PULP & PAPER · CHEMICALS & HEALTH · AGROCHEMICALS · OTHER CHEMICALS · INOR. SALTS & ACIDS · PETROCHEMICALS · LEATHER · MILK & CHEESE · ANIMAL FIBERS · MEAT & EGGS · FISH & SEAFOOD · TROPICAL AGRIC. · CEREALS & VEG. OILS · COTTON/RICE/SOY & OTHERS · TOBACCO · FRUIT · MISC. AGRICULTURE · NOT CLASSIFIED · TEXTILE & FABRICS · GARMENTS · FOOD PROCESSING · BEER/SPIRITS & CIGS. · PRECIOUS STONES · COAL · OIL · MINING

2010 EXPORT TREEMAP ▼ TOTAL: $ 5,419,211,610

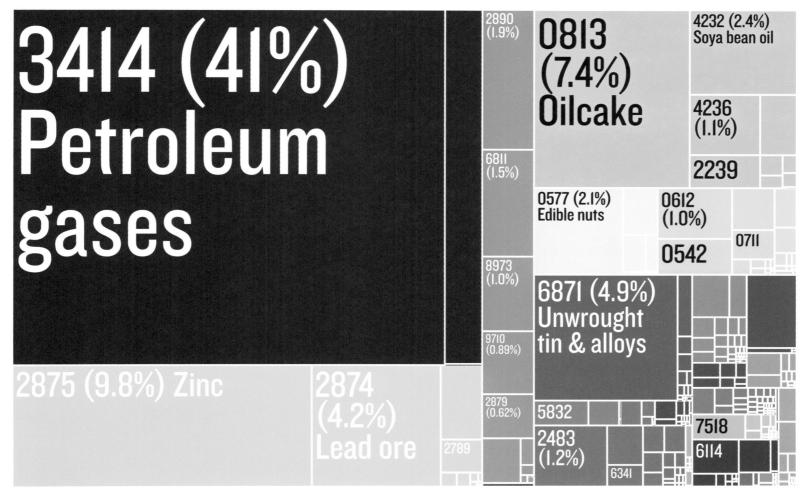

* Numbers indicate SITC-4 Rev 2 codes which can be found in the Appendix. Percentages next to the product codes indicate proportion of the product in the exports of the country. Treemap headers show the total trade of the country.

2010 EXPORT DESTINATIONS ▼ TOTAL: $ 5,419,211,610

2010 IMPORT SOURCES ▼ TOTAL: $ 4,875,172,100

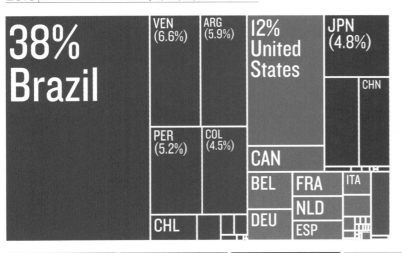

EAST ASIA & PACIFIC · EUROPE & CENTRAL ASIA · LATIN AMERICA & CARIBBEAN · MIDDLE EAST & NORTH AFRICA · NORTH AMERICA · SOUTH ASIA · SUB-SAHARAN AFRICA

BOSNIA AND HERZEGOVINA

ECONOMIC COMPLEXITY INDEX [2010] ▸ 0.627 (38) | COMPLEXITY OUTLOOK INDEX [2010] ▸ 0.903 (28) | EXPECTED GDPᴘᴄ GROWTH * ▸ 3.5% (8)

*Expected annual average for the 2010-2020 period.

2010 PRODUCT SPACE ▶

○ PRODUCTS EXPORTED WITH RCA > 1

● PRODUCTS NOT EXPORTED WITH RCA > 1

NODE SIZE IS PROPORTIONAL TO WORLD TRADE

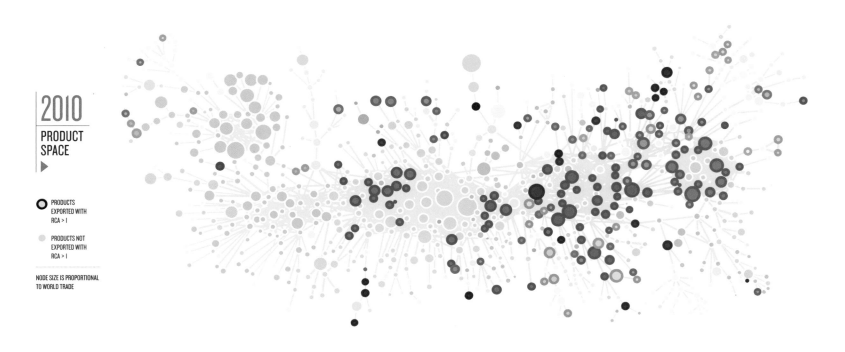

2010 EXPORT OPPORTUNITY SPECTRUM ◀

FRACTION OF PRODUCTS WITH RCA > 1

22% OF WORLD TRADE (WT)

6% OF WT

2% OF WT

0.8% OF WT

0.06% OF WT

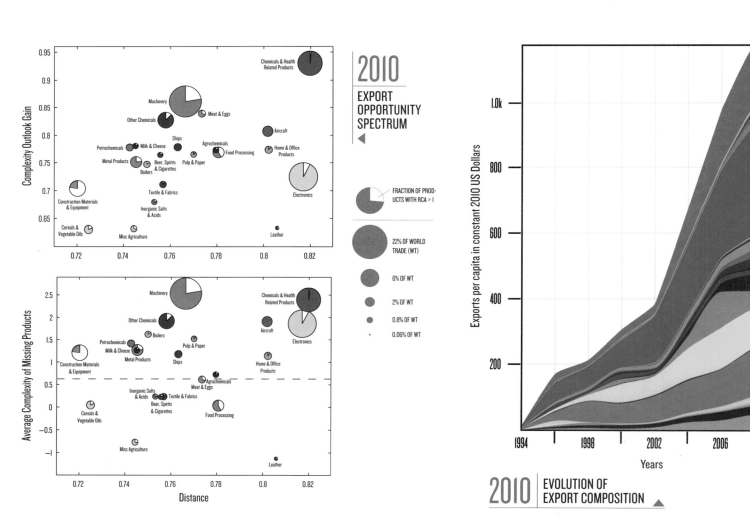

2010 | EVOLUTION OF EXPORT COMPOSITION ▲

| POPULATION ▸ 3.8 M / (108) |
| TOTAL EXPORTS ▸ USD 4.2 B / (97) |

| GDP ▸ USD 17 B / (100) |
| GDPᴘᴄ ▸ USD 4,427 / (75) |

| EXPORTS PER CAPITA ▸ USD 1,105 / (72) |
| EXPORTS AS SHARE OF GDP ▸ 25 % (64) |

* Data are from 2010. Numbers indicate:
Value (World Ranking among 128 countries)
Region: Eastern Europe and Central Asia.

ELECTRONICS · MACHINERY · AIRCRAFT · BOILERS · SHIPS · METAL PRODUCTS · CONSTR. MATL. & EQPT. · HOME & OFFICE · PULP & PAPER · CHEMICALS & HEALTH · AGROCHEMICALS · OTHER CHEMICALS · INOR. SALTS & ACIDS · PETROCHEMICALS · LEATHER · MILK & CHEESE · ANIMAL FIBERS · MEAT & EGGS · FISH & SEAFOOD · TROPICAL AGRIC. · CEREALS & VEG. OILS · COTTON/RICE/SOY & OTHERS · TOBACCO · FRUIT · MISC. AGRICULTURE · NOT CLASSIFIED · TEXTILE & FABRICS · GARMENTS · FOOD PROCESSING · BEER/SPIRITS & CIGS. · PRECIOUS STONES · COAL · OIL · MINING

2010 EXPORT TREEMAP ▾ TOTAL: $ 4,154,602,580

Treemap product codes: 3510 (3.8%) Electric current; 6842 (1.7%); 6911 (1.5%); 2483 (1.5%); 7432 (1.5%) Parts of pumps and compressors; 6991 (0.74%); 8510 (6.1%) Footwear; 8211 (2.6%); 2482 (1.2%); 7849 (1.4%); 7436; 7169; 7731 (1.1%); 8219 (2.0%); 2450 (0.92%); 6428; 7239; 6123 (1.7%) Non metal & non abestos footwear material; 6731 (1.1%); 7439; 7441; 8429; 6732 (1.8%); 6353 (0.87%); 6997; 6954; 8421; 8462; 8459; 6725 (1.1%); 8431; 8451; 6783; 6841 (6.5%) Unwrought aluminium & aluminium alloys; 2882 (1.3%); 2873 (2.7%) Aluminium ore; 3345 (2.1%); 5232 (1.3%); 2111 (0.92%); 4236 (0.67%); 2874; 2783; 5417; 6424; 2112; 0412; 5225; 8939; 0149; 3232 (5.0%) Coke & semi coke of coal; 2815; 2820 (1.7%); 9310 (1.1%); 6935 (1.1%); 0484; 1110; 0142; 3354; 8931; 0586; 0730

* Numbers indicate SITC-4 Rev 2 codes which can be found in the Appendix. Percentages next to the product codes indicate proportion of the product in the exports of the country. Treemap headers show the total trade of the country.

2010 EXPORT DESTINATIONS ▾ TOTAL: $ 4,154,602,580

14% Croatia; 12% Germany; SVN (9.5%); AUT (7.6%); 13% Italy; 13% Serbia; MNE (3.6%); FRA; POL; TUR; ESP; CHE; ROU; BEL; HUN; CZE; RUS

2010 IMPORT SOURCES ▾ TOTAL: $ 8,375,589,336

15% Croatia; ITA (8.9%); RUS (8.7%); SVN (5.9%); CHN (4.6%); DEU (11%); AUT (3.7%); USA (3.6%); SRB (11%); HUN (3.1%); GRC; NLD; ESP; ROU; TUR; MKD; GBR; SVK

EAST ASIA & PACIFIC · EUROPE & CENTRAL ASIA · LATIN AMERICA & CARIBBEAN · MIDDLE EAST & NORTH AFRICA · NORTH AMERICA · SOUTH ASIA · SUB-SAHARAN AFRICA

BOTSWANA

| ECONOMIC COMPLEXITY INDEX [2010] ▸ 0.201 (56) | COMPLEXITY OUTLOOK INDEX [2010] ▸ -0.631 (81) | EXPECTED GDPᴘᴄ GROWTH * ▸ 1.4% (89) |

*Expected annual average for the 2010-2020 period.

2010 PRODUCT SPACE ▶

○ PRODUCTS EXPORTED WITH RCA > 1

● PRODUCTS NOT EXPORTED WITH RCA > 1

NODE SIZE IS PROPORTIONAL TO WORLD TRADE

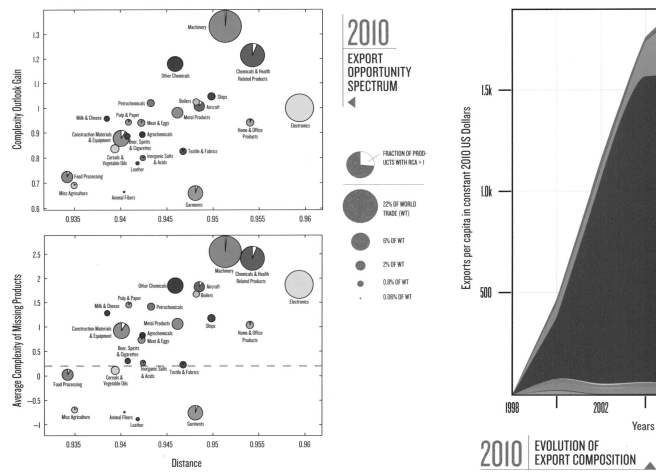

2010 EXPORT OPPORTUNITY SPECTRUM ◀

⊙ FRACTION OF PRODUCTS WITH RCA > 1

○ 22% OF WORLD TRADE (WT)

● 6% OF WT

● 2% OF WT

● 0.8% OF WT

· 0.06% OF WT

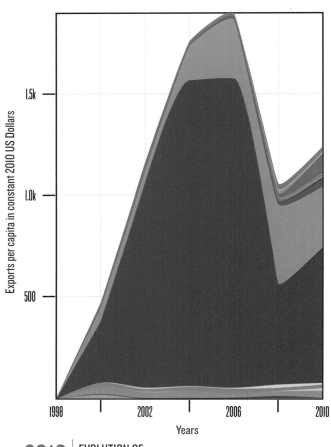

2010 EVOLUTION OF EXPORT COMPOSITION ▲

| POPULATION ▸ 2 M / (123) | GDP ▸ USD 15 B / (103) | EXPORTS PER CAPITA ▸ USD 1,238/ (67) |
| TOTAL EXPORTS ▸ USD 2.5 B / (106) | GDPᴘᴄ ▸ USD 7,427 / (58) | EXPORTS AS SHARE OF GDP ▸ 17 % (94) |

* Data are from 2010. Numbers indicate:
Value (World Ranking among 128 countries)
Region: Sub-Saharan Africa.

ELECTRONICS · MACHINERY · AIRCRAFT · BOILERS · SHIPS · METAL PRODUCTS · CONSTR. MATL. & EQPT. · HOME & OFFICE · PULP & PAPER · CHEMICALS & HEALTH · AGROCHEMICALS · OTHER CHEMICALS · INOR. SALTS & ACIDS · PETROCHEMICALS · LEATHER · MILK & CHEESE · ANIMAL FIBERS · MEAT & EGGS · FISH & SEAFOOD · TROPICAL AGRIC. · CEREALS & VEG. OILS · COTTON/RICE/SOY & OTHERS · TOBACCO · FRUIT · MISC. AGRICULTURE · NOT CLASSIFIED · TEXTILE & FABRICS · GARMENTS · FOOD PROCESSING · BEER/SPIRITS & CIGS. · PRECIOUS STONES · COAL · OIL · MINING

2010 EXPORT TREEMAP ▼ TOTAL: $ 2,484,287,298

6672 (52%) Unmounted diamonds

2872 (23%) Nickel

6624 (6.5%) Non refractory ceramic bricks

7731

0111 (2.6%) Bovine meat

0342

1110

5121

0470

6612

2871

8997 (0.66%)

8439

8451

2783

3354

3222

* Numbers indicate SITC-4 Rev 2 codes which can be found in the Appendix. Percentages next to the product codes indicate proportion of the product in the exports of the country. Treemap headers show the total trade of the country.

2010 EXPORT DESTINATIONS ▼ TOTAL: $ 2,484 287,298

31% United Kingdom

17% Norway

16% Nigeria

ZWE (9.0%)

ZAF

USA (6.2%)

BEL

DEU

2010 IMPORT SOURCES ▼ TOTAL: $ 834,616,099

44% China

DEU (6.2%)

BEL (5.2%)

ISR (13%)

GBR

FRA

ITA

SVK

USA (5.6%)

IND (4.1%)

JPN

THA

KOR

HKG

EAST ASIA & PACIFIC · EUROPE & CENTRAL ASIA · LATIN AMERICA & CARIBBEAN · MIDDLE EAST & NORTH AFRICA · NORTH AMERICA · SOUTH ASIA · SUB-SAHARAN AFRICA

BRAZIL

ECONOMIC COMPLEXITY INDEX [2010] ▸ 0.347 (46)	COMPLEXITY OUTLOOK INDEX [2010] ▸ 1.292 (10)	EXPECTED GDPᴘᴄ GROWTH * ▸ 2.4% (48)

*Expected annual average for the 2010-2020 period.

2010
PRODUCT SPACE ▶

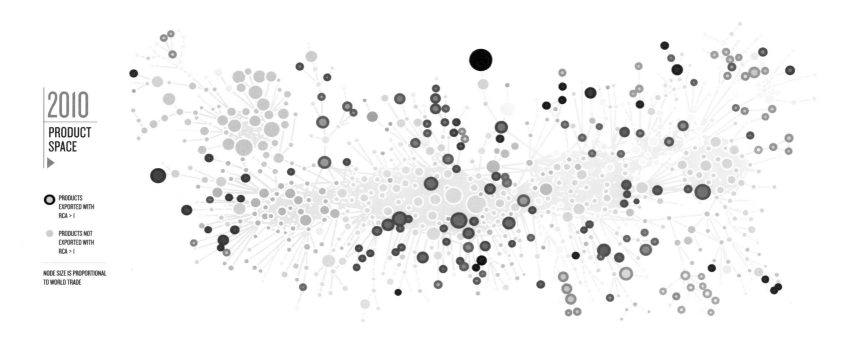

○ PRODUCTS EXPORTED WITH RCA > 1

○ PRODUCTS NOT EXPORTED WITH RCA > 1

NODE SIZE IS PROPORTIONAL TO WORLD TRADE

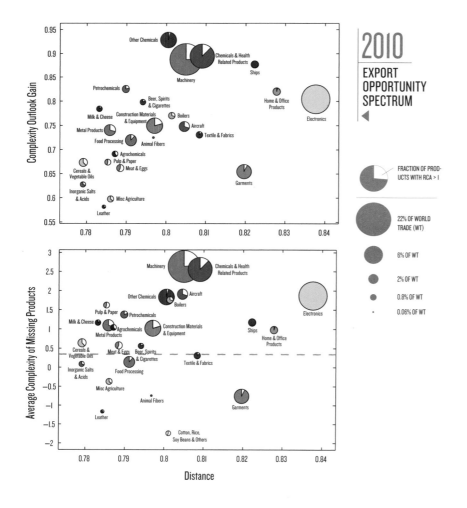

2010
EXPORT OPPORTUNITY SPECTRUM ◀

⊙ FRACTION OF PRODUCTS WITH RCA > 1

22% OF WORLD TRADE (WT)

6% OF WT

2% OF WT

0.8% OF WT

0.06% OF WT

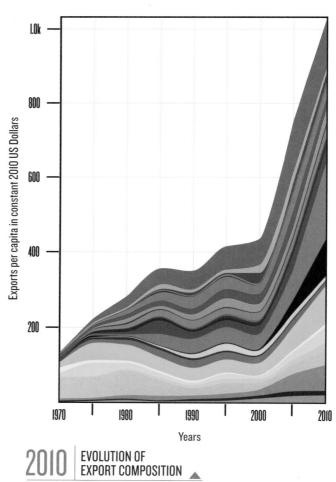

2010 | EVOLUTION OF EXPORT COMPOSITION ▲

* Data are from 2010. Numbers indicate:
Value (World Ranking among 128 countries)
Region: Latin America and the Caribbean.

POPULATION ▸ 195 M / (5)	GDP ▸ USD 2.1 T / (7)	EXPORTS PER CAPITA ▸ USD 1,032 / (74)
TOTAL EXPORTS ▸ USD 201 B / (20)	GDPᴘᴄ ▸ USD 10,993 / (43)	EXPORTS AS SHARE OF GDP ▸ 9.4 % (120)

ELECTRONICS · MACHINERY · AIRCRAFT · BOILERS · SHIPS · METAL PRODUCTS · CONSTR. MATL. & EQPT. · HOME & OFFICE · PULP & PAPER · CHEMICALS & HEALTH · AGROCHEMICALS · OTHER CHEMICALS · INOR. SALTS & ACIDS · PETROCHEMICALS · LEATHER · MILK & CHEESE · ANIMAL FIBERS · MEAT & EGGS · FISH & SEAFOOD · TROPICAL AGRIC. · CEREALS & VEG. OILS · COTTON/RICE/SOY & OTHERS · TOBACCO · FRUIT · MISC. AGRICULTURE · NOT CLASSIFIED · TEXTILE & FABRICS · GARMENTS · FOOD PROCESSING · BEER/SPIRITS & CIGS. · PRECIOUS STONES · COAL · OIL · MINING

2010 EXPORT TREEMAP ▾ TOTAL: $201,273,933,044

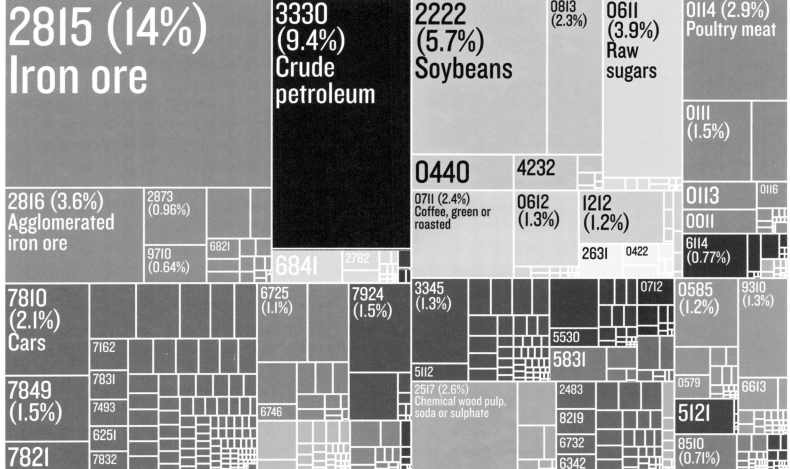

* Numbers indicate SITC-4 Rev 2 codes which can be found in the Appendix. Percentages next to the product codes indicate proportion of the product in the exports of the country. Treemap headers show the total trade of the country.

2010 EXPORT DESTINATIONS ▾ TOTAL: $ 201,273,933,044

2010 IMPORT SOURCES ▾ TOTAL: $ 161,294,364,520

EAST ASIA & PACIFIC · EUROPE & CENTRAL ASIA · LATIN AMERICA & CARIBBEAN · MIDDLE EAST & NORTH AFRICA · NORTH AMERICA · SOUTH ASIA · SUB-SAHARAN AFRICA

BULGARIA

ECONOMIC COMPLEXITY INDEX [2010] ▸ 0.619 (39) | COMPLEXITY OUTLOOK INDEX [2010] ▸ 1.666 (5) | EXPECTED GDPᴘᴄ GROWTH * ▸ 3.6% (7)

*Expected annual average for the 2010-2020 period.

2010 PRODUCT SPACE ▶

○ PRODUCTS EXPORTED WITH RCA > 1

● PRODUCTS NOT EXPORTED WITH RCA > 1

NODE SIZE IS PROPORTIONAL TO WORLD TRADE

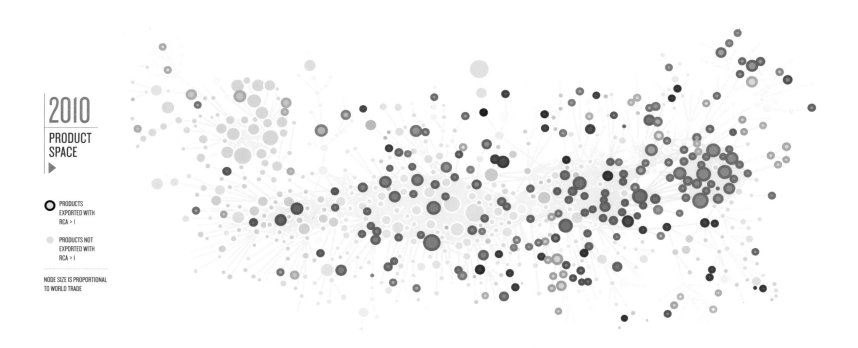

2010 EXPORT OPPORTUNITY SPECTRUM ◀

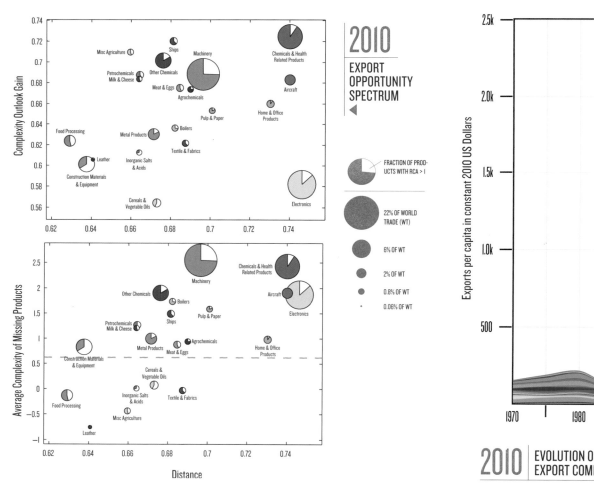

◐ FRACTION OF PRODUCTS WITH RCA > 1

● 22% OF WORLD TRADE (WT)

● 6% OF WT

● 2% OF WT

• 0.8% OF WT

· 0.06% OF WT

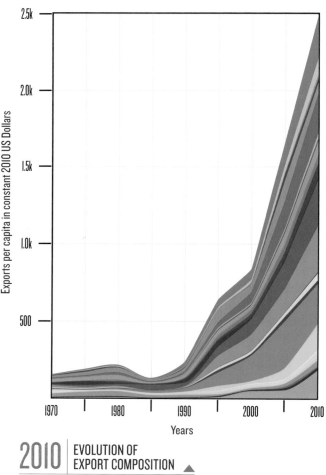

2010 EVOLUTION OF EXPORT COMPOSITION ▲

POPULATION ▸ 7.5 M / (81)
TOTAL EXPORTS ▸ USD 19 B / (65)

GDP ▸ USD 48 B / (73)
GDPPC ▸ USD 6,335 / (60)

EXPORTS PER CAPITA ▸ USD 2,501 / (47)
EXPORTS AS SHARE OF GDP ▸ 39 % (35)

* Data are from 2010. Numbers indicate:
Value (World Ranking among 128 countries)
Region: Eastern Europe and Central Asia.

ELECTRONICS · MACHINERY · AIRCRAFT · BOILERS · SHIPS · METAL PRODUCTS · CONSTR. MATL. & EQPT. · HOME & OFFICE · PULP & PAPER · CHEMICALS & HEALTH · AGROCHEMICALS · OTHER CHEMICALS · INOR. SALTS & ACIDS · PETROCHEMICALS · LEATHER · MILK & CHEESE · ANIMAL FIBERS · MEAT & EGGS · FISH & SEAFOOD · TROPICAL AGRIC. · CEREALS & VEG. OILS · COTTON/RICE/SOY & OTHERS · TOBACCO · FRUIT · MISC. AGRICULTURE · NOT CLASSIFIED · TEXTILE & FABRICS · GARMENTS · FOOD PROCESSING · BEER/SPIRITS & CIGS. · PRECIOUS STONES · COAL · OIL · MINING

2010 | EXPORT TREEMAP ▾ TOTAL: $ 18,841,613,297

7721 (1.3%)
7919
7810 (0.85%)
7821
7169
7492 (0.81%)
6991
7758
7129
7781 (0.73%)
8947
8942
7764
7611
7415

6822 (1.6%) Worked copper & copper alloys
6744 (0.66%)
7932

6821 (8.5%) Unwrought copper & copper alloys
2890 (1.0%)
2871 (0.84%)
6861
2879

7731 (1.5%)
3510 (1.4%)
6343
8219
8122
8211
8212
6652

8439 (1.0%)
8459 (1.0%)
8451 (0.82%)
8423 (0.63%)
8463
6123
8472
8422
8434
6514

3345 (9.5%) Lubricating petroleum oils
8745 (0.74%)
8822

5417 (2.2%) Medicaments
5530
0819
5232 (0.92%)
5832

6851 (0.74%)
2224 (1.8%)
0412 (1.7%)
2226 (1.1%)
0440

1211 (0.75%)
0612

9310 (4.5%) Unclassified transactions
2820 (1.7%) Iron & steel waste
6651

0484 (0.73%)
1121
8931
0730
0114 (0.62%)

* Numbers indicate SITC-4 Rev 2 codes which can be found in the Appendix. Percentages next to the product codes indicate proportion of the product in the exports of the country. Treemap headers show the total trade of the country.

2010 | EXPORT DESTINATIONS ▾ TOTAL: $ 18,841,613,297

11% Germany
10% Italy
ROU (9.3%)
8.3% Turkey
FRA (4.4%)
SRB
RUS
GIB
GRC (6.5%)
POL
UKR
NLD
HUN
BEL (5.6%)
SVK
CHN

2010 | IMPORT SOURCES ▾ TOTAL: $ 23,191,221,054

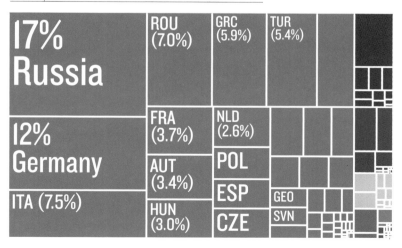

17% Russia
12% Germany
ITA (7.5%)
ROU (7.0%)
FRA (3.7%)
AUT (3.4%)
HUN (3.0%)
GRC (5.9%)
NLD (2.6%)
POL
ESP
CZE
TUR (5.4%)
GEO
SVN

EAST ASIA & PACIFIC | EUROPE & CENTRAL ASIA | LATIN AMERICA & CARIBBEAN | MIDDLE EAST & NORTH AFRICA | NORTH AMERICA | SOUTH ASIA | SUB-SAHARAN AFRICA

CAMBODIA

ECONOMIC COMPLEXITY INDEX [2010] ▸ -0.965 (104) COMPLEXITY OUTLOOK INDEX [2010] ▸ -1.087 (120) EXPECTED GDPᴘᴄ GROWTH * ▸ 1.9% (65)

*Expected annual average for the 2010-2020 period.

2010
PRODUCT SPACE ▶

○ PRODUCTS EXPORTED WITH RCA > 1

● PRODUCTS NOT EXPORTED WITH RCA > 1

NODE SIZE IS PROPORTIONAL TO WORLD TRADE

2010
EXPORT OPPORTUNITY SPECTRUM ◀

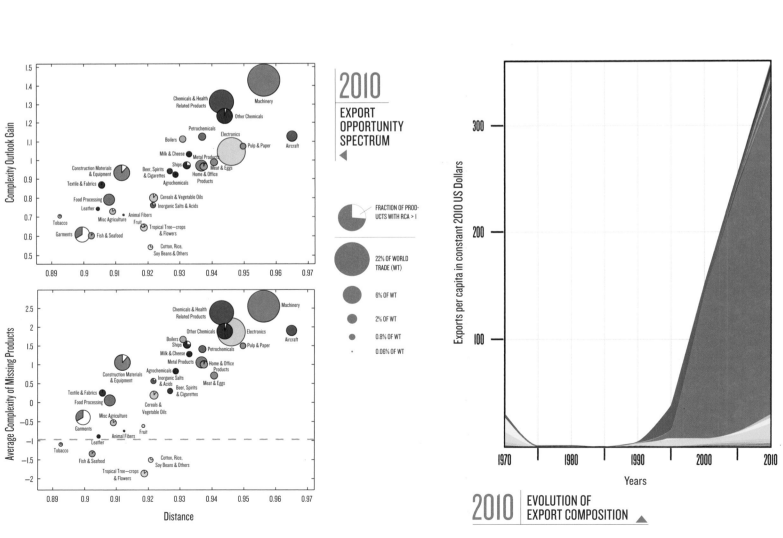

◔ FRACTION OF PRODUCTS WITH RCA > 1

● 22% OF WORLD TRADE (WT)

● 6% OF WT

● 2% OF WT

· 0.8% OF WT

· 0.06% OF WT

2010 | EVOLUTION OF EXPORT COMPOSITION ▲

POPULATION ▸ 14 M / (60)
TOTAL EXPORTS ▸ USD 5.1 B / (92)

GDP ▸ USD 11 B / (110)
GDPᴘᴄ ▸ USD 795 / (116)

EXPORTS PER CAPITA ▸ USD 362 / (101)
EXPORTS AS SHARE OF GDP ▸ 45 % (25)

* Data are from 2010. Numbers indicate:
Value (World Ranking among 128 countries)
Region: East Asia and Pacific.

ELECTRONICS · MACHINERY · AIRCRAFT · BOILERS · SHIPS · METAL PRODUCTS · CONSTR. MATL. & EQPT. · HOME & OFFICE · PULP & PAPER · CHEMICALS & HEALTH · AGROCHEMICALS · OTHER CHEMICALS · INORG. SALTS & ACIDS · PETROCHEMICALS · LEATHER · MILK & CHEESE · ANIMAL FIBERS · MEAT & EGGS · FISH & SEAFOOD · TROPICAL AGRIC. · CEREALS & VEG. OILS · COTTON/RICE/SOY & OTHERS · TOBACCO · FRUIT · MISC. AGRICULTURE · NOT CLASSIFIED · TEXTILE & FABRICS · GARMENTS · FOOD PROCESSING · BEER/SPIRITS & CIGS. · PRECIOUS STONES · COAL · OIL · MINING

2010 EXPORT TREEMAP ▾ TOTAL: $5,112,204,567

8451 (20%) Knit outerwear
8459 (18%) Other knit outerwear
8510 (9.2%) Footwear
8439 (8.6%) Other women's outerwear
8423 (5.5%) Men's trousers
8462 (8.6%) Knit undergarments of cotton
8463 (4.0%) Knit undergarments of synthetic fibers
8452 (2.4%)
8429 (1.6%) Other men outerwear
8441 (0.84%)
8435
2320 (3.5%) Natural rubber, latex & gums
0577
0422
0440 (0.60%)
2483 (0.97%)
7938 (1.4%)
7852 (1.3%)
7933
9710 (1.1%)
2733 (1.1%)
2882
0819

* Numbers indicate SITC-4 Rev 2 codes which can be found in the Appendix. Percentages next to the product codes indicate proportion of the product in the exports of the country. Treemap headers show the total trade of the country.

2010 EXPORT DESTINATIONS ▾ TOTAL: $5,112,204,567

42% United States
8.2% Germany
GBR (7.2%)
FRA (2.6%)
ESP (2.5%)
POL
ITA
NLD
MEX
VNM (5.0%)
JPN (3.7%)

2010 IMPORT SOURCES ▾ TOTAL: $5,919,926,926

27% Singapore
19% China
12% Thailand
9.4% Viet Nam
KOR
9.6% Hong Kong
JPN (2.5%)

EAST ASIA & PACIFIC · EUROPE & CENTRAL ASIA · LATIN AMERICA & CARIBBEAN · MIDDLE EAST & NORTH AFRICA · NORTH AMERICA · SOUTH ASIA · SUB-SAHARAN AFRICA

CAMEROON

ECONOMIC COMPLEXITY INDEX [2010] ▸ -1.749 (126)　　**COMPLEXITY OUTLOOK INDEX [2010]** ▸ -1.159 (124)　　**EXPECTED GDPPC GROWTH** * ▸ 0.4% (107)

*Expected annual average for the 2010-2020 period.

2010
PRODUCT SPACE ▶

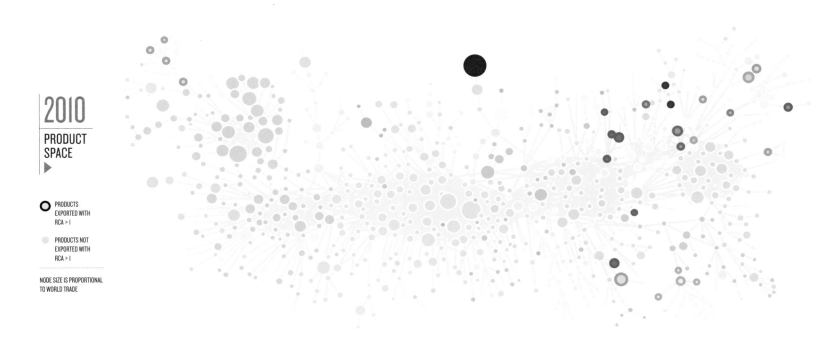

○ PRODUCTS EXPORTED WITH RCA > 1

● PRODUCTS NOT EXPORTED WITH RCA > 1

NODE SIZE IS PROPORTIONAL TO WORLD TRADE

2010
EXPORT OPPORTUNITY SPECTRUM ◀

◔ FRACTION OF PRODUCTS WITH RCA > 1

● 22% OF WORLD TRADE (WT)

● 6% OF WT

● 2% OF WT

● 0.8% OF WT

· 0.06% OF WT

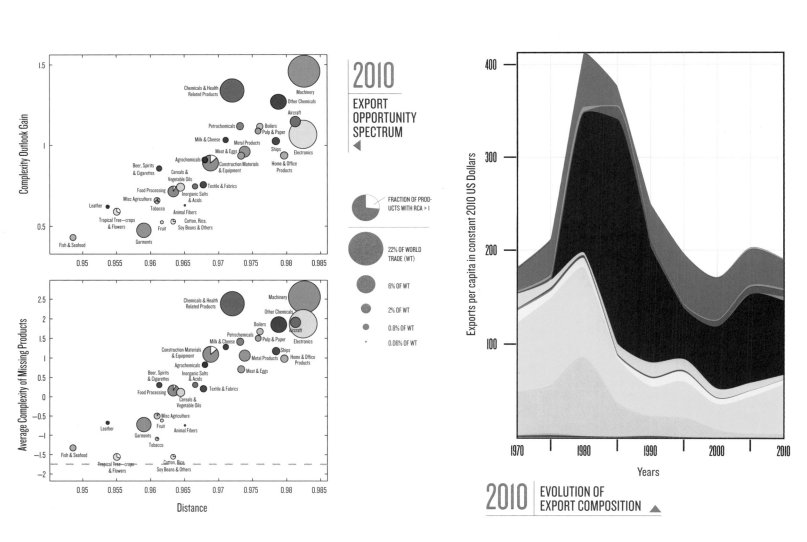

2010 | EVOLUTION OF EXPORT COMPOSITION ▲

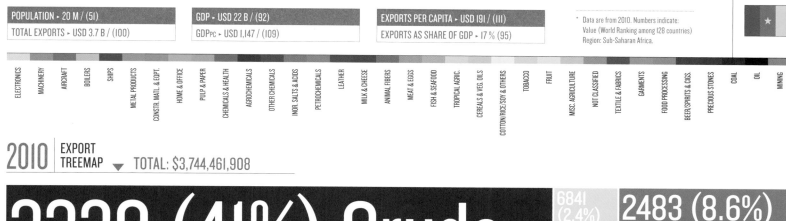

POPULATION ▸ 20 M / (51)
TOTAL EXPORTS ▸ USD 3.7 B / (100)

GDP ▸ USD 22 B / (92)
GDPᴘᴄ ▸ USD 1,147 / (109)

EXPORTS PER CAPITA ▸ USD 191 / (111)
EXPORTS AS SHARE OF GDP ▸ 17 % / (95)

* Data are from 2010. Numbers indicate:
Value (World Ranking among 128 countries)
Region: Sub-Saharan Africa.

ELECTRONICS · MACHINERY · AIRCRAFT · BOILERS · SHIPS · METAL PRODUCTS · CONSTR. MATL. & EQPT. · HOME & OFFICE · PULP & PAPER · CHEMICALS & HEALTH · AGROCHEMICALS · OTHER CHEMICALS · INOR. SALTS & ACIDS · PETROCHEMICALS · LEATHER · MILK & CHEESE · ANIMAL FIBERS · MEAT & EGGS · FISH & SEAFOOD · TROPICAL AGRIC. · CEREALS & VEG. OILS · COTTON/RICE/SOY & OTHERS · TOBACCO · FRUIT · MISC. AGRICULTURE · NOT CLASSIFIED · TEXTILE & FABRICS · GARMENTS · FOOD PROCESSING · BEER/SPIRITS & CIGS. · PRECIOUS STONES · COAL · OIL · MINING

2010 | EXPORT TREEMAP ▾ TOTAL: $3,744,461,908

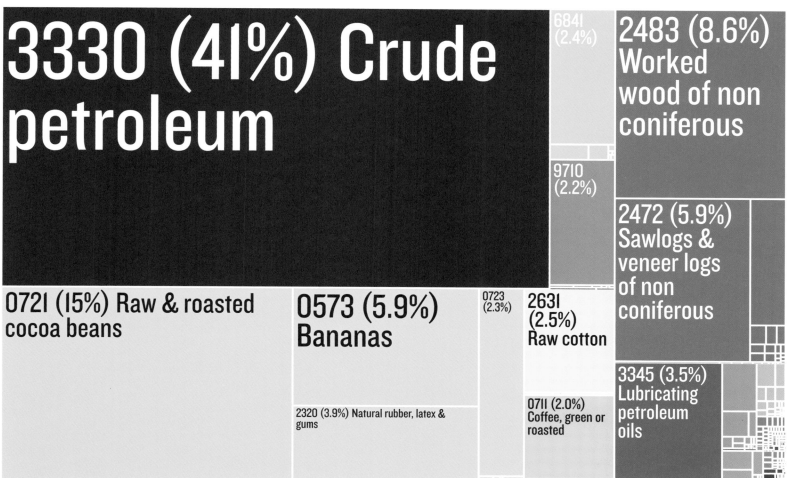

3330 (41%) Crude petroleum

684I (2.4%)

2483 (8.6%) Worked wood of non coniferous

9710 (2.2%)

2472 (5.9%) Sawlogs & veneer logs of non coniferous

0721 (15%) Raw & roasted cocoa beans

0573 (5.9%) Bananas

0723 (2.3%)

2631 (2.5%) Raw cotton

2320 (3.9%) Natural rubber, latex & gums

0711 (2.0%) Coffee, green or roasted

3345 (3.5%) Lubricating petroleum oils

* Numbers indicate SITC-4 Rev 2 codes which can be found in the Appendix. Percentages next to the product codes indicate proportion of the product in the exports of the country. Treemap headers show the total trade of the country.

2010 | EXPORT DESTINATIONS ▾ TOTAL: $ 3,744,461,908

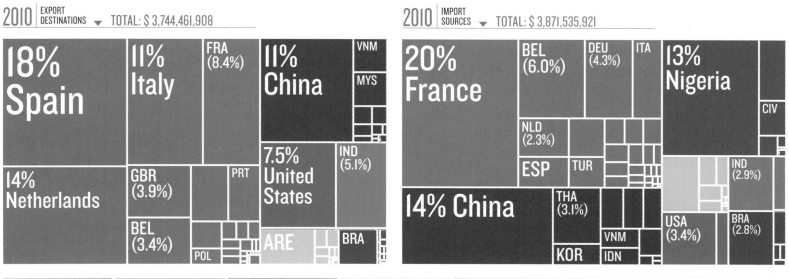

18% Spain

11% Italy

FRA (8.4%)

11% China

VNM
MYS

14% Netherlands

GBR (3.9%)
BEL (3.4%)
POL
PRT

7.5% United States

IND (5.1%)
ARE
BRA

2010 | IMPORT SOURCES ▾ TOTAL: $ 3,871,535,921

20% France

BEL (6.0%)
DEU (4.3%)
ITA

NLD (2.3%)
ESP
TUR

14% China

THA (3.1%)
VNM
KOR
IDN

13% Nigeria

CIV
IND (2.9%)
USA (3.4%)
BRA (2.8%)

EAST ASIA & PACIFIC · EUROPE & CENTRAL ASIA · LATIN AMERICA & CARIBBEAN · MIDDLE EAST & NORTH AFRICA · NORTH AMERICA · SOUTH ASIA · SUB-SAHARAN AFRICA

CANADA

ECONOMIC COMPLEXITY INDEX [2010] ► 0.775 (30) | COMPLEXITY OUTLOOK INDEX [2010] ► 1.254 (14) | EXPECTED GDPᴘᴄ GROWTH * ► 1.4% (88)

*Expected annual average for the 2010-2020 period.

2010 PRODUCT SPACE ►

○ PRODUCTS EXPORTED WITH RCA > 1

● PRODUCTS NOT EXPORTED WITH RCA > 1

NODE SIZE IS PROPORTIONAL TO WORLD TRADE

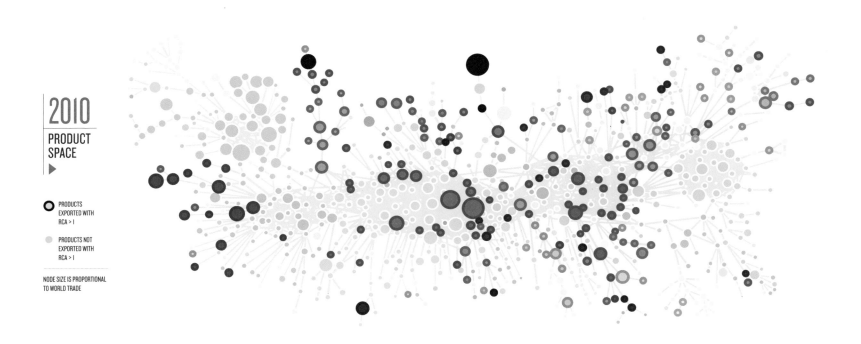

2010 EXPORT OPPORTUNITY SPECTRUM ◄

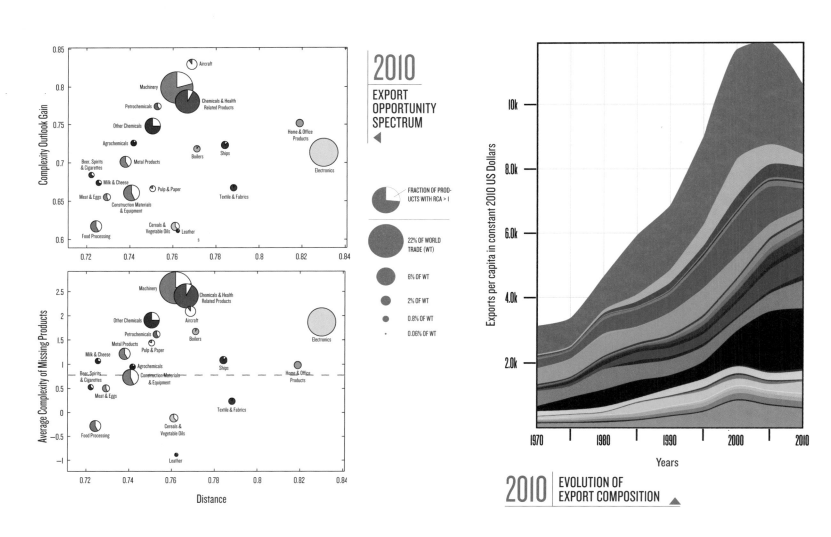

◕ FRACTION OF PRODUCTS WITH RCA > 1

⬤ 22% OF WORLD TRADE (WT)

● 6% OF WT

● 2% OF WT

• 0.8% OF WT

· 0.06% OF WT

2010 EVOLUTION OF EXPORT COMPOSITION ▲

POPULATION ▸ 34 M / (33)
TOTAL EXPORTS ▸ USD 362 B / (9)

GDP ▸ USD 1.6 T / (10)
GDPPC ▸ USD 46,212 / (9)

EXPORTS PER CAPITA ▸ USD 10,609 / (15)
EXPORTS AS SHARE OF GDP ▸ 23 % (72)

* Data are from 2010. Numbers indicate:
Value (World Ranking among 128 countries)
Region: North America.

ELECTRONICS | MACHINERY | AIRCRAFT | BOILERS | SHIPS | METAL PRODUCTS | CONSTR. MATL. & EQPT. | HOME & OFFICE | PULP & PAPER | CHEMICALS & HEALTH | AGROCHEMICALS | OTHER CHEMICALS | INOR. SALTS & ACIDS | PETROCHEMICALS | LEATHER | MILK & CHEESE | ANIMAL FIBERS | MEAT & EGGS | FISH & SEAFOOD | TROPICAL AGRIC. | CEREALS & VEG. OILS | COTTON/RICE/SOY & OTHERS | TOBACCO | FRUIT | MISC. AGRICULTURE | NOT CLASSIFIED | TEXTILE & FABRICS | GARMENTS | FOOD PROCESSING | BEER/SPIRITS & CIGS. | PRECIOUS STONES | COAL | OIL | MINING

2010 | EXPORT TREEMAP ▾ TOTAL: $ 362,046,592,324

7810 (9.6%) Cars
7849 (2.3%)
3330 (13%) Crude petroleum
3414 (3.4%)
9710 (3.6%) Gold, non monetary
6841 (1.6%)
3222 (1.4%)
6672
6831 | 6811
6821 | 5241
2815
7924 (1.3%)
6783
6725
6822
6252
3345 (3.7%) Lubricating petroleum oils
5111
5112
5417 (1.4%) | 8939 | 5530
5623 (1.4%)
9310 (4.4%) Unclassified transactions
0412 (0.97%) | 0542
2226 (0.82%)
041!
0813
2482 (1.2%)
6842
8211
6428
6343
2517 (1.3%)
6411
0113 (0.63%) | 0011
0111
0360
8931
0980
0484
5121

* Numbers indicate SITC-4 Rev 2 codes which can be found in the Appendix. Percentages next to the product codes indicate proportion of the product in the exports of the country. Treemap headers show the total trade of the country.

2010 | EXPORT DESTINATIONS ▾ TOTAL: $ 362,046,592,324

70% United States

GBR (5.7%)
DEU
CHN (3.7%)
KOR

2010 | IMPORT SOURCES ▾ TOTAL: $ 346,994,147,942

51% United States

11% China
FRA | ITA
JPN (3.3%)
KAZ
KOR
MEX (5.4%)

EAST ASIA & PACIFIC | EUROPE & CENTRAL ASIA | LATIN AMERICA & CARIBBEAN | MIDDLE EAST & NORTH AFRICA | NORTH AMERICA | SOUTH ASIA | SUB-SAHARAN AFRICA

CHILE

| ECONOMIC COMPLEXITY INDEX [2010] ▸ -0.118 (68) | COMPLEXITY OUTLOOK INDEX [2010] ▸ -0.302 (70) | EXPECTED GDPᴘᴄ GROWTH * ▸ 0.6% (103) |

*Expected annual average for the 2010-2020 period.

2010 PRODUCT SPACE ▸

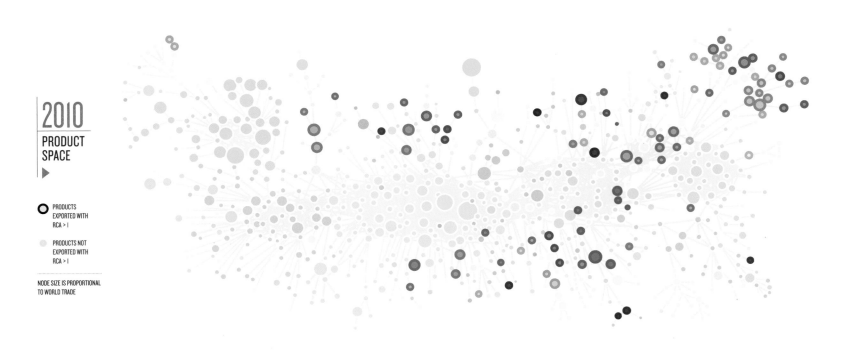

○ PRODUCTS EXPORTED WITH RCA > 1

○ PRODUCTS NOT EXPORTED WITH RCA > 1

NODE SIZE IS PROPORTIONAL TO WORLD TRADE

2010 EXPORT OPPORTUNITY SPECTRUM ◂

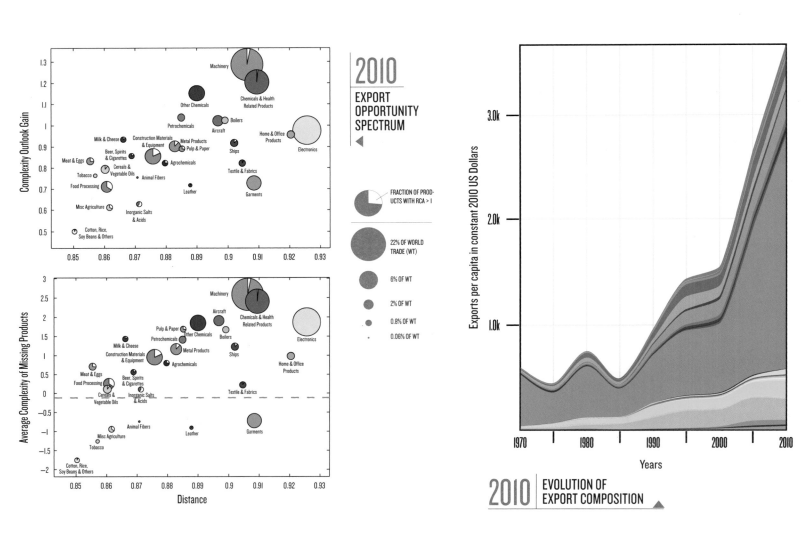

FRACTION OF PRODUCTS WITH RCA > 1

22% OF WORLD TRADE (WT)

6% OF WT

2% OF WT

0.8% OF WT

0.06% OF WT

2010 EVOLUTION OF EXPORT COMPOSITION ▲

POPULATION ▸ 17 M / (53)	GDP ▸ USD 216 B / (41)	EXPORTS PER CAPITA ▸ USD 3,679 / (40)	* Data are from 2010. Numbers indicate: Value (World Ranking among 128 countries) Region: Latin America and the Caribbean.
TOTAL EXPORTS ▸ USD 63 B / (41)	GDPᴘᴄ ▸ USD 12,640 / (39)	EXPORTS AS SHARE OF GDP ▸ 29 % (52)	

ELECTRONICS · MACHINERY · AIRCRAFT · BOILERS · SHIPS · METAL PRODUCTS · CONSTR. MATL. & EQPT. · HOME & OFFICE · PULP & PAPER · CHEMICALS & HEALTH · AGROCHEMICALS · OTHER CHEMICALS · INDR. SALTS & ACIDS · PETROCHEMICALS · LEATHER · MILK & CHEESE · ANIMAL FIBERS · MEAT & EGGS · FISH & SEAFOOD · TROPICAL AGRIC. · CEREALS & VEG. OILS · COTTON/RICE/SOY & OTHERS · TOBACCO · FRUIT · MISC. AGRICULTURE · NOT CLASSIFIED · TEXTILE & FABRICS · GARMENTS · FOOD PROCESSING · BEER/SPIRITS & CIGS. · PRECIOUS STONES · COAL · OIL · MINING

2010 EXPORT TREEMAP ▼ TOTAL: $ 62,968,069,145

* Numbers indicate SITC-4 Rev 2 codes which can be found in the Appendix. Percentages next to the product codes indicate proportion of the product in the exports of the country. Treemap headers show the total trade of the country.

2010 EXPORT DESTINATIONS ▼ TOTAL: $ 62,968,069,145

2010 IMPORT SOURCES ▼ TOTAL: $ 50,448,773,867

EAST ASIA & PACIFIC · EUROPE & CENTRAL ASIA · LATIN AMERICA & CARIBBEAN · MIDDLE EAST & NORTH AFRICA · NORTH AMERICA · SOUTH ASIA · SUB-SAHARAN AFRICA

CHINA

ECONOMIC COMPLEXITY INDEX [2010] ▸ 0.88 (26) | **COMPLEXITY OUTLOOK INDEX [2010]** ▸ 1.493 (7) | **EXPECTED GDPᴘᴄ GROWTH** * ▸ 4.2% (2)

*Expected annual average for the 2010-2020 period.

2010 PRODUCT SPACE ▶

○ PRODUCTS EXPORTED WITH RCA > 1

● PRODUCTS NOT EXPORTED WITH RCA > 1

NODE SIZE IS PROPORTIONAL TO WORLD TRADE

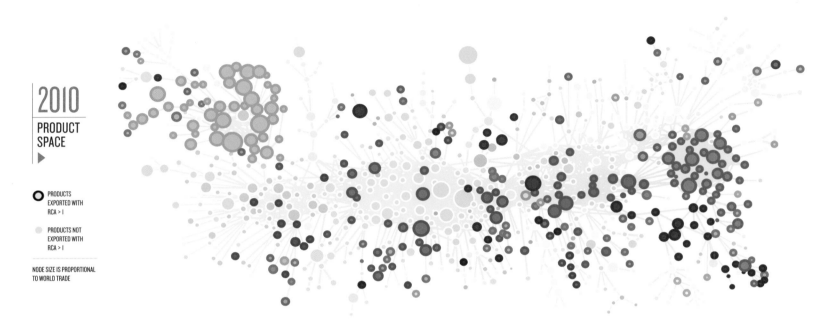

2010 EXPORT OPPORTUNITY SPECTRUM ◀

◐ FRACTION OF PRODUCTS WITH RCA > 1

● 22% OF WORLD TRADE (WT)

● 6% OF WT

● 2% OF WT

● 0.8% OF WT

· 0.06% OF WT

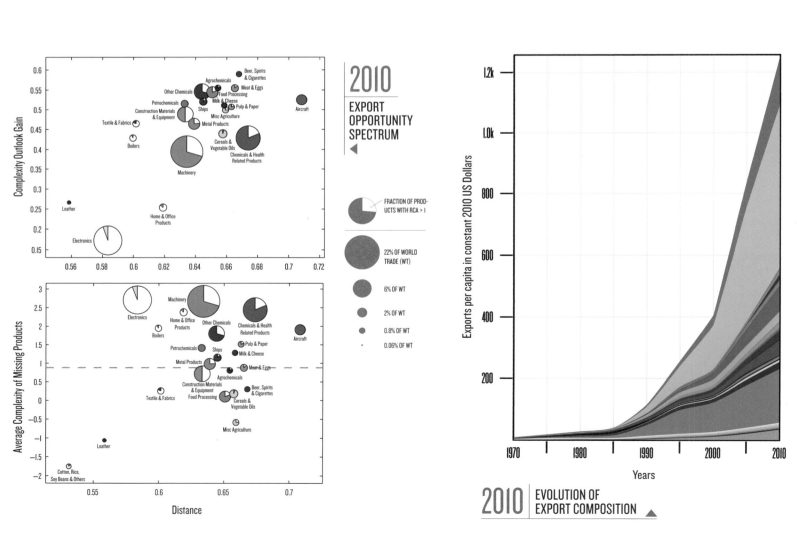

2010 | EVOLUTION OF EXPORT COMPOSITION ▲

POPULATION ▸ 1.34 B / (1)
TOTAL EXPORTS ▸ USD 1.7 T / (1)

GDP ▸ USD 5.9 T / (2)
GDPᴘᴄ ▸ USD 4,433 / (74)

EXPORTS PER CAPITA ▸ USD 1,256 / (65)
EXPORTS AS SHARE OF GDP ▸ 28 % (55)

* Data are from 2010. Numbers indicate:
Value (World Ranking among 128 countries)
Region: East Asia and Pacific.

ELECTRONICS | MACHINERY | AIRCRAFT | BOILERS | SHIPS | METAL PRODUCTS | CONSTR. MATL. & EQPT. | HOME & OFFICE | PULP & PAPER | CHEMICALS & HEALTH | AGROCHEMICALS | OTHER CHEMICALS | INOR. SALTS & ACIDS | PETROCHEMICALS | LEATHER | MILK & CHEESE | ANIMAL FIBERS | MEAT & EGGS | FISH & SEAFOOD | TROPICAL AGRIC. | CEREALS & VEG. OILS | COTTON/RICE/SOY & OTHERS | TOBACCO | FRUIT | MISC. AGRICULTURE | NOT CLASSIFIED | TEXTILE & FABRICS | GARMENTS | FOOD PROCESSING | BEER/SPIRITS & CIGS. | PRECIOUS STONES | COAL | OIL | MINING

2010 EXPORT TREEMAP ▾ TOTAL: $ 1,680,027,842,958

7522 (5.3%) Digital data processing machines

7649 (4.1%) Parts of telecom & sound equipment

7643 (3.7%) Television & radio transmitters

8942 (3.3%)

7721 (1.4%)
7758 (0.93%)
7849
7162 (0.54%)
7492
6991
7284
7442
7784
6940
7239
7452

7599 (2.9%) Parts of registers & calculating machines

7638 (1.6%)
7611 (1.4%)
7788 (1.4%)
7712 (1.4%)

7764 (2.6%) Electronic microcircuits

7518 (1.2%)
8124 (0.79%)
7641 (0.77%)
8947 (0.67%)

7525 (2.2%)
7763 (1.9%)

7528
8841
7768

6251
7431
7851
7491
7161

7932 (1.2%)

7711

8510 (2.6%) Footwear
8439 (1.1%)
8459 (1.1%)
8462
6522
8463
6589
8431
8433
6531
6514

8939 (1.0%)
9310 (0.80%)

8310 (1.4%)
8451 (1.3%)

8219 (1.1%)
7731 (0.91%)
8212
6842
6624
7752
6974
8851
8842

8211 (0.97%)

6613
8999
5823

6421

* Numbers indicate SITC-4 Rev 2 codes which can be found in the Appendix. Percentages next to the product codes indicate proportion of the product in the exports of the country. Treemap headers show the total trade of the country.

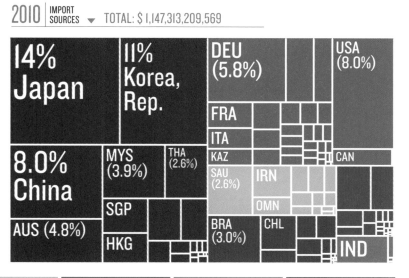

2010 EXPORT DESTINATIONS ▾ TOTAL: $ 1,680,027,842,958

10% Hong Kong
JPN (8.0%)
CHN (5.5%)
AUS
SGP
KOR (3.8%)
THA
MYS
IDN
20% United States
MEX
IND
BRA
ARE
DEU (5.2%)
GBR
FRA
RUS
NLD
ITA
ESP
TUR

2010 IMPORT SOURCES ▾ TOTAL: $ 1,147,313,209,569

14% Japan
8.0% China
AUS (4.8%)
11% Korea, Rep.
MYS (3.9%)
SGP
HKG
THA (2.6%)
DEU (5.8%)
FRA
ITA
KAZ
SAU (2.6%)
IRN
OMN
BRA (3.0%)
CHL
USA (8.0%)
CAN
IND

EAST ASIA & PACIFIC | EUROPE & CENTRAL ASIA | LATIN AMERICA & CARIBBEAN | MIDDLE EAST & NORTH AFRICA | NORTH AMERICA | SOUTH ASIA | SUB-SAHARAN AFRICA

COLOMBIA

ECONOMIC COMPLEXITY INDEX [2010] ▸ 0.118 (58) | COMPLEXITY OUTLOOK INDEX [2010] ▸ -0.016 (62) | EXPECTED GDPᴘᴄ GROWTH * ▸ 1.9% (68)

*Expected annual average for the 2010-2020 period.

2010 PRODUCT SPACE ▶

○ PRODUCTS EXPORTED WITH RCA > I

● PRODUCTS NOT EXPORTED WITH RCA > I

NODE SIZE IS PROPORTIONAL TO WORLD TRADE

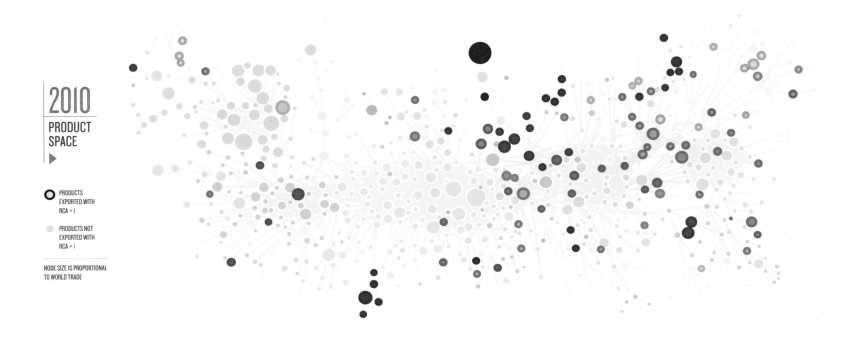

2010 EXPORT OPPORTUNITY SPECTRUM ◀

FRACTION OF PRODUCTS WITH RCA > I

22% OF WORLD TRADE (WT)

6% OF WT

2% OF WT

0.8% OF WT

0.06% OF WT

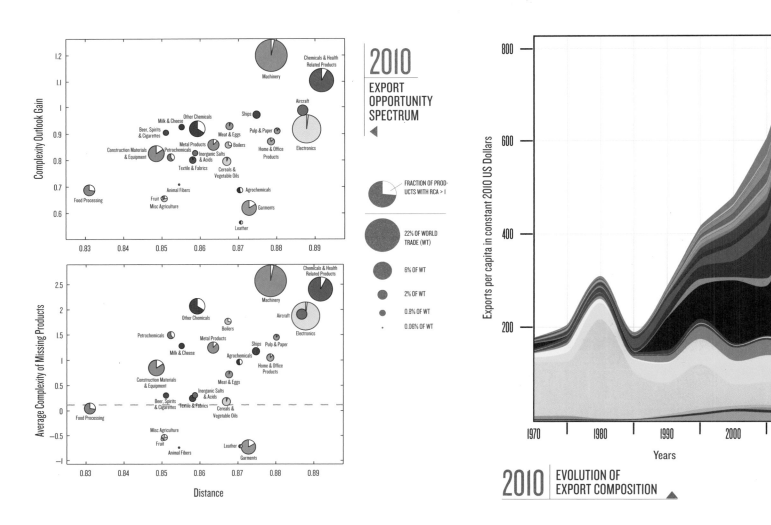

2010 | EVOLUTION OF EXPORT COMPOSITION ▲

POPULATION ▸ 46 M / (25)
TOTAL EXPORTS ▸ USD 38 B / (55)

GDP ▸ USD 289 B / (34)
GDPᴘᴄ ▸ USD 6,238 / (61)

EXPORTS PER CAPITA ▸ USD 828 / (78)
EXPORTS AS SHARE OF GDP ▸ 13 % (105)

* Data are from 2010. Numbers indicate:
Value (World Ranking among 128 countries)
Region: Latin America and the Caribbean.

ELECTRONICS | MACHINERY | AIRCRAFT | BOILERS | SHIPS | METAL PRODUCTS | CONSTR. MAT'L & EQPT. | HOME & OFFICE | PULP & PAPER | CHEMICALS & HEALTH | AGROCHEMICALS | OTHER CHEMICALS | INOR. SALTS & ACIDS | PETROCHEMICALS | LEATHER | MILK & CHEESE | ANIMAL FIBERS | MEAT & EGGS | FISH & SEAFOOD | TROPICAL AGRIC. | CEREALS & VEG. OILS | COTTON/RICE/SOY & OTHERS | TOBACCO | FRUIT | MISC. AGRICULTURE | NOT CLASSIFIED | TEXTILE & FABRICS | GARMENTS | FOOD PROCESSING | BEER/SPIRITS & CIGS. | PRECIOUS STONES | COAL | OIL | MINING

2010 | EXPORT TREEMAP ▼ TOTAL: $ 38,322,220,223

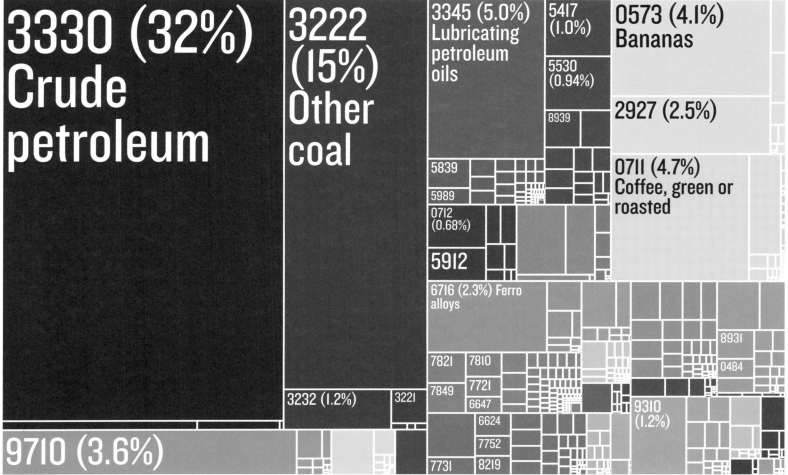

* Numbers indicate SITC-4 Rev 2 codes which can be found in the Appendix. Percentages next to the product codes indicate proportion of the product in the exports of the country. Treemap headers show the total trade of the country.

2010 | EXPORT DESTINATIONS ▼ TOTAL: $ 38,322,220,223

38% United States

BEL | FRA
ITA
ESP
CHN (5.0%)

ECU (4.9%) | CHL (3.7%) | BRA
VEN (3.9%) | PER (3.2%) | PAN
MEX | TTO | JPN
KOR

2010 | IMPORT SOURCES ▼ TOTAL: $ 34,541,685,266

MEX (9.9%) | ARG (3.9%)
BRA (6.0%) | CHL

27% United States

14% China | DEU (4.3%)
FRA (3.1%)

JPN (2.8%)
KOR
IND | ISR

EAST ASIA & PACIFIC | EUROPE & CENTRAL ASIA | LATIN AMERICA & CARIBBEAN | MIDDLE EAST & NORTH AFRICA | NORTH AMERICA | SOUTH ASIA | SUB-SAHARAN AFRICA

CONGO REPUBLIC

ECONOMIC COMPLEXITY INDEX [2010] ▸ -1.548 (122) | COMPLEXITY OUTLOOK INDEX [2010] ▸ -1.075 (119) | EXPECTED GDPᴘᴄ GROWTH * ▸ -0.3% (116)

*Expected annual average for the 2010-2020 period.

2010 PRODUCT SPACE ▸

○ PRODUCTS EXPORTED WITH RCA > 1

● PRODUCTS NOT EXPORTED WITH RCA > 1

NODE SIZE IS PROPORTIONAL TO WORLD TRADE

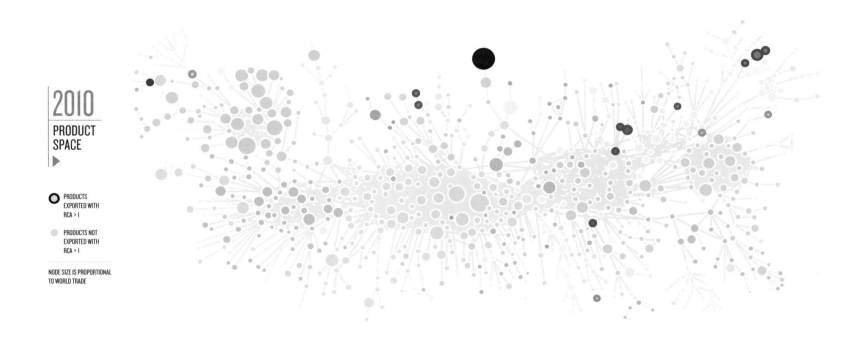

2010 EXPORT OPPORTUNITY SPECTRUM ◂

FRACTION OF PRODUCTS WITH RCA > 1

22% OF WORLD TRADE (WT)

6% OF WT

2% OF WT

0.8% OF WT

0.06% OF WT

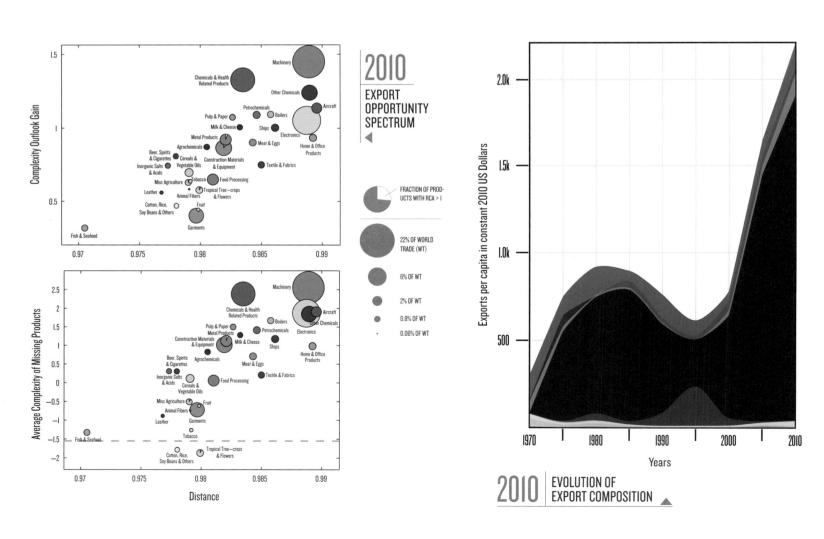

2010 | EVOLUTION OF EXPORT COMPOSITION ▲

POPULATION ▸ 4 M / (106)	GDP ▸ USD 12 B / (107)	EXPORTS PER CAPITA ▸ USD 2,214 / (52)	* Data are from 2010. Numbers indicate:
TOTAL EXPORTS ▸ USD 8.9 B / (76)	GDPpc ▸ USD 2,970 / (84)	EXPORTS AS SHARE OF GDP ▸ 75 % (4)	Value (World Ranking among 128 countries) Region: Sub-Saharan Africa.

ELECTRONICS · MACHINERY · AIRCRAFT · BOILERS · SHIPS · METAL PRODUCTS · CONSTR. MATL. & EQPT. · HOME & OFFICE · PULP & PAPER · CHEMICALS & HEALTH · AGROCHEMICALS · OTHER CHEMICALS · INOR. SALTS & ACIDS · PETROCHEMICALS · LEATHER · MILK & CHEESE · ANIMAL FIBERS · MEAT & EGGS · FISH & SEAFOOD · TROPICAL AGRIC. · CEREALS & VEG. OILS · COTTON/RICE/SOY & OTHERS · TOBACCO · FRUIT · MISC. AGRICULTURE · NOT CLASSIFIED · TEXTILE & FABRICS · GARMENTS · FOOD PROCESSING · BEER/SPIRITS & CIGS. · PRECIOUS STONES · COAL · OIL · MINING

2010 | EXPORT TREEMAP ▾ TOTAL: $ 8,949,393,473

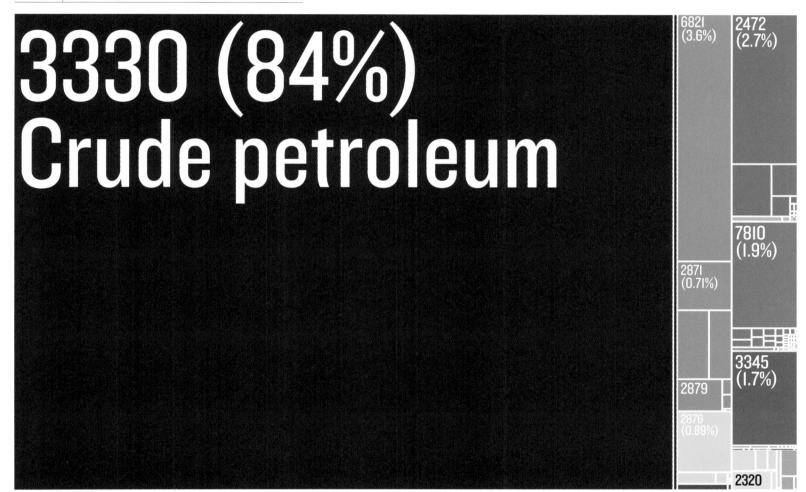

3330 (84%) Crude petroleum

6821 (3.6%) · 2472 (2.7%) · 7810 (1.9%) · 2871 (0.71%) · 3345 (1.7%) · 2879 · 2876 (0.89%) · 2320

* Numbers indicate SITC-4 Rev 2 codes which can be found in the Appendix. Percentages next to the product codes indicate proportion of the product in the exports of the country. Treemap headers show the total trade of the country.

2010 | EXPORT DESTINATIONS ▾ TOTAL: $ 8,949,393,473

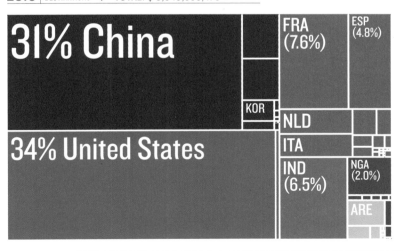

31% China · FRA (7.6%) · ESP (4.8%) · KOR · NLD · ITA · IND (6.5%) · NGA (2.0%) · 34% United States · ARE

2010 | IMPORT SOURCES ▾ TOTAL: $ 2,839,646,269

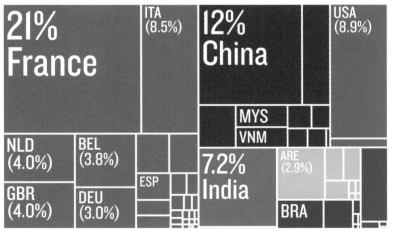

21% France · ITA (8.5%) · 12% China · USA (8.9%) · MYS · VNM · NLD (4.0%) · BEL (3.8%) · ESP · 7.2% India · ARE (2.9%) · GBR (4.0%) · DEU (3.0%) · BRA

EAST ASIA & PACIFIC · EUROPE & CENTRAL ASIA · LATIN AMERICA & CARIBBEAN · MIDDLE EAST & NORTH AFRICA · NORTH AMERICA · SOUTH ASIA · SUB-SAHARAN AFRICA

COSTA RICA

| ECONOMIC COMPLEXITY INDEX [2010] ▸ 0.191 (57) | COMPLEXITY OUTLOOK INDEX [2010] ▸ -0.367 (72) | EXPECTED GDPᴘᴄ GROWTH * ▸ 1.5% (85) |

*Expected annual average for the 2010-2020 period.

2010 PRODUCT SPACE ▸

○ PRODUCTS EXPORTED WITH RCA > 1

● PRODUCTS NOT EXPORTED WITH RCA > 1

NODE SIZE IS PROPORTIONAL TO WORLD TRADE

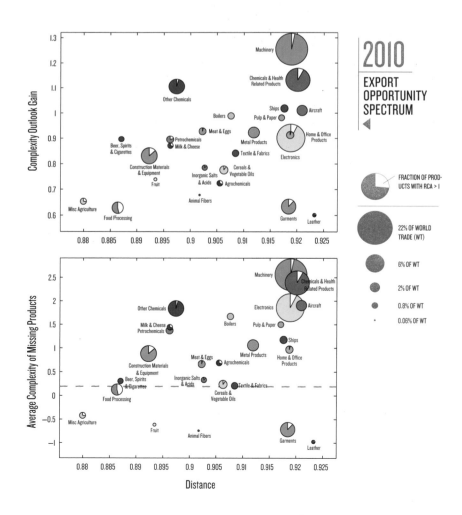

2010 EXPORT OPPORTUNITY SPECTRUM ◂

◔ FRACTION OF PRODUCTS WITH RCA > 1

⬤ 22% OF WORLD TRADE (WT)

⬤ 6% OF WT

● 2% OF WT

• 0.8% OF WT

· 0.06% OF WT

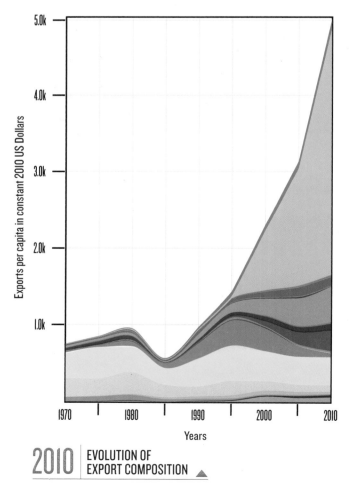

2010 EVOLUTION OF EXPORT COMPOSITION ▲

POPULATION ▸ 4.7 M / (100)
TOTAL EXPORTS ▸ USD 23 B / (60)

GDP ▸ USD 36 B / (82)
GDPᴘᴄ ▸ USD 7,774 / (54)

EXPORTS PER CAPITA ▸ USD 5,033 / (35)
EXPORTS AS SHARE OF GDP ▸ 65 % / (8)

* Data are from 2010. Numbers indicate:
Value (World Ranking among 128 countries)
Region: Latin America and the Caribbean.

ELECTRONICS · MACHINERY · AIRCRAFT · BOILERS · SHIPS · METAL PRODUCTS · CONSTR. MATL. & EQPT. · HOME & OFFICE · PULP & PAPER · CHEMICALS & HEALTH · AGROCHEMICALS · OTHER CHEMICALS · INOR. SALTS & ACIDS · PETROCHEMICALS · LEATHER · MILK & CHEESE · ANIMAL FIBERS · MEAT & EGGS · FISH & SEAFOOD · TROPICAL AGRIC. · CEREALS & VEG. OILS · COTTON/RICE/SOY & OTHERS · TOBACCO · FRUIT · MISC. AGRICULTURE · NOT CLASSIFIED · TEXTILE & FABRICS · GARMENTS · FOOD PROCESSING · BEER/SPIRITS & CIGS. · PRECIOUS STONES · COAL · OIL · MINING

2010 | EXPORT TREEMAP ▼ TOTAL: $ 23,448,846,641

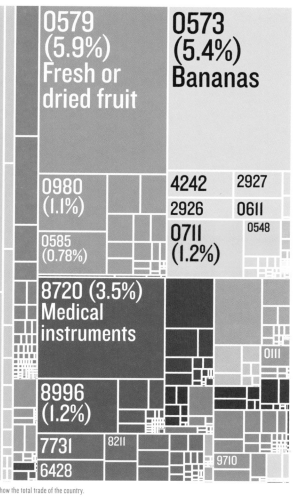

7764 (38%) Electronic microcircuits

7599 (25%) Parts of registers & calculating machines

0579 (5.9%) Fresh or dried fruit

0573 (5.4%) Bananas

0980 (1.1%)

0585 (0.78%)

4242 · 2927 · 2926 · 0611

0711 (1.2%) · 0548

8720 (3.5%) Medical instruments

8996 (1.2%)

0111

7731 · 8211

6428 · 9710

* Numbers indicate SITC-4 Rev 2 codes which can be found in the Appendix. Percentages next to the product codes indicate proportion of the product in the exports of the country. Treemap headers show the total trade of the country.

2010 | EXPORT DESTINATIONS ▼ TOTAL: $ 23,448,846,641

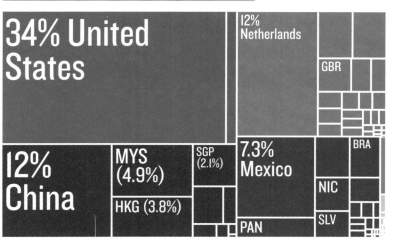

34% United States

12% China

MYS (4.9%)

HKG (3.8%)

SGP (2.1%)

12% Netherlands

GBR

7.3% Mexico

NIC

SLV

PAN

BRA

2010 | IMPORT SOURCES ▼ TOTAL: $ 12,207,867,986

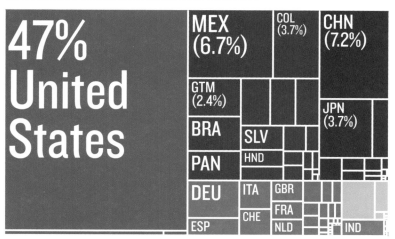

47% United States

MEX (6.7%)

GTM (2.4%)

BRA

PAN

DEU

ESP

SLV

HND

ITA

CHE

GBR

FRA

NLD

COL (3.7%)

CHN (7.2%)

JPN (3.7%)

IND

EAST ASIA & PACIFIC · EUROPE & CENTRAL ASIA · LATIN AMERICA & CARIBBEAN · MIDDLE EAST & NORTH AFRICA · NORTH AMERICA · SOUTH ASIA · SUB-SAHARAN AFRICA

CÔTE D'IVOIRE

ECONOMIC COMPLEXITY INDEX [2010] ▸ -1.27 (118) **COMPLEXITY OUTLOOK INDEX [2010] ▸ -1.015 (114)** **EXPECTED GDPᴘᴄ GROWTH * ▸ 1.1% (94)**

*Expected annual average for the 2010-2020 period.

2010 PRODUCT SPACE ▸

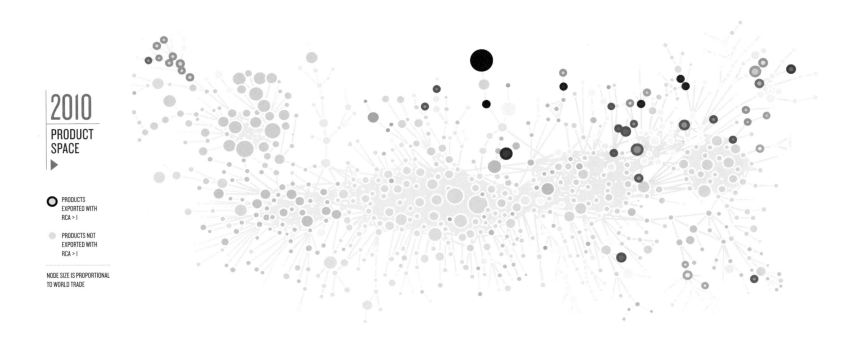

○ PRODUCTS EXPORTED WITH RCA > 1

○ PRODUCTS NOT EXPORTED WITH RCA > 1

NODE SIZE IS PROPORTIONAL TO WORLD TRADE

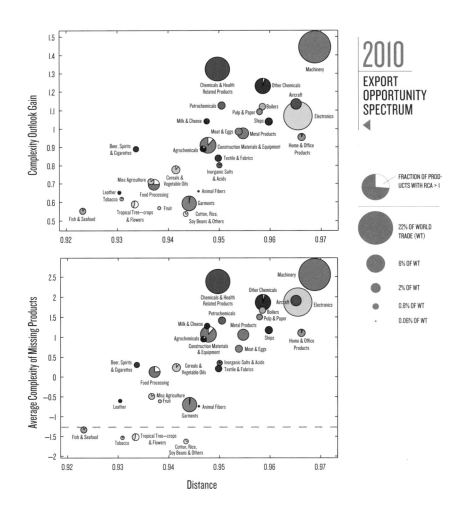

2010 EXPORT OPPORTUNITY SPECTRUM ◂

◔ FRACTION OF PRODUCTS WITH RCA > 1

○ 22% OF WORLD TRADE (WT)

○ 6% OF WT

○ 2% OF WT

○ 0.8% OF WT

· 0.06% OF WT

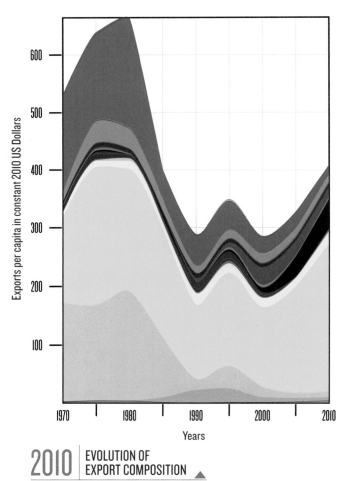

2010 EVOLUTION OF EXPORT COMPOSITION ▲

POPULATION ▸ 20 M / (50)
TOTAL EXPORTS ▸ USD 8.1 B / (79)

GDP ▸ USD 23 B / (90)
GDPᴘᴄ ▸ USD 1,161 / (107)

EXPORTS PER CAPITA ▸ USD 409 / (98)
EXPORTS AS SHARE OF GDP ▸ 35 % / (41)

* Data are from 2010. Numbers indicate:
Value (World Ranking among 128 countries)
Region: Sub-Saharan Africa.

ELECTRONICS · MACHINERY · AIRCRAFT · BOILERS · SHIPS · METAL PRODUCTS · CONSTR. MATL. & EQPT. · HOME & OFFICE · PULP & PAPER · CHEMICALS & HEALTH · AGROCHEMICALS · OTHER CHEMICALS · INOR. SALTS & ACIDS · PETROCHEMICALS · LEATHER · MILK & CHEESE · ANIMAL FIBERS · MEAT & EGGS · FISH & SEAFOOD · TROPICAL AGRIC. · CEREALS & VEG. OILS · COTTON/RICE/SOY & OTHERS · TOBACCO · FRUIT · MISC. AGRICULTURE · NOT CLASSIFIED · TEXTILE & FABRICS · GARMENTS · FOOD PROCESSING · BEER/SPIRITS & CIGS. · PRECIOUS STONES · COAL · OIL · MINING

2010 | EXPORT TREEMAP ▾ TOTAL: $ 8,073,460,503

0721 (32%) Raw & roasted cocoa beans

2320 (8.4%) Natural rubber, latex & gums

0723 (15%) Cocoa butter & paste

0573 (2.9%) Bananas

0722 (1.6%)

4242 (1.3%)

0577 (3.2%)

2631 (1.7%)

0711 (1.8%)

0712

5541

0460

3330 (12%) Crude petroleum

3345 (4.0%) Lubricating petroleum oils

2483 (1.7%) Worked wood of non coniferous

6341 (0.77%)

2472

0730 (0.87%)

0579 (0.75%)

0371 (1.4%)

8510

0980 (0.61%)

0483

8931

9310 (0.81%)

* Numbers indicate SITC-4 Rev 2 codes which can be found in the Appendix. Percentages next to the product codes indicate proportion of the product in the exports of the country. Treemap headers show the total trade of the country.

2010 | EXPORT DESTINATIONS ▾ TOTAL: $ 8,073,460,503

12% Germany

NLD (10%)

FRA (9.2%)

14% United States

CAN (4.6%)

ITA (4.9%)

GBR

ESP

RUS

TUR

EST

UKR

MYS

VNM

CHN

IND (2.9%)

DZA

BEL (4.0%)

2010 | IMPORT SOURCES ▾ TOTAL: $ 6,093,295,648

17% France

BEL (4.0%)

NLD (3.3%)

DEU (2.4%)

SWE

ESP (2.4%)

GBR

ROU

8.7% China

THA (6.1%)

VNM

KOR

IDN

20% Nigeria

ZAF

SEN

COL (3.5%)

BRA

IND

PAK

USA

EAST ASIA & PACIFIC · EUROPE & CENTRAL ASIA · LATIN AMERICA & CARIBBEAN · MIDDLE EAST & NORTH AFRICA · NORTH AMERICA · SOUTH ASIA · SUB-SAHARAN AFRICA

CROATIA

ECONOMIC COMPLEXITY INDEX [2010] ▸ 0.897 (25) | **COMPLEXITY OUTLOOK INDEX [2010]** ▸ 1.078 (20) | **EXPECTED GDP**PC **GROWTH** * ▸ 2.8% (29)

*Expected annual average for the 2010-2020 period.

2010 PRODUCT SPACE ▸

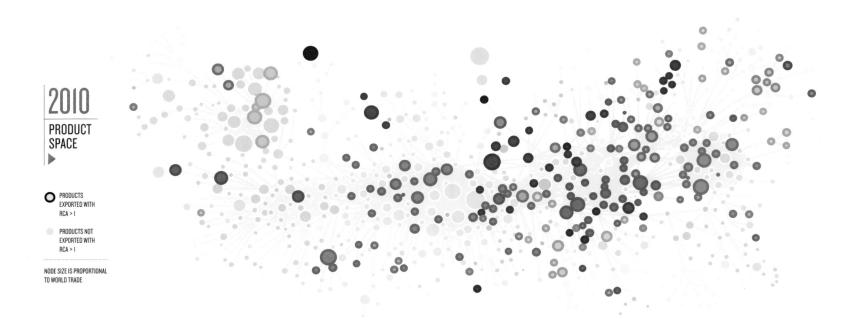

○ PRODUCTS EXPORTED WITH RCA > 1

○ PRODUCTS NOT EXPORTED WITH RCA > 1

NODE SIZE IS PROPORTIONAL TO WORLD TRADE

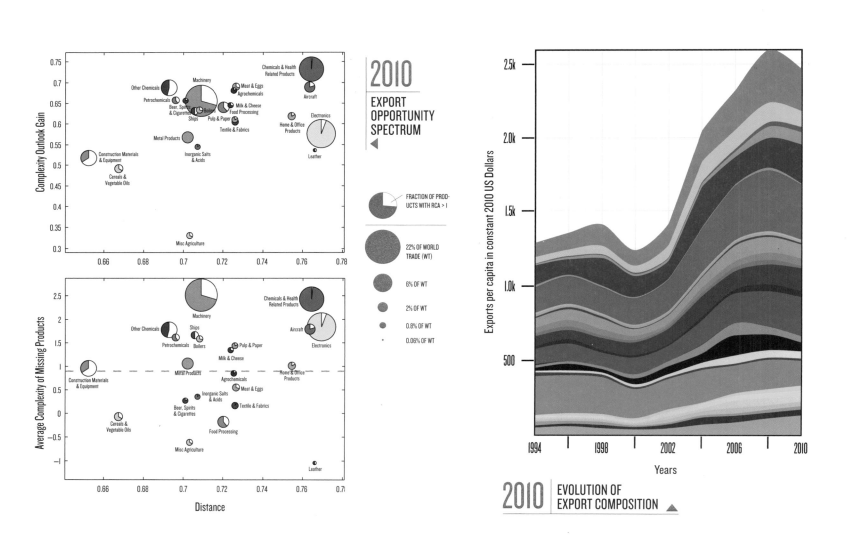

2010 EXPORT OPPORTUNITY SPECTRUM ◂

FRACTION OF PRODUCTS WITH RCA > 1

22% OF WORLD TRADE (WT)

6% OF WT

2% OF WT

0.8% OF WT

0.06% OF WT

2010 | EVOLUTION OF EXPORT COMPOSITION ▲

POPULATION ▸ 4.4 M / (103)
TOTAL EXPORTS ▸ USD 11 B / (72)

GDP ▸ USD 61 B / (64)
GDPᴘᴄ ▸ USD 13,774 / (36)

EXPORTS PER CAPITA ▸ USD 2,471 / (48)
EXPORTS AS SHARE OF GDP ▸ 18 % (87)

* Data are from 2010. Numbers indicate:
Value (World Ranking among 128 countries)
Region: Eastern Europe and Central Asia.

ELECTRONICS | MACHINERY | AIRCRAFT | BOILERS | SHIPS | METAL PRODUCTS | CONSTR. MATL. & EQPT. | HOME & OFFICE | PULP & PAPER | CHEMICALS & HEALTH | AGROCHEMICALS | OTHER CHEMICALS | INOR. SALTS & ACIDS | PETROCHEMICALS | LEATHER | MILK & CHEESE | ANIMAL FIBERS | MEAT & EGGS | FISH & SEAFOOD | TROPICAL AGRIC. | CEREALS & VEG. OILS | COTTON/RICE/SOY & OTHERS | TOBACCO | FRUIT | MISC. AGRICULTURE | NOT CLASSIFIED | TEXTILE & FABRICS | GARMENTS | FOOD PROCESSING | BEER/SPIRITS & CIGS. | PRECIOUS STONES | COAL | OIL | MINING

2010 | EXPORT TREEMAP ▾ TOTAL: $ 10,916,770,111

7721 (0.98%)
7239
6782
8743
7783
7284 (0.83%)
7499
7162
7212
7849 (0.80%)
9510
7491
7139
7452

7763 (1.1%)
7788
7768
7711 (2.4%) Electrical transformers

3510 (3.4%) Electric current
2483 (2.0%)
6842 (1.7%)
8510 (1.5%)

7731 (1.1%)
6353 (0.61%)
6624
6123
8424
8211
6911 (0.53%)
8212
8431
8219
2472 (0.52%)
6359
8422
2450
6514
6517

7932 (7.6%) Ships & boats
7938 (2.9%) Special floating structures
7149 (0.72%)
7144

3414 (1.2%)
3413 (0.97%)
6612 (1.1%)
0980 (1.1%)
1110

3345 (9.6%) Lubricating petroleum oils
5417 (3.5%) Medicaments
5621 (1.3%)
8922
8921
5831 (1.8%)

2882
6998
8973
0488
0730
2734
0484
1222 (0.72%)
6421
2820 (1.4%)
1123
6129 (0.64%)

9310 (1.2%)
5823
0344
0149
8928

* Numbers indicate SITC-4 Rev 2 codes which can be found in the Appendix. Percentages next to the product codes indicate proportion of the product in the exports of the country. Treemap headers show the total trade of the country.

2010 | EXPORT DESTINATIONS ▾ TOTAL: $ 10,916,770,111

17% Italy
12% Bosnia and Herzegovina
SVN (8.3%)

8.3% Germany
AUT (5.8%)
LUX (2.9%)
HUN
RUS
TUR
POL
CZE
MNE
CYP

USA (3.0%)
BMU

2010 | IMPORT SOURCES ▾ TOTAL: $ 18,444,579,250

15% Italy
13% Germany
RUS (9.3%)

SVN (5.8%)
AUT (4.9%)
TUR (2.9%)
HUN (2.8%)
CHE
FRA (2.7%)
BEL
NLD
SVK
SWE

CHN (6.7%)
JPN
KOR
USA (2.9%)

EAST ASIA & PACIFIC | EUROPE & CENTRAL ASIA | LATIN AMERICA & CARIBBEAN | MIDDLE EAST & NORTH AFRICA | NORTH AMERICA | SOUTH ASIA | SUB-SAHARAN AFRICA

CUBA

ECONOMIC COMPLEXITY INDEX [2010] ▸ -0.404 (77) | **COMPLEXITY OUTLOOK INDEX [2010]** ▸ -0.894 (98) | **EXPECTED GDPᴘᴄ GROWTH *** ▸ 0.7% (102)

*Expected annual average for the 2010-2020 period.

2010
PRODUCT SPACE ▶

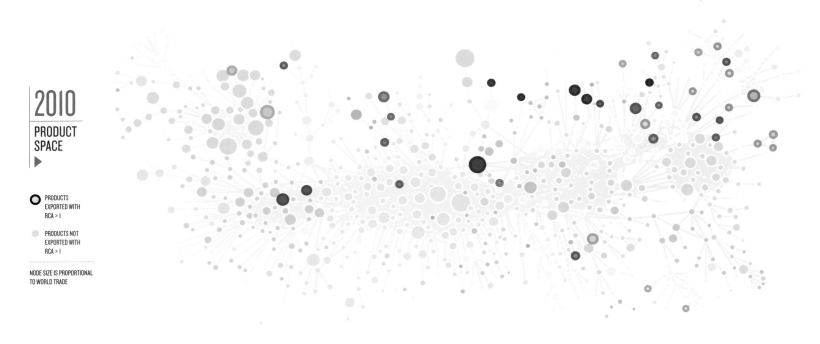

○ PRODUCTS EXPORTED WITH RCA > 1

○ PRODUCTS NOT EXPORTED WITH RCA > 1

NODE SIZE IS PROPORTIONAL TO WORLD TRADE

2010
EXPORT OPPORTUNITY SPECTRUM ◀

◐ FRACTION OF PRODUCTS WITH RCA > 1

⬤ 22% OF WORLD TRADE (WT)

⬤ 6% OF WT

● 2% OF WT

• 0.8% OF WT

· 0.06% OF WT

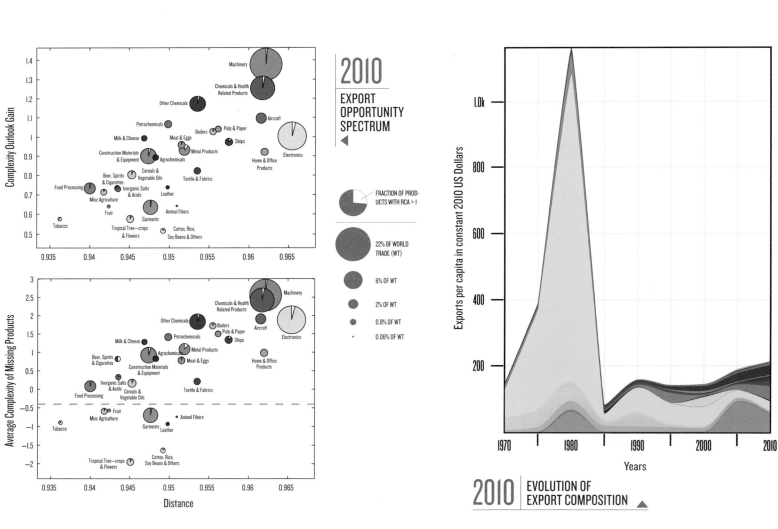

2010 | EVOLUTION OF EXPORT COMPOSITION ▲

POPULATION ‣ 11 M / (65)	GDP ‣ USD 61 B / (65)	EXPORTS PER CAPITA ‣ USD 214 / (108)	
TOTAL EXPORTS ‣ USD 2.4 B / (108)	GDPᴾᶜ ‣ USD 5,397 / (64)	EXPORTS AS SHARE OF GDP ‣ 4 % (128)	

* Data are from 2010. Numbers indicate:
Value (World Ranking among 128 countries)
Region: Latin America and the Caribbean.

ELECTRONICS · MACHINERY · AIRCRAFT · BOILERS · SHIPS · METAL PRODUCTS · CONSTR. MATL. & EQPT. · HOME & OFFICE · PULP & PAPER · CHEMICALS & HEALTH · AGROCHEMICALS · OTHER CHEMICALS · INOR. SALTS & ACIDS · PETROCHEMICALS · LEATHER · MILK & CHEESE · ANIMAL FIBERS · MEAT & EGGS · FISH & SEAFOOD · TROPICAL AGRIC. · CEREALS & VEG. OILS · COTTON/RICE/SOY & OTHERS · TOBACCO · FRUIT · MISC. AGRICULTURE · NOT CLASSIFIED · TEXTILE & FABRICS · GARMENTS · FOOD PROCESSING · BEER/SPIRITS & CIGS. · PRECIOUS STONES · COAL · OIL · MINING

2010 | EXPORT TREEMAP ▼ TOTAL: $ 2,404,595,089

9310 (26%) Unclassified transactions

2872 (17%) Nickel

2879 (2.0%)

2882 (1.6%)

3330 (1.1%)

1221 (8.4%) Cigars

1124 (4.9%) Alcoholic beverages

0585

0611 (12%) Raw sugars

3345 (4.1%) Lubricating petroleum oils

5416 (3.0%) Glycosides & vaccines

5417 (7.2%) Medicaments

6725 (1.3%)

0360 (2.5%)

7272

7938

0616

2450

6732

* Numbers indicate SITC-4 Rev 2 codes which can be found in the Appendix. Percentages next to the product codes indicate proportion of the product in the exports of the country. Treemap headers show the total trade of the country.

2010 | EXPORT DESTINATIONS ▼ TOTAL: $ 2,404,595,089

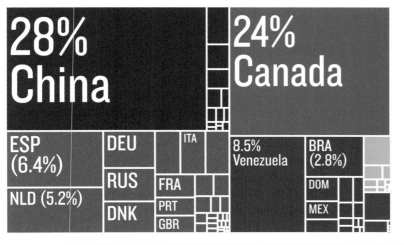

28% China

24% Canada

ESP (6.4%)

NLD (5.2%)

DEU

RUS

DNK

ITA

FRA

PRT

GBR

8.5% Venezuela

BRA (2.8%)

DOM

MEX

2010 | IMPORT SOURCES ▼ TOTAL: $ 5,077,536,324

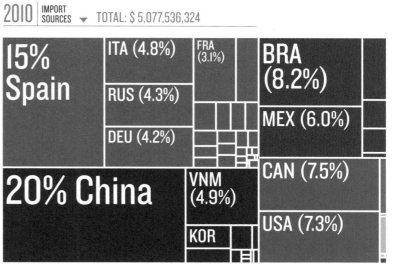

15% Spain

ITA (4.8%)

RUS (4.3%)

DEU (4.2%)

FRA (3.1%)

BRA (8.2%)

MEX (6.0%)

20% China

VNM (4.9%)

KOR

CAN (7.5%)

USA (7.3%)

EAST ASIA & PACIFIC · EUROPE & CENTRAL ASIA · LATIN AMERICA & CARIBBEAN · MIDDLE EAST & NORTH AFRICA · NORTH AMERICA · SOUTH ASIA · SUB-SAHARAN AFRICA

CZECH REPUBLIC

ECONOMIC COMPLEXITY INDEX [2010] ▸ 1.682 (8) | COMPLEXITY OUTLOOK INDEX [2010] ▸ -0.084 (66) | EXPECTED GDPᴘᴄ GROWTH * ▸ 2.7% (32)

*Expected annual average for the 2010-2020 period.

2010 PRODUCT SPACE ▶

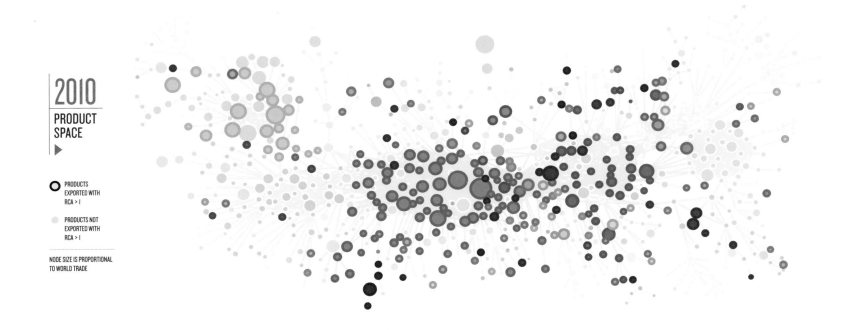

○ PRODUCTS EXPORTED WITH RCA > 1

● PRODUCTS NOT EXPORTED WITH RCA > 1

NODE SIZE IS PROPORTIONAL TO WORLD TRADE

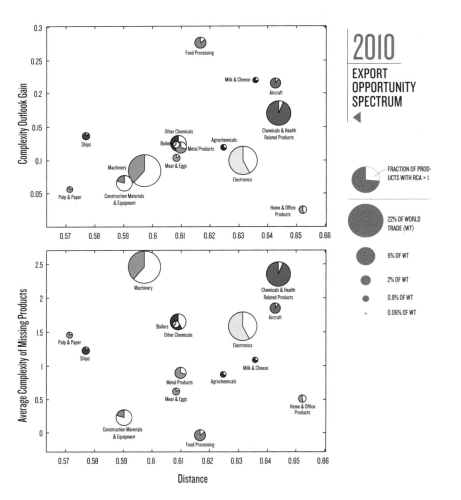

2010 EXPORT OPPORTUNITY SPECTRUM ◀

◖ FRACTION OF PRODUCTS WITH RCA > 1

● 22% OF WORLD TRADE (WT)

● 6% OF WT

● 2% OF WT

● 0.8% OF WT

· 0.06% OF WT

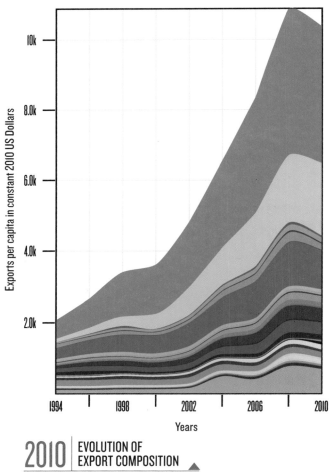

2010 EVOLUTION OF EXPORT COMPOSITION ▲

POPULATION ▸ 11 M / (69)
TOTAL EXPORTS ▸ USD 109 B / (30)

GDP ▸ USD 198 B / (45)
GDPᴘᴄ ▸ USD 18,789 / (31)

EXPORTS PER CAPITA ▸ USD 10,375 / (17)
EXPORTS AS SHARE OF GDP ▸ 55 % (15)

* Data are from 2010. Numbers indicate:
Value (World Ranking among 128 countries)
Region: Eastern Europe and Central Asia.

ELECTRONICS · MACHINERY · AIRCRAFT · BOILERS · SHIPS · METAL PRODUCTS · CONSTR. MATL. & EQPT. · HOME & OFFICE · PULP & PAPER · CHEMICALS & HEALTH · AGROCHEMICALS · OTHER CHEMICALS · INOR. SALTS & ACIDS · PETROCHEMICALS · LEATHER · MILK & CHEESE · ANIMAL FIBERS · MEAT & EGGS · FISH & SEAFOOD · TROPICAL AGRIC. · CEREALS & VEG. OILS · COTTON/RICE/SOY & OTHERS · TOBACCO · FRUIT · MISC. AGRICULTURE · NOT CLASSIFIED · TEXTILE & FABRICS · GARMENTS · FOOD PROCESSING · BEER/SPIRITS & CIGS. · PRECIOUS STONES · COAL · OIL · MINING

2010 EXPORT TREEMAP ▾ — TOTAL: $ 109,138,761,416

7810 (10%) Cars

7849 (7.0%) Other vehicle parts

7523 (3.4%) CPUs

7611 (2.4%)

3510 (1.6%)

7731 (1.6%)

8211 (1.1%)

8939 (0.98%)

5417 (0.76%)

3345 (0.82%)

6911 (0.71%)

6997 · 2471 · 6353 · 6732 · 6924 · 8720 · 5989 · 7414 · 6343

7522 (1.3%)

8942 (1.3%)

7415 (1.2%)

7721 (2.7%) Switchboards, relays & fuses

7431 · 6782 · 6731 · 7449 · 7842 · 7499 · 6289 · 7161 · 6760 · 7416 · 7784

6251 (0.98%)

7783 · 6991 · 7139 · 7436 · 7239

7599 (1.1%)

7421 (0.99%)

7525 (0.96%)

6413

5831

6210

9310 (4.5%) Unclassified transactions

7763 (0.82%)

7781

7649 · 7712 · 7621 · 7638 · 7643 · 7648 · 7528

1123

1222

2882 (0.59%) · 6998 · 6794

6744 · 6783 · 6770 · 6252 · 6259

3222 (0.96%)

3232

* Numbers indicate SITC-4 Rev 2 codes which can be found in the Appendix. Percentages next to the product codes indicate proportion of the product in the exports of the country. Treemap headers show the total trade of the country.

2010 EXPORT DESTINATIONS ▾ — TOTAL: $ 109,138,761,416

33% Germany

FRA (5.4%)

POL (5.4%)

GBR (5.1%)

ITA (4.9%)

CHN

AUT (4.7%)

ESP (2.4%)

NLD (3.5%)

CHE

SWE

SVK

BEL

ROU

2010 IMPORT SOURCES ▾ — TOTAL: $ 106,912,554,801

26% Germany

RUS (5.8%)

SVK (5.3%)

12% China

AUT (3.4%)

FRA (3.3%)

BEL

JPN (2.2%)

CHE

IRL

KOR

POL (6.5%)

NLD (3.2%)

AZE

NOR

EAST ASIA & PACIFIC · EUROPE & CENTRAL ASIA · LATIN AMERICA & CARIBBEAN · MIDDLE EAST & NORTH AFRICA · NORTH AMERICA · SOUTH ASIA · SUB-SAHARAN AFRICA

DENMARK

ECONOMIC COMPLEXITY INDEX [2010] ► 1.306 (18) | **COMPLEXITY OUTLOOK INDEX [2010]** ► 0.974 (26) | **EXPECTED GDPₚ꜀ GROWTH *** ► 1.7% (74)

*Expected annual average for the 2010-2020 period.

2010
PRODUCT SPACE ►

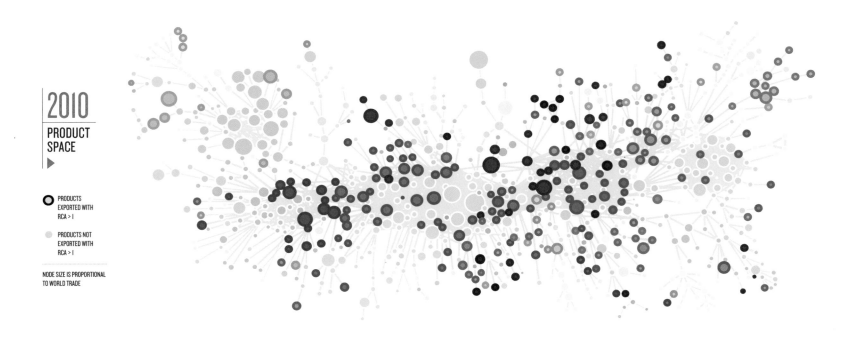

○ PRODUCTS EXPORTED WITH RCA > 1

● PRODUCTS NOT EXPORTED WITH RCA > 1

NODE SIZE IS PROPORTIONAL TO WORLD TRADE

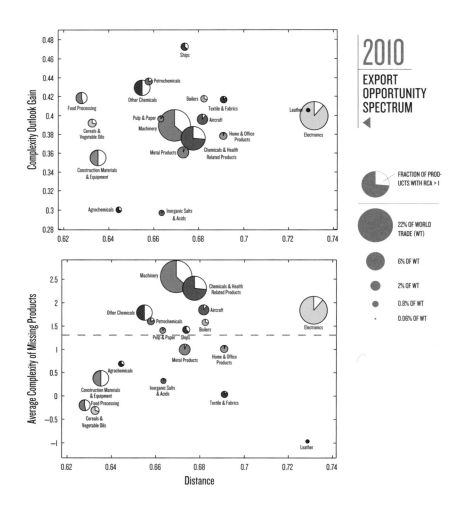

2010
EXPORT OPPORTUNITY SPECTRUM ◄

FRACTION OF PRODUCTS WITH RCA > 1

22% OF WORLD TRADE (WT)

6% OF WT

2% OF WT

0.8% OF WT

0.06% OF WT

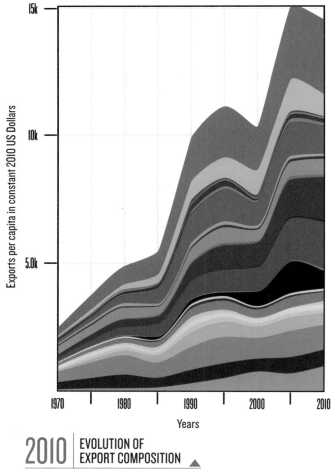

2010 | EVOLUTION OF EXPORT COMPOSITION ▲

POPULATION ▸ 5.5 M / (93)
TOTAL EXPORTS ▸ USD 81 B / (33)

GDP ▸ USD 312 B / (31)
GDPᴘᴄ ▸ USD 56,278 / (4)

EXPORTS PER CAPITA ▸ USD 14,592 / (11)
EXPORTS AS SHARE OF GDP ▸ 26 % (62)

* Data are from 2010. Numbers indicate:
Value (World Ranking among 128 countries)
Region: Western Europe.

ELECTRONICS MACHINERY AIRCRAFT BOILERS SHIPS METAL PRODUCTS CONSTR. MATL. & EQPT. HOME & OFFICE PULP & PAPER CHEMICALS & HEALTH AGROCHEMICALS OTHER CHEMICALS INOR. SALTS & ACIDS PETROCHEMICALS LEATHER MILK & CHEESE ANIMAL FIBERS MEAT & EGGS FISH & SEAFOOD TROPICAL AGRIC. CEREALS & VEG. OILS COTTON/RICE/SOY & OTHERS TOBACCO FRUIT MISC. AGRICULTURE NOT CLASSIFIED TEXTILE & FABRICS GARMENTS FOOD PROCESSING BEER/SPIRITS & CIGS. PRECIOUS STONES COAL OIL MINING

2010 EXPORT TREEMAP ▾ TOTAL: $ 80,952,198,505

7161 (3.1%) DC motors & generators
7492 (1.2%)
7169 (1.1%)
7721
7849
7436 7212 7493 7499 7162 6991 7783 7139 7219 7239
8942 (1.3%)
7522 7788 7599 7611
7932 (0.87%)
0113 (3.8%) Swine meat
0013 (0.66%) 0114 0111 0149
0341 0814
0240 (1.6%)
2120 (0.89%) 0230
0360 0350 0371 0344
8219 (1.2%)
6428 7414 8211 6997 6912
3510 (1.0%)

3345 (3.0%) Lubricating petroleum oils
5416 (1.5%) 8996 (1.4%)
5417 (7.9%) Medicaments
8939 (1.1%)
9310 (4.7%) Unclassified transactions
0980 (1.4%)
8931 0484 6421 1123
0612 0412 0430 2926 2925

5169 (1.1%)
5989 (0.93%)
5530
3330 (4.0%) Crude petroleum
5419
8973 8510 8451 8459 8462

8720 (1.0%) 5145 5415 5831

* Numbers indicate SITC-4 Rev 2 codes which can be found in the Appendix. Percentages next to the product codes indicate proportion of the product in the exports of the country. Treemap headers show the total trade of the country.

2010 EXPORT DESTINATIONS ▾ TOTAL: $ 80,952,198,505

16% Germany
14% Sweden
GBR (7.1%)
NOR (5.3%)
FRA (4.2%)
CHN (2.9%)
JPN (2.5%)
NLD (3.3%) FIN BEL
USA (6.8%)
ITA (3.1%)
IRL
ESP
POL
CHE
CZE

2010 IMPORT SOURCES ▾ TOTAL: $ 75,011,932,457

21% Germany
13% Sweden
NLD (7.1%)
GBR (5.8%)
7.6% China
ITA (3.5%)
POL (3.1%)
FIN
THA
SGP
BEL (3.4%)
RUS
IRL
USA (3.2%)
FRA (3.4%)
CZE
CHE

EAST ASIA & PACIFIC | EUROPE & CENTRAL ASIA | LATIN AMERICA & CARIBBEAN | MIDDLE EAST & NORTH AFRICA | NORTH AMERICA | SOUTH ASIA | SUB-SAHARAN AFRICA

DOMINICAN REPUBLIC

ECONOMIC COMPLEXITY INDEX [2010] ▸ -0.299 (74) | **COMPLEXITY OUTLOOK INDEX [2010]** ▸ -0.247 (69) | **EXPECTED GDPPC GROWTH** * ▸ 1.3% (91)

*Expected annual average for the 2010-2020 period.

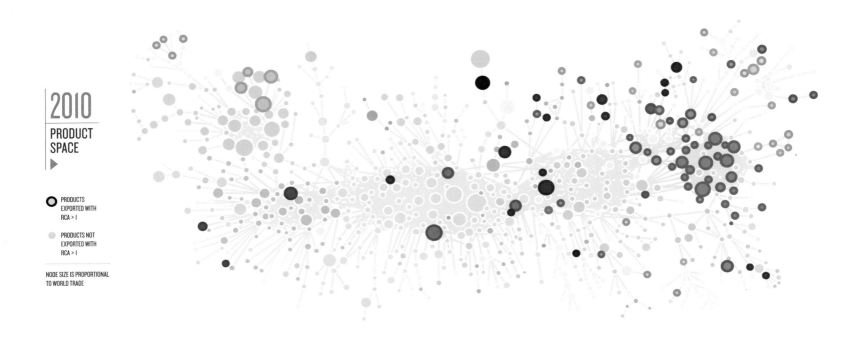

2010

PRODUCT SPACE ▶

○ PRODUCTS EXPORTED WITH RCA > 1

○ PRODUCTS NOT EXPORTED WITH RCA > 1

NODE SIZE IS PROPORTIONAL TO WORLD TRADE

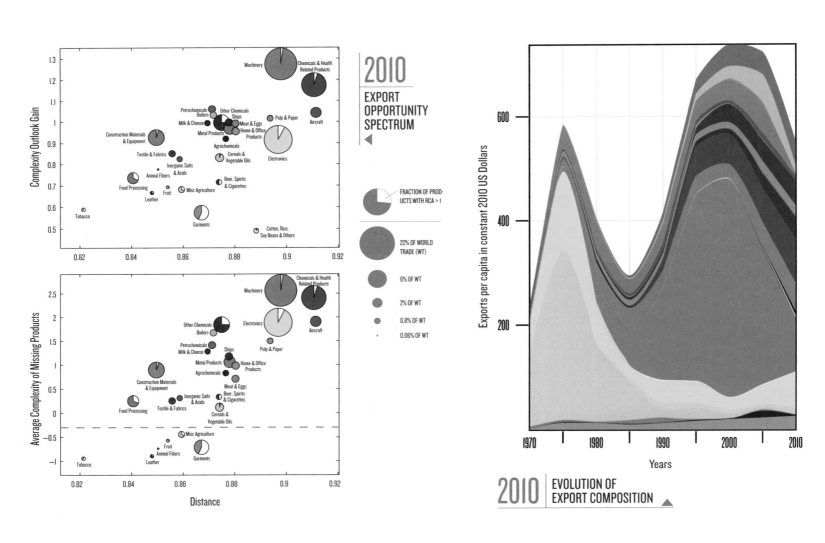

2010

EXPORT OPPORTUNITY SPECTRUM ◀

FRACTION OF PRODUCTS WITH RCA > 1

22% OF WORLD TRADE (WT)

6% OF WT

2% OF WT

0.8% OF WT

0.06% OF WT

2010 | **EVOLUTION OF EXPORT COMPOSITION** ▲

POPULATION ▸ 9.9 M / (73)
TOTAL EXPORTS ▸ USD 5.4 B / (89)

GDP ▸ USD 52 B / (71)
GDPᴘᴄ ▸ USD 5,195 / (67)

EXPORTS PER CAPITA ▸ USD 548 / (87)
EXPORTS AS SHARE OF GDP ▸ 11 % / (118)

* Data are from 2010. Numbers indicate:
Value (World Ranking among 128 countries)
Region: Latin America and the Caribbean.

ELECTRONICS · MACHINERY · AIRCRAFT · BOILERS · SHIPS · METAL PRODUCTS · CONSTR. MATL. & EQPT. · HOME & OFFICE · PULP & PAPER · CHEMICALS & HEALTH · AGROCHEMICALS · OTHER CHEMICALS · INOR. SALTS & ACIDS · PETROCHEMICALS · LEATHER · MILK & CHEESE · ANIMAL FIBERS · MEAT & EGGS · FISH & SEAFOOD · TROPICAL AGRIC. · CEREALS & VEG. OILS · COTTON/RICE/SOY & OTHERS · TOBACCO · FRUIT · MISC. AGRICULTURE · NOT CLASSIFIED · TEXTILE & FABRICS · GARMENTS · FOOD PROCESSING · BEER/SPIRITS & CIGS. · PRECIOUS STONES · COAL · OIL · MINING

2010 EXPORT TREEMAP ▾ — TOTAL: $ 5,436,778,263

8720 (13%) Medical instruments

3345 (1.4%) — 7741 (0.75%)

8510 (3.9%) Footwear

8462 (2.7%) Knit undergarments of cotton

8423 (2.0%) Men's trousers

8465 (1.4%)

8463 (0.84%)

6589 (1.8%)

8459 (0.70%)

6123

8431

8451 (1.6%)

8939 (4.3%) Miscellaneous articles of plastic

5419 (1.1%)

5530

0573 (6.1%) Bananas

0721 (3.1%) Raw & roasted cocoa beans

0611 (2.8%)

1223 (0.73%) · 1211 · 0615 · 0711 · 2929

7721 (6.5%) Switchboards, relays & fuses

8973 (4.1%) Precious jewellery

2871 (1.2%)

3413 (1.1%)

7788 (1.3%)

7781

7763

7711

9710 (3.6%)

6612 (0.79%)

1221 (5.7%) Cigars

1124 (2.6%) Alcoholic beverages

0980 (0.91%) — 0545 (0.67%)

0579 (0.69%)

9310 (3.4%) Unclassified transactions

2820 · 2511 · 6114

* Numbers indicate SITC-4 Rev 2 codes which can be found in the Appendix. Percentages next to the product codes indicate proportion of the product in the exports of the country. Treemap headers show the total trade of the country.

2010 EXPORT DESTINATIONS ▾ — TOTAL: $ 5,436,778,263

63% United States

BEL (3.8%)
GBR (3.0%)
NLD (3.0%)
FRA
ITA
MEX
ECU
CHN (2.1%)
JPN
KOR

2010 IMPORT SOURCES ▾ — TOTAL: $ 13,907,357,803

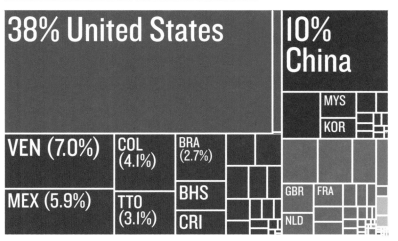

38% United States

VEN (7.0%)
MEX (5.9%)
COL (4.1%)
TTO (3.1%)
BRA (2.7%)
BHS
CRI
10% China
MYS
KOR
GBR · FRA
NLD

EAST ASIA & PACIFIC | EUROPE & CENTRAL ASIA | LATIN AMERICA & CARIBBEAN | MIDDLE EAST & NORTH AFRICA | NORTH AMERICA | SOUTH ASIA | SUB-SAHARAN AFRICA

ECUADOR

ECONOMIC COMPLEXITY INDEX [2010] ▸ -0.666 (92)	COMPLEXITY OUTLOOK INDEX [2010] ▸ -0.74 (89)	EXPECTED GDPᴘᴄ GROWTH * ▸ 0.8% (98)

*Expected annual average for the 2010-2020 period.

2010
PRODUCT SPACE ▸

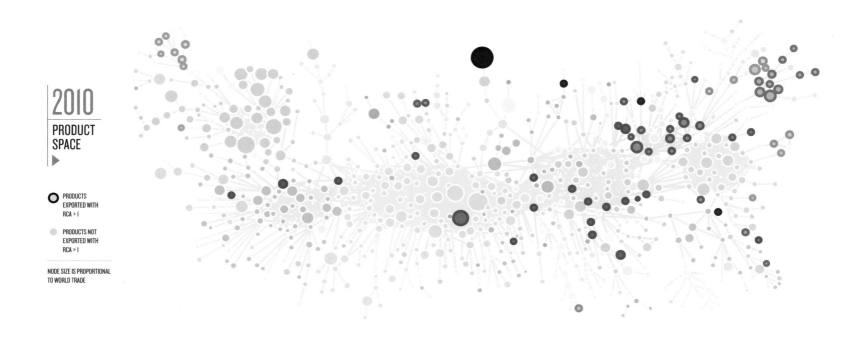

○ PRODUCTS EXPORTED WITH RCA > 1

○ PRODUCTS NOT EXPORTED WITH RCA > 1

NODE SIZE IS PROPORTIONAL TO WORLD TRADE

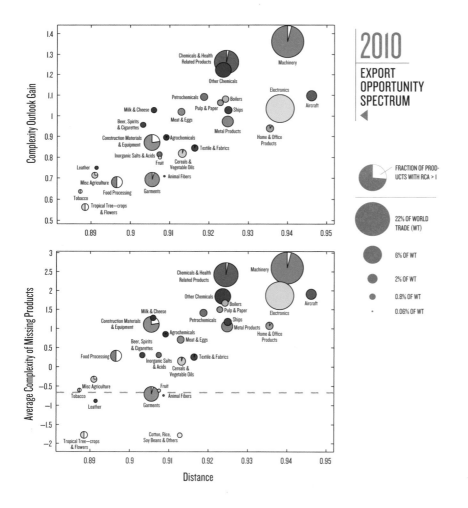

2010
EXPORT OPPORTUNITY SPECTRUM ◂

◐ FRACTION OF PRODUCTS WITH RCA > 1

● 22% OF WORLD TRADE (WT)

● 6% OF WT

● 2% OF WT

● 0.8% OF WT

· 0.06% OF WT

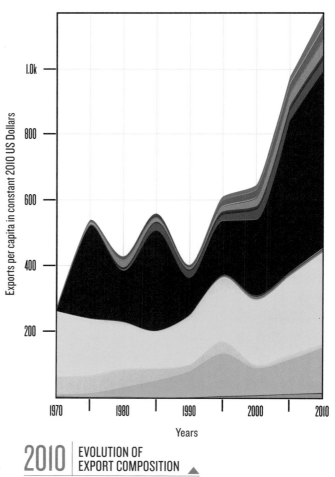

2010 | EVOLUTION OF EXPORT COMPOSITION ▲

POPULATION ▸ 14 M / (58)	GDP ▸ USD 58 B / (67)	EXPORTS PER CAPITA ▸ USD 1,174 / (69)	* Data are from 2010. Numbers indicate:
TOTAL EXPORTS ▸ USD 17 B / (67)	GDPᴘᴄ ▸ USD 4,008 / (79)	EXPORTS AS SHARE OF GDP ▸ 29 % / (51)	Value (World Ranking among 128 countries)
			Region: Latin America and the Caribbean.

ELECTRONICS · MACHINERY · AIRCRAFT · BOILERS · SHIPS · METAL PRODUCTS · CONSTR. MATL. & EQPT. · HOME & OFFICE · PULP & PAPER · CHEMICALS & HEALTH · AGROCHEMICALS · OTHER CHEMICALS · INOR. SALTS & ACIDS · PETROCHEMICALS · LEATHER · MILK & CHEESE · ANIMAL FIBERS · MEAT & EGGS · FISH & SEAFOOD · TROPICAL AGRIC. · CEREALS & VEG. OILS · COTTON/RICE/SOY & OTHERS · TOBACCO · FRUIT · MISC. AGRICULTURE · NOT CLASSIFIED · TEXTILE & FABRICS · GARMENTS · FOOD PROCESSING · BEER/SPIRITS & CIGS. · PRECIOUS STONES · COAL · OIL · MINING

2010 | EXPORT TREEMAP ▾ TOTAL: $ 16,980,863,589

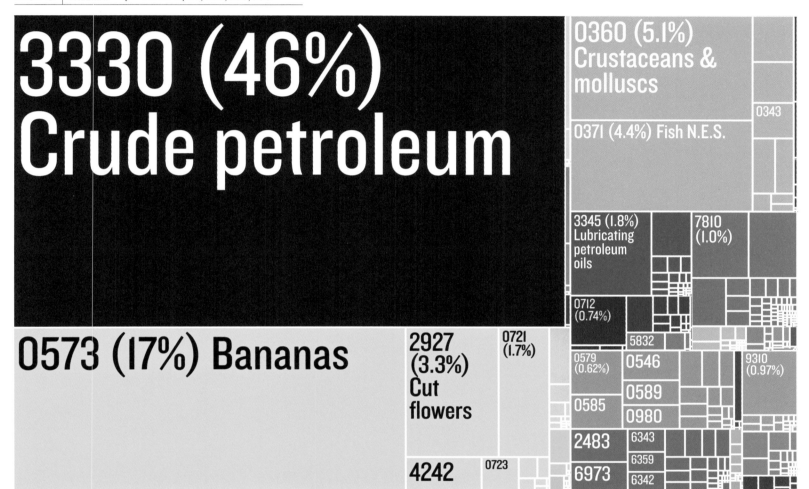

3330 (46%) Crude petroleum

0573 (17%) Bananas

2927 (3.3%) Cut flowers

0721 (1.7%)

4242

0723

0360 (5.1%) Crustaceans & molluscs

0343

0371 (4.4%) Fish N.E.S.

3345 (1.8%) Lubricating petroleum oils

7810 (1.0%)

0712 (0.74%)

5832

0579 (0.62%)

0546

0589

0585

0980

9310 (0.97%)

2483

6343

6359

6973

6342

* Numbers indicate SITC-4 Rev 2 codes which can be found in the Appendix. Percentages next to the product codes indicate proportion of the product in the exports of the country. Treemap headers show the total trade of the country.

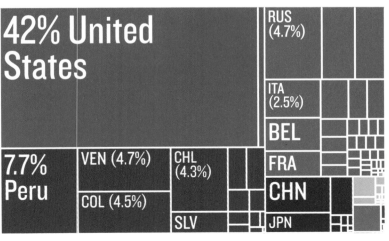

2010 | EXPORT DESTINATIONS ▾ TOTAL: $ 16,980,863,589

42% United States

7.7% Peru

VEN (4.7%)

COL (4.5%)

CHL (4.3%)

SLV

RUS (4.7%)

ITA (2.5%)

BEL

FRA

CHN

JPN

2010 | IMPORT SOURCES ▾ TOTAL: $ 18,624,513,008

10% Colombia

PER (5.1%)

27% United States

BRA (5.0%)

PAN (4.9%)

VEN (2.6%)

MEX

BHS

7.5% China

KOR (4.4%)

JPN (3.3%)

THA

DEU (2.8%)

ITA

BEL

ESP

EAST ASIA & PACIFIC · EUROPE & CENTRAL ASIA · LATIN AMERICA & CARIBBEAN · MIDDLE EAST & NORTH AFRICA · NORTH AMERICA · SOUTH ASIA · SUB-SAHARAN AFRICA

EGYPT

ECONOMIC COMPLEXITY INDEX [2010] ▸ -0.102 (67) | **COMPLEXITY OUTLOOK INDEX [2010]** ▸ 1.463 (8) | **EXPECTED GDPᴘᴄ GROWTH** * ▸ 3.4% (12)

*Expected annual average for the 2010-2020 period.

2010
PRODUCT SPACE ▶

- ⬤ PRODUCTS EXPORTED WITH RCA > 1
- ⬤ PRODUCTS NOT EXPORTED WITH RCA > 1

NODE SIZE IS PROPORTIONAL TO WORLD TRADE

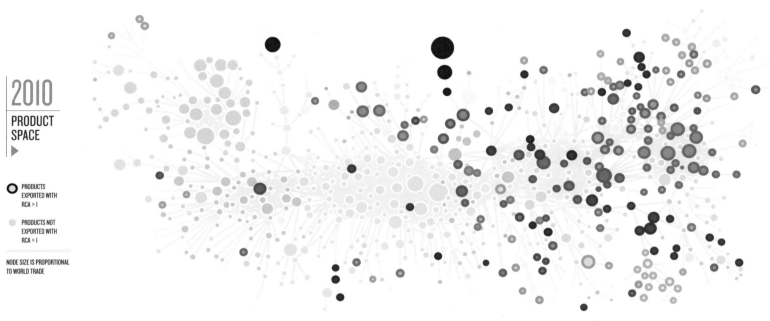

2010
EXPORT OPPORTUNITY SPECTRUM ◀

FRACTION OF PRODUCTS WITH RCA > 1

- 22% OF WORLD TRADE (WT)
- 6% OF WT
- 2% OF WT
- 0.8% OF WT
- 0.06% OF WT

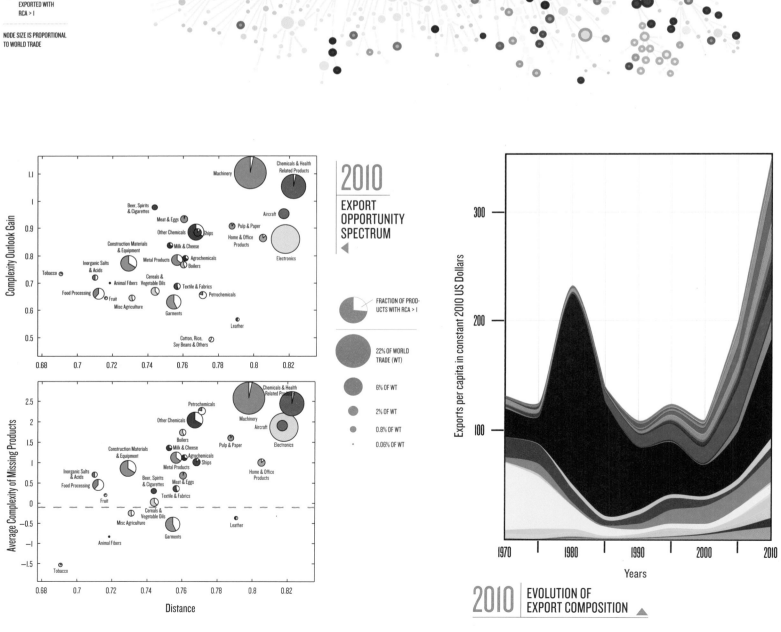

2010 | EVOLUTION OF EXPORT COMPOSITION ▲

POPULATION ▸ 81 M/ (16)
TOTAL EXPORTS ▸ USD 29 B / (57)

GDP ▸ USD 219 B / (39)
GDPᴘᴄ ▸ USD 2,698 / (90)

EXPORTS PER CAPITA ▸ USD 355 / (103)
EXPORTS AS SHARE OF GDP ▸ 13 % (106)

* Data are from 2010. Numbers indicate:
  Value (World Ranking among 128 countries)
  Region: Middle East and North Africa.

ELECTRONICS · MACHINERY · AIRCRAFT · BOILERS · SHIPS · METAL PRODUCTS · CONSTR. MATL. & EQPT. · HOME & OFFICE · PULP & PAPER · CHEMICALS & HEALTH · AGROCHEMICALS · OTHER CHEMICALS · INOR. SALTS & ACIDS · PETROCHEMICALS · LEATHER · MILK & CHEESE · ANIMAL FIBERS · MEAT & EGGS · FISH & SEAFOOD · TROPICAL AGRIC. · CEREALS & VEG. OILS · COTTON/RICE/SOY & OTHERS · TOBACCO · FRUIT · MISC. AGRICULTURE · NOT CLASSIFIED · TEXTILE & FABRICS · GARMENTS · FOOD PROCESSING · BEER/SPIRITS & DIGS. · PRECIOUS STONES · COAL · OIL · MINING

2010 | EXPORT TREEMAP ▾ TOTAL: $ 28,814,207,698

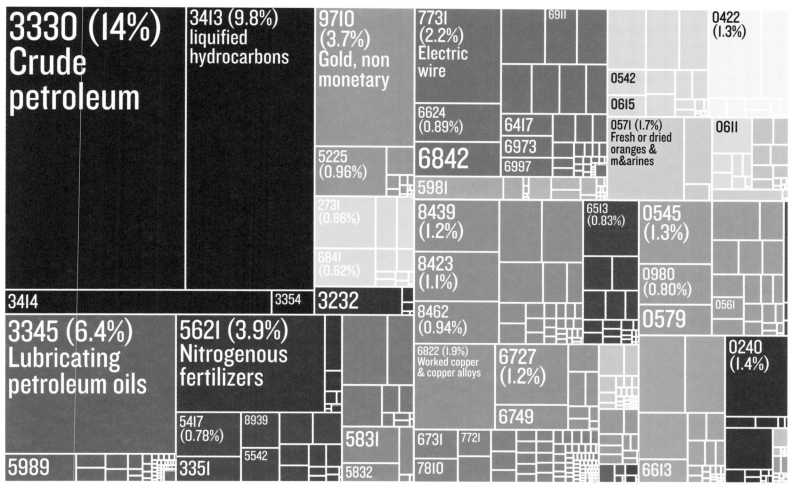

* Numbers indicate SITC-4 Rev 2 codes which can be found in the Appendix. Percentages next to the product codes indicate proportion of the product in the exports of the country. Treemap headers show the total trade of the country.

2010 | EXPORT DESTINATIONS ▾ TOTAL: $ 28,814,207,698

2010 | IMPORT SOURCES ▾ TOTAL: $ 50,661,524,214

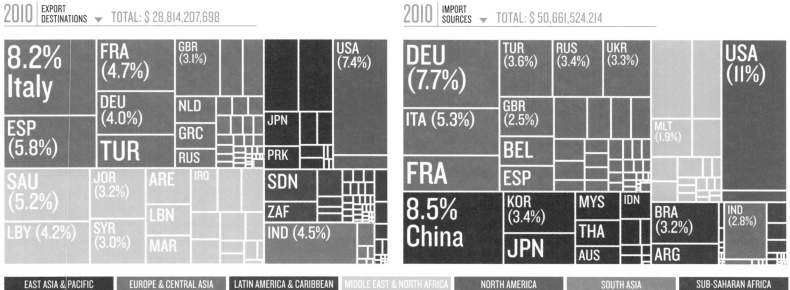

EAST ASIA & PACIFIC · EUROPE & CENTRAL ASIA · LATIN AMERICA & CARIBBEAN · MIDDLE EAST & NORTH AFRICA · NORTH AMERICA · SOUTH ASIA · SUB-SAHARAN AFRICA

EL SALVADOR

ECONOMIC COMPLEXITY INDEX [2010] ▸ 0.037 (61) COMPLEXITY OUTLOOK INDEX [2010] ▸ 0.233 (53) EXPECTED GDPᴘᴄ GROWTH * ▸ 2.5% (42)

*Expected annual average for the 2010-2020 period.

2010 PRODUCT SPACE ▶

◯ PRODUCTS EXPORTED WITH RCA > 1

○ PRODUCTS NOT EXPORTED WITH RCA > 1

NODE SIZE IS PROPORTIONAL TO WORLD TRADE

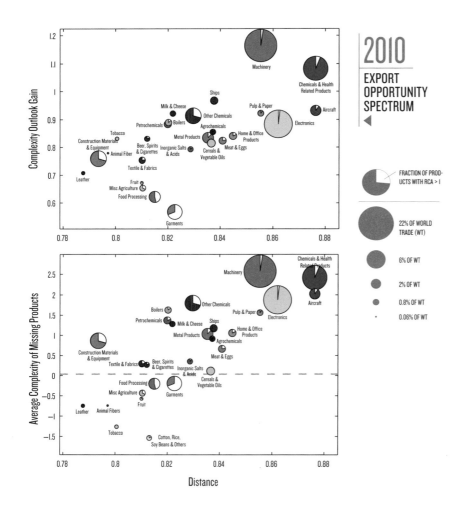

2010 EXPORT OPPORTUNITY SPECTRUM ◀

◐ FRACTION OF PRODUCTS WITH RCA > 1

◯ 22% OF WORLD TRADE (WT)

● 6% OF WT

● 2% OF WT

• 0.8% OF WT

· 0.06% OF WT

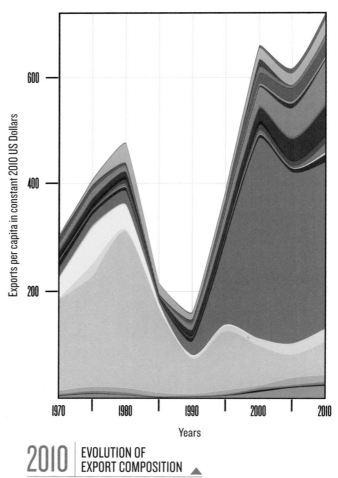

2010 | EVOLUTION OF EXPORT COMPOSITION ▲

POPULATION ▸ 6.2 M / (90)
TOTAL EXPORTS ▸ USD 4.5 B / (94)

GDP ▸ USD 21 B / (93)
GDPᴘᴄ ▸ USD 3,460 / (82)

EXPORTS PER CAPITA ▸ USD 719 / (82)
EXPORTS AS SHARE OF GDP ▸ 21 % (78)

* Data are from 2010. Numbers indicate:
Value (World Ranking among 128 countries)
Region: Latin America and the Caribbean.

ELECTRONICS · MACHINERY · AIRCRAFT · BOILERS · SHIPS · METAL PRODUCTS · CONSTR. MATL. & EQPT. · HOME & OFFICE · PULP & PAPER · CHEMICALS & HEALTH · AGROCHEMICALS · OTHER CHEMICALS · INOR. SALTS & ACIDS · PETROCHEMICALS · LEATHER · MILK & CHEESE · ANIMAL FIBERS · MEAT & EGGS · FISH & SEAFOOD · TROPICAL AGRIC. · CEREALS & VEG. OILS · COTTON/RICE/SOY & OTHERS · TOBACCO · FRUIT · MISC. AGRICULTURE · NOT CLASSIFIED · TEXTILE & FABRICS · GARMENTS · FOOD PROCESSING · BEER/SPIRITS & CIGS. · PRECIOUS STONES · COAL · OIL · MINING

2010 EXPORT TREEMAP ▾ TOTAL: $ 4,452,895,189

8462 (15%) Knit undergarments of cotton
8451 (6.8%) Knit outerwear
0711 (5.2%) Coffee, green or roasted
8931 (2.6%) Closable plastic packing
1110 (2.4%)
5417 (2.4%)
6424 (2.0%)
0481 (0.97%)
0612
0484 (1.6%)
6421 (1.3%)
8939 (1.2%)
5542 (0.94%)
8459 (5.4%) Other knit outerwear
8472 (2.7%) Knit clothing accessories
8465 (1.2%)
6584 (1.0%)
0611 (2.9%) Raw sugars
0585
0589
4312
3345 (1.2%)
8510 (1.0%)
0620
8463 (3.7%) Knit undergarments of synthetic fibers
8441 (0.98%)
8433
7788 (3.2%) Other electrical machinery & equipment N.E.S.
6732 (0.76%)
6842
8212
9710 (2.0%)
0371 (1.5%)
6552 (0.91%)
8423
8219
9310 (1.8%) Unclassified transactions
6513
6514
6534
8997
6746 (0.75%)
6770
2882
2789

* Numbers indicate SITC-4 Rev 2 codes which can be found in the Appendix. Percentages next to the product codes indicate proportion of the product in the exports of the country. Treemap headers show the total trade of the country.

2010 EXPORT DESTINATIONS ▾ TOTAL: $ 4,452,895,189

46% United States
14% Guatemala
13% Honduras
NIC (4.0%)
CRI (3.2%)
HKG

2010 IMPORT SOURCES ▾ TOTAL: $ 7,657,761,070

GTM (9.6%)
HND (4.5%)
NIC
CHN (5.6%)
MEX (8.9%)
CRI
ECU
ANT
VEN
COL
JPN
KOR
36% United States
ITA

EAST ASIA & PACIFIC · EUROPE & CENTRAL ASIA · LATIN AMERICA & CARIBBEAN · MIDDLE EAST & NORTH AFRICA · NORTH AMERICA · SOUTH ASIA · SUB-SAHARAN AFRICA

ESTONIA

ECONOMIC COMPLEXITY INDEX [2010] ▸ 0.813 (27)	COMPLEXITY OUTLOOK INDEX [2010] ▸ 1.279 (11)	EXPECTED GDPᴘᴄ GROWTH * ▸ 2.8% (30)

*Expected annual average for the 2010-2020 period.

2010 PRODUCT SPACE ▸

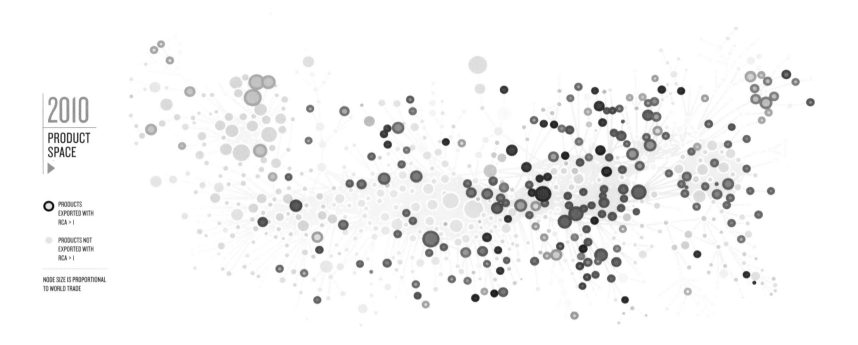

- ⬤ PRODUCTS EXPORTED WITH RCA > 1
- ○ PRODUCTS NOT EXPORTED WITH RCA > 1

NODE SIZE IS PROPORTIONAL TO WORLD TRADE

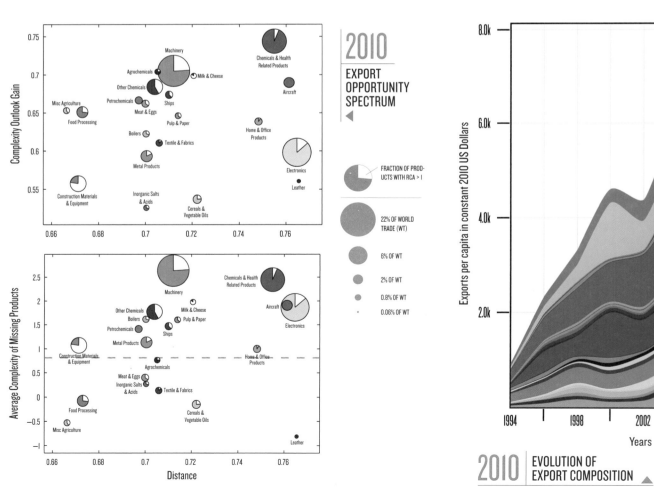

2010 EXPORT OPPORTUNITY SPECTRUM ◂

- FRACTION OF PRODUCTS WITH RCA > 1
- 22% OF WORLD TRADE (WT)
- 6% OF WT
- 2% OF WT
- 0.8% OF WT
- 0.06% OF WT

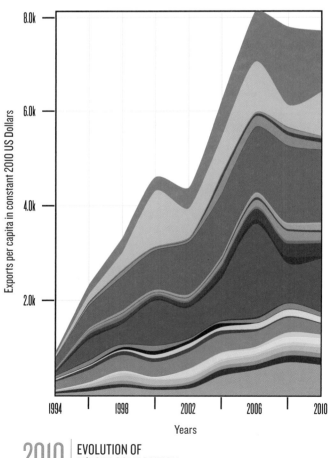

2010 EVOLUTION OF EXPORT COMPOSITION ▲

POPULATION ▸ 1.3 M / (127)
TOTAL EXPORTS ▸ USD 10 B / (73)

GDP ▸ USD 19 B / (97)
GDPᴘᴄ ▸ USD 14,045 / (35)

EXPORTS PER CAPITA ▸ USD 7,726 / (26)
EXPORTS AS SHARE OF GDP ▸ 55 % (16)

* Data are from 2010. Numbers indicate:
Value (World Ranking among 128 countries)
Region: Eastern Europe and Central Asia.

ELECTRONICS · MACHINERY · AIRCRAFT · BOILERS · SHIPS · METAL PRODUCTS · CONSTR. MATL. & EQPT. · HOME & OFFICE · PULP & PAPER · CHEMICALS & HEALTH · AGROCHEMICALS · OTHER CHEMICALS · INOR. SALTS & ACIDS · PETROCHEMICALS · LEATHER · MILK & CHEESE · ANIMAL FIBERS · MEAT & EGGS · FISH & SEAFOOD · TROPICAL AGRIC. · CEREALS & VEG. OILS · COTTON/RICE/SOY & OTHERS · TOBACCO · FRUIT · MISC. AGRICULTURE · NOT CLASSIFIED · TEXTILE & FABRICS · GARMENTS · FOOD PROCESSING · BEER/SPIRITS & CIGS. · PRECIOUS STONES · COAL · OIL · MINING

2010 | EXPORT TREEMAP ▼ TOTAL: $ 10,354,731,241

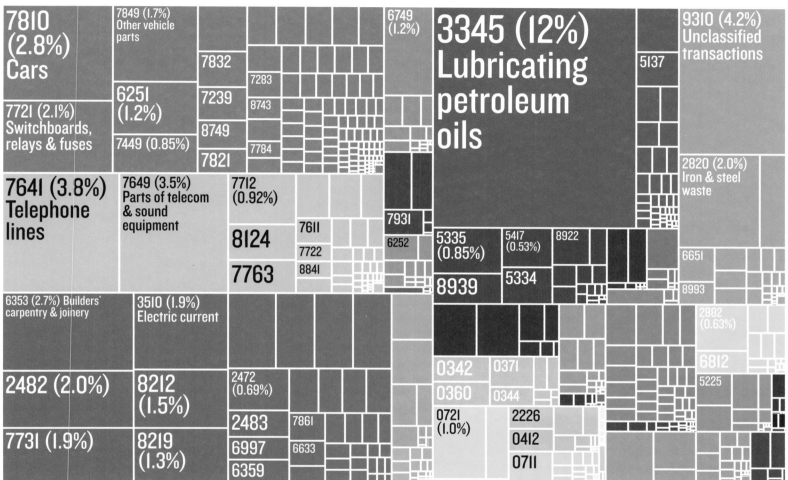

* Numbers indicate SITC-4 Rev 2 codes which can be found in the Appendix. Percentages next to the product codes indicate proportion of the product in the exports of the country. Treemap headers show the total trade of the country.

2010 | EXPORT DESTINATIONS ▼ TOTAL: $ 10,354,731,241

2010 | IMPORT SOURCES ▼ TOTAL: $ 11,978,142,519

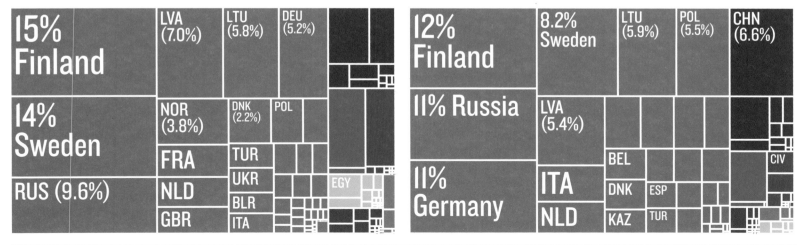

EAST ASIA & PACIFIC · EUROPE & CENTRAL ASIA · LATIN AMERICA & CARIBBEAN · MIDDLE EAST & NORTH AFRICA · NORTH AMERICA · SOUTH ASIA · SUB-SAHARAN AFRICA

ETHIOPIA

ECONOMIC COMPLEXITY INDEX [2010] ▸ -1.415 (120) | COMPLEXITY OUTLOOK INDEX [2010] ▸ -1.167 (125) | EXPECTED GDPᴘᴄ GROWTH * ▸ 2.1% (59)

*Expected annual average for the 2010-2020 period.

2010 PRODUCT SPACE ▶

○ PRODUCTS EXPORTED WITH RCA > 1

● PRODUCTS NOT EXPORTED WITH RCA > 1

NODE SIZE IS PROPORTIONAL TO WORLD TRADE

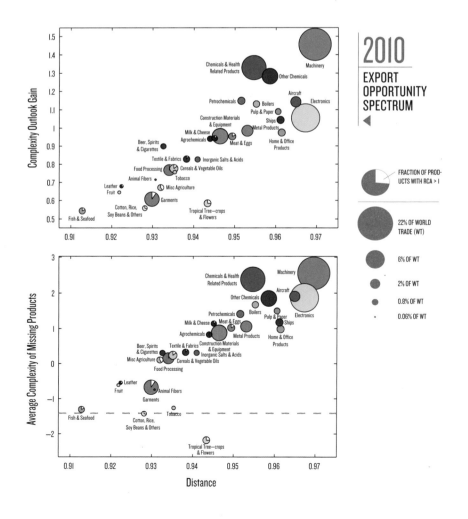

2010 EXPORT OPPORTUNITY SPECTRUM ◀

◔ FRACTION OF PRODUCTS WITH RCA > 1

⬤ 22% OF WORLD TRADE (WT)

● 6% OF WT

● 2% OF WT

• 0.8% OF WT

· 0.06% OF WT

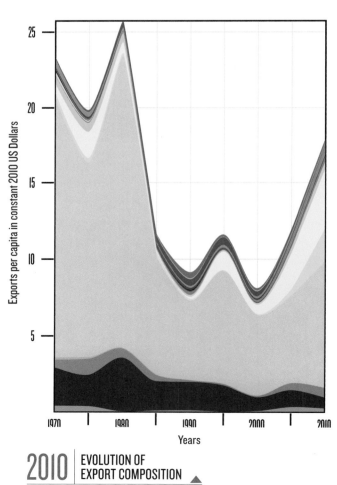

2010 EVOLUTION OF EXPORT COMPOSITION ▲

POPULATION ▸ 83 M / (14)	GDP ▸ USD 30 B / (86)	EXPORTS PER CAPITA ▸ USD 18 / (128)
TOTAL EXPORTS ▸ USD 1.5 B / (117)	GDPpc ▸ USD 358 / (126)	EXPORTS AS SHARE OF GDP ▸ 5 % (127)

* Data are from 2010. Numbers indicate:
  Value (World Ranking among 128 countries)
  Region: Sub-Saharan Africa.

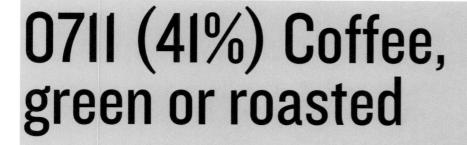

ELECTRONICS · MACHINERY · AIRCRAFT · BOILERS · SHIPS · METAL PRODUCTS · CONSTR. MATL. & EQPT. · HOME & OFFICE · PULP & PAPER · CHEMICALS & HEALTH · AGROCHEMICALS · OTHER CHEMICALS · INOR. SALTS & ACIDS · PETROCHEMICALS · LEATHER · MILK & CHEESE · ANIMAL FIBERS · MEAT & EGGS · FISH & SEAFOOD · TROPICAL AGRIC. · CEREALS & VEG. OILS · COTTON/RICE/SOY & OTHERS · TOBACCO · FRUIT · MISC. AGRICULTURE · NOT CLASSIFIED · TEXTILE & FABRICS · GARMENTS · FOOD PROCESSING · BEER/SPIRITS & CIGS. · PRECIOUS STONES · COAL · OIL · MINING

2010 EXPORT TREEMAP ▾   TOTAL: $ 1,485,000,922

0711 (41%) Coffee, green or roasted

2225 (21%) Sesame seeds

0542 (4.9%)

0752

2927 (10%) Cut flowers

2926 (1.4%)

2238 (2.2%) Oil seeds & fruits N.E.S.

6115 (2.4%) Sheep & lamb leather

6116

0112 (3.0%) Sheep & goat meat

9710 (2.0%) Gold, non monetary

2879 (0.81%)

6851

6513

9310 (1.3%)

0545 (0.72%)

* Numbers indicate SITC-4 Rev 2 codes which can be found in the Appendix. Percentages next to the product codes indicate proportion of the product in the exports of the country. Treemap headers show the total trade of the country.

2010 EXPORT DESTINATIONS ▾   TOTAL: $ 1,485,000,922

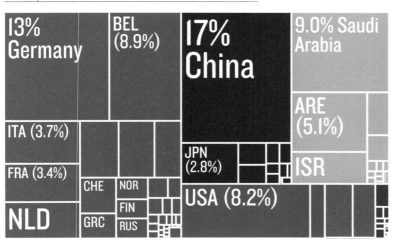

13% Germany — BEL (8.9%) — 17% China — 9.0% Saudi Arabia — ITA (3.7%) — ARE (5.1%) — JPN (2.8%) — ISR — FRA (3.4%) — CHE — NOR — USA (8.2%) — NLD — GRC — FIN — RUS

2010 IMPORT SOURCES ▾   TOTAL: $ 7,866,845,779

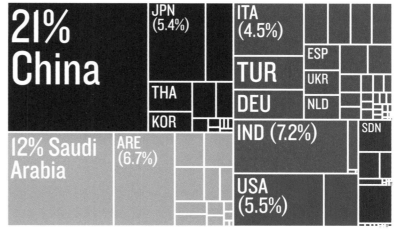

21% China — JPN (5.4%) — ITA (4.5%) — ESP — THA — TUR — UKR — KOR — DEU — NLD — 12% Saudi Arabia — ARE (6.7%) — IND (7.2%) — SDN — USA (5.5%)

EAST ASIA & PACIFIC · EUROPE & CENTRAL ASIA · LATIN AMERICA & CARIBBEAN · MIDDLE EAST & NORTH AFRICA · NORTH AMERICA · SOUTH ASIA · SUB-SAHARAN AFRICA

FINLAND

ECONOMIC COMPLEXITY INDEX [2010] ▸ 1.686 (7) | COMPLEXITY OUTLOOK INDEX [2010] ▸ 1.043 (22) | EXPECTED GDPᴘᴄ GROWTH * ▸ 2.6% (40)

*Expected annual average for the 2010-2020 period.

2010 PRODUCT SPACE ▶

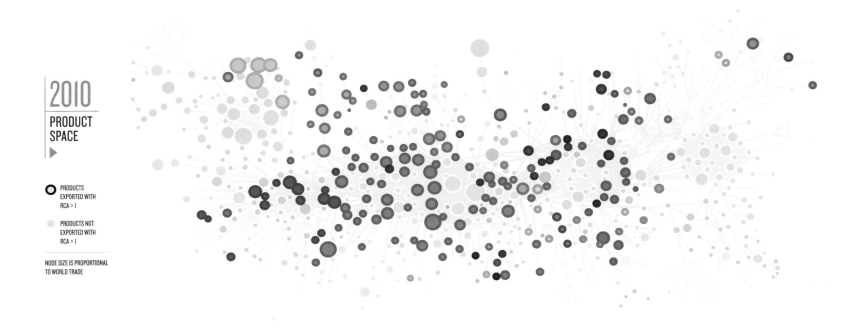

○ PRODUCTS EXPORTED WITH RCA > 1

○ PRODUCTS NOT EXPORTED WITH RCA > 1

NODE SIZE IS PROPORTIONAL TO WORLD TRADE

2010 EXPORT OPPORTUNITY SPECTRUM ◀

○ FRACTION OF PRODUCTS WITH RCA > 1

22% OF WORLD TRADE (WT)

6% OF WT

2% OF WT

0.8% OF WT

0.06% OF WT

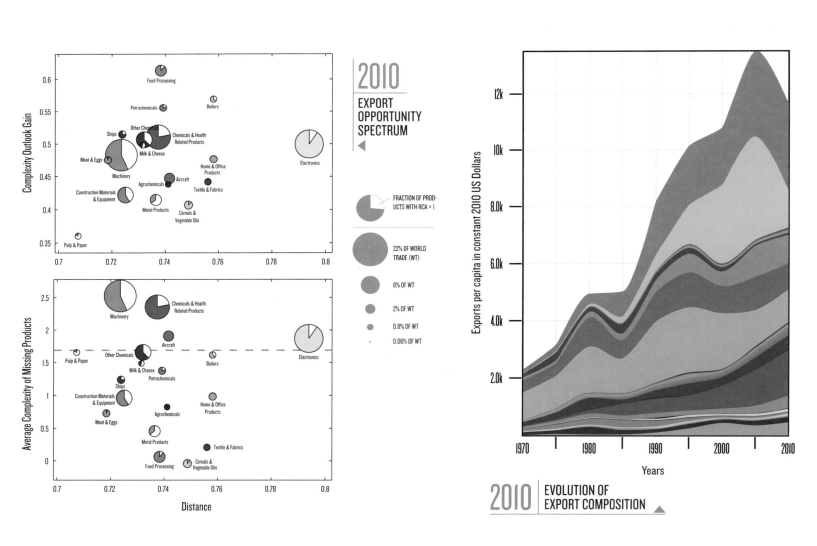

2010 EVOLUTION OF EXPORT COMPOSITION ▲

POPULATION ▸ 5.4 M / (96)
TOTAL EXPORTS ▸ USD 62 B / (42)

GDP ▸ USD 237 B / (36)
GDPᴘᴄ ▸ USD 44,091 / (13)

EXPORTS PER CAPITA ▸ USD 11,598 / (14)
EXPORTS AS SHARE OF GDP ▸ 26 % / (61)

* Data are from 2010. Numbers indicate:
Value (World Ranking among 128 countries)
Region: Western Europe.

ELECTRONICS | MACHINERY | AIRCRAFT | BOILERS | SHIPS | METAL PRODUCTS | CONSTR. MATL. & EQPT. | HOME & OFFICE | PULP & PAPER | CHEMICALS & HEALTH | AGROCHEMICALS | OTHER CHEMICALS | INOR. SALTS & ACIDS | PETROCHEMICALS | LEATHER | MILK & CHEESE | ANIMAL FIBERS | MEAT & EGGS | FISH & SEAFOOD | TROPICAL AGRIC. | CEREALS & VEG. OILS | COTTON/RICE/SOY & OTHERS | TOBACCO | FRUIT | MISC. AGRICULTURE | NOT CLASSIFIED | TEXTILE & FABRICS | GARMENTS | FOOD PROCESSING | BEER/SPIRITS & CIGS. | PRECIOUS STONES | COAL | OIL | MINING

2010 EXPORT TREEMAP ▾ TOTAL: $ 62,202,122,584

6418 (3.3%) Rolls/sheets of coated paper

7162 (2.1%) AC electric motors & generators

7442 (1.2%)

7643 (4.5%) Television & radio transmitters

3345 (7.6%) Lubricating petroleum oils

6412 (3.1%) Printing & writing paper in rolls or seets

6415 (2.6%) Paper & paperboad in rolls or sheets

7284 (1.0%) 7239 (0.93%) 7234 (0.92%)

7139 7493

7283 7219

7224 7849

7492 7259 8741

7251 8743 7373 7783

7416 7169 7822 6991

6746 (3.1%) Iron/steel <3mm tick sheets

6727 (1.1%) 6783 (0.94%)

6749 6822 6744

7649 (2.2%) 7712 (1.4%)

7788 7711 7924

5989 5123

8720 5839 5162 7741

5169 5331 8742

5417 (2.1%) Medicaments

5831 (1.0%)

8939

6831 (0.98%) 6861 (0.97%)

9310 (2.8%) Unclassified transactions

9710

2517 (2.2%) Chemical wood pulp, soda or sulphate

6413 (0.90%) 2519

2482 (2.3%) Worked wood of coniferous

7731

6342 6353 2471

2120 (0.69%)

* Numbers indicate SITC-4 Rev 2 codes which can be found in the Appendix. Percentages next to the product codes indicate proportion of the product in the exports of the country. Treemap headers show the total trade of the country.

2010 EXPORT DESTINATIONS ▾ TOTAL: $ 62,202,122,584

11% Sweden

10% Germany

RUS (6.7%)

NLD (5.9%)

GBR (4.3%)

BEL (2.9%)

NOR (2.9%)

ITA

POL

CZE

CHN (5.7%)

JPN

USA (5.4%)

CAN

IND

2010 IMPORT SOURCES ▾ TOTAL: $ 61,321,138,888

18% Russia

13% Germany

SWE (10%)

NLD (5.4%)

FRA (4.0%)

NOR

POL

ESP

CZE CHE

IRL

TUR

PRT

7.1% China

JPN

KOR

USA (3.2%)

BRA

IND

EAST ASIA & PACIFIC | EUROPE & CENTRAL ASIA | LATIN AMERICA & CARIBBEAN | MIDDLE EAST & NORTH AFRICA | NORTH AMERICA | SOUTH ASIA | SUB-SAHARAN AFRICA

FRANCE

| ECONOMIC COMPLEXITY INDEX [2010] ▸ 1.53 (11) | COMPLEXITY OUTLOOK INDEX [2010] ▸ -0.051 (65) | EXPECTED GDPᴘᴄ GROWTH * ▸ 1.8% (72) |

*Expected annual average for the 2010-2020 period.

2010
PRODUCT SPACE ▸

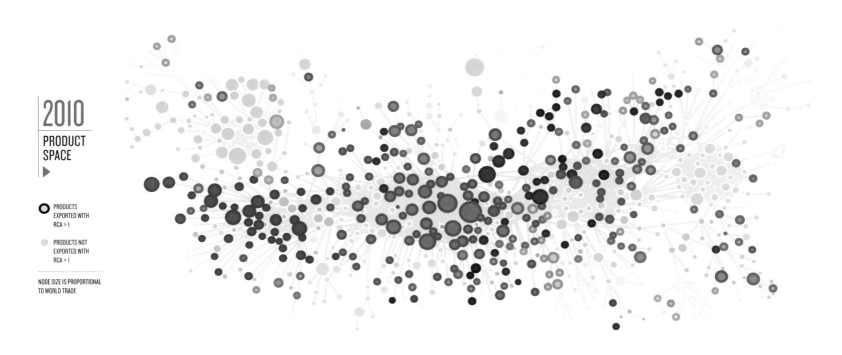

○ PRODUCTS EXPORTED WITH RCA > 1

○ PRODUCTS NOT EXPORTED WITH RCA > 1

NODE SIZE IS PROPORTIONAL TO WORLD TRADE

2010
EXPORT OPPORTUNITY SPECTRUM ◂

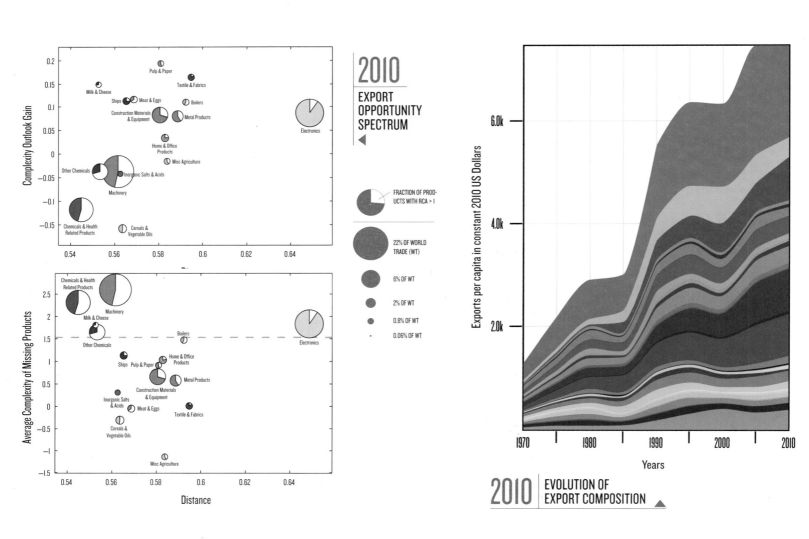

◔ FRACTION OF PRODUCTS WITH RCA > 1

⬤ 22% OF WORLD TRADE (WT)

● 6% OF WT

● 2% OF WT

● 0.8% OF WT

· 0.06% OF WT

2010 | EVOLUTION OF EXPORT COMPOSITION ▲

POPULATION ▸ 65 M / (20)

TOTAL EXPORTS ▸ USD 487 B / (5)

GDP ▸ USD 2.5 T / (5)

GDPᴘᴄ ▸ USD 39,170 / (19)

EXPORTS PER CAPITA ▸ USD 7,479 / (28)

EXPORTS AS SHARE OF GDP ▸ 19 % (80)

* Data are from 2010. Numbers indicate:
Value (World Ranking among 128 countries)
Region: Western Europe.

ELECTRONICS · MACHINERY · AIRCRAFT · BOILERS · SHIPS · METAL PRODUCTS · CONSTR. MATL. & EQPT. · HOME & OFFICE · PULP & PAPER · CHEMICALS & HEALTH · AGROCHEMICALS · OTHER CHEMICALS · INOR. SALTS & ACIDS · PETROCHEMICALS · LEATHER · MILK & CHEESE · ANIMAL FIBERS · MEAT & EGGS · FISH & SEAFOOD · TROPICAL AGRIC. · CEREALS & VEG. OILS · COTTON/RICE/SOY & OTHERS · TOBACCO · FRUIT · MISC. AGRICULTURE · NOT CLASSIFIED · TEXTILE & FABRICS · GARMENTS · FOOD PROCESSING · BEER/SPIRITS & CIGS. · PRECIOUS STONES · COAL · OIL · MINING

2010 | EXPORT TREEMAP ▾ TOTAL: $ 486,717,519,751

7810 (4.6%) Cars

7849 (3.6%) Other vehicle parts

7721 (1.6%)

7924 (7.0%) Aircrafts of more than 15 tons

3510 (0.78%)

1121 (1.7%) Wine

6732 · 7414

8219 · 6911

8211

8931

0484

1110

1124 (0.89%)

7821 (0.85%) · 7239 · 7783 · 7442

7132 · 8743 · 7452

7492 · 7493 · 7416 · 7758

7139 · 7162

7284 · 8741 · 7441

7929 (1.7%)

7149 · 7148

6749 · 6746

6822 · 6725

9310 (3.4%) Unclassified transactions

2820

8928

0240 (0.67%) · 0113

0224

8973 (0.65%)

5241 · 3413

0411

8310 (0.76%)

5417 (5.5%) Medicaments

5542

5530 (2.7%)

3345 (2.2%) Lubricating petroleum oils

5416 (1.3%)

5989

5156 (0.79%)

8996

5514

2331

5148

7742

2010 | EXPORT DESTINATIONS ▾ TOTAL: $ 486,717,519,751

15% Germany

BEL (8.1%)

ITA (7.9%)

GBR (6.9%)

NLD (3.1%)

POL · PRT

FRA · AUT

SWE · CZE · ROU

ESP (6.2%)

CHN (3.2%)

SGP

AUS

KOR

DZA

SAU

MAR

USA (7.2%)

2010 | IMPORT SOURCES ▾ TOTAL: $ 535,125,544,019

18% Germany

BEL (8.0%)

ITA (7.6%)

ESP (6.3%)

RUS (2.7%)

CHE (2.5%)

NOR

POL

IRL

KAZ

SVK

CHN (7.9%)

USA (5.9%)

JPN

LBY

* Numbers indicate SITC-4 Rev 2 codes which can be found in the Appendix. Percentages next to the product codes indicate proportion of the product in the exports of the country. Treemap headers show the total trade of the country.

EAST ASIA & PACIFIC · EUROPE & CENTRAL ASIA · LATIN AMERICA & CARIBBEAN · MIDDLE EAST & NORTH AFRICA · NORTH AMERICA · SOUTH ASIA · SUB-SAHARAN AFRICA

GABON

| ECONOMIC COMPLEXITY INDEX [2010] ▸ -1.141 (114) | COMPLEXITY OUTLOOK INDEX [2010] ▸ -0.961 (104) | EXPECTED GDPᴘᴄ GROWTH * ▸ -0.8% (123) |

*Expected annual average for the 2010-2020 period.

2010 PRODUCT SPACE ▶

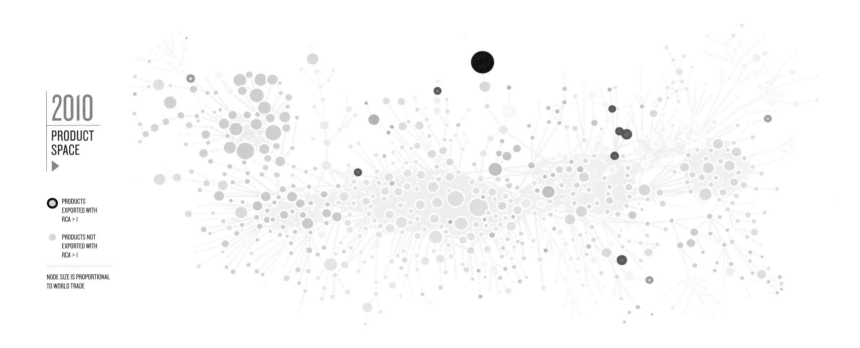

○ PRODUCTS EXPORTED WITH RCA > 1

○ PRODUCTS NOT EXPORTED WITH RCA > 1

NODE SIZE IS PROPORTIONAL TO WORLD TRADE

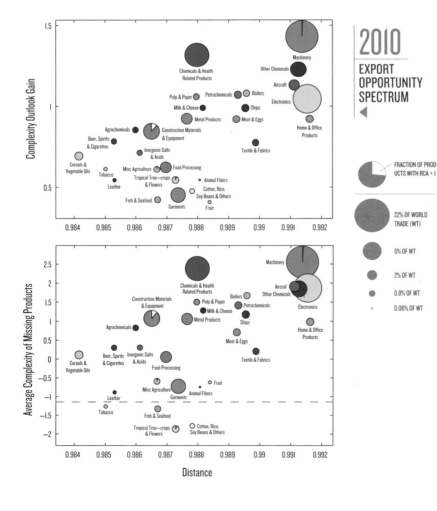

2010 EXPORT OPPORTUNITY SPECTRUM ◀

◑ FRACTION OF PRODUCTS WITH RCA > 1

○ 22% OF WORLD TRADE (WT)

○ 6% OF WT

○ 2% OF WT

○ 0.8% OF WT

· 0.06% OF WT

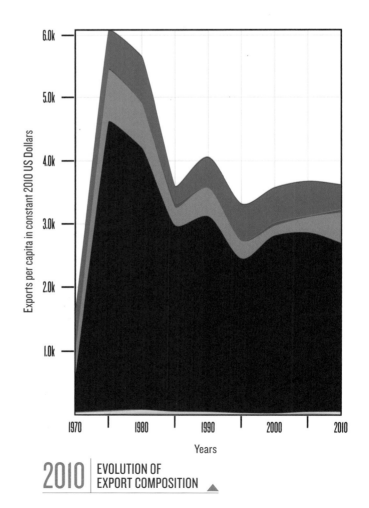

2010 EVOLUTION OF EXPORT COMPOSITION ▲

POPULATION ► 1.5 M / (125)
TOTAL EXPORTS ► USD 5.5 B / (88)

GDP ► USD 13 B / (105)
GDPᴘᴄ ► USD 8,768 / (52)

EXPORTS PER CAPITA ► USD 3,630 / (41)
EXPORTS AS SHARE OF GDP ► 41 % (31)

* Data are from 2010. Numbers indicate:
Value (World Ranking among 128 countries)
Region: Sub-Saharan Africa.

ELECTRONICS · MACHINERY · AIRCRAFT · BOILERS · SHIPS · METAL PRODUCTS · CONSTR. MATL. & EQPT. · HOME & OFFICE · PULP & PAPER · CHEMICALS & HEALTH · AGROCHEMICALS · OTHER CHEMICALS · INOR. SALTS & ACIDS · PETROCHEMICALS · LEATHER · MILK & CHEESE · ANIMAL FIBERS · MEAT & EGGS · FISH & SEAFOOD · TROPICAL AGRIC. · CEREALS & VEG. OILS · COTTON/RICE/SOY & OTHERS · TOBACCO · FRUIT · MISC. AGRICULTURE · NOT CLASSIFIED · TEXTILE & FABRICS · GARMENTS · FOOD PROCESSING · BEER/SPIRITS & CIGS. · PRECIOUS STONES · COAL · OIL · MINING

2010 | EXPORT TREEMAP ▼ TOTAL: $ 5,465,186,535

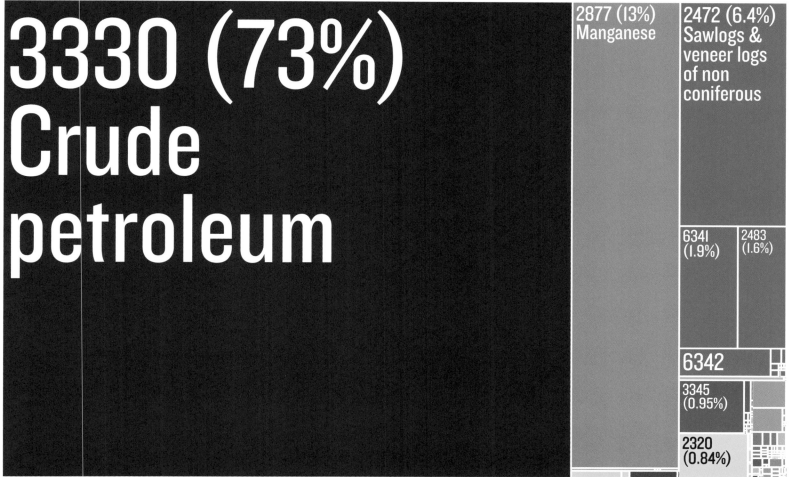

3330 (73%) Crude petroleum

2877 (13%) Manganese

2472 (6.4%) Sawlogs & veneer logs of non coniferous

6341 (1.9%)

2483 (1.6%)

6342

3345 (0.95%)

2320 (0.84%)

* Numbers indicate SITC-4 Rev 2 codes which can be found in the Appendix. Percentages next to the product codes indicate proportion of the product in the exports of the country. Treemap headers show the total trade of the country.

2010 | EXPORT DESTINATIONS ▼ TOTAL: $ 5,465,186,535

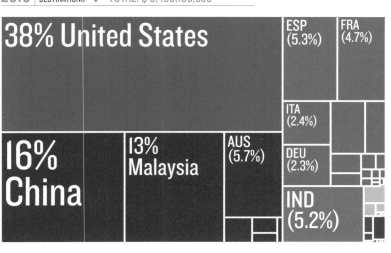

38% United States

ESP (5.3%)

FRA (4.7%)

ITA (2.4%)

DEU (2.3%)

AUS (5.7%)

16% China

13% Malaysia

IND (5.2%)

2010 | IMPORT SOURCES ▼ TOTAL: $ 2,185,568,203

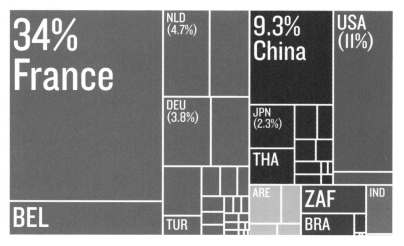

34% France

NLD (4.7%)

9.3% China

USA (11%)

DEU (3.8%)

JPN (2.3%)

THA

ARE

ZAF

IND

BEL

TUR

BRA

EAST ASIA & PACIFIC · EUROPE & CENTRAL ASIA · LATIN AMERICA & CARIBBEAN · MIDDLE EAST & NORTH AFRICA · NORTH AMERICA · SOUTH ASIA · SUB-SAHARAN AFRICA

GEORGIA

| ECONOMIC COMPLEXITY INDEX [2010] ▸ -0.324 (75) | COMPLEXITY OUTLOOK INDEX [2010] ▸ -0.506 (76) | EXPECTED GDPᴘᴄ GROWTH * ▸ 1.9% (67) |

*Expected annual average for the 2010-2020 period.

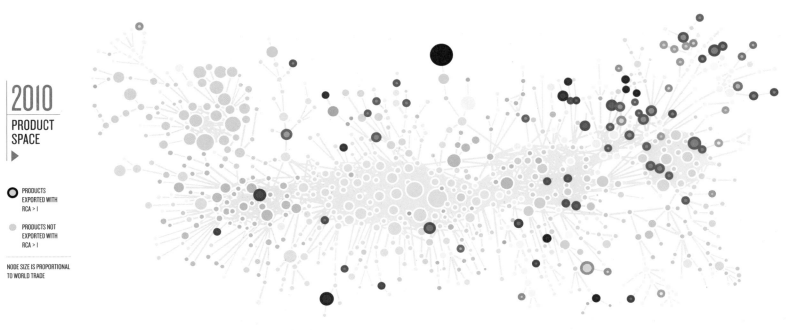

2010 PRODUCT SPACE ▸

○ PRODUCTS EXPORTED WITH RCA > 1

○ PRODUCTS NOT EXPORTED WITH RCA > 1

NODE SIZE IS PROPORTIONAL TO WORLD TRADE

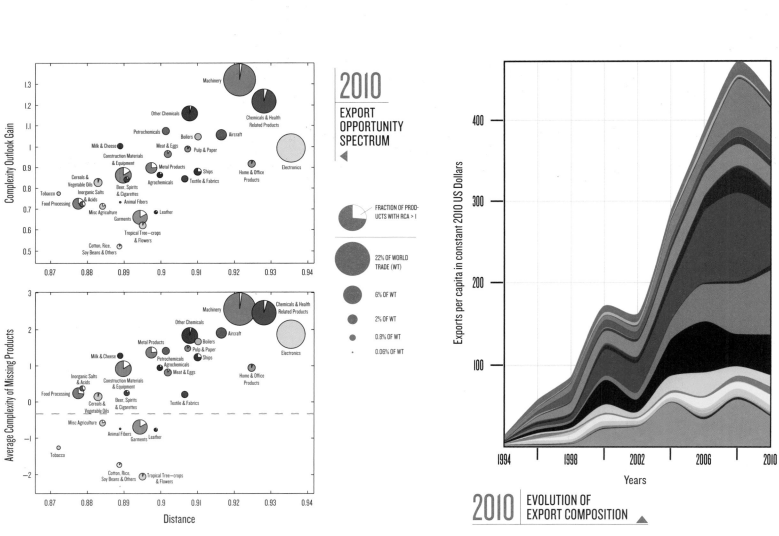

2010 EXPORT OPPORTUNITY SPECTRUM ◂

◐ FRACTION OF PRODUCTS WITH RCA > 1

● 22% OF WORLD TRADE (WT)

● 6% OF WT

● 2% OF WT

• 0.8% OF WT

· 0.06% OF WT

2010 EVOLUTION OF EXPORT COMPOSITION ▲

POPULATION ▸ 4.5 M / (102)
TOTAL EXPORTS ▸ USD 1.9 B / (111)

GDP ▸ USD 12 B / (109)
GDPᴘᴄ ▸ USD 2,614 / (91)

EXPORTS PER CAPITA ▸ USD 433 / (96)
EXPORTS AS SHARE OF GDP ▸ 17 % (97)

* Data are from 2010. Numbers indicate:
Value (World Ranking among 128 countries)
Region: Eastern Europe and Central Asia.

ELECTRONICS | MACHINERY | AIRCRAFT | BOILERS | SHIPS | METAL PRODUCTS | CONSTR. MATL. & EQPT. | HOME & OFFICE | PULP & PAPER | CHEMICALS & HEALTH | AGROCHEMICALS | OTHER CHEMICALS | INOR. SALTS & ACIDS | PETROCHEMICALS | LEATHER | MILK & CHEESE | ANIMAL FIBERS | MEAT & EGGS | FISH & SEAFOOD | TROPICAL AGRIC. | CEREALS & VEG. OILS | COTTON/RICE/SOY & OTHERS | TOBACCO | FRUIT | MISC. AGRICULTURE | NOT CLASSIFIED | TEXTILE & FABRICS | GARMENTS | FOOD PROCESSING | BEER/SPIRITS & CIGS. | PRECIOUS STONES | COAL | OIL | MINING

2010 | EXPORT TREEMAP ▾ TOTAL: $ 1,926,999,344

2871 (10%) Copper

9710 (5.3%) Gold, non monetary

2882 (2.4%)

2877 | **6821**
2890 | **2879**

6716 (10%) Ferro alloys

2820 (7.7%) Iron & steel waste

3330 (11%) Crude petroleum

3222 (1.4%)

7911 (0.74%)

7431

9310

3345 (14%) Lubricating petroleum oils

5621 (4.7%) Nitrogenous fertilizers

1110 (2.6%) Non alcoholic beverages N.E.S.

1121 (1.9%)

1124 (1.6%)

5121

3510 (1.4%) | **6732 (1.4%)**

2483
8219

0577 (2.9%) Edible nuts

0571 (0.96%)

2925

5417 (0.90%)

* Numbers indicate SITC-4 Rev 2 codes which can be found in the Appendix. Percentages next to the product codes indicate proportion of the product in the exports of the country. Treemap headers show the total trade of the country.

2010 | EXPORT DESTINATIONS ▾ TOTAL: $ 1,926,999,344

14% Turkey

UKR (6.4%)

DEU (3.7%)

USA (9.4%)

AZE | **CYP**

CAN (6.0%)

BGR (9.6%)

LBN (6.4%)

IRN

RUS

GBR (8.9%)

NLD | **FRA**

CHN

ITA

KOR

2010 | IMPORT SOURCES ▾ TOTAL: $ 4,751,141,261

17% Turkey

DEU (6.2%)

RUS (5.3%)

CHN (6.3%)

UKR (11%)

KAZ

ARE (3.0%)

USA (4.2%)

GRC | **POL**

IRN

AZE (8.9%)

FRA | **ARM**

GBR | **BLR**

EAST ASIA & PACIFIC | EUROPE & CENTRAL ASIA | LATIN AMERICA & CARIBBEAN | MIDDLE EAST & NORTH AFRICA | NORTH AMERICA | SOUTH ASIA | SUB-SAHARAN AFRICA

GERMANY

| ECONOMIC COMPLEXITY INDEX [2010] ► 1.956 (2) | COMPLEXITY OUTLOOK INDEX [2010] ► -3.871 (128) | EXPECTED GDPᴘᴄ GROWTH * ► -0.2% (115) |

*Expected annual average for the 2010-2020 period.

2010 PRODUCT SPACE ▶

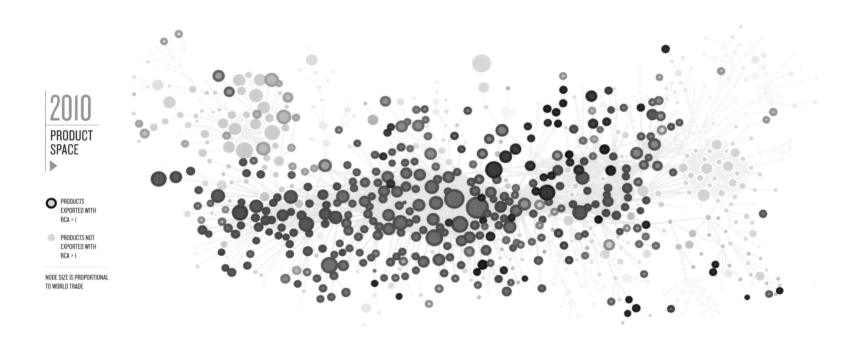

- ⬤ PRODUCTS EXPORTED WITH RCA > 1
- ⬤ PRODUCTS NOT EXPORTED WITH RCA > 1

NODE SIZE IS PROPORTIONAL TO WORLD TRADE

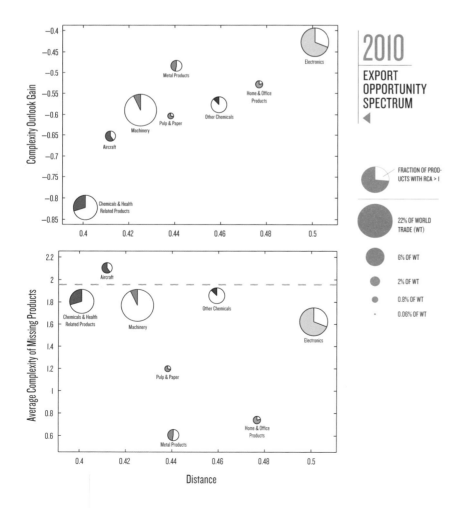

2010 EXPORT OPPORTUNITY SPECTRUM ◀

FRACTION OF PRODUCTS WITH RCA > 1

22% OF WORLD TRADE (WT)

6% OF WT

2% OF WT

0.8% OF WT

0.06% OF WT

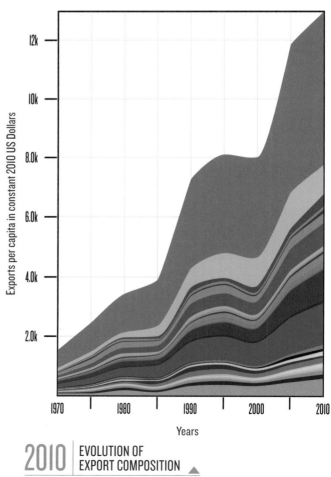

2010 EVOLUTION OF EXPORT COMPOSITION ▲

POPULATION ▸ 82 M / (15)
TOTAL EXPORTS ▸ USD 1.1 T / (3)

GDP ▸ USD 3.3 T / (4)
GDPᴘᴄ ▸ USD 39,852 / (17)

EXPORTS PER CAPITA ▸ USD 12,993 / (13)
EXPORTS AS SHARE OF GDP ▸ 33 % (46)

* Data are from 2010. Numbers indicate:
Value (World Ranking among 128 countries)
Region: Western Europe.

ELECTRONICS · MACHINERY · AIRCRAFT · BOILERS · SHIPS · METAL PRODUCTS · CONSTR. MATL. & EQPT. · HOME & OFFICE · PULP & PAPER · CHEMICALS & HEALTH · AGROCHEMICALS · OTHER CHEMICALS · INOR. SALTS & ACIDS · PETROCHEMICALS · LEATHER · MILK & CHEESE · ANIMAL FIBERS · MEAT & EGGS · FISH & SEAFOOD · TROPICAL AGRIC. · CEREALS & VEG. OILS · COTTON/RICE/SOY & OTHERS · TOBACCO · FRUIT · MISC. AGRICULTURE · NOT CLASSIFIED · TEXTILE & FABRICS · GARMENTS · FOOD PROCESSING · BEER/SPIRITS & CIGS. · PRECIOUS STONES · COAL · OIL · MINING

2010 | EXPORT TREEMAP ▾ TOTAL: $ 1,062,556,066,165

7810 (11%) Cars

7849 (4.1%) Other vehicle parts

7764 (0.78%)
7763 (0.71%)
7649
7518
7525
7522
7643
8710
8124
7788
7421

7721 (2.0%) Switchboards, relays & fuses
7284 (1.5%)
7139 (1.1%)
7493 (0.85%)
7452 (0.70%)
7132
8743
7442
6991
7436
7224
7822
7272
7283
7919
7758
7281
6289
7212
7441
7413

7924 (1.9%) Aircrafts of more than 15 tons
7144
6822 (0.69%)
6746
6749

5989 (1.3%)
3345 (1.2%)
8720 (0.77%)
5156
8744
8748
2331
5311
5112
5824
8996
5831
5834
6210
5832
9310 (2.3%) Unclassified transactions
9710

5417 (4.4%) Medicaments
8939 (0.89%)
5334
5419
0730
6421
0113
0223
5922
6415

* Numbers indicate SITC-4 Rev 2 codes which can be found in the Appendix. Percentages next to the product codes indicate proportion of the product in the exports of the country. Treemap headers show the total trade of the country.

2010 | EXPORT DESTINATIONS ▾ TOTAL: $ 1,062,556,066,165

8.8% France
ITA (6.5%)
GBR (6.2%)
NLD (5.8%)
BEL (5.4%)
POL (3.2%)
ESP (3.1%)
CZE
RUS
AUT (4.9%)
CHE (4.9%)
NOR
FIN
CHN (6.3%)
JPN
7.1% United States
BRA
MEX
IND
ZAF

2010 | IMPORT SOURCES ▾ TOTAL: $ 924,900,011,149

NLD (8.1%)
FRA (8.0%)
ITA (5.6%)
GBR (4.9%)
BEL (4.5%)
CZE (3.9%)
POL (3.7%)
RUS
ESP
AUT (4.4%)
SVK
ROU
CHE (4.3%)
IRL
9.5% China
KOR
USA (5.7%)
BRA

EAST ASIA & PACIFIC · EUROPE & CENTRAL ASIA · LATIN AMERICA & CARIBBEAN · MIDDLE EAST & NORTH AFRICA · NORTH AMERICA · SOUTH ASIA · SUB-SAHARAN AFRICA

GHANA

ECONOMIC COMPLEXITY INDEX [2010] ▸ -1.088 (113) | **COMPLEXITY OUTLOOK INDEX [2010] ▸ -0.975 (106)** | **EXPECTED GDPᴘᴄ GROWTH * ▸ 1.3% (92)**

*Expected annual average for the 2010-2020 period.

2010
PRODUCT SPACE ▶

◯ PRODUCTS EXPORTED WITH RCA > 1

◯ PRODUCTS NOT EXPORTED WITH RCA > 1

NODE SIZE IS PROPORTIONAL TO WORLD TRADE

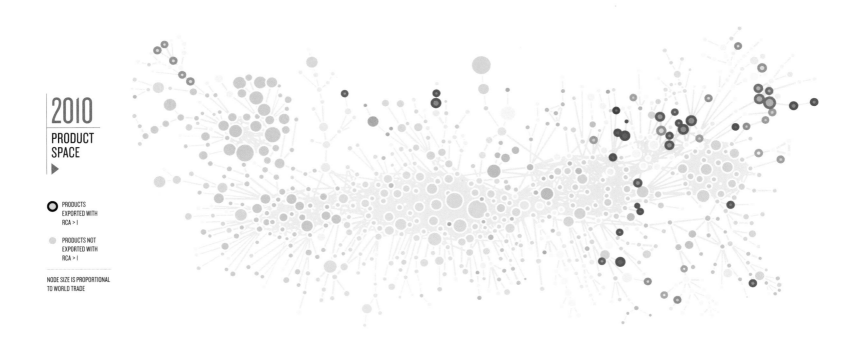

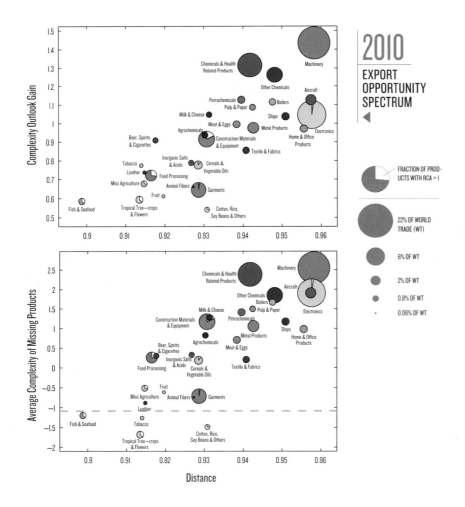

2010
EXPORT OPPORTUNITY SPECTRUM ◀

◐ FRACTION OF PRODUCTS WITH RCA > 1

⬤ 22% OF WORLD TRADE (WT)

⬤ 6% OF WT

● 2% OF WT

• 0.8% OF WT

· 0.06% OF WT

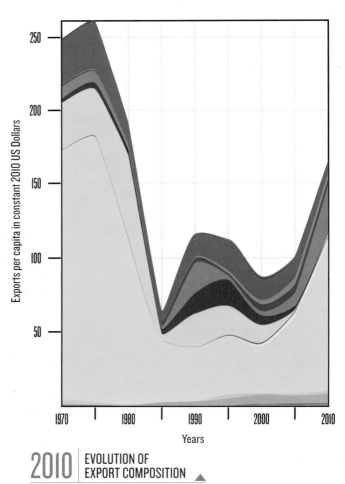

2010 | EVOLUTION OF EXPORT COMPOSITION ▲

POPULATION ▸ 24 M / (42)
TOTAL EXPORTS ▸ USD 4.1 B / (98)

GDP ▸ USD 32 B / (84)
GDPᴘᴄ ▸ USD 1,319 / (102)

EXPORTS PER CAPITA ▸ USD 166 / (115)
EXPORTS AS SHARE OF GDP ▸ 13 % / (118)

* Data are from 2010. Numbers indicate:
Value (World Ranking among 128 countries)
Region: Sub-Saharan Africa.

ELECTRONICS | MACHINERY | AIRCRAFT | BOILERS | SHIPS | METAL PRODUCTS | CONSTR. MATL. & EQPT. | HOME & OFFICE | PULP & PAPER | CHEMICALS & HEALTH | AGROCHEMICALS | OTHER CHEMICALS | INOR. SALTS & ACIDS | PETROCHEMICALS | LEATHER | MILK & CHEESE | ANIMAL FIBERS | MEAT & EGGS | FISH & SEAFOOD | TROPICAL AGRIC. | CEREALS & VEG. OILS | COTTON/RICE/SOY & OTHERS | TOBACCO | FRUIT | MISC. AGRICULTURE | NOT CLASSIFIED | TEXTILE & FABRICS | GARMENTS | FOOD PROCESSING | BEER/SPIRITS & CIGS. | PRECIOUS STONES | COAL | OIL | MINING

2010 | EXPORT TREEMAP ▾ TOTAL: $ 4,052,850,523

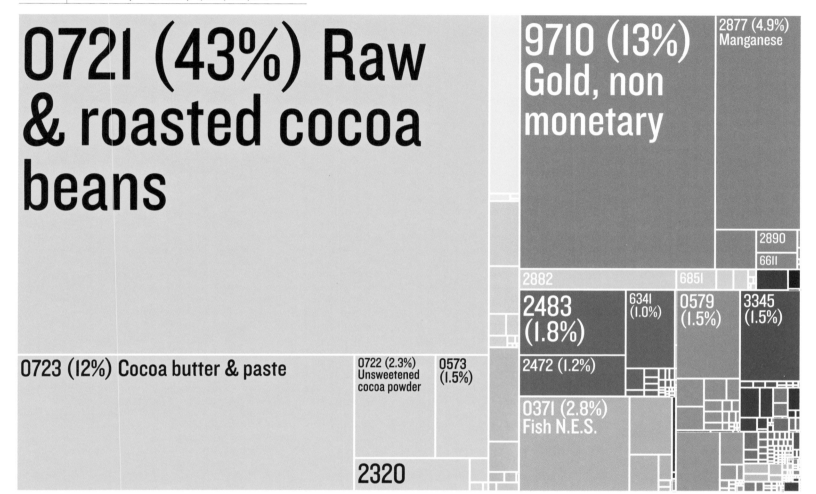

* Numbers indicate SITC-4 Rev 2 codes which can be found in the Appendix. Percentages next to the product codes indicate proportion of the product in the exports of the country. Treemap headers show the total trade of the country.

2010 | EXPORT DESTINATIONS ▾ TOTAL: $ 4,052,850,523

2010 | IMPORT SOURCES ▾ TOTAL: $ 7,248,699,486

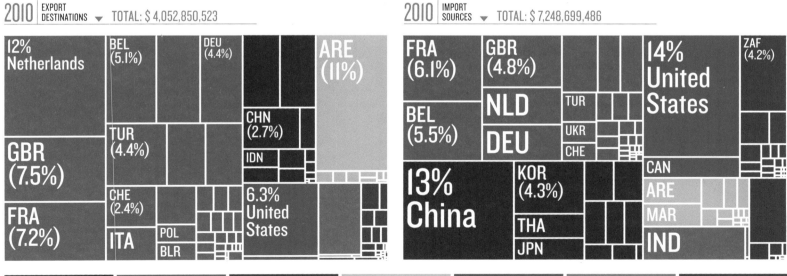

EAST ASIA & PACIFIC | EUROPE & CENTRAL ASIA | LATIN AMERICA & CARIBBEAN | MIDDLE EAST & NORTH AFRICA | NORTH AMERICA | SOUTH ASIA | SUB-SAHARAN AFRICA

GREECE

ECONOMIC COMPLEXITY INDEX [2010] ► 0.279 (49)   COMPLEXITY OUTLOOK INDEX [2010] ► 1.689 (4)   EXPECTED GDPᴘᴄ GROWTH * ► 1.6% (78)

*Expected annual average for the 2010-2020 period.

2010 PRODUCT SPACE ▶

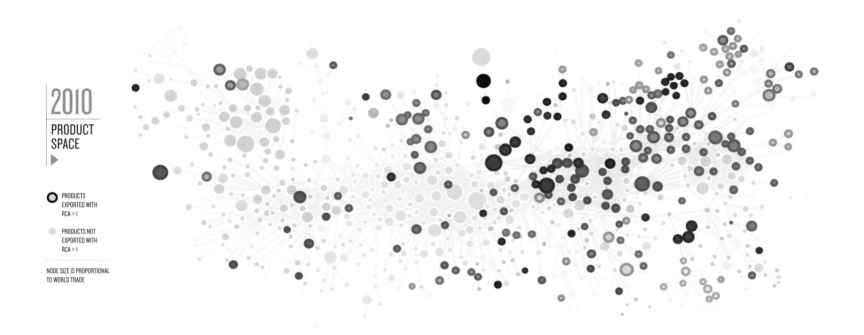

- ○ PRODUCTS EXPORTED WITH RCA > 1
- ○ PRODUCTS NOT EXPORTED WITH RCA > 1

NODE SIZE IS PROPORTIONAL TO WORLD TRADE

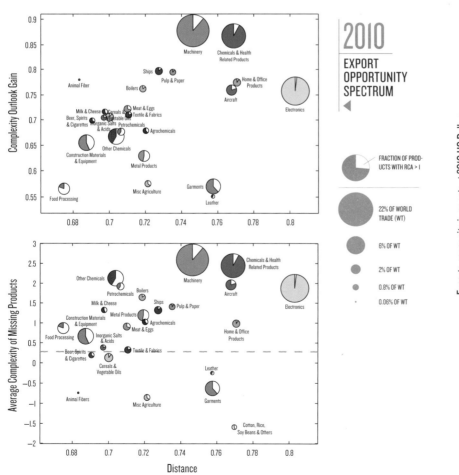

2010 EXPORT OPPORTUNITY SPECTRUM ◀

FRACTION OF PRODUCTS WITH RCA > 1

- 22% OF WORLD TRADE (WT)
- 6% OF WT
- 2% OF WT
- 0.8% OF WT
- 0.06% OF WT

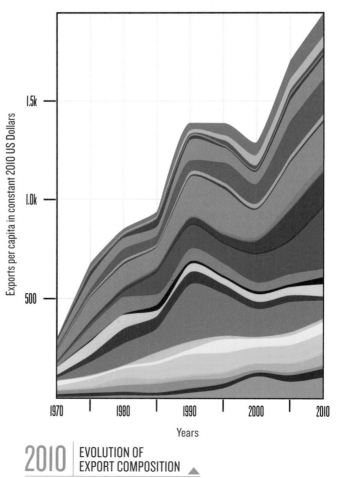

2010 EVOLUTION OF EXPORT COMPOSITION ▲

POPULATION ▸ 11 M / (64)	GDP ▸ USD 299 B / (32)	EXPORTS PER CAPITA ▸ USD 1,950 / (55)	* Data are from 2010. Numbers indicate:
TOTAL EXPORTS ▸ USD 22 B / (61)	GDPPC ▸ USD 26,433 / (26)	EXPORTS AS SHARE OF GDP ▸ 7.4 % (122)	Value (World Ranking among 128 countries) Region: Western Europe.

ELECTRONICS · MACHINERY · AIRCRAFT · BOILERS · SHIPS · METAL PRODUCTS · CONSTR. MATL. & EQPT. · HOME & OFFICE · PULP & PAPER · CHEMICALS & HEALTH · AGROCHEMICALS · OTHER CHEMICALS · INOR. SALTS & ACIDS · PETROCHEMICALS · LEATHER · MILK & CHEESE · ANIMAL FIBERS · MEAT & EGGS · FISH & SEAFOOD · TROPICAL AGRIC. · CEREALS & VEG. OILS · COTTON/RICE/SOY & OTHERS · TOBACCO · FRUIT · MISC. AGRICULTURE · NOT CLASSIFIED · TEXTILE & FABRICS · GARMENTS · FOOD PROCESSING · BEER/SPIRITS & CIGS. · PRECIOUS STONES · COAL · OIL · MINING

2010 | EXPORT TREEMAP ▾ TOTAL: $ 22,066,497,471

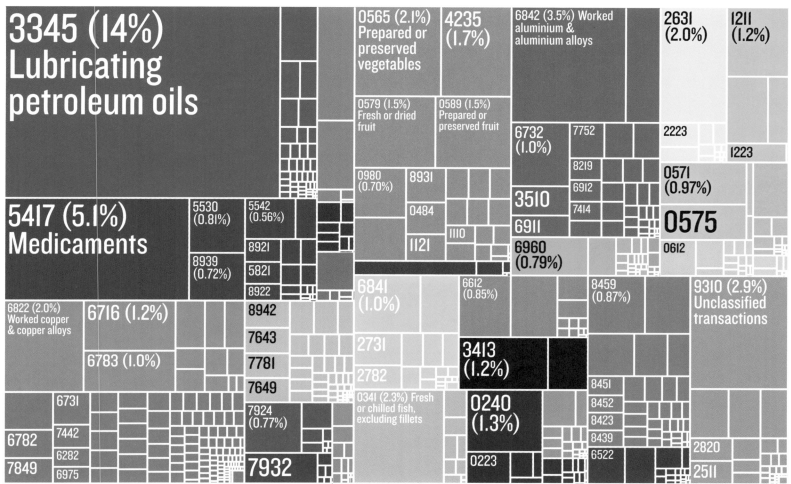

* Numbers indicate SITC-4 Rev 2 codes which can be found in the Appendix. Percentages next to the product codes indicate proportion of the product in the exports of the country. Treemap headers show the total trade of the country.

2010 | EXPORT DESTINATIONS ▾ TOTAL: $ 22,066,497,471

- 11% Germany
- 11% Italy
- TUR (6.8%)
- CYP (6.6%)
- ROU (3.4%)
- FRA (3.4%)
- ESP
- ALB
- BGR (6.3%)
- SRB
- CHE
- DNK
- MNE
- SVK
- POL
- PRT
- GBR (4.3%)
- LBY
- MAR
- ISR
- CHN
- USA (3.7%)

2010 | IMPORT SOURCES ▾ TOTAL: $ 57,847,517,729

- 10% Germany
- 9.8% Italy
- 9.7% Russia
- FRA (5.1%)
- KAZ
- CHE
- AUT
- NLD (5.0%)
- CYP
- DNK
- ROU
- IRL
- CHN (5.9%)
- KOR (3.8%)
- LBY (2.9%)
- USA (2.5%)
- IRN
- SGP
- JPN
- EGY
- PAN
- IND

| EAST ASIA & PACIFIC | EUROPE & CENTRAL ASIA | LATIN AMERICA & CARIBBEAN | MIDDLE EAST & NORTH AFRICA | NORTH AMERICA | SOUTH ASIA | SUB-SAHARAN AFRICA |

GUATEMALA

ECONOMIC COMPLEXITY INDEX [2010] ▸ -0.42 (79) COMPLEXITY OUTLOOK INDEX [2010] ▸ 0.04 (59) EXPECTED GDPᴘᴄ GROWTH * ▸ 2.0% (60)

*Expected annual average for the 2010-2020 period.

2010 PRODUCT SPACE ▶

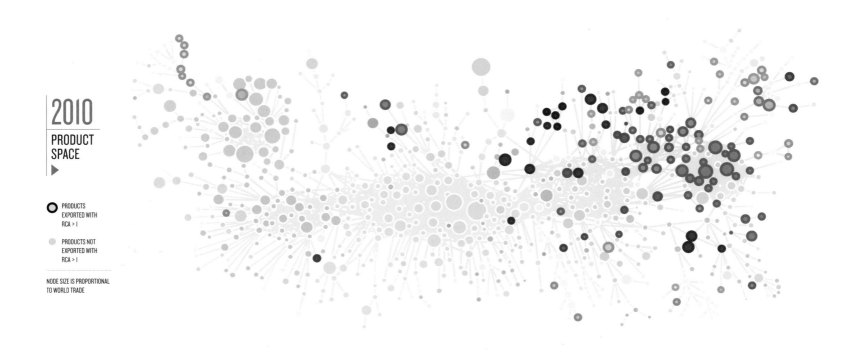

○ PRODUCTS EXPORTED WITH RCA > 1

○ PRODUCTS NOT EXPORTED WITH RCA > 1

NODE SIZE IS PROPORTIONAL TO WORLD TRADE

2010 EXPORT OPPORTUNITY SPECTRUM ◀

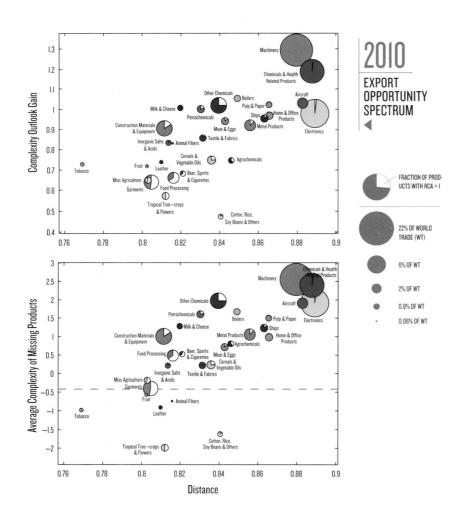

⬤ FRACTION OF PROD-UCTS WITH RCA > 1

⬤ 22% OF WORLD TRADE (WT)

⬤ 6% OF WT

⬤ 2% OF WT

⬤ 0.8% OF WT

• 0.06% OF WT

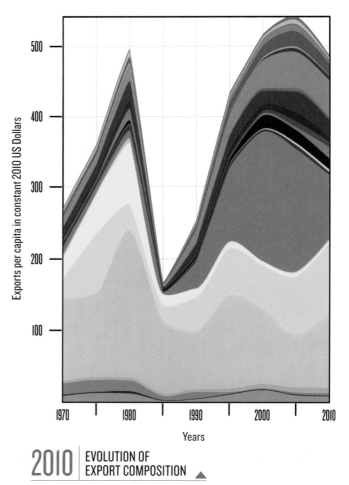

2010 EVOLUTION OF EXPORT COMPOSITION ▲

POPULATION ▸ 14 M / (59)
TOTAL EXPORTS ▸ USD 7 B / (84)

GDP ▸ USD 41 B / (76)
GDPᴾᶜ ▸ USD 2,873 / (87)

EXPORTS PER CAPITA ▸ USD 487 / (92)
EXPORTS AS SHARE OF GDP ▸ 17 % (93)

* Data are from 2010. Numbers indicate:
Value (World Ranking among 128 countries)
Region: Latin America and the Caribbean.

ELECTRONICS · MACHINERY · AIRCRAFT · BOILERS · SHIPS · METAL PRODUCTS · CONSTR. MATL. & EQPT. · HOME & OFFICE · PULP & PAPER · CHEMICALS & HEALTH · AGROCHEMICALS · OTHER CHEMICALS · INOR. SALTS & ACIDS · PETROCHEMICALS · LEATHER · MILK & CHEESE · ANIMAL FIBERS · MEAT & EGGS · FISH & SEAFOOD · TROPICAL AGRIC. · CEREALS & VEG. OILS · COTTON/RICE/SOY & OTHERS · TOBACCO · FRUIT · MISC. AGRICULTURE · NOT CLASSIFIED · TEXTILE & FABRICS · GARMENTS · FOOD PROCESSING · BEER/SPIRITS & CIGS. · PRECIOUS STONES · COAL · OIL · MINING

2010 EXPORT TREEMAP ▾ TOTAL: $ 7,003,757,849

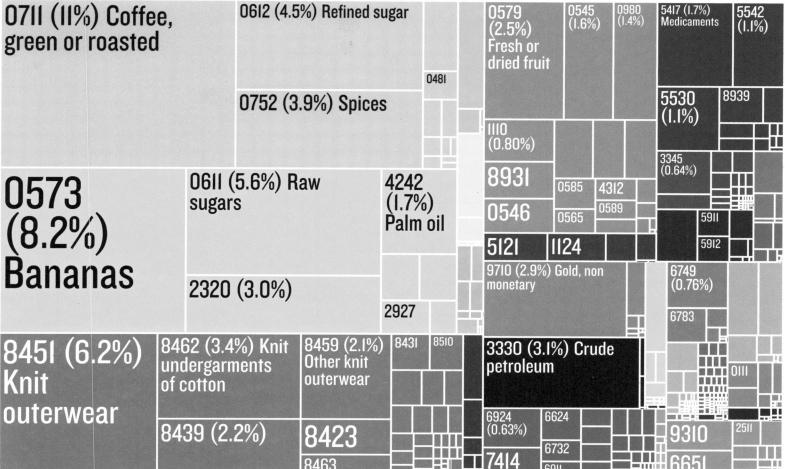

* Numbers indicate SITC-4 Rev 2 codes which can be found in the Appendix. Percentages next to the product codes indicate proportion of the product in the exports of the country. Treemap headers show the total trade of the country.

2010 EXPORT DESTINATIONS ▾ TOTAL: $ 7,003,757,849

44% United States
10% El Salvador
MEX (6.4%)
CRI
NIC (3.4%)
PAN (2.6%)
ITA
GBR
JPN (2.3%)
KOR

2010 IMPORT SOURCES ▾ TOTAL: $ 12,643,325,226

39% United States
11% Mexico
SLV (4.9%)
PAN (3.1%)
CRI (3.0%)
COL
HND
CHL
NIC
CHN (6.6%)
HKG
THA
DEU (1.9%)
ESP
BEL
IND

EAST ASIA & PACIFIC · EUROPE & CENTRAL ASIA · LATIN AMERICA & CARIBBEAN · MIDDLE EAST & NORTH AFRICA · NORTH AMERICA · SOUTH ASIA · SUB-SAHARAN AFRICA

GUINEA

ECONOMIC COMPLEXITY INDEX [2010] ▸ -1.694 (125)	COMPLEXITY OUTLOOK INDEX [2010] ▸ -1.099 (121)	EXPECTED GDPᴘᴄ GROWTH * ▸ 1.5% (87)

*Expected annual average for the 2010-2020 period.

2010
PRODUCT SPACE ▸

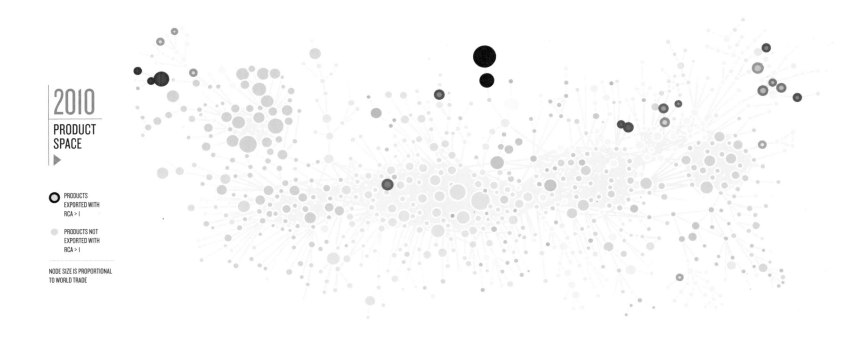

○ PRODUCTS EXPORTED WITH RCA > 1

● PRODUCTS NOT EXPORTED WITH RCA > 1

NODE SIZE IS PROPORTIONAL TO WORLD TRADE

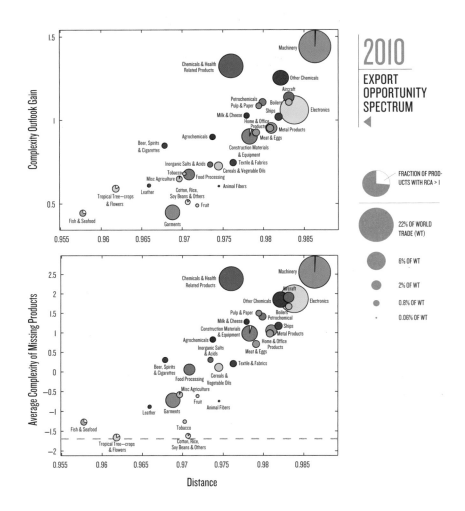

2010
EXPORT OPPORTUNITY SPECTRUM ◂

◔ FRACTION OF PRODUCTS WITH RCA > 1

⬤ 22% OF WORLD TRADE (WT)

● 6% OF WT

● 2% OF WT

• 0.8% OF WT

· 0.06% OF WT

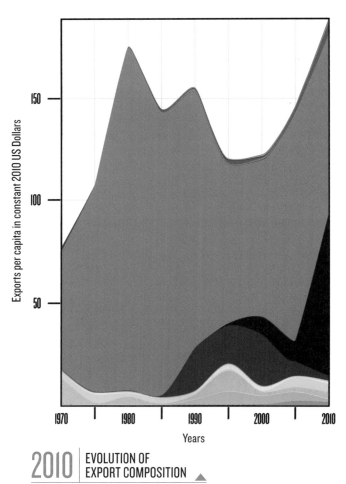

2010 | EVOLUTION OF EXPORT COMPOSITION ▲

POPULATION ▸ 10 M / (71)
TOTAL EXPORTS ▸ USD 1.9 B / (112)

GDP ▸ USD 4.7 B / (126)
GDPᴘᴄ ▸ USD 474 / (123)

EXPORTS PER CAPITA ▸ USD 190 / (112)
EXPORTS AS SHARE OF GDP ▸ 40 % (33)

* Data are from 2010. Numbers indicate:
Value (World Ranking among 128 countries)
Region: Sub-Saharan Africa.

ELECTRONICS · MACHINERY · AIRCRAFT · BOILERS · SHIPS · METAL PRODUCTS · CONSTR. MATL. & EQPT. · HOME & OFFICE · PULP & PAPER · CHEMICALS & HEALTH · AGROCHEMICALS · OTHER CHEMICALS · INOR. SALTS & ACIDS · PETROCHEMICALS · LEATHER · MILK & CHEESE · ANIMAL FIBERS · MEAT & EGGS · FISH & SEAFOOD · TROPICAL AGRIC. · CEREALS & VEG. OILS · COTTON/RICE/SOY & OTHERS · TOBACCO · FRUIT · MISC. AGRICULTURE · NOT CLASSIFIED · TEXTILE & FABRICS · GARMENTS · FOOD PROCESSING · BEER/SPIRITS & CIGS. · PRECIOUS STONES · COAL · OIL · MINING

2010 | EXPORT TREEMAP ▾ TOTAL: $ 1,891,629,929

2873 (39%)
Aluminium ore

3413 (21%)
liquified hydrocarbons

3330 (21%)
Crude petroleum

9710 (4.6%)
Gold, non monetary

2871 (2.6%)
Copper

2320 (1.4%)

0721

0711 (1.8%)
Coffee, green or roasted

0577

2472 (2.7%)
Sawlogs & veneer logs of non coniferous

0350

0342

* Numbers indicate SITC-4 Rev 2 codes which can be found in the Appendix. Percentages next to the product codes indicate proportion of the product in the exports of the country. Treemap headers show the total trade of the country.

2010 | EXPORT DESTINATIONS ▾ TOTAL: $ 1,891,629,929

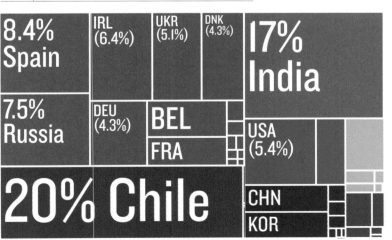

8.4% Spain
7.5% Russia
20% Chile
IRL (6.4%)
DEU (4.3%)
UKR (5.1%)
DNK (4.3%)
BEL
FRA
17% India
USA (5.4%)
CHN
KOR

2010 | IMPORT SOURCES ▾ TOTAL: $ 1,822,475,525

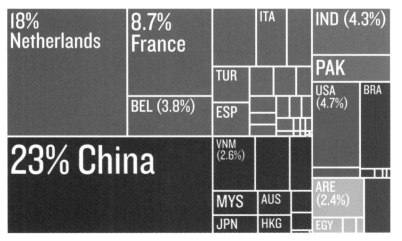

18% Netherlands
8.7% France
BEL (3.8%)
23% China
ITA
TUR
ESP
VNM (2.6%)
MYS
JPN
AUS
HKG
IND (4.3%)
PAK
USA (4.7%)
BRA
ARE (2.4%)
EGY

EAST ASIA & PACIFIC | EUROPE & CENTRAL ASIA | LATIN AMERICA & CARIBBEAN | MIDDLE EAST & NORTH AFRICA | NORTH AMERICA | SOUTH ASIA | SUB-SAHARAN AFRICA

HONDURAS

ECONOMIC COMPLEXITY INDEX [2010] ▸ -0.663 (91) | COMPLEXITY OUTLOOK INDEX [2010] ▸ -0.509 (77) | EXPECTED GDPPC GROWTH * ▸ 1.7% (76)

*Expected annual average for the 2010-2020 period.

2010 PRODUCT SPACE ▶

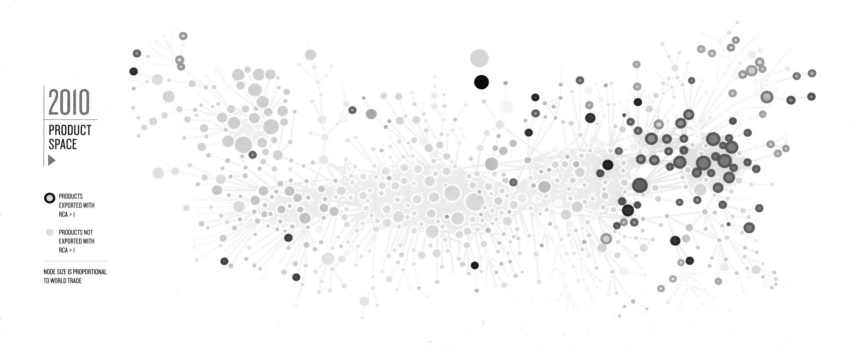

○ PRODUCTS EXPORTED WITH RCA > 1

○ PRODUCTS NOT EXPORTED WITH RCA > 1

NODE SIZE IS PROPORTIONAL TO WORLD TRADE

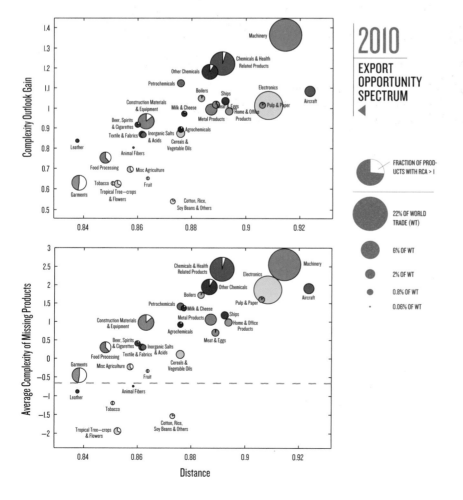

2010 EXPORT OPPORTUNITY SPECTRUM ◀

FRACTION OF PRODUCTS WITH RCA > 1

22% OF WORLD TRADE (WT)

6% OF WT

2% OF WT

0.8% OF WT

0.06% OF WT

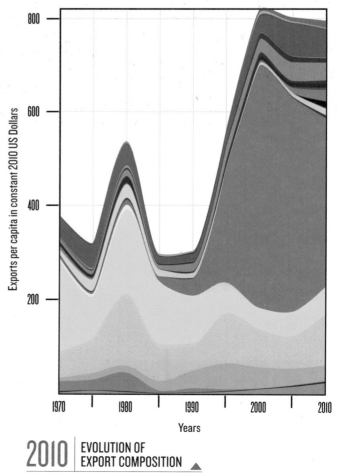

2010 | EVOLUTION OF EXPORT COMPOSITION ▲

POPULATION ▸ 7.6 M / (80)
TOTAL EXPORTS ▸ USD 6 B / (85)

GDP ▸ USD 15 B / (102)
GDPᴾᶜ ▸ USD 2,019 / (95)

EXPORTS PER CAPITA ▸ USD 793 / (80)
EXPORTS AS SHARE OF GDP ▸ 39 % (36)

* Data are from 2010. Numbers indicate:
Value (World Ranking among 128 countries)
Region: Latin America and the Caribbean.

ELECTRONICS · MACHINERY · AIRCRAFT · BOILERS · SHIPS · METAL PRODUCTS · CONSTR. MATL. & EQPT. · HOME & OFFICE · PULP & PAPER · CHEMICALS & HEALTH · AGROCHEMICALS · OTHER CHEMICALS · INOR. SALTS & ACIDS · PETROCHEMICALS · LEATHER · MILK & CHEESE · ANIMAL FIBERS · MEAT & EGGS · FISH & SEAFOOD · TROPICAL AGRIC. · CEREALS & VEG. OILS · COTTON/RICE/SOY & OTHERS · TOBACCO · FRUIT · MISC. AGRICULTURE · NOT CLASSIFIED · TEXTILE & FABRICS · GARMENTS · FOOD PROCESSING · BEER/SPIRITS & CIGS. · PRECIOUS STONES · COAL · OIL · MINING

2010 EXPORT TREEMAP ▼ TOTAL: $ 6,030,839,035

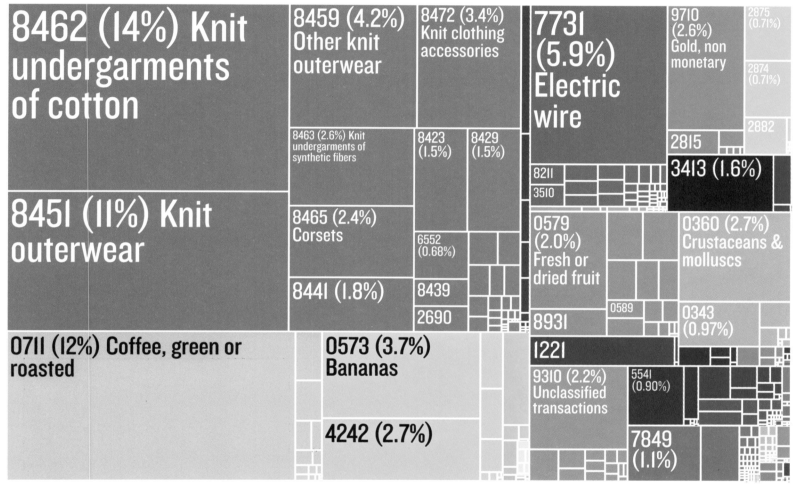

8462 (14%) Knit undergarments of cotton

8451 (11%) Knit outerwear

0711 (12%) Coffee, green or roasted

8459 (4.2%) Other knit outerwear

8463 (2.6%) Knit undergarments of synthetic fibers

8465 (2.4%) Corsets

8441 (1.8%)

8439

2690

0573 (3.7%) Bananas

4242 (2.7%)

8472 (3.4%) Knit clothing accessories

8423 (1.5%)

8429 (1.5%)

6552 (0.68%)

7731 (5.9%) Electric wire

8211

3510

0579 (2.0%) Fresh or dried fruit

0589

8931

1221

9310 (2.2%) Unclassified transactions

5541 (0.90%)

7849 (1.1%)

9710 (2.6%) Gold, non monetary

2815

3413 (1.6%)

0360 (2.7%) Crustaceans & molluscs

0343 (0.97%)

2875 (0.71%)

2874 (0.71%)

2882

* Numbers indicate SITC-4 Rev 2 codes which can be found in the Appendix. Percentages next to the product codes indicate proportion of the product in the exports of the country. Treemap headers show the total trade of the country.

2010 EXPORT DESTINATIONS ▼ TOTAL: $ 6,030,839,035

61% United States

SLV (5.7%)

MEX (4.1%)

NIC

GTM (4.6%)

DEU (4.2%)

BEL

CHN

KOR

FRA

NLD

ESP

ITA

2010 IMPORT SOURCES ▼ TOTAL: $ 7,106,738,192

65% United States

SLV (8.1%)

MEX (5.9%)

BRA

CHN (4.4%)

KOR

ITA

ESP

EAST ASIA & PACIFIC · EUROPE & CENTRAL ASIA · LATIN AMERICA & CARIBBEAN · MIDDLE EAST & NORTH AFRICA · NORTH AMERICA · SOUTH ASIA · SUB-SAHARAN AFRICA

HUNGARY

ECONOMIC COMPLEXITY INDEX [2010] ▸ 1.436 (13)	COMPLEXITY OUTLOOK INDEX [2010] ▸ 0.859 (30)	EXPECTED GDPᴘᴄ GROWTH * ▸ 3.4% (11)

*Expected annual average for the 2010-2020 period.

2010 PRODUCT SPACE ▸

● PRODUCTS EXPORTED WITH RCA > 1

○ PRODUCTS NOT EXPORTED WITH RCA > 1

NODE SIZE IS PROPORTIONAL TO WORLD TRADE

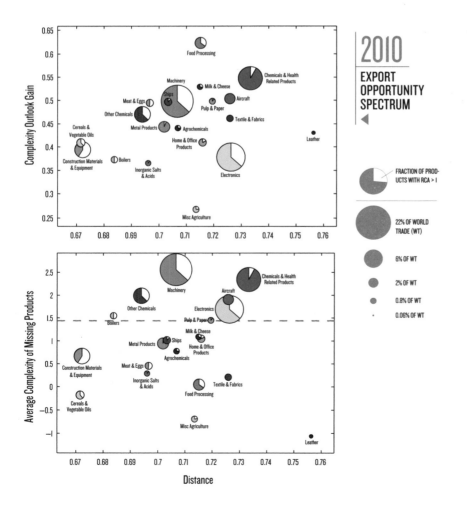

2010 EXPORT OPPORTUNITY SPECTRUM ◂

FRACTION OF PRODUCTS WITH RCA > 1

22% OF WORLD TRADE (WT)

6% OF WT

2% OF WT

0.8% OF WT

0.06% OF WT

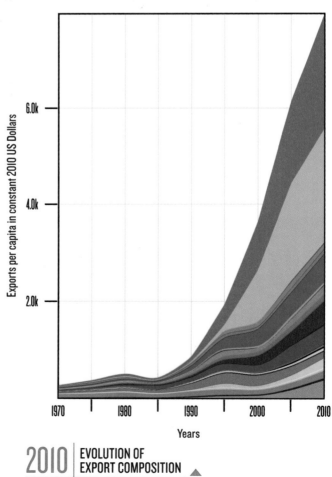

2010 EVOLUTION OF EXPORT COMPOSITION ▲

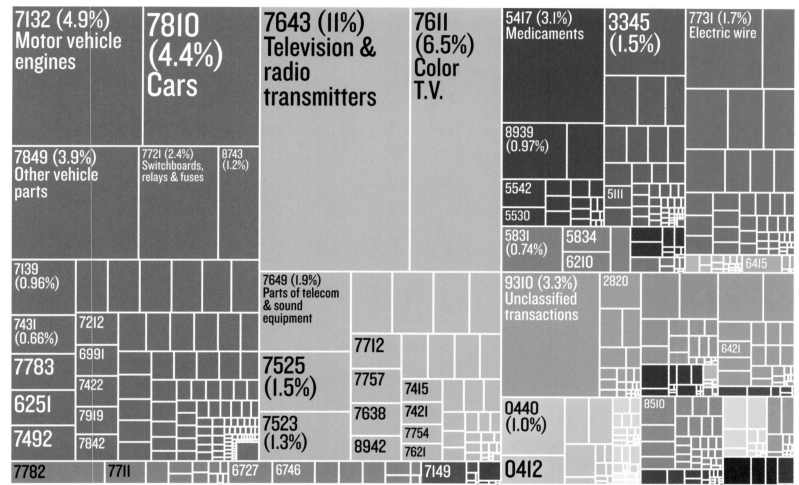

ELECTRONICS · MACHINERY · AIRCRAFT · BOILERS · SHIPS · METAL PRODUCTS · CONSTR. MATL. & EQPT. · HOME & OFFICE · PULP & PAPER · CHEMICALS & HEALTH · AGROCHEMICALS · OTHER CHEMICALS · INOR. SALTS & ACIDS · PETROCHEMICALS · LEATHER · MILK & CHEESE · ANIMAL FIBERS · MEAT & EGGS · FISH & SEAFOOD · TROPICAL AGRIC. · CEREALS & VEG. OILS · COTTON/RICE/SOY & OTHERS · TOBACCO · FRUIT · MISC. AGRICULTURE · NOT CLASSIFIED · TEXTILE & FABRICS · GARMENTS · FOOD PROCESSING · BEER/SPIRITS & CIGS. · PRECIOUS STONES · COAL · OIL · MINING

2010 | EXPORT TREEMAP ▾ TOTAL: $ 79,687,477,173

7132 (4.9%) Motor vehicle engines

7810 (4.4%) Cars

7643 (11%) Television & radio transmitters

7611 (6.5%) Color T.V.

5417 (3.1%) Medicaments

3345 (1.5%)

7731 (1.7%) Electric wire

7849 (3.9%) Other vehicle parts

7721 (2.4%) Switchboards, relays & fuses

8743 (1.2%)

8939 (0.97%)

5542

5530

5111

5831 (0.74%)

5834

6210

6415

7139 (0.96%)

7649 (1.9%) Parts of telecom & sound equipment

9310 (3.3%) Unclassified transactions

2820

7431 (0.66%)

7212

6991

7422

7712

6421

7525 (1.5%)

7757

7415

8510

7783

6251

7919

7523 (1.3%)

7638

7421

0440 (1.0%)

7492

7842

8942

7754

7621

7782

7711

6727

6746

7149

0412

*Numbers indicate SITC-4 Rev 2 codes which can be found in the Appendix. Percentages next to the product codes indicate proportion of the product in the exports of the country. Treemap headers show the total trade of the country.

2010 | EXPORT DESTINATIONS ▾ TOTAL: $ 79,687,477,173

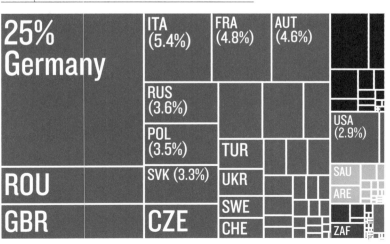

25% Germany

ITA (5.4%)

FRA (4.8%)

AUT (4.6%)

RUS (3.6%)

USA (2.9%)

POL (3.5%)

TUR

SAU

ROU

SVK (3.3%)

UKR

ARE

GBR

CZE

SWE

CHE

ZAF

2010 | IMPORT SOURCES ▾ TOTAL: $ 71,295,271,721

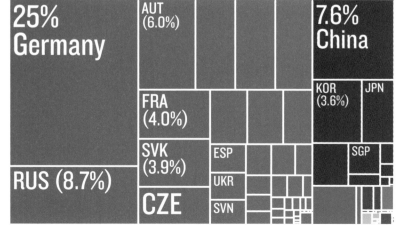

25% Germany

AUT (6.0%)

7.6% China

KOR (3.6%)

JPN

FRA (4.0%)

SVK (3.9%)

ESP

SGP

UKR

RUS (8.7%)

CZE

SVN

EAST ASIA & PACIFIC · EUROPE & CENTRAL ASIA · LATIN AMERICA & CARIBBEAN · MIDDLE EAST & NORTH AFRICA · NORTH AMERICA · SOUTH ASIA · SUB-SAHARAN AFRICA

INDIA

ECONOMIC COMPLEXITY INDEX [2010] ▸ 0.211 (55) | **COMPLEXITY OUTLOOK INDEX [2010] ▸ 3.286 (1)** | **EXPECTED GDPᴘᴄ GROWTH * ▸ 5.8% (1)**

*Expected annual average for the 2010-2020 period.

2010 PRODUCT SPACE ▸

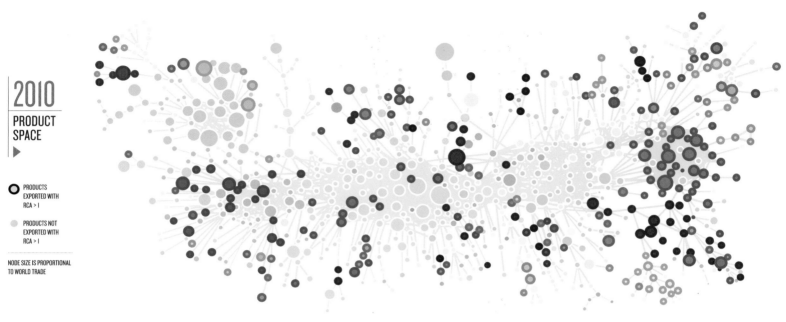

○ PRODUCTS EXPORTED WITH RCA > 1

○ PRODUCTS NOT EXPORTED WITH RCA > 1

NODE SIZE IS PROPORTIONAL TO WORLD TRADE

2010 EXPORT OPPORTUNITY SPECTRUM ◂

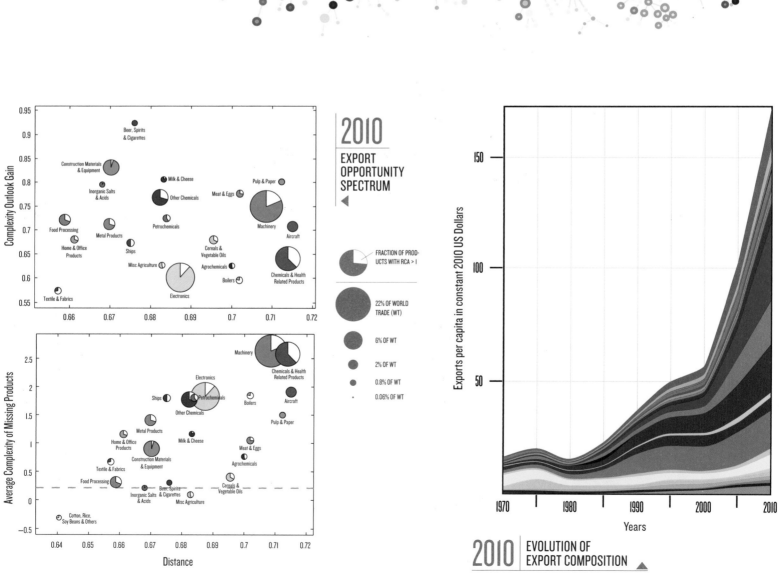

⬤ FRACTION OF PRODUCTS WITH RCA > 1

⬤ 22% OF WORLD TRADE (WT)

⬤ 6% OF WT

⬤ 2% OF WT

⬤ 0.8% OF WT

· 0.06% OF WT

2010 EVOLUTION OF EXPORT COMPOSITION ▲

POPULATION ▸ 1.23 B / (2)
TOTAL EXPORTS ▸ USD 211 B / (17)

GDP ▸ USD 1.7 T / (9)
GDPPC ▸ USD 1,375 / (101)

EXPORTS PER CAPITA ▸ USD 172 / (113)
EXPORTS AS SHARE OF GDP ▸ 13 % (109)

* Data are from 2010. Numbers indicate:
Value (World Ranking among 128 countries)
Region: South Asia.

ELECTRONICS | MACHINERY | AIRCRAFT | BOILERS | SHIPS | METAL PRODUCTS | CONSTR. MATL. & EQPT. | HOME & OFFICE | PULP & PAPER | CHEMICALS & HEALTH | AGROCHEMICALS | OTHER CHEMICALS | INOR. SALTS & ACIDS | PETROCHEMICALS | LEATHER | MILK & CHEESE | ANIMAL FIBERS | MEAT & EGGS | FISH & SEAFOOD | TROPICAL AGRIC. | CEREALS & VEG. OILS | COTTON/RICE/SOY & OTHERS | TOBACCO | FRUIT | MISC. AGRICULTURE | NOT CLASSIFIED | TEXTILE & FABRICS | GARMENTS | FOOD PROCESSING | BEER/SPIRITS & CIGS. | PRECIOUS STONES | COAL | OIL | MINING

2010 | EXPORT TREEMAP ▾ TOTAL: $ 211,138,299,999

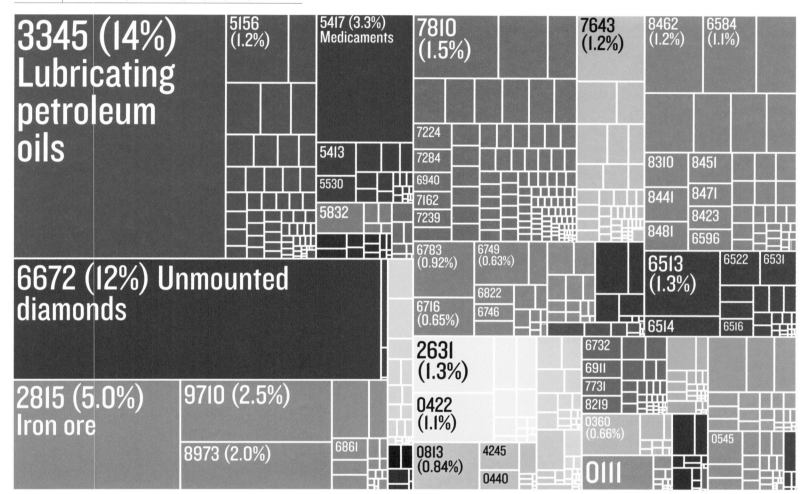

* Numbers indicate SITC-4 Rev 2 codes which can be found in the Appendix. Percentages next to the product codes indicate proportion of the product in the exports of the country. Treemap headers show the total trade of the country.

2010 | EXPORT DESTINATIONS ▾ TOTAL: $ 211,138,299,999

8.9% China | HKG (3.9%) | 10% United Arab Emirates | 13% United States
SGP | IDN | THA | SAU |
| MYS | VNM | |
GBR (3.6%) | FRA | ZAF | BRA (1.8%) | BHS
| | | | MEX
DEU (3.5%) | ITA | | BGD | NPL
| BEL | | | LKA

2010 | IMPORT SOURCES ▾ TOTAL: $ 308,950,475,958

12% China | AUS (3.5%) | CHE (6.7%)
| KOR | SGP | THA | RUS
| IDN | MYS | DEU (3.3%) | FRA
ARE (9.1%) | IRN (3.2%) | QAT | NGA | AGO | VEN
SAU (6.0%) | KWT | | ZAF |
| IRQ | | USA (5.5%) |

EAST ASIA & PACIFIC | EUROPE & CENTRAL ASIA | LATIN AMERICA & CARIBBEAN | MIDDLE EAST & NORTH AFRICA | NORTH AMERICA | SOUTH ASIA | SUB-SAHARAN AFRICA

INDONESIA

ECONOMIC COMPLEXITY INDEX [2010] ▸ -0.077 (65) | COMPLEXITY OUTLOOK INDEX [2010] ▸ 1.65 (6) | EXPECTED GDPᴘᴄ GROWTH * ▸ 3.5% (10)

*Expected annual average for the 2010-2020 period.

2010 PRODUCT SPACE ▶

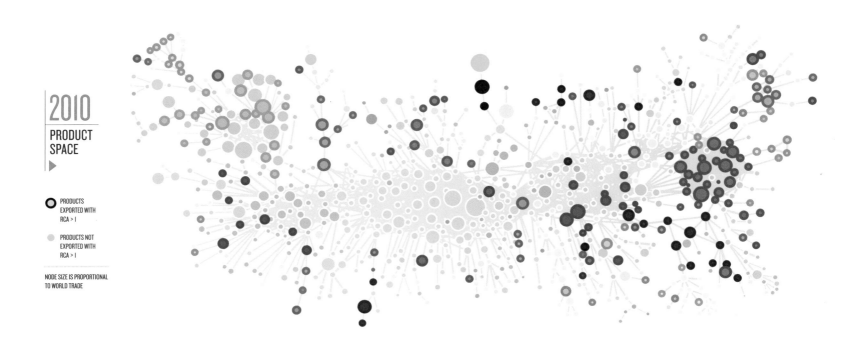

○ PRODUCTS EXPORTED WITH RCA > 1

○ PRODUCTS NOT EXPORTED WITH RCA > 1

NODE SIZE IS PROPORTIONAL TO WORLD TRADE

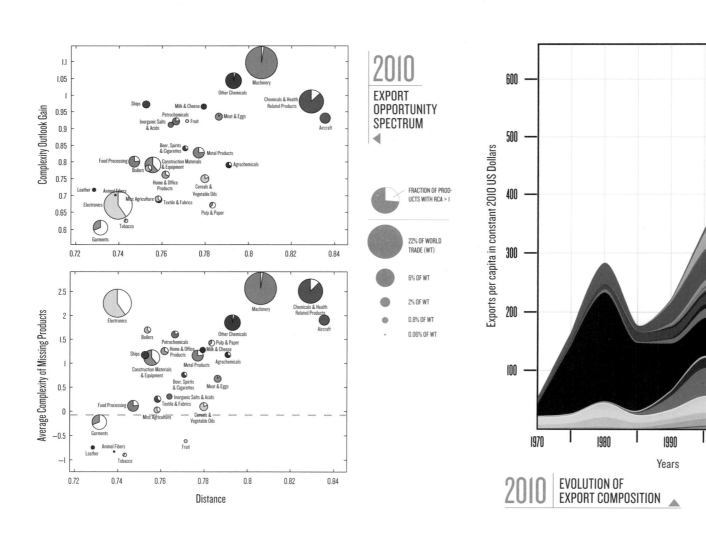

2010 EXPORT OPPORTUNITY SPECTRUM ◀

◔ FRACTION OF PRODUCTS WITH RCA > 1

⬤ 22% OF WORLD TRADE (WT)

⬤ 6% OF WT

● 2% OF WT

• 0.8% OF WT

· 0.06% OF WT

2010 | EVOLUTION OF EXPORT COMPOSITION ▲

POPULATION ▸ 240 M / (4)	**GDP ▸ USD 708 B / (18)**
TOTAL EXPORTS ▸ USD 158 B / (23)	GDPᴘᴄ ▸ USD 2,952 / (85)

EXPORTS PER CAPITA ▸ USD 659 / (84)
EXPORTS AS SHARE OF GDP ▸ 22 % (75)

Data are from 2010. Numbers indicate:
Value (World Ranking among 128 countries)
Region: East Asia and Pacific.

ELECTRONICS · MACHINERY · AIRCRAFT · BOILERS · SHIPS · METAL PRODUCTS · CONSTR. MATL. & EQPT. · HOME & OFFICE · PULP & PAPER · CHEMICALS & HEALTH · AGROCHEMICALS · OTHER CHEMICALS · INOR. SALTS & ACIDS · PETROCHEMICALS · LEATHER · MILK & CHEESE · ANIMAL FIBERS · MEAT & EGGS · FISH & SEAFOOD · TROPICAL AGRIC. · CEREALS & VEG. OILS · COTTON/RICE/SOY & OTHERS · TOBACCO · FRUIT · MISC. AGRICULTURE · NOT CLASSIFIED · TEXTILE & FABRICS · GARMENTS · FOOD PROCESSING · BEER/SPIRITS & CIGS. · PRECIOUS STONES · COAL · OIL · MINING

2010 EXPORT TREEMAP ▾ TOTAL: $ 158,159,866,457

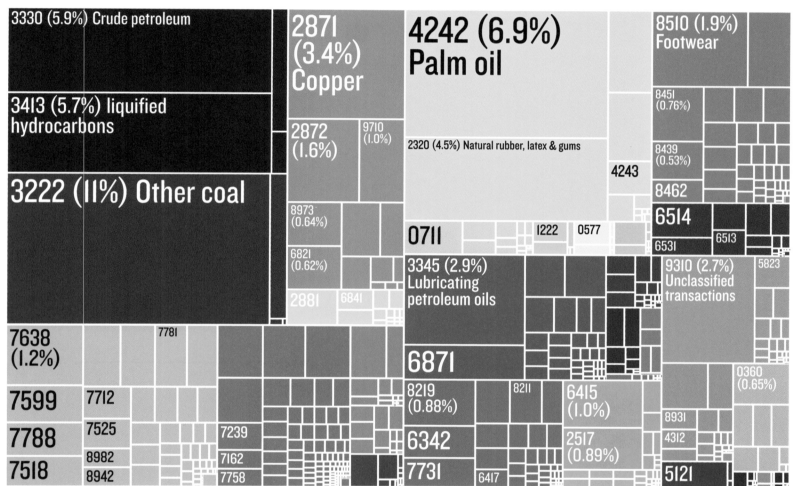

3330 (5.9%) Crude petroleum
3413 (5.7%) liquified hydrocarbons
3222 (11%) Other coal
7638 (1.2%)
7599
7788
7518
7781
7712
7525
8982
8942
7239
7162
7758

2871 (3.4%) Copper
2872 (1.6%)
9710 (1.0%)
8973 (0.64%)
6821 (0.62%)
2881
6841

4242 (6.9%) Palm oil
2320 (4.5%) Natural rubber, latex & gums
4243
0711
1222
0577
3345 (2.9%) Lubricating petroleum oils
6871
8219 (0.88%)
8211
6415 (1.0%)
6342
2517 (0.89%)
7731
6417
5121

8510 (1.9%) Footwear
8451 (0.76%)
8439 (0.53%)
8462
6514
6531
6513
9310 (2.7%) Unclassified transactions
5823
0360 (0.65%)
8931
4312

*Numbers indicate SITC-4 Rev 2 codes which can be found in the Appendix. Percentages next to the product codes indicate proportion of the product in the exports of the country. Treemap headers show the total trade of the country.

2010 EXPORT DESTINATIONS ▾ TOTAL: $ 158,159,866,457

16% Japan
CHN (12%)
SGP (9.5%)
8.0% Korea, Rep.
MYS (5.3%)
AUS (2.7%)
HKG
USA (9.8%)
ESP
BEL
IND (5.5%)

2010 IMPORT SOURCES ▾ TOTAL: $ 119,868,731,167

15% Singapore
15% China
JPN (13%)
THA (5.6%)
HKG
VNM
MYS (6.6%)
KOR (5.8%)
DEU (2.2%)
ITA
SAU (3.3%)
USA (7.1%)
BRA

EAST ASIA & PACIFIC · EUROPE & CENTRAL ASIA · LATIN AMERICA & CARIBBEAN · MIDDLE EAST & NORTH AFRICA · NORTH AMERICA · SOUTH ASIA · SUB-SAHARAN AFRICA

ISLAMIC REPUBLIC OF IRAN

ECONOMIC COMPLEXITY INDEX [2010] ▸ -0.798 (96) | **COMPLEXITY OUTLOOK INDEX [2010]** ▸ -0.882 (94) | **EXPECTED GDPᴘᴄ GROWTH** * ▸ 0.4% (108)

*Expected annual average for the 2010-2020 period.

2010 PRODUCT SPACE ▶

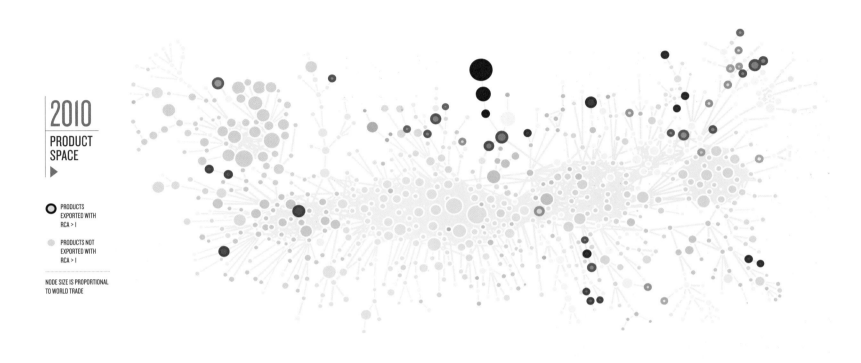

◯ PRODUCTS EXPORTED WITH RCA > 1

◯ PRODUCTS NOT EXPORTED WITH RCA > 1

NODE SIZE IS PROPORTIONAL TO WORLD TRADE

2010 EXPORT OPPORTUNITY SPECTRUM ◀

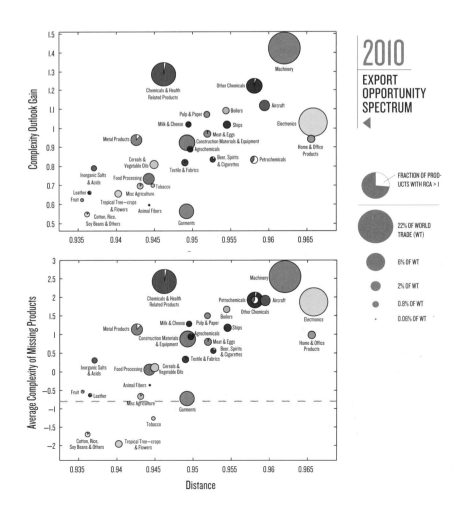

FRACTION OF PRODUCTS WITH RCA > 1

22% OF WORLD TRADE (WT)

6% OF WT

2% OF WT

0.8% OF WT

0.06% OF WT

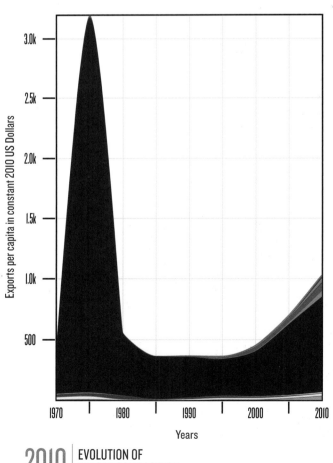

2010 | EVOLUTION OF EXPORT COMPOSITION ▲

POPULATION ▸ 74 M / (17)	GDP ▸ USD 331 B / (29)
TOTAL EXPORTS ▸ USD 77 B / (35)	GDPPC ▸ USD 4,526 / (72)

EXPORTS PER CAPITA ▸ USD 1,044 / (73)
EXPORTS AS SHARE OF GDP ▸ 23 % (68)

* Data are from 2010. Numbers indicate:
Value (World Ranking among 128 countries)
Region: Middle East and North Africa.

ELECTRONICS · MACHINERY · AIRCRAFT · BOILERS · SHIPS · METAL PRODUCTS · CONSTR. MATL. & EQPT. · HOME & OFFICE · PULP & PAPER · CHEMICALS & HEALTH · AGROCHEMICALS · OTHER CHEMICALS · INOR. SALTS & ACIDS · PETROCHEMICALS · LEATHER · MILK & CHEESE · ANIMAL FIBERS · MEAT & EGGS · FISH & SEAFOOD · TROPICAL AGRIC. · CEREALS & VEG. OILS · COTTON/RICE/SOY & OTHERS · TOBACCO · FRUIT · MISC. AGRICULTURE · NOT CLASSIFIED · TEXTILE & FABRICS · GARMENTS · FOOD PROCESSING · BEER/SPIRITS & CIGS. · PRECIOUS STONES · COAL · OIL · MINING

2010 | EXPORT TREEMAP ▾ TOTAL: $ 77,200,364,745

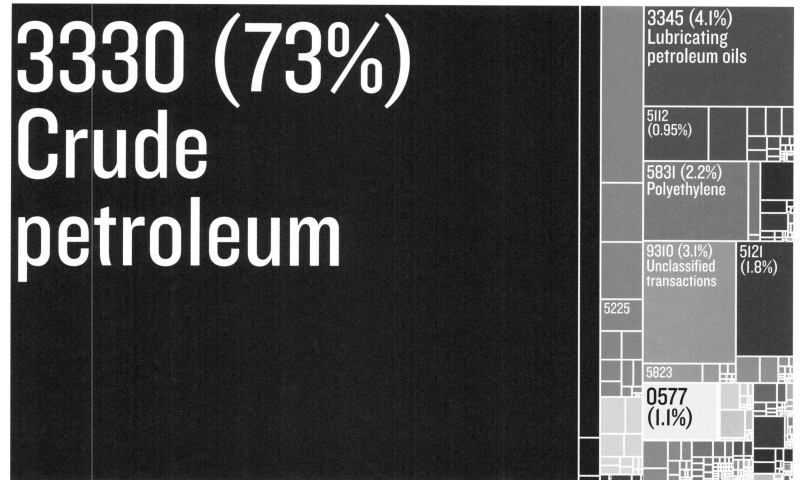

3330 (73%) Crude petroleum

3345 (4.1%) Lubricating petroleum oils

5112 (0.95%)

5831 (2.2%) Polyethylene

9310 (3.1%) Unclassified transactions

5121 (1.8%)

5225

5823

0577 (1.1%)

* Numbers indicate SITC-4 Rev 2 codes which can be found in the Appendix. Percentages next to the product codes indicate proportion of the product in the exports of the country. Treemap headers show the total trade of the country.

2010 | EXPORT DESTINATIONS ▾ TOTAL: $ 77,200,364,745

21% China
13% Japan
KOR (8.1%)
SGP
13% India
9.0% Turkey
ITA (7.4%)
ESP
FRA
PAK
LKA
ZAF (3.7%)
ARE

2010 | IMPORT SOURCES ▾ TOTAL: $ 51,015,587,123

8.0% Germany
CHE (3.8%)
RUS (3.2%)
CHN (10%)
KOR (6.7%)
FRA (3.6%)
SWE
TUR (4.2%)
ITA (3.3%)
AUT
BEL
28% United Arab Emirates
JPN
SGP
IND (2.5%)
BRA (1.9%)

EAST ASIA & PACIFIC · EUROPE & CENTRAL ASIA · LATIN AMERICA & CARIBBEAN · MIDDLE EAST & NORTH AFRICA · NORTH AMERICA · SOUTH ASIA · SUB-SAHARAN AFRICA

IRELAND

ECONOMIC COMPLEXITY INDEX [2010] ▸ 1.358 (17)   **COMPLEXITY OUTLOOK INDEX [2010] ▸ 0.369 (46)**   **EXPECTED GDPᴘᴄ GROWTH * ▸ 1.6% (77)**

*Expected annual average for the 2010-2020 period.

2010
PRODUCT SPACE ▸

○ PRODUCTS EXPORTED WITH RCA > 1

○ PRODUCTS NOT EXPORTED WITH RCA > 1

NODE SIZE IS PROPORTIONAL TO WORLD TRADE

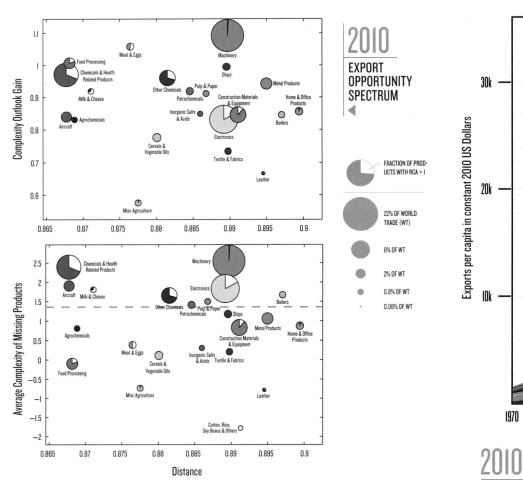

2010
EXPORT OPPORTUNITY SPECTRUM ◂

◔ FRACTION OF PRODUCTS WITH RCA > 1

⬤ 22% OF WORLD TRADE (WT)

● 6% OF WT

● 2% OF WT

● 0.8% OF WT

· 0.06% OF WT

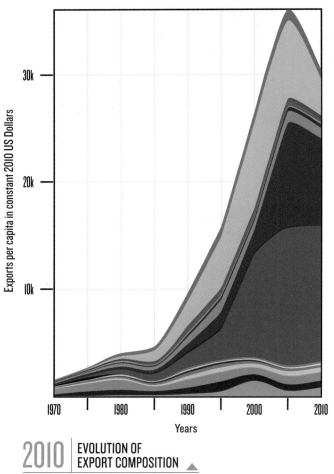

2010 | EVOLUTION OF EXPORT COMPOSITION ▲

POPULATION ▸ 4.5 M / (101)
TOTAL EXPORTS ▸ USD 136 B / (25)

GDP ▸ USD 205 B / (43)
GDPᴘᴄ ▸ USD 45,873 / (10)

EXPORTS PER CAPITA ▸ USD 30,298 / (3)
EXPORTS AS SHARE OF GDP ▸ 66 % (6)

* Data are from 2010. Numbers indicate:
  Value (World Ranking among 128 countries)
  Region: Western Europe.

ELECTRONICS • MACHINERY • AIRCRAFT • BOILERS • SHIPS • METAL PRODUCTS • CONSTR. MATL. & EQPT. • HOME & OFFICE • PULP & PAPER • CHEMICALS & HEALTH • AGROCHEMICALS • OTHER CHEMICALS • INOR. SALTS & ACIDS • PETROCHEMICALS • LEATHER • MILK & CHEESE • ANIMAL FIBERS • MEAT & EGGS • FISH & SEAFOOD • TROPICAL AGRIC. • CEREALS & VEG. OILS • COTTON/RICE/SOY & OTHERS • TOBACCO • FRUIT • MISC. AGRICULTURE • NOT CLASSIFIED • TEXTILE & FABRICS • GARMENTS • FOOD PROCESSING • BEER/SPIRITS & CIGS. • PRECIOUS STONES • COAL • OIL • MINING

2010 | EXPORT TREEMAP ▾ TOTAL: $ 135,561,950,284

5156 (14%) Heterocyclic compound; nucleic acids

5148 (6.7%) Other nitrogen function compounds

5417 (24%) Medicaments

8996 (4.4%) Orthopaedic appliances

8720 (2.6%) Medical instruments

5989 (1.5%)

5514 (4.0%) Odoriferous substances

5157 (1.2%)

5415

3345

5416 (3.4%) Glycosides & vaccines

7643 (1.6%)   7764 (1.5%)   7523 (1.4%)

7525 (1.2%)   7599 (0.71%)

8841 (1.0%)   7638

8942

7522 (0.89%)   7528

7924

0111 (1.3%)

0149

0015

0113

0224

5922

0980 (2.1%) Edible products N.E.S.

1124   1123

9310 (2.3%) Unclassified transactions

0488 (0.80%)

0819

* Numbers indicate SITC-4 Rev 2 codes which can be found in the Appendix. Percentages next to the product codes indicate proportion of the product in the exports of the country. Treemap headers show the total trade of the country.

2010 | EXPORT DESTINATIONS ▾ TOTAL: $ 135,561,950,284

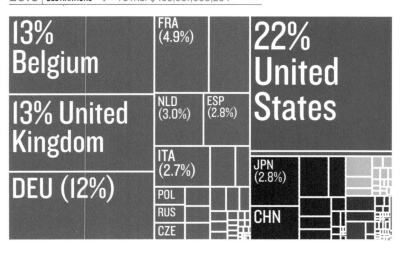

13% Belgium

13% United Kingdom

DEU (12%)

FRA (4.9%)

NLD (3.0%)   ESP (2.8%)

ITA (2.7%)

POL

RUS

CZE

22% United States

JPN (2.8%)

CHN

2010 | IMPORT SOURCES ▾ TOTAL: $ 53,410,098,471

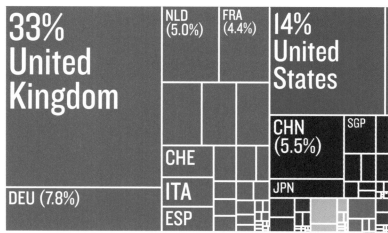

33% United Kingdom

DEU (7.8%)

CHE

ITA

ESP

NLD (5.0%)   FRA (4.4%)

14% United States

CHN (5.5%)   SGP

JPN

EAST ASIA & PACIFIC   EUROPE & CENTRAL ASIA   LATIN AMERICA & CARIBBEAN   MIDDLE EAST & NORTH AFRICA   NORTH AMERICA   SOUTH ASIA   SUB-SAHARAN AFRICA

ISRAEL

ECONOMIC COMPLEXITY INDEX [2010] ▸ 1.209 (20) | **COMPLEXITY OUTLOOK INDEX [2010]** ▸ 0.816 (31) | **EXPECTED GDPᴘᴄ GROWTH** * ▸ 2.2% (52)

*Expected annual average for the 2010-2020 period.

2010
PRODUCT SPACE ▶

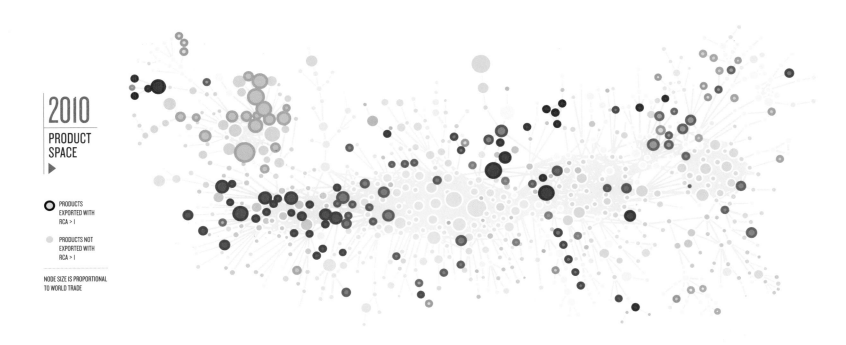

○ PRODUCTS EXPORTED WITH RCA > 1

○ PRODUCTS NOT EXPORTED WITH RCA > 1

NODE SIZE IS PROPORTIONAL TO WORLD TRADE

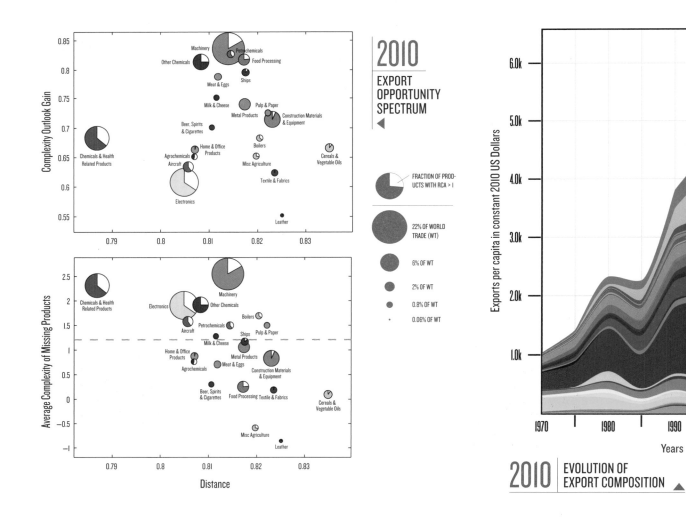

2010
EXPORT OPPORTUNITY SPECTRUM ◀

FRACTION OF PRODUCTS WITH RCA > 1

22% OF WORLD TRADE (WT)

6% OF WT

2% OF WT

0.8% OF WT

0.06% OF WT

2010 | EVOLUTION OF EXPORT COMPOSITION ▲

POPULATION ▸ 7.6 M / (79)
TOTAL EXPORTS ▸ USD 50 B / (49)

GDP ▸ USD 217 B / (40)
GDPᴘᴄ ▸ USD 28,522 / (25)

EXPORTS PER CAPITA ▸ USD 6,593 / (30)
EXPORTS AS SHARE OF GDP ▸ 23 % (70)

* Data are from 2010. Numbers indicate:
Value (World Ranking among 128 countries)
Region: Middle East and North Africa.

ELECTRONICS | MACHINERY | AIRCRAFT | BOILERS | SHIPS | METAL PRODUCTS | CONSTR. MATL. & EQPT. | HOME & OFFICE | PULP & PAPER | CHEMICALS & HEALTH | AGROCHEMICALS | OTHER CHEMICALS | INOR. SALTS & ACIDS | PETROCHEMICALS | LEATHER | MILK & CHEESE | ANIMAL FIBERS | MEAT & EGGS | FISH & SEAFOOD | TROPICAL AGRIC. | CEREALS & VEG. OILS | COTTON/RICE/SOY & OTHERS | TOBACCO | FRUIT | MISC. AGRICULTURE | NOT CLASSIFIED | TEXTILE & FABRICS | GARMENTS | FOOD PROCESSING | BEER/SPIRITS & CIGS. | PRECIOUS STONES | COAL | OIL | MINING

2010 | EXPORT TREEMAP ▼ TOTAL: $ 50,265,597,060

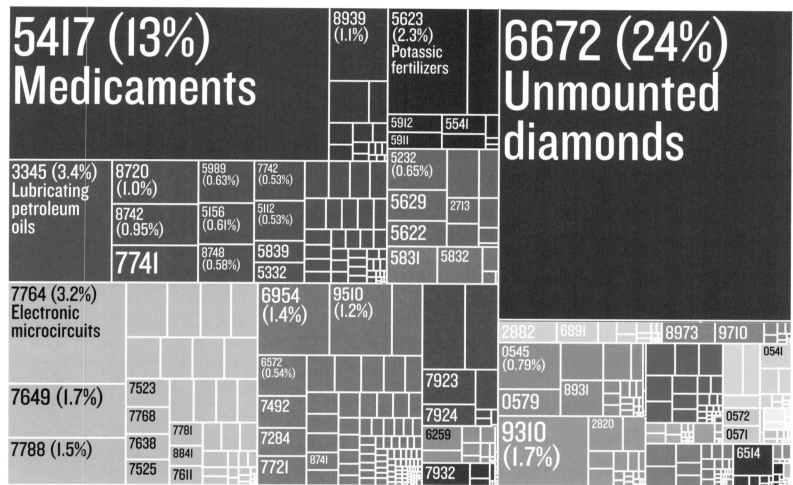

* Numbers indicate SITC-4 Rev 2 codes which can be found in the Appendix. Percentages next to the product codes indicate proportion of the product in the exports of the country. Treemap headers show the total trade of the country.

2010 | EXPORT DESTINATIONS ▼ TOTAL: $ 50,265,597,060

2010 | IMPORT SOURCES ▼ TOTAL: $ 44,241,831,646

EAST ASIA & PACIFIC | EUROPE & CENTRAL ASIA | LATIN AMERICA & CARIBBEAN | MIDDLE EAST & NORTH AFRICA | NORTH AMERICA | SOUTH ASIA | SUB-SAHARAN AFRICA

ITALY

| ECONOMIC COMPLEXITY INDEX [2010] ▸ 1.398 (16) | COMPLEXITY OUTLOOK INDEX [2010] ▸ -0.44 (75) | EXPECTED GDPᴘᴄ GROWTH * ▸ 1.5% (83) |

*Expected annual average for the 2010-2020 period.

2010 PRODUCT SPACE ▶

○ PRODUCTS EXPORTED WITH RCA > 1

○ PRODUCTS NOT EXPORTED WITH RCA > 1

NODE SIZE IS PROPORTIONAL TO WORLD TRADE

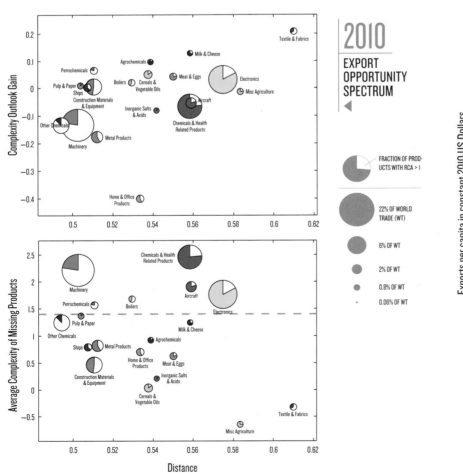

2010 EXPORT OPPORTUNITY SPECTRUM ◀

○ FRACTION OF PRODUCTS WITH RCA > 1

22% OF WORLD TRADE (WT)

6% OF WT

2% OF WT

0.8% OF WT

0.06% OF WT

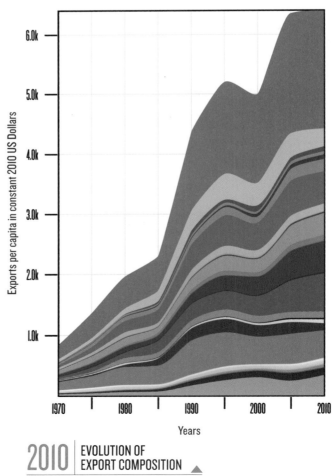

2010 EVOLUTION OF EXPORT COMPOSITION ▲

POPULATION ‣ 60 M / (22)	GDP ‣ USD 2 T / (8)	EXPORTS PER CAPITA ‣ USD 6,416 / (32)	* Data are from 2010. Numbers indicate:
TOTAL EXPORTS ‣ USD 388 B / (7)	GDPᴘᴄ ‣ USD 33,788 / (21)	EXPORTS AS SHARE OF GDP ‣ 19 % (83)	Value (World Ranking among 128 countries) Region: Western Europe.

ELECTRONICS · MACHINERY · AIRCRAFT · BOILERS · SHIPS · METAL PRODUCTS · CONSTR. MATL. & EQPT. · HOME & OFFICE · PULP & PAPER · CHEMICALS & HEALTH · AGROCHEMICALS · OTHER CHEMICALS · INOR. SALTS & ACIDS · PETROCHEMICALS · LEATHER · MILK & CHEESE · ANIMAL FIBERS · MEAT & EGGS · FISH & SEAFOOD · TROPICAL AGRIC. · CEREALS & VEG. OILS · COTTON/RICE/SOY & OTHERS · TOBACCO · FRUIT · MISC. AGRICULTURE · NOT CLASSIFIED · TEXTILE & FABRICS · GARMENTS · FOOD PROCESSING · BEER/SPIRITS & CIGS. · PRECIOUS STONES · COAL · OIL · MINING

2010 | EXPORT TREEMAP ▼ TOTAL: $ 388,082,453,210

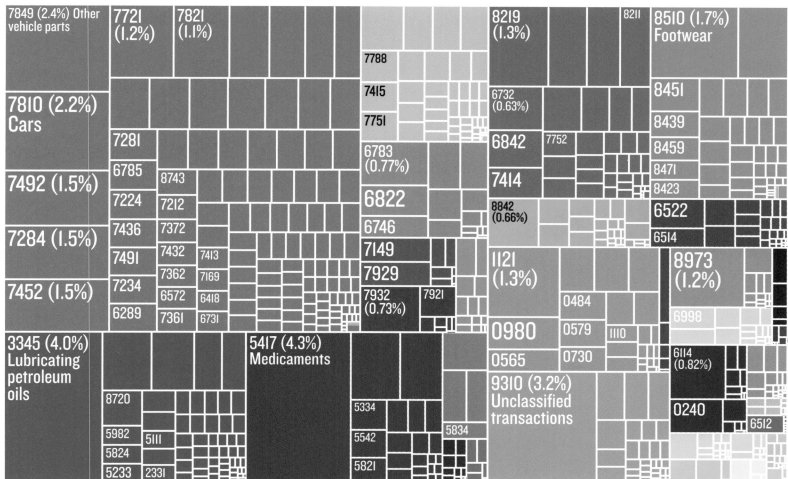

* Numbers indicate SITC-4 Rev 2 codes which can be found in the Appendix. Percentages next to the product codes indicate proportion of the product in the exports of the country. Treemap headers show the total trade of the country.

2010 | EXPORT DESTINATIONS ▼ TOTAL: $ 388,082,453,210   2010 | IMPORT SOURCES ▼ TOTAL: $ 432,889,497,963

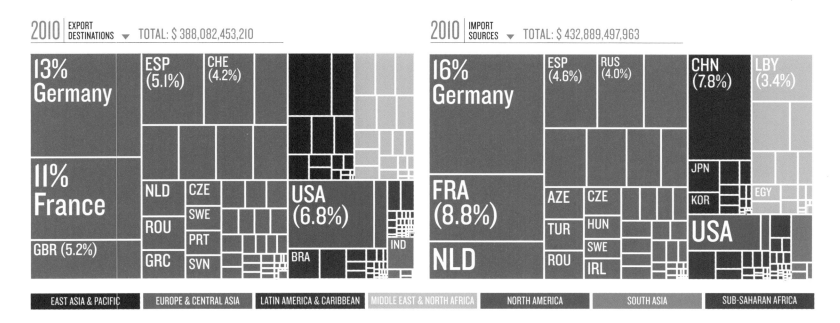

EAST ASIA & PACIFIC · EUROPE & CENTRAL ASIA · LATIN AMERICA & CARIBBEAN · MIDDLE EAST & NORTH AFRICA · NORTH AMERICA · SOUTH ASIA · SUB-SAHARAN AFRICA

JAMAICA

| ECONOMIC COMPLEXITY INDEX [2010] ▸ -0.41 (78) | COMPLEXITY OUTLOOK INDEX [2010] ▸ -0.897 (99) | EXPECTED GDPᴘᴄ GROWTH * ▸ 0.8% (99) |

*Expected annual average for the 2010-2020 period.

2010 PRODUCT SPACE ▶

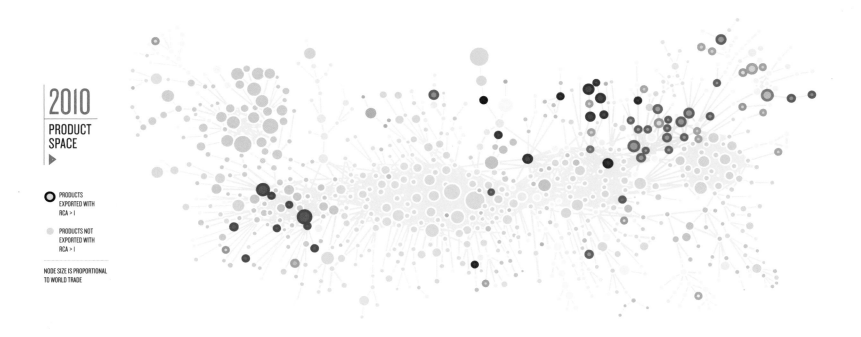

○ PRODUCTS EXPORTED WITH RCA > 1

○ PRODUCTS NOT EXPORTED WITH RCA > 1

NODE SIZE IS PROPORTIONAL TO WORLD TRADE

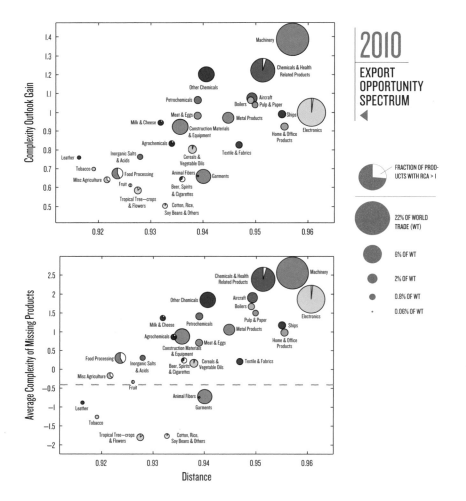

2010 EXPORT OPPORTUNITY SPECTRUM ◀

◐ FRACTION OF PRODUCTS WITH RCA > 1

● 22% OF WORLD TRADE (WT)

● 6% OF WT

● 2% OF WT

● 0.8% OF WT

· 0.06% OF WT

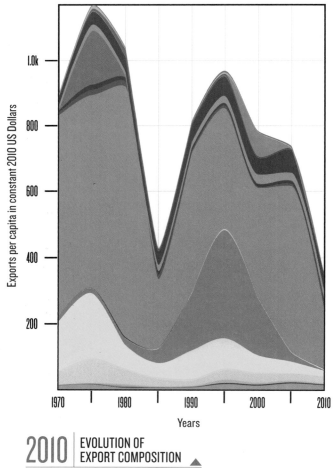

2010 | EVOLUTION OF EXPORT COMPOSITION ▲

POPULATION ▸ 2.7 M / (118)
TOTAL EXPORTS ▸ USD 943 M / (124)

GDP ▸ USD 14 B / (104)
GDPᴘᴄ ▸ USD 5,133 / (108)

EXPORTS PER CAPITA ▸ USD 349 / (104)
EXPORTS AS SHARE OF GDP ▸ 6.8 % / (123)

* Data are from 2010. Numbers indicate:
Value (World Ranking among 128 countries)
Region: Latin America and the Caribbean.

ELECTRONICS · MACHINERY · AIRCRAFT · BOILERS · SHIPS · METAL PRODUCTS · CONSTR. MATL. & EQPT. · HOME & OFFICE · PULP & PAPER · CHEMICALS & HEALTH · AGROCHEMICALS · OTHER CHEMICALS · INOR. SALTS & ACIDS · PETROCHEMICALS · LEATHER · MILK & CHEESE · ANIMAL FIBERS · MEAT & EGGS · FISH & SEAFOOD · TROPICAL AGRIC. · CEREALS & VEG. OILS · COTTON/RICE/SOY & OTHERS · TOBACCO · FRUIT · MISC. AGRICULTURE · NOT CLASSIFIED · TEXTILE & FABRICS · GARMENTS · FOOD PROCESSING · BEER/SPIRITS & CIGS. · PRECIOUS STONES · COAL · OIL · MINING

2010 | EXPORT TREEMAP ▾ TOTAL: $ 943,069,430

2873 (45%) Aluminium ore

9710 (3.4%)

5225 (1.0%)

6612

2732

2890

8973

1124 (5.5%) Alcoholic beverages

1123 (4.4%) Beer

5121 (2.8%)

0548 (2.3%)

0711 (2.3%)

0751

0488

0611 (4.3%) Raw sugars

0980 (2.1%) Edible products N.E.S.

0484 (1.1%)

0589

0565

1121

0571

1110 (1.2%)

3345 (2.6%) Lubricating petroleum oils

5156 (1.6%)

9310 (2.8%) Unclassified transactions

2820 (1.5%)

5989 (0.82%)

5147

5148

* Numbers indicate SITC-4 Rev 2 codes which can be found in the Appendix. Percentages next to the product codes indicate proportion of the product in the exports of the country. Treemap headers show the total trade of the country.

2010 | EXPORT DESTINATIONS ▾ TOTAL: $ 943,069,430

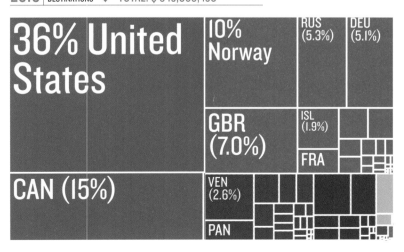

36% United States

10% Norway

RUS (5.3%)

DEU (5.1%)

CAN (15%)

GBR (7.0%)

ISL (1.9%)

FRA

VEN (2.6%)

PAN

2010 | IMPORT SOURCES ▾ TOTAL: $ 4,638,020,112

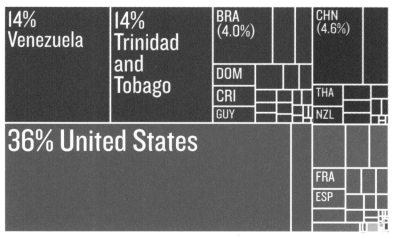

14% Venezuela

14% Trinidad and Tobago

BRA (4.0%)

CHN (4.6%)

DOM

CRI

GUY

THA

NZL

36% United States

FRA

ESP

EAST ASIA & PACIFIC   EUROPE & CENTRAL ASIA   LATIN AMERICA & CARIBBEAN   MIDDLE EAST & NORTH AFRICA   NORTH AMERICA   SOUTH ASIA   SUB-SAHARAN AFRICA

JAPAN

ECONOMIC COMPLEXITY INDEX [2010] ▸ 2.169 (1) | COMPLEXITY OUTLOOK INDEX [2010] ▸ -0.346 (71) | EXPECTED GDPᴘᴄ GROWTH * ▸ 2.3% (49)

*Expected annual average for the 2010-2020 period.

2010
PRODUCT SPACE ▶

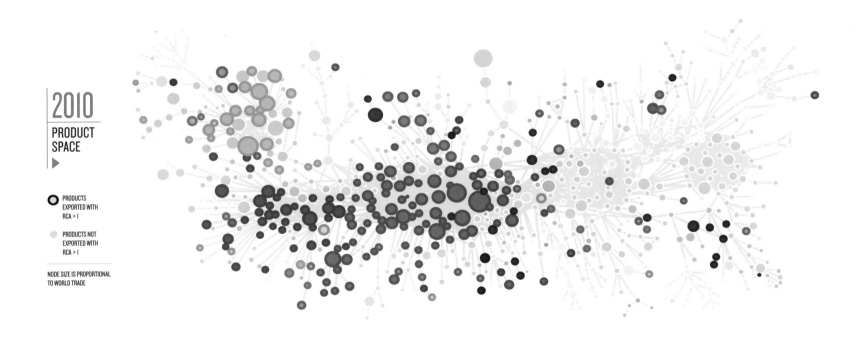

○ PRODUCTS EXPORTED WITH RCA > 1

◯ PRODUCTS NOT EXPORTED WITH RCA > 1

NODE SIZE IS PROPORTIONAL TO WORLD TRADE

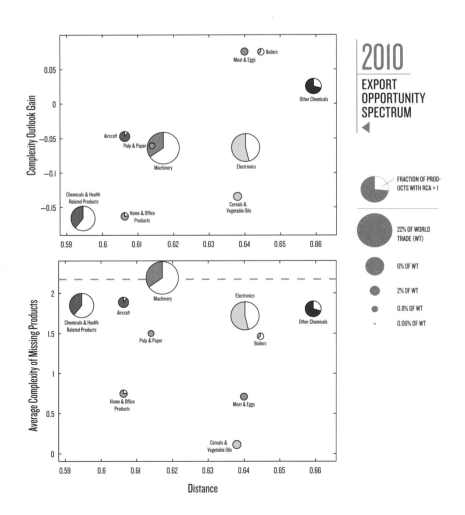

2010
EXPORT OPPORTUNITY SPECTRUM ◀

⬤ FRACTION OF PRODUCTS WITH RCA > 1

⬤ 22% OF WORLD TRADE (WT)

⬤ 6% OF WT

● 2% OF WT

• 0.8% OF WT

· 0.06% OF WT

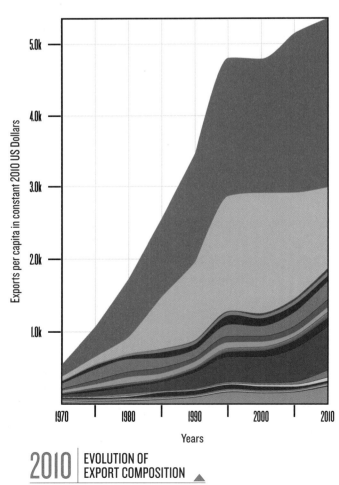

2010 | EVOLUTION OF EXPORT COMPOSITION ▲

POPULATION ▸ 128 M / (10)	GDP ▸ USD 5.5 T / (3)	EXPORTS PER CAPITA ▸ USD 5,352 / (34)	* Data are from 2010. Numbers indicate:
TOTAL EXPORTS ▸ USD 682 B / (4)	GDPᴘᴄ ▸ USD 43,063 / (14)	EXPORTS AS SHARE OF GDP ▸ 12 % (111)	Value (World Ranking among 128 countries) Region: East Asia and Pacific.

ELECTRONICS — MACHINERY — AIRCRAFT — BOILERS — SHIPS — METAL PRODUCTS — CONSTR. MATL. & EQPT. — HOME & OFFICE — PULP & PAPER — CHEMICALS & HEALTH — AGROCHEMICALS — OTHER CHEMICALS — INOR. SALTS & ACIDS — PETROCHEMICALS — LEATHER — MILK & CHEESE — ANIMAL FIBERS — MEAT & EGGS — FISH & SEAFOOD — TROPICAL AGRIC. — CEREALS & VEG. OILS — COTTON/RICE/SOY & OTHERS — TOBACCO — FRUIT — MISC. AGRICULTURE — NOT CLASSIFIED — TEXTILE & FABRICS — GARMENTS — FOOD PROCESSING — BEER/SPIRITS & CIGS. — PRECIOUS STONES — COAL — OIL — MINING

2010 EXPORT TREEMAP ▼ TOTAL: $ 682,060,606,138

7810 (13%) Cars

7849 (4.7%) Other vehicle parts

7284 (3.4%) Specialized industry machinery & parts N.E.S

7139 (0.97%)
7239 (0.62%)
7493
8743
7491
7431
7132
7367
7492
7851
7783
7361
6940

7721 (2.2%) Switchboards, relays & fuses

7416 7161
7224 7245
7452
7441
7188
6731

7234 (1.5%)
7821 (1.2%)

6727 (1.0%)
6749 (0.89%)
6745
6725
7932 (1.2%)

3345 (1.6%) Lubricating petroleum oils

5989 (1.4%)
8822
7742
5839
5836
5112
5843
5417
5831
8939
9310 (2.3%) Unclassified transactions
7731
6842
6997

2820
8928

7764 (4.4%) Electronic microcircuits

7788 (1.9%)

7649 (1.7%)
7638 (1.6%)
7763 (1.4%)

8710 (1.3%)
7768 (1.2%)
8841 (1.1%)

7518 7415
7611 7525
7421
8942 7522

7929
7149

* Numbers indicate SITC-4 Rev 2 codes which can be found in the Appendix. Percentages next to the product codes indicate proportion of the product in the exports of the country. Treemap headers show the total trade of the country.

2010 EXPORT DESTINATIONS ▼ TOTAL: $ 682,060,606,138

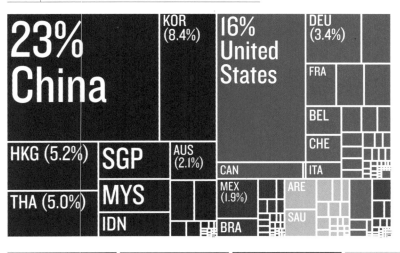

23% China
KOR (8.4%)
HKG (5.2%)
THA (5.0%)
SGP
MYS
IDN
AUS (2.1%)
16% United States
DEU (3.4%)
FRA
BEL
CHE
CAN
ITA
MEX (1.9%)
ARE
SAU
BRA

2010 IMPORT SOURCES ▼ TOTAL: $ 599,061,506,946

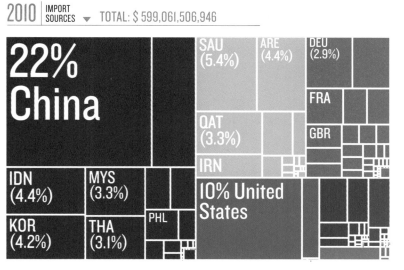

22% China
IDN (4.4%)
KOR (4.2%)
MYS (3.3%)
THA (3.1%)
PHL
SAU (5.4%)
ARE (4.4%)
DEU (2.9%)
QAT (3.3%)
FRA
IRN
GBR
10% United States

EAST ASIA & PACIFIC — EUROPE & CENTRAL ASIA — LATIN AMERICA & CARIBBEAN — MIDDLE EAST & NORTH AFRICA — NORTH AMERICA — SOUTH ASIA — SUB-SAHARAN AFRICA

JORDAN

ECONOMIC COMPLEXITY INDEX [2010] ▸ 0.364 (45) | COMPLEXITY OUTLOOK INDEX [2010] ▸ -0.034 (64) | EXPECTED GDPᴘᴄ GROWTH * ▸ 2.6% (41)

*Expected annual average for the 2010-2020 period.

2010 PRODUCT SPACE ▶

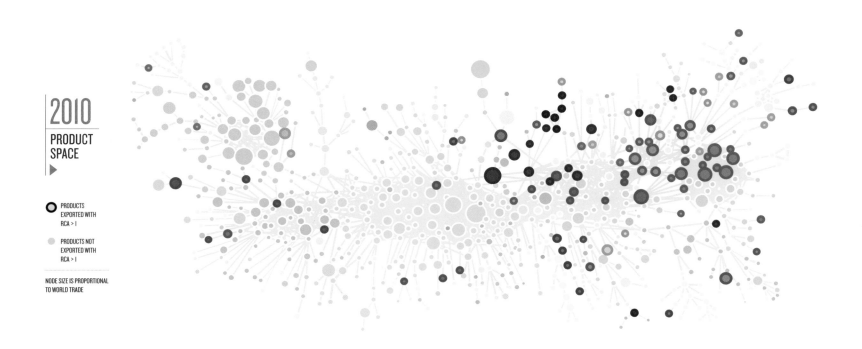

- ● PRODUCTS EXPORTED WITH RCA > 1
- ● PRODUCTS NOT EXPORTED WITH RCA > 1

NODE SIZE IS PROPORTIONAL TO WORLD TRADE

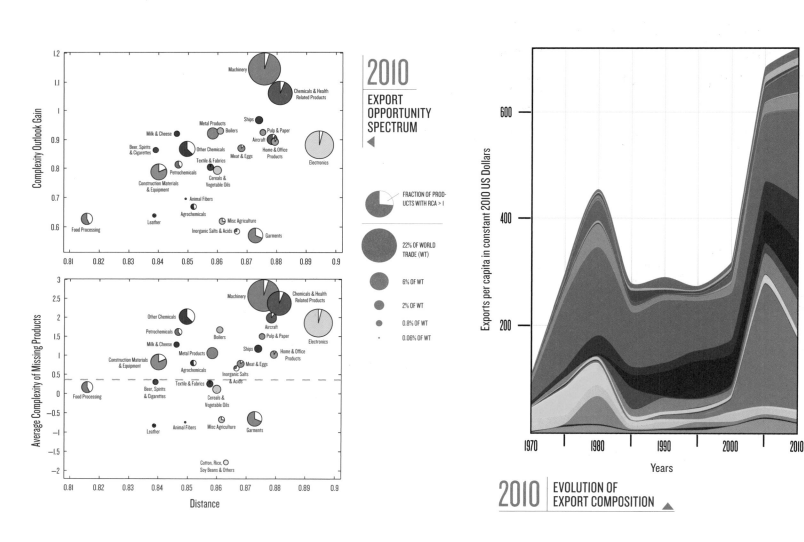

2010 EXPORT OPPORTUNITY SPECTRUM ◀

- FRACTION OF PRODUCTS WITH RCA > 1
- 22% OF WORLD TRADE (WT)
- 6% OF WT
- 2% OF WT
- 0.8% OF WT
- 0.06% OF WT

2010 EVOLUTION OF EXPORT COMPOSITION ▲

POPULATION ▸ 6 M / (91)
TOTAL EXPORTS ▸ USD 4.4 B / (95)

GDP ▸ USD 26 B / (88)
GDPᴘᴄ ▸ USD 4,370 / (76)

EXPORTS PER CAPITA ▸ USD 724 / (81)
EXPORTS AS SHARE OF GDP ▸ 17 % (96)

* Data are from 2010. Numbers indicate:
Value (World Ranking among 128 countries)
Region: Middle East and North Africa.

ELECTRONICS · MACHINERY · AIRCRAFT · BOILERS · SHIPS · METAL PRODUCTS · CONSTR. MATL. & EQPT. · HOME & OFFICE · PULP & PAPER · CHEMICALS & HEALTH · AGROCHEMICALS · OTHER CHEMICALS · INOR. SALTS & ACIDS · PETROCHEMICALS · LEATHER · MILK & CHEESE · ANIMAL FIBERS · MEAT & EGGS · FISH & SEAFOOD · TROPICAL AGRIC. · CEREALS & VEG. OILS · COTTON/RICE/SOY & OTHERS · TOBACCO · FRUIT · MISC. AGRICULTURE · NOT CLASSIFIED · TEXTILE & FABRICS · GARMENTS · FOOD PROCESSING · BEER/SPIRITS & CIGS. · PRECIOUS STONES · COAL · OIL · MINING

2010 | EXPORT TREEMAP ▾ TOTAL: $ 4,375,537,035

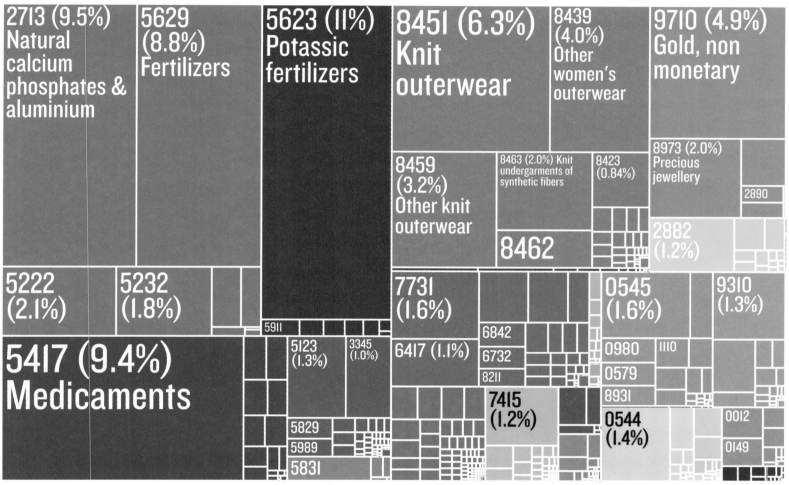

2713 (9.5%) Natural calcium phosphates & aluminium

5629 (8.8%) Fertilizers

5623 (11%) Potassic fertilizers

8451 (6.3%) Knit outerwear

8439 (4.0%) Other women's outerwear

9710 (4.9%) Gold, non monetary

8459 (3.2%) Other knit outerwear

8463 (2.0%) Knit undergarments of synthetic fibers

8423 (0.84%)

8973 (2.0%) Precious jewellery

2890

8462

2882 (1.2%)

5222 (2.1%)

5232 (1.8%)

7731 (1.6%)

0545 (1.6%)

9310 (1.3%)

5911

5417 (9.4%) Medicaments

5123 (1.3%)

3345 (1.0%)

6417 (1.1%)

6842

6732

8211

0980

0579

8931

1110

7415 (1.2%)

0544 (1.4%)

0012

0149

5829

5989

5831

* Numbers indicate SITC-4 Rev 2 codes which can be found in the Appendix. Percentages next to the product codes indicate proportion of the product in the exports of the country. Treemap headers show the total trade of the country.

2010 | EXPORT DESTINATIONS ▾ TOTAL: $ 4,375,537,035

13% Saudi Arabia

LBN (4.8%)

SYR (3.7%)

17% India

IDN

DZA (2.8%)

JPN

ARE (5.9%)

EGY (2.5%)

PSE

KOR

21% United States

ITA

ETH (2.1%)

NLD

GBR

2010 | IMPORT SOURCES ▾ TOTAL: $ 14,826,265,364

19% Saudi Arabia

EGY (6.2%)

ARE

10% China

BHR

IRQ

JPN (2.9%)

MYS

ISR

KWT

THA

DEU (6.0%)

ITA (3.3%)

USA (5.6%)

UKR

CHE

IRL

TUR

FRA

ESP

SWE

BRA

ARG

BEL

EAST ASIA & PACIFIC · EUROPE & CENTRAL ASIA · LATIN AMERICA & CARIBBEAN · MIDDLE EAST & NORTH AFRICA · NORTH AMERICA · SOUTH ASIA · SUB-SAHARAN AFRICA

KAZAKHSTAN

| ECONOMIC COMPLEXITY INDEX [2010] ▸ -0.562 (87) | COMPLEXITY OUTLOOK INDEX [2010] ▸ -0.671 (84) | EXPECTED GDPᴘᴄ GROWTH * ▸ 0.1% (114) |

*Expected annual average for the 2010-2020 period.

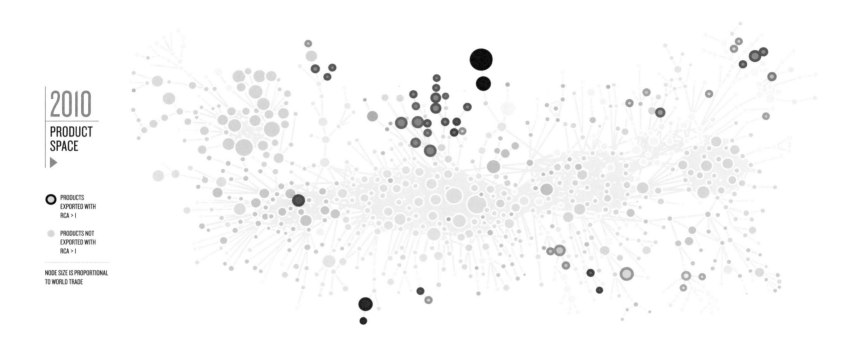

2010
PRODUCT SPACE
▶

○ PRODUCTS EXPORTED WITH RCA > 1

○ PRODUCTS NOT EXPORTED WITH RCA > 1

NODE SIZE IS PROPORTIONAL TO WORLD TRADE

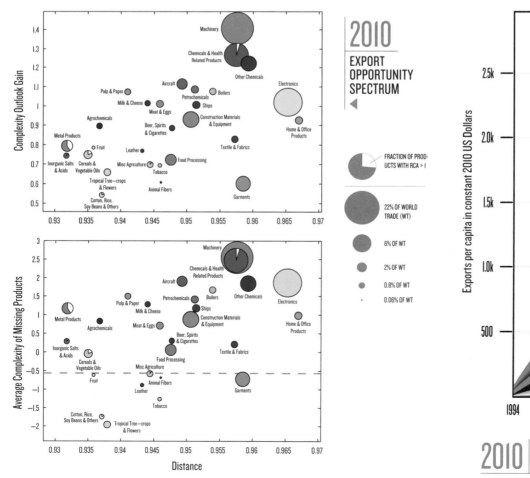

2010
EXPORT OPPORTUNITY SPECTRUM
◀

⊙ FRACTION OF PRODUCTS WITH RCA > 1

● 22% OF WORLD TRADE (WT)

● 6% OF WT

● 2% OF WT

● 0.8% OF WT

· 0.06% OF WT

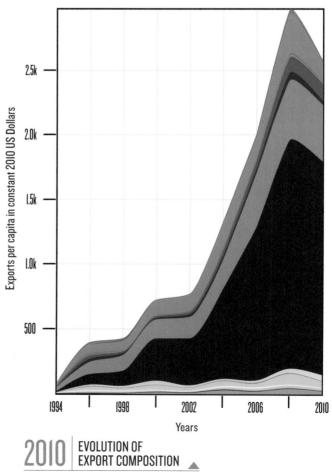

2010 | EVOLUTION OF EXPORT COMPOSITION ▲

POPULATION ‣ 16 M / (55)	GDP ‣ USD 148 B / (51)	EXPORTS PER CAPITA ‣ USD 2,577 / (45)	* Data are from 2010. Numbers indicate:
TOTAL EXPORTS ‣ USD 42 B / (54)	GDPᴾᶜ ‣ USD 9,070 / (51)	EXPORTS AS SHARE OF GDP ‣ 28 % (54)	Value (World Ranking among 128 countries) Region: Eastern Europe and Central Asia.

ELECTRONICS · MACHINERY · AIRCRAFT · BOILERS · SHIPS · METAL PRODUCTS · CONSTR. MATL. & EQPT. · HOME & OFFICE · PULP & PAPER · CHEMICALS & HEALTH · AGROCHEMICALS · OTHER CHEMICALS · INOR. SALTS & ACIDS · PETROCHEMICALS · LEATHER · MILK & CHEESE · ANIMAL FIBERS · MEAT & EGGS · FISH & SEAFOOD · TROPICAL AGRIC. · CEREALS & VEG. OILS · COTTON/RICE/SOY & OTHERS · TOBACCO · FRUIT · MISC. AGRICULTURE · NOT CLASSIFIED · TEXTILE & FABRICS · GARMENTS · FOOD PROCESSING · BEER/SPIRITS & CIGS. · PRECIOUS STONES · COAL · OIL · MINING

2010 | EXPORT TREEMAP ▼ TOTAL: $ 42,068,475,345

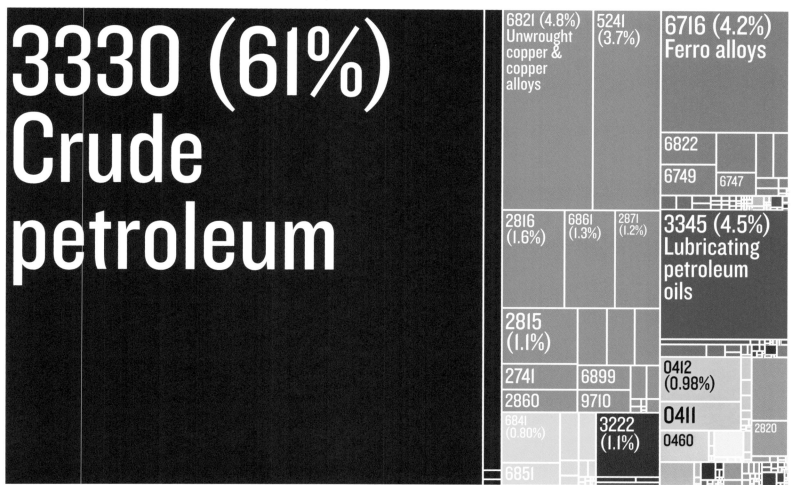

3330 (61%) Crude petroleum

6821 (4.8%) Unwrought copper & copper alloys

5241 (3.7%)

6716 (4.2%) Ferro alloys

6822

6749 · 6747

2816 (1.6%) · 6861 (1.3%) · 2871 (1.2%)

3345 (4.5%) Lubricating petroleum oils

2815 (1.1%)

2741 · 6899

2860 · 9710

0412 (0.98%)

0411 · 0460 · 2820

6841 (0.80%)

3222 (1.1%)

6851

*Numbers indicate SITC-4 Rev 2 codes which can be found in the Appendix. Percentages next to the product codes indicate proportion of the product in the exports of the country. Treemap headers show the total trade of the country.

2010 | EXPORT DESTINATIONS ▼ TOTAL: $ 42,068,475,345

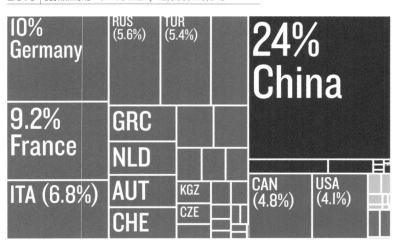

10% Germany · RUS (5.6%) · TUR (5.4%) · 24% China

9.2% France · GRC · NLD · AUT · KGZ · CZE · CAN (4.8%) · USA (4.1%)

ITA (6.8%) · CHE

2010 | IMPORT SOURCES ▼ TOTAL: $ 24,564,542,865

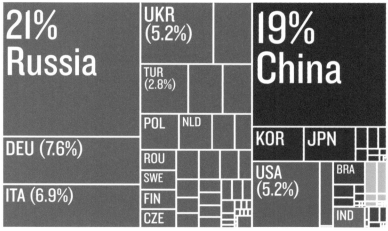

21% Russia · UKR (5.2%) · TUR (2.8%) · 19% China

POL · NLD

DEU (7.6%) · ROU · KOR · JPN

SWE · USA (5.2%) · BRA

ITA (6.9%) · FIN · IND

CZE

EAST ASIA & PACIFIC · EUROPE & CENTRAL ASIA · LATIN AMERICA & CARIBBEAN · MIDDLE EAST & NORTH AFRICA · NORTH AMERICA · SOUTH ASIA · SUB-SAHARAN AFRICA

KENYA

ECONOMIC COMPLEXITY INDEX [2010] ▸ -0.503 (85) | **COMPLEXITY OUTLOOK INDEX [2010] ▸ 0.272 (50)** | **EXPECTED GDPᴘᴄ GROWTH * ▸ 3.4% (13)**

Expected annual average for the 2010-2020 period.

2010
PRODUCT SPACE ▶

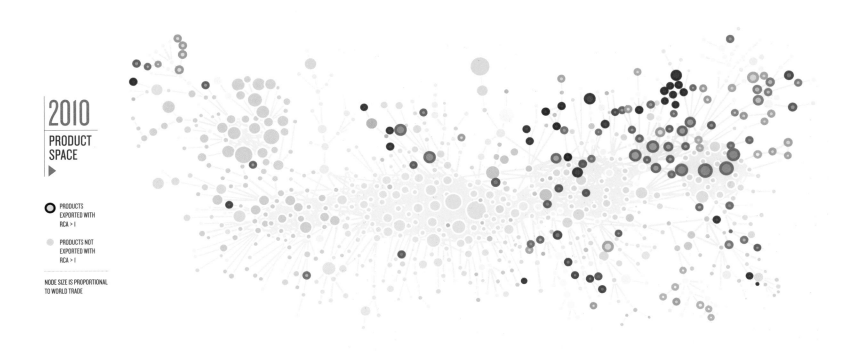

○ PRODUCTS EXPORTED WITH RCA > 1

○ PRODUCTS NOT EXPORTED WITH RCA > 1

NODE SIZE IS PROPORTIONAL TO WORLD TRADE

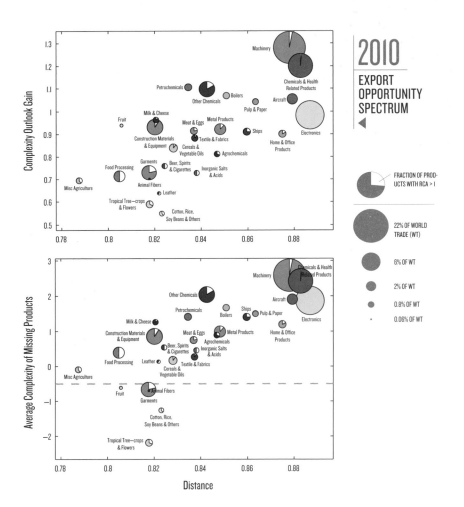

2010
EXPORT OPPORTUNITY SPECTRUM ◀

◐ FRACTION OF PRODUCTS WITH RCA > 1

● 22% OF WORLD TRADE (WT)

● 6% OF WT

● 2% OF WT

● 0.8% OF WT

· 0.06% OF WT

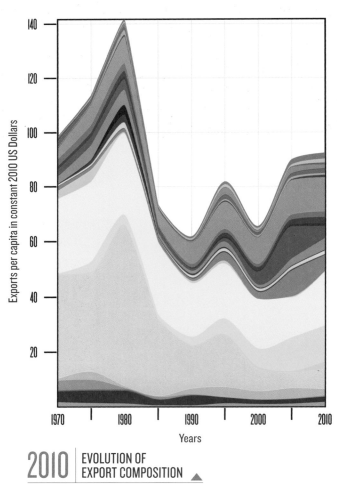

2010
EVOLUTION OF EXPORT COMPOSITION ▲

POPULATION ‣ 41 M / (29)	GDP ‣ USD 32 B / (83)	EXPORTS PER CAPITA ‣ USD 92 / (122)	* Data are from 2010. Numbers indicate:
TOTAL EXPORTS ‣ USD 3.7 B / (99)	GDPᴘᴄ ‣ USD 795 / (117)	EXPORTS AS SHARE OF GDP ‣ 12 % / (115)	Value (World Ranking among 128 countries) Region: Sub-Saharan Africa.

ELECTRONICS · MACHINERY · AIRCRAFT · BOILERS · SHIPS · METAL PRODUCTS · CONSTR. MATL. & EQPT. · HOME & OFFICE · PULP & PAPER · CHEMICALS & HEALTH · AGROCHEMICALS · OTHER CHEMICALS · INOR. SALTS & ACIDS · PETROCHEMICALS · LEATHER · MILK & CHEESE · ANIMAL FIBERS · MEAT & EGGS · FISH & SEAFOOD · TROPICAL AGRIC. · CEREALS & VEG. OILS · COTTON/RICE/SOY & OTHERS · TOBACCO · FRUIT · MISC. AGRICULTURE · NOT CLASSIFIED · TEXTILE & FABRICS · GARMENTS · FOOD PROCESSING · BEER/SPIRITS & CIGS. · PRECIOUS STONES · COAL · OIL · MINING

2010 EXPORT TREEMAP ▼ TOTAL: $ 3,745,974,311

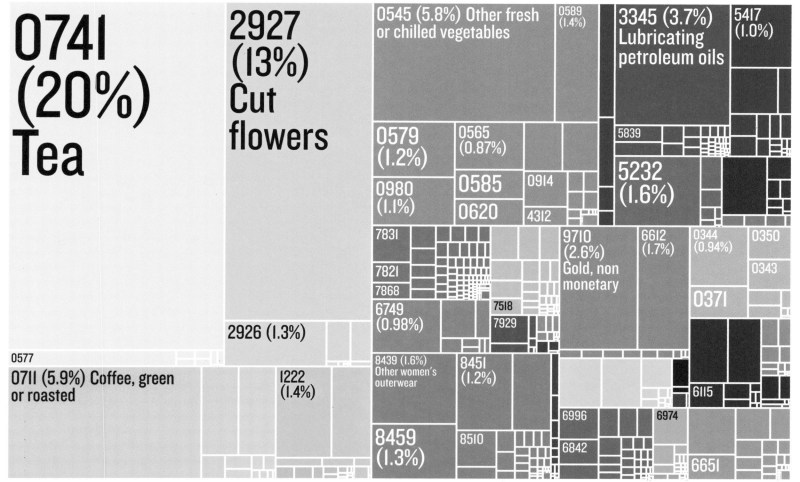

0741 (20%) Tea

2927 (13%) Cut flowers

2926 (1.3%)

0577

0711 (5.9%) Coffee, green or roasted

1222 (1.4%)

0545 (5.8%) Other fresh or chilled vegetables

0589 (1.4%)

0579 (1.2%)

0565 (0.87%)

0980 (1.1%)

0585

0914

0620

4312

7831

7821

7868

6749 (0.98%)

7518

7929

8439 (1.6%) Other women's outerwear

8451 (1.2%)

8459 (1.3%)

8510

9710 (2.6%) Gold, non monetary

6612 (1.7%)

6996

6842

6974

3345 (3.7%) Lubricating petroleum oils

5417 (1.0%)

5839

5232 (1.6%)

0344 (0.94%)

0350

0343

0371

6115

6651

* Numbers indicate SITC-4 Rev 2 codes which can be found in the Appendix. Percentages next to the product codes indicate proportion of the product in the exports of the country. Treemap headers show the total trade of the country.

2010 EXPORT DESTINATIONS ▼ TOTAL: $ 3,745,974,311

12% United Kingdom

NLD (11%)

12% Uganda

DEU (3.0%)

ITA

BEL

FIN

KAZ

TZA (6.7%)

ETH

ZWE

EGY (5.0%)

PAK (5.2%)

ARE (4.0%)

USA (7.8%)

SGP

HKG

JPN

CHN

2010 IMPORT SOURCES ▼ TOTAL: $ 10,912,869,462

12% China

JPN (6.2%)

GBR (5.2%)

DEU

FRA

NLD

FIN

ITA

BEL

IRL

SWE

SGP (3.4%)

KOR (2.0%)

THA

12% United Arab Emirates

SAU (3.4%)

ZAF (6.2%)

IND (11%)

USA (4.0%)

BRA

EAST ASIA & PACIFIC · EUROPE & CENTRAL ASIA · LATIN AMERICA & CARIBBEAN · MIDDLE EAST & NORTH AFRICA · NORTH AMERICA · SOUTH ASIA · SUB-SAHARAN AFRICA

KOREA, REPUBLIC

ECONOMIC COMPLEXITY INDEX [2010] ▸ 1.691 (6) | COMPLEXITY OUTLOOK INDEX [2010] ▸ 0.948 (27) | EXPECTED GDPᴘᴄ GROWTH * ▸ 3.3% (16)

*Expected annual average for the 2010-2020 period.

2010 PRODUCT SPACE ▶

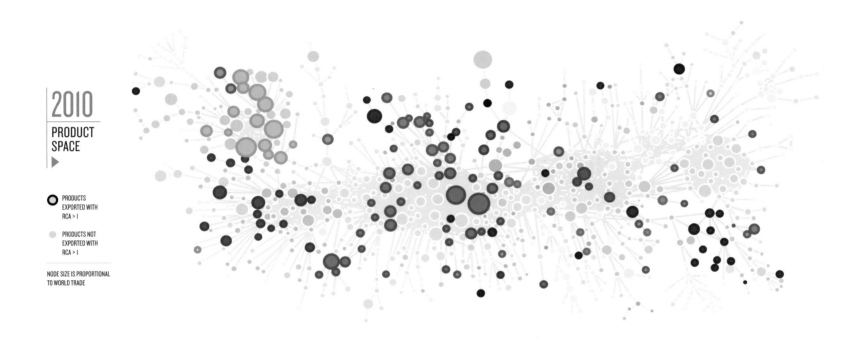

○ PRODUCTS EXPORTED WITH RCA > 1

● PRODUCTS NOT EXPORTED WITH RCA > 1

NODE SIZE IS PROPORTIONAL TO WORLD TRADE

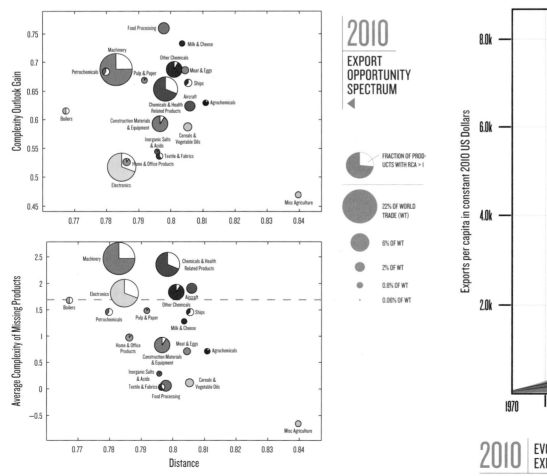

2010 EXPORT OPPORTUNITY SPECTRUM ◀

◑ FRACTION OF PRODUCTS WITH RCA > 1

● 22% OF WORLD TRADE (WT)

● 6% OF WT

● 2% OF WT

● 0.8% OF WT

• 0.06% OF WT

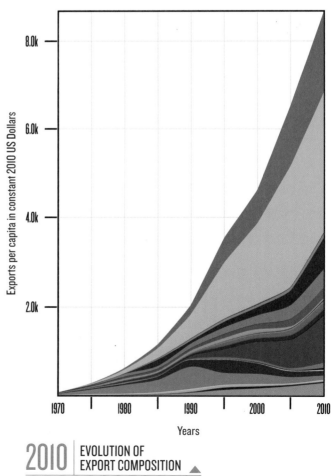

2010 | EVOLUTION OF EXPORT COMPOSITION ▲

POPULATION ▸ 49 M / (24)	GDP ▸ USD 1 T / (15)	EXPORTS PER CAPITA ▸ USD 8,689 / (22)	* Data are from 2010. Numbers indicate:
TOTAL EXPORTS ▸ USD 429 B / (6)	GDPᴘᴄ ▸ USD 20,540 / (30)	EXPORTS AS SHARE OF GDP ▸ 42 % / (30)	Value (World Ranking among 128 countries) Region: East Asia and Pacific.

ELECTRONICS · MACHINERY · AIRCRAFT · BOILERS · SHIPS · METAL PRODUCTS · CONSTR. MATL. & EQPT. · HOME & OFFICE · PULP & PAPER · CHEMICALS & HEALTH · AGROCHEMICALS · OTHER CHEMICALS · INOR. SALTS & ACIDS · PETROCHEMICALS · LEATHER · MILK & CHEESE · ANIMAL FIBERS · MEAT & EGGS · FISH & SEAFOOD · TROPICAL AGRIC. · CEREALS & VEG. OILS · COTTON/RICE/SOY & OTHERS · TOBACCO · FRUIT · MISC. AGRICULTURE · NOT CLASSIFIED · TEXTILE & FABRICS · GARMENTS · FOOD PROCESSING · BEER/SPIRITS & CIGS. · PRECIOUS STONES · COAL · OIL · MINING

2010 EXPORT TREEMAP ▼ TOTAL: $ 429,341,500,538

7764 (13%) Electronic microcircuits

8710 (4.8%) Optical instruments

7810 (6.3%) Cars

7849 (2.6%) Other vehicle parts

7284 (0.96%)

7721

7234 (0.66%)

6251 · 7162

7247 · 7442

7239 · 7493

7821 · 7783

7416 · 6954

7649 (4.6%) Parts of telecom & sound equipment

7599 (2.0%) Parts of registers & calculating machines

7763 (0.82%)

7781 (0.71%)

7788 (0.87%)

7768 (0.71%)

7518

7522

7611 (0.86%)

7525

7641

7643 (3.4%) Television & radio transmitters

7932 (5.9%) Ships & boats

7938 (1.8%)

6749 (1.1%)

6746 (0.85%)

6822 (0.65%)

7711

6770

3345 (6.0%) Lubricating petroleum oils

5138

5831

5832

9310 (0.92%) · 5833 (0.92%)

5823 (0.80%)

6911

6552

5112 (0.86%)

5148

5121

*Numbers indicate SITC-4 Rev 2 codes which can be found in the Appendix. Percentages next to the product codes indicate proportion of the product in the exports of the country. Treemap headers show the total trade of the country.

2010 EXPORT DESTINATIONS ▼ TOTAL: $ 429,341,500,538

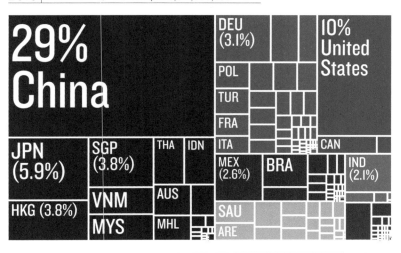

29% China

JPN (5.9%) · SGP (3.8%) · HKG (3.8%) · VNM · MYS · THA · IDN · AUS · MHL

DEU (3.1%) · POL · TUR · FRA · ITA · MEX (2.6%) · SAU · ARE · BRA

10% United States · CAN · IND (2.1%)

2010 IMPORT SOURCES ▼ TOTAL: $ 369,075,560,733

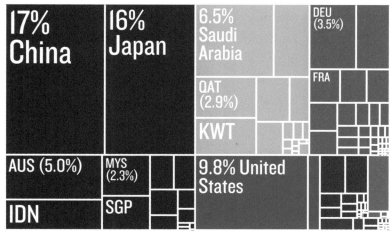

17% China · **16% Japan** · AUS (5.0%) · MYS (2.3%) · IDN · SGP

6.5% Saudi Arabia · QAT (2.9%) · KWT · 9.8% United States

DEU (3.5%) · FRA

EAST ASIA & PACIFIC · EUROPE & CENTRAL ASIA · LATIN AMERICA & CARIBBEAN · MIDDLE EAST & NORTH AFRICA · NORTH AMERICA · SOUTH ASIA · SUB-SAHARAN AFRICA

KUWAIT

| ECONOMIC COMPLEXITY INDEX [2010] ▸ -0.033 (64) | COMPLEXITY OUTLOOK INDEX [2010] ▸ -0.814 (92) | EXPECTED GDPᴘᴄ GROWTH * ▸ -1.0% (124) |

*Expected annual average for the 2010-2020 period.

2010
PRODUCT SPACE ▶

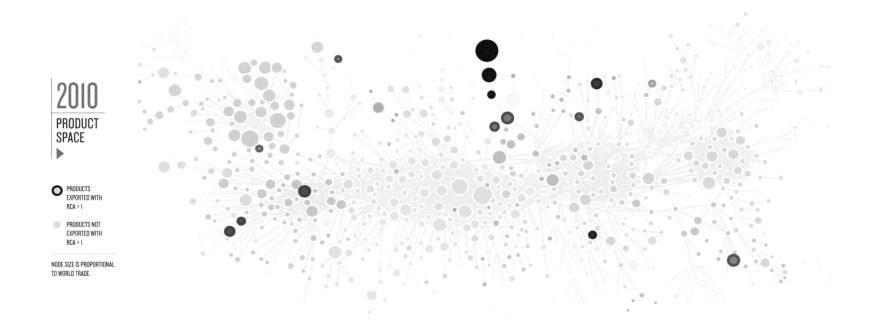

○ PRODUCTS EXPORTED WITH RCA > 1

○ PRODUCTS NOT EXPORTED WITH RCA > 1

NODE SIZE IS PROPORTIONAL TO WORLD TRADE

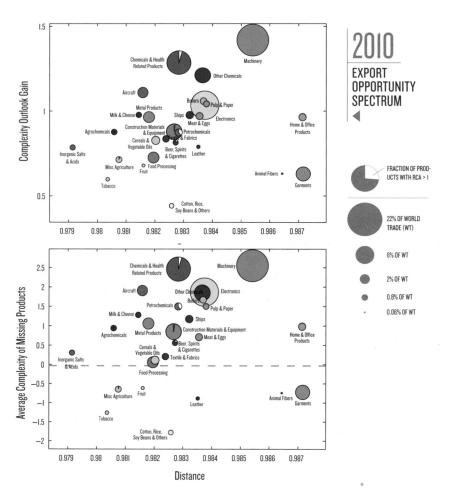

2010
EXPORT OPPORTUNITY SPECTRUM ◀

FRACTION OF PRODUCTS WITH RCA > 1

22% OF WORLD TRADE (WT)

6% OF WT

2% OF WT

0.8% OF WT

0.06% OF WT

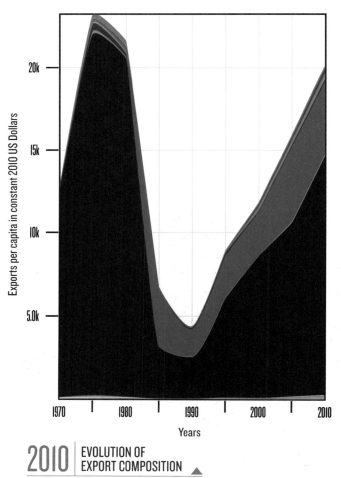

2010 | EVOLUTION OF EXPORT COMPOSITION ▲

POPULATION ▸ 2.7 M / (117)
TOTAL EXPORTS ▸ USD 55 B / (45)

GDP ▸ USD 124 B / (56)
GDPₚc ▸ USD 45,437 / (11)

EXPORTS PER CAPITA ▸ USD 20,243 / (9)
EXPORTS AS SHARE OF GDP ▸ 45 % (28)

* Data are from 2010. Numbers indicate:
Value (World Ranking among 128 countries)
Region: Middle East and North Africa.

ELECTRONICS · MACHINERY · AIRCRAFT · BOILERS · SHIPS · METAL PRODUCTS · CONSTR. MATL. & EQPT. · HOME & OFFICE · PULP & PAPER · CHEMICALS & HEALTH · AGROCHEMICALS · OTHER CHEMICALS · INOR. SALTS & ACIDS · PETROCHEMICALS · LEATHER · MILK & CHEESE · ANIMAL FIBERS · MEAT & EGGS · FISH & SEAFOOD · TROPICAL AGRIC. · CEREALS & VEG. OILS · COTTON/RICE/SOY & OTHERS · TOBACCO · FRUIT · MISC. AGRICULTURE · NOT CLASSIFIED · TEXTILE & FABRICS · GARMENTS · FOOD PROCESSING · BEER/SPIRITS & CIGS. · PRECIOUS STONES · COAL · OIL · MINING

2010 | EXPORT TREEMAP ▾ TOTAL: $ 55,400,629,620

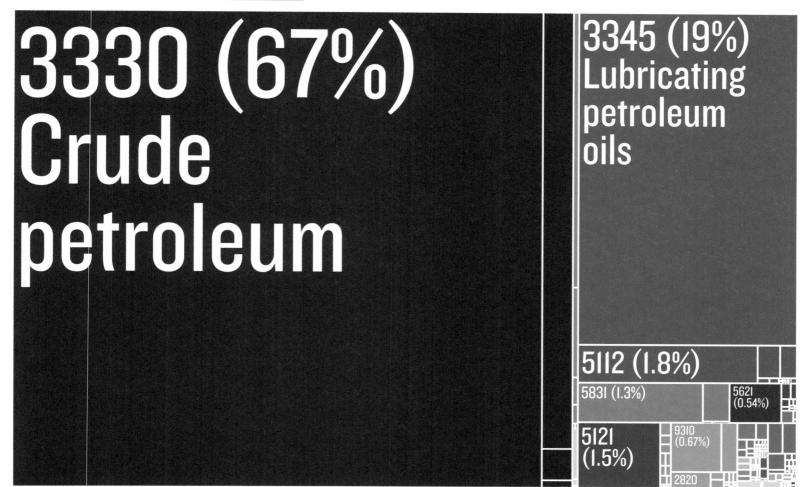

3330 (67%) Crude petroleum

3345 (19%) Lubricating petroleum oils

5112 (1.8%)

5831 (1.3%)

5621 (0.54%)

5121 (1.5%)

9310 (0.67%)

2820

* Numbers indicate SITC-4 Rev 2 codes which can be found in the Appendix. Percentages next to the product codes indicate proportion of the product in the exports of the country. Treemap headers show the total trade of the country.

2010 | EXPORT DESTINATIONS ▾ TOTAL: $55,400.629,620

18% Korea, Rep.

17% Japan

15% India

USA (9.1%)

PAK

11% China

SGP (4.3%)

NLD (3.8%)

EGY (2.5%)

IDN

GBR

ARE

ZMB

2010 | IMPORT SOURCES ▾ TOTAL: $18,677,712,644

8.4% Germany

GBR (4.4%)

15% United States

IND (8.8%)

ITA (4.9%)

FRA (3.4%)

BEL

ESP

CHE

RUS

CHN (9.7%)

KOR (5.6%)

JPN (7.6%)

THA

ARE (7.3%)

MYS

EAST ASIA & PACIFIC · EUROPE & CENTRAL ASIA · LATIN AMERICA & CARIBBEAN · MIDDLE EAST & NORTH AFRICA · NORTH AMERICA · SOUTH ASIA · SUB-SAHARAN AFRICA

KYRGYZ REPUBLIC

ECONOMIC COMPLEXITY INDEX [2010] ▸ -0.532 (86) | COMPLEXITY OUTLOOK INDEX [2010] ▸ -0.229 (68) | EXPECTED GDPᴘᴄ GROWTH * ▸ 2.9% (27)

*Expected annual average for the 2010-2020 period.

2010
PRODUCT SPACE ▶

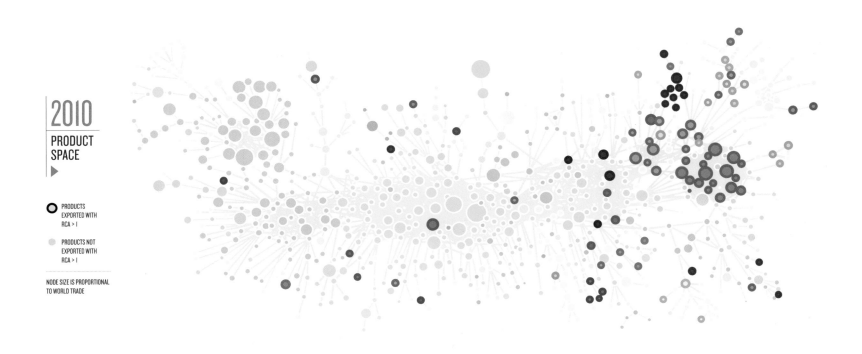

○ PRODUCTS EXPORTED WITH RCA > I

○ PRODUCTS NOT EXPORTED WITH RCA > I

NODE SIZE IS PROPORTIONAL TO WORLD TRADE

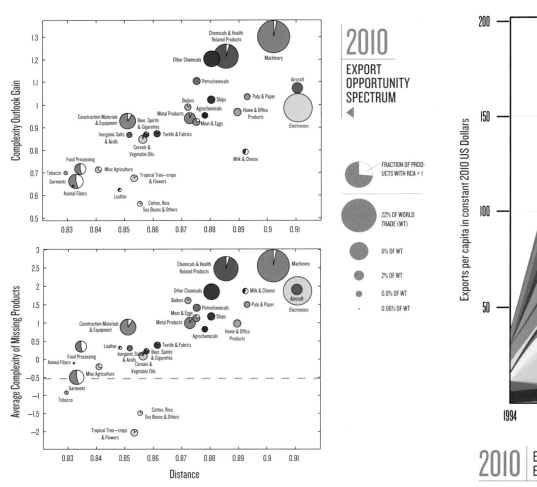

2010
EXPORT OPPORTUNITY SPECTRUM ◀

◔ FRACTION OF PROD-UCTS WITH RCA > I

⬤ 22% OF WORLD TRADE (WT)

⬤ 6% OF WT

● 2% OF WT

• 0.8% OF WT

· 0.06% OF WT

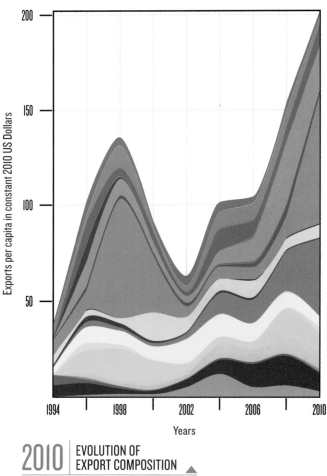

2010 | EVOLUTION OF EXPORT COMPOSITION ▲

POPULATION ▸ 5.4 M / (94)
TOTAL EXPORTS ▸ USD 1.1 B / (121)

GDP ▸ USD 4.8 B / (125)
GDPₚ𝒸 ▸ USD 880 / (114)

EXPORTS PER CAPITA ▸ USD 202 / (109)
EXPORTS AS SHARE OF GDP ▸ 23 % (73)

* Data are from 2010. Numbers indicate:
Value (World Ranking among 128 countries)
Region: Eastern Europe and Central Asia.

ELECTRONICS · MACHINERY · AIRCRAFT · BOILERS · SHIPS · METAL PRODUCTS · CONSTR. MATL. & EQPT. · HOME & OFFICE · PULP & PAPER · CHEMICALS & HEALTH · AGROCHEMICALS · OTHER CHEMICALS · INOR. SALTS & ACIDS · PETROCHEMICALS · LEATHER · MILK & CHEESE · ANIMAL FIBERS · MEAT & EGGS · FISH & SEAFOOD · TROPICAL AGRIC. · CEREALS & VEG. OILS · COTTON/RICE/SOY & OTHERS · TOBACCO · FRUIT · MISC. AGRICULTURE · NOT CLASSIFIED · TEXTILE & FABRICS · GARMENTS · FOOD PROCESSING · BEER/SPIRITS & CIGS. · PRECIOUS STONES · COAL · OIL · MINING

2010 EXPORT TREEMAP ▾ TOTAL: $ 1,098,720,992

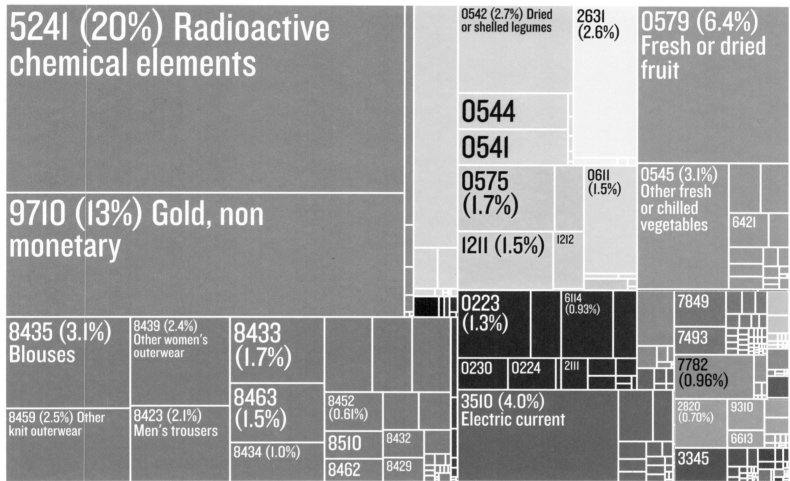

* Numbers indicate SITC-4 Rev 2 codes which can be found in the Appendix. Percentages next to the product codes indicate proportion of the product in the exports of the country. Treemap headers show the total trade of the country.

2010 EXPORT DESTINATIONS ▾ TOTAL: $1,098,720,992

32% Russia
20% France
14% Kazakhstan
13% United Arab Emirates
GBR (6.4%)
CHN (6.0%)
BLR

2010 IMPORT SOURCES ▾ TOTAL: $ 2,954,637,787

33% Russia
21% China
KAZ (12%)
POL
BEL
JPN
KOR
USA (5.9%)

EAST ASIA & PACIFIC | EUROPE & CENTRAL ASIA | LATIN AMERICA & CARIBBEAN | MIDDLE EAST & NORTH AFRICA | NORTH AMERICA | SOUTH ASIA | SUB-SAHARAN AFRICA

LAO PDR

ECONOMIC COMPLEXITY INDEX [2010] ▸ -0.817 (98) | COMPLEXITY OUTLOOK INDEX [2010] ▸ -0.681 (86) | EXPECTED GDPᴘᴄ GROWTH * ▸ 2.0% (62)

*Expected annual average for the 2010-2020 period.

2010 PRODUCT SPACE ▶

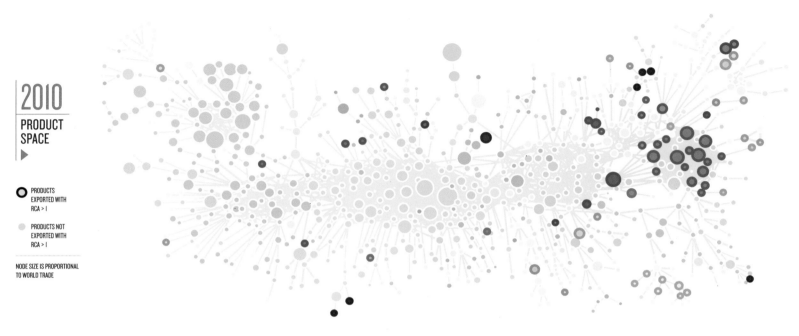

- ◉ PRODUCTS EXPORTED WITH RCA > 1
- ● PRODUCTS NOT EXPORTED WITH RCA > 1

NODE SIZE IS PROPORTIONAL TO WORLD TRADE

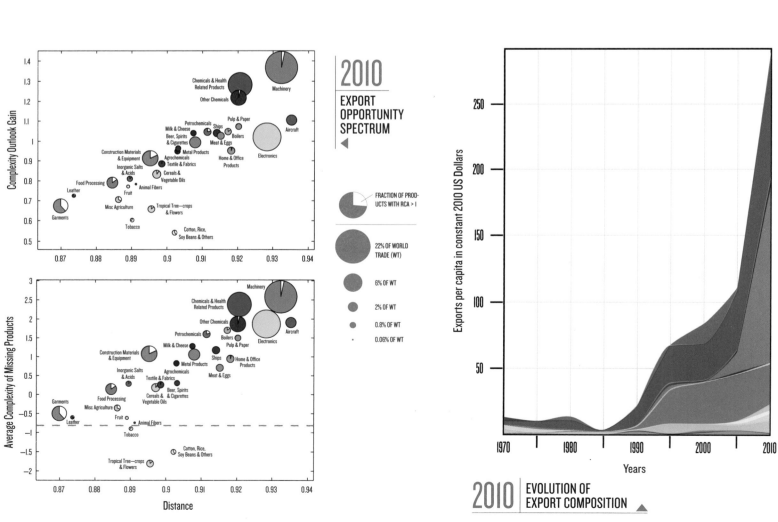

2010 EXPORT OPPORTUNITY SPECTRUM ◀

FRACTION OF PRODUCTS WITH RCA > 1

- 22% OF WORLD TRADE (WT)
- 6% OF WT
- 2% OF WT
- 0.8% OF WT
- 0.06% OF WT

2010 EVOLUTION OF EXPORT COMPOSITION ▲

POPULATION ▸ 6.2 M / (89)	GDP ▸ USD 7.2 B / (119)	EXPORTS PER CAPITA ▸ USD 292 / (106)	* Data are from 2010. Numbers indicate:
TOTAL EXPORTS ▸ USD 1.8 B / (115)	GDPPc ▸ USD 1,158 / (108)	EXPORTS AS SHARE OF GDP ▸ 25 % (63)	Value (World Ranking among 128 countries) Region: East Asia and Pacific.

ELECTRONICS · MACHINERY · AIRCRAFT · BOILERS · SHIPS · METAL PRODUCTS · CONSTR. MATL. & EQPT. · HOME & OFFICE · PULP & PAPER · CHEMICALS & HEALTH · AGROCHEMICALS · OTHER CHEMICALS · INOR. SALTS & ACIDS · PETROCHEMICALS · LEATHER · MILK & CHEESE · ANIMAL FIBERS · MEAT & EGGS · FISH & SEAFOOD · TROPICAL AGRIC. · CEREALS & VEG. OILS · COTTON/RICE/SOY & OTHERS · TOBACCO · FRUIT · MISC. AGRICULTURE · NOT CLASSIFIED · TEXTILE & FABRICS · GARMENTS · FOOD PROCESSING · BEER/SPIRITS & CIGS. · PRECIOUS STONES · COAL · OIL · MINING

2010 EXPORT TREEMAP ▾ TOTAL: $ 1,813,066,968

* Numbers indicate SITC-4 Rev 2 codes which can be found in the Appendix. Percentages next to the product codes indicate proportion of the product in the exports of the country. Treemap headers show the total trade of the country.

2010 EXPORT DESTINATIONS ▾ TOTAL: $ 1,813,066,968

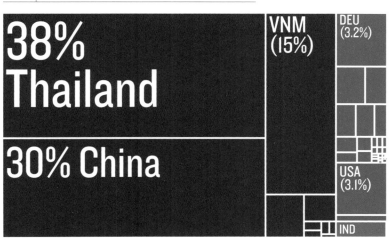

2010 IMPORT SOURCES ▾ TOTAL: $ 3,221,838,101

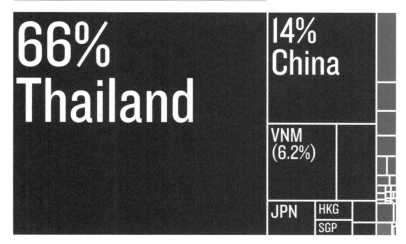

EAST ASIA & PACIFIC · EUROPE & CENTRAL ASIA · LATIN AMERICA & CARIBBEAN · MIDDLE EAST & NORTH AFRICA · NORTH AMERICA · SOUTH ASIA · SUB-SAHARAN AFRICA

LATVIA

ECONOMIC COMPLEXITY INDEX [2010] ▸ 0.674 (36) | COMPLEXITY OUTLOOK INDEX [2010] ▸ 0.994 (24) | EXPECTED GDPᴘᴄ GROWTH * ▸ 2.7% (37)

*Expected annual average for the 2010-2020 period.

2010 PRODUCT SPACE ▶

○ PRODUCTS EXPORTED WITH RCA > 1

○ PRODUCTS NOT EXPORTED WITH RCA > 1

NODE SIZE IS PROPORTIONAL TO WORLD TRADE

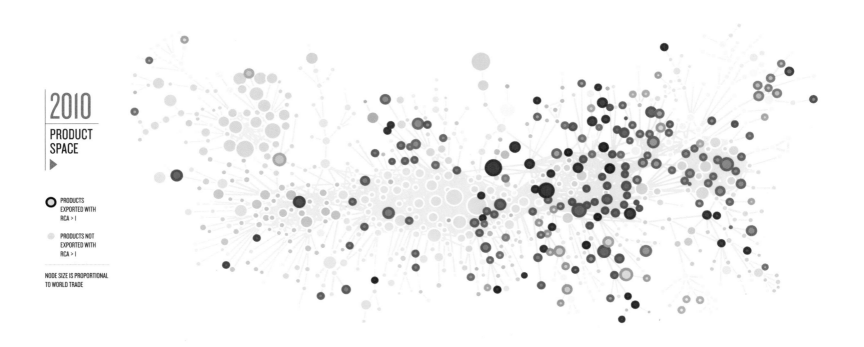

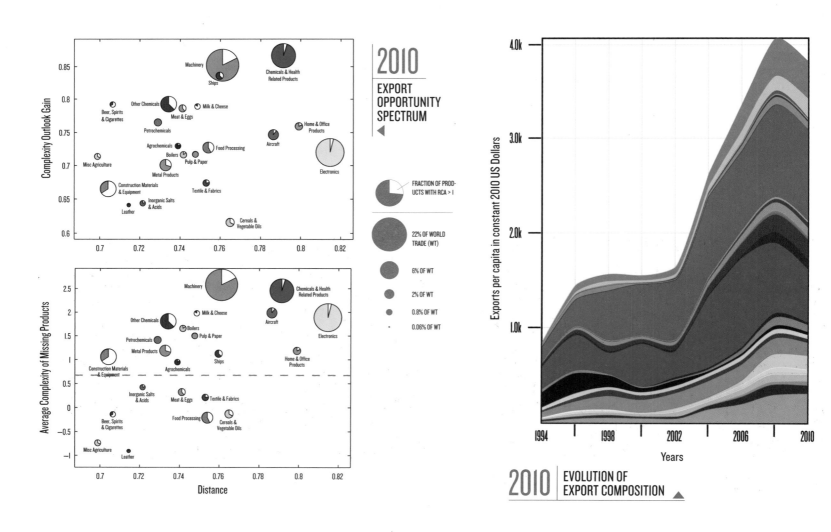

2010 EXPORT OPPORTUNITY SPECTRUM ◀

○ FRACTION OF PRODUCTS WITH RCA > 1

● 22% OF WORLD TRADE (WT)

● 6% OF WT

● 2% OF WT

● 0.8% OF WT

· 0.06% OF WT

2010 | EVOLUTION OF EXPORT COMPOSITION ▲

POPULATION ▸ 2.2 M / (120)
TOTAL EXPORTS ▸ USD 8.6 B / (78)

GDP ▸ USD 24 B / (89)
GDPᴘᴄ ▸ USD 10,723 / (44)

EXPORTS PER CAPITA ▸ USD 3,821 / (39)
EXPORTS AS SHARE OF GDP ▸ 36 % (40)

* Data are from 2010. Numbers indicate:
Value (World Ranking among 128 countries)
Region: Eastern Europe and Central Asia.

ELECTRONICS | MACHINERY | AIRCRAFT | BOILERS | SHIPS | METAL PRODUCTS | CONSTR. MATL. & EQPT. | HOME & OFFICE | PULP & PAPER | CHEMICALS & HEALTH | AGROCHEMICALS | OTHER CHEMICALS | INOR. SALTS & ACIDS | PETROCHEMICALS | LEATHER | MILK & CHEESE | ANIMAL FIBERS | MEAT & EGGS | FISH & SEAFOOD | TROPICAL AGRIC. | CEREALS & VEG. OILS | COTTON/RICE/SOY & OTHERS | TOBACCO | FRUIT | MISC. AGRICULTURE | NOT CLASSIFIED | TEXTILE & FABRICS | GARMENTS | FOOD PROCESSING | BEER/SPIRITS & CIGS. | PRECIOUS STONES | COAL | OIL | MINING

2010 EXPORT TREEMAP ▾ TOTAL: $ 8,555,460,872

2482 (5.3%) Worked wood of coniferous

2460 (1.9%)

6343 (1.7%)

6342 (1.6%)

2471 (1.5%)

7810 (1.7%) Cars

6822

9310 (4.7%) Unclassified transactions

7436
7239
7919
7821
7234
6251

6732 (2.1%)

6353 (1.2%)

6911 (0.82%)

6359 (0.73%)

7721

7849

3224 (1.2%)

8219 (1.2%)

6416

8211

7284

2820 (1.1%)

2472 (2.0%)

2450

7731

7611 (1.8%) Color T.V.

7643 (0.73%)

8841

3510 (1.1%)

6633

6618

7599

7144

6997

7522

3345 (13%) Lubricating petroleum oils

5417 (2.5%) Medicaments

5542

0412 (2.2%) Other wheat, unmilled

0411

6841

8939

2226

5623 (1.6%)

0223 (0.81%)

0240

6519

6514

5629

0224

5621

0371 (0.79%)

0342

0484

8931

1124 (0.96%)

0980

1110

6421

0341

* Numbers indicate SITC-4 Rev 2 codes which can be found in the Appendix. Percentages next to the product codes indicate proportion of the product in the exports of the country. Treemap headers show the total trade of the country.

2010 EXPORT DESTINATIONS ▾ TOTAL: $ 8,555,460,872

15% Lithuania

RUS (7.8%)

EST (7.6%)

GBR (6.3%)

EGY

DEU (8.7%)

DNK (3.4%)

IND

FIN (3.3%)

BLR

SWE (8.7%)

NOR (3.1%)

ESP

TUR

BEL

KAZ

2010 IMPORT SOURCES ▾ TOTAL: $ 10,222,142,207

17% Lithuania

7.8% Poland

7.1% Estonia

FIN (4.7%)

NLD (3.8%)

ITA (3.3%)

DEU (11%)

SWE (3.4%)

BEL

HUN

RUS (10%)

BLR (3.4%)

GBR

ESP

UKR

CHE

AUT

EAST ASIA & PACIFIC | EUROPE & CENTRAL ASIA | LATIN AMERICA & CARIBBEAN | MIDDLE EAST & NORTH AFRICA | NORTH AMERICA | SOUTH ASIA | SUB-SAHARAN AFRICA

LEBANON

| ECONOMIC COMPLEXITY INDEX [2010] ▸ 0.331 (47) | COMPLEXITY OUTLOOK INDEX [2010] ▸ 1.109 (17) | EXPECTED GDPᴘᴄ GROWTH * ▸ 2.5% (45) |

*Expected annual average for the 2010-2020 period.

2010 PRODUCT SPACE ▶

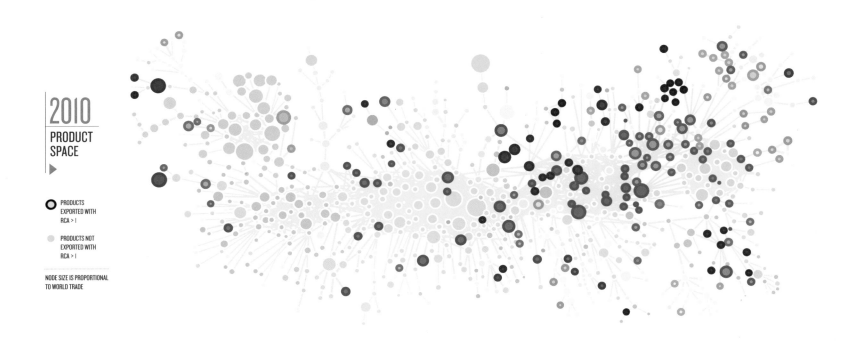

○ PRODUCTS EXPORTED WITH RCA > 1

○ PRODUCTS NOT EXPORTED WITH RCA > 1

NODE SIZE IS PROPORTIONAL TO WORLD TRADE

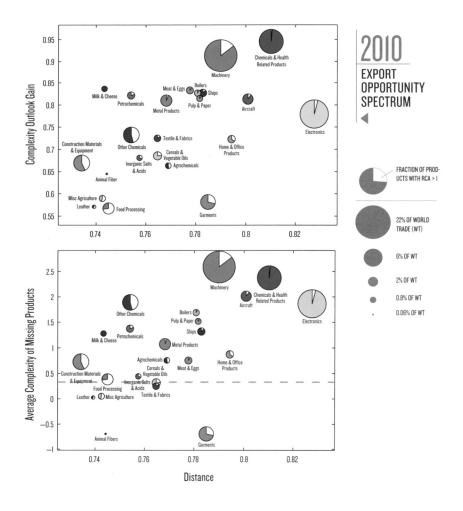

2010 EXPORT OPPORTUNITY SPECTRUM ◀

⊙ FRACTION OF PRODUCTS WITH RCA > 1

22% OF WORLD TRADE (WT)

6% OF WT

2% OF WT

0.8% OF WT

0.06% OF WT

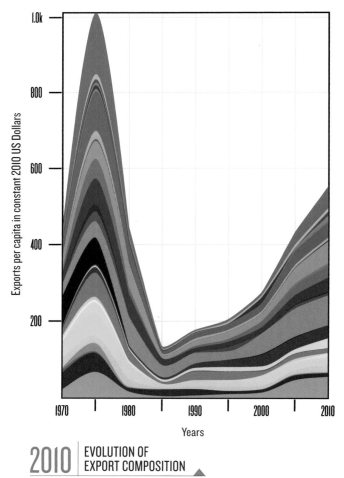

2010 EVOLUTION OF EXPORT COMPOSITION ▲

POPULATION ▸ 4.2 M / (105)	GDP ▸ USD 39 B / (79)	EXPORTS PER CAPITA ▸ USD 554 / (86)
TOTAL EXPORTS ▸ USD 2.3 B / (109)	GDPᴘᴄ ▸ USD 9,227 / (48)	EXPORTS AS SHARE OF GDP ▸ 6 % / (125)

* Data are from 2010. Numbers indicate:
Value (World Ranking among 128 countries)
Region: Middle East and North Africa.

ELECTRONICS — MACHINERY — AIRCRAFT — BOILERS — SHIPS — METAL PRODUCTS — CONSTR. MATL. & EQPT. — HOME & OFFICE — PULP & PAPER — CHEMICALS & HEALTH — AGROCHEMICALS — OTHER CHEMICALS — INOR. SALTS & ACIDS — PETROCHEMICALS — LEATHER — MILK & CHEESE — ANIMAL FIBERS — MEAT & EGGS — FISH & SEAFOOD — TROPICAL AGRIC. — CEREALS & VEG. OILS — COTTON/RICE/SOY & OTHERS — TOBACCO — FRUIT — MISC. AGRICULTURE — NOT CLASSIFIED — TEXTILE & FABRICS — GARMENTS — FOOD PROCESSING — BEER/SPIRITS & CIGS. — PRECIOUS STONES — COAL — OIL — MINING

2010 | EXPORT TREEMAP ▾ — TOTAL: $ 2,341,813,108

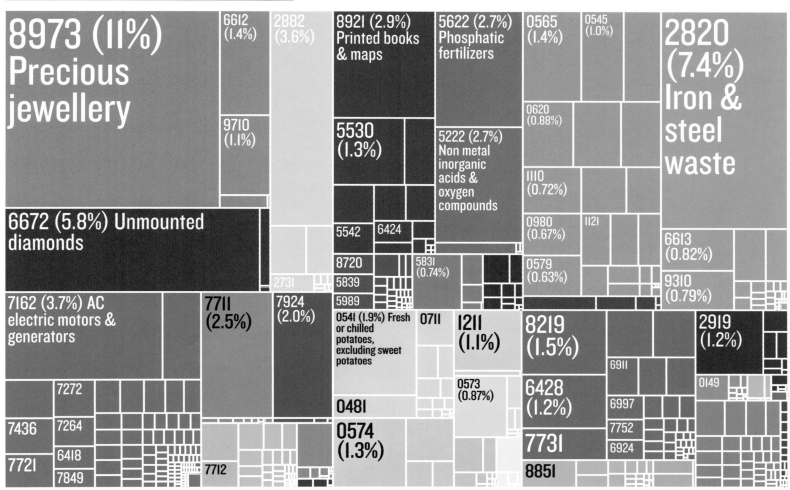

* Numbers indicate SITC-4 Rev 2 codes which can be found in the Appendix. Percentages next to the product codes indicate proportion of the product in the exports of the country. Treemap headers show the total trade of the country.

2010 | EXPORT DESTINATIONS ▾ — TOTAL: $ 2,341,813,108

- 12% United Arab Emirates
- 11% Saudi Arabia
- 8.8% Turkey
- BEL (3.9%)
- DEU
- NLD
- CHE (7.1%)
- ITA
- GRC
- 7.2% Syrian Arab Republic
- QAT (4.0%)
- EGY (3.9%)
- IRN (2.9%)
- IDN (2.3%)
- NGA (2.3%)
- USA (3.4%)
- JOR (4.2%)
- DZA
- KOR
- CIV
- IND

2010 | IMPORT SOURCES ▾ — TOTAL: $ 16,986,725,568

- ITA (7.4%)
- DEU (7.3%)
- FRA (6.3%)
- 8.4% China
- EGY (2.7%)
- JPN (3.3%)
- KOR
- JOR
- UKR (5.8%)
- RUS (2.9%)
- GBR (2.8%)
- TUR (3.7%)
- NLD
- GRC
- 10% United States
- BRA
- CHE
- BEL
- IND

EAST ASIA & PACIFIC — EUROPE & CENTRAL ASIA — LATIN AMERICA & CARIBBEAN — MIDDLE EAST & NORTH AFRICA — NORTH AMERICA — SOUTH ASIA — SUB-SAHARAN AFRICA

LIBYA

ECONOMIC COMPLEXITY INDEX [2010] ► -1.245 (116) | COMPLEXITY OUTLOOK INDEX [2010] ► -0.988 (111) | EXPECTED GDPᴘᴄ GROWTH * ► -1.1% (126)

*Expected annual average for the 2010-2020 period.

2010 PRODUCT SPACE ►

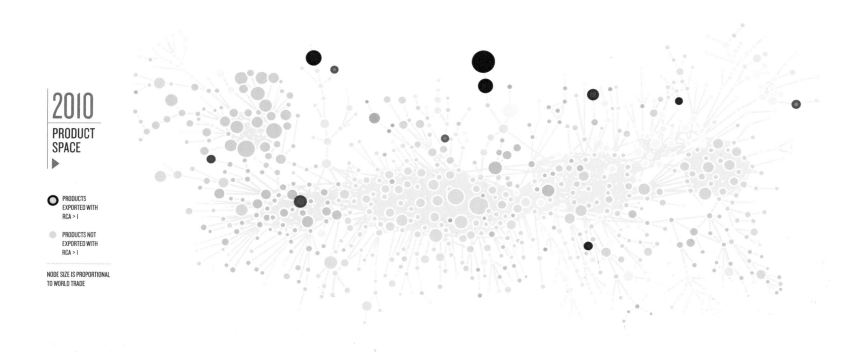

○ PRODUCTS EXPORTED WITH RCA > 1

● PRODUCTS NOT EXPORTED WITH RCA > 1

NODE SIZE IS PROPORTIONAL TO WORLD TRADE

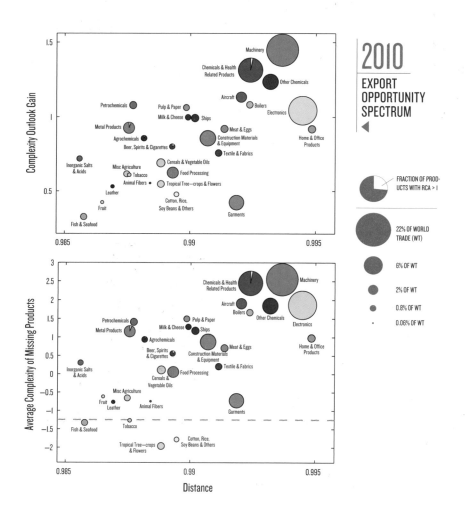

2010 EXPORT OPPORTUNITY SPECTRUM ◄

◔ FRACTION OF PRODUCTS WITH RCA > 1

● 22% OF WORLD TRADE (WT)

● 6% OF WT

● 2% OF WT

● 0.8% OF WT

· 0.06% OF WT

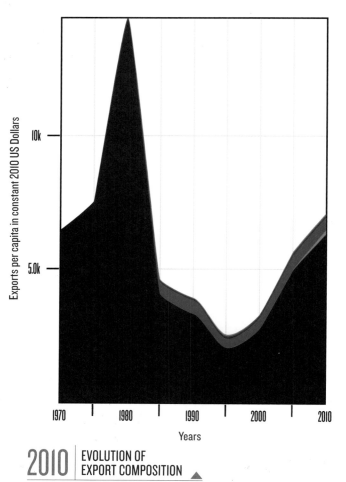

2010 EVOLUTION OF EXPORT COMPOSITION ▲

POPULATION ▸ 6.4 M/ (88)	GDP ▸ USD 62 B / (63)	EXPORTS PER CAPITA ▸ USD 7,118 / (29)	* Data are from 2010. Numbers indicate:
TOTAL EXPORTS ▸ USD 45 B / (50)	GDPᴘᴄ ▸ USD 9,957 / (47)	EXPORTS AS SHARE OF GDP ▸ 73 % (5)	Value (World Ranking among 128 countries)
			Region: Middle East and North Africa.

ELECTRONICS · MACHINERY · AIRCRAFT · BOILERS · SHIPS · METAL PRODUCTS · CONSTR. MATL. & EQPT. · HOME & OFFICE · PULP & PAPER · CHEMICALS & HEALTH · AGROCHEMICALS · OTHER CHEMICALS · INOR. SALTS & ACIDS · PETROCHEMICALS · LEATHER · MILK & CHEESE · ANIMAL FIBERS · MEAT & EGGS · FISH & SEAFOOD · TROPICAL AGRIC. · CEREALS & VEG. OILS · COTTON/RICE/SOY & OTHERS · TOBACCO · FRUIT · MISC. AGRICULTURE · NOT CLASSIFIED · TEXTILE & FABRICS · GARMENTS · FOOD PROCESSING · BEER/SPIRITS & CIGS. · PRECIOUS STONES · COAL · OIL · MINING

2010 | EXPORT TREEMAP ▼ — TOTAL: $ 45,235,556,731

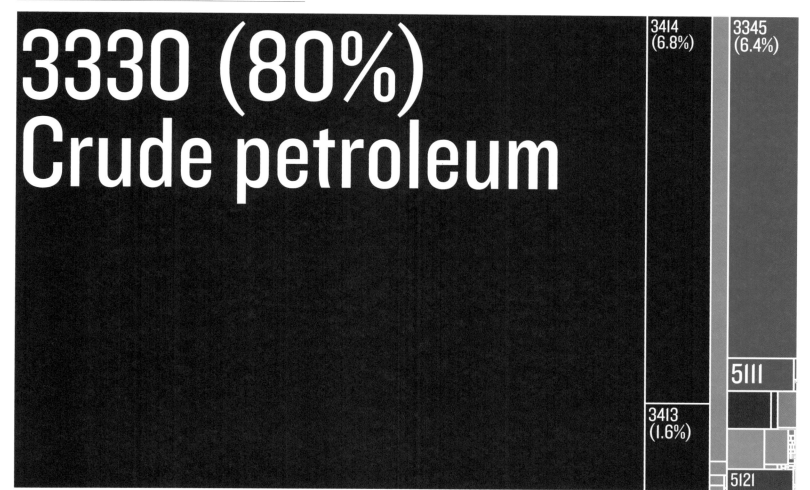

3330 (80%) Crude petroleum

3414 (6.8%)

3345 (6.4%)

3413 (1.6%)

5111

5121

* Numbers indicate SITC-4 Rev 2 codes which can be found in the Appendix. Percentages next to the product codes indicate proportion of the product in the exports of the country. Treemap headers show the total trade of the country.

2010 | EXPORT DESTINATIONS ▼ TOTAL: $ 45,235,556,731

33% Italy

FRA (13%)

ESP (8.9%)

DEU (8.2%)

9.0% China

AUS

GBR (3.9%)

USA (4.4%)

GRC (3.7%)

NLD

CHE

IRL

IND

2010 | IMPORT SOURCES ▼ TOTAL: $ 19,709,878,651

18% Italy

DEU (6.7%)

FRA (6.5%)

9.8% Turkey

GRC

SWE

UKR

RUS

AUT

10% China

KOR (7.2%)

THA

USA (3.4%)

EGY (6.2%)

TUN (3.7%)

ARE (3.1%)

EAST ASIA & PACIFIC · EUROPE & CENTRAL ASIA · LATIN AMERICA & CARIBBEAN · MIDDLE EAST & NORTH AFRICA · NORTH AMERICA · SOUTH ASIA · SUB-SAHARAN AFRICA

LITHUANIA

ECONOMIC COMPLEXITY INDEX [2010] ▸ 0.674 (37)	COMPLEXITY OUTLOOK INDEX [2010] ▸ 1.047 (21)	EXPECTED GDPᴘᴄ GROWTH * ▸ 2.7% (36)

*Expected annual average for the 2010-2020 period.

2010 PRODUCT SPACE ▸

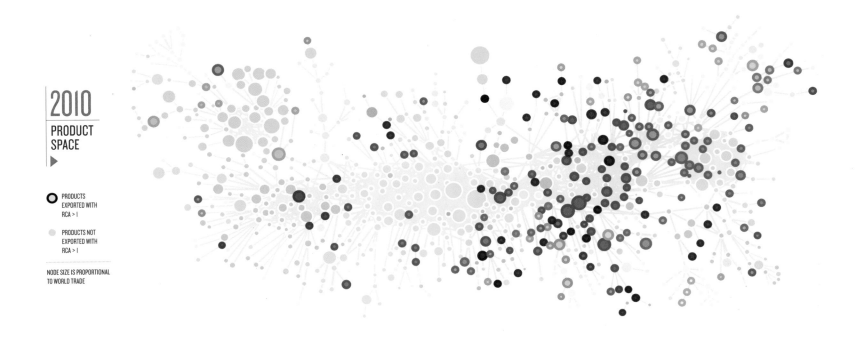

○ PRODUCTS EXPORTED WITH RCA > 1

● PRODUCTS NOT EXPORTED WITH RCA > 1

NODE SIZE IS PROPORTIONAL TO WORLD TRADE

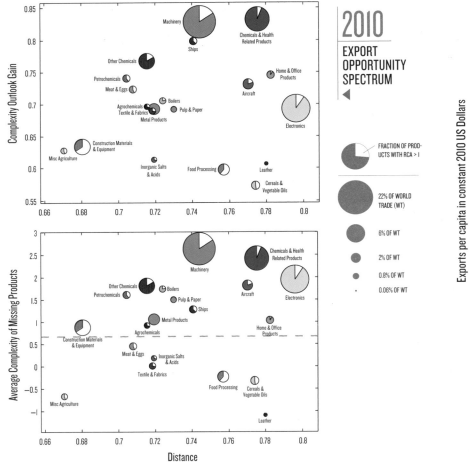

2010 EXPORT OPPORTUNITY SPECTRUM ◂

⬤ FRACTION OF PRODUCTS WITH RCA > 1

⬤ 22% OF WORLD TRADE (WT)

⬤ 6% OF WT

⬤ 2% OF WT

• 0.8% OF WT

· 0.06% OF WT

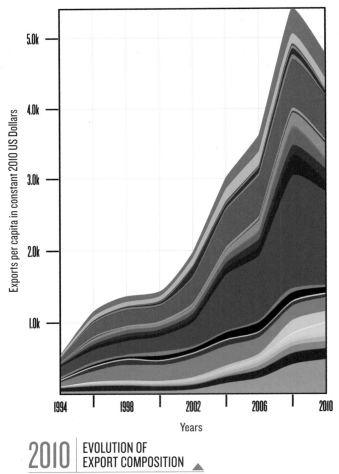

2010 EVOLUTION OF EXPORT COMPOSITION ▲

POPULATION ▸ 3.3 M / (113)
TOTAL EXPORTS ▸ USD 16 B / (70)

GDP ▸ USD 36 B / (81)
GDPpc ▸ USD 11,046 / (42)

EXPORTS PER CAPITA ▸ USD 4,788 / (37)
EXPORTS AS SHARE OF GDP ▸ 43 % (29)

* Data are from 2010. Numbers indicate:
Value (World Ranking among 128 countries)
Region: Eastern Europe and Central Asia.

ELECTRONICS · MACHINERY · AIRCRAFT · BOILERS · SHIPS · METAL PRODUCTS · CONSTR. MATL. & EQPT. · HOME & OFFICE · PULP & PAPER · CHEMICALS & HEALTH · AGROCHEMICALS · OTHER CHEMICALS · INOR. SALTS & ACIDS · PETROCHEMICALS · LEATHER · MILK & CHEESE · ANIMAL FIBERS · MEAT & EGGS · FISH & SEAFOOD · TROPICAL AGRIC. · CEREALS & VEG. OILS · COTTON/RICE/SOY & OTHERS · TOBACCO · FRUIT · MISC. AGRICULTURE · NOT CLASSIFIED · TEXTILE & FABRICS · GARMENTS · FOOD PROCESSING · BEER/SPIRITS & CIGS. · PRECIOUS STONES · COAL · OIL · MINING

2010 EXPORT TREEMAP ▾ TOTAL: $ 15,737,237,579

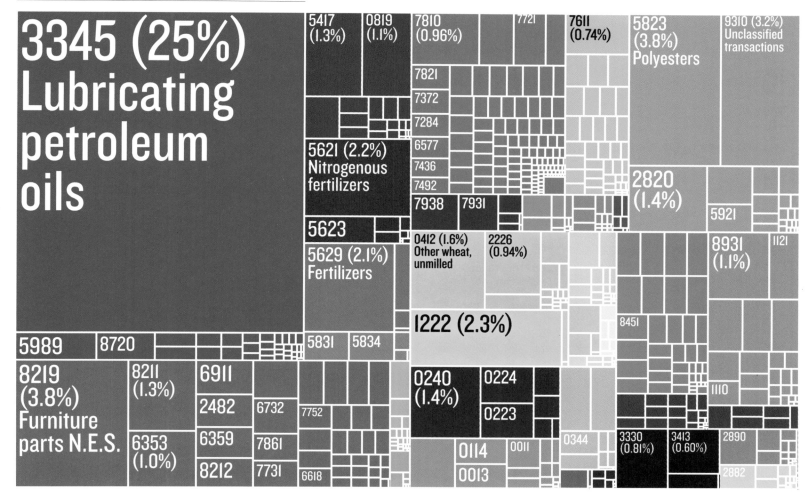

* Numbers indicate SITC-4 Rev 2 codes which can be found in the Appendix. Percentages next to the product codes indicate proportion of the product in the exports of the country. Treemap headers show the total trade of the country.

2010 EXPORT DESTINATIONS ▾ TOTAL: $ 15,737,237,579

12% Germany
11% Latvia
RUS (7.3%)
POL (6.0%)
NLD (5.9%)
GBR (5.3%)
FRA (4.6%)
USA (3.8%)
CAN (2.2%)
SWE (4.6%)
DNK (3.2%)
NOR (3.1%)
ITA
EST (4.5%)
FIN (1.9%)
ESP
UKR (3.7%)
BLR
TUR
KAZ
IND

2010 IMPORT SOURCES ▾ TOTAL: $ 21,560,123,316

33% Russia
DEU (11%)
8.8% Poland
LVA (6.1%)
ITA (3.3%)
BEL (3.2%)
FIN
ESP
SWE (3.2%)
GBR
AUT
CZE

EAST ASIA & PACIFIC | EUROPE & CENTRAL ASIA | LATIN AMERICA & CARIBBEAN | MIDDLE EAST & NORTH AFRICA | NORTH AMERICA | SOUTH ASIA | SUB-SAHARAN AFRICA

MACEDONIA, FYR

ECONOMIC COMPLEXITY INDEX [2010] ▸ -0.02 (62) | COMPLEXITY OUTLOOK INDEX [2010] ▸ 0.243 (51) | EXPECTED GDPᴘᴄ GROWTH * ▸ 2.2% (55)

*Expected annual average for the 2010-2020 period.

2010 PRODUCT SPACE ▶

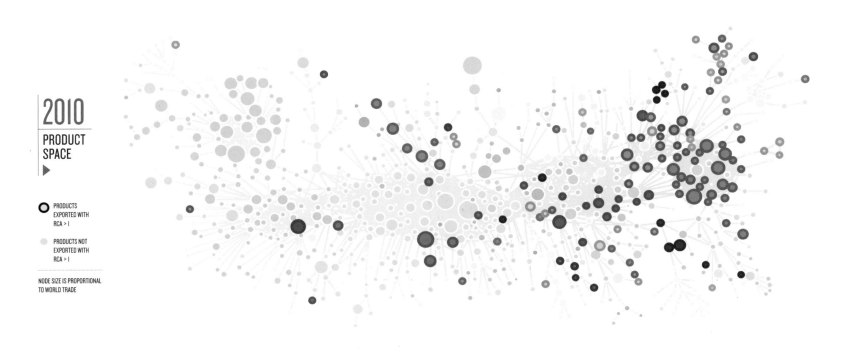

○ PRODUCTS EXPORTED WITH RCA > 1

● PRODUCTS NOT EXPORTED WITH RCA > 1

NODE SIZE IS PROPORTIONAL TO WORLD TRADE

2010 EXPORT OPPORTUNITY SPECTRUM ◀

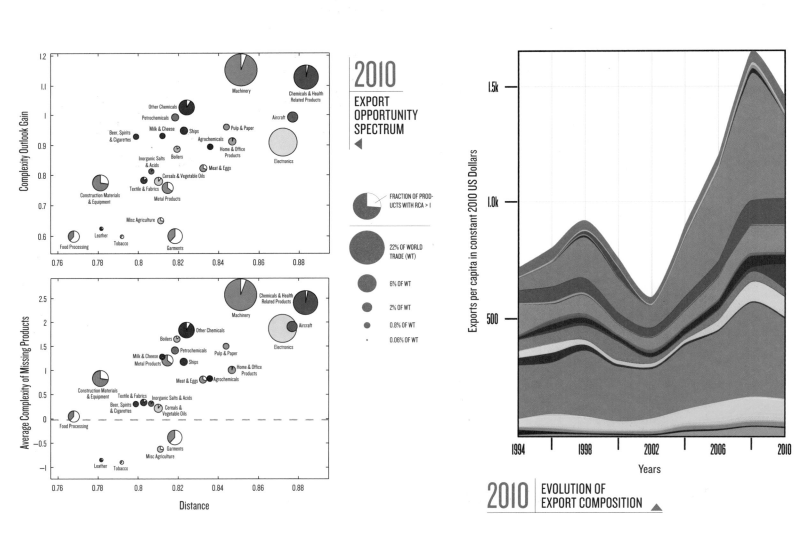

◔ FRACTION OF PRODUCTS WITH RCA > 1

● 22% OF WORLD TRADE (WT)

● 6% OF WT

● 2% OF WT

● 0.8% OF WT

· 0.06% OF WT

2010 EVOLUTION OF EXPORT COMPOSITION ▲

POPULATION ▸ 2.1 M / (121)	GDP ▸ USD 9.1 B / (116)	EXPORTS PER CAPITA ▸ USD 1,457 / (63)	* Data are from 2010. Numbers indicate:
TOTAL EXPORTS ▸ USD 3 B / (102)	GDPᴘᴄ ▸ USD 4,434 / (73)	EXPORTS AS SHARE OF GDP ▸ 33 % (44)	Value (World Ranking among 128 countries) Region: Eastern Europe and Central Asia.

ELECTRONICS · MACHINERY · AIRCRAFT · BOILERS · SHIPS · METAL PRODUCTS · CONSTR. MATL. & EQPT. · HOME & OFFICE · PULP & PAPER · CHEMICALS & HEALTH · AGROCHEMICALS · OTHER CHEMICALS · INOR. SALTS & ACIDS · PETROCHEMICALS · LEATHER · MILK & CHEESE · ANIMAL FIBERS · MEAT & EGGS · FISH & SEAFOOD · TROPICAL AGRIC. · CEREALS & VEG. OILS · COTTON/RICE/SOY & OTHERS · TOBACCO · FRUIT · MISC. AGRICULTURE · NOT CLASSIFIED · TEXTILE & FABRICS · GARMENTS · FOOD PROCESSING · BEER/SPIRITS & CIGS. · PRECIOUS STONES · COAL · OIL · MINING

2010 EXPORT TREEMAP ▾ TOTAL: $ 3,003,234,593

6716 (11%) Ferro alloys

6744 (6.4%) Iron/steel >=4.75mm tick sheets

6749 (3.0%) Other worked iron/steel sheets

6783 (2.8%) Other iron or steel tubes & pipes

6746

7721 (1.3%)

7919

8720 3345

7781
7643
6623

5989 (6.7%) Chemical products

5417 (1.9%)

2874 (2.5%) Lead ore

2882 (0.73%)

2875 (1.2%)

2871 (2.0%)

1121 (1.6%) Wine

0484 (0.97%)

1211 (2.9%) Raw tobacco

8439 (3.0%) Other women's outerwear

8510 (2.0%) Footwear

8423 (1.8%) Men's trousers

8441 (2.9%)

8459 (1.9%)

8435 (2.6%)

8431 (1.9%)

8462 (0.75%)

6123 (0.67%)

8433 (0.66%)

6589

6584

8451

0545 (1.4%)

0546

0620

0730

0586

3510 (3.7%) Electric current

8211

6732

7731

1222 1212

0575 0574 4236

9310 (1.1%)

2820 (0.86%)

*Numbers indicate SITC-4 Rev 2 codes which can be found in the Appendix. Percentages next to the product codes indicate proportion of the product in the exports of the country. Treemap headers show the total trade of the country.

2010 EXPORT DESTINATIONS ▾ TOTAL: $ 3,003,234,593

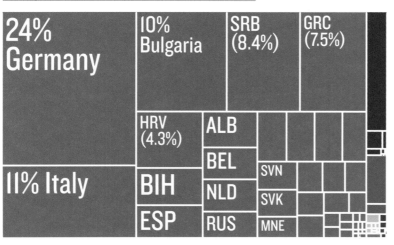

24% Germany

10% Bulgaria

SRB (8.4%)

GRC (7.5%)

HRV (4.3%)

ALB

BEL

SVN

11% Italy

BIH

NLD

SVK

ESP

RUS

MNE

2010 IMPORT SOURCES ▾ TOTAL: $ 4,292,815,537

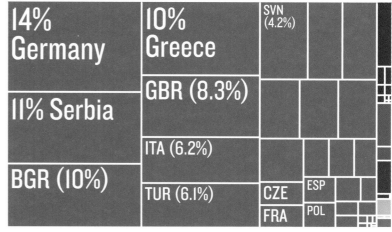

14% Germany

10% Greece

SVN (4.2%)

GBR (8.3%)

11% Serbia

ITA (6.2%)

BGR (10%)

TUR (6.1%)

CZE

ESP

FRA

POL

EAST ASIA & PACIFIC · EUROPE & CENTRAL ASIA · LATIN AMERICA & CARIBBEAN · MIDDLE EAST & NORTH AFRICA · NORTH AMERICA · SOUTH ASIA · SUB-SAHARAN AFRICA

MADAGASCAR

ECONOMIC COMPLEXITY INDEX [2010] ▸ -1.051 (111) | **COMPLEXITY OUTLOOK INDEX [2010]** ▸ -0.709 (87) | **EXPECTED GDP**ᴘᴄ **GROWTH** * ▸ 2.7% (35)

*Expected annual average for the 2010-2020 period.

2010
PRODUCT SPACE ▶

○ PRODUCTS EXPORTED WITH RCA > 1

○ PRODUCTS NOT EXPORTED WITH RCA > 1

NODE SIZE IS PROPORTIONAL TO WORLD TRADE

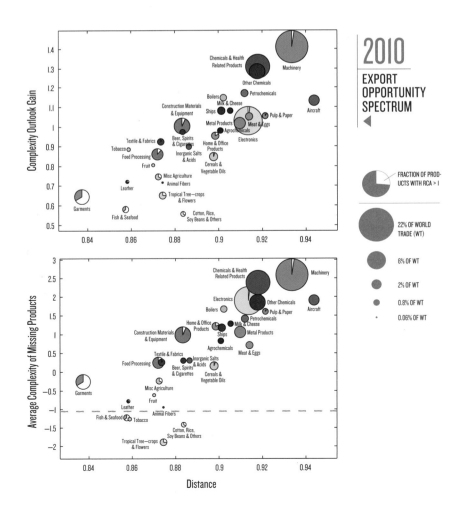

2010
EXPORT OPPORTUNITY SPECTRUM ◀

○ FRACTION OF PRODUCTS WITH RCA > 1

⬤ 22% OF WORLD TRADE (WT)

⬤ 6% OF WT

● 2% OF WT

● 0.8% OF WT

· 0.06% OF WT

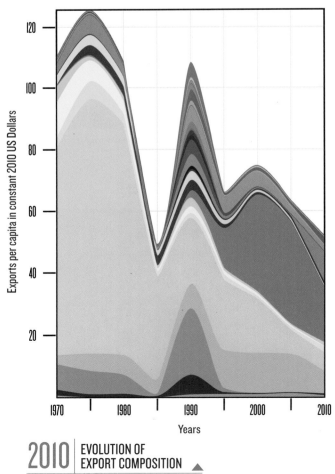

2010 | EVOLUTION OF EXPORT COMPOSITION ▲

POPULATION ▸ 21 M / (47)
TOTAL EXPORTS ▸ USD 1.1 B / (122)

GDP ▸ USD 8.7 B / (117)
GDPᴘᴄ ▸ USD 421 / (124)

EXPORTS PER CAPITA ▸ USD 52 / (125)
EXPORTS AS SHARE OF GDP ▸ 12 % / (112)

* Data are from 2010. Numbers indicate:
Value (World Ranking among 128 countries)
Region: Sub-Saharan Africa.

ELECTRONICS | MACHINERY | AIRCRAFT | BOILERS | SHIPS | METAL PRODUCTS | CONSTR. MATL. & EQPT. | HOME & OFFICE | PULP & PAPER | CHEMICALS & HEALTH | AGROCHEMICALS | OTHER CHEMICALS | INOR. SALTS & ACIDS | PETROCHEMICALS | LEATHER | MILK & CHEESE | ANIMAL FIBERS | MEAT & EGGS | FISH & SEAFOOD | TROPICAL AGRIC. | CEREALS & VEG. OILS | COTTON/RICE/SOY & OTHERS | TOBACCO | FRUIT | MISC. AGRICULTURE | NOT CLASSIFIED | TEXTILE & FABRICS | GARMENTS | FOOD PROCESSING | BEER/SPIRITS & CIGS. | PRECIOUS STONES | COAL | OIL | MINING

2010 EXPORT TREEMAP ▾ TOTAL: $ 1,076,708,880

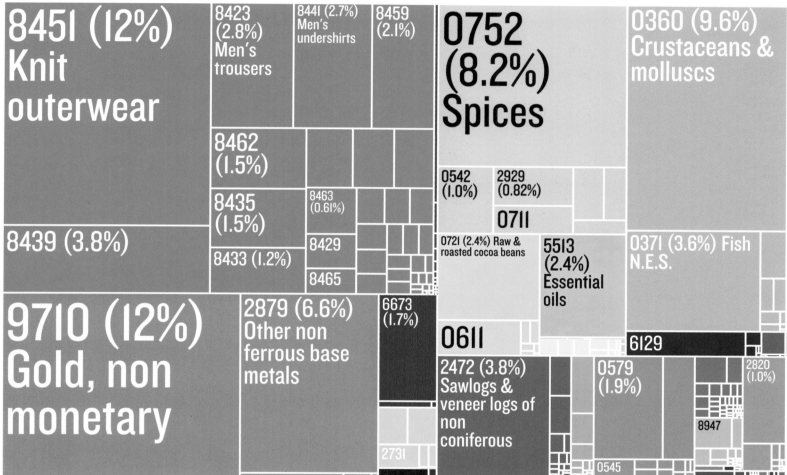

* Numbers indicate SITC-4 Rev 2 codes which can be found in the Appendix. Percentages next to the product codes indicate proportion of the product in the exports of the country. Treemap headers show the total trade of the country.

2010 EXPORT DESTINATIONS ▾ TOTAL: $ 1,076,708,880

29% France
DEU (7.7%)
9.4% United States
CAN (4.1%)
8.4% China
SGP
JPN
ZAF
12% United Arab Emirates
IND
ESP (4.4%)
ITA (3.1%)
BEL
GBR
NLD

2010 IMPORT SOURCES ▾ TOTAL: $ 1,899,854,180

21% China
16% France
SGP (5.8%)
THA
HKG
IDN
AUS
ITA
DEU (2.7%)
BEL
ESP
9.1% South Africa
MUS (4.3%)
USA (6.1%)
CAN (4.3%)
IND
PAK

EAST ASIA & PACIFIC | EUROPE & CENTRAL ASIA | LATIN AMERICA & CARIBBEAN | MIDDLE EAST & NORTH AFRICA | NORTH AMERICA | SOUTH ASIA | SUB-SAHARAN AFRICA

MALAWI

ECONOMIC COMPLEXITY INDEX [2010] ▸ -0.832 (99) | COMPLEXITY OUTLOOK INDEX [2010] ▸ -0.893 (97) | EXPECTED GDPᴘᴄ GROWTH * ▸ 3.1% (22)

*Expected annual average for the 2010-2020 period.

2010 PRODUCT SPACE ▶

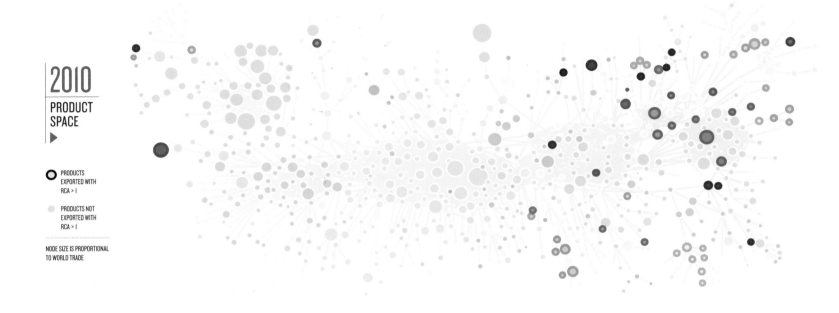

○ PRODUCTS EXPORTED WITH RCA > 1

○ PRODUCTS NOT EXPORTED WITH RCA > 1

·········

NODE SIZE IS PROPORTIONAL TO WORLD TRADE

2010 EXPORT OPPORTUNITY SPECTRUM ◀

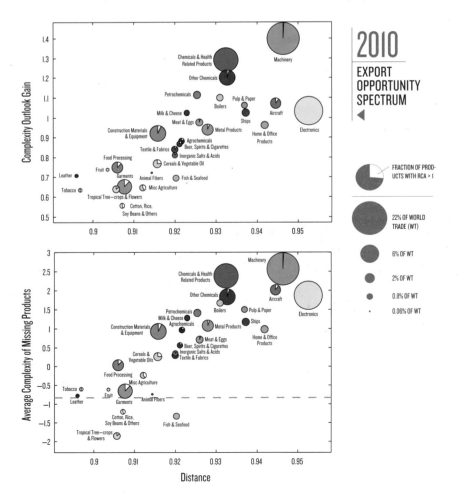

FRACTION OF PRODUCTS WITH RCA > 1

22% OF WORLD TRADE (WT)

6% OF WT

2% OF WT

0.8% OF WT

0.06% OF WT

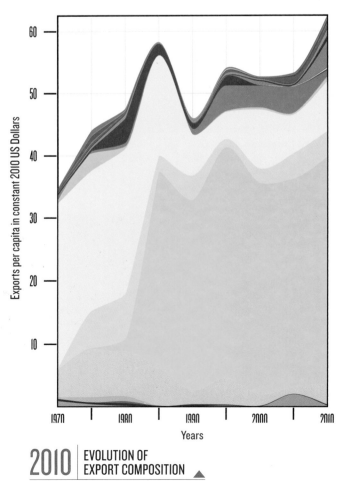

2010 EVOLUTION OF EXPORT COMPOSITION ▲

POPULATION ▸ 15 M / (57)	GDP ▸ USD 5.1 B / (124)	EXPORTS PER CAPITA ▸ USD 63 / (123)
TOTAL EXPORTS ▸ USD 932 M / (126)	GDPᴘᴄ ▸ USD 339 / (127)	EXPORTS AS SHARE OF GDP ▸ 18 % (84)

* Data are from 2010. Numbers indicate:
  Value (World Ranking among 128 countries)
  Region: Sub-Saharan Africa.

ELECTRONICS · MACHINERY · AIRCRAFT · BOILERS · SHIPS · METAL PRODUCTS · CONSTR. MATL. & EQPT. · HOME & OFFICE · PULP & PAPER · CHEMICALS & HEALTH · AGROCHEMICALS · OTHER CHEMICALS · INOR. SALTS & ACIDS · PETROCHEMICALS · LEATHER · MILK & CHEESE · ANIMAL FIBERS · MEAT & EGGS · FISH & SEAFOOD · TROPICAL AGRIC. · CEREALS & VEG. OILS · COTTON/RICE/SOY & OTHERS · TOBACCO · FRUIT · MISC. AGRICULTURE · NOT CLASSIFIED · TEXTILE & FABRICS · GARMENTS · FOOD PROCESSING · BEER/SPIRITS & CIGS. · PRECIOUS STONES · COAL · OIL · MINING

2010 | EXPORT TREEMAP ▼ TOTAL: $ 932,077,164

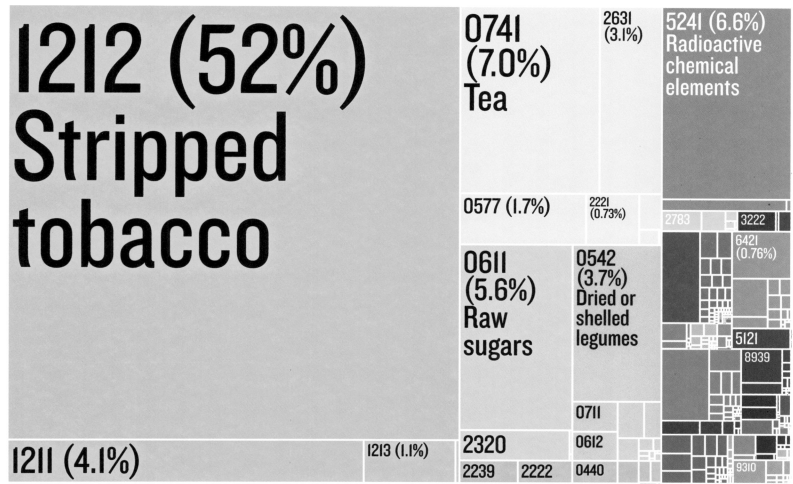

1212 (52%) Stripped tobacco
1211 (4.1%)
1213 (1.1%)
0741 (7.0%) Tea
2631 (3.1%)
5241 (6.6%) Radioactive chemical elements
0577 (1.7%)
2221 (0.73%)
0611 (5.6%) Raw sugars
0542 (3.7%) Dried or shelled legumes
2783
3222
6421 (0.76%)
5121
8939
0711
0612
2320
2239
2222
0440
9310

* Numbers indicate SITC-4 Rev 2 codes which can be found in the Appendix. Percentages next to the product codes indicate proportion of the product in the exports of the country. Treemap headers show the total trade of the country.

2010 | EXPORT DESTINATIONS ▼ TOTAL: $ 932,077,164

12% Germany
RUS (7.9%)
ZWE (7.7%)
ZAF (6.2%)
USA (7.4%)
NLD (5.6%)
UKR
TUR
ZMB
TZA
JPN (3.7%)
EGY (3.9%)
GBR (3.9%)
ESP
CHE
CHN (3.1%)
BEL
GRC

2010 | IMPORT SOURCES ▼ TOTAL: $ 1,954,290,918

30% South Africa
8.9% China
GBR (3.8%)
FRA (3.0%)
CHE
IDN
AUS
NLD
HKG
KOR
DEU
ZMB (5.7%)
KEN (2.3%)
7.7% India
ARE (5.0%)
USA (3.3%)
TZA
NAM
ARG

EAST ASIA & PACIFIC · EUROPE & CENTRAL ASIA · LATIN AMERICA & CARIBBEAN · MIDDLE EAST & NORTH AFRICA · NORTH AMERICA · SOUTH ASIA · SUB-SAHARAN AFRICA

MALAYSIA

ECONOMIC COMPLEXITY INDEX [2010] ▸ 0.744 (32) | COMPLEXITY OUTLOOK INDEX [2010] ▸ 0.567 (43) | EXPECTED GDPᴘᴄ GROWTH * ▸ 2.8% (31)

*Expected annual average for the 2010-2020 period.

2010 PRODUCT SPACE ▶

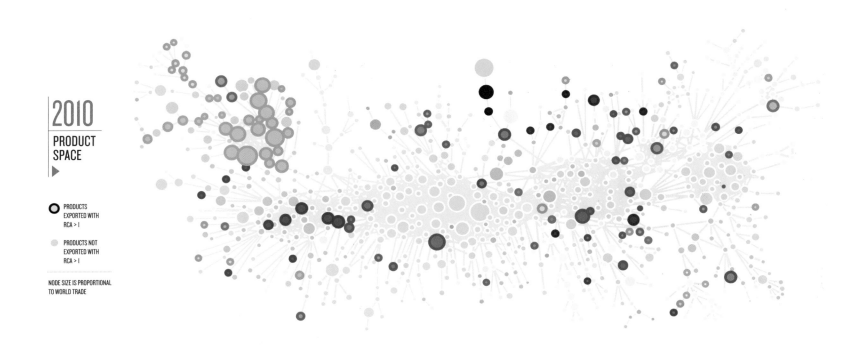

○ PRODUCTS EXPORTED WITH RCA > 1

○ PRODUCTS NOT EXPORTED WITH RCA > 1

NODE SIZE IS PROPORTIONAL TO WORLD TRADE

2010 EXPORT OPPORTUNITY SPECTRUM ◀

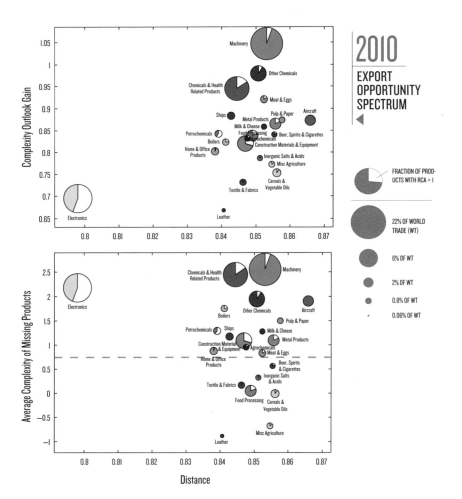

○ FRACTION OF PRODUCTS WITH RCA > 1

● 22% OF WORLD TRADE (WT)

● 6% OF WT

● 2% OF WT

● 0.8% OF WT

· 0.06% OF WT

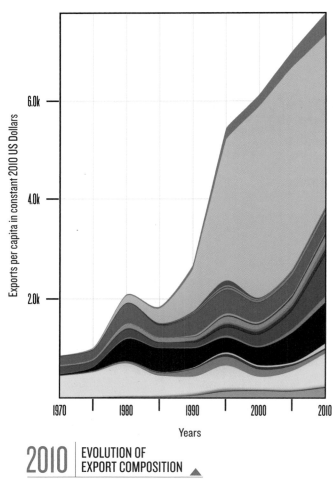

2010 | EVOLUTION OF EXPORT COMPOSITION ▲

POPULATION ▸ 28 M / (40)	GDP ▸ USD 238 B / (35)	EXPORTS PER CAPITA ▸ USD 7,789 / (25)	* Data are from 2010. Numbers indicate:
TOTAL EXPORTS ▸ USD 221 B / (14)	GDPᴘᴄ ▸ USD 8,373 / (53)	EXPORTS AS SHARE OF GDP ▸ 93 % (2)	Value (World Ranking among 128 countries) Region: East Asia and Pacific.

ELECTRONICS · MACHINERY · AIRCRAFT · BOILERS · SHIPS · METAL PRODUCTS · CONSTR. MATL. & EQPT. · HOME & OFFICE · PULP & PAPER · CHEMICALS & HEALTH · AGROCHEMICALS · OTHER CHEMICALS · INOR. SALTS & ACIDS · PETROCHEMICALS · LEATHER · MILK & CHEESE · ANIMAL FIBERS · MEAT & EGGS · FISH & SEAFOOD · TROPICAL AGRIC. · CEREALS & VEG. OILS · COTTON/RICE/SOY & OTHERS · TOBACCO · FRUIT · MISC. AGRICULTURE · NOT CLASSIFIED · TEXTILE & FABRICS · GARMENTS · FOOD PROCESSING · BEER/SPIRITS & CIGS. · PRECIOUS STONES · COAL · OIL · MINING

2010 | EXPORT TREEMAP ▼ TOTAL: $ 221,211,941,555

7764 (20%) Electronic microcircuits

7599 (4.5%) Parts of registers & calculating machines

3345 (6.8%) Lubricating petroleum oils

3330 (5.4%) Crude petroleum

3413 (4.9%) liquified hydrocarbons

7763 (3.5%) Diodes & transistors

7649 (2.1%) Parts of telecom & sound equipment

7788 (1.0%)

7611 (1.8%)

7525 (2.6%) Peripheral computer hardware

8482 (1.2%)

7522 (0.71%)

7518 (0.69%)

7528

7523

7415

7628

7757

7712

8748 (0.61%)

5989

5137

6871

8720

5112

8742

6210

5831

8939

4242 (5.2%) Palm oil

8973 (0.93%)

9710

2320 (1.4%)

4244

0723

9310 (1.3%)

8931

4312

0980

5121 (0.64%)

7721 (1.1%)

7849

8743

8749

7758

8219 (0.80%)

6342

2483

7731

2472

8211

*Numbers indicate SITC-4 Rev 2 codes which can be found in the Appendix. Percentages next to the product codes indicate proportion of the product in the exports of the country. Treemap headers show the total trade of the country.

2010 | EXPORT DESTINATIONS ▼ TOTAL: $ 221,211,941,555

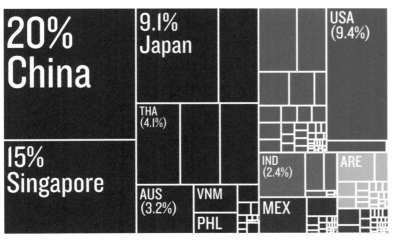

20% China

15% Singapore

9.1% Japan

THA (4.1%)

AUS (3.2%)

VNM

PHL

USA (9.4%)

IND (2.4%)

ARE

MEX

2010 | IMPORT SOURCES ▼ TOTAL: $ 141,380,050,249

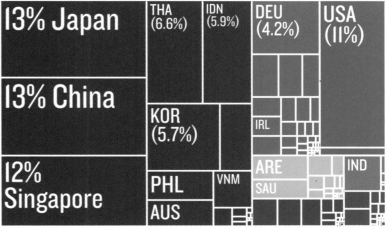

13% Japan

13% China

12% Singapore

THA (6.6%)

KOR (5.7%)

PHL

AUS

IDN (5.9%)

VNM

DEU (4.2%)

IRL

ARE

SAU

USA (11%)

IND

EAST ASIA & PACIFIC · EUROPE & CENTRAL ASIA · LATIN AMERICA & CARIBBEAN · MIDDLE EAST & NORTH AFRICA · NORTH AMERICA · SOUTH ASIA · SUB-SAHARAN AFRICA

MALI

| ECONOMIC COMPLEXITY INDEX [2010] ▸ -0.999 (107) | COMPLEXITY OUTLOOK INDEX [2010] ▸ -0.979 (108) | EXPECTED GDPᴘᴄ GROWTH * ▸ 2.2% (54) |

*Expected annual average for the 2010-2020 period.

2010 PRODUCT SPACE ▸

○ PRODUCTS EXPORTED WITH RCA > 1

○ PRODUCTS NOT EXPORTED WITH RCA > 1

NODE SIZE IS PROPORTIONAL TO WORLD TRADE

2010 EXPORT OPPORTUNITY SPECTRUM ◂

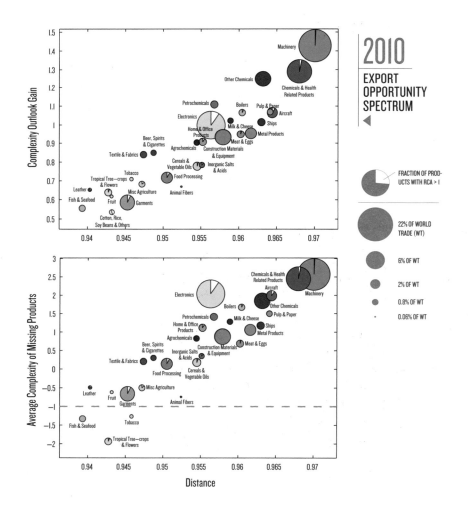

FRACTION OF PRODUCTS WITH RCA > 1

22% OF WORLD TRADE (WT)

6% OF WT

2% OF WT

0.8% OF WT

0.06% OF WT

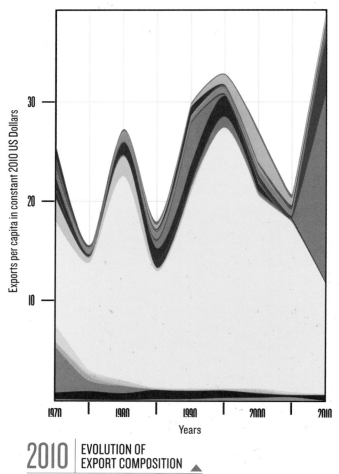

2010 EVOLUTION OF EXPORT COMPOSITION ▲

POPULATION ▸ 15 M / (56)	GDP ▸ USD 9.4 B / (114)	EXPORTS PER CAPITA ▸ USD 39 / (126)
TOTAL EXPORTS ▸ USD 605 M / (128)	GDPₚ𝒸 ▸ USD 613 / (119)	EXPORTS AS SHARE OF GDP ▸ 6.4 % (124)

* Data are from 2010. Numbers indicate:
Value (World Ranking among 128 countries)
Region: Sub-Saharan Africa.

ELECTRONICS · MACHINERY · AIRCRAFT · BOILERS · SHIPS · METAL PRODUCTS · CONSTR. MATL. & EQPT. · HOME & OFFICE · PULP & PAPER · CHEMICALS & HEALTH · AGROCHEMICALS · OTHER CHEMICALS · INOR. SALTS & ACIDS · PETROCHEMICALS · LEATHER · MILK & CHEESE · ANIMAL FIBERS · MEAT & EGGS · FISH & SEAFOOD · TROPICAL AGRIC. · CEREALS & VEG. OILS · COTTON/RICE/SOY & OTHERS · TOBACCO · FRUIT · MISC. AGRICULTURE · NOT CLASSIFIED · TEXTILE & FABRICS · GARMENTS · FOOD PROCESSING · BEER/SPIRITS & CIGS. · PRECIOUS STONES · COAL · OIL · MINING

2010 EXPORT TREEMAP ▾ TOTAL: $ 604,706,430

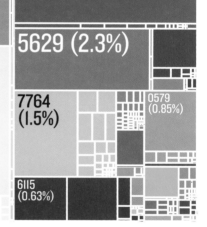

9710 (48%) Gold, non monetary

2631 (24%) Raw cotton

2225 (3.8%) Sesame seeds

3345 (14%) Lubricating petroleum oils

5629 (2.3%)

7764 (1.5%)

0579 (0.85%)

6115 (0.63%)

* Numbers indicate SITC-4 Rev 2 codes which can be found in the Appendix. Percentages next to the product codes indicate proportion of the product in the exports of the country. Treemap headers show the total trade of the country.

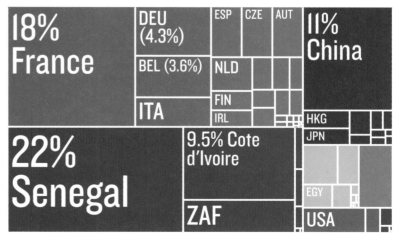

2010 EXPORT DESTINATIONS ▾ TOTAL: $ 604,706,430

47% United Arab Emirates

ITA
DEU
PAK (5.3%)

14% Korea, Rep.

11% China

VNM (3.6%)
IDN (3.1%)
BFA (2.5%)

THA

2010 IMPORT SOURCES ▾ TOTAL: $ 2,040,810,189

18% France

DEU (4.3%)
BEL (3.6%)
ITA

ESP
CZE
AUT
NLD
FIN
IRL

11% China

22% Senegal

9.5% Cote d'Ivoire

ZAF

HKG
JPN
EGY
USA

EAST ASIA & PACIFIC · EUROPE & CENTRAL ASIA · LATIN AMERICA & CARIBBEAN · MIDDLE EAST & NORTH AFRICA · NORTH AMERICA · SOUTH ASIA · SUB-SAHARAN AFRICA

MAURITANIA

ECONOMIC COMPLEXITY INDEX [2010] ▸ -1.576 (123)	COMPLEXITY OUTLOOK INDEX [2010] ▸ -1.151 (123)	EXPECTED GDPPC GROWTH * ▸ 0.7% (101)

*Expected annual average for the 2010-2020 period.

2010
PRODUCT SPACE ▶

- ○ PRODUCTS EXPORTED WITH RCA > 1
- ○ PRODUCTS NOT EXPORTED WITH RCA > 1

NODE SIZE IS PROPORTIONAL TO WORLD TRADE

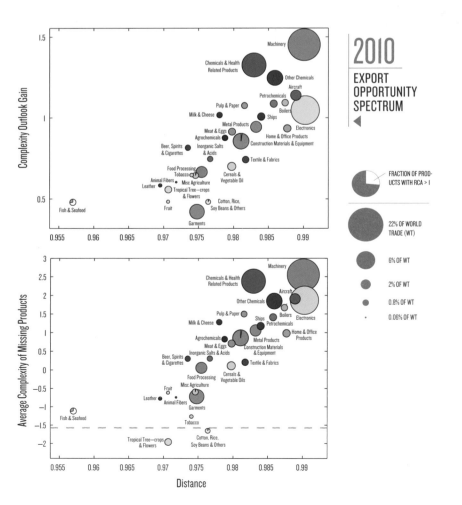

2010
EXPORT OPPORTUNITY SPECTRUM ◀

- FRACTION OF PRODUCTS WITH RCA > 1
- 22% OF WORLD TRADE (WT)
- 6% OF WT
- 2% OF WT
- 0.8% OF WT
- 0.06% OF WT

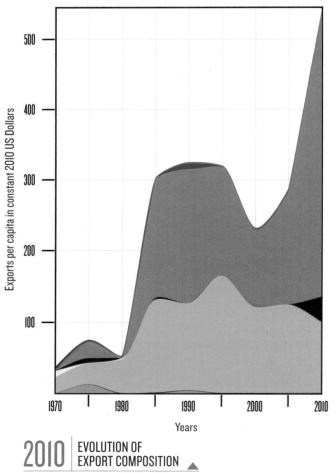

2010
EVOLUTION OF EXPORT COMPOSITION ▲

* Data are from 2010. Numbers indicate:
Value (World Ranking among 128 countries)
Region: Sub-Saharan Africa.

POPULATION ► 3.5 M / (111)
TOTAL EXPORTS ► USD 1.9 B / (113)

GDP ► USD 3.6 B / (127)
GDPᴘᴄ ► USD 1,045 / (111)

EXPORTS PER CAPITA ► USD 545 / (89)
EXPORTS AS SHARE OF GDP ► 52 % (18)

ELECTRONICS · MACHINERY · AIRCRAFT · BOILERS · SHIPS · METAL PRODUCTS · CONSTR. MATL. & EQPT. · HOME & OFFICE · PULP & PAPER · CHEMICALS & HEALTH · AGROCHEMICALS · OTHER CHEMICALS · INOR. SALTS & ACIDS · PETROCHEMICALS · LEATHER · MILK & CHEESE · ANIMAL FIBERS · MEAT & EGGS · FISH & SEAFOOD · TROPICAL AGRIC. · CEREALS & VEG. OILS · COTTON/RICE/SOY & OTHERS · TOBACCO · FRUIT · MISC. AGRICULTURE · NOT CLASSIFIED · TEXTILE & FABRICS · GARMENTS · FOOD PROCESSING · BEER/SPIRITS & CIGS. · PRECIOUS STONES · COAL · OIL · MINING

2010 | EXPORT TREEMAP ▼ TOTAL: $ 1,886,427,087

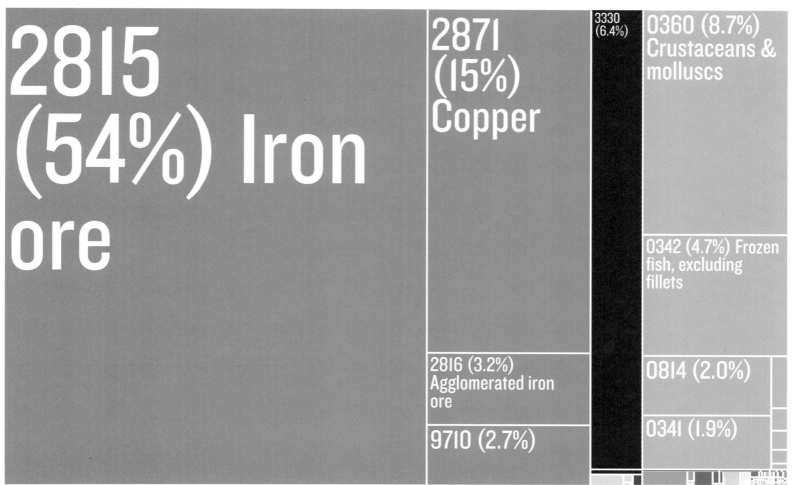

2815 (54%) Iron ore

2871 (15%) Copper

2816 (3.2%) Agglomerated iron ore

9710 (2.7%)

3330 (6.4%)

0360 (8.7%) Crustaceans & molluscs

0342 (4.7%) Frozen fish, excluding fillets

0814 (2.0%)

0341 (1.9%)

* Numbers indicate SITC-4 Rev 2 codes which can be found in the Appendix. Percentages next to the product codes indicate proportion of the product in the exports of the country. Treemap headers show the total trade of the country.

2010 | EXPORT DESTINATIONS ▼ TOTAL: $ 1,886,427,087

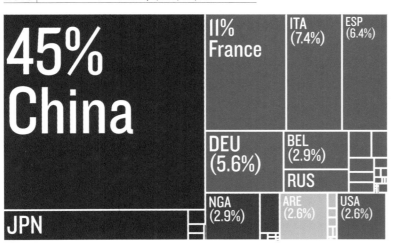

45% China

JPN

11% France

ITA (7.4%)

ESP (6.4%)

DEU (5.6%)

BEL (2.9%)

RUS

NGA (2.9%)

ARE (2.6%)

USA (2.6%)

2010 | IMPORT SOURCES ▼ TOTAL: $ 2,007,255,098

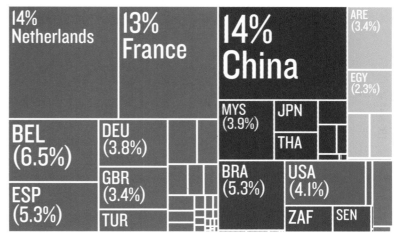

14% Netherlands

13% France

14% China

ARE (3.4%)

EGY (2.3%)

BEL (6.5%)

DEU (3.8%)

MYS (3.9%)

JPN

THA

ESP (5.3%)

GBR (3.4%)

TUR

BRA (5.3%)

USA (4.1%)

ZAF

SEN

EAST ASIA & PACIFIC   EUROPE & CENTRAL ASIA   LATIN AMERICA & CARIBBEAN   MIDDLE EAST & NORTH AFRICA   NORTH AMERICA   SOUTH ASIA   SUB-SAHARAN AFRICA

MAURITIUS

ECONOMIC COMPLEXITY INDEX [2010] ► -0.272 (72) | COMPLEXITY OUTLOOK INDEX [2010] ► -0.418 (74) | EXPECTED GDPᴘᴄ GROWTH * ► 0.9% (96)

*Expected annual average for the 2010-2020 period.

2010 PRODUCT SPACE ►

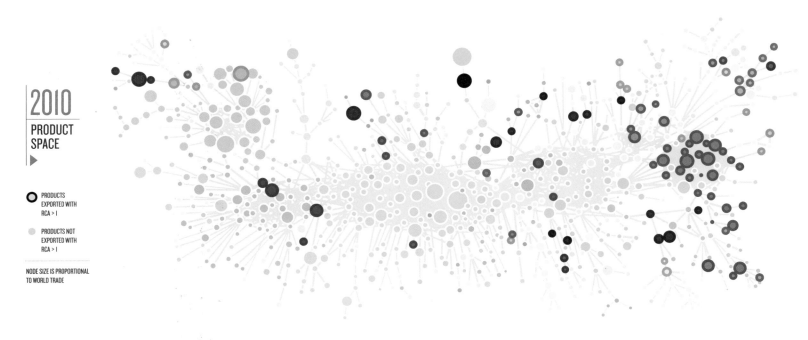

○ PRODUCTS EXPORTED WITH RCA > 1

● PRODUCTS NOT EXPORTED WITH RCA > 1

NODE SIZE IS PROPORTIONAL TO WORLD TRADE

2010 EXPORT OPPORTUNITY SPECTRUM ◄

FRACTION OF PRODUCTS WITH RCA > 1

22% OF WORLD TRADE (WT)

6% OF WT

2% OF WT

0.8% OF WT

0.06% OF WT

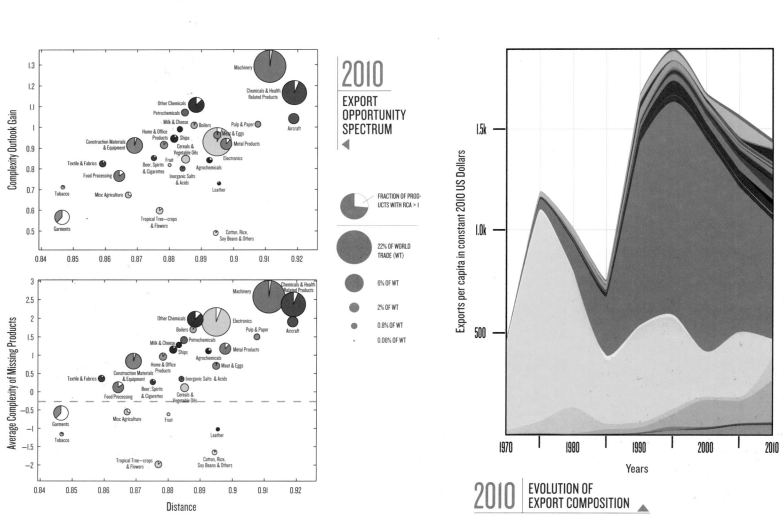

2010 EVOLUTION OF EXPORT COMPOSITION ▲

POPULATION ▸ 1.3 M / (128)
TOTAL EXPORTS ▸ USD 1.9 B / (114)
GDP ▸ USD 9.7 B / (112)
GDPpc ▸ USD 7,584 / (56)
EXPORTS PER CAPITA ▸ USD 1,447 / (64)
EXPORTS AS SHARE OF GDP ▸ 19 % (82)

* Data are from 2010. Numbers indicate:
Value (World Ranking among 128 countries)
Region: Sub-Saharan Africa.

2010 EXPORT TREEMAP — TOTAL: $ 1,853,024,509

* Numbers indicate SITC-4 Rev 2 codes which can be found in the Appendix. Percentages next to the product codes indicate proportion of the product in the exports of the country. Treemap headers show the total trade of the country.

2010 EXPORT DESTINATIONS — TOTAL: $ 1,853,024,509

2010 IMPORT SOURCES — TOTAL: $ 4,031,888,732

MEXICO

ECONOMIC COMPLEXITY INDEX [2010] ▸ 0.979 (24) | COMPLEXITY OUTLOOK INDEX [2010] ▸ 0.794 (36) | EXPECTED GDPᴘᴄ GROWTH * ▸ 3.1% (20)

*Expected annual average for the 2010-2020 period.

2010 PRODUCT SPACE ▶

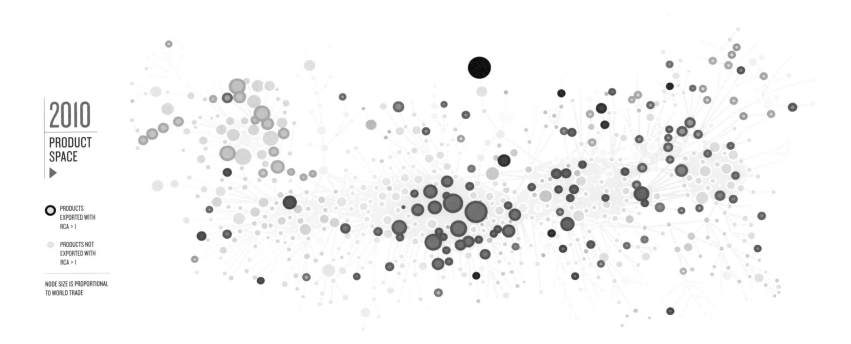

○ PRODUCTS EXPORTED WITH RCA > 1

● PRODUCTS NOT EXPORTED WITH RCA > 1

NODE SIZE IS PROPORTIONAL TO WORLD TRADE

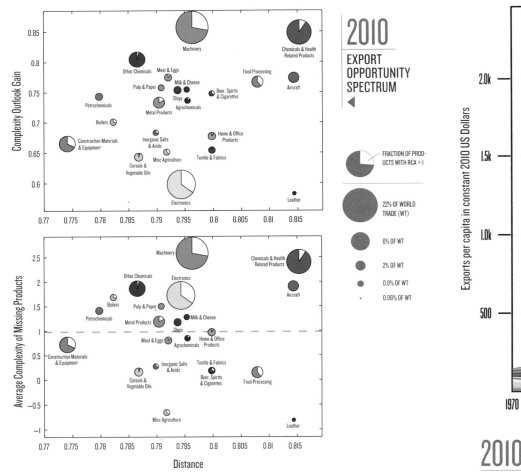

2010 EXPORT OPPORTUNITY SPECTRUM ◀

◔ FRACTION OF PRODUCTS WITH RCA > 1

● 22% OF WORLD TRADE (WT)

● 6% OF WT

● 2% OF WT

● 0.8% OF WT

· 0.06% OF WT

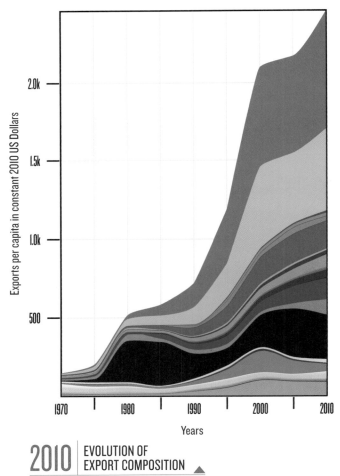

2010 EVOLUTION OF EXPORT COMPOSITION ▲

POPULATION ▸ 113 M / (11)
TOTAL EXPORTS ▸ USD 279 B / (12)

GDP ▸ USD 1 T / (14)
GDP$_{PC}$ ▸ USD 9,133 / (49)

EXPORTS PER CAPITA ▸ USD 2,464 / (49)
EXPORTS AS SHARE OF GDP ▸ 27 % (59)

* Data are from 2010. Numbers indicate:
Value (World Ranking among 128 countries)
Region: Latin America and the Caribbean.

ELECTRONICS · MACHINERY · AIRCRAFT · BOILERS · SHIPS · METAL PRODUCTS · CONSTR. MATL. & EQPT. · HOME & OFFICE · PULP & PAPER · CHEMICALS & HEALTH · AGROCHEMICALS · OTHER CHEMICALS · INOR. SALTS & ACIDS · PETROCHEMICALS · LEATHER · MILK & CHEESE · ANIMAL FIBERS · MEAT & EGGS · FISH & SEAFOOD · TROPICAL AGRIC. · CEREALS & VEG. OILS · COTTON/RICE/SOY & OTHERS · TOBACCO · FRUIT · MISC. AGRICULTURE · NOT CLASSIFIED · TEXTILE & FABRICS · GARMENTS · FOOD PROCESSING · BEER/SPIRITS & CIGS. · PRECIOUS STONES · COAL · OIL · MINING

2010 EXPORT TREEMAP ▾ TOTAL: $ 279,440,490,489

7810 (7.7%) Cars
7849 (4.5%) Other vehicle parts
7611 (6.2%) Color T.V.
7523 (4.0%)
3330 (11%) Crude petroleum
8720 (1.9%)
3345 (1.5%)

7821 (4.2%) Trucks & vans
7721 (2.2%)
5138

7139 (1.0%)
7162 (0.59%)
7643 (3.5%) Television & radio transmitters
7649 (1.1%)
9710 (2.0%) Gold, non monetary
6811 (0.87%)
2871

7132 (0.83%)
7492 (0.59%)
7788 (0.72%)
7731 (2.2%) Electric wire
7752 (0.90%)
9310 (2.5%) Unclassified transactions

7783
7239
7525
7712
8219
6973

6991
7415
7528
8841
8211 (1.5%)
6911
6428
5823

8743
7436
7621
7763
7421
0545 (0.87%)
1123 (0.70%)
0575

6725
7711
7149
0579
1124
0711

* Numbers indicate SITC-4 Rev 2 codes which can be found in the Appendix. Percentages next to the product codes indicate proportion of the product in the exports of the country. Treemap headers show the total trade of the country.

2010 EXPORT DESTINATIONS ▾ TOTAL: $ 279,440,490,489

74% United States
COL
ARG

2010 IMPORT SOURCES ▾ TOTAL: $ 261,909,615,090

49% United States
15% China
KOR (4.3%)
JPN
DEU (3.8%)
BRA
ITA

EAST ASIA & PACIFIC | EUROPE & CENTRAL ASIA | LATIN AMERICA & CARIBBEAN | MIDDLE EAST & NORTH AFRICA | NORTH AMERICA | SOUTH ASIA | SUB-SAHARAN AFRICA

MOLDOVA

| ECONOMIC COMPLEXITY INDEX [2010] ▸ -0.029 (63) | COMPLEXITY OUTLOOK INDEX [2010] ▸ 0.037 (60) | EXPECTED GDPᴘᴄ GROWTH * ▸ 3.1% (21) |

*Expected annual average for the 2010-2020 period.

2010 PRODUCT SPACE ▶

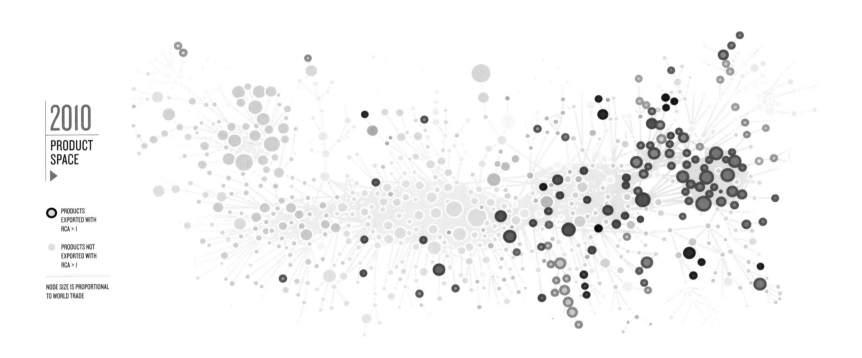

○ PRODUCTS EXPORTED WITH RCA > 1

○ PRODUCTS NOT EXPORTED WITH RCA > 1

NODE SIZE IS PROPORTIONAL TO WORLD TRADE

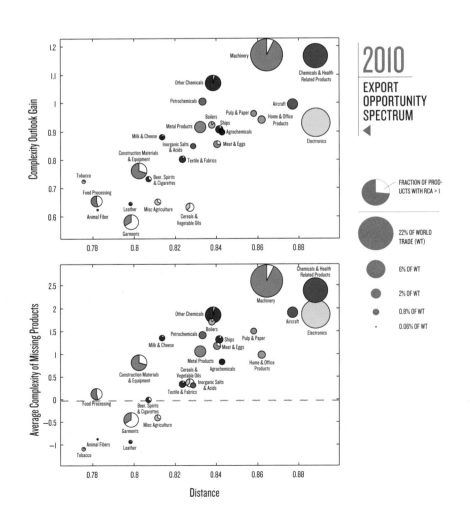

2010 EXPORT OPPORTUNITY SPECTRUM ◀

◔ FRACTION OF PRODUCTS WITH RCA > 1

⬤ 22% OF WORLD TRADE (WT)

⬤ 6% OF WT

● 2% OF WT

• 0.8% OF WT

· 0.06% OF WT

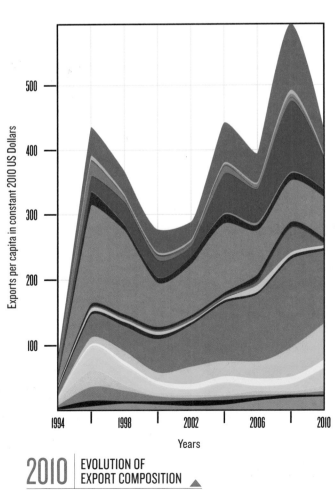

2010 EVOLUTION OF EXPORT COMPOSITION ▲

POPULATION ‣ 3.6 M / (109)
TOTAL EXPORTS ‣ USD 1.5 B / (116)

GDP ‣ USD 5.8 B / (122)
GDPᴘᴄ ‣ USD 1,632 / (97)

EXPORTS PER CAPITA ‣ USD 431 / (97)
EXPORTS AS SHARE OF GDP ‣ 26 % (60)

* Data are from 2010. Numbers indicate:
Value (World Ranking among 128 countries)
Region: Eastern Europe and Central Asia.

ELECTRONICS · MACHINERY · AIRCRAFT · BOILERS · SHIPS · METAL PRODUCTS · CONSTR. MATL. & EQPT. · HOME & OFFICE · PULP & PAPER · CHEMICALS & HEALTH · AGROCHEMICALS · OTHER CHEMICALS · INOR. SALTS & ACIDS · PETROCHEMICALS · LEATHER · MILK & CHEESE · ANIMAL FIBERS · MEAT & EGGS · FISH & SEAFOOD · TROPICAL AGRIC. · CEREALS & VEG. OILS · COTTON/RICE/SOY & OTHERS · TOBACCO · FRUIT · MISC. AGRICULTURE · NOT CLASSIFIED · TEXTILE & FABRICS · GARMENTS · FOOD PROCESSING · BEER/SPIRITS & CIGS. · PRECIOUS STONES · COAL · OIL · MINING

2010 | EXPORT TREEMAP ▾ — TOTAL: $ 1,535,895,370

8510 (4.3%) Footwear
8431 (1.8%)
8439 (1.6%)
8429 (1.5%)
8435 (1.3%)
1121 (8.2%) Wine
7731 (3.5%) Electric wire
6732 (3.1%)

6584 (3.1%) Linens & furnishings
8310 (1.2%)
8462 (0.90%)
8451 (1.2%)
8433
8441
8997
8421
8481
0579 (1.4%)
3510 (1.2%)
6911

8459 (2.3%)
8452 (1.0%)
6589
0565
0484
8211 (1.0%)
6924
8212

1124 (2.5%)

2224 (3.4%) Sunflower seeds
4236 (2.7%) Sunflower seed oil
0574 (3.7%) Fresh apples
0577 (2.9%)
6731 (5.0%) Iron/steel wire rod
6651 (1.9%) Glass bottles
7162
7423
0112

2820 (1.2%)
2111

2226 (1.5%)
0430 (1.0%)
0575 (1.2%)
2882 (1.0%)

0412 (1.5%)
2222
4232
0612 (1.4%)
1211 (1.0%)
8942
8731
8939

* Numbers indicate SITC-4 Rev 2 codes which can be found in the Appendix. Percentages next to the product codes indicate proportion of the product in the exports of the country. Treemap headers show the total trade of the country.

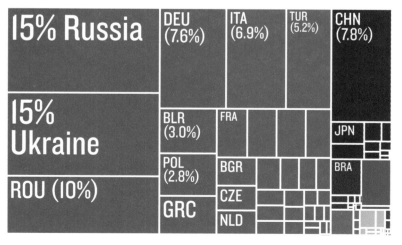

2010 | EXPORT DESTINATIONS ▾ — TOTAL: $ 1,535,895,370

25% Russia
11% Romania
DEU (7.0%)
TUR (6.5%)

13% Italy
BLR (4.9%)
POL (3.0%)

UKR (4.4%)
GRC
SRB
GBR
CZE
AUT · LTU

2010 | IMPORT SOURCES ▾ — TOTAL: $ 3,576,570,823

15% Russia
DEU (7.6%)
ITA (6.9%)
TUR (5.2%)
CHN (7.8%)

15% Ukraine
BLR (3.0%)
FRA
JPN

POL (2.8%)
BGR
BRA

ROU (10%)
GRC
CZE
NLD

EAST ASIA & PACIFIC · EUROPE & CENTRAL ASIA · LATIN AMERICA & CARIBBEAN · MIDDLE EAST & NORTH AFRICA · NORTH AMERICA · SOUTH ASIA · SUB-SAHARAN AFRICA

MONGOLIA

ECONOMIC COMPLEXITY INDEX [2010] ▸ -1.142 (115) | **COMPLEXITY OUTLOOK INDEX [2010]** ▸ -1.071 (117) | **EXPECTED GDPᴾᶜ GROWTH** * ▸ 0.6% (104)

*Expected annual average for the 2010-2020 period.

2010 PRODUCT SPACE ▸

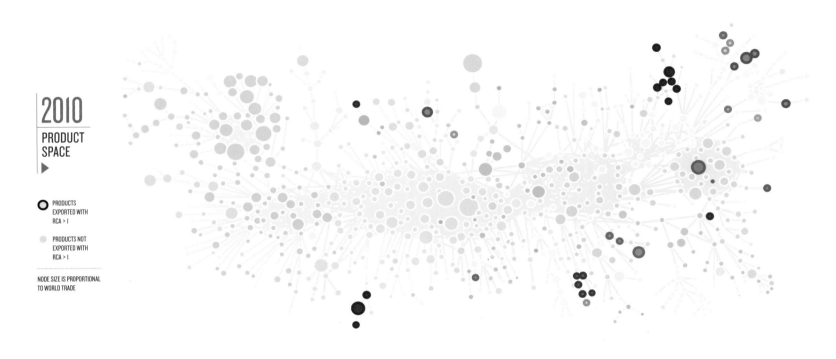

○ PRODUCTS EXPORTED WITH RCA > 1

○ PRODUCTS NOT EXPORTED WITH RCA > 1

NODE SIZE IS PROPORTIONAL TO WORLD TRADE

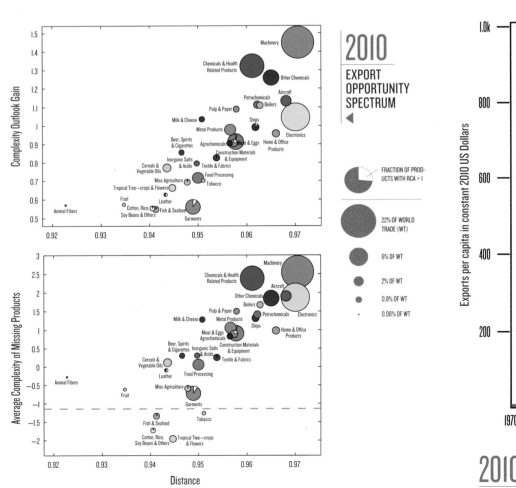

2010 EXPORT OPPORTUNITY SPECTRUM ◂

FRACTION OF PRODUCTS WITH RCA > 1

22% OF WORLD TRADE (WT)

6% OF WT

2% OF WT

0.8% OF WT

0.06% OF WT

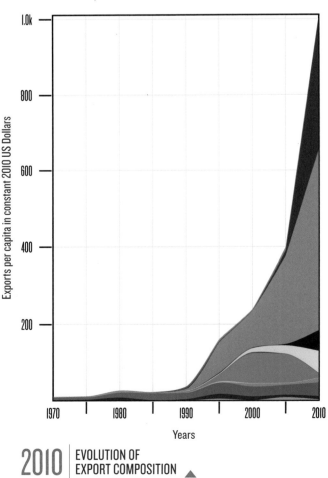

2010 EVOLUTION OF EXPORT COMPOSITION ▸

POPULATION ▸ 2.8 M / (116)	GDP ▸ USD 6.2 B / (121)
TOTAL EXPORTS ▸ USD 2.8 B / (104)	GDPPC ▸ USD 2,250 / (93)

EXPORTS PER CAPITA ▸ USD 1,011 / (75)
EXPORTS AS SHARE OF GDP ▸ 45 % (27)

* Data are from 2010. Numbers indicate:
Value (World Ranking among 128 countries)
Region: East Asia and Pacific.

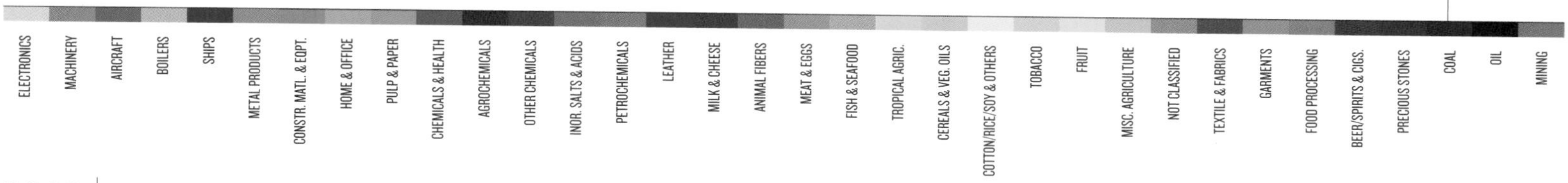

ELECTRONICS MACHINERY AIRCRAFT BOILERS SHIPS METAL PRODUCTS CONSTR. MATL. & EQPT. HOME & OFFICE PULP & PAPER CHEMICALS & HEALTH AGROCHEMICALS OTHER CHEMICALS INOR. SALTS & ACIDS PETROCHEMICALS LEATHER MILK & CHEESE ANIMAL FIBERS MEAT & EGGS FISH & SEAFOOD TROPICAL AGRIC. CEREALS & VEG. OILS COTTON/RICE/SOY & OTHERS TOBACCO FRUIT MISC. AGRICULTURE NOT CLASSIFIED TEXTILE & FABRICS GARMENTS FOOD PROCESSING BEER/SPIRITS & CIGS. PRECIOUS STONES COAL OIL MINING

2010 EXPORT TREEMAP ▾ TOTAL: $ 2,785,683,136

2871 (29%) Copper

3222 (34%) Other coal

9710 (7.5%) Gold, non monetary

2879 (2.4%)

2815 (7.2%) Iron ore

6821 (0.65%)

2785 (2.7%) Quartz metal family

2875 (2.6%) Zinc

2874

3330 (5.4%) Crude petroleum

2683 (2.8%)

2687

2682

0115 (0.70%)

0111

2111

8451 (0.66%)

* Numbers indicate SITC-4 Rev 2 codes which can be found in the Appendix. Percentages next to the product codes indicate proportion of the product in the exports of the country. Treemap headers show the total trade of the country.

2010 EXPORT DESTINATIONS ▾ TOTAL: $ 2,785,683,136

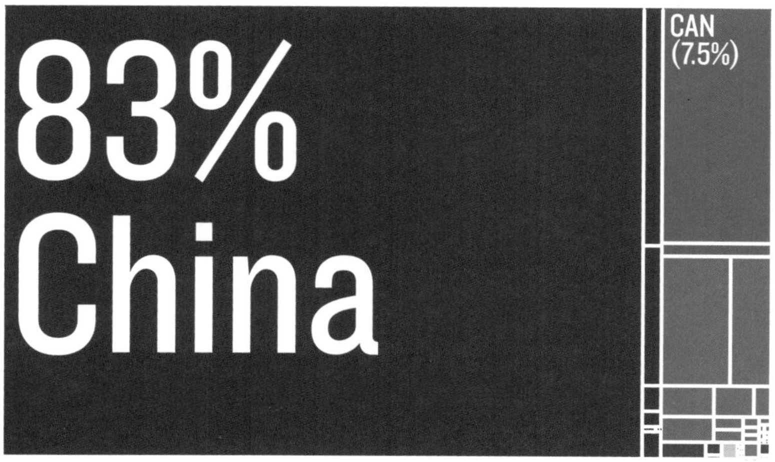

83% China

CAN (7.5%)

2010 IMPORT SOURCES ▾ TOTAL: $ 3,420,162,649

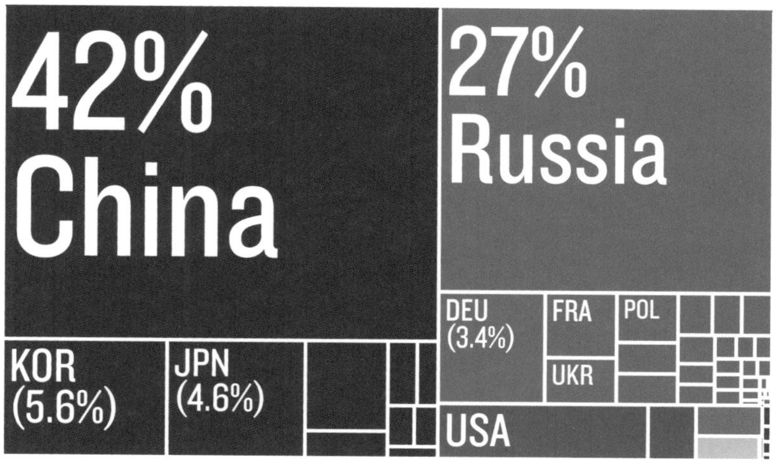

42% China

27% Russia

DEU (3.4%)

FRA

POL

UKR

KOR (5.6%)

JPN (4.6%)

USA

| EAST ASIA & PACIFIC | EUROPE & CENTRAL ASIA | LATIN AMERICA & CARIBBEAN | MIDDLE EAST & NORTH AFRICA | NORTH AMERICA | SOUTH ASIA | SUB-SAHARAN AFRICA |

MOROCCO

| ECONOMIC COMPLEXITY INDEX [2010] ▸ -0.485 (84) | COMPLEXITY OUTLOOK INDEX [2010] ▸ -0.197 (67) | EXPECTED GDPᴘᴄ GROWTH * ▸ 1.8% (71) |

*Expected annual average for the 2010-2020 period.

2010 PRODUCT SPACE ▶

○ PRODUCTS EXPORTED WITH RCA > 1

○ PRODUCTS NOT EXPORTED WITH RCA > 1

NODE SIZE IS PROPORTIONAL TO WORLD TRADE

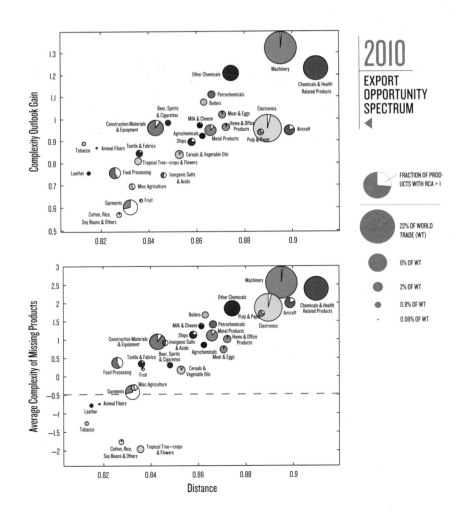

2010 EXPORT OPPORTUNITY SPECTRUM ◀

FRACTION OF PRODUCTS WITH RCA > 1

22% OF WORLD TRADE (WT)

6% OF WT

2% OF WT

0.8% OF WT

0.06% OF WT

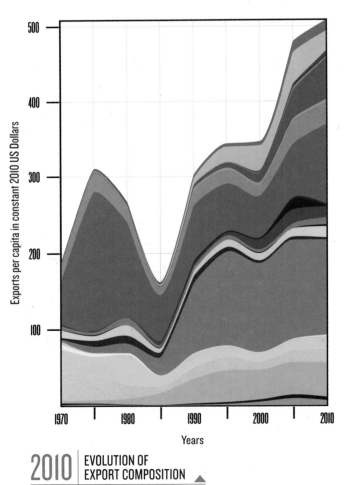

2010 EVOLUTION OF EXPORT COMPOSITION ▲

POPULATION ▸ 32 M / (36)	GDP ▸ USD 91 B / (59)	EXPORTS PER CAPITA ▸ USD 508 / (91)	* Data are from 2010. Numbers indicate:
TOTAL EXPORTS ▸ USD 16 B / (68)	GDPPc ▸ USD 2,795 / (89)	EXPORTS AS SHARE OF GDP ▸18 % (88)	Value (World Ranking among 128 countries) Region: Middle East and North Africa.

ELECTRONICS · MACHINERY · AIRCRAFT · BOILERS · SHIPS · METAL PRODUCTS · CONSTR. MATL. & EQPT. · HOME & OFFICE · PULP & PAPER · CHEMICALS & HEALTH · AGROCHEMICALS · OTHER CHEMICALS · INOR. SALTS & ACIDS · PETROCHEMICALS · LEATHER · MILK & CHEESE · ANIMAL FIBERS · MEAT & EGGS · FISH & SEAFOOD · TROPICAL AGRIC. · CEREALS & VEG. OILS · COTTON/RICE/SOY & OTHERS · TOBACCO · FRUIT · MISC. AGRICULTURE · NOT CLASSIFIED · TEXTILE & FABRICS · GARMENTS · FOOD PROCESSING · BEER/SPIRITS & CIGS. · PRECIOUS STONES · COAL · OIL · MINING

2010 EXPORT TREEMAP ▾ TOTAL: $ 16,237,430,039

8439 (3.8%) Other women's outerwear
8431 (1.9%)
8462 (1.8%)
8435 (1.7%)
8433 (1.7%)
7731 (9.6%) Electric wire
7764 (3.5%) Electronic microcircuits
0360 (2.8%)
0371 (2.3%)
8510 (2.2%)
8459 (1.4%)
8465 (0.77%)
8451 (1.1%)
8452 (0.76%)
6123
8423 (2.2%)
8463
8434 (0.71%)
8424
7763 (1.1%)
7721 (0.97%)
0342 (0.96%)
0372 (0.90%)
4111
5222 (7.6%) Non metal inorganic acids & oxygen compounds
2713 (5.5%) Natural calcium phosphates & aluminium
3345 (2.4%)
8211
8122
2517
6749
0814
2919
0240
9710 (0.95%)
0544 (2.8%) Tomatoes
0571 (3.0%) Fresh or dried oranges & m&arines
2874
2875
6851
5629 (6.3%) Fertilizers
5622 (1.2%)
0545 (2.4%) Other fresh or chilled vegetables
0565 (0.94%)
0579
9310

* Numbers indicate SITC-4 Rev 2 codes which can be found in the Appendix. Percentages next to the product codes indicate proportion of the product in the exports of the country. Treemap headers show the total trade of the country.

2010 EXPORT DESTINATIONS ▾ TOTAL: $ 16,237,430,039

21% France · 20% Spain · DEU (4.0%) · ITA (3.9%) · CHN (2.5%) · IND (4.8%) · SGP · KOR · HKG · PAK · BRA (3.7%) · USA (4.1%) · MEX · ARE · DZA

2010 IMPORT SOURCES ▾ TOTAL: $ 32,291,747,687

15% France · ESP (11%) · SAU (5.9%) · 8.3% China · IRQ (2.0%) · KOR · DEU (4.6%) · TUR · BEL · EGY · JPN · GBR · RUS (3.8%) · NLD · GRC · 7.0% United States

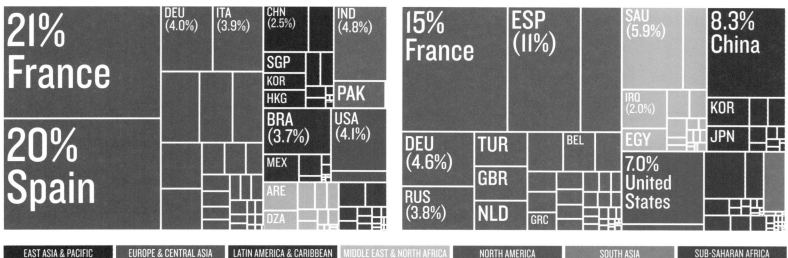

EAST ASIA & PACIFIC · EUROPE & CENTRAL ASIA · LATIN AMERICA & CARIBBEAN · MIDDLE EAST & NORTH AFRICA · NORTH AMERICA · SOUTH ASIA · SUB-SAHARAN AFRICA

MOZAMBIQUE

ECONOMIC COMPLEXITY INDEX [2010] ▸ -1.259 (117) | **COMPLEXITY OUTLOOK INDEX [2010] ▸ -1.03 (115)** | **EXPECTED GDPᴘᴄ GROWTH * ▸ 2.3% (51)**

*Expected annual average for the 2010-2020 period.

2010
PRODUCT SPACE ▶

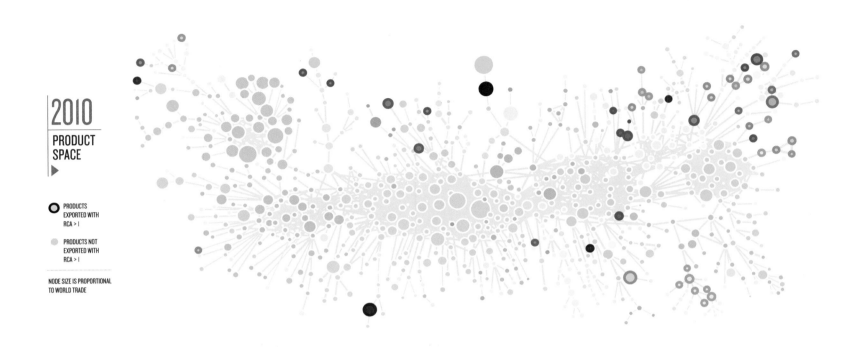

○ PRODUCTS EXPORTED WITH RCA > 1

○ PRODUCTS NOT EXPORTED WITH RCA > 1

NODE SIZE IS PROPORTIONAL TO WORLD TRADE

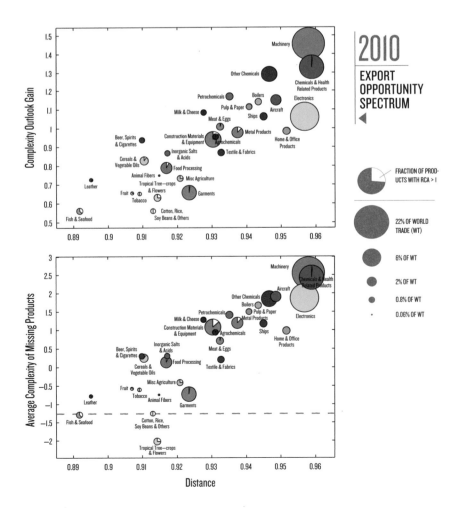

2010
EXPORT OPPORTUNITY SPECTRUM ◀

◔ FRACTION OF PRODUCTS WITH RCA > 1

⬤ 22% OF WORLD TRADE (WT)

⬤ 6% OF WT

● 2% OF WT

• 0.8% OF WT

· 0.06% OF WT

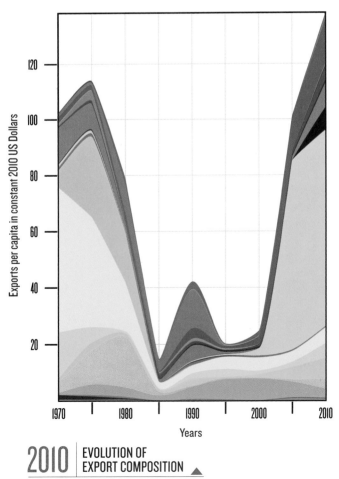

2010 | EVOLUTION OF EXPORT COMPOSITION ▲

POPULATION ▸ 23 M / (44)	GDP ▸ USD 9.2 B / (115)	EXPORTS PER CAPITA ▸ USD 138 / (117)
TOTAL EXPORTS ▸ USD 3.2 B / (101)	GDPpc ▸ USD 394 / (125)	EXPORTS AS SHARE OF GDP ▸ 35 % (42)

* Data are from 2010. Numbers indicate:
Value (World Ranking among 128 countries)
Region: Sub-Saharan Africa.

ELECTRONICS · MACHINERY · AIRCRAFT · BOILERS · SHIPS · METAL PRODUCTS · CONSTR. MATL. & EQPT. · HOME & OFFICE · PULP & PAPER · CHEMICALS & HEALTH · AGROCHEMICALS · OTHER CHEMICALS · INOR. SALTS & ACIDS · PETROCHEMICALS · LEATHER · MILK & CHEESE · ANIMAL FIBERS · MEAT & EGGS · FISH & SEAFOOD · TROPICAL AGRIC. · CEREALS & VEG. OILS · COTTON/RICE/SOY & OTHERS · TOBACCO · FRUIT · MISC. AGRICULTURE · NOT CLASSIFIED · TEXTILE & FABRICS · GARMENTS · FOOD PROCESSING · BEER/SPIRITS & CIGS. · PRECIOUS STONES · COAL · OIL · MINING

2010 EXPORT TREEMAP ▾ TOTAL: $ 3,235,381,347

6841 (49%) Unwrought aluminium & aluminium alloys

2879 (3.1%) Other non ferrous base metals

1212 (4.7%) Stripped tobacco

0577 (1.4%)

3510 (7.3%) Electric current

2872 (2.4%) Nickel

1211

2221

6821

0611 (3.3%) Raw sugars

3413 (4.9%) liquified hydrocarbons

2472 (2.8%) Sawlogs & veneer logs of non coniferous

0542 (1.3%)

0460 (0.55%)

0615

2483 (1.1%)

3345 (3.6%) Lubricating petroleum oils

0360 (2.1%) Crustaceans & molluscs

3330

3222

* Numbers indicate SITC-4 Rev 2 codes which can be found in the Appendix. Percentages next to the product codes indicate proportion of the product in the exports of the country. Treemap headers show the total trade of the country.

2010 EXPORT DESTINATIONS ▾ TOTAL: $ 3,235,381,347

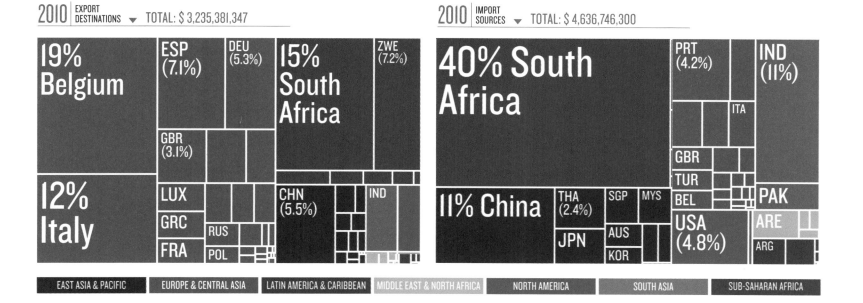

19% Belgium

ESP (7.1%)

DEU (5.3%)

15% South Africa

ZWE (7.2%)

GBR (3.1%)

12% Italy

LUX

GRC

FRA

RUS

POL

CHN (5.5%)

IND

2010 IMPORT SOURCES ▾ TOTAL: $ 4,636,746,300

40% South Africa

PRT (4.2%)

IND (11%)

ITA

GBR

TUR

BEL

11% China

THA (2.4%)

SGP

MYS

JPN

AUS

KOR

USA (4.8%)

PAK

ARE

ARG

EAST ASIA & PACIFIC · EUROPE & CENTRAL ASIA · LATIN AMERICA & CARIBBEAN · MIDDLE EAST & NORTH AFRICA · NORTH AMERICA · SOUTH ASIA · SUB-SAHARAN AFRICA

NAMIBIA

ECONOMIC COMPLEXITY INDEX [2010] ▸ -0.836 (100)   COMPLEXITY OUTLOOK INDEX [2010] ▸ -0.983 (110)   EXPECTED GDPᴘᴄ GROWTH * ▸ 0.2% (112)

*Expected annual average for the 2010-2020 period.

2010 PRODUCT SPACE ▶

○ PRODUCTS EXPORTED WITH RCA > 1

○ PRODUCTS NOT EXPORTED WITH RCA > 1

NODE SIZE IS PROPORTIONAL TO WORLD TRADE

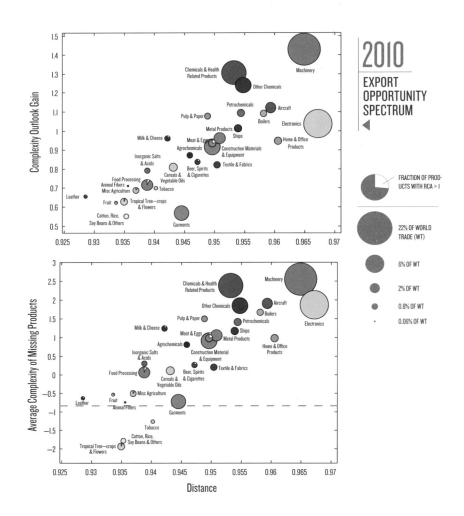

2010 EXPORT OPPORTUNITY SPECTRUM ◀

FRACTION OF PRODUCTS WITH RCA > 1

22% OF WORLD TRADE (WT)

6% OF WT

2% OF WT

0.8% OF WT

0.06% OF WT

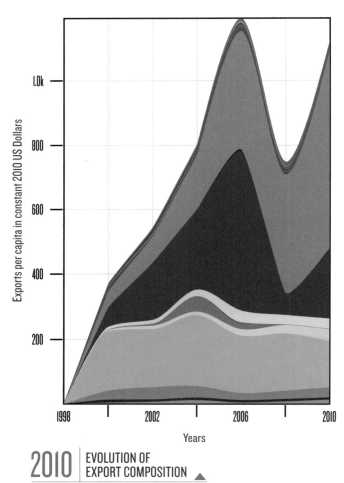

2010 | EVOLUTION OF EXPORT COMPOSITION ▲

POPULATION ▸ 2.3 M / (119)	GDP ▸ USD 11 B / (111)	EXPORTS PER CAPITA ▸ USD 1,131 / (71)	* Data are from 2010. Numbers indicate:
TOTAL EXPORTS ▸ USD 2.6 B / (105)	GDPᴘᴄ ▸ USD 4,876 / (69)	EXPORTS AS SHARE OF GDP ▸ 23 % (69)	Value (World Ranking among 128 countries) Region: Sub-Saharan Africa.

ELECTRONICS · MACHINERY · AIRCRAFT · BOILERS · SHIPS · METAL PRODUCTS · CONSTR. MATL. & EQPT. · HOME & OFFICE · PULP & PAPER · CHEMICALS & HEALTH · AGROCHEMICALS · OTHER CHEMICALS · INOR. SALTS & ACIDS · PETROCHEMICALS · LEATHER · MILK & CHEESE · ANIMAL FIBERS · MEAT & EGGS · FISH & SEAFOOD · TROPICAL AGRIC. · CEREALS & VEG. OILS · COTTON/RICE/SOY & OTHERS · TOBACCO · FRUIT · MISC. AGRICULTURE · NOT CLASSIFIED · TEXTILE & FABRICS · GARMENTS · FOOD PROCESSING · BEER/SPIRITS & CIGS. · PRECIOUS STONES · COAL · OIL · MINING

2010 EXPORT TREEMAP ▾ TOTAL: $ 2,582,063,733

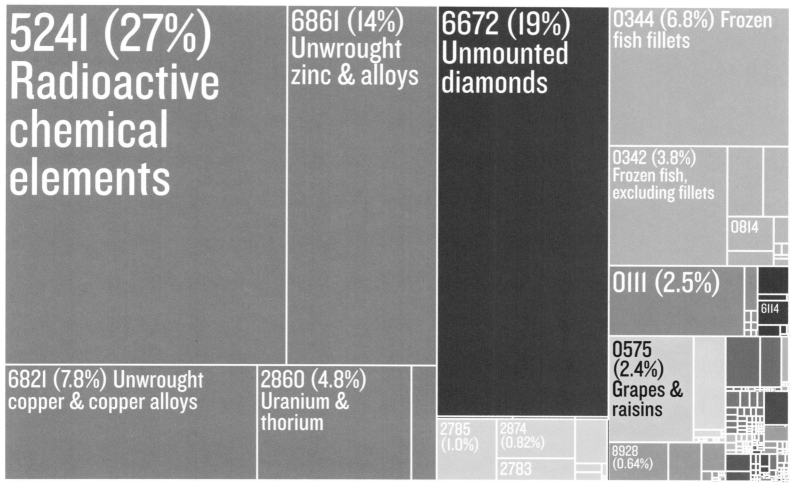

5241 (27%) Radioactive chemical elements

6861 (14%) Unwrought zinc & alloys

6672 (19%) Unmounted diamonds

0344 (6.8%) Frozen fish fillets

0342 (3.8%) Frozen fish, excluding fillets

0814

0111 (2.5%)

6114

0575 (2.4%) Grapes & raisins

6821 (7.8%) Unwrought copper & copper alloys

2860 (4.8%) Uranium & thorium

2785 (1.0%) · 2874 (0.82%) · 2783

8928 (0.64%)

* Numbers indicate SITC-4 Rev 2 codes which can be found in the Appendix. Percentages next to the product codes indicate proportion of the product in the exports of the country. Treemap headers show the total trade of the country.

2010 EXPORT DESTINATIONS ▾ TOTAL: $ 2,582,063,733

2010 IMPORT SOURCES ▾ TOTAL: $ 1,184,293,453

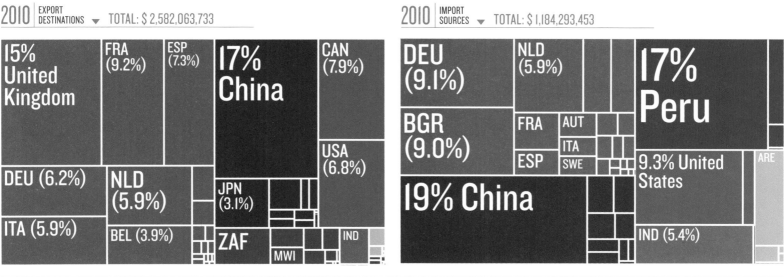

Export destinations: 15% United Kingdom · FRA (9.2%) · ESP (7.3%) · 17% China · CAN (7.9%) · DEU (6.2%) · NLD (5.9%) · USA (6.8%) · JPN (3.1%) · ITA (5.9%) · BEL (3.9%) · ZAF · MWI · IND

Import sources: DEU (9.1%) · NLD (5.9%) · 17% Peru · BGR (9.0%) · FRA · AUT · ITA · ESP · SWE · 9.3% United States · ARE · 19% China · IND (5.4%)

EAST ASIA & PACIFIC · EUROPE & CENTRAL ASIA · LATIN AMERICA & CARIBBEAN · MIDDLE EAST & NORTH AFRICA · NORTH AMERICA · SOUTH ASIA · SUB-SAHARAN AFRICA

NETHERLANDS

| ECONOMIC COMPLEXITY INDEX [2010] ▸ 1.082 (22) | COMPLEXITY OUTLOOK INDEX [2010] ▸ 1.226 (15) | EXPECTED GDP PC GROWTH * ▸ 1.8% (70) |

*Expected annual average for the 2010-2020 period.

2010 PRODUCT SPACE ▸

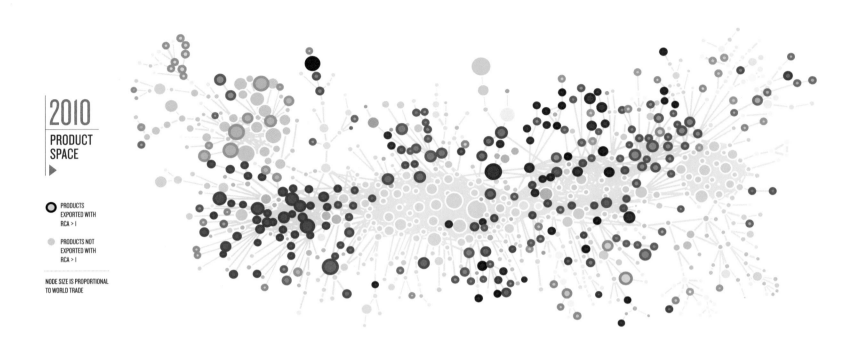

- ◉ PRODUCTS EXPORTED WITH RCA > 1
- ○ PRODUCTS NOT EXPORTED WITH RCA > 1

NODE SIZE IS PROPORTIONAL TO WORLD TRADE

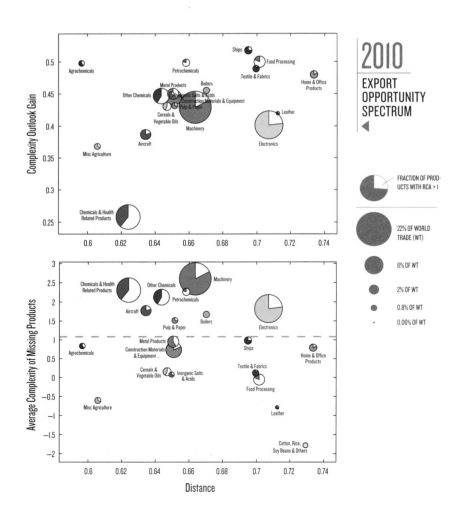

2010 EXPORT OPPORTUNITY SPECTRUM ◀

- FRACTION OF PRODUCTS WITH RCA > 1
- 22% OF WORLD TRADE (WT)
- 6% OF WT
- 2% OF WT
- 0.8% OF WT
- 0.06% OF WT

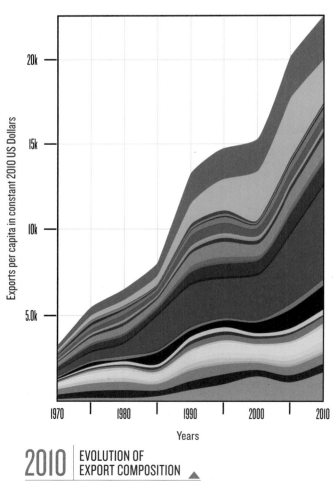

2010 EVOLUTION OF EXPORT COMPOSITION ▲

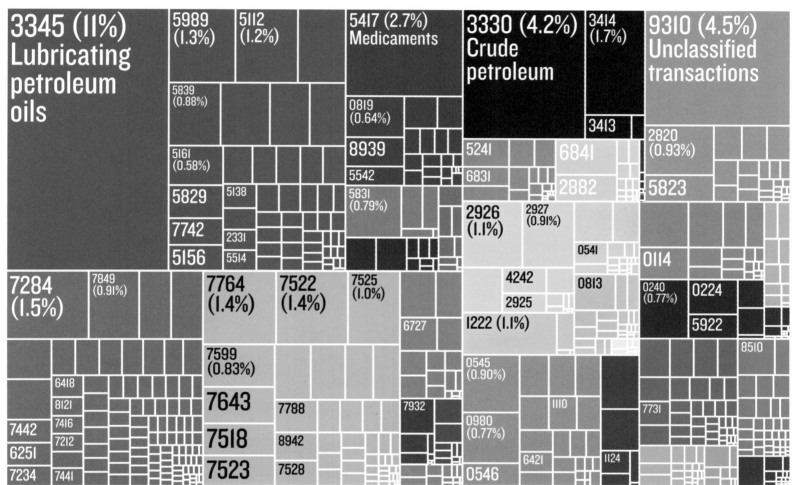

POPULATION ▸ 17 M / (54)
TOTAL EXPORTS ▸ USD 375 B / (8)
GDP ▸ USD 774 B / (16)
GDPᴘᴄ ▸ USD 46,597 / (8)
EXPORTS PER CAPITA ▸ USD 22,536 / (7)
EXPORTS AS SHARE OF GDP ▸ 48 % (20)

2010 EXPORT TREEMAP ▾ TOTAL: $ 374,451,601,468

* Numbers indicate SITC-4 Rev 2 codes which can be found in the Appendix. Percentages next to the product codes indicate proportion of the product in the exports of the country. Treemap headers show the total trade of the country.

2010 EXPORT DESTINATIONS ▾ TOTAL: $ 374,451,601,468

2010 IMPORT SOURCES ▾ TOTAL: $ 358,732,020,509

EAST ASIA & PACIFIC   EUROPE & CENTRAL ASIA   LATIN AMERICA & CARIBBEAN   MIDDLE EAST & NORTH AFRICA   NORTH AMERICA   SOUTH ASIA   SUB-SAHARAN AFRICA

NEW ZEALAND

| ECONOMIC COMPLEXITY INDEX [2010] ▸ 0.261 (50) | COMPLEXITY OUTLOOK INDEX [2010] ▸ 0.713 (41) | EXPECTED GDPᴘᴄ GROWTH * ▸ 0.7% (100) |

*Expected annual average for the 2010-2020 period.

2010 PRODUCT SPACE ▶

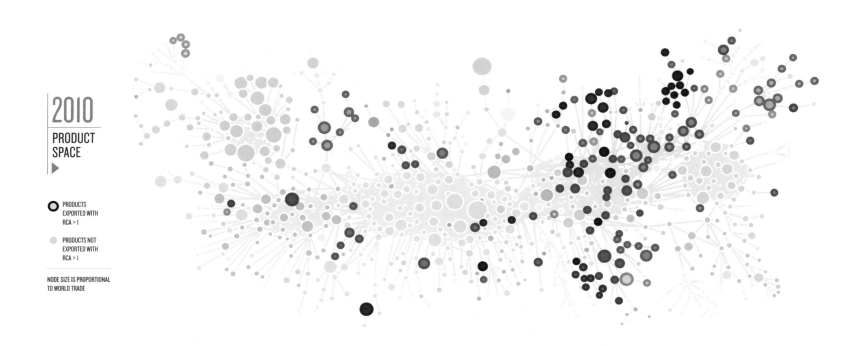

○ PRODUCTS EXPORTED WITH RCA > 1

● PRODUCTS NOT EXPORTED WITH RCA > 1

NODE SIZE IS PROPORTIONAL TO WORLD TRADE

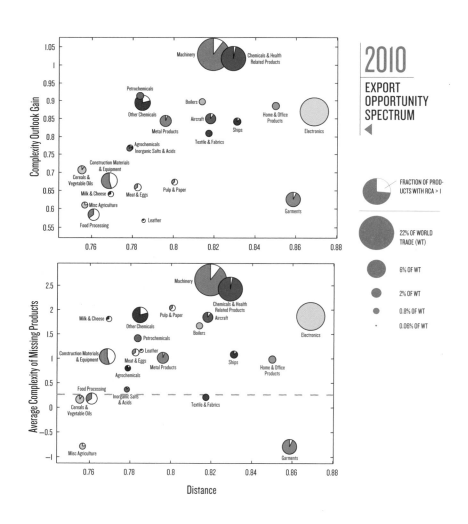

2010 EXPORT OPPORTUNITY SPECTRUM ◀

FRACTION OF PRODUCTS WITH RCA > 1

22% OF WORLD TRADE (WT)

6% OF WT

2% OF WT

0.8% OF WT

0.06% OF WT

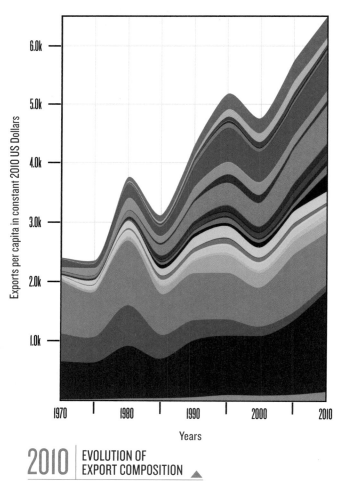

2010 | EVOLUTION OF EXPORT COMPOSITION ▲

POPULATION ▸ 4.4 M / (104)	GDP ▸ USD 143 B / (52)	EXPORTS PER CAPITA ▸ USD 6,502 / (31)	* Data are from 2010. Numbers indicate:
TOTAL EXPORTS ▸ USD 28 B / (58)	GDPᴘᴄ ▸ USD 32,620 / (22)	EXPORTS AS SHARE OF GDP ▸ 20 % (79)	Value (World Ranking among 128 countries) Region: East Asia and Pacific.

ELECTRONICS · MACHINERY · AIRCRAFT · BOILERS · SHIPS · METAL PRODUCTS · CONSTR. MATL. & EQPT. · HOME & OFFICE · PULP & PAPER · CHEMICALS & HEALTH · AGROCHEMICALS · OTHER CHEMICALS · INOR. SALTS & ACIDS · PETROCHEMICALS · LEATHER · MILK & CHEESE · ANIMAL FIBERS · MEAT & EGGS · FISH & SEAFOOD · TROPICAL AGRIC. · CEREALS & VEG. OILS · COTTON/RICE/SOY & OTHERS · TOBACCO · FRUIT · MISC. AGRICULTURE · NOT CLASSIFIED · TEXTILE & FABRICS · GARMENTS · FOOD PROCESSING · BEER/SPIRITS & CIGS. · PRECIOUS STONES · COAL · OIL · MINING

2010 EXPORT TREEMAP ▾ TOTAL: $ 28,397,440,120

* Numbers indicate SITC-4 Rev 2 codes which can be found in the Appendix. Percentages next to the product codes indicate proportion of the product in the exports of the country. Treemap headers show the total trade of the country.

2010 EXPORT DESTINATIONS ▾ TOTAL: $ 28,397,440,120

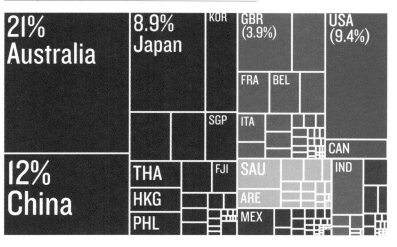

2010 IMPORT SOURCES ▾ TOTAL: $ 26,259,720,479

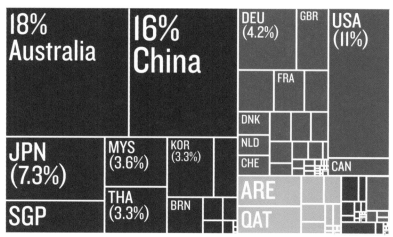

EAST ASIA & PACIFIC | EUROPE & CENTRAL ASIA | LATIN AMERICA & CARIBBEAN | MIDDLE EAST & NORTH AFRICA | NORTH AMERICA | SOUTH ASIA | SUB-SAHARAN AFRICA

NICARAGUA

ECONOMIC COMPLEXITY INDEX [2010] ► -0.991 (106) | **COMPLEXITY OUTLOOK INDEX [2010] ► -0.884 (96)** | **EXPECTED GDPᴘᴄ GROWTH * ► 1.6% (79)**

*Expected annual average for the 2010-2020 period.

2010
PRODUCT SPACE ▶

○ PRODUCTS EXPORTED WITH RCA > 1

● PRODUCTS NOT EXPORTED WITH RCA > 1

NODE SIZE IS PROPORTIONAL TO WORLD TRADE

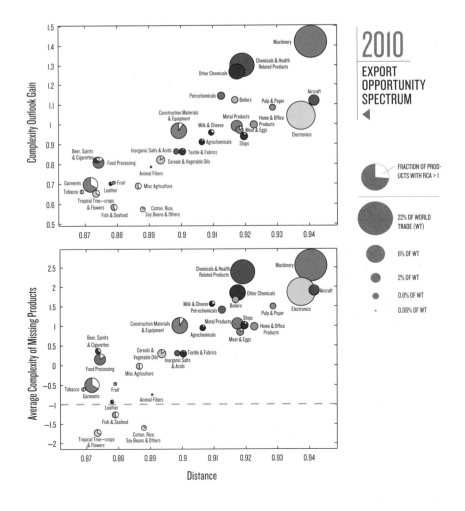

2010
EXPORT OPPORTUNITY SPECTRUM ◀

◔ FRACTION OF PRODUCTS WITH RCA > 1

● 22% OF WORLD TRADE (WT)

● 6% OF WT

● 2% OF WT

● 0.8% OF WT

· 0.06% OF WT

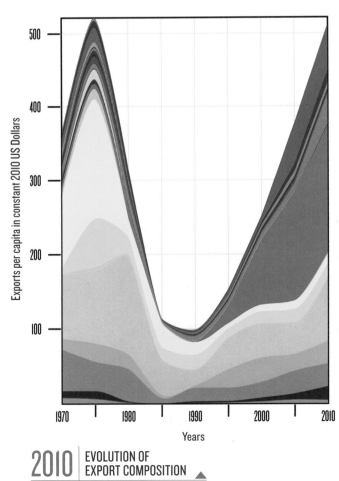

2010 | EVOLUTION OF EXPORT COMPOSITION ▲

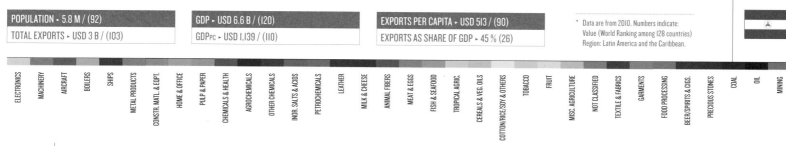

POPULATION ‣ 5.8 M / (92)
TOTAL EXPORTS ‣ USD 3 B / (103)

GDP ‣ USD 6.6 B / (120)
GDPᵖᶜ ‣ USD 1,139 / (110)

EXPORTS PER CAPITA ‣ USD 513 / (90)
EXPORTS AS SHARE OF GDP ‣ 45 % (26)

* Data are from 2010. Numbers indicate:
Value (World Ranking among 128 countries)
Region: Latin America and the Caribbean.

ELECTRONICS | MACHINERY | AIRCRAFT | BOILERS | SHIPS | METAL PRODUCTS | CONSTR. MATL. & EQPT. | HOME & OFFICE | PULP & PAPER | CHEMICALS & HEALTH | AGROCHEMICALS | OTHER CHEMICALS | INOR. SALTS & ACIDS | PETROCHEMICALS | LEATHER | MILK & CHEESE | ANIMAL FIBERS | MEAT & EGGS | FISH & SEAFOOD | TROPICAL AGRIC. | CEREALS & VEG. OILS | COTTON/RICE/SOY & OTHERS | TOBACCO | FRUIT | MISC. AGRICULTURE | NOT CLASSIFIED | TEXTILE & FABRICS | GARMENTS | FOOD PROCESSING | BEER/SPIRITS & CIGS. | PRECIOUS STONES | COAL | OIL | MINING

2010 | EXPORT TREEMAP ▾ TOTAL: $ 2,968,741,208

8451 (10%) Knit outerwear

8462 (7.2%) Knit undergarments of cotton

0711 (12%) Coffee, green or roasted

8423 (5.8%) Men's trousers

8463 (2.4%) Knit undergarments of synthetic fibers

8441 (1.3%)

8439 (1.6%)

8452

0542 (1.5%)

0615 (1.1%)

0611 (2.2%) Raw sugars

0573 (0.71%)

0548

4242

4234

2221 (2.0%)

8459 (3.4%) Other knit outerwear

0111 (5.4%) Bovine meat

0011 | 0116

0240 (2.0%)

9710 (7.5%) Gold, non monetary

0360 (4.4%) Crustaceans & molluscs

0342

0341

0224 (0.98%)

7731 (11%) Electric wire

8211 | 2483

1221 (2.7%) Cigars

1124

9310 (0.54%)

3345

0712

* Numbers indicate SITC-4 Rev 2 codes which can be found in the Appendix. Percentages next to the product codes indicate proportion of the product in the exports of the country. Treemap headers show the total trade of the country.

2010 | EXPORT DESTINATIONS ▾ TOTAL: $ 2,968,741,208

64% United States

SLV (5.6%)

MEX (3.8%)

CRI

VEN

GTM

ESP (2.0%)

FRA

BEL

2010 | IMPORT SOURCES ▾ TOTAL: $ 3,900,282,823

17% Venezuela

MEX (7.4%)

GTM (6.0%)

CRI (8.1%)

SLV (4.5%)

BRA

ANT

20% United States

ESP

DEU

7.9% China

KOR (5.7%)

THA

EAST ASIA & PACIFIC | EUROPE & CENTRAL ASIA | LATIN AMERICA & CARIBBEAN | MIDDLE EAST & NORTH AFRICA | NORTH AMERICA | SOUTH ASIA | SUB-SAHARAN AFRICA

NIGERIA

ECONOMIC COMPLEXITY INDEX [2010] ▸ -2.312 (128)	COMPLEXITY OUTLOOK INDEX [2010] ▸ -1.141 (122)	EXPECTED GDPᴘᴄ GROWTH * ▸ -0.4% (119)

*Expected annual average for the 2010-2020 period.

2010
PRODUCT SPACE ▸

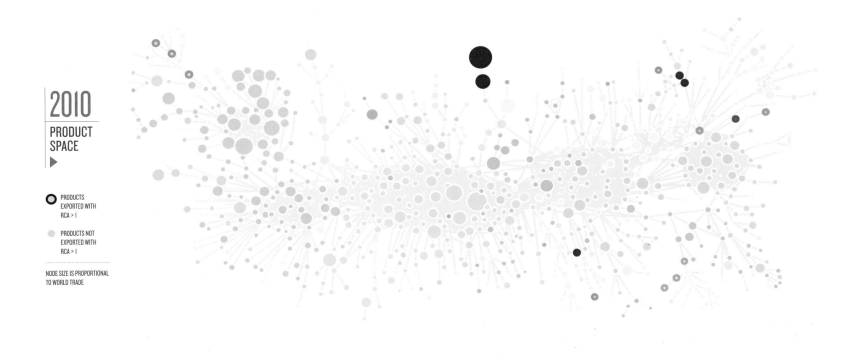

○ PRODUCTS EXPORTED WITH RCA > 1

◉ PRODUCTS NOT EXPORTED WITH RCA > 1

NODE SIZE IS PROPORTIONAL TO WORLD TRADE

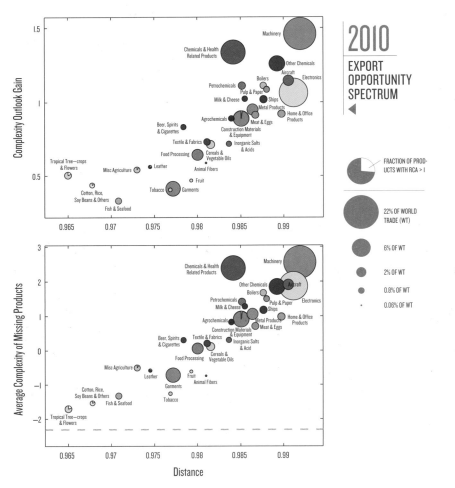

2010
EXPORT OPPORTUNITY SPECTRUM ◂

⬕ FRACTION OF PRODUCTS WITH RCA > 1

◯ 22% OF WORLD TRADE (WT)

◯ 6% OF WT

○ 2% OF WT

○ 0.8% OF WT

· 0.06% OF WT

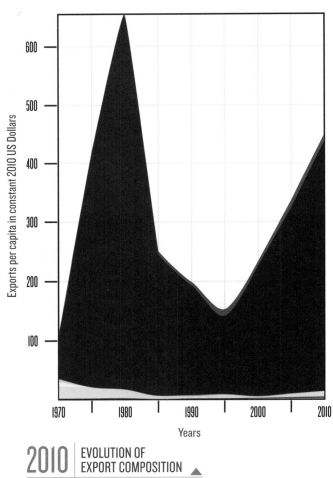

2010
EVOLUTION OF EXPORT COMPOSITION ▲

POPULATION ▸ 158 M / (7)
TOTAL EXPORTS ▸ USD 71 B / (37)

GDP ▸ USD 197 B / (46)
GDPPC ▸ USD 1,242 / (105)

EXPORTS PER CAPITA ▸ USD 451 / (93)
EXPORTS AS SHARE OF GDP ▸ 36 % (38)

* Data are from 2010. Numbers indicate:
Value (World Ranking among 128 countries)
Region: Sub-Saharan Africa.

ELECTRONICS · MACHINERY · AIRCRAFT · BOILERS · SHIPS · METAL PRODUCTS · CONSTR. MATL. & EQPT. · HOME & OFFICE · PULP & PAPER · CHEMICALS & HEALTH · AGROCHEMICALS · OTHER CHEMICALS · INOR. SALTS & ACIDS · PETROCHEMICALS · LEATHER · MILK & CHEESE · ANIMAL FIBERS · MEAT & EGGS · FISH & SEAFOOD · TROPICAL AGRIC. · CEREALS & VEG. OILS · COTTON/RICE/SOY & OTHERS · TOBACCO · FRUIT · MISC. AGRICULTURE · NOT CLASSIFIED · TEXTILE & FABRICS · GARMENTS · FOOD PROCESSING · BEER/SPIRITS & CIGS. · PRECIOUS STONES · COAL · OIL · MINING

2010 | EXPORT TREEMAP ▾ TOTAL: $ 71,428,776,877

3330 (86%) Crude petroleum

3413 (8.5%)

6115

6116

* Numbers indicate SITC-4 Rev 2 codes which can be found in the Appendix. Percentages next to the product codes indicate proportion of the product in the exports of the country. Treemap headers show the total trade of the country.

2010 | EXPORT DESTINATIONS ▾ TOTAL: $ 71,428,776,877

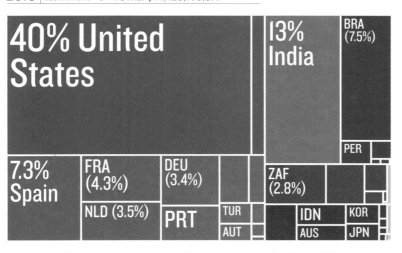

40% United States

7.3% Spain

FRA (4.3%)

NLD (3.5%)

DEU (3.4%)

PRT

TUR

AUT

13% India

BRA (7.5%)

PER

ZAF (2.8%)

IDN

AUS

KOR

JPN

2010 | IMPORT SOURCES ▾ TOTAL: $ 42,226,055,938

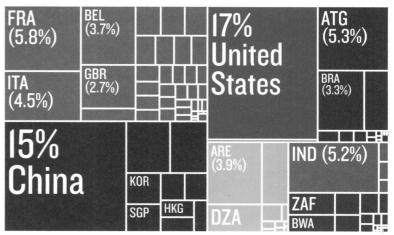

FRA (5.8%)

ITA (4.5%)

BEL (3.7%)

GBR (2.7%)

15% China

KOR

SGP

HKG

17% United States

ARE (3.9%)

DZA

ATG (5.3%)

BRA (3.3%)

IND (5.2%)

ZAF

BWA

EAST ASIA & PACIFIC · EUROPE & CENTRAL ASIA · LATIN AMERICA & CARIBBEAN · MIDDLE EAST & NORTH AFRICA · NORTH AMERICA · SOUTH ASIA · SUB-SAHARAN AFRICA

NORWAY

| ECONOMIC COMPLEXITY INDEX [2010] ▸ 0.592 (41) | COMPLEXITY OUTLOOK INDEX [2010] ▸ -0.015 (61) | EXPECTED GDPᴘᴄ GROWTH * ▸ -0.3% (118) |

*Expected annual average for the 2010-2020 period.

2010 PRODUCT SPACE ▸

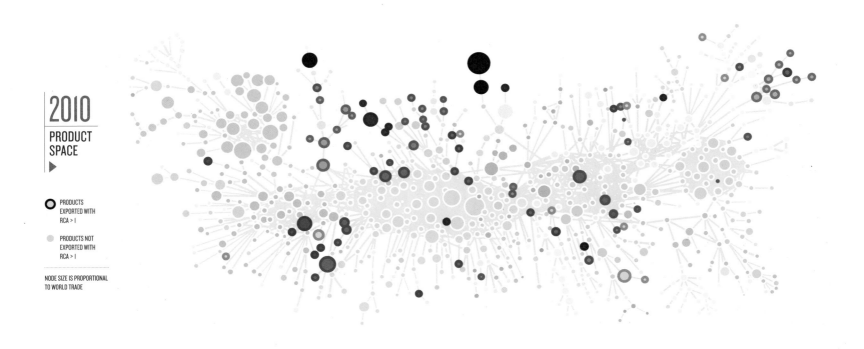

- ● PRODUCTS EXPORTED WITH RCA > 1
- ● PRODUCTS NOT EXPORTED WITH RCA > 1

NODE SIZE IS PROPORTIONAL TO WORLD TRADE

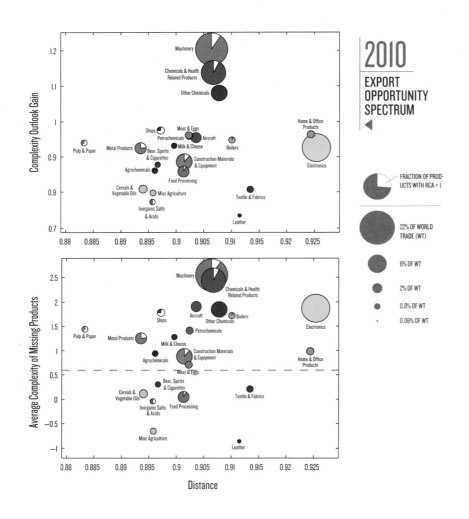

2010 EXPORT OPPORTUNITY SPECTRUM ◂

◔ FRACTION OF PRODUCTS WITH RCA > 1

⬤ 22% OF WORLD TRADE (WT)

● 6% OF WT

● 2% OF WT

• 0.8% OF WT

· 0.06% OF WT

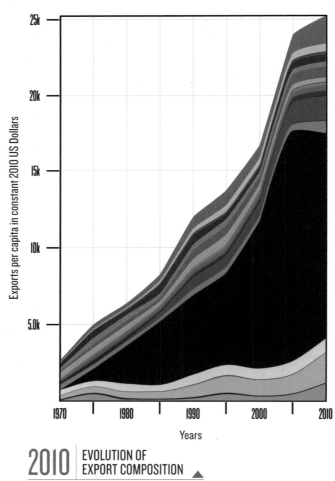

2010 | EVOLUTION OF EXPORT COMPOSITION ▲

POPULATION ▸ 4.9 M / (99)
TOTAL EXPORTS ▸ USD 123 B / (29)

GDP ▸ USD 418 B / (24)
GDPᴘᴄ ▸ USD 85,443 / (1)

EXPORTS PER CAPITA ▸ USD 25,175 / (6)
EXPORTS AS SHARE OF GDP ▸ 29 % (50)

* Data are from 2010. Numbers indicate:
   Value (World Ranking among 128 countries)
   Region: Western Europe.

ELECTRONICS · MACHINERY · AIRCRAFT · BOILERS · SHIPS · METAL PRODUCTS · CONSTR. MATL. & EQPT. · HOME & OFFICE · PULP & PAPER · CHEMICALS & HEALTH · AGROCHEMICALS · OTHER CHEMICALS · INOR. SALTS & ACIDS · PETROCHEMICALS · LEATHER · MILK & CHEESE · ANIMAL FIBERS · MEAT & EGGS · FISH & SEAFOOD · TROPICAL AGRIC. · CEREALS & VEG. OILS · COTTON/RICE/SOY & OTHERS · TOBACCO · FRUIT · MISC. AGRICULTURE · NOT CLASSIFIED · TEXTILE & FABRICS · GARMENTS · FOOD PROCESSING · BEER/SPIRITS & CIGS. · PRECIOUS STONES · COAL · OIL · MINING

2010 | EXPORT TREEMAP ▾ TOTAL: $ 123,085,656,476

3330 (34%) Crude petroleum

3414 (16%) Petroleum gases

6841 (2.5%)   2734   6812   6831 (1.9%)   2815   6821

7284 (0.82%)   7188   7428
7442
7239   9510   8743
7721   7234
7763   7788   7643   6716 (1.0%)
7932 (1.2%)

3345 (4.0%) Lubricating petroleum oils
5989 (0.70%)
5111   5113
5417 (0.73%)
8211
7731   6997

0341 (3.8%) Fresh or chilled fish, excluding fillets
0342 (1.4%)
0350
0343

9310 (4.1%) Unclassified transactions

* Numbers indicate SITC-4 Rev 2 codes which can be found in the Appendix. Percentages next to the product codes indicate proportion of the product in the exports of the country. Treemap headers show the total trade of the country.

2010 | EXPORT DESTINATIONS ▾ TOTAL: $ 123,085,656,476

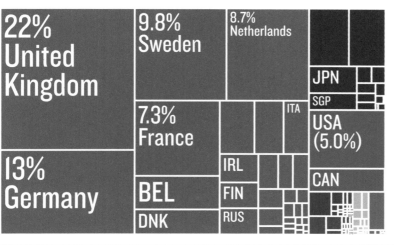

22% United Kingdom
13% Germany
9.8% Sweden
7.3% France
BEL
DNK
8.7% Netherlands
ITA
IRL
FIN
RUS
JPN
SGP
USA (5.0%)
CAN

2010 | IMPORT SOURCES ▾ TOTAL: $ 69,495,220,373

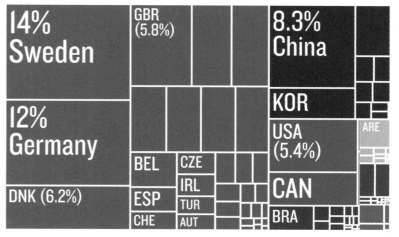

14% Sweden
12% Germany
DNK (6.2%)
GBR (5.8%)
BEL
ESP
CHE
CZE
IRL
TUR
AUT
8.3% China
KOR
USA (5.4%)
CAN
BRA
ARE

EAST ASIA & PACIFIC   EUROPE & CENTRAL ASIA   LATIN AMERICA & CARIBBEAN   MIDDLE EAST & NORTH AFRICA   NORTH AMERICA   SOUTH ASIA   SUB-SAHARAN AFRICA

OMAN

ECONOMIC COMPLEXITY INDEX [2010] ▸ -0.276 (73) | COMPLEXITY OUTLOOK INDEX [2010] ▸ -0.847 (93) | EXPECTED GDPᴘᴄ GROWTH * ▸ -0.5% (120)

*Expected annual average for the 2010-2020 period.

2010 PRODUCT SPACE ▶

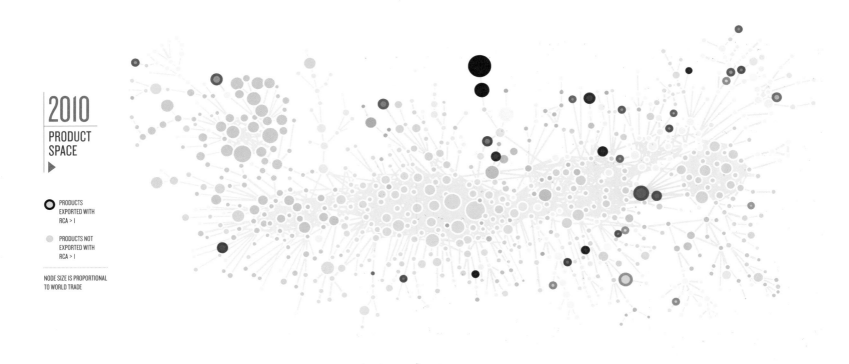

● PRODUCTS EXPORTED WITH RCA > 1

● PRODUCTS NOT EXPORTED WITH RCA > 1

NODE SIZE IS PROPORTIONAL TO WORLD TRADE

2010 EXPORT OPPORTUNITY SPECTRUM ◀

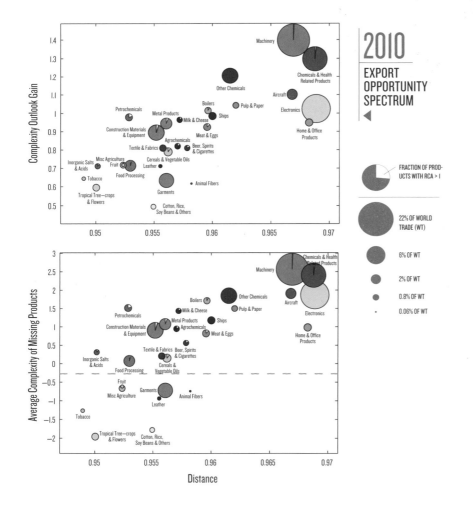

FRACTION OF PRODUCTS WITH RCA > 1

22% OF WORLD TRADE (WT)

6% OF WT

2% OF WT

0.8% OF WT

0.06% OF WT

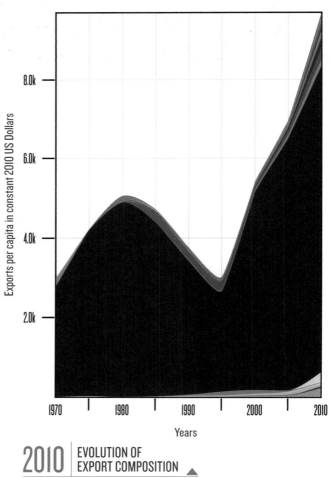

2010 | EVOLUTION OF EXPORT COMPOSITION ▲

POPULATION ▸ 2.8 M / (115)	GDP ▸ USD 58 B / (68)	EXPORTS PER CAPITA ▸ USD 9,725 / (20)	* Data are from 2010. Numbers indicate:
TOTAL EXPORTS ▸ USD 27 B / (59)	GDPᴘᴄ ▸ USD 20,791 / (29)	EXPORTS AS SHARE OF GDP ▸ 47 % / (21)	Value (World Ranking among 128 countries) Region: Middle East and North Africa.

ELECTRONICS · MACHINERY · AIRCRAFT · BOILERS · SHIPS · METAL PRODUCTS · CONSTR. MAT. & EQPT. · HOME & OFFICE · PULP & PAPER · CHEMICALS & HEALTH · AGROCHEMICALS · OTHER CHEMICALS · INOR. SALTS & ACIDS · PETROCHEMICALS · LEATHER · MILK & CHEESE · ANIMAL FIBERS · MEAT & EGGS · FISH & SEAFOOD · TROPICAL AGRIC. · CEREALS & VEG. OILS · COTTON/RICE/SOY & OTHERS · TOBACCO · FRUIT · MISC. AGRICULTURE · NOT CLASSIFIED · TEXTILE & FABRICS · GARMENTS · FOOD PROCESSING · BEER/SPIRITS & CIGS. · PRECIOUS STONES · COAL · OIL · MINING

2010 | EXPORT TREEMAP ▼ TOTAL: $ 27,058,636,228

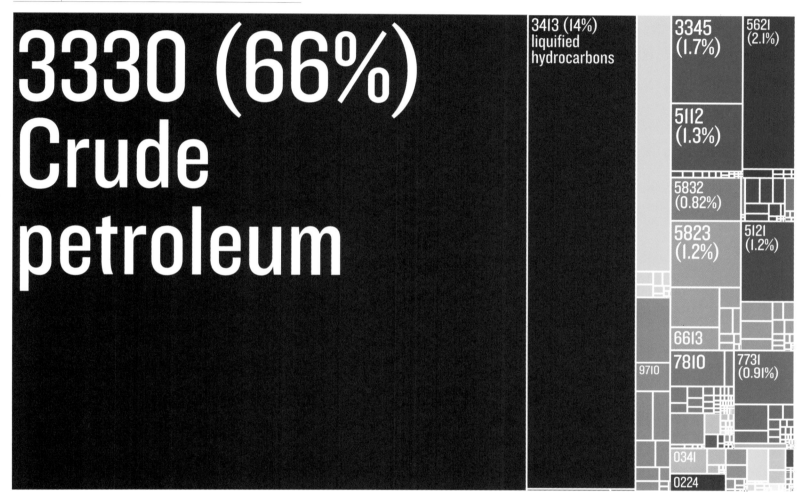

3330 (66%) Crude petroleum

3413 (14%) liquified hydrocarbons

3345 (1.7%)

5621 (2.1%)

5112 (1.3%)

5832 (0.82%)

5823 (1.2%)

5121 (1.2%)

6613

9710

7810

7731 (0.91%)

0341

0224

*Numbers indicate SITC-4 Rev 2 codes which can be found in the Appendix. Percentages next to the product codes indicate proportion of the product in the exports of the country. Treemap headers show the total trade of the country.

2010 | EXPORT DESTINATIONS ▼ TOTAL: $ 27,058,636,228

33% China

15% Japan

14% Korea, Rep.

8.0% Thailand

IDN

12% India

ARE (3.5%)

QAT

2010 | IMPORT SOURCES ▼ TOTAL: $ 16,873,360,576

27% United Arab Emirates

17% Japan

CHN (4.6%)

KOR

THA

SAU (3.1%)

FRA (3.9%)

DEU (3.8%)

ITA

CHE

NLD

BEL

RUS

DNK

USA (5.3%)

IND (4.4%)

EAST ASIA & PACIFIC · EUROPE & CENTRAL ASIA · LATIN AMERICA & CARIBBEAN · MIDDLE EAST & NORTH AFRICA · NORTH AMERICA · SOUTH ASIA · SUB-SAHARAN AFRICA

PAKISTAN

ECONOMIC COMPLEXITY INDEX [2010] ▸ -0.621 (90) | COMPLEXITY OUTLOOK INDEX [2010] ▸ 0.738 (40) | EXPECTED GDPᴘᴄ GROWTH * ▸ 3.3% (17)

*Expected annual average for the 2010-2020 period.

2010 PRODUCT SPACE ▶

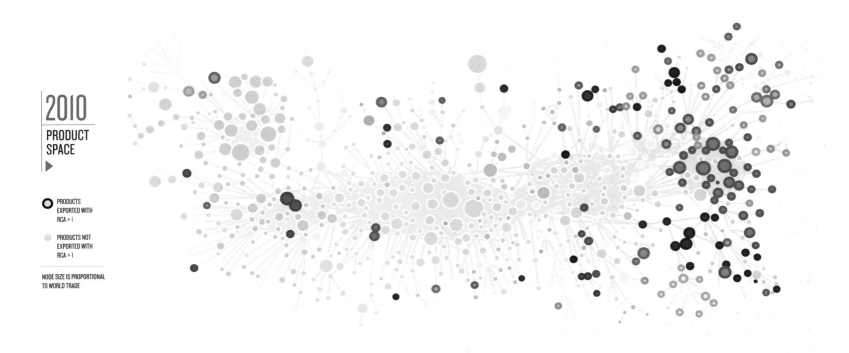

- ● PRODUCTS EXPORTED WITH RCA > 1
- ○ PRODUCTS NOT EXPORTED WITH RCA > 1

NODE SIZE IS PROPORTIONAL TO WORLD TRADE

2010 EXPORT OPPORTUNITY SPECTRUM ◀

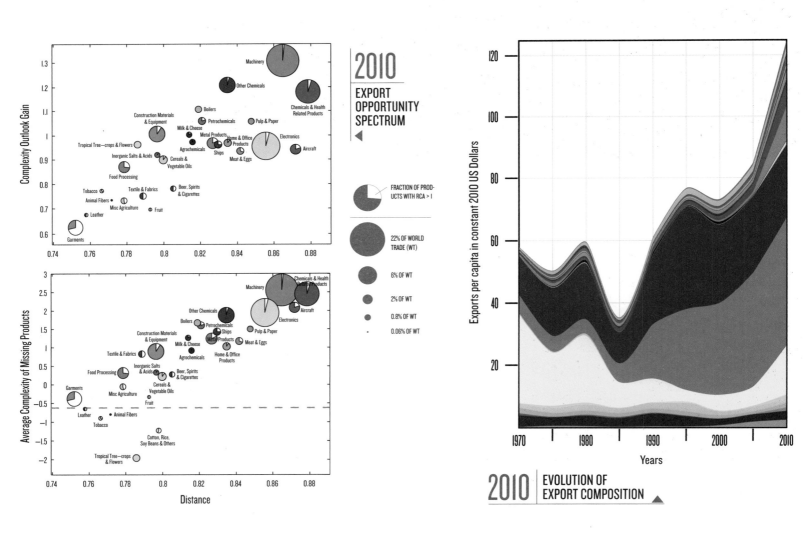

FRACTION OF PRODUCTS WITH RCA > 1

- 22% OF WORLD TRADE (WT)
- 6% OF WT
- 2% OF WT
- 0.8% OF WT
- 0.06% OF WT

2010 EVOLUTION OF EXPORT COMPOSITION ▲

POPULATION ▸ 174 M / (6)	GDP ▸ USD 177 B / (47)	EXPORTS PER CAPITA ▸ USD 125 / (118)	* Data are from 2010. Numbers indicate:
TOTAL EXPORTS ▸ USD 22 B / (62)	GDPᴘᴄ ▸ USD 1,019 / (113)	EXPORTS AS SHARE OF GDP ▸ 12 % / (113)	Value (World Ranking among 128 countries) Region: Middle East and North Africa.

ELECTRONICS · MACHINERY · AIRCRAFT · BOILERS · SHIPS · METAL PRODUCTS · CONSTR. MATL. & EQPT. · HOME & OFFICE · PULP & PAPER · CHEMICALS & HEALTH · AGROCHEMICALS · OTHER CHEMICALS · INOR. SALTS & ACIDS · PETROCHEMICALS · LEATHER · MILK & CHEESE · ANIMAL FIBERS · MEAT & EGGS · FISH & SEAFOOD · TROPICAL AGRIC. · CEREALS & VEG. OILS · COTTON/RICE/SOY & OTHERS · TOBACCO · FRUIT · MISC. AGRICULTURE · NOT CLASSIFIED · TEXTILE & FABRICS · GARMENTS · FOOD PROCESSING · BEER/SPIRITS & CIGS. · PRECIOUS STONES · COAL · OIL · MINING

2010 EXPORT TREEMAP ▾ TOTAL: $ 21,668,594,166

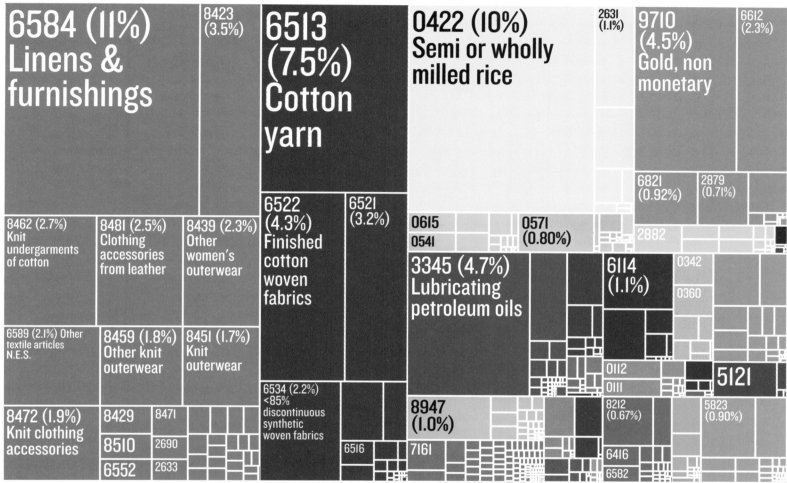

* Numbers indicate SITC-4 Rev 2 codes which can be found in the Appendix. Percentages next to the product codes indicate proportion of the product in the exports of the country. Treemap headers show the total trade of the country.

2010 EXPORT DESTINATIONS ▾ TOTAL: $ 21,668,594,166

2010 IMPORT SOURCES ▾ TOTAL: $ 34,025,948,796

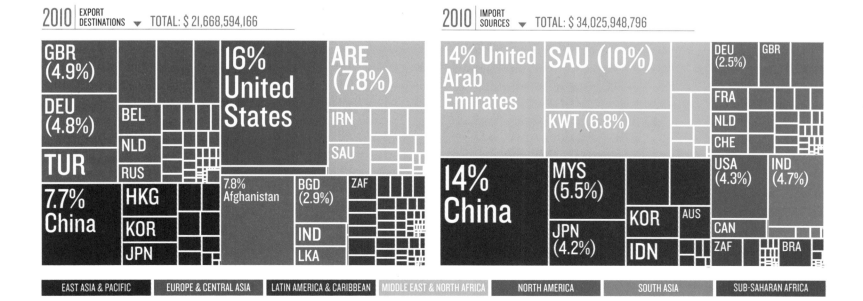

EAST ASIA & PACIFIC — EUROPE & CENTRAL ASIA — LATIN AMERICA & CARIBBEAN — MIDDLE EAST & NORTH AFRICA — NORTH AMERICA — SOUTH ASIA — SUB-SAHARAN AFRICA

PANAMA

ECONOMIC COMPLEXITY INDEX [2010] ▸ 0.454 (43) | COMPLEXITY OUTLOOK INDEX [2010] ▸ 0.526 (44) | EXPECTED GDPPC GROWTH * ▸ 2.4% (46)

*Expected annual average for the 2010-2020 period.

2010 PRODUCT SPACE ▶

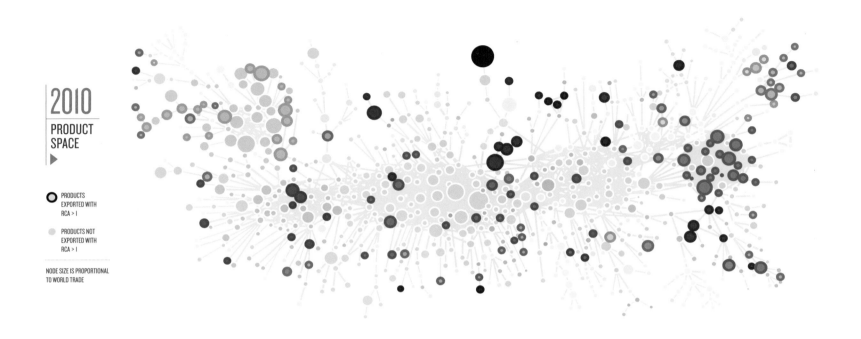

● PRODUCTS EXPORTED WITH RCA > 1

● PRODUCTS NOT EXPORTED WITH RCA > 1

NODE SIZE IS PROPORTIONAL TO WORLD TRADE

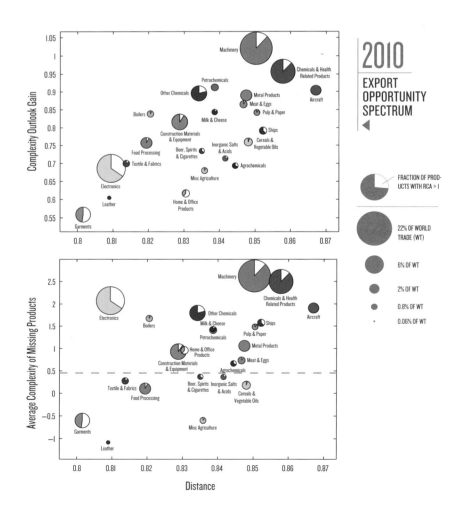

2010 EXPORT OPPORTUNITY SPECTRUM ◀

◖ FRACTION OF PRODUCTS WITH RCA > 1

● 22% OF WORLD TRADE (WT)

● 6% OF WT

● 2% OF WT

● 0.8% OF WT

· 0.06% OF WT

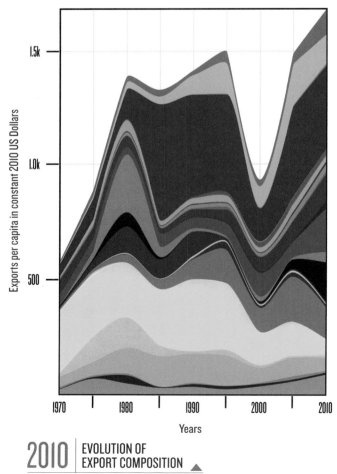

2010 EVOLUTION OF EXPORT COMPOSITION ▲

POPULATION ▸ 3.5 M / (110)
TOTAL EXPORTS ▸ USD 5.9 B / (86)

GDP ▸ USD 27 B / (87)
GDPᴘᴄ ▸ USD 7,614 / (55)

EXPORTS PER CAPITA ▸ USD 1,686 / (58)
EXPORTS AS SHARE OF GDP ▸ 22 % (76)

* Data are from 2010. Numbers indicate:
Value (World Ranking among 128 countries)
Region: Latin America and the Caribbean.

ELECTRONICS · MACHINERY · AIRCRAFT · BOILERS · SHIPS · METAL PRODUCTS · CONSTR. MATL. & EQPT. · HOME & OFFICE · PULP & PAPER · CHEMICALS & HEALTH · AGROCHEMICALS · OTHER CHEMICALS · INOR. SALTS & ACIDS · PETROCHEMICALS · LEATHER · MILK & CHEESE · ANIMAL FIBERS · MEAT & EGGS · FISH & SEAFOOD · TROPICAL AGRIC. · CEREALS & VEG. OILS · COTTON/RICE/SOY & OTHERS · TOBACCO · FRUIT · MISC. AGRICULTURE · NOT CLASSIFIED · TEXTILE & FABRICS · GARMENTS · FOOD PROCESSING · BEER/SPIRITS & CIGS. · PRECIOUS STONES · COAL · OIL · MINING

2010 | EXPORT TREEMAP ▾ — TOTAL: $ 5,930,135,556

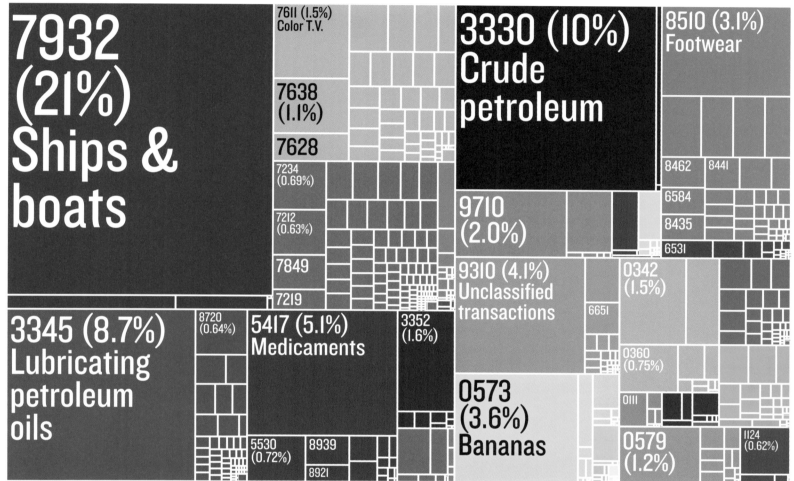

* Numbers indicate SITC-4 Rev 2 codes which can be found in the Appendix. Percentages next to the product codes indicate proportion of the product in the exports of the country. Treemap headers show the total trade of the country.

2010 | EXPORT DESTINATIONS ▾ — TOTAL: $ 5,930,135,556

16% Ecuador
11% Venezuela
8.8% Korea, Rep.
GRC (6.0%)
JPN (6.3%)
BEL
ITA
GTM (6.6%)
CRI (3.6%)
SLV (3.4%)
USA (6.1%)
IND (4.3%)
PER (4.5%)
COL

2010 | IMPORT SOURCES ▾ — TOTAL: $ 24,537,599,303

37% Singapore
FRA (3.1%)
12% United States
GBR
ITA
COL (3.7%)
CHN (15%)
MEX

EAST ASIA & PACIFIC · EUROPE & CENTRAL ASIA · LATIN AMERICA & CARIBBEAN · MIDDLE EAST & NORTH AFRICA · NORTH AMERICA · SOUTH ASIA · SUB-SAHARAN AFRICA

PAPUA NEW GUINEA

ECONOMIC COMPLEXITY INDEX [2010] ▸ **-1.314 (119)** | **COMPLEXITY OUTLOOK INDEX [2010]** ▸ **-1.073 (118)** | **EXPECTED GDPPC GROWTH** * ▸ **0.8% (97)**

*Expected annual average for the 2010-2020 period.

2010 PRODUCT SPACE ▶

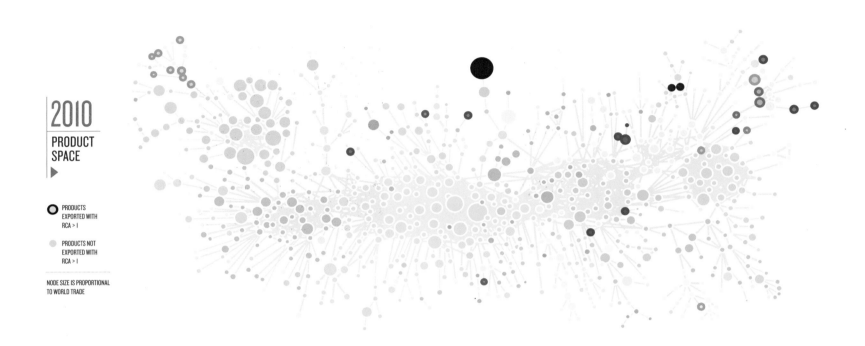

○ PRODUCTS EXPORTED WITH RCA > 1

○ PRODUCTS NOT EXPORTED WITH RCA > 1

NODE SIZE IS PROPORTIONAL TO WORLD TRADE

2010 EXPORT OPPORTUNITY SPECTRUM ◀

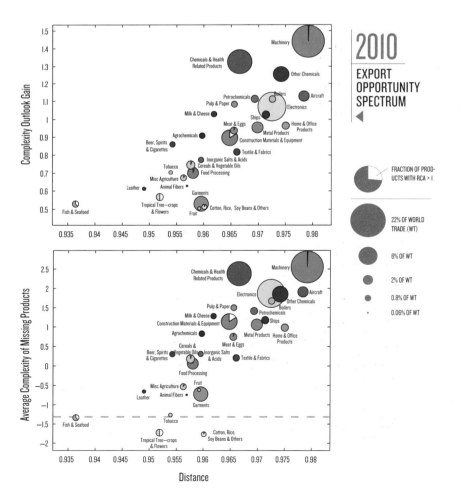

FRACTION OF PRODUCTS WITH RCA > 1

22% OF WORLD TRADE (WT)

6% OF WT

2% OF WT

0.8% OF WT

0.06% OF WT

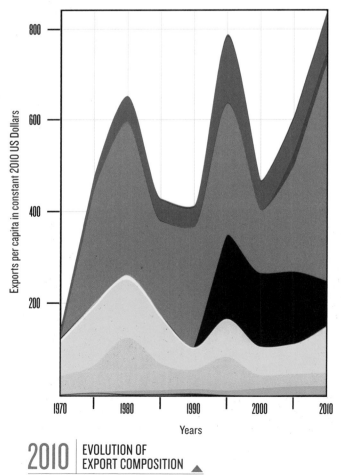

2010 EVOLUTION OF EXPORT COMPOSITION ▲

POPULATION ▸ 6.9 M / (86)
TOTAL EXPORTS ▸ USD 5.8 B / (87)

GDP ▸ USD 9.5 B / (113)
GDPpc ▸ USD 1,382 / (99)

EXPORTS PER CAPITA ▸ USD 841 / (77)
EXPORTS AS SHARE OF GDP ▸ 61 % / (12)

* Data are from 2010. Numbers indicate:
Value (World Ranking among 128 countries)
Region: East Asia and Pacific.

ELECTRONICS | MACHINERY | AIRCRAFT | BOILERS | SHIPS | METAL PRODUCTS | CONSTR. MATL. & EQPT. | HOME & OFFICE | PULP & PAPER | CHEMICALS & HEALTH | AGROCHEMICALS | OTHER CHEMICALS | INOR. SALTS & ACIDS | PETROCHEMICALS | LEATHER | MILK & CHEESE | ANIMAL FIBERS | MEAT & EGGS | FISH & SEAFOOD | TROPICAL AGRIC. | CEREALS & VEG. OILS | COTTON/RICE/SOY & OTHERS | TOBACCO | FRUIT | MISC. AGRICULTURE | NOT CLASSIFIED | TEXTILE & FABRICS | GARMENTS | FOOD PROCESSING | BEER/SPIRITS & CIGS. | PRECIOUS STONES | COAL | OIL | MINING

2010 | EXPORT TREEMAP ▼ TOTAL: $ 5,769,279,532

9710 (33%) Gold, non monetary

2871 (22%) Copper

3330 (12%) Crude petroleum

4242 (6.3%) Palm oil

4243 4244

2472 (8.9%) Sawlogs & veneer logs of non coniferous

0721 (3.1%)

0711 (3.3%)

3345 (3.3%)

0371 (1.2%)

0342 (0.90%)

* Numbers indicate SITC-4 Rev 2 codes which can be found in the Appendix. Percentages next to the product codes indicate proportion of the product in the exports of the country. Treemap headers show the total trade of the country.

2010 | EXPORT DESTINATIONS ▼ TOTAL: $ 5,769,279,532

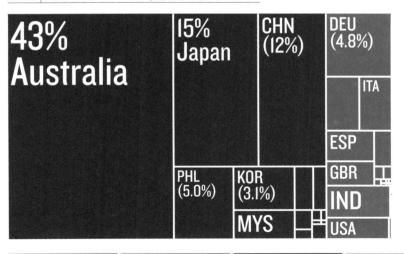

43% Australia

15% Japan

CHN (12%)

DEU (4.8%)

ITA

ESP

GBR

IND

USA

PHL (5.0%)

KOR (3.1%)

MYS

2010 | IMPORT SOURCES ▼ TOTAL: $ 4,368,624,360

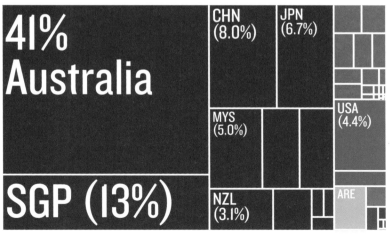

41% Australia

SGP (13%)

CHN (8.0%)

JPN (6.7%)

MYS (5.0%)

NZL (3.1%)

USA (4.4%)

ARE

EAST ASIA & PACIFIC | EUROPE & CENTRAL ASIA | LATIN AMERICA & CARIBBEAN | MIDDLE EAST & NORTH AFRICA | NORTH AMERICA | SOUTH ASIA | SUB-SAHARAN AFRICA

PARAGUAY

ECONOMIC COMPLEXITY INDEX [2010] ▸ -0.476 (83) | COMPLEXITY OUTLOOK INDEX [2010] ▸ -0.629 (80) | EXPECTED GDPᴾᶜ GROWTH * ▸ 1.5% (84)

*Expected annual average for the 2010-2020 period.

2010 PRODUCT SPACE ▶

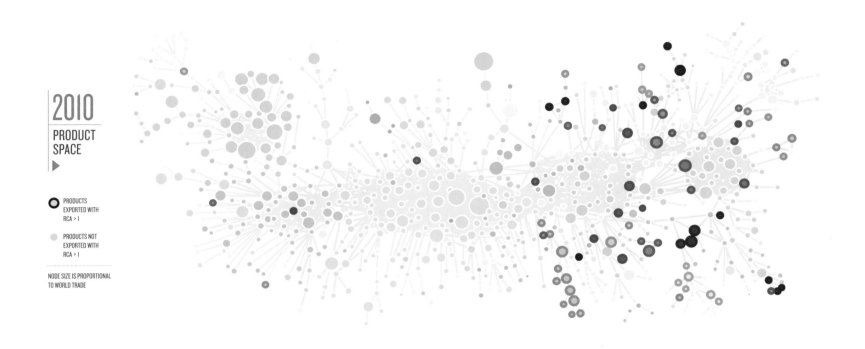

○ PRODUCTS EXPORTED WITH RCA > 1

○ PRODUCTS NOT EXPORTED WITH RCA > 1

NODE SIZE IS PROPORTIONAL TO WORLD TRADE

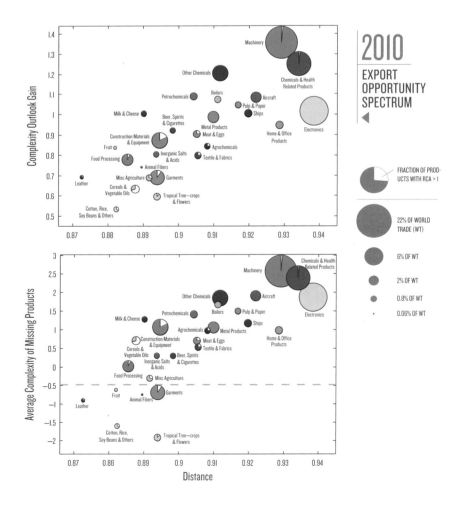

2010 EXPORT OPPORTUNITY SPECTRUM ◀

◐ FRACTION OF PRODUCTS WITH RCA > 1

⬤ 22% OF WORLD TRADE (WT)

● 6% OF WT

● 2% OF WT

• 0.8% OF WT

· 0.06% OF WT

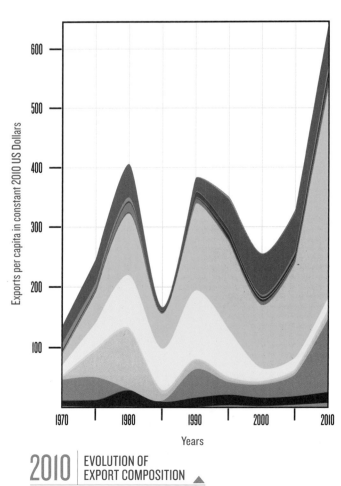

2010 | EVOLUTION OF EXPORT COMPOSITION ▲

POPULATION ▸ 6.5 M / (87)
TOTAL EXPORTS ▸ USD 4.2 B / (96)

GDP ▸ USD 18 B / (98)
GDPᴘᴄ ▸ USD 2,840 / (88)

EXPORTS PER CAPITA ▸ USD 645 / (85)
EXPORTS AS SHARE OF GDP ▸ 23 % (74)

* Data are from 2010. Numbers indicate:
Value (World Ranking among 128 countries)
Region: Latin America and the Caribbean.

ELECTRONICS · MACHINERY · AIRCRAFT · BOILERS · SHIPS · METAL PRODUCTS · CONSTR. MATL. & EQPT. · HOME & OFFICE · PULP & PAPER · CHEMICALS & HEALTH · AGROCHEMICALS · OTHER CHEMICALS · INOR. SALTS & ACIDS · PETROCHEMICALS · LEATHER · MILK & CHEESE · ANIMAL FIBERS · MEAT & EGGS · FISH & SEAFOOD · TROPICAL AGRIC. · CEREALS & VEG. OILS · COTTON/RICE/SOY & OTHERS · TOBACCO · FRUIT · MISC. AGRICULTURE · NOT CLASSIFIED · TEXTILE & FABRICS · GARMENTS · FOOD PROCESSING · BEER/SPIRITS & CIGS. · PRECIOUS STONES · COAL · OIL · MINING

2010 | EXPORT TREEMAP ▼ TOTAL: $ 4,164,535,925

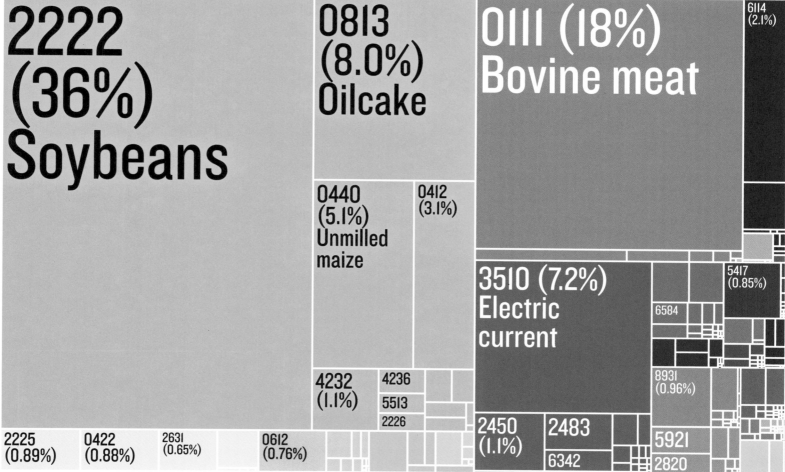

2222 (36%) Soybeans

0813 (8.0%) Oilcake

0111 (18%) Bovine meat

6114 (2.1%)

0440 (5.1%) Unmilled maize

0412 (3.1%)

3510 (7.2%) Electric current

5417 (0.85%)

6584

8931 (0.96%)

4232 (1.1%)

4236

5513

2226

2450 (1.1%)

2483

6342

5921

2820

2225 (0.89%)

0422 (0.88%)

2631 (0.65%)

0612 (0.76%)

* Numbers indicate SITC-4 Rev 2 codes which can be found in the Appendix. Percentages next to the product codes indicate proportion of the product in the exports of the country. Treemap headers show the total trade of the country.

2010 | EXPORT DESTINATIONS ▼ TOTAL: $ 4,164,535,925

14% Chile

13% Brazil

9.6% Argentina

VEN

ISR

MEX

PER (5.2%)

RUS (9.8%)

NLD (5.5%)

TUR (4.8%)

GRC

ITA (6.2%)

DEU (5.0%)

ESP (4.6%)

PRT

SVN

USA

2010 | IMPORT SOURCES ▼ TOTAL: $ 8,922,700,102

25% Brazil

16% Argentina

VEN (2.3%)

DEU

32% China

JPN (3.5%)

USA (4.7%)

KOR

THA

IND

EAST ASIA & PACIFIC · EUROPE & CENTRAL ASIA · LATIN AMERICA & CARIBBEAN · MIDDLE EAST & NORTH AFRICA · NORTH AMERICA · SOUTH ASIA · SUB-SAHARAN AFRICA

PERU

ECONOMIC COMPLEXITY INDEX [2010] ▸ -0.476 (82) | COMPLEXITY OUTLOOK INDEX [2010] ▸ 0.208 (55) | EXPECTED GDPᴘᴄ GROWTH * ▸ 1.4% (90)

*Expected annual average for the 2010-2020 period.

2010 PRODUCT SPACE ▶

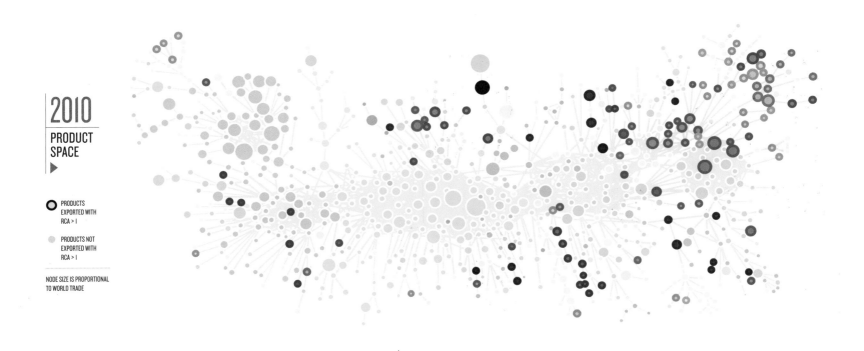

○ PRODUCTS EXPORTED WITH RCA > 1

○ PRODUCTS NOT EXPORTED WITH RCA > 1

NODE SIZE IS PROPORTIONAL TO WORLD TRADE

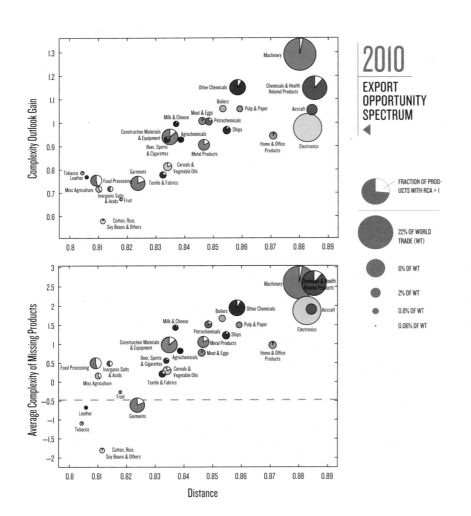

2010 EXPORT OPPORTUNITY SPECTRUM ◀

FRACTION OF PRODUCTS WITH RCA > 1

22% OF WORLD TRADE (WT)

6% OF WT

2% OF WT

0.8% OF WT

0.06% OF WT

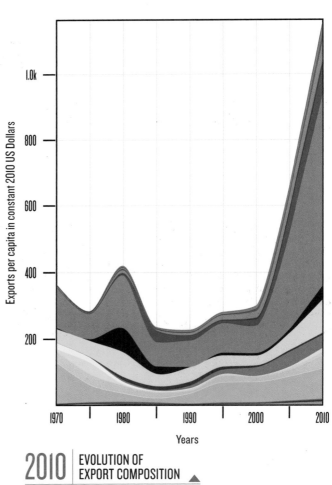

2010 EVOLUTION OF EXPORT COMPOSITION ▲

POPULATION ▸ 29 M / (37)
TOTAL EXPORTS ▸ USD 34 B / (56)

GDP ▸ USD 154 B / (50)
GDPₚᴄ ▸ USD 5,292 / (65)

EXPORTS PER CAPITA ▸ USD 1,165 / (70)
EXPORTS AS SHARE OF GDP ▸ 22 % (77)

* Data are from 2010. Numbers indicate:
Value (World Ranking among 128 countries)
Region: Latin America and the Caribbean.

ELECTRONICS · MACHINERY · AIRCRAFT · BOILERS · SHIPS · METAL PRODUCTS · CONSTR. MATL. & EQPT. · HOME & OFFICE · PULP & PAPER · CHEMICALS & HEALTH · AGROCHEMICALS · OTHER CHEMICALS · INOR. SALTS & ACIDS · PETROCHEMICALS · LEATHER · MILK & CHEESE · ANIMAL FIBERS · MEAT & EGGS · FISH & SEAFOOD · TROPICAL AGRIC. · CEREALS & VEG. OILS · COTTON/RICE/SOY & OTHERS · TOBACCO · FRUIT · MISC. AGRICULTURE · NOT CLASSIFIED · TEXTILE & FABRICS · GARMENTS · FOOD PROCESSING · BEER/SPIRITS & CIGS. · PRECIOUS STONES · COAL · OIL · MINING

2010 | EXPORT TREEMAP ▾ TOTAL: $ 33,873,822,804

9710 (20%) Gold, non monetary

2871 (18%) Copper

2875 (4.8%) Zinc

2874 (3.4%) Lead ore

3413 (2.1%) liquified hydrocarbons

3330 (1.5%)

6821 (6.5%) Unwrought copper & copper alloys

2815 (2.2%) Iron ore

2879 (1.1%)

6861 (0.73%)

2890 (0.68%)

3345 (4.0%) Lubricating petroleum oils

6871 (2.1%)

5322

0711 (2.7%) Coffee, green or roasted

0573

0751

0545 (1.6%) Other fresh or chilled vegetables

0579 (0.77%)

8931

0565 (1.1%)

0814 (5.1%) Meat and fish flour

0360 (0.99%)

4111

0344

0224

8462 (1.3%)

6822 (1.0%)

2483

9310

6732

6624

* Numbers indicate SITC-4 Rev 2 codes which can be found in the Appendix. Percentages next to the product codes indicate proportion of the product in the exports of the country. Treemap headers show the total trade of the country.

2010 | EXPORT DESTINATIONS ▾ TOTAL: $ 33,873,822,804

11% Switzerland

DEU

17% China

ESP (3.6%)

NLD · GBR
FRA · SWE
FIN · BGR

JPN (5.6%)

CHL (3.7%)

ECU (2.8%)

14% United States

CAN (9.6%)

BRA (2.7%)

VEN

BOL

2010 | IMPORT SOURCES ▾ TOTAL: $ 26,713,049,869

7.4% Brazil

ECU (4.9%)

17% China

COL (4.5%)

ARG (4.3%)

MEX

JPN (4.5%)

PRY

THA

CHL (3.7%)

19% United States

DEU (3.0%)

ITA

ESP

AGO

EAST ASIA & PACIFIC · EUROPE & CENTRAL ASIA · LATIN AMERICA & CARIBBEAN · MIDDLE EAST & NORTH AFRICA · NORTH AMERICA · SOUTH ASIA · SUB-SAHARAN AFRICA

PHILIPPINES

| ECONOMIC COMPLEXITY INDEX [2010] ► 0.245 (52) | COMPLEXITY OUTLOOK INDEX [2010] ► 0.242 (52) | EXPECTED GDP PC GROWTH * ► 3.3% (15) |

*Expected annual average for the 2010-2020 period.

2010 PRODUCT SPACE ▶

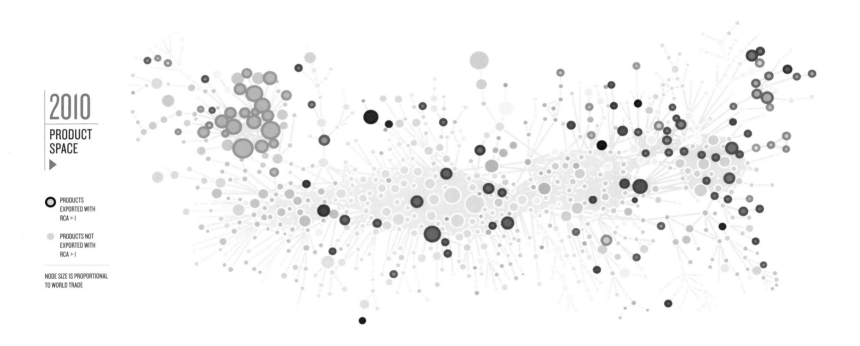

- ● PRODUCTS EXPORTED WITH RCA > 1
- ● PRODUCTS NOT EXPORTED WITH RCA > 1

NODE SIZE IS PROPORTIONAL TO WORLD TRADE

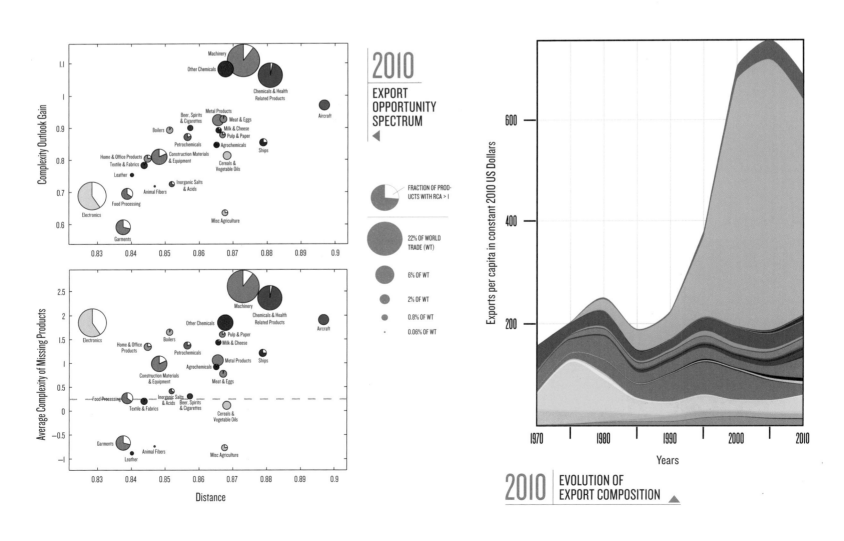

2010 EXPORT OPPORTUNITY SPECTRUM ◀

○ FRACTION OF PRODUCTS WITH RCA > 1

● 22% OF WORLD TRADE (WT)
● 6% OF WT
● 2% OF WT
● 0.8% OF WT
· 0.06% OF WT

2010 | EVOLUTION OF EXPORT COMPOSITION ▲

POPULATION ▸ 93 M / (12)
TOTAL EXPORTS ▸ USD 64 B / (40)

GDP ▸ USD 200 B / (44)
GDPᴘᴄ ▸ USD 2,140 / (94)

EXPORTS PER CAPITA ▸ USD 690 / (83)
EXPORTS AS SHARE OF GDP ▸ 32 % (48)

* Data are from 2010. Numbers indicate:
 Value (World Ranking among 128 countries)
 Region: East Asia and Pacific.

ELECTRONICS · MACHINERY · AIRCRAFT · BOILERS · SHIPS · METAL PRODUCTS · CONSTR. MATL. & EQPT. · HOME & OFFICE · PULP & PAPER · CHEMICALS & HEALTH · AGROCHEMICALS · OTHER CHEMICALS · INOR. SALTS & ACIDS · PETROCHEMICALS · LEATHER · MILK & CHEESE · ANIMAL FIBERS · MEAT & EGGS · FISH & SEAFOOD · TROPICAL AGRIC. · CEREALS & VEG. OILS · COTTON/RICE/SOY & OTHERS · TOBACCO · FRUIT · MISC. AGRICULTURE · NOT CLASSIFIED · TEXTILE & FABRICS · GARMENTS · FOOD PROCESSING · BEER/SPIRITS & CIGS. · PRECIOUS STONES · COAL · OIL · MINING

2010 | EXPORT TREEMAP ▾ | TOTAL: $ 64,380,113,886

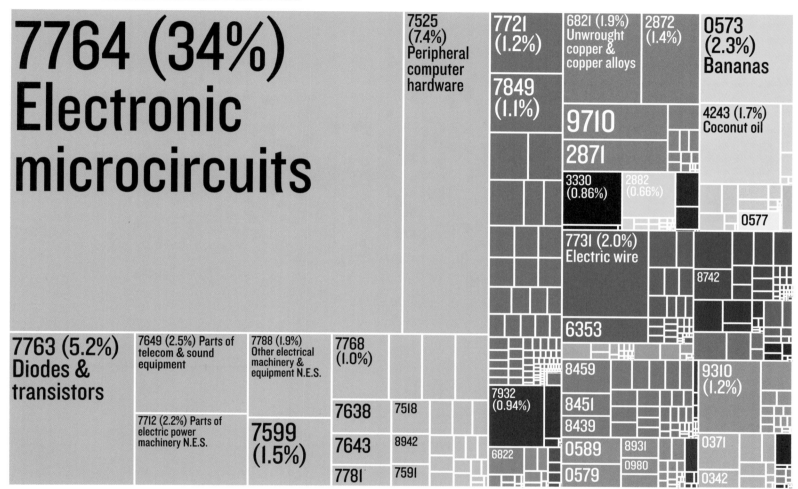

7764 (34%) Electronic microcircuits

7763 (5.2%) Diodes & transistors

7649 (2.5%) Parts of telecom & sound equipment

7712 (2.2%) Parts of electric power machinery N.E.S.

7788 (1.9%) Other electrical machinery & equipment N.E.S.

7599 (1.5%)

7768 (1.0%)

7638 · 7518
7643 · 8942
7781 · 7591

7525 (7.4%) Peripheral computer hardware

7721 (1.2%)
7849 (1.1%)

6821 (1.9%) Unwrought copper & copper alloys
2872 (1.4%)
0573 (2.3%) Bananas

9710
2871
3330 (0.86%) · 2882 (0.66%)

4243 (1.7%) Coconut oil
0577

7731 (2.0%) Electric wire
8742

6353

8459 · 9310 (1.2%)
7932 (0.94%) · 8451
8439
6822 · 0589 · 8931 · 0980 · 0371
0579 · 0342

* Numbers indicate SITC-4 Rev 2 codes which can be found in the Appendix. Percentages next to the product codes indicate proportion of the product in the exports of the country. Treemap headers show the total trade of the country.

2010 | EXPORT DESTINATIONS ▾ | TOTAL: $ 64,380,113,886

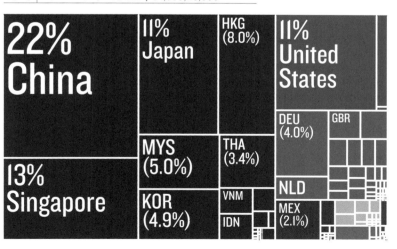

22% China
13% Singapore
11% Japan
HKG (8.0%)
MYS (5.0%)
KOR (4.9%)
THA (3.4%)
VNM
IDN
11% United States
DEU (4.0%)
GBR
NLD
MEX (2.1%)

2010 | IMPORT SOURCES ▾ | TOTAL: $ 51,432,872,056

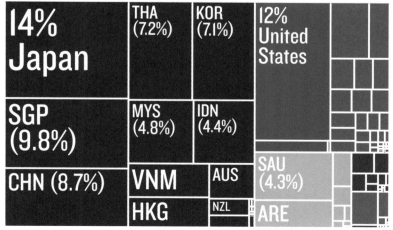

14% Japan
SGP (9.8%)
CHN (8.7%)
HKG
THA (7.2%)
MYS (4.8%)
VNM
KOR (7.1%)
IDN (4.4%)
AUS
NZL
12% United States
SAU (4.3%)
ARE

EAST ASIA & PACIFIC · EUROPE & CENTRAL ASIA · LATIN AMERICA & CARIBBEAN · MIDDLE EAST & NORTH AFRICA · NORTH AMERICA · SOUTH ASIA · SUB-SAHARAN AFRICA

POLAND

ECONOMIC COMPLEXITY INDEX [2010] ▸ 1.131 (21)   **COMPLEXITY OUTLOOK INDEX [2010] ▸ 0.799 (34)**   **EXPECTED GDPPC GROWTH * ▸ 3.0% (23)**

*Expected annual average for the 2010-2020 period.

2010
PRODUCT SPACE ▶

○ PRODUCTS EXPORTED WITH RCA > 1

○ PRODUCTS NOT EXPORTED WITH RCA > 1

NODE SIZE IS PROPORTIONAL TO WORLD TRADE

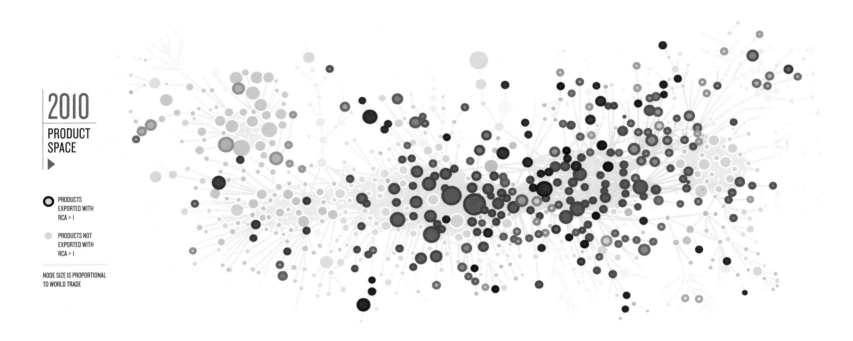

2010
EXPORT OPPORTUNITY SPECTRUM ◀

FRACTION OF PRODUCTS WITH RCA > 1

22% OF WORLD TRADE (WT)

6% OF WT

2% OF WT

0.8% OF WT

0.06% OF WT

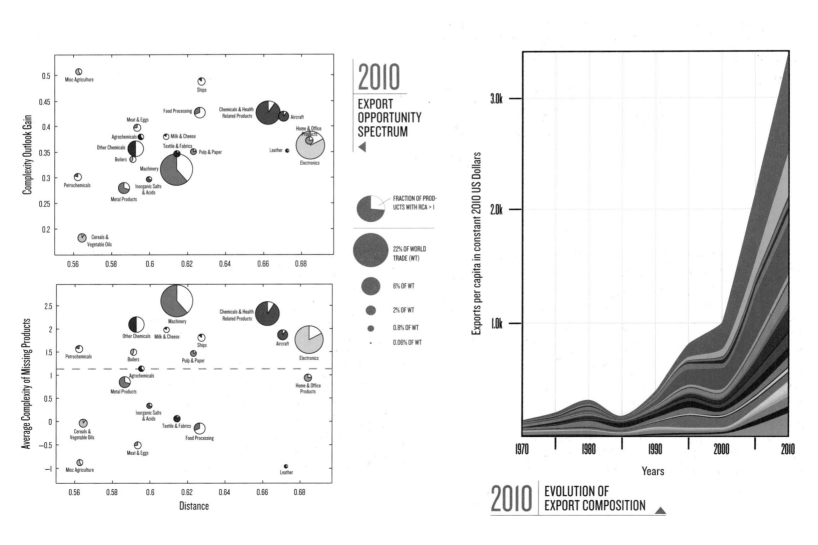

2010 | EVOLUTION OF EXPORT COMPOSITION ▲

POPULATION ‣ 38 M / (31)	GDP ‣ USD 470 B / (20)	EXPORTS PER CAPITA ‣ USD 3,413 / (43)	* Data are from 2010. Numbers indicate:
TOTAL EXPORTS ‣ USD 130 B / (27)	GDPᴘᴄ ‣ USD 12,303 / (40)	EXPORTS AS SHARE OF GDP ‣ 28 % (56)	Value (World Ranking among 128 countries) Region: Eastern Europe and Central Asia.

ELECTRONICS · MACHINERY · AIRCRAFT · BOILERS · SHIPS · METAL PRODUCTS · CONSTR. MATL. & EQPT. · HOME & OFFICE · PULP & PAPER · CHEMICALS & HEALTH · AGROCHEMICALS · OTHER CHEMICALS · INOR. SALTS & ACIDS · PETROCHEMICALS · LEATHER · MILK & CHEESE · ANIMAL FIBERS · MEAT & EGGS · FISH & SEAFOOD · TROPICAL AGRIC. · CEREALS & VEG. OILS · COTTON/RICE/SOY & OTHERS · TOBACCO · FRUIT · MISC. AGRICULTURE · NOT CLASSIFIED · TEXTILE & FABRICS · GARMENTS · FOOD PROCESSING · BEER/SPIRITS & CIGS. · PRECIOUS STONES · COAL · OIL · MINING

2010 | EXPORT TREEMAP ▼ TOTAL: $ 130,310,102,853

7849 (5.0%) Other vehicle parts

7810 (4.6%) Cars

7611 (3.7%) Color T.V.

7523 (1.8%)

5417 (1.5%)

5530 (1.4%)

3345 (1.1%)

6821 (1.5%)

6811

7132 (2.0%) Motor vehicle engines

7751 (1.1%)

8939 (1.2%)

5821

5334

3232 (1.7%)

7491

5542

7649 (0.77%)

7757

7522

8124

7712

7415

7721 (1.0%)

7493

7832

7452

6210

5834

7139

6418

7284

7162

7416

7431

6251

8121

7821

6647

6760

6822 (0.84%)

6733

7782

7711

7932 (1.1%)

7149 (0.61%)

9310 (3.9%) Unclassified transactions

0111 (0.66%)

0114 (0.60%)

0350

0240

0223

0224

2120

1222 (1.1%)

0412

8211 (2.4%)

8219 (2.0%)

7731 (1.5%)

6911 (0.73%)

6997

6359

6842

6732

7861

3510

0980 (0.71%)

8931 (0.63%)

0730

6415

6413

0586

0546

0585

8510

8212 (0.62%)

6428 (0.81%)

6353

* Numbers indicate SITC-4 Rev 2 codes which can be found in the Appendix. Percentages next to the product codes indicate proportion of the product in the exports of the country. Treemap headers show the total trade of the country.

2010 | EXPORT DESTINATIONS ▼ TOTAL: $ 130,310,102,853

26% Germany

GBR (6.5%)

FRA (6.3%)

CZE (5.3%)

CHN

NLD (3.8%)

BEL (2.6%)

SWE (3.0%)

HUN

ROU

UKR

LTU

ITA (6.6%)

ESP (2.8%)

SVK

NOR

2010 | IMPORT SOURCES ▼ TOTAL: $ 154,374,562,521

22% Germany

ITA (5.7%)

FRA (4.3%)

CZE (3.8%)

9.2% China

NLD (3.7%)

AUT

KOR (2.8%)

GBR

JPN

11% Russia

BEL

UKR

USA (2.8%)

SVK

FIN

CHE

IRL

EAST ASIA & PACIFIC · EUROPE & CENTRAL ASIA · LATIN AMERICA & CARIBBEAN · MIDDLE EAST & NORTH AFRICA · NORTH AMERICA · SOUTH ASIA · SUB-SAHARAN AFRICA

PORTUGAL

ECONOMIC COMPLEXITY INDEX [2010] ▸ 0.676 (35)	COMPLEXITY OUTLOOK INDEX [2010] ▸ 1.846 (3)	EXPECTED GDPᴘᴄ GROWTH * ▸ 2.5% (44)

*Expected annual average for the 2010-2020 period.

2010 PRODUCT SPACE ▸

○ PRODUCTS EXPORTED WITH RCA > 1

● PRODUCTS NOT EXPORTED WITH RCA > 1

NODE SIZE IS PROPORTIONAL TO WORLD TRADE

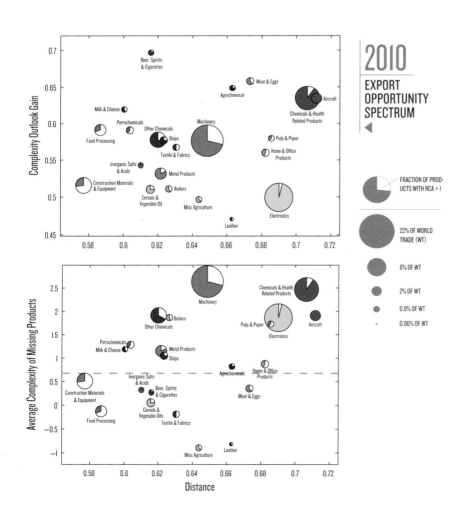

2010 EXPORT OPPORTUNITY SPECTRUM ◂

◖ FRACTION OF PRODUCTS WITH RCA > 1

● 22% OF WORLD TRADE (WT)

● 6% OF WT

● 2% OF WT

● 0.8% OF WT

· 0.06% OF WT

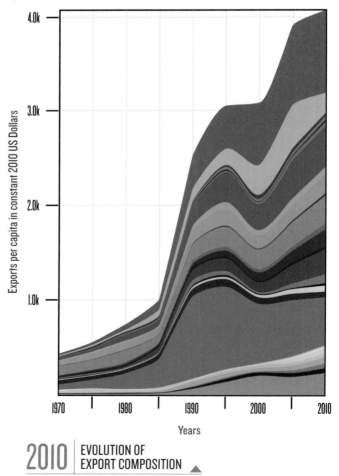

2010 | EVOLUTION OF EXPORT COMPOSITION ▲

POPULATION ▸ 11 M / (67)	GDP ▸ USD 227 B / (37)	EXPORTS PER CAPITA ▸ USD 4,077 / (38)	* Data are from 2010. Numbers indicate:
TOTAL EXPORTS ▸ USD 43 B / (53)	GDPᴘᴄ ▸ USD 21,358 / (28)	EXPORTS AS SHARE OF GDP ▸ 19 % / (81)	Value (World Ranking among 128 countries) Region: Western Europe.

ELECTRONICS · MACHINERY · AIRCRAFT · BOILERS · SHIPS · METAL PRODUCTS · CONSTR. MATL. & EQPT. · HOME & OFFICE · PULP & PAPER · CHEMICALS & HEALTH · AGROCHEMICALS · OTHER CHEMICALS · INOR. SALTS & ACIDS · PETROCHEMICALS · LEATHER · MILK & CHEESE · ANIMAL FIBERS · MEAT & EGGS · FISH & SEAFOOD · TROPICAL AGRIC. · CEREALS & VEG. OILS · COTTON/RICE/SOY & OTHERS · TOBACCO · FRUIT · MISC. AGRICULTURE · NOT CLASSIFIED · TEXTILE & FABRICS · GARMENTS · FOOD PROCESSING · BEER/SPIRITS & CIGS. · PRECIOUS STONES · COAL · OIL · MINING

2010 EXPORT TREEMAP ▾ TOTAL: $ 43,367,388,556

7849 (4.3%) Other vehicle parts

7810 (3.9%) Cars

7621 (1.5%)

8510 (3.6%) Footwear

8462 (1.5%)

3345 (3.3%) Lubricating petroleum oils

5417 (1.4%)

7721 (1.7%) Switchboards, relays & fuses

7781
7648
7522
8841
6749   7711

8459 (0.75%)   8439

8451   6575

8463   8472

8441

6522

8939 (0.87%)

5989 (0.69%)
5111 (0.68%)
5112

5821
5334
6573

6251 (1.5%)

7758
7436
7284

7431
7162
7491
7283
7831

6330 (1.9%) Cork manufactures

2871 (1.1%)

7821 (1.1%)   7783

6911 (0.85%)

6415 (2.4%) Paper & paperboad in rolls or sheets

1121 (1.7%)

0980   1110

8931

0484

9710

7442

7731 (1.5%)

6973

2517 (1.7%)

9310 (2.4%) Unclassified transactions

6651 (0.70%)

0223

8211 (1.3%)

8122   7414
6924   6997
6633

9410

1222 (0.90%)

8219 (1.0%)

6842

6613

* Numbers indicate SITC-4 Rev 2 codes which can be found in the Appendix. Percentages next to the product codes indicate proportion of the product in the exports of the country. Treemap headers show the total trade of the country.

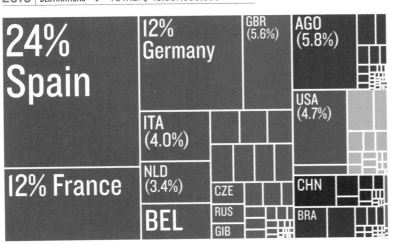

2010 EXPORT DESTINATIONS ▾ TOTAL: $ 43,367,388,556

24% Spain

12% Germany

GBR (5.6%)

AGO (5.8%)

USA (4.7%)

ITA (4.0%)

NLD (3.4%)

CZE

CHN

12% France

BEL

RUS
GIB

BRA

2010 IMPORT SOURCES ▾ TOTAL: $ 68,615,549,103

31% Spain

7.1% France

ITA (5.7%)

CHN (2.7%)

KOR

NGA (2.4%)   LBY

NLD (4.9%)

BEL

DEU (14%)

KAZ   IRL
NOR   RUS
SWE   CHE

USA

EAST ASIA & PACIFIC   EUROPE & CENTRAL ASIA   LATIN AMERICA & CARIBBEAN   MIDDLE EAST & NORTH AFRICA   NORTH AMERICA   SOUTH ASIA   SUB-SAHARAN AFRICA

QATAR

ECONOMIC COMPLEXITY INDEX [2010] ▸ -0.101 (66)   COMPLEXITY OUTLOOK INDEX [2010] ▸ -0.811 (91)   EXPECTED GDPᴘᴄ GROWTH * ▸ -1.6% (127)

*Expected annual average for the 2010-2020 period.

2010 PRODUCT SPACE ▶

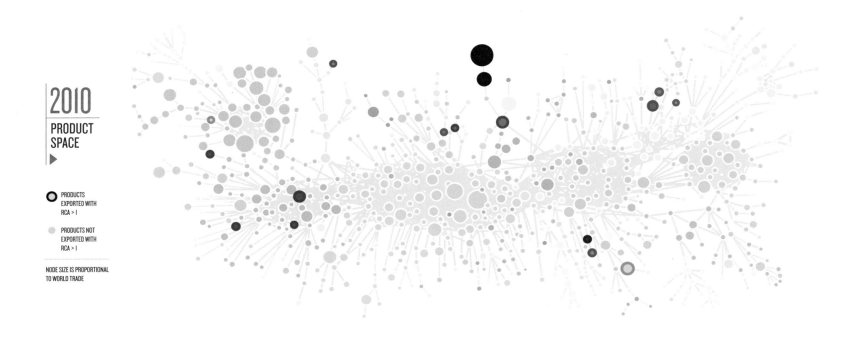

- ● PRODUCTS EXPORTED WITH RCA > 1
- ● PRODUCTS NOT EXPORTED WITH RCA > 1

NODE SIZE IS PROPORTIONAL TO WORLD TRADE

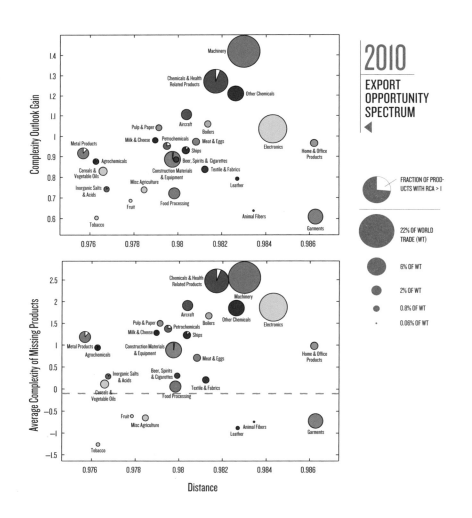

2010 EXPORT OPPORTUNITY SPECTRUM ◀

FRACTION OF PRODUCTS WITH RCA > 1

- 22% OF WORLD TRADE (WT)
- 6% OF WT
- 2% OF WT
- 0.8% OF WT
- 0.06% OF WT

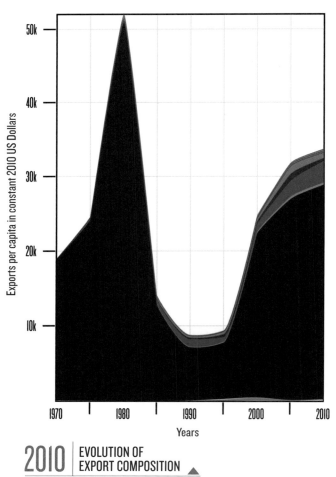

2010 | EVOLUTION OF EXPORT COMPOSITION ▲

POPULATION ► 1.8 M / (124)	GDP ► USD 127 B / (55)	EXPORTS PER CAPITA ► USD 33,731 / (2)	* Data are from 2010. Numbers indicate:
TOTAL EXPORTS ► USD 59 B / (43)	GDPPc ► USD 72,398 / (2)	EXPORTS AS SHARE OF GDP ► 47 % (22)	Value (World Ranking among 128 countries) Region: Middle East and North Africa.

ELECTRONICS · MACHINERY · AIRCRAFT · BOILERS · SHIPS · METAL PRODUCTS · CONSTR. MATL. & EQPT. · HOME & OFFICE · PULP & PAPER · CHEMICALS & HEALTH · AGROCHEMICALS · OTHER CHEMICALS · INOR. SALTS & ACIDS · PETROCHEMICALS · LEATHER · MILK & CHEESE · ANIMAL FIBERS · MEAT & EGGS · FISH & SEAFOOD · TROPICAL AGRIC. · CEREALS & VEG. OILS · COTTON/RICE/SOY & OTHERS · TOBACCO · FRUIT · MISC. AGRICULTURE · NOT CLASSIFIED · TEXTILE & FABRICS · GARMENTS · FOOD PROCESSING · BEER/SPIRITS & CIGS. · PRECIOUS STONES · COAL · OIL · MINING

2010 | EXPORT TREEMAP ▼ — TOTAL: $ 59,326,138,183

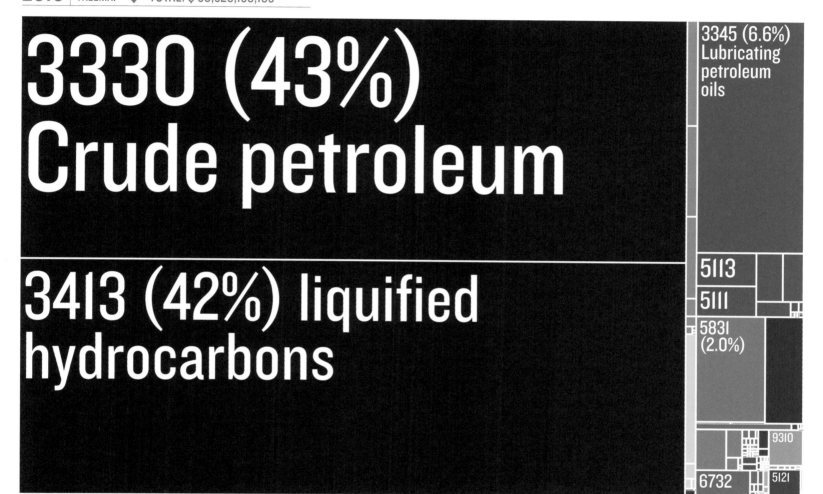

3330 (43%) Crude petroleum

3413 (42%) liquified hydrocarbons

3345 (6.6%) Lubricating petroleum oils

5113

5111

5831 (2.0%)

9310

6732

5121

* Numbers indicate SITC-4 Rev 2 codes which can be found in the Appendix. Percentages next to the product codes indicate proportion of the product in the exports of the country. Treemap headers show the total trade of the country.

2010 | EXPORT DESTINATIONS ▼ — TOTAL: $ 59,326,138,183

2010 | IMPORT SOURCES ▼ — TOTAL: $ 21,615,653,313

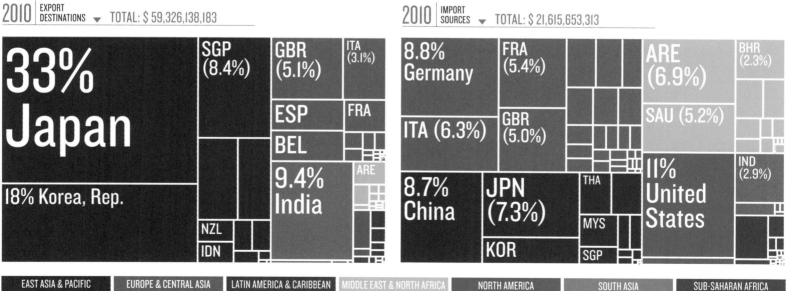

33% Japan

18% Korea, Rep.

SGP (8.4%)

GBR (5.1%)

ITA (3.1%)

ESP

FRA

BEL

9.4% India

ARE

NZL

IDN

8.8% Germany

FRA (5.4%)

ITA (6.3%)

GBR (5.0%)

8.7% China

JPN (7.3%)

KOR

THA

MYS

SGP

ARE (6.9%)

SAU (5.2%)

11% United States

BHR (2.3%)

IND (2.9%)

EAST ASIA & PACIFIC · EUROPE & CENTRAL ASIA · LATIN AMERICA & CARIBBEAN · MIDDLE EAST & NORTH AFRICA · NORTH AMERICA · SOUTH ASIA · SUB-SAHARAN AFRICA

ROMANIA

| ECONOMIC COMPLEXITY INDEX [2010] ▸ 0.785 (29) | COMPLEXITY OUTLOOK INDEX [2010] ▸ 1.276 (12) | EXPECTED GDPᴘᴄ GROWTH * ▸ 3.4% (14) |

*Expected annual average for the 2010-2020 period.

2010
PRODUCT SPACE ▶

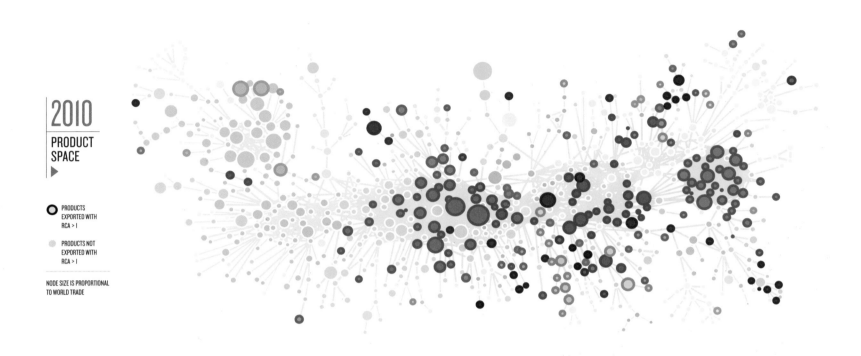

○ PRODUCTS EXPORTED WITH RCA > 1

○ PRODUCTS NOT EXPORTED WITH RCA > 1

NODE SIZE IS PROPORTIONAL TO WORLD TRADE

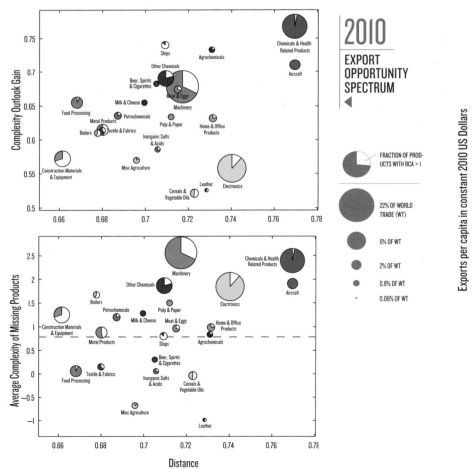

2010
EXPORT OPPORTUNITY SPECTRUM ◀

⊙ FRACTION OF PRODUCTS WITH RCA > 1

⊙ 22% OF WORLD TRADE (WT)

⊙ 6% OF WT

○ 2% OF WT

○ 0.8% OF WT

· 0.06% OF WT

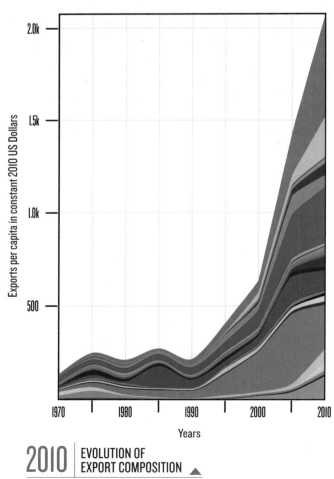

2010 | EVOLUTION OF EXPORT COMPOSITION ▲

| POPULATION ▸ 21 M / (46) | GDP ▸ USD 162 B / (49) | EXPORTS PER CAPITA ▸ USD 2,076 / (54) |
| TOTAL EXPORTS ▸ USD 45 B / (52) | GDPPC ▸ USD 7,539 / (57) | EXPORTS AS SHARE OF GDP ▸ 28 % (58) |

* Data are from 2010. Numbers indicate:
Value (World Ranking among 128 countries)
Region: Eastern Europe and Central Asia.

ELECTRONICS · MACHINERY · AIRCRAFT · BOILERS · SHIPS · METAL PRODUCTS · CONSTR. MATL. & EQPT. · HOME & OFFICE · PULP & PAPER · CHEMICALS & HEALTH · AGROCHEMICALS · OTHER CHEMICALS · INOR. SALTS & ACIDS · PETROCHEMICALS · LEATHER · MILK & CHEESE · ANIMAL FIBERS · MEAT & EGGS · FISH & SEAFOOD · TROPICAL AGRIC. · CEREALS & VEG. OILS · COTTON/RICE/SOY & OTHERS · TOBACCO · FRUIT · MISC. AGRICULTURE · NOT CLASSIFIED · TEXTILE & FABRICS · GARMENTS · FOOD PROCESSING · BEER/SPIRITS & CIGS. · PRECIOUS STONES · COAL · OIL · MINING

2010 | EXPORT TREEMAP ▼ TOTAL: $ 44,508,446,085

7810 (5.4%) Cars

7849 (4.8%) Other vehicle parts

7721 (2.4%)

7643 (5.1%) Television & radio transmitters

7611 (0.85%)

7649

7415

6251 (1.8%) Car tires

7783 · 8743
7493 · 7169
7492 · 7284
6991 · 6289 · 7132
7162 · 7784

7932 (1.3%)
7931 (0.97%)
7921

6727 (1.1%)
6713

7491 (1.5%)

7731 (5.3%) Electric wire

8211 (1.9%)

7752
6353
6416
6911

3345 (3.7%) Lubricating petroleum oils

5829
5138

9310 (3.1%) Unclassified transactions

5417 (1.4%)

5831
5832

2820 (2.2%) Iron & steel waste

8510 (2.8%) Footwear

8451 (0.73%)

6123
8431
8435

8441
8429
8310
8424

6514

2224
0430
1222 (1.1%)

* Numbers indicate SITC-4 Rev 2 codes which can be found in the Appendix. Percentages next to the product codes indicate proportion of the product in the exports of the country. Treemap headers show the total trade of the country.

2010 | EXPORT DESTINATIONS ▼ TOTAL: $ 44,508,446,085

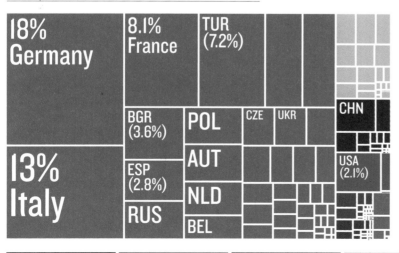

18% Germany

13% Italy

8.1% France

BGR (3.6%)
ESP (2.8%)
RUS

TUR (7.2%)

POL
AUT
NLD
BEL

CZE · UKR

CHN

USA (2.1%)

2010 | IMPORT SOURCES ▼ TOTAL: $ 55,586,469,048

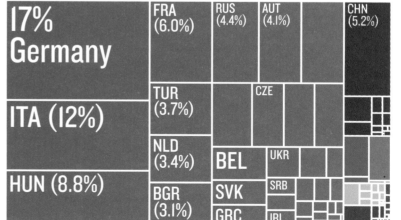

17% Germany

ITA (12%)

HUN (8.8%)

FRA (6.0%)

TUR (3.7%)

NLD (3.4%)

BGR (3.1%)

RUS (4.4%)

AUT (4.1%)

CZE

BEL

SVK
GRC

UKR
SRB
IRL

CHN (5.2%)

EAST ASIA & PACIFIC · EUROPE & CENTRAL ASIA · LATIN AMERICA & CARIBBEAN · MIDDLE EAST & NORTH AFRICA · NORTH AMERICA · SOUTH ASIA · SUB-SAHARAN AFRICA

RUSSIAN FEDERATION

ECONOMIC COMPLEXITY INDEX [2010] ▸ 0.4 (44) | COMPLEXITY OUTLOOK INDEX [2010] ▸ 0.089 (58) | EXPECTED GDPᴘᴄ GROWTH * ▸ 1.7% (73)

*Expected annual average for the 2010-2020 period.

2010
PRODUCT SPACE ▸

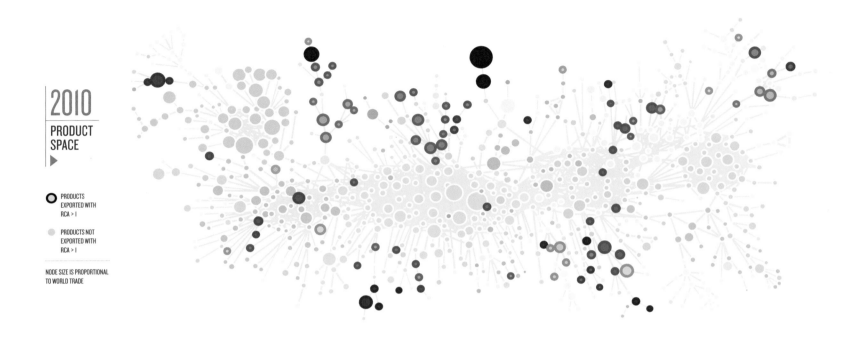

○ PRODUCTS EXPORTED WITH RCA > 1

○ PRODUCTS NOT EXPORTED WITH RCA > 1

NODE SIZE IS PROPORTIONAL TO WORLD TRADE

2010
EXPORT OPPORTUNITY SPECTRUM ◂

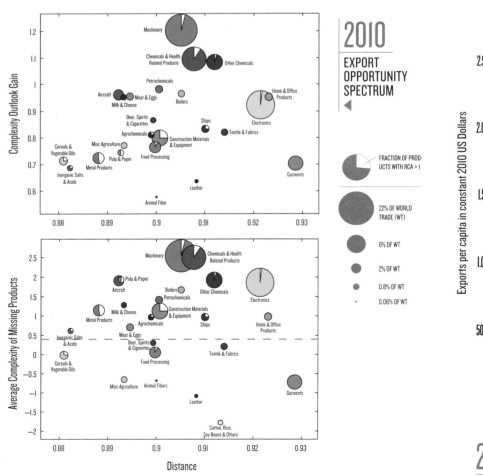

⬤ FRACTION OF PRODUCTS WITH RCA > 1

⬤ 22% OF WORLD TRADE (WT)

⬤ 6% OF WT

● 2% OF WT

• 0.8% OF WT

· 0.06% OF WT

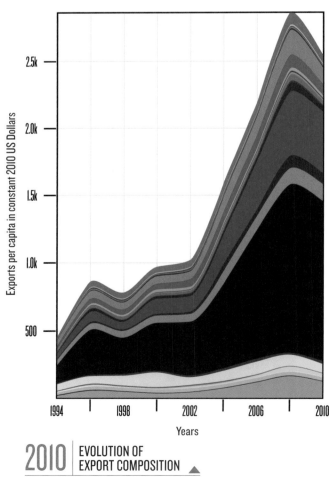

2010 | EVOLUTION OF EXPORT COMPOSITION ▲

POPULATION ▸ 142 M / (9)
TOTAL EXPORTS ▸ USD 360 B / (10)

GDP ▸ USD 1.5 T / (11)
GDPₚc ▸ USD 10,481 / (45)

EXPORTS PER CAPITA ▸ USD 2,540 / (46)
EXPORTS AS SHARE OF GDP ▸ 24 % (65)

* Data are from 2010. Numbers indicate:
Value (World Ranking among 128 countries)
Region: Eastern Europe and Central Asia.

ELECTRONICS | MACHINERY | AIRCRAFT | BOILERS | SHIPS | METAL PRODUCTS | CONSTR. MATL. & EQPT. | HOME & OFFICE | PULP & PAPER | CHEMICALS & HEALTH | AGROCHEMICALS | OTHER CHEMICALS | INOR. SALTS & ACIDS | PETROCHEMICALS | LEATHER | MILK & CHEESE | ANIMAL FIBERS | MEAT & EGGS | FISH & SEAFOOD | TROPICAL AGRIC. | CEREALS & VEG. OILS | COTTON/RICE/SOY & OTHERS | TOBACCO | FRUIT | MISC. AGRICULTURE | NOT CLASSIFIED | TEXTILE & FABRICS | GARMENTS | FOOD PROCESSING | BEER/SPIRITS & CIGS. | PRECIOUS STONES | COAL | OIL | MINING

2010 | EXPORT TREEMAP ▼ TOTAL: $ 360,435,751,552

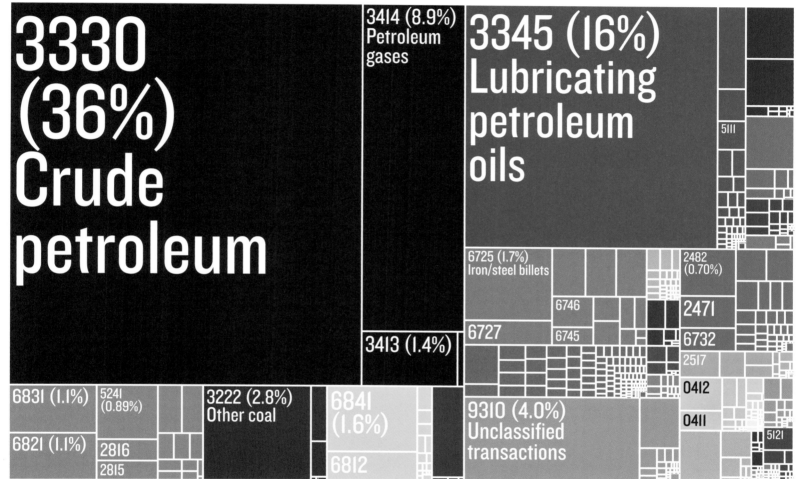

* Numbers indicate SITC-4 Rev 2 codes which can be found in the Appendix. Percentages next to the product codes indicate proportion of the product in the exports of the country. Treemap headers show the total trade of the country.

2010 | EXPORT DESTINATIONS ▼ TOTAL: $ 360,435,751,552

2010 | IMPORT SOURCES ▼ TOTAL: $ 192,501,771,701

EAST ASIA & PACIFIC | EUROPE & CENTRAL ASIA | LATIN AMERICA & CARIBBEAN | MIDDLE EAST & NORTH AFRICA | NORTH AMERICA | SOUTH ASIA | SUB-SAHARAN AFRICA

SAUDI ARABIA

ECONOMIC COMPLEXITY INDEX [2010] ▸ 0.11 (59) | COMPLEXITY OUTLOOK INDEX [2010] ▸ -0.678 (85) | EXPECTED GDPᴘᴄ GROWTH * ▸ 0.4% (109)

*Expected annual average for the 2010-2020 period.

2010 PRODUCT SPACE ▶

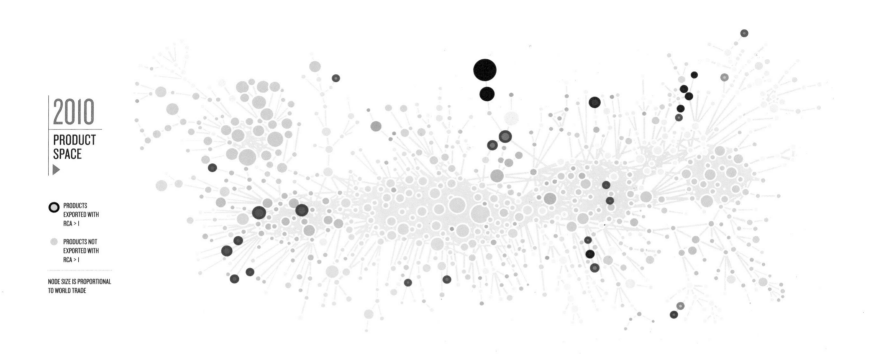

○ PRODUCTS EXPORTED WITH RCA > 1

○ PRODUCTS NOT EXPORTED WITH RCA > 1

NODE SIZE IS PROPORTIONAL TO WORLD TRADE

2010 EXPORT OPPORTUNITY SPECTRUM ◀

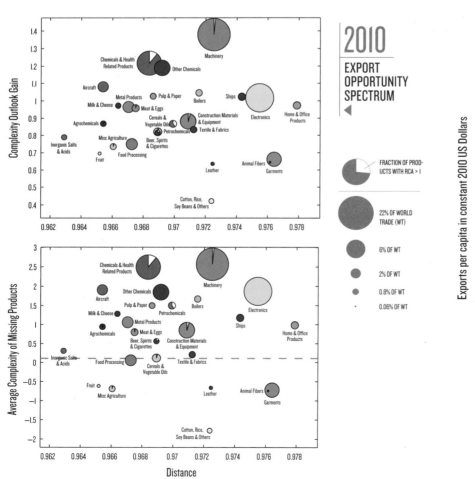

○ FRACTION OF PRODUCTS WITH RCA > 1

● 22% OF WORLD TRADE (WT)

● 6% OF WT

● 2% OF WT

● 0.8% OF WT

· 0.06% OF WT

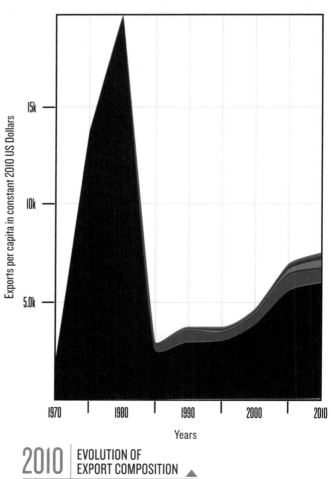

2010 EVOLUTION OF EXPORT COMPOSITION ▲

POPULATION ▸ 27 M / (41)	GDP ▸ USD 451 B / (23)	EXPORTS PER CAPITA ▸ USD 7,553 / (27)
TOTAL EXPORTS ▸ USD 207 B / (18)	GDPPC ▸ USD 16,423 / (32)	EXPORTS AS SHARE OF GDP ▸ 46 % (23)

* Data are from 2010. Numbers indicate:
Value (World Ranking among 128 countries)
Region: Middle East and North Africa.

ELECTRONICS · MACHINERY · AIRCRAFT · BOILERS · SHIPS · METAL PRODUCTS · CONSTR. MATL. & EQPT. · HOME & OFFICE · PULP & PAPER · CHEMICALS & HEALTH · AGROCHEMICALS · OTHER CHEMICALS · INOR. SALTS & ACIDS · PETROCHEMICALS · LEATHER · MILK & CHEESE · ANIMAL FIBERS · MEAT & EGGS · FISH & SEAFOOD · TROPICAL AGRIC. · CEREALS & VEG. OILS · COTTON/RICE/SOY & OTHERS · TOBACCO · FRUIT · MISC. AGRICULTURE · NOT CLASSIFIED · TEXTILE & FABRICS · GARMENTS · FOOD PROCESSING · BEER/SPIRITS & CIGS. · PRECIOUS STONES · COAL · OIL · MINING

2010 EXPORT TREEMAP ▾ TOTAL: $ 207,321,415,766

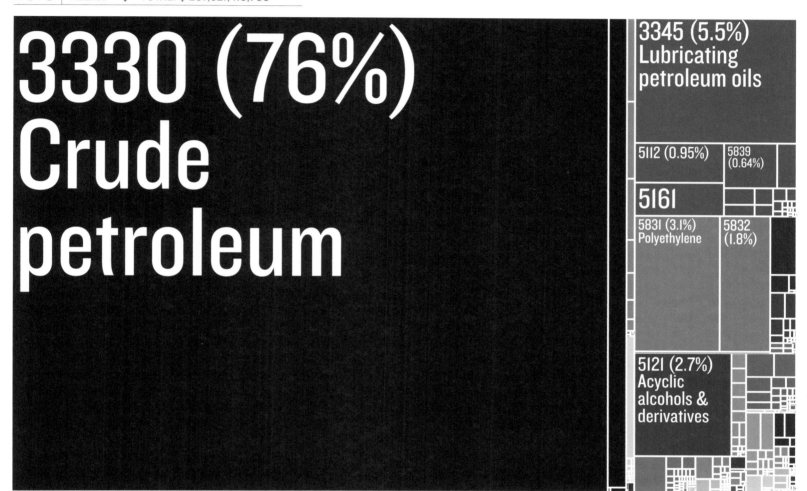

3330 (76%) Crude petroleum

3345 (5.5%) Lubricating petroleum oils

5112 (0.95%) · 5839 (0.64%)

5161

5831 (3.1%) Polyethylene · 5832 (1.8%)

5121 (2.7%) Acyclic alcohols & derivatives

* Numbers indicate SITC-4 Rev 2 codes which can be found in the Appendix. Percentages next to the product codes indicate proportion of the product in the exports of the country. Treemap headers show the total trade of the country.

2010 EXPORT DESTINATIONS ▾ TOTAL: $ 207,321,415,766

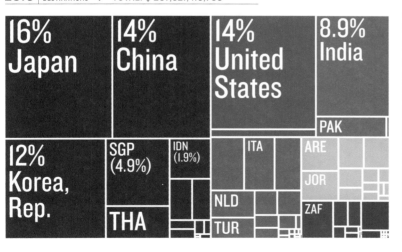

16% Japan · 14% China · 14% United States · 8.9% India
12% Korea, Rep. · SGP (4.9%) · IDN (1.9%) · ITA · ARE · PAK
· JOR · NLD · ZAF · THA · TUR

2010 IMPORT SOURCES ▾ TOTAL: $ 97,272,958,942

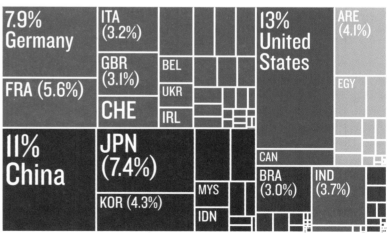

7.9% Germany · ITA (3.2%) · GBR (3.1%) · BEL · 13% United States · ARE (4.1%)
FRA (5.6%) · UKR · CHE · IRL · EGY
11% China · JPN (7.4%) · CAN · BRA (3.0%) · IND (3.7%)
· KOR (4.3%) · MYS · IDN

| EAST ASIA & PACIFIC | EUROPE & CENTRAL ASIA | LATIN AMERICA & CARIBBEAN | MIDDLE EAST & NORTH AFRICA | NORTH AMERICA | SOUTH ASIA | SUB-SAHARAN AFRICA |

SENEGAL

ECONOMIC COMPLEXITY INDEX [2010] ▸ -0.977 (105) | **COMPLEXITY OUTLOOK INDEX [2010]** ▸ -0.882 (95) | **EXPECTED GDPᴘᴄ GROWTH** * ▸ 1.7% (75)

*Expected annual average for the 2010-2020 period.

2010
PRODUCT SPACE ▶

○ PRODUCTS EXPORTED WITH RCA > 1

○ PRODUCTS NOT EXPORTED WITH RCA > 1

NODE SIZE IS PROPORTIONAL TO WORLD TRADE

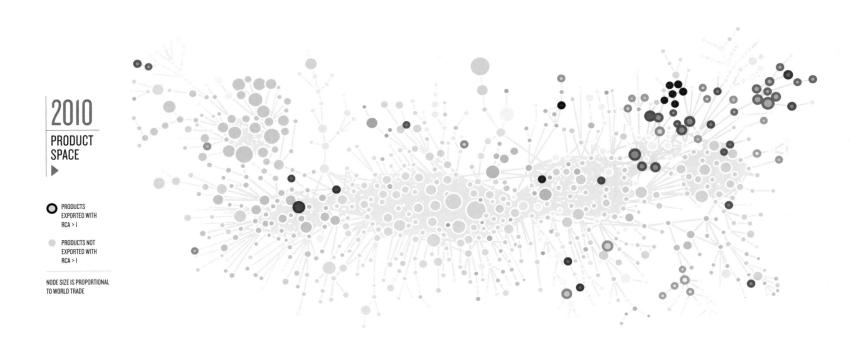

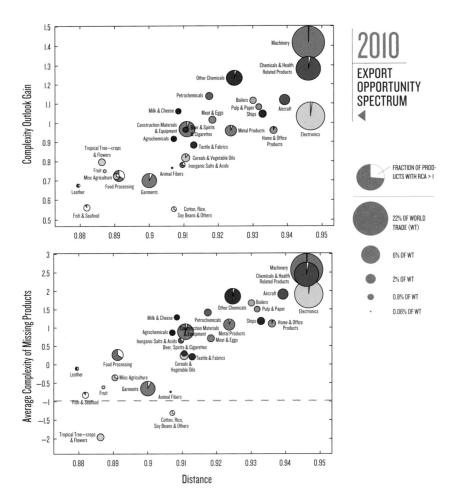

2010
EXPORT OPPORTUNITY SPECTRUM ◀

◔ FRACTION OF PRODUCTS WITH RCA > 1

● 22% OF WORLD TRADE (WT)

● 6% OF WT

● 2% OF WT

● 0.8% OF WT

· 0.06% OF WT

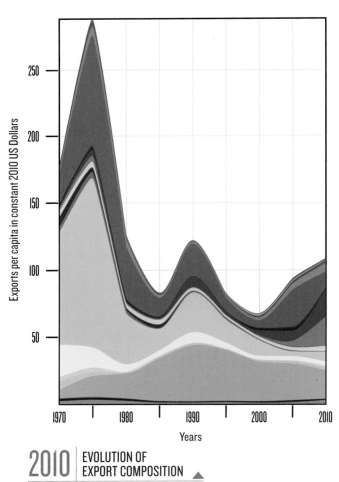

2010 | EVOLUTION OF EXPORT COMPOSITION ▲

POPULATION ▸ 12 M / (63)
TOTAL EXPORTS ▸ USD 1.4 B / (119)

GDP ▸ USD 13 B / (106)
GDPᴘᴄ ▸ USD 1,034 / (112)

EXPORTS PER CAPITA ▸ USD 109 / (120)
EXPORTS AS SHARE OF GDP ▸ 11 % / (119)

* Data are from 2010. Numbers indicate:
Value (World Ranking among 128 countries)
Region: Sub-Saharan Africa.

ELECTRONICS · MACHINERY · AIRCRAFT · BOILERS · SHIPS · METAL PRODUCTS · CONSTR. MATL. & EQPT. · HOME & OFFICE · PULP & PAPER · CHEMICALS & HEALTH · AGROCHEMICALS · OTHER CHEMICALS · INOR. SALTS & ACIDS · PETROCHEMICALS · LEATHER · MILK & CHEESE · ANIMAL FIBERS · MEAT & EGGS · FISH & SEAFOOD · TROPICAL AGRIC. · CEREALS & VEG. OILS · COTTON/RICE/SOY & OTHERS · TOBACCO · FRUIT · MISC. AGRICULTURE · NOT CLASSIFIED · TEXTILE & FABRICS · GARMENTS · FOOD PROCESSING · BEER/SPIRITS & CIGS. · PRECIOUS STONES · COAL · OIL · MINING

2010 EXPORT TREEMAP ▾ TOTAL: $ 1,354,504,274

3345 (18%) Lubricating petroleum oils

5222 (10%) Non metal inorganic acids & oxygen compounds

0342 (6.2%) Frozen fish, excluding fillets

0360 (5.6%) Crustaceans & molluscs

4234 (5.1%) Peanut oil

0813 (1.6%)

2631 (1.8%) Raw cotton

0341 (4.2%) Fresh or chilled fish, excluding fillets

0344 (1.2%)

0343 (1.0%)

0350

0372

1222

1223

5417

6612 (12%) Cement

9710 (8.6%) Gold, non monetary

2882 (1.4%)

2783 (1.1%)

2782 (0.91%)

2789

0980 (2.0%) Edible products N.E.S.

0579 (0.90%)

2820 (2.3%) Iron & steel waste

6732 (0.98%)

0545 (1.6%)

7821

* Numbers indicate SITC-4 Rev 2 codes which can be found in the Appendix. Percentages next to the product codes indicate proportion of the product in the exports of the country. Treemap headers show the total trade of the country.

2010 EXPORT DESTINATIONS ▾ TOTAL: $ 1,354,504,274

32% Mali

CMR

BFA

12% India

ARE (7.8%)

CHN (3.4%)

FRA (7.2%)

ESP (4.4%)

ITA

BEL (4.0%)

PRT

CHE

2010 IMPORT SOURCES ▾ TOTAL: $ 5,255,053,704

18% France

15% United Kingdom

9.3% China

NGA (3.6%)

VNM

JPN

NLD (5.8%)

ESP (3.3%)

USA (4.1%)

BEL

ITA (2.7%)

UKR

IRL

IND (4.0%)

ARG

EGY

EAST ASIA & PACIFIC | EUROPE & CENTRAL ASIA | LATIN AMERICA & CARIBBEAN | MIDDLE EAST & NORTH AFRICA | NORTH AMERICA | SOUTH ASIA | SUB-SAHARAN AFRICA

SERBIA

ECONOMIC COMPLEXITY INDEX [2010] ▸ 0.69 (34)   COMPLEXITY OUTLOOK INDEX [2010] ▸ 1.339 (9)   EXPECTED GDPᴘᴄ GROWTH * ▸ 3.7% (6)

*Expected annual average for the 2010-2020 period.

2010 PRODUCT SPACE ▸

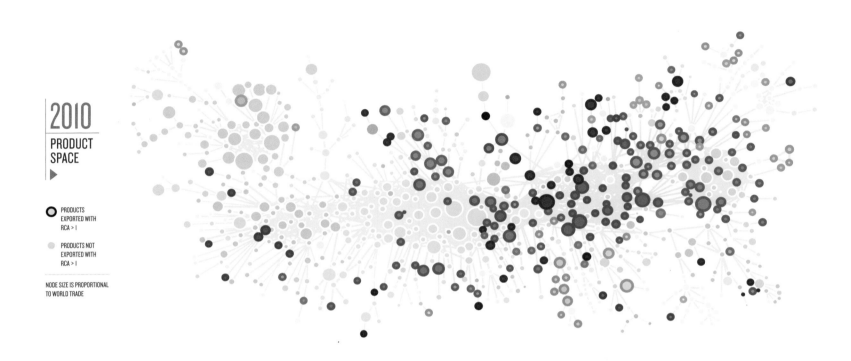

○ PRODUCTS EXPORTED WITH RCA > 1

○ PRODUCTS NOT EXPORTED WITH RCA > 1

NODE SIZE IS PROPORTIONAL TO WORLD TRADE

2010 EXPORT OPPORTUNITY SPECTRUM ◂

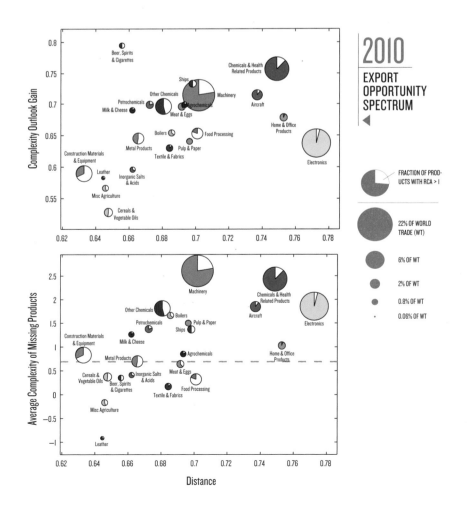

FRACTION OF PRODUCTS WITH RCA > 1

22% OF WORLD TRADE (WT)

6% OF WT

2% OF WT

0.8% OF WT

0.06% OF WT

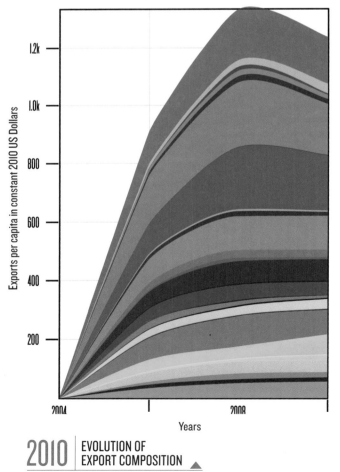

2010 | EVOLUTION OF EXPORT COMPOSITION ▲

POPULATION ▸ 7.3 M / (83)
TOTAL EXPORTS ▸ USD 9 B / (75)

GDP ▸ USD 38 B / (80)
GDPpc ▸ USD 5,273 / (66)

EXPORTS PER CAPITA ▸ USD 1,238 / (66)
EXPORTS AS SHARE OF GDP ▸ 23 % (67)

* Data are from 2010. Numbers indicate:
Value (World Ranking among 128 countries)
Region: Eastern Europe and Central Asia.

ELECTRONICS · MACHINERY · AIRCRAFT · BOILERS · SHIPS · METAL PRODUCTS · CONSTR. MATL. & EQPT. · HOME & OFFICE · PULP & PAPER · CHEMICALS & HEALTH · AGROCHEMICALS · OTHER CHEMICALS · INOR. SALTS & ACIDS · PETROCHEMICALS · LEATHER · MILK & CHEESE · ANIMAL FIBERS · MEAT & EGGS · FISH & SEAFOOD · TROPICAL AGRIC. · CEREALS & VEG. OILS · COTTON/RICE/SOY & OTHERS · TOBACCO · FRUIT · MISC. AGRICULTURE · NOT CLASSIFIED · TEXTILE & FABRICS · GARMENTS · FOOD PROCESSING · BEER/SPIRITS & CIGS. · PRECIOUS STONES · COAL · OIL · MINING

2010 EXPORT TREEMAP ▼ TOTAL: $ 9,029,787,911

6727 (5.1%) Iron/steel coils
6822 (3.7%) Worked copper & copper alloys
6747 (1.7%)
6716 (1.1%)
7611
6746 (0.81%)
6745
6744
6251 (1.7%)
7721 (0.83%)
7758
7849 (0.76%)
7919
7432
7162 (1.2%)
9510
7284
6418 (1.5%)
3510 (3.4%) Electric current
6842 (1.8%) Worked aluminium & aluminium alloys
8211 (1.0%)
6924
6997
6973
6359
8219
2483
6912
7731 (2.1%)
5852
7931
7922
5417 (1.9%) Medicaments
8939 (1.3%)
3345 (1.2%)
5111
5542 (0.69%)
8922
5334
5335
0819
5831 (1.7%)
0440 (2.8%) Unmilled maize
0548
0412
4232
8463 (1.7%)
8510 (1.2%)
8472
8439
0612 (1.8%) Refined sugar
6123 (0.86%)
0586 (2.6%) Temporarily preserved fruit
0980 (1.0%)
0484 (0.81%)
0579 (0.59%)
0730 (0.71%)
8931
0585
1121
1123
5121
9310 (2.0%) Unclassified transactions
2820 (1.6%)
6821
0011 (0.61%)
3354
0223
2111

* Numbers indicate SITC-4 Rev 2 codes which can be found in the Appendix. Percentages next to the product codes indicate proportion of the product in the exports of the country. Treemap headers show the total trade of the country.

2010 EXPORT DESTINATIONS ▼ TOTAL: $ 9,029,787,911

2010 IMPORT SOURCES ▼ TOTAL: $ 15,120,572,762

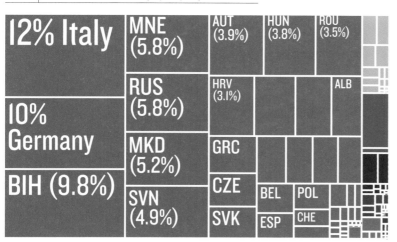

12% Italy
10% Germany
BIH (9.8%)
MNE (5.8%)
RUS (5.8%)
MKD (5.2%)
SVN (4.9%)
AUT (3.9%)
HUN (3.8%)
ROU (3.5%)
HRV (3.1%)
ALB
GRC
CZE
BEL
POL
SVK
ESP
CHE

13% Russia
11% Germany
ITA (8.6%)
HUN (5.0%)
AUT (3.1%)
SVN (3.1%)
FRA
HRV
ROU (3.6%)
BGR (3.6%)
BIH (3.5%)
CHN (6.8%)
TUR
UKR
BEL
GRC
MKD
GBR
NLD
SWE
MNE
LBY

EAST ASIA & PACIFIC · EUROPE & CENTRAL ASIA · LATIN AMERICA & CARIBBEAN · MIDDLE EAST & NORTH AFRICA · NORTH AMERICA · SOUTH ASIA · SUB-SAHARAN AFRICA

SINGAPORE

ECONOMIC COMPLEXITY INDEX [2010] ► 1.651 (10)	COMPLEXITY OUTLOOK INDEX [2010] ► 0.81 (33)	EXPECTED GDPᴘᴄ GROWTH * ► 2.4% (47)

*Expected annual average for the 2010-2020 period.

2010
PRODUCT SPACE ►

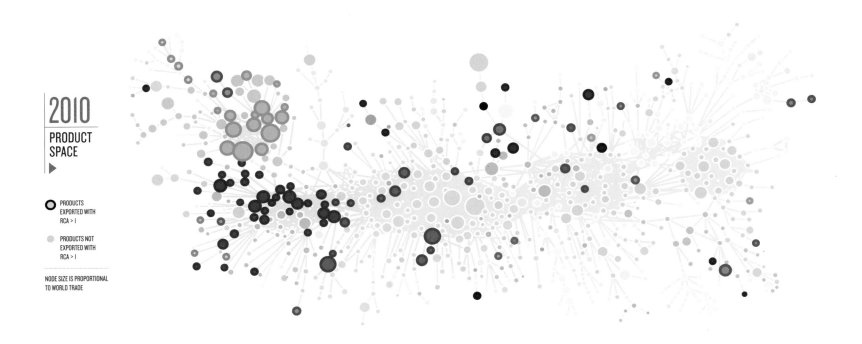

○ PRODUCTS EXPORTED WITH RCA > 1

○ PRODUCTS NOT EXPORTED WITH RCA > 1

NODE SIZE IS PROPORTIONAL TO WORLD TRADE

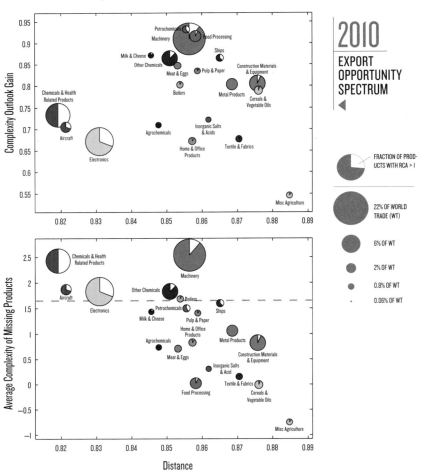

2010
EXPORT OPPORTUNITY SPECTRUM ◄

◖ FRACTION OF PRODUCTS WITH RCA > 1

● 22% OF WORLD TRADE (WT)

● 6% OF WT

● 2% OF WT

● 0.8% OF WT

· 0.06% OF WT

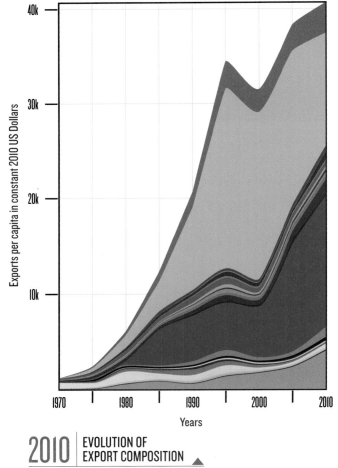

2010 | EVOLUTION OF EXPORT COMPOSITION ▲

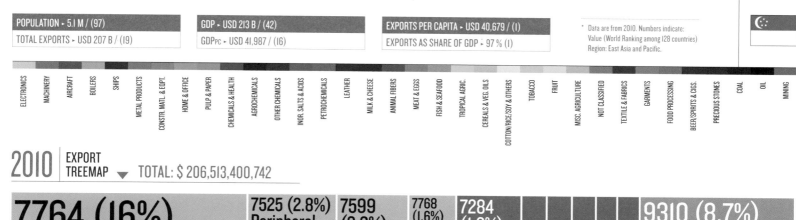

* Data are from 2010. Numbers indicate:
Value (World Ranking among 128 countries)
Region: East Asia and Pacific.

POPULATION ▸ 5.1 M / (97)	GDP ▸ USD 213 B / (42)	EXPORTS PER CAPITA ▸ USD 40,679 / (1)
TOTAL EXPORTS ▸ USD 207 B / (19)	GDPᴘᴄ ▸ USD 41,987 / (16)	EXPORTS AS SHARE OF GDP ▸ 97 % (1)

2010 EXPORT TREEMAP ▾ TOTAL: $ 206,513,400,742

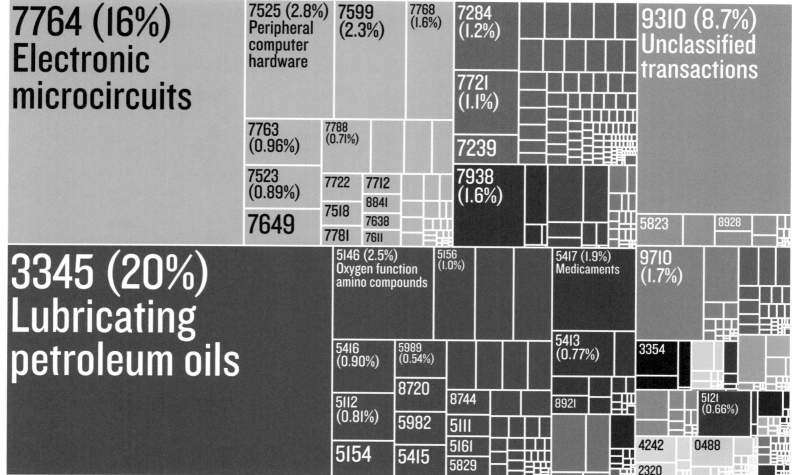

* Numbers indicate SITC-4 Rev 2 codes which can be found in the Appendix. Percentages next to the product codes indicate proportion of the product in the exports of the country. Treemap headers show the total trade of the country.

2010 EXPORT DESTINATIONS ▾ TOTAL: $ 206,513,400,742

2010 IMPORT SOURCES ▾ TOTAL: $ 258,195,293,703

EAST ASIA & PACIFIC   EUROPE & CENTRAL ASIA   LATIN AMERICA & CARIBBEAN   MIDDLE EAST & NORTH AFRICA ▸   NORTH AMERICA   SOUTH ASIA   SUB-SAHARAN AFRICA

SLOVAK REPUBLIC

ECONOMIC COMPLEXITY INDEX [2010] ► 1.433 (15) | **COMPLEXITY OUTLOOK INDEX [2010]** ► 0.798 (35) | **EXPECTED GDPᴘᴄ GROWTH** * ► 3.1% (19)

*Expected annual average for the 2010-2020 period.

2010
PRODUCT SPACE ▶

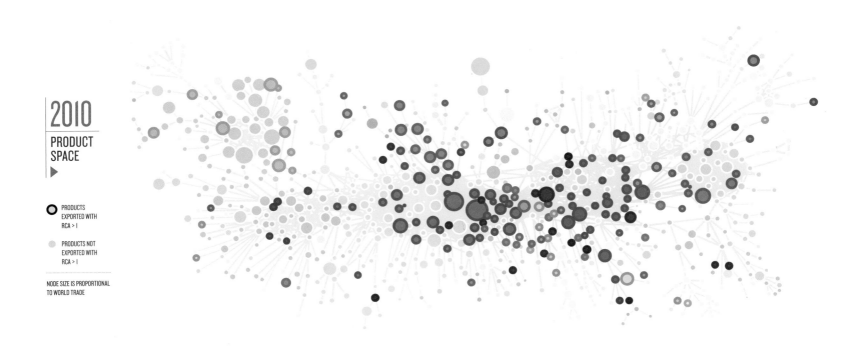

○ PRODUCTS EXPORTED WITH RCA > 1

● PRODUCTS NOT EXPORTED WITH RCA > 1

NODE SIZE IS PROPORTIONAL TO WORLD TRADE

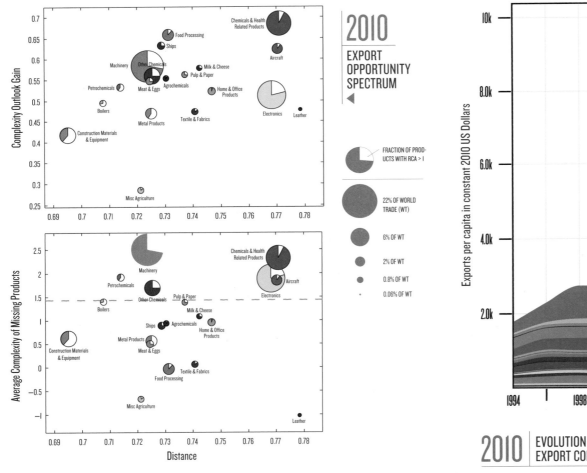

2010
EXPORT OPPORTUNITY SPECTRUM ◀

◔ FRACTION OF PRODUCTS WITH RCA > 1

⬤ 22% OF WORLD TRADE (WT)

● 6% OF WT

● 2% OF WT

● 0.8% OF WT

· 0.06% OF WT

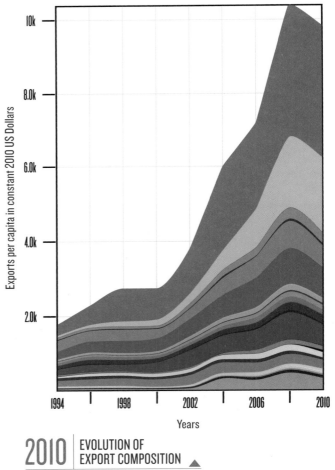

2010
EVOLUTION OF EXPORT COMPOSITION ▲

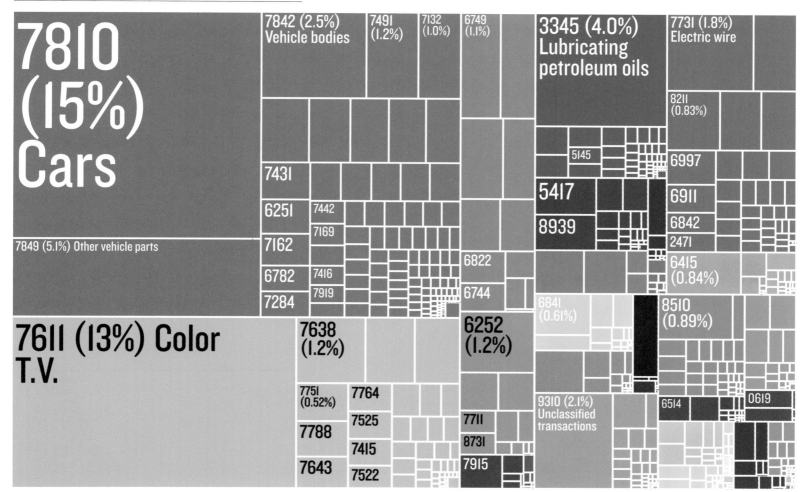

POPULATION ▸ 5.4 M / (95)
TOTAL EXPORTS ▸ USD 53 B / (47)

GDP ▸ USD 87 B / (60)
GDPᴘᴄ ▸ USD 16,036 / (33)

EXPORTS PER CAPITA ▸ USD 9,849 / (19)
EXPORTS AS SHARE OF GDP ▸ 61 % / (10)

* Data are from 2010. Numbers indicate:
Value (World Ranking among 128 countries)
Region: Eastern Europe and Central Asia.

ELECTRONICS · MACHINERY · AIRCRAFT · BOILERS · SHIPS · METAL PRODUCTS · CONSTR. MATL. & EQPT. · HOME & OFFICE · PULP & PAPER · CHEMICALS & HEALTH · AGROCHEMICALS · OTHER CHEMICALS · INOR. SALTS & ACIDS · PETROCHEMICALS · LEATHER · MILK & CHEESE · ANIMAL FIBERS · MEAT & EGGS · FISH & SEAFOOD · TROPICAL AGRIC. · CEREALS & VEG. OILS · COTTON/RICE/SOY & OTHERS · TOBACCO · FRUIT · MISC. AGRICULTURE · NOT CLASSIFIED · TEXTILE & FABRICS · GARMENTS · FOOD PROCESSING · BEER/SPIRITS & CIGS. · PRECIOUS STONES · COAL · OIL · MINING

2010 | EXPORT TREEMAP ▾ TOTAL: $ 53,482,619,803

7810 (15%) Cars

7849 (5.1%) Other vehicle parts

7611 (13%) Color T.V.

7842 (2.5%) Vehicle bodies

7491 (1.2%)

7132 (1.0%)

6749 (1.1%)

7431

6251 · 7442

7169

7162

6782 · 7416

7919

7284

7638 (1.2%)

7751 (0.52%) · 7764

7788 · 7525

7415

7643 · 7522

6822

6744

6252 (1.2%)

7711

8731

7915

3345 (4.0%) Lubricating petroleum oils

5145

5417

8939

9310 (2.1%) Unclassified transactions

6841 (0.61%)

7731 (1.8%) Electric wire

8211 (0.83%)

6997

6911

6842

2471

6415 (0.84%)

8510 (0.89%)

6514

0619

* Numbers indicate SITC-4 Rev 2 codes which can be found in the Appendix. Percentages next to the product codes indicate proportion of the product in the exports of the country. Treemap headers show the total trade of the country.

2010 | EXPORT DESTINATIONS ▾ TOTAL: $ 53,482,619,803

21% Germany

11% Czech Republic

FRA (6.8%)

POL (6.2%)

AUT (6.0%)

ITA (5.8%)

CHN

HUN (5.2%)

ESP (3.6%)

TUR

ROU

USA

RUS (4.3%)

NLD

GBR (4.2%)

SWE

BEL

2010 | IMPORT SOURCES ▾ TOTAL: $ 52,299,906,156

20% Germany

CZE (13%)

RUS (11%)

HUN (5.0%)

POL (4.8%)

ITA (3.8%)

AUT (2.9%)

NLD

UKR

BEL

TUR

ESP

ROU

CHE

8.8% Korea, Rep.

CHN (6.7%)

JPN (1.9%)

USA

EAST ASIA & PACIFIC · EUROPE & CENTRAL ASIA · LATIN AMERICA & CARIBBEAN · MIDDLE EAST & NORTH AFRICA · NORTH AMERICA · SOUTH ASIA · SUB-SAHARAN AFRICA

SLOVENIA

ECONOMIC COMPLEXITY INDEX [2010] ▸ 1.436 (14) | **COMPLEXITY OUTLOOK INDEX [2010]** ▸ 0.751 (39) | **EXPECTED GDPᴘᴄ GROWTH** * ▸ 2.7% (33)

*Expected annual average for the 2010-2020 period.

2010
PRODUCT SPACE ▸

○ PRODUCTS EXPORTED WITH RCA > 1

○ PRODUCTS NOT EXPORTED WITH RCA > 1

NODE SIZE IS PROPORTIONAL TO WORLD TRADE

2010
EXPORT OPPORTUNITY SPECTRUM ◂

FRACTION OF PRODUCTS WITH RCA > 1

22% OF WORLD TRADE (WT)

6% OF WT

2% OF WT

0.8% OF WT

0.06% OF WT

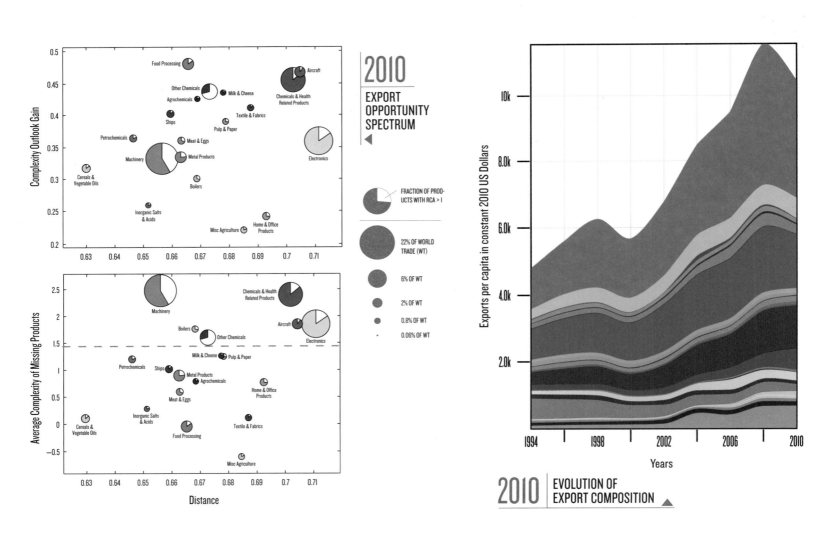

2010 | EVOLUTION OF EXPORT COMPOSITION ▲

POPULATION ▸ 2 M / (122)
TOTAL EXPORTS ▸ USD 21 B / (63)

GDP ▸ USD 47 B / (74)
GDPPC ▸ USD 22,898 / (27)

EXPORTS PER CAPITA ▸ USD 10,459 / (16)
EXPORTS AS SHARE OF GDP ▸ 46 % (24)

* Data are from 2010. Numbers indicate:
Value (World Ranking among 128 countries)
Region: Eastern Europe and Central Asia.

ELECTRONICS · MACHINERY · AIRCRAFT · BOILERS · SHIPS · METAL PRODUCTS · CONSTR. MATL. & EQPT. · HOME & OFFICE · PULP & PAPER · CHEMICALS & HEALTH · AGROCHEMICALS · OTHER CHEMICALS · INOR. SALTS & ACIDS · PETROCHEMICALS · LEATHER · MILK & CHEESE · ANIMAL FIBERS · MEAT & EGGS · FISH & SEAFOOD · TROPICAL AGRIC. · CEREALS & VEG. OILS · COTTON/RICE/SOY & OTHERS · TOBACCO · FRUIT · MISC. AGRICULTURE · NOT CLASSIFIED · TEXTILE & FABRICS · GARMENTS · FOOD PROCESSING · BEER/SPIRITS & CIGS. · PRECIOUS STONES · COAL · OIL · MINING

2010 | EXPORT TREEMAP ▼ TOTAL: $ 21,426,115,582

7810 (9.0%) Cars

7758 (1.9%) Electro thermal home appliances N.E.S.

6251 (1.2%)

7821 (1.1%)

7757 (1.4%)

8211 (2.2%) Chairs & seats

8219 (1.3%)

7721 (0.93%)

3510 (1.9%) Electric current

6911

8942

6418 (0.63%)

7723

7773 | 6416
2483
7861 | 7414
6428 | 6359
6973 | 8932

6415

8947

7849 (2.8%)

7493 | 7188

6572

6842 (1.8%)

6411

7162

6289

6744 (1.2%)

7711

7432

7434

8731

9310 (4.1%) Unclassified transactions

0813 (0.69%)

7783 (2.1%)

6954 | 7161

2222

5822

5417 (7.9%) Medicaments

5530 (0.94%)

8939 (0.87%)

3345 (2.5%) Lubricating petroleum oils

8720

2820 | 6635
5823
8928 | 7853

6514 (0.78%)

5334 (0.58%)

6210

6841 (0.71%)

0223

5335

5331

6998

8931

5542

5416

0980

* Numbers indicate SITC-4 Rev 2 codes which can be found in the Appendix. Percentages next to the product codes indicate proportion of the product in the exports of the country. Treemap headers show the total trade of the country.

2010 | EXPORT DESTINATIONS ▼ TOTAL: $ 21,426,115,582

22% Germany

FRA (7.7%)

AUT (7.0%)

HRV (5.0%)

HUN (3.5%)

BIH

POL (2.9%)

SRB | CHE

12% Italy

CZE | BEL
DNK

GBR

ROU | SWE

2010 | IMPORT SOURCES ▼ TOTAL: $ 23,934,344,413

18% Germany

8.2% Austria

FRA (5.5%)

CHN (5.1%)

HUN (2.9%)

CHE | SRB

KOR

JPN

16% Italy

ESP

BIH | SVK

CZE

BEL

POL

GBR | BGR

IND

EAST ASIA & PACIFIC · EUROPE & CENTRAL ASIA · LATIN AMERICA & CARIBBEAN · MIDDLE EAST & NORTH AFRICA · NORTH AMERICA · SOUTH ASIA · SUB-SAHARAN AFRICA

SOUTH AFRICA

ECONOMIC COMPLEXITY INDEX [2010] ▸ 0.238 (54)	COMPLEXITY OUTLOOK INDEX [2010] ▸ 1.013 (23)	EXPECTED GDPᴘᴄ GROWTH * ▸ 2.5% (43)

*Expected annual average for the 2010-2020 period.

2010 PRODUCT SPACE ▸

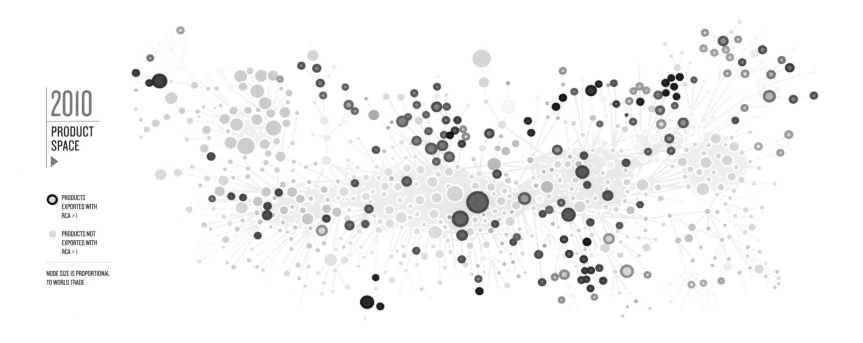

○ PRODUCTS EXPORTED WITH RCA > 1

○ PRODUCTS NOT EXPORTED WITH RCA > 1

NODE SIZE IS PROPORTIONAL TO WORLD TRADE

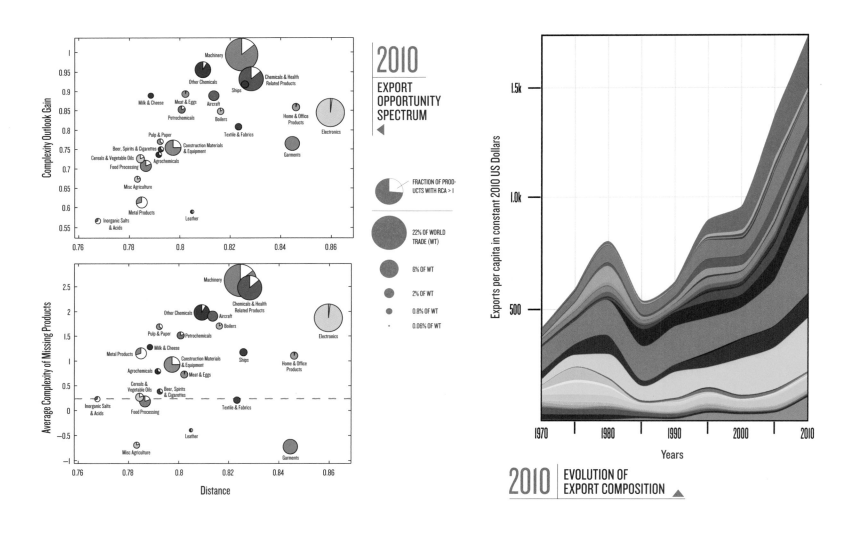

2010 EXPORT OPPORTUNITY SPECTRUM ◂

◔ FRACTION OF PRODUCTS WITH RCA > 1

⬤ 22% OF WORLD TRADE (WT)

⬤ 6% OF WT

● 2% OF WT

• 0.8% OF WT

· 0.06% OF WT

2010 EVOLUTION OF EXPORT COMPOSITION ▲

POPULATION ▸ 50 M / (23)	GDP ▸ USD 364 B / (28)	EXPORTS PER CAPITA ▸ USD 1,738 / (57)
TOTAL EXPORTS ▸ USD 87 B / (32)	GDPᴘᴄ ▸ USD 7,272 / (59)	EXPORTS AS SHARE OF GDP ▸ 24 % (66)

* Data are from 2010. Numbers indicate:
Value (World Ranking among 128 countries)
Region: Sub-Saharan Africa.

ELECTRONICS · MACHINERY · AIRCRAFT · BOILERS · SHIPS · METAL PRODUCTS · CONSTR. MATL. & EQPT. · HOME & OFFICE · PULP & PAPER · CHEMICALS & HEALTH · AGROCHEMICALS · OTHER CHEMICALS · INOR. SALTS & ACIDS · PETROCHEMICALS · LEATHER · MILK & CHEESE · ANIMAL FIBERS · MEAT & EGGS · FISH & SEAFOOD · TROPICAL AGRIC. · CEREALS & VEG. OILS · COTTON/RICE/SOY & OTHERS · TOBACCO · FRUIT · MISC. AGRICULTURE · NOT CLASSIFIED · TEXTILE & FABRICS · GARMENTS · FOOD PROCESSING · BEER/SPIRITS & CIGS. · PRECIOUS STONES · COAL · OIL · MINING

2010 EXPORT TREEMAP ▾ TOTAL: $ 86,865,326,995

- 9710 (6.9%) Gold, non monetary
- 2815 (5.8%) Iron ore
- 6812 (11%) Unwrought metals of platinum
- 7810 (4.1%) Cars
- 7436 (2.0%)
- 6716 (4.5%) Ferro alloys
- 7821 (1.2%)
- 7132
- 7239
- 7139
- 7234
- 7721
- 7849 (0.75%)
- 6727 (0.74%)
- 6746
- 6749
- 3345 (1.3%)
- 5989
- 5137
- 5162
- 5832
- 2816 (2.1%) Agglomerated iron ore
- 2877 (1.8%)
- 2879 (1.8%) Other non ferrous base metals
- 2871
- 6821
- 6831
- 6841 (1.4%)
- 2882
- 2881
- 2786
- 9310 (4.6%) Unclassified transactions
- 8928 (0.65%)
- 2820
- 0571 (1.1%)
- 0575
- 0980
- 0589
- 0585
- 3222 (6.0%) Other coal
- 6672 (6.1%) Unmounted diamonds
- 6842
- 2460
- 6911
- 8211
- 5121
- 2681

* Numbers indicate SITC-4 Rev 2 codes which can be found in the Appendix. Percentages next to the product codes indicate proportion of the product in the exports of the country. Treemap headers show the total trade of the country.

2010 EXPORT DESTINATIONS ▾ TOTAL: $ 86,865,326,995

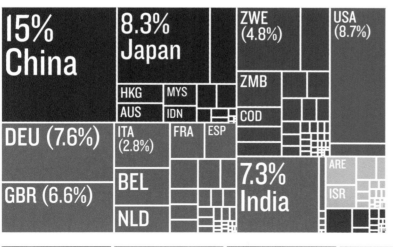

- 15% China
- 8.3% Japan
- ZWE (4.8%)
- USA (8.7%)
- HKG
- MYS
- AUS
- IDN
- ZMB
- COD
- DEU (7.6%)
- ITA (2.8%)
- FRA
- ESP
- GBR (6.6%)
- BEL
- NLD
- 7.3% India
- ARE
- ISR

2010 IMPORT SOURCES ▾ TOTAL: $ 70,193,810,693

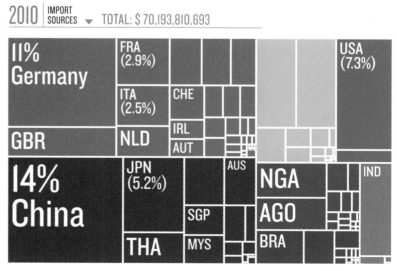

- 11% Germany
- FRA (2.9%)
- ITA (2.5%)
- CHE
- IRL
- AUT
- USA (7.3%)
- GBR
- NLD
- 14% China
- JPN (5.2%)
- AUS
- NGA
- IND
- SGP
- AGO
- THA
- MYS
- BRA

EAST ASIA & PACIFIC · EUROPE & CENTRAL ASIA · LATIN AMERICA & CARIBBEAN · MIDDLE EAST & NORTH AFRICA · NORTH AMERICA · SOUTH ASIA · SUB-SAHARAN AFRICA

SPAIN

ECONOMIC COMPLEXITY INDEX [2010] ► 1.047 (23)   COMPLEXITY OUTLOOK INDEX [2010] ► 1.103 (18)   EXPECTED GDPᴘᴄ GROWTH * ► 2.2% (57)

*Expected annual average for the 2010-2020 period.

2010 PRODUCT SPACE ►

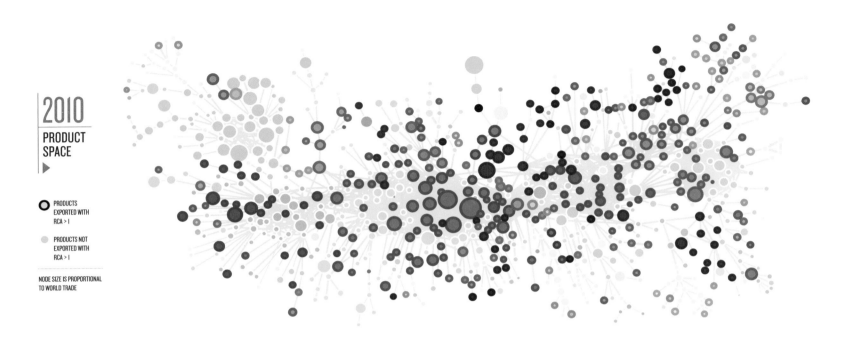

○ PRODUCTS EXPORTED WITH RCA > 1

○ PRODUCTS NOT EXPORTED WITH RCA > 1

NODE SIZE IS PROPORTIONAL TO WORLD TRADE

2010 EXPORT OPPORTUNITY SPECTRUM ◄

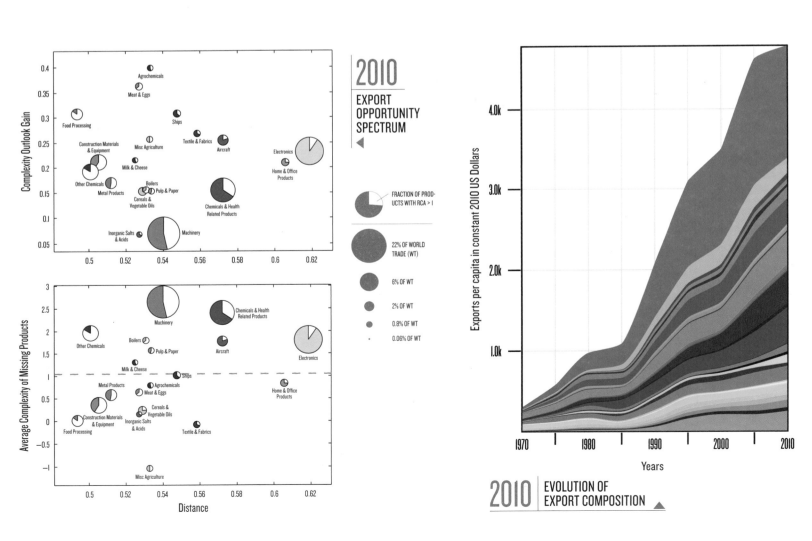

FRACTION OF PRODUCTS WITH RCA > 1

22% OF WORLD TRADE (WT)

6% OF WT

2% OF WT

0.8% OF WT

0.06% OF WT

2010 EVOLUTION OF EXPORT COMPOSITION ▲

POPULATION ▸ 46 M / (26)
TOTAL EXPORTS ▸ USD 221 B / (15)

GDP ▸ USD 1.4 T / (12)
GDPPC ▸ USD 30,026 / (24)

EXPORTS PER CAPITA ▸ USD 4,791 / (36)
EXPORTS AS SHARE OF GDP ▸ 16 % (99)

* Data are from 2010. Numbers indicate:
Value (World Ranking among 128 countries)
Region: Western Europe.

ELECTRONICS · MACHINERY · AIRCRAFT · BOILERS · SHIPS · METAL PRODUCTS · CONSTR. MATL. & EQPT. · HOME & OFFICE · PULP & PAPER · CHEMICALS & HEALTH · AGROCHEMICALS · OTHER CHEMICALS · INOR. SALTS & ACIDS · PETROCHEMICALS · LEATHER · MILK & CHEESE · ANIMAL FIBERS · MEAT & EGGS · FISH & SEAFOOD · TROPICAL AGRIC. · CEREALS & VEG. OILS · COTTON/RICE/SOY & OTHERS · TOBACCO · FRUIT · MISC. AGRICULTURE · NOT CLASSIFIED · TEXTILE & FABRICS · GARMENTS · FOOD PROCESSING · BEER/SPIRITS & CIGS. · PRECIOUS STONES · COAL · OIL · MINING

2010 | EXPORT TREEMAP ▾ TOTAL: $ 220,725,696,179

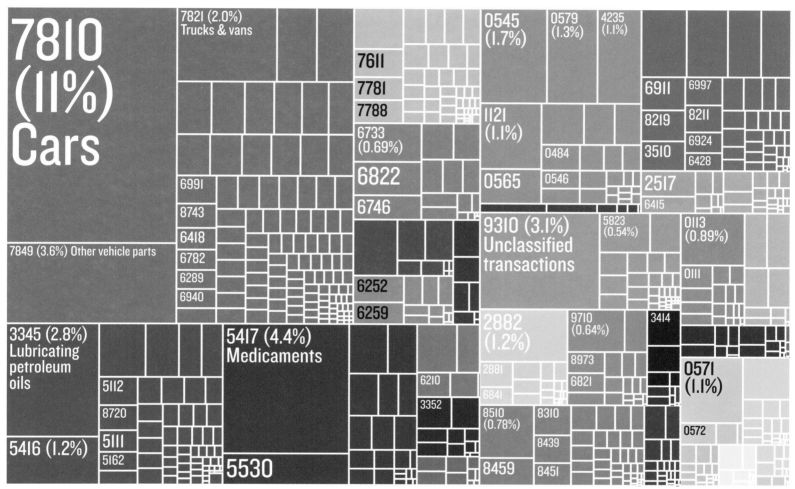

7810 (11%) Cars

7821 (2.0%) Trucks & vans

7611

7781

7788

6733 (0.69%)

6822

6746

6991

8743

6418

6782

6289

6940

6252

6259

7849 (3.6%) Other vehicle parts

0545 (1.7%)

0579 (1.3%)

4235 (1.1%)

1121 (1.1%)

0484

0565

0546

9310 (3.1%) Unclassified transactions

5823 (0.54%)

6911

6997

8219

8211

3510

6924

6428

2517

6415

0113 (0.89%)

0111

3345 (2.8%) Lubricating petroleum oils

5112

8720

5111

5162

5416 (1.2%)

5417 (4.4%) Medicaments

6210

3352

5530

2882 (1.2%)

2881

6841

9710 (0.64%)

8973

6821

3414

0571 (1.1%)

0572

8510 (0.78%)

8310

8439

8451

8459

* Numbers indicate SITC-4 Rev 2 codes which can be found in the Appendix. Percentages next to the product codes indicate proportion of the product in the exports of the country. Treemap headers show the total trade of the country.

2010 | EXPORT DESTINATIONS ▾ TOTAL: $ 220,725,696,179

15% France

12% Germany

PRT (9.7%)

9.1% Italy

NLD (3.5%)

BEL (3.4%)

GIB

TUR

GBR (6.5%)

CHN (2.6%)

JPN

2010 | IMPORT SOURCES ▾ TOTAL: $ 278,448,957,213

12% Germany

11% France

ITA (7.1%)

GBR (4.5%)

PRT (3.7%)

IRL

TUR

POL

CHE

AUT

NLD (4.5%)

7.9% China

LBY

JPN

IDN

BRA

NGA

MEX

USA (4.0%)

IND

EAST ASIA & PACIFIC · EUROPE & CENTRAL ASIA · LATIN AMERICA & CARIBBEAN · MIDDLE EAST & NORTH AFRICA · NORTH AMERICA · SOUTH ASIA · SUB-SAHARAN AFRICA

SRI LANKA

ECONOMIC COMPLEXITY INDEX [2010] ▸ -0.455 (80)   COMPLEXITY OUTLOOK INDEX [2010] ▸ 0.111 (57)   EXPECTED GDPᴘᴄ GROWTH * ▸ 2.2% (56)

*Expected annual average for the 2010-2020 period.

2010 PRODUCT SPACE ▶

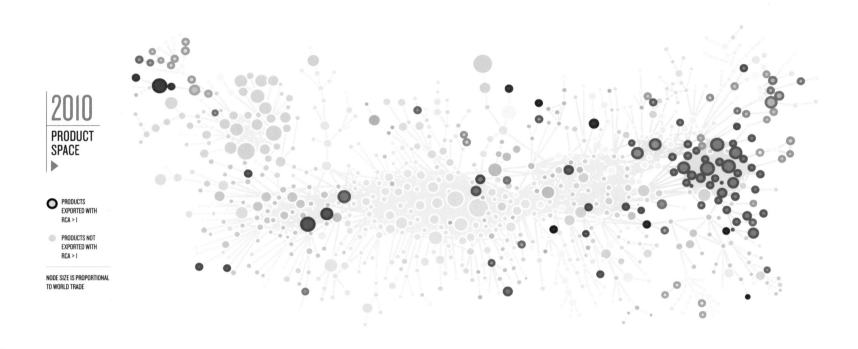

○ PRODUCTS EXPORTED WITH RCA > I

○ PRODUCTS NOT EXPORTED WITH RCA > I

NODE SIZE IS PROPORTIONAL TO WORLD TRADE

2010 EXPORT OPPORTUNITY SPECTRUM ◀

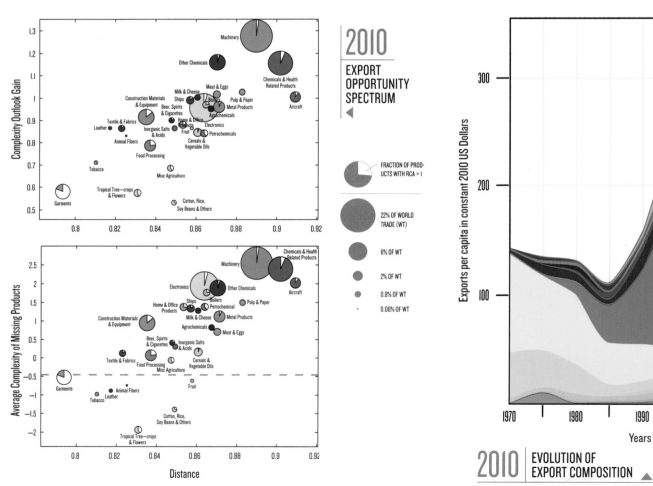

FRACTION OF PRODUCTS WITH RCA > I

22% OF WORLD TRADE (WT)

6% OF WT

2% OF WT

0.8% OF WT

0.06% OF WT

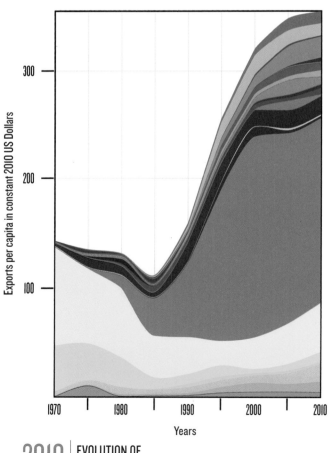

2010 EVOLUTION OF EXPORT COMPOSITION ▲

POPULATION ▸ 21 M / (48)
TOTAL EXPORTS ▸ USD 7.3 B / (81)

GDP ▸ USD 50 B / (72)
GDPₚc ▸ USD 2,400 / (92)

EXPORTS PER CAPITA ▸ USD 355 / (102)
EXPORTS AS SHARE OF GDP ▸ 15 % (101)

* Data are from 2010. Numbers indicate:
Value (World Ranking among 128 countries)
Region: South Asia.

ELECTRONICS | MACHINERY | AIRCRAFT | BOILERS | SHIPS | METAL PRODUCTS | CONSTR. MATL. & EQPT. | HOME & OFFICE | PULP & PAPER | CHEMICALS & HEALTH | AGROCHEMICALS | OTHER CHEMICALS | INOR. SALTS & ACIDS | PETROCHEMICALS | LEATHER | MILK & CHEESE | ANIMAL FIBERS | MEAT & EGGS | FISH & SEAFOOD | TROPICAL AGRIC. | CEREALS & VEG. OILS | COTTON/RICE/SOY & OTHERS | TOBACCO | FRUIT | MISC. AGRICULTURE | NOT CLASSIFIED | TEXTILE & FABRICS | GARMENTS | FOOD PROCESSING | BEER/SPIRITS & CIGS. | PRECIOUS STONES | COAL | OIL | MINING

2010 | EXPORT TREEMAP ▾ TOTAL: $ 7,339,588,366

8462 (7.7%) Knit undergarments of cotton

8459 (5.9%) Other knit outerwear

8439 (5.8%) Other women's outerwear

0741 (12%) Tea

6259 (4.4%) Other tires articles

7711

8482 (1.9%) Clothing accessories from rubber

8423 (4.9%) Men's trousers

8451 (2.8%) Knit outerwear

8441 (2.2%)

8472 (2.2%)

0752 (1.7%) Spices

2320 (2.1%) Natural rubber, latex & gums

7452

7441

8465 (4.4%) Corsets

8435 (1.4%)

8452 (0.93%)

0460 (1.1%)

0723

8947

8433 (1.3%)

8429

1212

5513

7938 (0.73%)

6672 (3.2%) Unmounted diamonds

6673 (1.5%)

0343 (1.5%)

0344

8463 (3.1%)

8431

5989 (0.74%)

0819

8434 (1.0%)

8481

7731 (0.55%)

7852 (1.2%)

8443

6582

* Numbers indicate SITC-4 Rev 2 codes which can be found in the Appendix. Percentages next to the product codes indicate proportion of the product in the exports of the country. Treemap headers show the total trade of the country.

2010 | EXPORT DESTINATIONS ▾ TOTAL: $ 7,339,588,366

13% United Kingdom

DEU (6.5%)

22% United States

JPN (2.7%)

IDN

MYS

CHN

BEL (4.4%)

FRA (3.0%)

6.4% India

ARE (2.8%)

MEX

RUS (3.8%)

TUR

NLD

2010 | IMPORT SOURCES ▾ TOTAL: $ 11,131,725,480

13% Singapore

JPN (4.8%)

HKG (4.7%)

GBR (2.4%)

ITA

BEL

NLD

MYS (3.2%)

DEU

RUS

CHN (10%)

THA

IRN (5.3%)

21% India

USA

SAU

EAST ASIA & PACIFIC | EUROPE & CENTRAL ASIA | LATIN AMERICA & CARIBBEAN | MIDDLE EAST & NORTH AFRICA | NORTH AMERICA | SOUTH ASIA | SUB-SAHARAN AFRICA

SUDAN

ECONOMIC COMPLEXITY INDEX [2010] ▸ -1.664 (124) | COMPLEXITY OUTLOOK INDEX [2010] ▸ -1.171 (126) | EXPECTED GDP PC GROWTH * ▸ 0.2% (113)

*Expected annual average for the 2010-2020 period.

2010 PRODUCT SPACE ▶

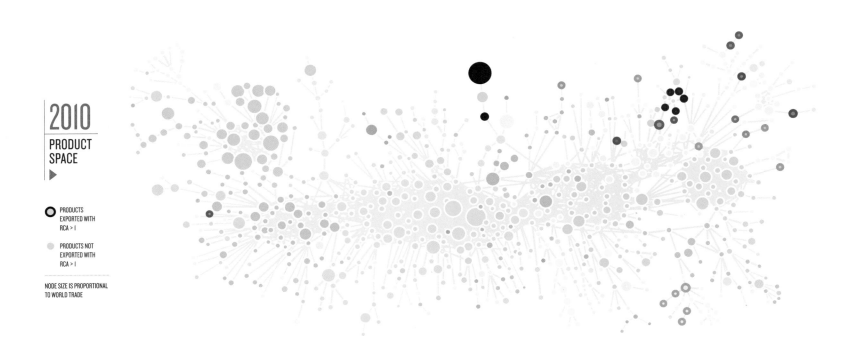

- ● PRODUCTS EXPORTED WITH RCA > 1
- ○ PRODUCTS NOT EXPORTED WITH RCA > 1

NODE SIZE IS PROPORTIONAL TO WORLD TRADE

2010 EXPORT OPPORTUNITY SPECTRUM ◀

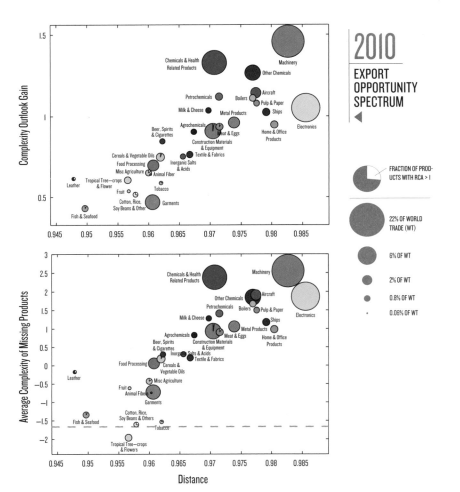

FRACTION OF PRODUCTS WITH RCA > 1

- 22% OF WORLD TRADE (WT)
- 6% OF WT
- 2% OF WT
- 0.8% OF WT
- 0.06% OF WT

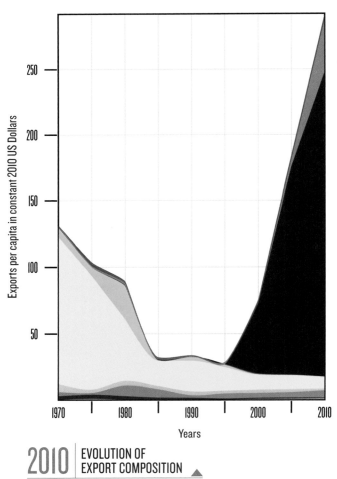

2010 EVOLUTION OF EXPORT COMPOSITION ▲

| POPULATION ▸ 34 M / (34) | GDP ▸ USD 67 B / (62) | EXPORTS PER CAPITA ▸ USD 292 / (107) | * Data are from 2010. Numbers indicate: |
| TOTAL EXPORTS ▸ USD 9.8 B / (74) | GDPᴘᴄ ▸ USD 1,538 / (98) | EXPORTS AS SHARE OF GDP ▸ 15 % (103) | Value (World Ranking among 128 countries) Region: Sub-Saharan Africa. |

ELECTRONICS · MACHINERY · AIRCRAFT · BOILERS · SHIPS · METAL PRODUCTS · CONSTR. MATL. & EQPT. · HOME & OFFICE · PULP & PAPER · CHEMICALS & HEALTH · AGROCHEMICALS · OTHER CHEMICALS · INOR. SALTS & ACIDS · PETROCHEMICALS · LEATHER · MILK & CHEESE · ANIMAL FIBERS · MEAT & EGGS · FISH & SEAFOOD · TROPICAL AGRIC. · CEREALS & VEG. OILS · COTTON/RICE/SOY & OTHERS · TOBACCO · FRUIT · MISC. AGRICULTURE · NOT CLASSIFIED · TEXTILE & FABRICS · GARMENTS · FOOD PROCESSING · BEER/SPIRITS & CIGS. · PRECIOUS STONES · COAL · OIL · MINING

2010 | EXPORT TREEMAP ▾ | TOTAL: $ 9,800,479,412

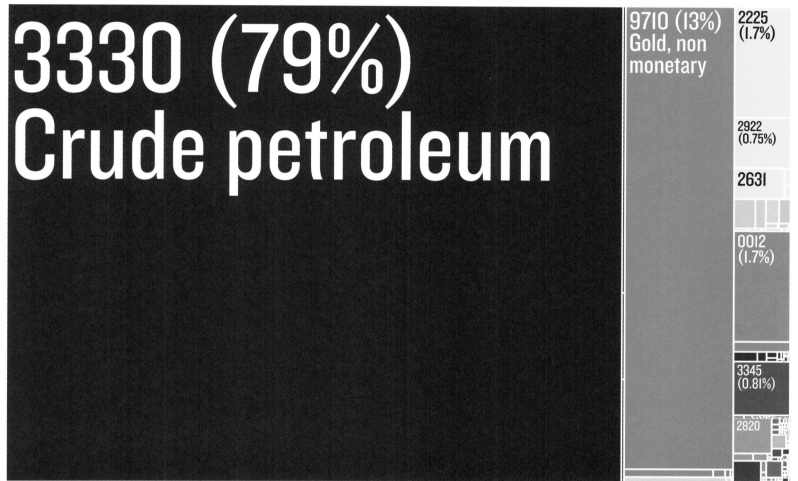

3330 (79%) Crude petroleum

9710 (13%) Gold, non monetary

2225 (1.7%)

2922 (0.75%)

2631

0012 (1.7%)

3345 (0.81%)

2820

* Numbers indicate SITC-4 Rev 2 codes which can be found in the Appendix. Percentages next to the product codes indicate proportion of the product in the exports of the country. Treemap headers show the total trade of the country.

2010 | EXPORT DESTINATIONS ▾ | TOTAL: $ 9,800,479,412

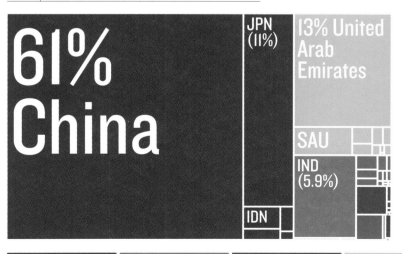

61% China

JPN (11%)

13% United Arab Emirates

SAU

IND (5.9%)

IDN

2010 | IMPORT SOURCES ▾ | TOTAL: $ 6,618,824,491

29% China

EGY (8.4%)

ARE (6.9%)

NZL

7.3% India

DEU (4.7%)

GBR (3.2%)

RUS (2.7%)

TUR (3.4%)

ITA (3.1%)

FRA

NLD

FIN

USA

CAN

EAST ASIA & PACIFIC · EUROPE & CENTRAL ASIA · LATIN AMERICA & CARIBBEAN · MIDDLE EAST & NORTH AFRICA · NORTH AMERICA · SOUTH ASIA · SUB-SAHARAN AFRICA

SWEDEN

ECONOMIC COMPLEXITY INDEX [2010] ▸ 1.706 (5) **COMPLEXITY OUTLOOK INDEX [2010]** ▸ 0.505 (45) **EXPECTED GDPᴘᴄ GROWTH *** ▸ 2.1% (58)

Expected annual average for the 2010-2020 period.

2010
PRODUCT SPACE ▸

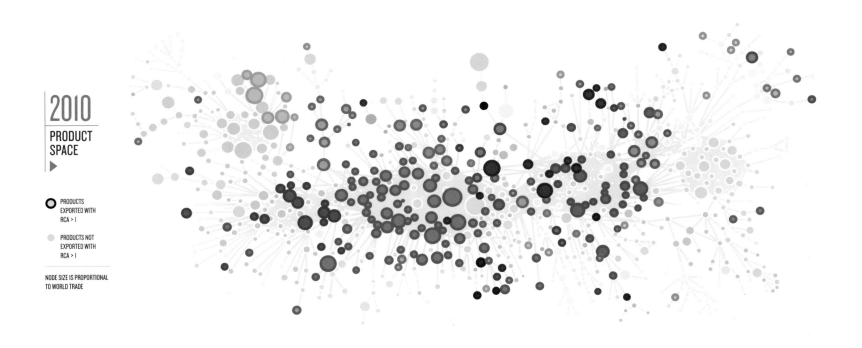

○ PRODUCTS EXPORTED WITH RCA > 1

○ PRODUCTS NOT EXPORTED WITH RCA > 1

NODE SIZE IS PROPORTIONAL TO WORLD TRADE

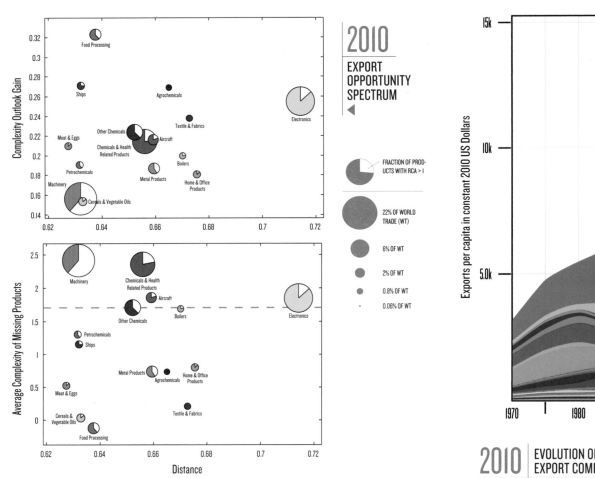

2010
EXPORT OPPORTUNITY SPECTRUM ◂

◖ FRACTION OF PRODUCTS WITH RCA > 1

● 22% OF WORLD TRADE (WT)

● 6% OF WT

● 2% OF WT

● 0.8% OF WT

· 0.06% OF WT

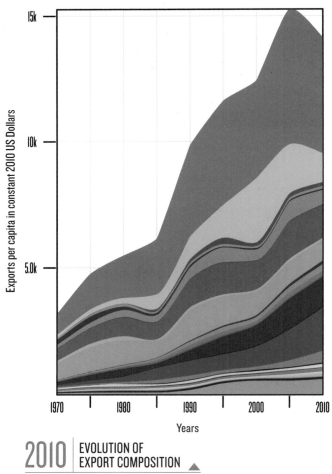

2010 | EVOLUTION OF EXPORT COMPOSITION ▲

POPULATION ▸ 9.4 M / (75)
TOTAL EXPORTS ▸ USD 132 B / (26)

GDP ▸ USD 462 B / (22)
GDPᴘᴄ ▸ USD 49,257 / (6)

EXPORTS PER CAPITA ▸ USD 14,101 / (12)
EXPORTS AS SHARE OF GDP ▸ 29 % (53)

* Data are from 2010. Numbers indicate:
Value (World Ranking among 128 countries)
Region: Western Europe.

ELECTRONICS · MACHINERY · AIRCRAFT · BOILERS · SHIPS · METAL PRODUCTS · CONSTR. MATL. & EQPT. · HOME & OFFICE · PULP & PAPER · CHEMICALS & HEALTH · AGROCHEMICALS · OTHER CHEMICALS · INOR. SALTS & ACIDS · PETROCHEMICALS · LEATHER · MILK & CHEESE · ANIMAL FIBERS · MEAT & EGGS · FISH & SEAFOOD · TROPICAL AGRIC. · CEREALS & VEG. OILS · COTTON/RICE/SOY & OTHERS · TOBACCO · FRUIT · MISC. AGRICULTURE · NOT CLASSIFIED · TEXTILE & FABRICS · GARMENTS · FOOD PROCESSING · BEER/SPIRITS & CIGS. · PRECIOUS STONES · COAL · OIL · MINING

2010 | EXPORT TREEMAP ▾ — TOTAL: $ 132,241,085,449

7810 (3.4%) Cars

7849 (3.1%) Other vehicle parts

6418 (1.8%)

7132 (1.4%)

7821 (1.4%)
7832 (0.82%)
7239 (0.80%)
7491 (0.71%)
7416 (0.69%)
7441
7442

7721 (1.1%)
6940 · 7439
7758 · 6991
8743 · 7161
9510
7422 · 7449
7283 · 7133
7138

6954 (1.1%)

7234 (1.0%)

7649 (1.9%) Parts of telecom & sound equipment

7788 · 7712
7764 · 7638
7763 · 7415
7611 · 7522

6713
6749
6727

7641 (1.2%)

7149
7711
7932

2482 (2.0%) Worked wood of coniferous

6428
6353
6997

2816 (1.3%)

2815

8219 (1.0%)

2517 (1.5%)
6413 (1.4%)

6415 (1.0%)

6412
2516

9310 (3.1%) Unclassified transactions

2882 · 2820
2874 · 6841

5121

3345 (6.2%) Lubricating petroleum oils

5989 (0.81%)
8996 (0.62%)
8744
5416

5417 (5.6%) Medicaments

8939 (0.82%)

* Numbers indicate SITC-4 Rev 2 codes which can be found in the Appendix. Percentages next to the product codes indicate proportion of the product in the exports of the country. Treemap headers show the total trade of the country.

2010 | EXPORT DESTINATIONS ▾ — TOTAL: $ 132,241,085,449

12% Germany

DNK (7.5%)

NOR (7.3%)

GBR (7.1%)

BEL (5.0%)
FRA (5.0%)
NLD (4.3%)
ITA
POL
ESP

FIN (4.7%)
RUS (1.9%)
CZE

CHN (3.9%)
JPN

CAN
ZAF
BRA

USA (6.9%)

2010 | IMPORT SOURCES ▾ — TOTAL: $ 132,314,901,100

18% Germany

NOR (9.1%)

DNK (8.3%)

NLD (6.3%)
RUS (5.2%)
FRA (4.6%)
BEL (3.9%)

GBR (5.5%)
ITA (2.9%)
ESP
IRL
CZE
AUT · LVA

FIN (5.4%)
POL (2.9%)

CHN (4.0%)
KOR
USA (3.2%)
IND

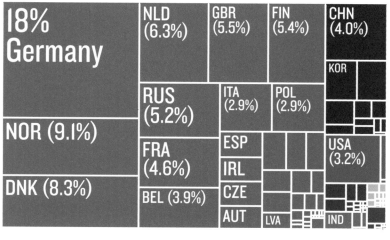

EAST ASIA & PACIFIC · EUROPE & CENTRAL ASIA · LATIN AMERICA & CARIBBEAN · MIDDLE EAST & NORTH AFRICA · NORTH AMERICA · SOUTH ASIA · SUB-SAHARAN AFRICA

SWITZERLAND

ECONOMIC COMPLEXITY INDEX [2010] ▸ 1.898 (3) | COMPLEXITY OUTLOOK INDEX [2010] ▸ 0.792 (38) | EXPECTED GDPᴘᴄ GROWTH * ▸ 2.2% (53)

*Expected annual average for the 2010-2020 period.

2010 PRODUCT SPACE ▸

○ PRODUCTS EXPORTED WITH RCA > I

○ PRODUCTS NOT EXPORTED WITH RCA > I

NODE SIZE IS PROPORTIONAL TO WORLD TRADE

2010 EXPORT OPPORTUNITY SPECTRUM ◂

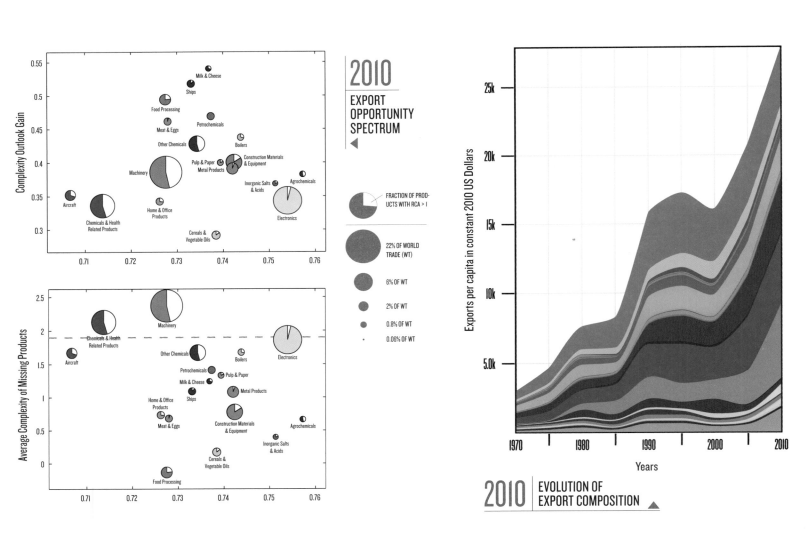

FRACTION OF PRODUCTS WITH RCA > I

22% OF WORLD TRADE (WT)

6% OF WT

2% OF WT

0.8% OF WT

0.06% OF WT

2010 EVOLUTION OF EXPORT COMPOSITION ▲

POPULATION ▸ 7.8 M / (78)
TOTAL EXPORTS ▸ USD 218 B / (16)

GDP ▸ USD 529 B / (19)
GDPᴘᴄ ▸ USD 67,644 / (3)

EXPORTS PER CAPITA ▸ USD 27,845 / (4)
EXPORTS AS SHARE OF GDP ▸ 41 % (32)

* Data are from 2010. Numbers indicate:
Value (World Ranking among 128 countries)
Region: Western Europe.

ELECTRONICS | MACHINERY | AIRCRAFT | BOILERS | SHIPS | METAL PRODUCTS | CONSTR. MATL. & EQPT. | HOME & OFFICE | PULP & PAPER | CHEMICALS & HEALTH | AGROCHEMICALS | OTHER CHEMICALS | INOR. SALTS & ACIDS | PETROCHEMICALS | LEATHER | MILK & CHEESE | ANIMAL FIBERS | MEAT & EGGS | FISH & SEAFOOD | TROPICAL AGRIC. | CEREALS & VEG. OILS | COTTON/RICE/SOY & OTHERS | TOBACCO | FRUIT | MISC. AGRICULTURE | NOT CLASSIFIED | TEXTILE & FABRICS | GARMENTS | FOOD PROCESSING | BEER/SPIRITS & CIGS. | PRECIOUS STONES | COAL | OIL | MINING

2010 | EXPORT TREEMAP ▾ TOTAL: $ 217,916,829,270

5416 (3.9%) Glycosides & vaccines
8996 (2.6%) Orthopaedic appliances
5156 (1.5%)
5417 (11%) Medicaments
7284 (1.8%) Specialized industry machinery & parts N.E.S
7721 (1.5%) Switchboards, relays & fuses
8851 (6.8%) Watches

5148 (1.3%)
5415 (0.84%)
7416
7849
7369
7162
7499
8749
8743
7449

8720 (1.1%)
8748
8742
5411
5311
5332
5413
5530 (0.56%)
8939
5419
7361
7784
7431
7161
8960 (0.77%)

5147 (0.85%)
8744
5146
0712
6842

9710 (17%) Gold, non monetary
6812 (1.7%) Unwrought metals of platinum
7712
7764
7788
7711
3510
7731

2882
8974
6672 (1.2%)
9310 (5.3%) Unclassified transactions
1222
0980
1110
0240
0730
5922

* Numbers indicate SITC-4 Rev 2 codes which can be found in the Appendix. Percentages next to the product codes indicate proportion of the product in the exports of the country. Treemap headers show the total trade of the country.

2010 | EXPORT DESTINATIONS ▾ TOTAL: $ 217,916,829,270

18% Germany
FRA (6.1%)
CHN (7.1%)
HKG (3.7%)
IND (9.4%)
JPN
ITA (5.7%)
AUT (3.4%)
THA
ARE
BEL
8.1% United States
ISR
GBR (3.9%)
RUS
BRA

2010 | IMPORT SOURCES ▾ TOTAL: $ 176,669,461,939

29% Germany
FRA (8.1%)
JPN (4.3%)
VNM
GBR (3.8%)
ESP (2.4%)
USA (5.5%)
IRL (2.9%)
ITA (9.3%)
BEL

EAST ASIA & PACIFIC | EUROPE & CENTRAL ASIA | LATIN AMERICA & CARIBBEAN | MIDDLE EAST & NORTH AFRICA | NORTH AMERICA | SOUTH ASIA | SUB-SAHARAN AFRICA

SYRIAN ARAB REPUBLIC

ECONOMIC COMPLEXITY INDEX [2010] ▸ -0.271 (71) | **COMPLEXITY OUTLOOK INDEX [2010] ▸ 0.208 (54)** | **EXPECTED GDPᴘᴄ GROWTH * ▸ 2.3% (50)**

*Expected annual average for the 2010-2020 period.

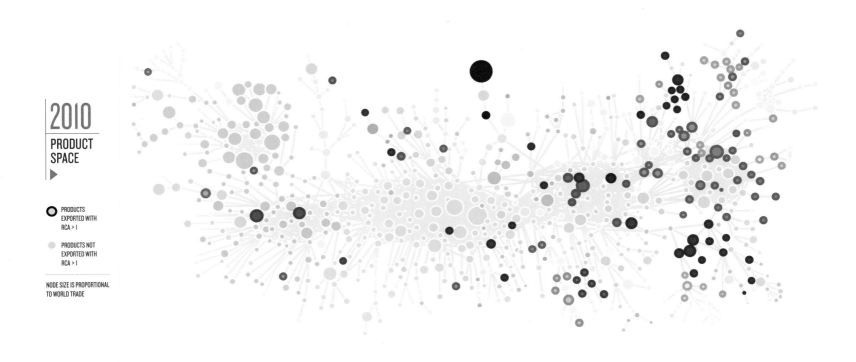

2010 PRODUCT SPACE ▶

- ○ PRODUCTS EXPORTED WITH RCA > 1
- ● PRODUCTS NOT EXPORTED WITH RCA > 1

NODE SIZE IS PROPORTIONAL TO WORLD TRADE

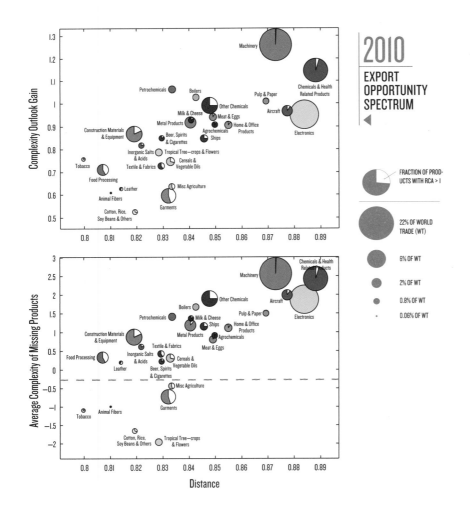

2010 EXPORT OPPORTUNITY SPECTRUM ◀

FRACTION OF PRODUCTS WITH RCA > 1

- 22% OF WORLD TRADE (WT)
- 6% OF WT
- 2% OF WT
- 0.8% OF WT
- 0.06% OF WT

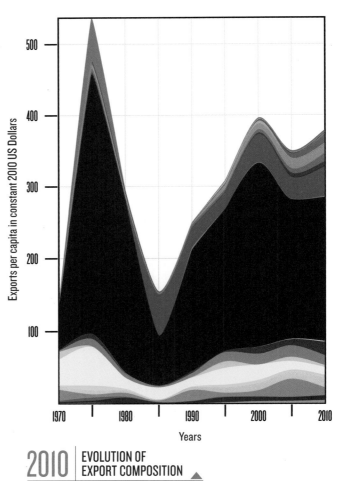

2010 | EVOLUTION OF EXPORT COMPOSITION ▲

POPULATION ▸ 20 M / (49)

TOTAL EXPORTS ▸ USD 7.8 B / (80)

GDP ▸ USD 59 B / (66)

GDPᴘᴄ ▸ USD 2,893 / (86)

EXPORTS PER CAPITA ▸ USD 379 / (100)

EXPORTS AS SHARE OF GDP ▸ 13 % / (107)

* Data are from 2010. Numbers indicate:
Value (World Ranking among 128 countries)
Region: Middle East and North Africa.

ELECTRONICS · MACHINERY · AIRCRAFT · BOILERS · SHIPS · METAL PRODUCTS · CONSTR. MATL. & EQPT. · HOME & OFFICE · PULP & PAPER · CHEMICALS & HEALTH · AGROCHEMICALS · OTHER CHEMICALS · INOR. SALTS & ACIDS · PETROCHEMICALS · LEATHER · MILK & CHEESE · ANIMAL FIBERS · MEAT & EGGS · FISH & SEAFOOD · TROPICAL AGRIC. · CEREALS & VEG. OILS · COTTON/RICE/SOY & OTHERS · TOBACCO · FRUIT · MISC. AGRICULTURE · NOT CLASSIFIED · TEXTILE & FABRICS · GARMENTS · FOOD PROCESSING · BEER/SPIRITS & CIGS. · PRECIOUS STONES · COAL · OIL · MINING

2010 EXPORT TREEMAP ▼ TOTAL: $ 7,754,782,575

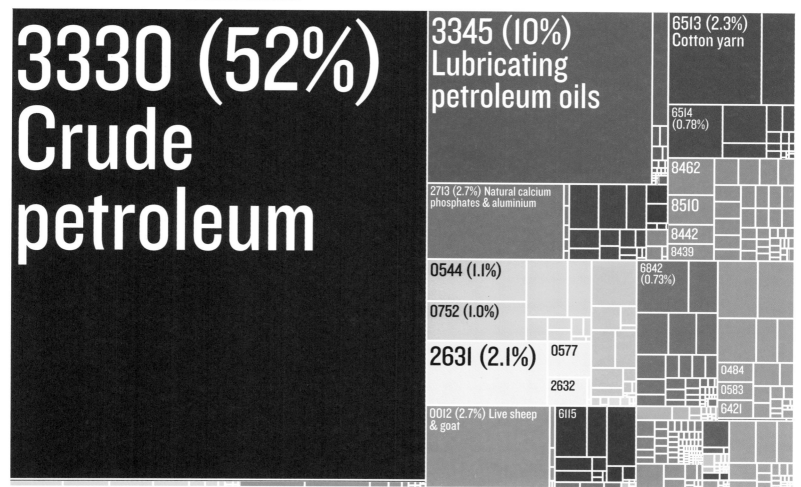

* Numbers indicate SITC-4 Rev 2 codes which can be found in the Appendix. Percentages next to the product codes indicate proportion of the product in the exports of the country. Treemap headers show the total trade of the country.

2010 EXPORT DESTINATIONS ▼ TOTAL: $ 7,754,782,575

2010 IMPORT SOURCES ▼ TOTAL: $ 16,442,479,244

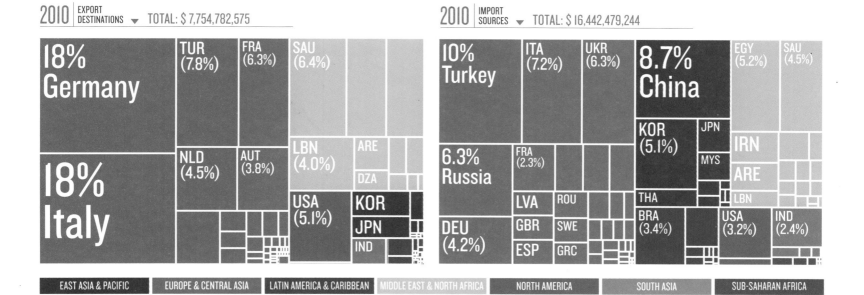

EAST ASIA & PACIFIC · EUROPE & CENTRAL ASIA · LATIN AMERICA & CARIBBEAN · MIDDLE EAST & NORTH AFRICA · NORTH AMERICA · SOUTH ASIA · SUB-SAHARAN AFRICA

TAJIKISTAN

| ECONOMIC COMPLEXITY INDEX [2010] ► -1.037 (110) | COMPLEXITY OUTLOOK INDEX [2010] ► -0.983 (109) | EXPECTED GDPᴘᴄ GROWTH * ► 1.8% (69) |

*Expected annual average for the 2010-2020 period.

2010 PRODUCT SPACE ▶

○ PRODUCTS EXPORTED WITH RCA > 1

○ PRODUCTS NOT EXPORTED WITH RCA > 1

NODE SIZE IS PROPORTIONAL TO WORLD TRADE

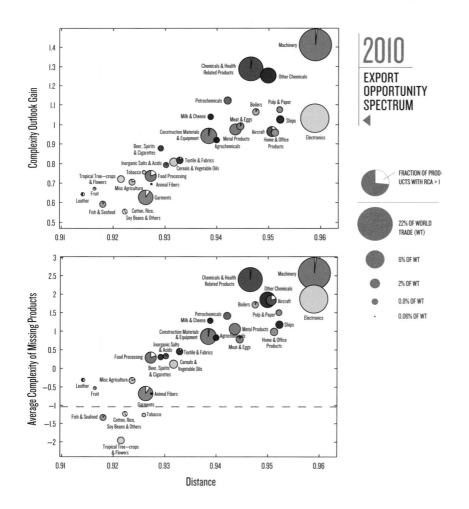

2010 EXPORT OPPORTUNITY SPECTRUM ◀

⊙ FRACTION OF PRODUCTS WITH RCA > 1

● 22% OF WORLD TRADE (WT)

● 6% OF WT

● 2% OF WT

● 0.8% OF WT

· 0.06% OF WT

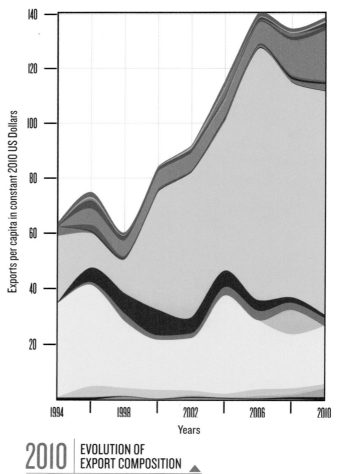

2010 | EVOLUTION OF EXPORT COMPOSITION ▲

POPULATION ▸ 6.9 M / (85)	GDP ▸ USD 5.6 B / (123)	EXPORTS PER CAPITA ▸ USD 139 / (116)
TOTAL EXPORTS ▸ USD 958 M / (123)	GDPᴘᴄ ▸ USD 820 / (115)	EXPORTS AS SHARE OF GDP ▸ 17 % (91)

* Data are from 2010. Numbers indicate:
Value (World Ranking among 128 countries)
Region: Eastern Europe and Central Asia.

ELECTRONICS · MACHINERY · AIRCRAFT · BOILERS · SHIPS · METAL PRODUCTS · CONSTR. MATL. & EQPT. · HOME & OFFICE · PULP & PAPER · CHEMICALS & HEALTH · AGROCHEMICALS · OTHER CHEMICALS · INOR. SALTS & ACIDS · PETROCHEMICALS · LEATHER · MILK & CHEESE · ANIMAL FIBERS · MEAT & EGGS · FISH & SEAFOOD · TROPICAL AGRIC. · CEREALS & VEG. OILS · COTTON/RICE/SOY & OTHERS · TOBACCO · FRUIT · MISC. AGRICULTURE · NOT CLASSIFIED · TEXTILE & FABRICS · GARMENTS · FOOD PROCESSING · BEER/SPIRITS & CIGS. · PRECIOUS STONES · COAL · OIL · MINING

2010 | EXPORT TREEMAP ▾ TOTAL: $ 958,314,403

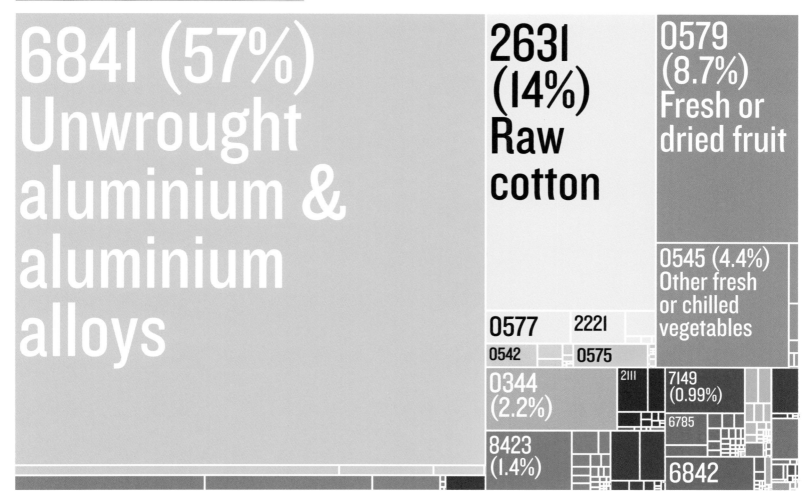

6841 (57%) Unwrought aluminium & aluminium alloys

2631 (14%) Raw cotton

0577 · 2221 · 0542 · 0575

0344 (2.2%) · 2111 · 8423 (1.4%)

0579 (8.7%) Fresh or dried fruit

0545 (4.4%) Other fresh or chilled vegetables

7149 (0.99%) · 6785 · 6842

* Numbers indicate SITC-4 Rev 2 codes which can be found in the Appendix. Percentages next to the product codes indicate proportion of the product in the exports of the country. Treemap headers show the total trade of the country.

2010 | EXPORT DESTINATIONS ▾ TOTAL: $ 958,314,403

27% Turkey

20% Russia

NOR (5.6%)

ITA (3.1%)

KAZ

9.8% Korea, Rep.

CHN (5.4%)

VNM

DZA (4.8%)

QAT (4.5%)

2010 | IMPORT SOURCES ▾ TOTAL: $ 2,630,863,024

52% China

25% Russia

TUR (5.5%)

UKR (2.8%)

LTU

DEU

USA · ARE · IND

EAST ASIA & PACIFIC · EUROPE & CENTRAL ASIA · LATIN AMERICA & CARIBBEAN · MIDDLE EAST & NORTH AFRICA · NORTH AMERICA · SOUTH ASIA · SUB-SAHARAN AFRICA

TANZANIA

ECONOMIC COMPLEXITY INDEX [2010] ▸ -1.019 (108) | COMPLEXITY OUTLOOK INDEX [2010] ▸ -0.022 (63) | EXPECTED GDPᴘᴄ GROWTH * ▸ 3.0% (26)

*Expected annual average for the 2010-2020 period.

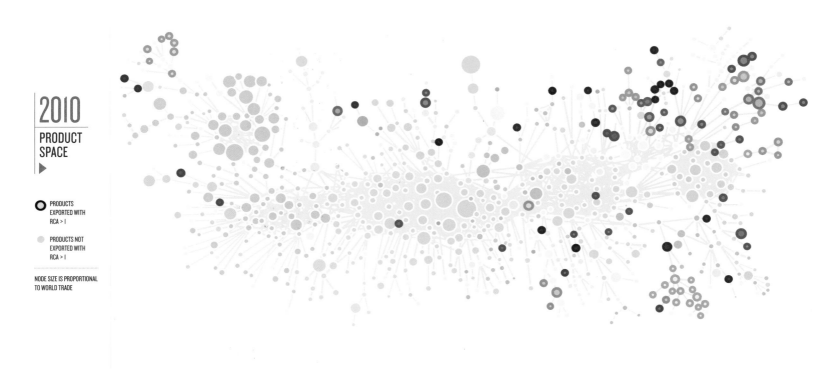

2010 PRODUCT SPACE ▶

- ⬤ PRODUCTS EXPORTED WITH RCA > 1
- ⬤ PRODUCTS NOT EXPORTED WITH RCA > 1

NODE SIZE IS PROPORTIONAL TO WORLD TRADE

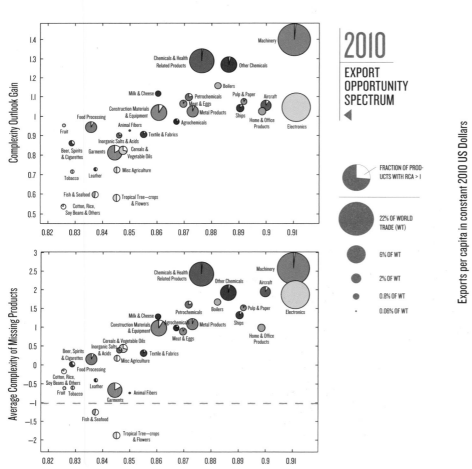

2010 EXPORT OPPORTUNITY SPECTRUM ◀

◔ FRACTION OF PRODUCTS WITH RCA > 1

- ⬤ 22% OF WORLD TRADE (WT)
- ⬤ 6% OF WT
- ⬤ 2% OF WT
- ⬤ 0.8% OF WT
- · 0.06% OF WT

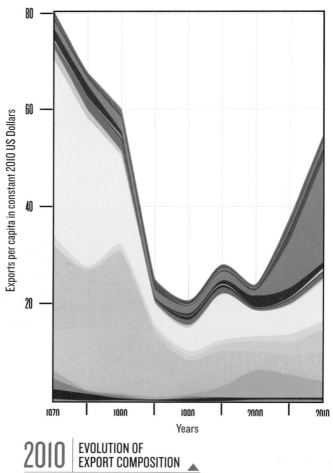

2010 | EVOLUTION OF EXPORT COMPOSITION ▲

POPULATION ▸ 45 M / (28)
TOTAL EXPORTS ▸ USD 2.5 B / (107)

GDP ▸ USD 23 B / (91)
GDPᴘᴄ ▸ USD 527 / (121)

EXPORTS PER CAPITA ▸ USD 55 / (124)
EXPORTS AS SHARE OF GDP ▸ 11 % (117)

* Data are from 2010. Numbers indicate:
  Value (World Ranking among 128 countries)
  Region: Sub-Saharan Africa.

ELECTRONICS · MACHINERY · AIRCRAFT · BOILERS · SHIPS · METAL PRODUCTS · CONSTR. MATL. & EQPT. · HOME & OFFICE · PULP & PAPER · CHEMICALS & HEALTH · AGROCHEMICALS · OTHER CHEMICALS · INOR. SALTS & ACIDS · PETROCHEMICALS · LEATHER · MILK & CHEESE · ANIMAL FIBERS · MEAT & EGGS · FISH & SEAFOOD · TROPICAL AGRIC. · CEREALS & VEG. OILS · COTTON/RICE/SOY & OTHERS · TOBACCO · FRUIT · MISC. AGRICULTURE · NOT CLASSIFIED · TEXTILE & FABRICS · GARMENTS · FOOD PROCESSING · BEER/SPIRITS & CIGS. · PRECIOUS STONES · COAL · OIL · MINING

2010 EXPORT TREEMAP ▼ TOTAL: $ 2,467,509,182

9710 (20%) Gold, non monetary

2890 (11%) Ores and precious metals

6821 (6.0%) Unwrought copper & copper alloys

6673 (1.4%)

6851

0343 (2.5%) Fresh or chilled fish fillets

0344 (2.4%) Frozen fish fillets

0360

0342

2919

3345 (2.4%) Lubricating petroleum oils

6589 (1.1%)

0577 (5.4%) Edible nuts

2631 (4.9%) Raw cotton

2225 (2.9%) Sesame seeds

0741 (1.0%)

0711 (5.0%) Coffee, green or roasted

0812 (0.85%)

0752 (0.66%)

0542 (4.3%) Dried or shelled legumes

1212 (6.8%) Stripped tobacco

0721 (1.2%)

2926

2927 (0.62%)

2925

5621

7148

9310

2820

* Numbers indicate SITC-4 Rev 2 codes which can be found in the Appendix. Percentages next to the product codes indicate proportion of the product in the exports of the country. Treemap headers show the total trade of the country.

2010 EXPORT DESTINATIONS ▼ TOTAL: $ 2,467,509,182

15% China

21% United Arab Emirates

JPN (5.6%)

VNM (2.6%)

IDN

KOR

NLD (4.0%)

ITA

BEL

ESP

CHE

POL

IND (10%)

DEU (3.9%)

KEN (4.8%)

UGA

ZMB

MWI

2010 IMPORT SOURCES ▼ TOTAL: $ 7,222,189,241

11% China

JPN (7.1%)

7.0% Switzerland

GBR

SGP (5.5%)

KOR

IDN

DEU (2.3%)

NLD

BEL

ITA

TUR

UKR

SWE

9.5% South Africa

KEN (3.5%)

11% India

8.3% United Arab Emirates

SAU (2.5%)

EAST ASIA & PACIFIC · EUROPE & CENTRAL ASIA · LATIN AMERICA & CARIBBEAN · MIDDLE EAST & NORTH AFRICA · NORTH AMERICA · SOUTH ASIA · SUB-SAHARAN AFRICA

THAILAND

ECONOMIC COMPLEXITY INDEX [2010] ▸ 0.8 (28) | COMPLEXITY OUTLOOK INDEX [2010] ▸ 1.257 (13) | EXPECTED GDPᴘᴄ GROWTH * ▸ 3.9% (4)

*Expected annual average for the 2010-2020 period.

2010
PRODUCT
SPACE
▸

⬤ PRODUCTS
EXPORTED WITH
RCA > 1

◯ PRODUCTS NOT
EXPORTED WITH
RCA > 1

NODE SIZE IS PROPORTIONAL
TO WORLD TRADE

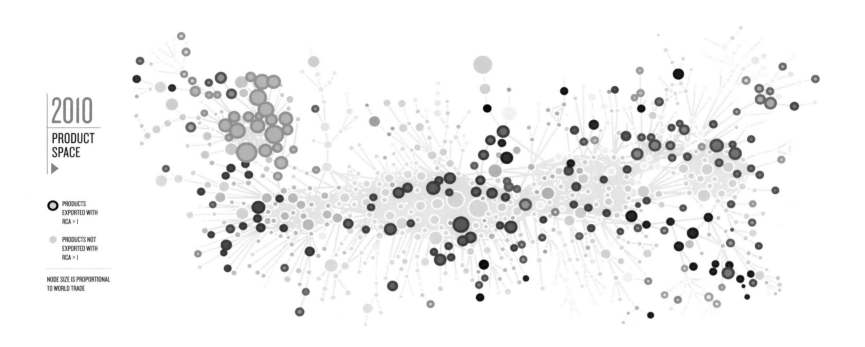

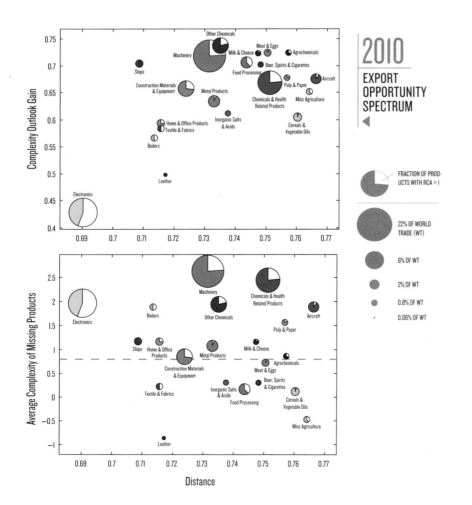

2010
EXPORT
OPPORTUNITY
SPECTRUM
◂

◐ FRACTION OF PROD-
UCTS WITH RCA > 1

⬤ 22% OF WORLD
TRADE (WT)

⬤ 6% OF WT

⬤ 2% OF WT

• 0.8% OF WT

· 0.06% OF WT

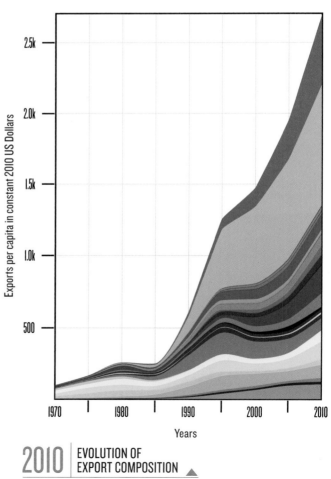

2010 | EVOLUTION OF
EXPORT COMPOSITION ▲

POPULATION ▸ 69 M / (19)
TOTAL EXPORTS ▸ USD 187 B / (22)

GDP ▸ USD 319 B / (30)
GDPᴘᴄ ▸ USD 4,614 / (70)

EXPORTS PER CAPITA ▸ USD 2,699 / (44)
EXPORTS AS SHARE OF GDP ▸ 59 % (14)

* Data are from 2010. Numbers indicate:
Value (World Ranking among 128 countries)
Region: East Asia and Pacific.

ELECTRONICS · MACHINERY · AIRCRAFT · BOILERS · SHIPS · METAL PRODUCTS · CONSTR. MATL. & EQPT. · HOME & OFFICE · PULP & PAPER · CHEMICALS & HEALTH · AGROCHEMICALS · OTHER CHEMICALS · INOR. SALTS & ACIDS · PETROCHEMICALS · LEATHER · MILK & CHEESE · ANIMAL FIBERS · MEAT & EGGS · FISH & SEAFOOD · TROPICAL AGRIC. · CEREALS & VEG. OILS · COTTON/RICE/SOY & OTHERS · TOBACCO · FRUIT · MISC. AGRICULTURE · NOT CLASSIFIED · TEXTILE & FABRICS · GARMENTS · FOOD PROCESSING · BEER/SPIRITS & CIGS. · PRECIOUS STONES · COAL · OIL · MINING

2010 | EXPORT TREEMAP ▾ TOTAL: $ 186,564,165,927

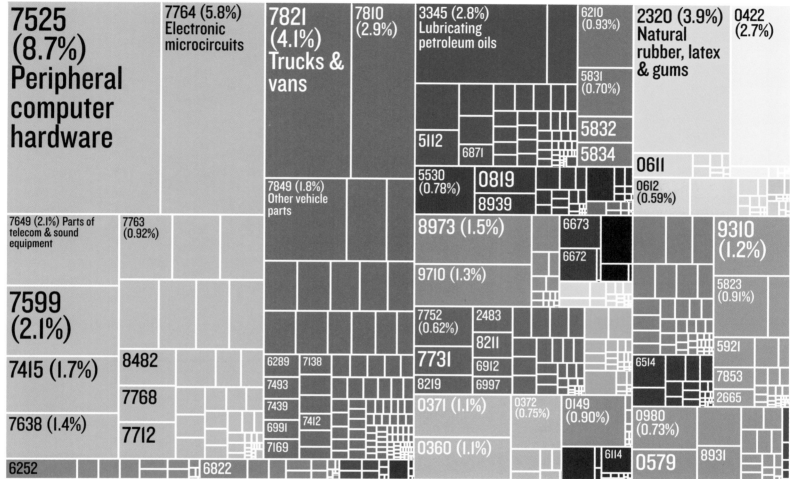

* Numbers indicate SITC-4 Rev 2 codes which can be found in the Appendix. Percentages next to the product codes indicate proportion of the product in the exports of the country. Treemap headers show the total trade of the country.

2010 | EXPORT DESTINATIONS ▾ TOTAL: $ 186,564,165,927

2010 | IMPORT SOURCES ▾ TOTAL: $ 157,546,698,352

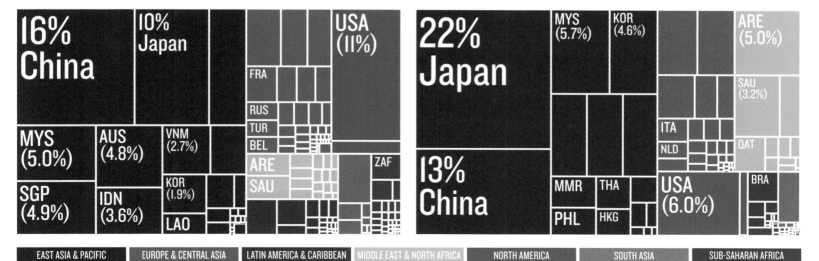

EAST ASIA & PACIFIC · EUROPE & CENTRAL ASIA · LATIN AMERICA & CARIBBEAN · MIDDLE EAST & NORTH AFRICA · NORTH AMERICA · SOUTH ASIA · SUB-SAHARAN AFRICA

TRINIDAD AND TOBAGO

| ECONOMIC COMPLEXITY INDEX [2010] ▸ -0.467 (81) | COMPLEXITY OUTLOOK INDEX [2010] ▸ -0.936 (103) | EXPECTED GDPᴘᴄ GROWTH * ▸ -0.5% (121) |

*Expected annual average for the 2010-2020 period.

2010
PRODUCT SPACE ▶

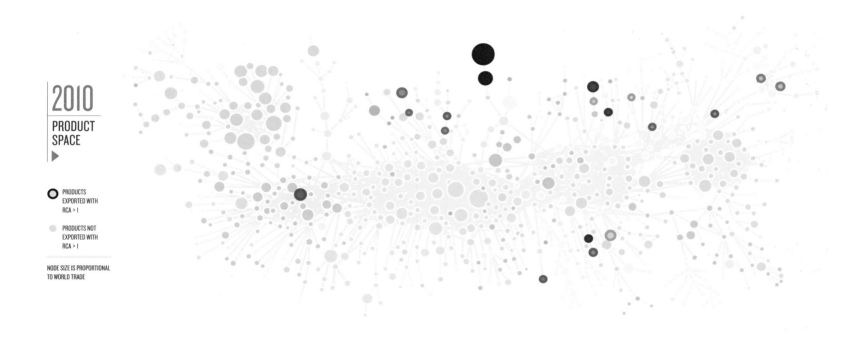

○ PRODUCTS EXPORTED WITH RCA > 1

○ PRODUCTS NOT EXPORTED WITH RCA > 1

NODE SIZE IS PROPORTIONAL TO WORLD TRADE

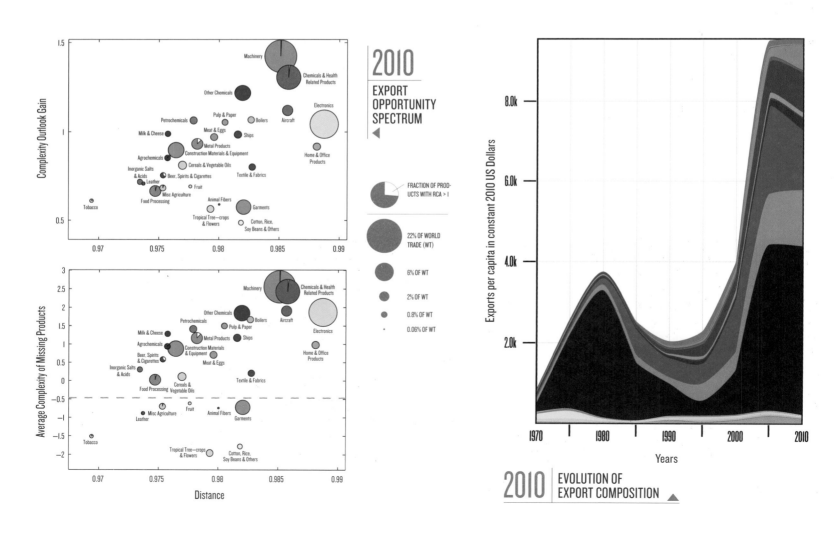

2010
EXPORT OPPORTUNITY SPECTRUM ◀

◔ FRACTION OF PRODUCTS WITH RCA > 1

◯ 22% OF WORLD TRADE (WT)

● 6% OF WT

● 2% OF WT

• 0.8% OF WT

· 0.06% OF WT

2010 | EVOLUTION OF EXPORT COMPOSITION ▲

POPULATION ▸ 1.3 M / (126)	GDP ▸ USD 21 B / (94)	EXPORTS PER CAPITA ▸ USD 9,549 / (21)	* Data are from 2010. Numbers indicate:
TOTAL EXPORTS ▸ USD 13 B / (71)	GDPᴘᴄ ▸ USD 15,614 / (34)	EXPORTS AS SHARE OF GDP ▸ 61 % (11)	Value (World Ranking among 128 countries) Region: Latin America and the Caribbean.

ELECTRONICS · MACHINERY · AIRCRAFT · BOILERS · SHIPS · METAL PRODUCTS · CONSTR. MAT. & EQPT. · HOME & OFFICE · PULP & PAPER · CHEMICALS & HEALTH · AGROCHEMICALS · OTHER CHEMICALS · INOR. SALTS & ACIDS · PETROCHEMICALS · LEATHER · MILK & CHEESE · ANIMAL FIBERS · MEAT & EGGS · FISH & SEAFOOD · TROPICAL AGRIC. · CEREALS & VEG. OILS · COTTON/RICE/SOY & OTHERS · TOBACCO · FRUIT · MISC. AGRICULTURE · NOT CLASSIFIED · TEXTILE & FABRICS · GARMENTS · FOOD PROCESSING · BEER/SPIRITS & CIGS. · PRECIOUS STONES · COAL · OIL · MINING

2010 | EXPORT TREEMAP ▾ TOTAL: $ 12,810,076,542

3413 (34%) liquified hydrocarbons

3330 (9.4%) Crude petroleum

3345 (15%) Lubricating petroleum oils

5121 (10%) Acyclic alcohols & derivatives

5621 (3.0%)

5225 (14%) Inorganic bases & metallic oxides

6713 (6.1%) Iron & steel powders

1110

0980

6731 (1.1%)

9310 (0.98%)

*Numbers indicate SITC-4 Rev 2 codes which can be found in the Appendix. Percentages next to the product codes indicate proportion of the product in the exports of the country. Treemap headers show the total trade of the country.

2010 | EXPORT DESTINATIONS ▾ TOTAL: $ 12,810,076,542

49% United States

JAM (5.0%)

ARG (3.6%)

ESP (6.8%)

DOM (3.3%)

CHL (2.2%)

SUR

ITA

DEU

KOR

2010 | IMPORT SOURCES ▾ TOTAL: $ 4,705,744,195

40% United States

11% Brazil

DEU (3.6%)

MEX

CHN (6.1%)

JPN (3.5%)

CAN

THA

EAST ASIA & PACIFIC · EUROPE & CENTRAL ASIA · LATIN AMERICA & CARIBBEAN · MIDDLE EAST & NORTH AFRICA · NORTH AMERICA · SOUTH ASIA · SUB-SAHARAN AFRICA

TUNISIA

ECONOMIC COMPLEXITY INDEX [2010] ▸ 0.239 (53) | COMPLEXITY OUTLOOK INDEX [2010] ▸ 0.648 (42) | EXPECTED GDPᴘᴄ GROWTH * ▸ 2.9% (28)

*Expected annual average for the 2010-2020 period.

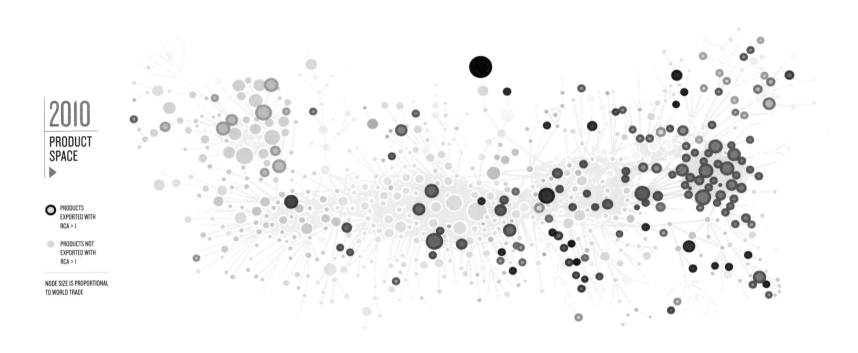

2010 PRODUCT SPACE ▶

○ PRODUCTS EXPORTED WITH RCA > 1

○ PRODUCTS NOT EXPORTED WITH RCA > 1

NODE SIZE IS PROPORTIONAL TO WORLD TRADE

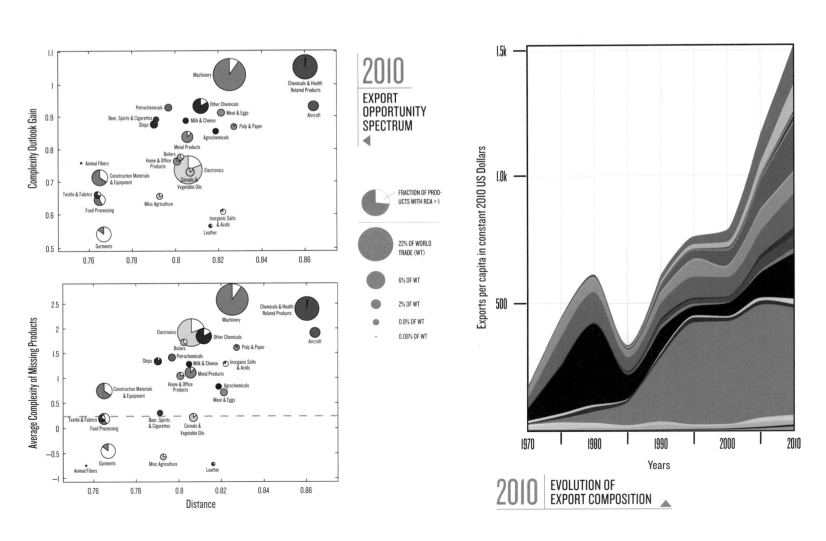

2010 EXPORT OPPORTUNITY SPECTRUM ◀

FRACTION OF PRODUCTS WITH RCA > 1

22% OF WORLD TRADE (WT)

6% OF WT

2% OF WT

0.8% OF WT

0.06% OF WT

2010 EVOLUTION OF EXPORT COMPOSITION ▲

POPULATION ▸ 11 M / (68)
TOTAL EXPORTS ▸ USD 16 B / (69)

GDP ▸ USD 44 B / (75)
GDPᴘᴄ ▸ USD 4,194 / (78)

EXPORTS PER CAPITA ▸ USD 1,520 / (60)
EXPORTS AS SHARE OF GDP ▸ 36 % (39)

* Data are from 2010. Numbers indicate:
Value (World Ranking among 128 countries)
Region: Middle East and North Africa.

ELECTRONICS · MACHINERY · AIRCRAFT · BOILERS · SHIPS · METAL PRODUCTS · CONSTR. MATL. & EQPT. · HOME & OFFICE · PULP & PAPER · CHEMICALS & HEALTH · AGROCHEMICALS · OTHER CHEMICALS · INOR. SALTS & ACIDS · PETROCHEMICALS · LEATHER · MILK & CHEESE · ANIMAL FIBERS · MEAT & EGGS · FISH & SEAFOOD · TROPICAL AGRIC. · CEREALS & VEG. OILS · COTTON/RICE/SOY & OTHERS · TOBACCO · FRUIT · MISC. AGRICULTURE · NOT CLASSIFIED · TEXTILE & FABRICS · GARMENTS · FOOD PROCESSING · BEER/SPIRITS & CIGS. · PRECIOUS STONES · COAL · OIL · MINING

2010 EXPORT TREEMAP ▾ TOTAL: $ 16,031,014,516

8423 (4.7%) Men's trousers

8459 (1.7%) Other knit outerwear

8451 (1.7%) Knit outerwear

8462 (1.2%)

3330 (12%) Crude petroleum

5629 (3.2%) Fertilizers

5222 (1.5%)

5232 (1.2%)

8439 (4.3%) Other women's outerwear

8463 (1.1%)

8429 (1.0%)

8465 (1.0%)

8431

8510 (3.4%) Footwear

6123 (0.95%)

6589

8424

5622 (1.8%)

5231

3345 (2.1%) Lubricating petroleum oils

8939 (0.77%)

2882 (0.72%)

7721 (3.5%) Switchboards, relays & fuses

7849 (1.3%)

7611 (1.0%)

7638 (0.95%)

7643

7781

7788 (0.91%)

7648

7649

7731 (8.3%) Electric wire

4235 (1.8%)

0579 (1.4%)

7162 (0.84%)

7436

7169

6994

8749

7938 (0.81%)

6749 (0.67%)

7711

7112

8743

7139

7783

7929

4232

4249

* Numbers indicate SITC-4 Rev 2 codes which can be found in the Appendix. Percentages next to the product codes indicate proportion of the product in the exports of the country. Treemap headers show the total trade of the country.

2010 EXPORT DESTINATIONS ▾ TOTAL: $ 16,031,014,516

25% France

18% Italy

10% Germany

GBR (5.6%)

LBY (4.6%)

DZA

MAR

ESP (4.8%)

TUR

CHE

IND

BEL

NLD

2010 IMPORT SOURCES ▾ TOTAL: $ 19,868,420,112

19% France

18% Italy

8.3% Germany

ESP (4.8%)

CHN (5.8%)

JPN

KOR

RUS (4.6%)

BEL

DZA (2.9%)

NLD

MLT

GBR

EGY

UKR

BRA

IND

EAST ASIA & PACIFIC · EUROPE & CENTRAL ASIA · LATIN AMERICA & CARIBBEAN · MIDDLE EAST & NORTH AFRICA · NORTH AMERICA · SOUTH ASIA · SUB-SAHARAN AFRICA

TURKEY

ECONOMIC COMPLEXITY INDEX [2010] ▸ 0.469 (42)   **COMPLEXITY OUTLOOK INDEX [2010]** ▸ 2.223 (2)   **EXPECTED GDPᴘᴄ GROWTH** * ▸ 3.3% (18)

Expected annual average for the 2010-2020 period.

2010
PRODUCT SPACE ▶

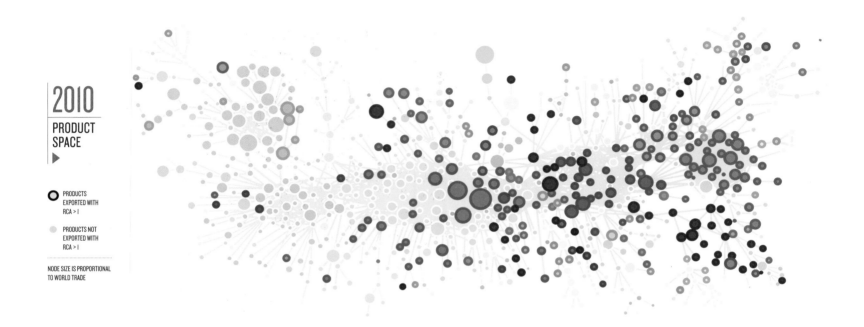

○ PRODUCTS EXPORTED WITH RCA > 1

○ PRODUCTS NOT EXPORTED WITH RCA > 1

NODE SIZE IS PROPORTIONAL TO WORLD TRADE

2010
EXPORT OPPORTUNITY SPECTRUM ◀

⊙ FRACTION OF PRODUCTS WITH RCA > 1

● 22% OF WORLD TRADE (WT)

● 6% OF WT

● 2% OF WT

● 0.8% OF WT

· 0.06% OF WT

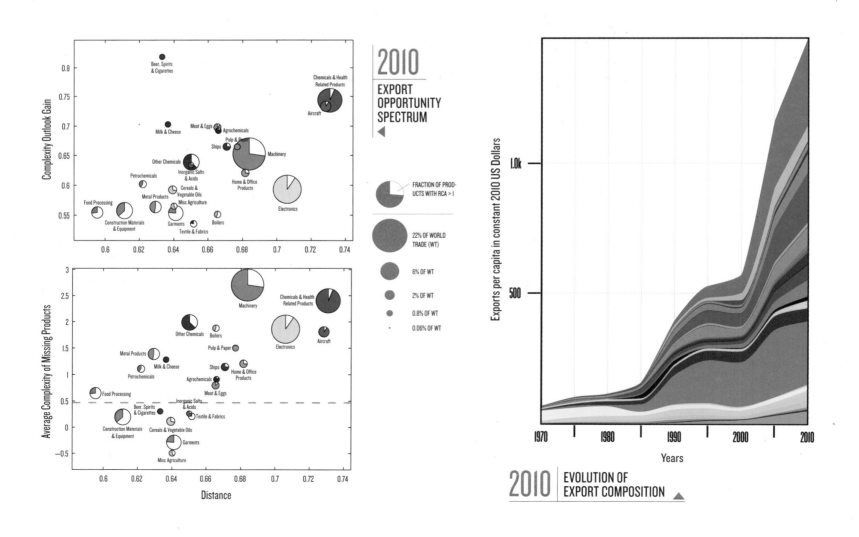

2010 | EVOLUTION OF EXPORT COMPOSITION ▲

POPULATION ▸ 73 M / (18)
TOTAL EXPORTS ▸ USD 108 B / (31)

GDP ▸ USD 731 B / (17)
GDPᴘᴄ ▸ USD 10,050 / (46)

EXPORTS PER CAPITA ▸ USD 1,483 / (62)
EXPORTS AS SHARE OF GDP ▸ 15 % / (102)

* Data are from 2010. Numbers indicate:
Value (World Ranking among 128 countries)
Region: Eastern Europe and Central Asia.

ELECTRONICS | MACHINERY | AIRCRAFT | BOILERS | SHIPS | METAL PRODUCTS | CONSTR. MATL. & EQPT. | HOME & OFFICE | PULP & PAPER | CHEMICALS & HEALTH | AGROCHEMICALS | OTHER CHEMICALS | INOR. SALTS & ACIDS | PETROCHEMICALS | LEATHER | MILK & CHEESE | ANIMAL FIBERS | MEAT & EGGS | FISH & SEAFOOD | TROPICAL AGRIC. | CEREALS & VEG. OILS | COTTON/RICE/SOY & OTHERS | TOBACCO | FRUIT | MISC. AGRICULTURE | NOT CLASSIFIED | TEXTILE & FABRICS | GARMENTS | FOOD PROCESSING | BEER/SPIRITS & CIGS. | PRECIOUS STONES | COAL | OIL | MINING

2010 EXPORT TREEMAP ▾ TOTAL: $ 107,919,189,552

7810 (5.1%) Cars
7821 (3.0%) Trucks & vans
7849 (2.6%)
6783 (1.2%)
6733 (0.72%)
6732 (3.0%) Iron/steel rods
7731 (1.8%)
7752 (1.1%)
3345 (2.3%) Lubricating petroleum oils
8939 (0.92%)

7139 (1.2%)
6727
6725 (1.0%)
6749
6724
7611 (1.5%) Color T.V.
6842 (0.95%)
8211 (0.61%)
5989
5112

7721 (0.76%)
6251
7132
6911 (0.84%)
6428
6210

7831
6991
7753
8219
6624
5831
5541

7758
7492
7452
7649
7415
6652
6974
6997

7932 (0.89%)
7149
7929
6612 (1.1%)
8973 (1.0%)
2731 (0.71%)
0589 (0.61%)
0579 (0.57%)
0730

8462 (2.4%) Knit undergarments of cotton
8451 (1.3%)
9710
2879
3330 (0.62%)
3413
0980
6421
0545

8459 (1.7%)
8423 (1.1%)
8435
8510
0460
0544
0577 (0.89%)
1211
1222
9310 (1.1%)

8439 (1.5%)
6584 (1.1%)
8441
8481
6581
8433
8431
0575 (0.65%)
0571
0572
6595
5823

* Numbers indicate SITC-4 Rev 2 codes which can be found in the Appendix. Percentages next to the product codes indicate proportion of the product in the exports of the country. Treemap headers show the total trade of the country.

2010 EXPORT DESTINATIONS ▾ TOTAL: $ 107,919,189,552

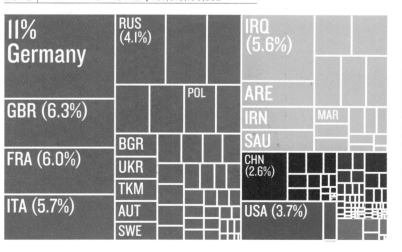

11% Germany | RUS (4.1%) | IRQ (5.6%)
GBR (6.3%) | POL | ARE | IRN | MAR | SAU
FRA (6.0%) | BGR | UKR | TKM | CHN (2.6%)
ITA (5.7%) | AUT | SWE | USA (3.7%)

2010 IMPORT SOURCES ▾ TOTAL: $ 164,102,767,349

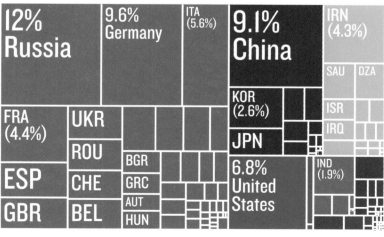

12% Russia | 9.6% Germany | ITA (5.6%) | 9.1% China | IRN (4.3%)
FRA (4.4%) | UKR | ROU | KOR (2.6%) | SAU | DZA
ESP | CHE | BGR | GRC | JPN | ISR | IRQ
GBR | BEL | AUT | HUN | 6.8% United States | IND (1.9%)

EAST ASIA & PACIFIC | EUROPE & CENTRAL ASIA | LATIN AMERICA & CARIBBEAN | MIDDLE EAST & NORTH AFRICA | NORTH AMERICA | SOUTH ASIA | SUB-SAHARAN AFRICA

TURKMENISTAN

| ECONOMIC COMPLEXITY INDEX [2010] ▸ -0.896 (101) | COMPLEXITY OUTLOOK INDEX [2010] ▸ -0.989 (112) | EXPECTED GDPᴘᴄ GROWTH * ▸ 0.3% (110) |

*Expected annual average for the 2010-2020 period.

2010
PRODUCT SPACE ▶

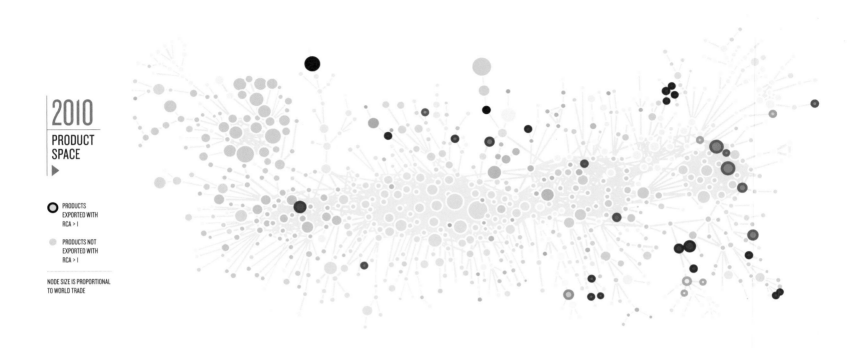

○ PRODUCTS EXPORTED WITH RCA > 1

○ PRODUCTS NOT EXPORTED WITH RCA > 1

NODE SIZE IS PROPORTIONAL TO WORLD TRADE

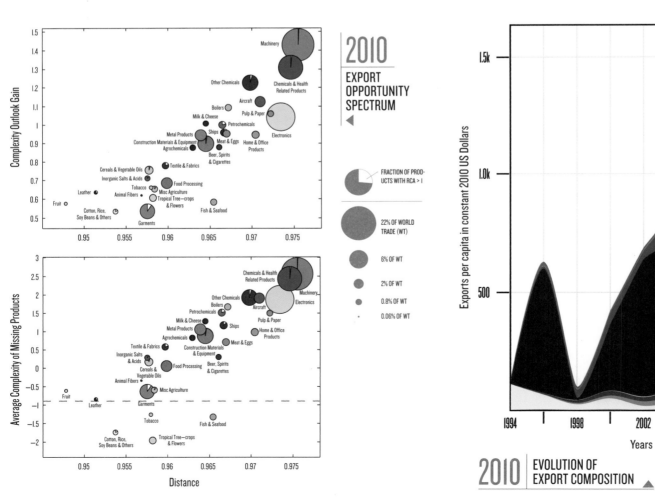

2010
EXPORT OPPORTUNITY SPECTRUM ◀

FRACTION OF PRODUCTS WITH RCA > 1

22% OF WORLD TRADE (WT)

6% OF WT

2% OF WT

0.8% OF WT

0.06% OF WT

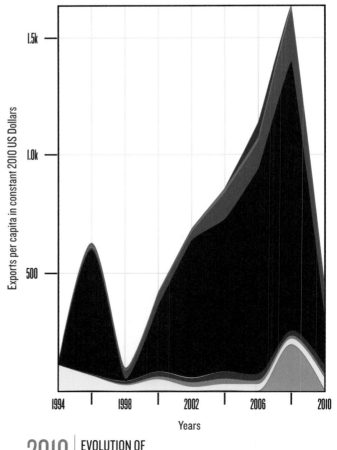

2010 | EVOLUTION OF EXPORT COMPOSITION ▲

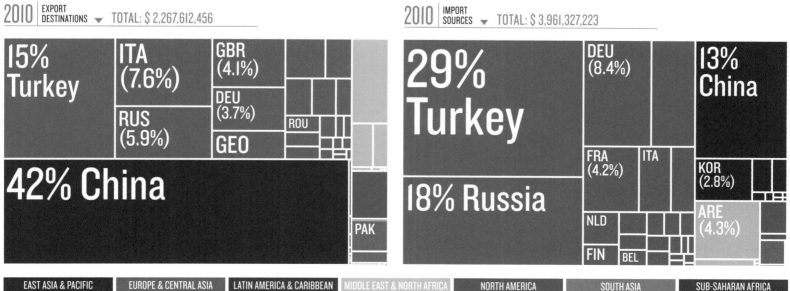

POPULATION ▸ 5 M / (98)
TOTAL EXPORTS ▸ USD 2.3 B / (110)

GDP ▸ USD 20 B / (95)
GDPPC ▸ USD 3,967 / (80)

EXPORTS PER CAPITA ▸ USD 450 / (94)
EXPORTS AS SHARE OF GDP ▸ 11 % (116)

* Data are from 2010. Numbers indicate:
Value (World Ranking among 128 countries)
Region: Eastern Europe and Central Asia.

ELECTRONICS · MACHINERY · AIRCRAFT · BOILERS · SHIPS · METAL PRODUCTS · CONSTR. MATL. & EQPT. · HOME & OFFICE · PULP & PAPER · CHEMICALS & HEALTH · AGROCHEMICALS · OTHER CHEMICALS · INOR. SALTS & ACIDS · PETROCHEMICALS · LEATHER · MILK & CHEESE · ANIMAL FIBERS · MEAT & EGGS · FISH & SEAFOOD · TROPICAL AGRIC. · CEREALS & VEG. OILS · COTTON/RICE/SOY & OTHERS · TOBACCO · FRUIT · MISC. AGRICULTURE · NOT CLASSIFIED · TEXTILE & FABRICS · GARMENTS · FOOD PROCESSING · BEER/SPIRITS & DIGS. · PRECIOUS STONES · COAL · OIL · MINING

2010 | EXPORT TREEMAP ▼ — TOTAL: $ 2,267,612,456

3414 (40%) Petroleum gases

3330 (3.5%)

2631 (9.8%) Raw cotton

3413 (0.68%)

3345 (24%) Lubricating petroleum oils

5832 (3.8%) Polypropylene

0813

2929

6513 (5.2%) Cotton yarn

6521 (2.1%) Unbleached cotton woven fabrics

6522 (0.92%)

6584 (1.3%)

8439 (0.89%)

6552

8462

9310 (0.97%)

3510 (0.74%)

5221

* Numbers indicate SITC-4 Rev 2 codes which can be found in the Appendix. Percentages next to the product codes indicate proportion of the product in the exports of the country. Treemap headers show the total trade of the country.

2010 | EXPORT DESTINATIONS ▼ TOTAL: $ 2,267,612,456

15% Turkey

ITA (7.6%)

RUS (5.9%)

GBR (4.1%)

DEU (3.7%)

GEO

ROU

42% China

PAK

2010 | IMPORT SOURCES ▼ TOTAL: $ 3,961,327,223

29% Turkey

18% Russia

DEU (8.4%)

FRA (4.2%)

ITA

NLD

FIN

BEL

13% China

KOR (2.8%)

ARE (4.3%)

EAST ASIA & PACIFIC · EUROPE & CENTRAL ASIA · LATIN AMERICA & CARIBBEAN · MIDDLE EAST & NORTH AFRICA · NORTH AMERICA · SOUTH ASIA · SUB-SAHARAN AFRICA

UGANDA

ECONOMIC COMPLEXITY INDEX [2010] ▸ -0.917 (102) | COMPLEXITY OUTLOOK INDEX [2010] ▸ -0.635 (82) | EXPECTED GDPᴘᴄ GROWTH * ▸ 2.7% (34)

*Expected annual average for the 2010-2020 period.

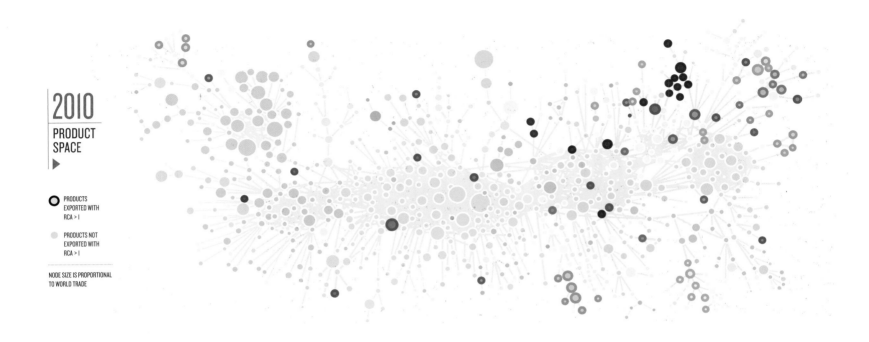

2010
PRODUCT SPACE ▶

○ PRODUCTS EXPORTED WITH RCA > 1

● PRODUCTS NOT EXPORTED WITH RCA > 1

NODE SIZE IS PROPORTIONAL TO WORLD TRADE

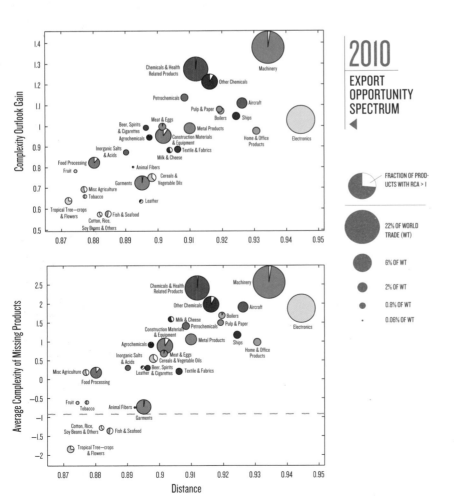

2010
EXPORT OPPORTUNITY SPECTRUM ◀

⬭ FRACTION OF PRODUCTS WITH RCA > 1

● 22% OF WORLD TRADE (WT)

● 6% OF WT

● 2% OF WT

● 0.8% OF WT

· 0.06% OF WT

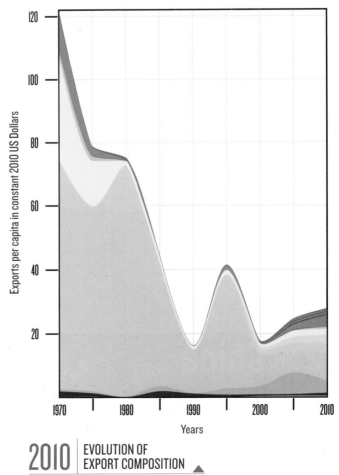

2010 | EVOLUTION OF EXPORT COMPOSITION ▲

POPULATION ▸ 33 M / (35)
TOTAL EXPORTS ▸ USD 935 M / (125)

GDP ▸ USD 17 B / (99)
GDPᴘᴄ ▸ USD 515 / (122)

EXPORTS PER CAPITA ▸ USD 28 / (127)
EXPORTS AS SHARE OF GDP ▸ 5.4 % / (126)

* Data are from 2010. Numbers indicate:
  Value (World Ranking among 128 countries)
  Region: Sub-Saharan Africa.

ELECTRONICS · MACHINERY · AIRCRAFT · BOILERS · SHIPS · METAL PRODUCTS · CONSTR. MAT. & EQPT. · HOME & OFFICE · PULP & PAPER · CHEMICALS & HEALTH · AGROCHEMICALS · OTHER CHEMICALS · INOR. SALTS & ACIDS · PETROCHEMICALS · LEATHER · MILK & CHEESE · ANIMAL FIBERS · MEAT & EGGS · FISH & SEAFOOD · TROPICAL AGRIC. · CEREALS & VEG. OILS · COTTON/RICE/SOY & OTHERS · TOBACCO · FRUIT · MISC. AGRICULTURE · NOT CLASSIFIED · TEXTILE & FABRICS · GARMENTS · FOOD PROCESSING · BEER/SPIRITS & CIGS. · PRECIOUS STONES · COAL · OIL · MINING

2010 | EXPORT TREEMAP ▾ TOTAL: $ 935,275,670

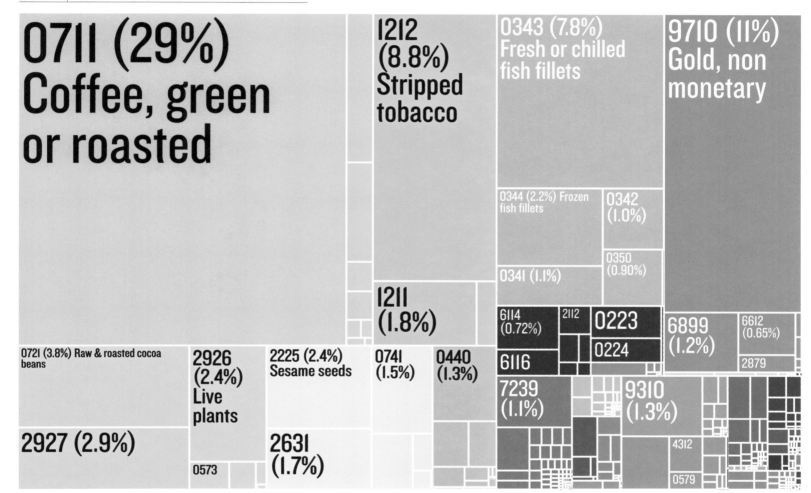

* Numbers indicate SITC-4 Rev 2 codes which can be found in the Appendix. Percentages next to the product codes indicate proportion of the product in the exports of the country. Treemap headers show the total trade of the country.

2010 | EXPORT DESTINATIONS ▾ TOTAL: $ 935,275,670

11% Germany · NLD (9.4%) · BEL (7.8%) · 11% Kenya · 11% United Arab Emirates · ITA (5.2%) · PRT · RUS (1.8%) · BDI · TZA · ISR · CHN (2.6%) · USA (5.8%) · IND · FRA · TUR · ESP (4.8%) · POL · IDN

2010 | IMPORT SOURCES ▾ TOTAL: $ 4,218,448,307

8.7% China · 11% Kenya · ARE (8.2%) · JPN (6.5%) · THA · ZAF (5.3%) · TZA · KWT · NLD · 15% India · USA (2.3%) · GBR · FRA · DEU · BEL · BRA

EAST ASIA & PACIFIC · EUROPE & CENTRAL ASIA · LATIN AMERICA & CARIBBEAN · MIDDLE EAST & NORTH AFRICA · NORTH AMERICA · SOUTH ASIA · SUB-SAHARAN AFRICA

UKRAINE

ECONOMIC COMPLEXITY INDEX [2010] ▸ 0.704 (33)   COMPLEXITY OUTLOOK INDEX [2010] ▸ 1.088 (19)   EXPECTED GDPᴘᴄ GROWTH * ▸ 4.2% (3)

*Expected annual average for the 2010-2020 period.

2010 PRODUCT SPACE ▶

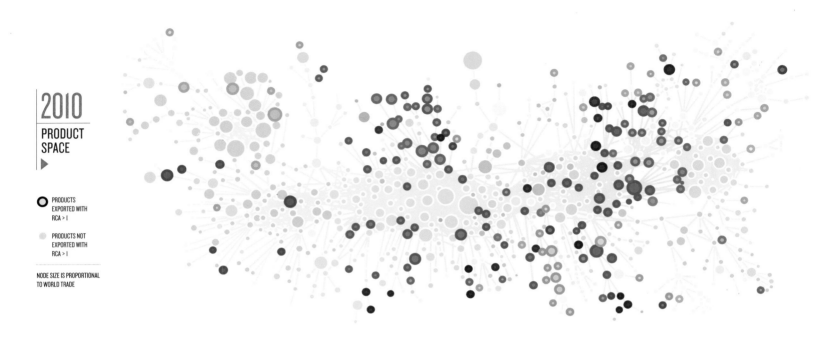

○ PRODUCTS EXPORTED WITH RCA > 1

○ PRODUCTS NOT EXPORTED WITH RCA > 1

NODE SIZE IS PROPORTIONAL TO WORLD TRADE

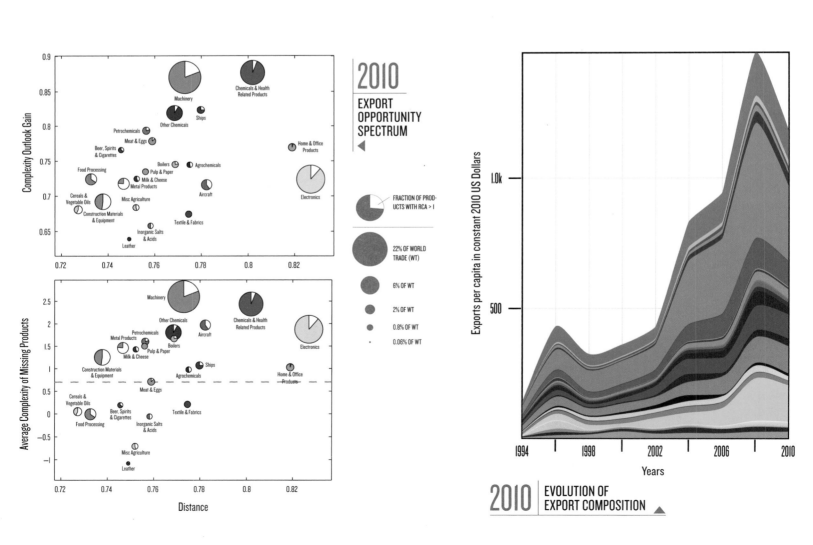

2010 EXPORT OPPORTUNITY SPECTRUM ◀

◗ FRACTION OF PRODUCTS WITH RCA > 1

22% OF WORLD TRADE (WT)

6% OF WT

2% OF WT

0.8% OF WT

0.06% OF WT

2010 EVOLUTION OF EXPORT COMPOSITION ▲

POPULATION ▸ 46 M / (27)
TOTAL EXPORTS ▸ USD 54 B / (46)

GDP ▸ USD 136 B / (53)
GDPᴘᴄ ▸ USD 2,974 / (83)

EXPORTS PER CAPITA ▸ USD 1,183 / (68)
EXPORTS AS SHARE OF GDP ▸ 40 % (34)

* Data are from 2010. Numbers indicate:
Value (World Ranking among 128 countries)
Region: Eastern Europe and Central Asia.

ELECTRONICS · MACHINERY · AIRCRAFT · BOILERS · SHIPS · METAL PRODUCTS · CONSTR. MATL. & EQPT. · HOME & OFFICE · PULP & PAPER · CHEMICALS & HEALTH · AGROCHEMICALS · OTHER CHEMICALS · INOR. SALTS & ACIDS · PETROCHEMICALS · LEATHER · MILK & CHEESE · ANIMAL FIBERS · MEAT & EGGS · FISH & SEAFOOD · TROPICAL AGRIC. · CEREALS & VEG. OILS · COTTON/RICE/SOY & OTHERS · TOBACCO · FRUIT · MISC. AGRICULTURE · NOT CLASSIFIED · TEXTILE & FABRICS · GARMENTS · FOOD PROCESSING · BEER/SPIRITS & CIGS. · PRECIOUS STONES · COAL · OIL · MINING

2010 | EXPORT TREEMAP ▾ TOTAL: $ 54,278,860,266

6725 (11%) Iron/steel billets

6716 (3.2%)

6727 (2.6%) Iron/steel coils

6744 (2.2%)

6712 (1.3%)   6746 (0.90%)

6783 (1.1%)

6733 (1.0%)

7915 (3.2%) Railway for freight

7932

4236 (3.9%) Sunflower seed oil

0412 (1.7%) Other wheat, unmilled

0440 (1.3%)

1222

2226 (1.2%)

0411

2224

2222

0430 (1.8%)

3345 (6.3%) Lubricating petroleum oils

5331   5156
5989

5621 (1.5%)

5417

6731 (1.3%)

7919 (0.58%)

7239

6782 (0.92%)

7721

6418

7810

7372

7431

7161

2815 (4.0%) Iron ore

2816 (2.4%) Agglomerated iron ore

5225

2873 (0.75%)

3221 (1.2%)

3222

3232 (0.77%)

2734

6841

6732 (2.7%) Iron/steel rods

6911

3510

2471

8219

2482

2483

8211

7731 (1.2%)

0730 (0.94%)

0980

6421

1124

0240 (0.72%)

9310 (0.97%)

1123

* Numbers indicate SITC-4 Rev 2 codes which can be found in the Appendix. Percentages next to the product codes indicate proportion of the product in the exports of the country. Treemap headers show the total trade of the country.

2010 | EXPORT DESTINATIONS ▾ TOTAL: $ 54,278,860,266

24% Russia

TUR (6.5%)

ITA

DEU (3.6%)

BLR (3.1%)

CZE

ROU

ESP

AUT

SVK

NLD

AZE

GBR

EGY (3.1%)

SYR

LBN

CHN (3.6%)

KOR

SGP

USA

SAU

THA   IND

IDN

2010 | IMPORT SOURCES ▾ TOTAL: $ 55,927,916,840

36% Russia

DEU (7.6%)

POL (4.6%)

NLD

GBR

CZE

KAZ

BLR (4.2%)

CHE

SVK

ESP

ITA

7.5% China

JPN

KOR

USA (2.9%)   IND

EAST ASIA & PACIFIC · EUROPE & CENTRAL ASIA · LATIN AMERICA & CARIBBEAN · MIDDLE EAST & NORTH AFRICA · NORTH AMERICA · SOUTH ASIA · SUB-SAHARAN AFRICA

UNITED ARAB EMIRATES

ECONOMIC COMPLEXITY INDEX [2010] ▸ 0.329 (48) | COMPLEXITY OUTLOOK INDEX [2010] ▸ 0.158 (56) | EXPECTED GDPᴘᴄ GROWTH * ▸ 0.3% (III)

*Expected annual average for the 2010-2020 period.

2010 PRODUCT SPACE ▶

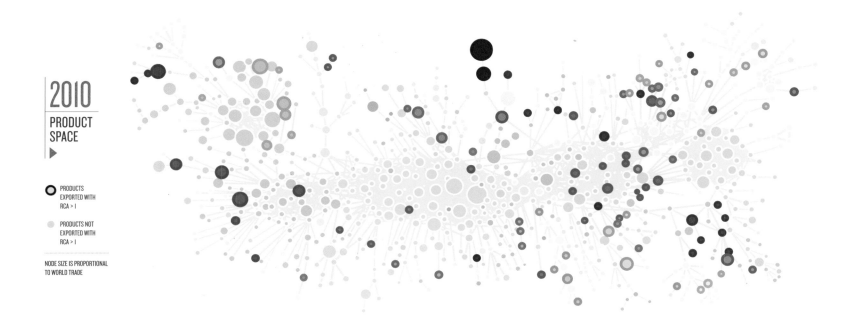

○ PRODUCTS EXPORTED WITH RCA > 1

○ PRODUCTS NOT EXPORTED WITH RCA > 1

NODE SIZE IS PROPORTIONAL TO WORLD TRADE

2010 EXPORT OPPORTUNITY SPECTRUM ◀

FRACTION OF PRODUCTS WITH RCA > 1

22% OF WORLD TRADE (WT)

6% OF WT

2% OF WT

0.8% OF WT

0.06% OF WT

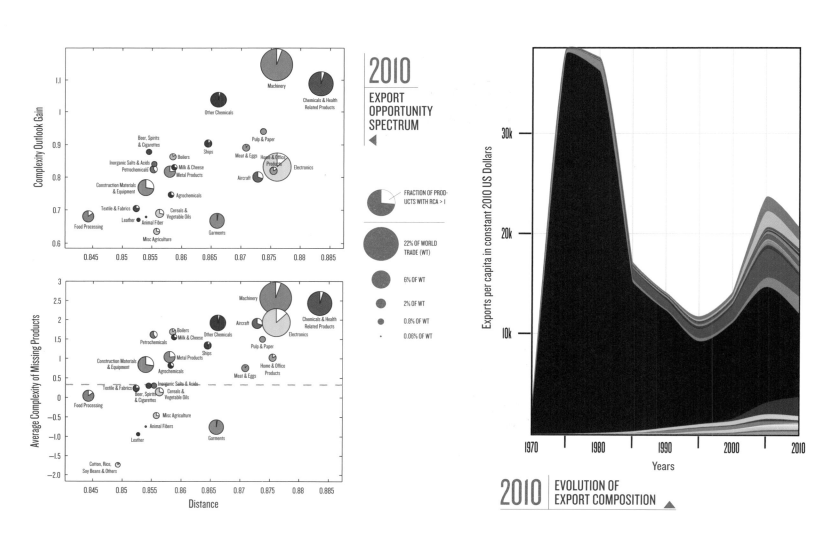

2010 EVOLUTION OF EXPORT COMPOSITION ▲

POPULATION ▸ 7.5 M / (82)
TOTAL EXPORTS ▸ USD 155 B / (24)

GDP ▸ USD 298 B / (33)
GDPᴘᴄ ▸ USD 39,625 / (18)

EXPORTS PER CAPITA ▸ USD 20,640 / (8)
EXPORTS AS SHARE OF GDP ▸ 52 % (19)

* Data are from 2010. Numbers indicate:
Value (World Ranking among 128 countries)
Region: Middle East and North Africa.

ELECTRONICS · MACHINERY · AIRCRAFT · BOILERS · SHIPS · METAL PRODUCTS · CONSTR. MATL. & EQPT. · HOME & OFFICE · PULP & PAPER · CHEMICALS & HEALTH · AGROCHEMICALS · OTHER CHEMICALS · INOR. SALTS & ACIDS · PETROCHEMICALS · LEATHER · MILK & CHEESE · ANIMAL FIBERS · MEAT & EGGS · FISH & SEAFOOD · TROPICAL AGRIC. · CEREALS & VEG. OILS · COTTON/RICE/SOY & OTHERS · TOBACCO · FRUIT · MISC. AGRICULTURE · NOT CLASSIFIED · TEXTILE & FABRICS · GARMENTS · FOOD PROCESSING · BEER/SPIRITS & CIGS. · PRECIOUS STONES · COAL · OIL · MINING

2010 EXPORT TREEMAP ▾ TOTAL: $ 155,039,720,546

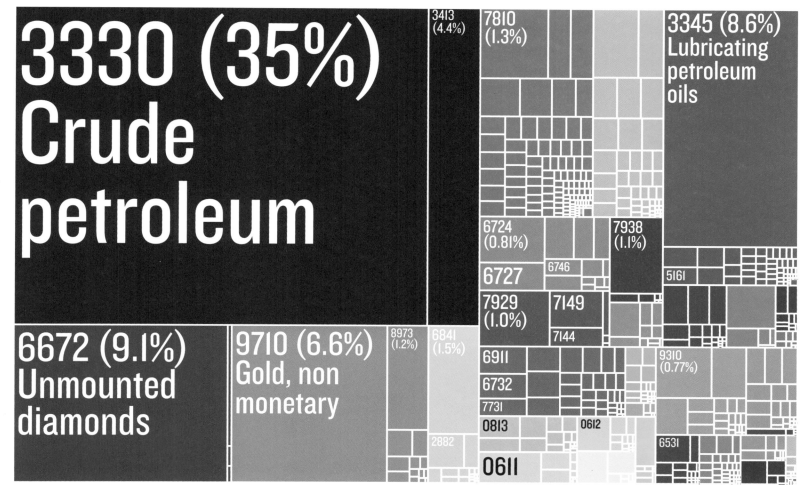

3330 (35%) Crude petroleum

3413 (4.4%)

7810 (1.3%)

3345 (8.6%) Lubricating petroleum oils

6724 (0.81%)

6727

6746

7938 (1.1%)

7929 (1.0%)

7149

7144

5161

6911

6732

7731

9310 (0.77%)

0813

0612

6531

6672 (9.1%) Unmounted diamonds

9710 (6.6%) Gold, non monetary

8973 (1.2%)

6841 (1.5%)

2882

0611

* Numbers indicate SITC-4 Rev 2 codes which can be found in the Appendix. Percentages next to the product codes indicate proportion of the product in the exports of the country. Treemap headers show the total trade of the country.

2010 EXPORT DESTINATIONS ▾ TOTAL: $ 155,039,720,546

17% Japan

THA (5.1%)

CHN (2.7%)

MYS

KOR (7.1%)

18% India

PAK (3.1%)

AFG

9.2% Iran

IRQ

SAU

BEL

NLD

FRA

GBR

NGA

KEN

2010 IMPORT SOURCES ▾ TOTAL: $ 132,486,555,515

12% China

JPN (5.8%)

KOR

IDN

16% India

USA (8.4%)

7.5% Germany

FRA (3.4%)

ITA (3.1%)

ESP

GBR

CHE

IRQ

EAST ASIA & PACIFIC · EUROPE & CENTRAL ASIA · LATIN AMERICA & CARIBBEAN · MIDDLE EAST & NORTH AFRICA · NORTH AMERICA · SOUTH ASIA · SUB-SAHARAN AFRICA

UNITED KINGDOM

ECONOMIC COMPLEXITY INDEX [2010] ▸ 1.666 (9)	COMPLEXITY OUTLOOK INDEX [2010] ▸ 0.811 (32)	EXPECTED GDPᴘᴄ GROWTH * ▸ 2.6% (38)

*Expected annual average for the 2010-2020 period.

2010 PRODUCT SPACE ▶

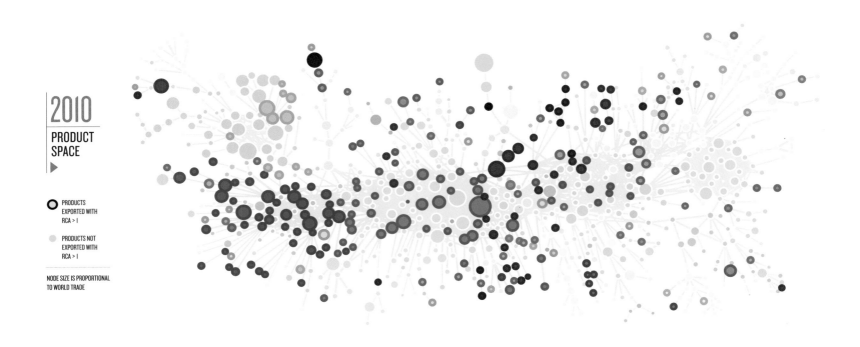

○ PRODUCTS EXPORTED WITH RCA > 1

● PRODUCTS NOT EXPORTED WITH RCA > 1

NODE SIZE IS PROPORTIONAL TO WORLD TRADE

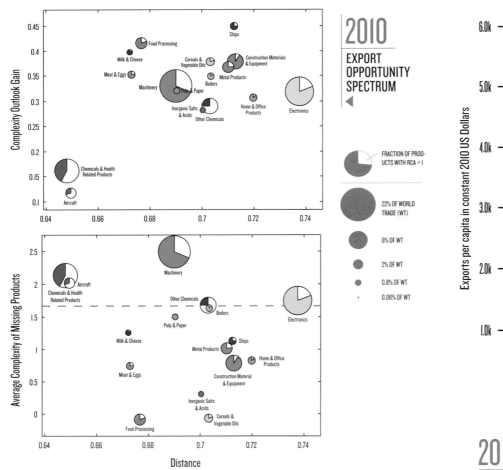

2010 EXPORT OPPORTUNITY SPECTRUM ◀

◔ FRACTION OF PRODUCTS WITH RCA > 1

● 22% OF WORLD TRADE (WT)

● 6% OF WT

● 2% OF WT

● 0.8% OF WT

· 0.06% OF WT

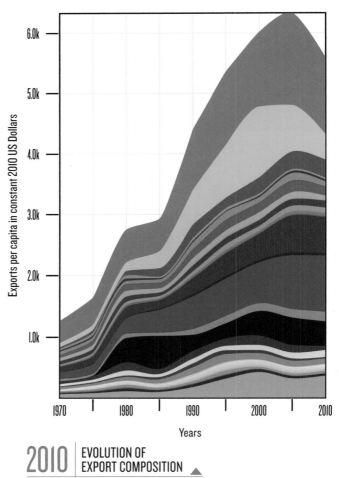

2010 | EVOLUTION OF EXPORT COMPOSITION ▲

POPULATION ▸ 62 M / (21)
TOTAL EXPORTS ▸ USD 348 B / (11)

GDP ▸ USD 2.3 T / (6)
GDPᴘᴄ ▸ USD 36,186 / (20)

EXPORTS PER CAPITA ▸ USD 5,586 / (33)
EXPORTS AS SHARE OF GDP ▸ 15 % / (100)

* Data are from 2010. Numbers indicate:
Value (World Ranking among 128 countries)
Region: Western Europe.

ELECTRONICS · MACHINERY · AIRCRAFT · BOILERS · SHIPS · METAL PRODUCTS · CONSTR. MATL. & EQPT. · HOME & OFFICE · PULP & PAPER · CHEMICALS & HEALTH · AGROCHEMICALS · OTHER CHEMICALS · INOR. SALTS & ACIDS · PETROCHEMICALS · LEATHER · MILK & CHEESE · ANIMAL FIBERS · MEAT & EGGS · FISH & SEAFOOD · TROPICAL AGRIC. · CEREALS & VEG. OILS · COTTON/RICE/SOY & OTHERS · TOBACCO · FRUIT · MISC. AGRICULTURE · NOT CLASSIFIED · TEXTILE & FABRICS · GARMENTS · FOOD PROCESSING · BEER/SPIRITS & CIGS. · PRECIOUS STONES · COAL · OIL · MINING

2010 | EXPORT TREEMAP ▾ TOTAL: $ 347,628,222,999

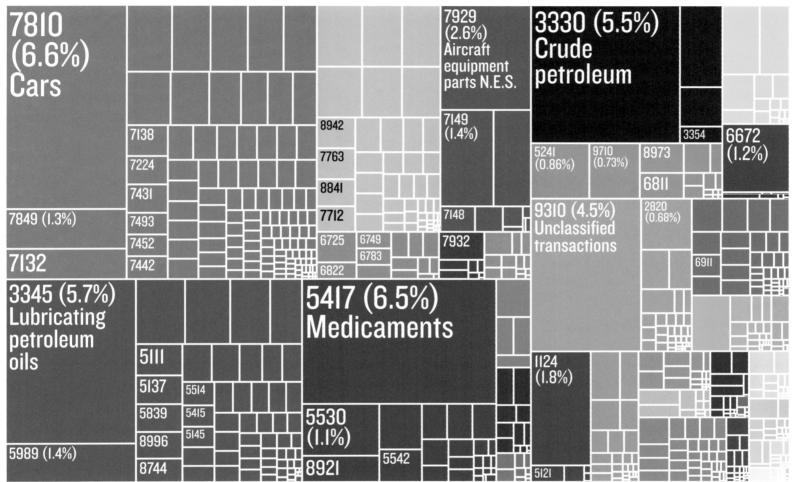

* Numbers indicate SITC-4 Rev 2 codes which can be found in the Appendix. Percentages next to the product codes indicate proportion of the product in the exports of the country. Treemap headers show the total trade of the country.

2010 | EXPORT DESTINATIONS ▾ TOTAL: $ 347,628,222,999

2010 | IMPORT SOURCES ▾ TOTAL: $ 525,822,255,962

EAST ASIA & PACIFIC · EUROPE & CENTRAL ASIA · LATIN AMERICA & CARIBBEAN · MIDDLE EAST & NORTH AFRICA · NORTH AMERICA · SOUTH ASIA · SUB-SAHARAN AFRICA

UNITED STATES OF AMERICA

ECONOMIC COMPLEXITY INDEX [2010] ▸ 1.507 (12) | COMPLEXITY OUTLOOK INDEX [2010] ▸ -0.649 (83) | EXPECTED GDPᴘᴄ GROWTH * ▸ 1.2% (93)

*Expected annual average for the 2010-2020 period.

2010 PRODUCT SPACE ▸

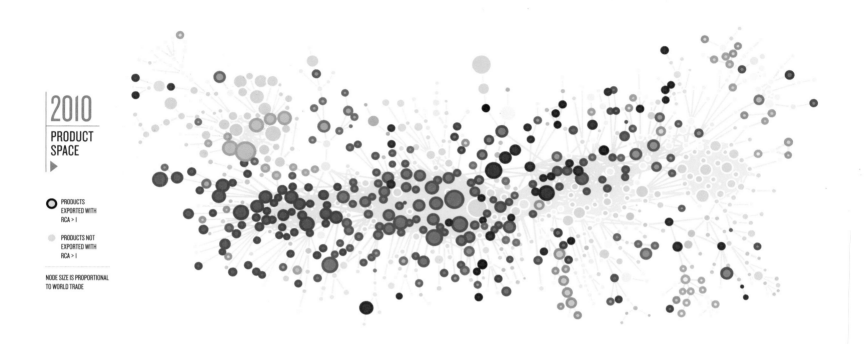

○ PRODUCTS EXPORTED WITH RCA > 1

○ PRODUCTS NOT EXPORTED WITH RCA > 1

NODE SIZE IS PROPORTIONAL TO WORLD TRADE

2010 EXPORT OPPORTUNITY SPECTRUM ◂

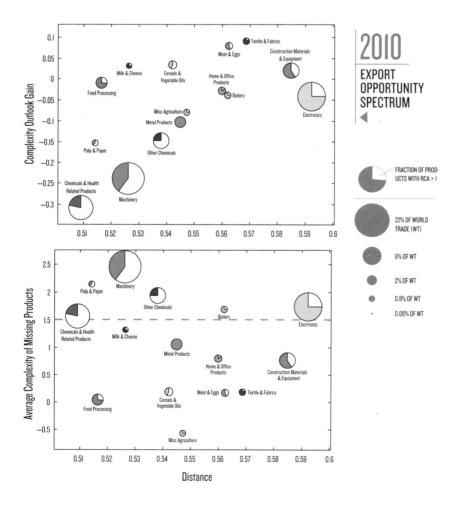

⊘ FRACTION OF PRODUCTS WITH RCA > 1

◯ 22% OF WORLD TRADE (WT)

○ 6% OF WT

○ 2% OF WT

• 0.8% OF WT

· 0.06% OF WT

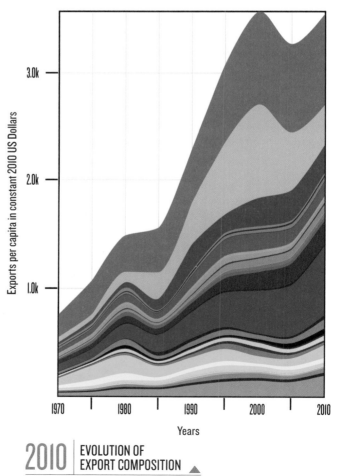

2010 | EVOLUTION OF EXPORT COMPOSITION ▲

POPULATION ▸ 309 M / (3)
TOTAL EXPORTS ▸ USD 1.1 T / (2)

GDP ▸ USD 14 T / (1)
GDPPC ▸ USD 46,702 / (7)

EXPORTS PER CAPITA ▸ USD 3,564 / (42)
EXPORTS AS SHARE OF GDP ▸ 7.6 % (121)

* Data are from 2010. Numbers indicate:
Value (World Ranking among 128 countries)
Region: North America.

ELECTRONICS · MACHINERY · AIRCRAFT · BOILERS · SHIPS · METAL PRODUCTS · CONSTR. MATL. & EQPT. · HOME & OFFICE · PULP & PAPER · CHEMICALS & HEALTH · AGROCHEMICALS · OTHER CHEMICALS · INOR. SALTS & ACIDS · PETROCHEMICALS · LEATHER · MILK & CHEESE · ANIMAL FIBERS · MEAT & EGGS · FISH & SEAFOOD · TROPICAL AGRIC. · CEREALS & VEG. OILS · COTTON/RICE/SOY & OTHERS · TOBACCO · FRUIT · MISC. AGRICULTURE · NOT CLASSIFIED · TEXTILE & FABRICS · GARMENTS · FOOD PROCESSING · BEER/SPIRITS & CIGS. · PRECIOUS STONES · COAL · OIL · MINING

2010 EXPORT TREEMAP ▾ TOTAL: $ 1,102,566,930,430

7810 (3.0%) Cars

7849 (2.3%) Other vehicle parts

7284 (1.4%)

7821 (1.2%)

7764 (2.8%) Electronic microcircuits

7924 (2.1%)

7149 (1.8%)

9710 (1.0%)

2222 (1.5%)

7721 (1.2%)

7139

7239 (0.79%)

7492

7234

7132

8743

7436

7493

7431

8741

7162

7161

7416

6954

7188

7138

7783

7499

7643

7763

7525

8841

6822

7528

7421

7415

6749

6783

7929 (1.6%)

7148

7921

7131

5241

2882

3222

9310 (3.4%) Unclassified transactions

7148

8211

7861

0813

3345 (4.3%) Lubricating petroleum oils

8720 (1.5%)

5989 (1.5%)

5416 (1.5%)

8996 (0.87%)

7741

7742

5112

5161

2331

5148

5137

5982

5415

5417 (2.6%) Medicaments

8939

5831

5834

5542

8921

5221

5121

5823

8931

2511

2517

6413

0114

0111

8219

8960

0113

* Numbers indicate SITC-4 Rev 2 codes which can be found in the Appendix. Percentages next to the product codes indicate proportion of the product in the exports of the country. Treemap headers show the total trade of the country.

2010 EXPORT DESTINATIONS ▾ TOTAL: $ 1,102,566,930,430

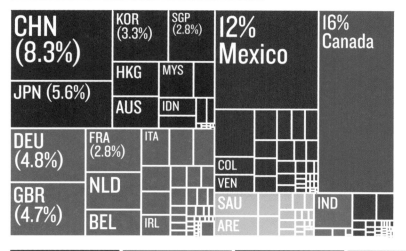

CHN (8.3%) | KOR (3.3%) | SGP (2.8%) | 12% Mexico | 16% Canada
JPN (5.6%) | HKG | MYS | |
| AUS | IDN | |
DEU (4.8%) | FRA (2.8%) | ITA | COL |
| NLD | | VEN | IND
GBR (4.7%) | BEL | IRL | SAU | ARE

2010 IMPORT SOURCES ▾ TOTAL: $ 1,704,961,595,230

19% China | JPN (6.2%) | 12% Mexico | 15% Canada
MYS	VEN
THA	
DEU (4.4%)	FRA	RUS	BRA
IRL	BEL	SAU	NGA
GBR | ITA | ISR

EAST ASIA & PACIFIC · EUROPE & CENTRAL ASIA · LATIN AMERICA & CARIBBEAN · MIDDLE EAST & NORTH AFRICA · NORTH AMERICA · SOUTH ASIA · SUB-SAHARAN AFRICA

URUGUAY

ECONOMIC COMPLEXITY INDEX [2010] ▸ 0.253 (51)	COMPLEXITY OUTLOOK INDEX [2010] ▸ 0.291 (49)	EXPECTED GDPᴘᴄ GROWTH * ▸ 1.6% (82)

*Expected annual average for the 2010-2020 period.

2010
PRODUCT SPACE
▶

○ PRODUCTS EXPORTED WITH RCA > 1

○ PRODUCTS NOT EXPORTED WITH RCA > 1

NODE SIZE IS PROPORTIONAL TO WORLD TRADE

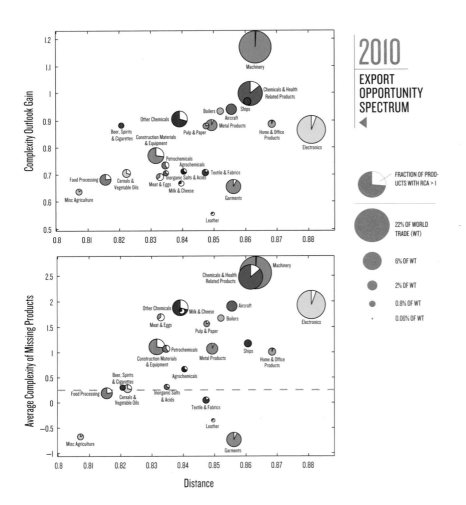

2010
EXPORT OPPORTUNITY SPECTRUM
◀

⬤ FRACTION OF PRODUCTS WITH RCA > 1

⬤ 22% OF WORLD TRADE (WT)

⬤ 6% OF WT

● 2% OF WT

• 0.8% OF WT

· 0.06% OF WT

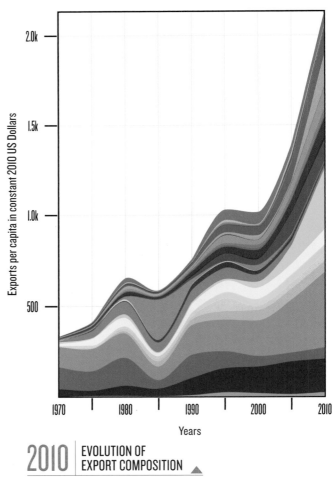

2010 | EVOLUTION OF EXPORT COMPOSITION ▲

POPULATION ▸ 3.4 M / (112)
TOTAL EXPORTS ▸ USD 7.2 B / (82)

GDP ▸ USD 39 B / (77)
GDPpc ▸ USD 11,742 / (41)

EXPORTS PER CAPITA ▸ USD 2,135 / (53)
EXPORTS AS SHARE OF GDP ▸ 18 % (85)

* Data are from 2010. Numbers indicate:
Value (World Ranking among 128 countries)
Region: Latin America and the Caribbean.

ELECTRONICS · MACHINERY · AIRCRAFT · BOILERS · SHIPS · METAL PRODUCTS · CONSTR. MATL. & EQPT. · HOME & OFFICE · PULP & PAPER · CHEMICALS & HEALTH · AGROCHEMICALS · OTHER CHEMICALS · INOR. SALTS & ACIDS · PETROCHEMICALS · LEATHER · MILK & CHEESE · ANIMAL FIBERS · MEAT & EGGS · FISH & SEAFOOD · TROPICAL AGRIC. · CEREALS & VEG. OILS · COTTON/RICE/SOY & OTHERS · TOBACCO · FRUIT · MISC. AGRICULTURE · NOT CLASSIFIED · TEXTILE & FABRICS · GARMENTS · FOOD PROCESSING · BEER/SPIRITS & CIGS. · PRECIOUS STONES · COAL · OIL · MINING

2010 EXPORT TREEMAP ▾ TOTAL: $ 7,165,504,397

0111 (13%) Bovine meat

0011 (2.5%) Live bovines

0112 (1.0%)

0116 (0.75%)

0115

0616

2222 (11%) Soybeans

0240 (2.1%)

0224 (1.7%)

0223

0230

2682

6512 (1.8%)

0342 (1.4%)

0814

0371

6114 (2.7%) Bovine & equine leather

2111

0412 (4.0%) Other wheat, unmilled

0440

0422 (3.2%) Semi or wholly milled rice

0421

0571 (1.3%)

1222

0482 (1.8%)

2517 (8.2%) Chemical wood pulp, soda or sulphate

2460 (2.1%) Pulpwood

3510 (1.0%)

2472

0980 (2.2%) Edible products N.E.S.

8931 (1.9%)

7849 (1.1%)

6416

0914 (0.68%)

0579

0585

5514 (2.5%) Odoriferous substances

5416 (0.68%)

3345 (1.1%)

5417 (2.9%) Medicaments

5542 (0.80%)

6210 (1.1%)

5231

5834

7832

7821

6612

* Numbers indicate SITC-4 Rev 2 codes which can be found in the Appendix. Percentages next to the product codes indicate proportion of the product in the exports of the country. Treemap headers show the total trade of the country.

2010 EXPORT DESTINATIONS ▾ TOTAL: $ 7,165,504,397

20% Brazil

ARG (7.3%)

VEN (4.0%)

MEX

DEU (7.2%)

ESP (2.6%)

NLD (2.6%)

RUS

TUR

ITA

GBR

PRT

14% China

JPN

HKG

USA

ISR

TUN

2010 IMPORT SOURCES ▾ TOTAL: $ 8,231,523,800

19% Argentina

BRA (18%)

18% China

KOR (1.9%)

SGP

DEU (3.7%)

ESP (2.0%)

CHE

GBR

NLD

BEL

11% United States

EAST ASIA & PACIFIC · EUROPE & CENTRAL ASIA · LATIN AMERICA & CARIBBEAN · MIDDLE EAST & NORTH AFRICA · NORTH AMERICA · SOUTH ASIA · SUB-SAHARAN AFRICA

UZBEKISTAN

ECONOMIC COMPLEXITY INDEX [2010] ▸ -0.358 (76) | COMPLEXITY OUTLOOK INDEX [2010] ▸ -0.414 (73) | EXPECTED GDPᴘᴄ GROWTH * ▸ 2.6% (39)

*Expected annual average for the 2010-2020 period.

2010 PRODUCT SPACE ▸

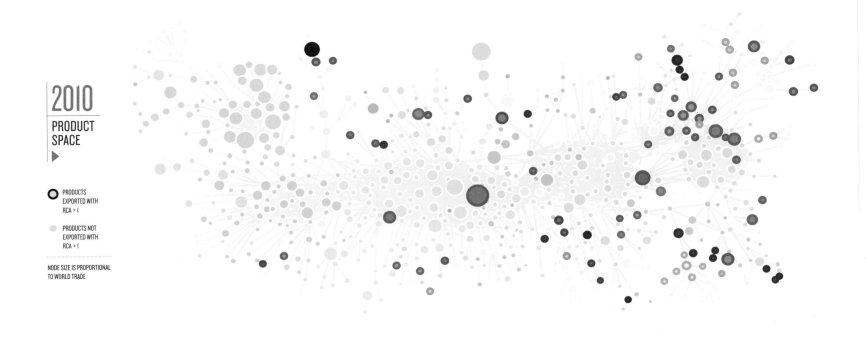

○ PRODUCTS EXPORTED WITH RCA > 1

○ PRODUCTS NOT EXPORTED WITH RCA > 1

NODE SIZE IS PROPORTIONAL TO WORLD TRADE

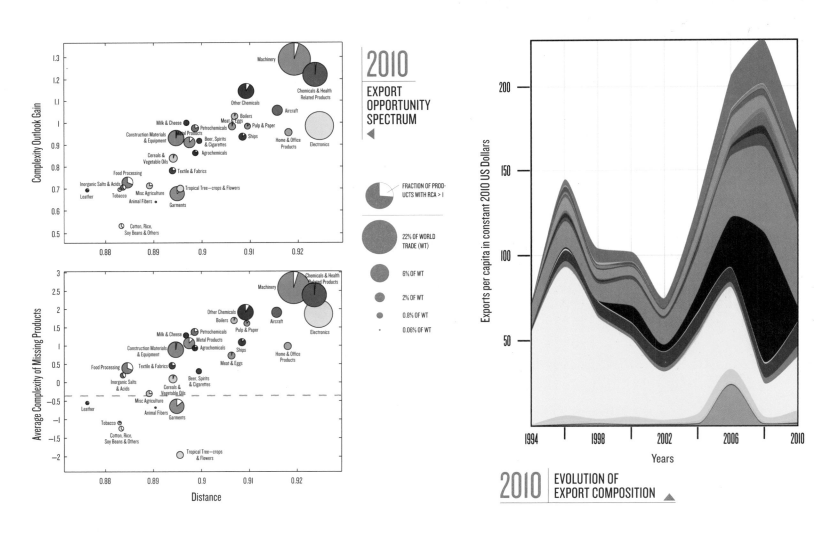

2010 EXPORT OPPORTUNITY SPECTRUM ◂

◔ FRACTION OF PRODUCTS WITH RCA > 1

● 22% OF WORLD TRADE (WT)

● 6% OF WT

● 2% OF WT

● 0.8% OF WT

· 0.06% OF WT

2010 | EVOLUTION OF EXPORT COMPOSITION ▲

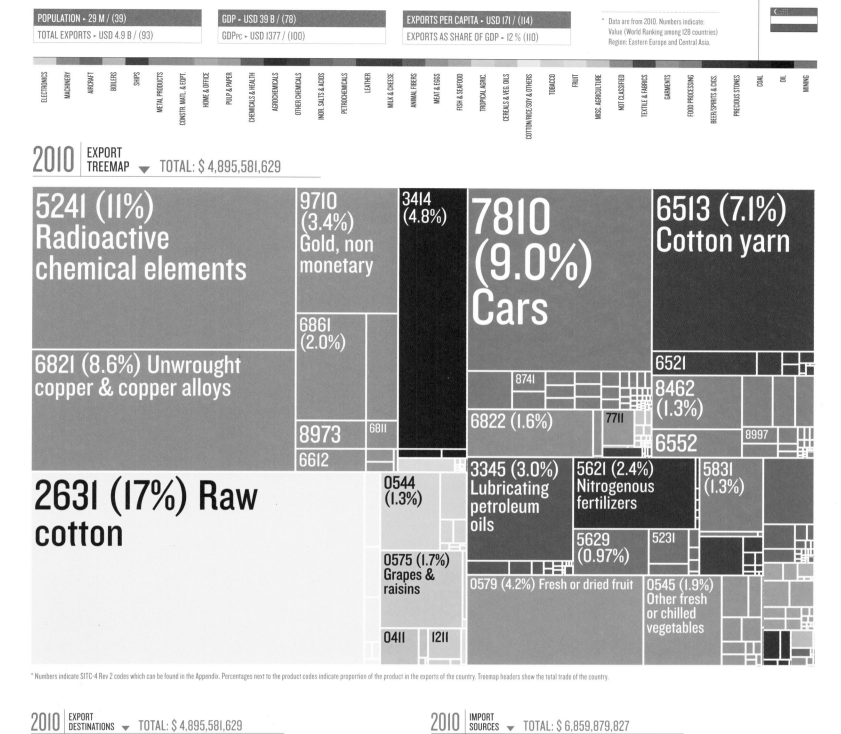

POPULATION ▸ 29 M / (39)
TOTAL EXPORTS ▸ USD 4.9 B / (93)

GDP ▸ USD 39 B / (78)
GDPᴘᴄ ▸ USD 1377 / (100)

EXPORTS PER CAPITA ▸ USD 171 / (114)
EXPORTS AS SHARE OF GDP ▸ 12 % / (110)

* Data are from 2010. Numbers indicate:
Value (World Ranking among 128 countries)
Region: Eastern Europe and Central Asia.

ELECTRONICS · MACHINERY · AIRCRAFT · BOILERS · SHIPS · METAL PRODUCTS · CONSTR. MATL. & EQPT. · HOME & OFFICE · PULP & PAPER · CHEMICALS & HEALTH · AGROCHEMICALS · OTHER CHEMICALS · INOR. SALTS & ACIDS · PETROCHEMICALS · LEATHER · MILK & CHEESE · ANIMAL FIBERS · MEAT & EGGS · FISH & SEAFOOD · TROPICAL AGRIC. · CEREALS & VEG. OILS · COTTON/RICE/SOY & OTHERS · TOBACCO · FRUIT · MISC. AGRICULTURE · NOT CLASSIFIED · TEXTILE & FABRICS · GARMENTS · FOOD PROCESSING · BEER/SPIRITS & CIGS. · PRECIOUS STONES · COAL · OIL · MINING

2010 | EXPORT TREEMAP ▾ TOTAL: $ 4,895,581,629

5241 (11%) Radioactive chemical elements

6821 (8.6%) Unwrought copper & copper alloys

9710 (3.4%) Gold, non monetary

6861 (2.0%)

8973 · 6811

6612

3414 (4.8%)

7810 (9.0%) Cars

8741

6822 (1.6%) · 7711

2631 (17%) Raw cotton

0544 (1.3%)

0575 (1.7%) Grapes & raisins

0411 · 1211

3345 (3.0%) Lubricating petroleum oils

5621 (2.4%) Nitrogenous fertilizers

5629 (0.97%) · 5231

0579 (4.2%) Fresh or dried fruit

6513 (7.1%) Cotton yarn

6521

8462 (1.3%)

6552 · 8997

5831 (1.3%)

0545 (1.9%) Other fresh or chilled vegetables

* Numbers indicate SITC-4 Rev 2 codes which can be found in the Appendix. Percentages next to the product codes indicate proportion of the product in the exports of the country. Treemap headers show the total trade of the country.

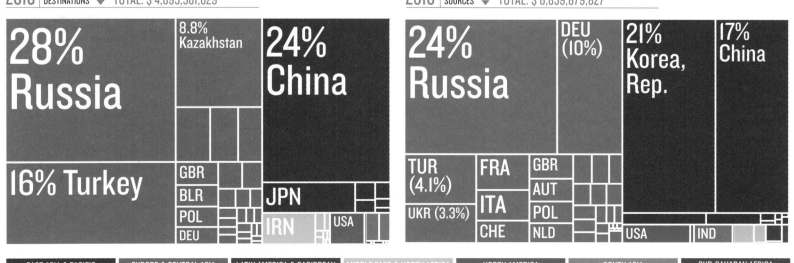

2010 | EXPORT DESTINATIONS ▾ TOTAL: $ 4,895,581,629

28% Russia

16% Turkey

8.8% Kazakhstan

GBR
BLR
POL
DEU

24% China

JPN

IRN · USA

2010 | IMPORT SOURCES ▾ TOTAL: $ 6,859,879,827

24% Russia

TUR (4.1%)
UKR (3.3%)

FRA
ITA
CHE

DEU (10%)

GBR
AUT
POL
NLD

21% Korea, Rep.

USA

17% China

IND

EAST ASIA & PACIFIC · EUROPE & CENTRAL ASIA · LATIN AMERICA & CARIBBEAN · MIDDLE EAST & NORTH AFRICA · NORTH AMERICA · SOUTH ASIA · SUB-SAHARAN AFRICA

VENEZUELA, RB

ECONOMIC COMPLEXITY INDEX [2010] ▸ -0.937 (103) | COMPLEXITY OUTLOOK INDEX [2010] ▸ -0.976 (107) | EXPECTED GDPPc GROWTH * ▸ -1.0% (125)

*Expected annual average for the 2010-2020 period.

2010 PRODUCT SPACE ▶

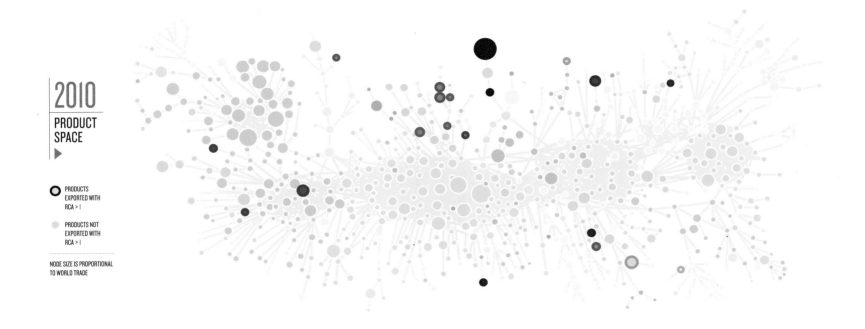

○ PRODUCTS EXPORTED WITH RCA > 1

○ PRODUCTS NOT EXPORTED WITH RCA > 1

NODE SIZE IS PROPORTIONAL TO WORLD TRADE

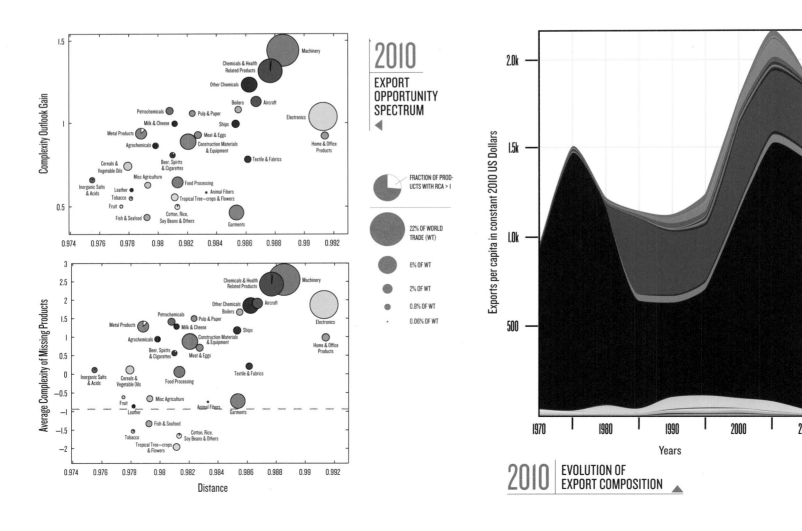

2010 EXPORT OPPORTUNITY SPECTRUM ◀

FRACTION OF PRODUCTS WITH RCA > 1

22% OF WORLD TRADE (WT)

6% OF WT

2% OF WT

0.8% OF WT

0.06% OF WT

2010 EVOLUTION OF EXPORT COMPOSITION ▲

POPULATION ▸ 29 M / (38)	GDP ▸ USD 394 B / (25)	EXPORTS PER CAPITA ▸ USD 1,925 / (56)	* Data are from 2010. Numbers indicate:
TOTAL EXPORTS ▸ USD 56 B / (44)	GDPPC ▸ USD 13,658 / (37)	EXPORTS AS SHARE OF GDP ▸ 14 % (104)	Value (World Ranking among 128 countries) Region: Latin America and the Caribbean.

ELECTRONICS · MACHINERY · AIRCRAFT · BOILERS · SHIPS · METAL PRODUCTS · CONSTR. MATL. & EQPT. · HOME & OFFICE · PULP & PAPER · CHEMICALS & HEALTH · AGROCHEMICALS · OTHER CHEMICALS · INOR. SALTS & ACIDS · PETROCHEMICALS · LEATHER · MILK & CHEESE · ANIMAL FIBERS · MEAT & EGGS · FISH & SEAFOOD · TROPICAL AGRIC. · CEREALS & VEG. OILS · COTTON/RICE/SOY & OTHERS · TOBACCO · FRUIT · MISC. AGRICULTURE · NOT CLASSIFIED · TEXTILE & FABRICS · GARMENTS · FOOD PROCESSING · BEER/SPIRITS & CIGS. · PRECIOUS STONES · COAL · OIL · MINING

2010 | EXPORT TREEMAP ▼ TOTAL: $ 55,500,881,992

3330 (72%) Crude petroleum

3345 (18%) Lubricating petroleum oils

5621

6713 (1.1%)

*Numbers indicate SITC-4 Rev 2 codes which can be found in the Appendix. Percentages next to the product codes indicate proportion of the product in the exports of the country. Treemap headers show the total trade of the country.

2010 | EXPORT DESTINATIONS ▼ TOTAL: $ 55,500,881,992

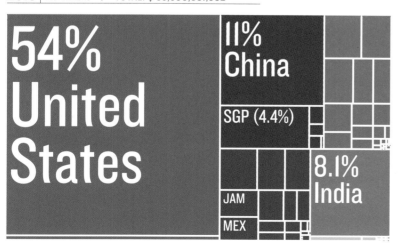

54% United States

11% China

SGP (4.4%)

8.1% India

JAM

MEX

2010 | IMPORT SOURCES ▼ TOTAL: $ 30,833,384,225

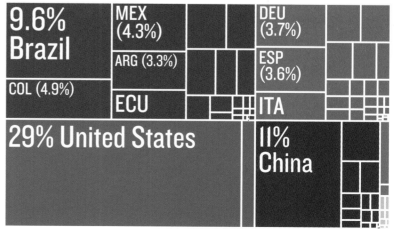

9.6% Brazil

MEX (4.3%)

ARG (3.3%)

COL (4.9%)

ECU

DEU (3.7%)

ESP (3.6%)

ITA

29% United States

11% China

EAST ASIA & PACIFIC · EUROPE & CENTRAL ASIA · LATIN AMERICA & CARIBBEAN · MIDDLE EAST & NORTH AFRICA · NORTH AMERICA · SOUTH ASIA · SUB-SAHARAN AFRICA

VIETNAM

ECONOMIC COMPLEXITY INDEX [2010] ► -0.248 (70) | **COMPLEXITY OUTLOOK INDEX [2010] ► 0.99 (25)** | **EXPECTED GDPᴘᴄ GROWTH * ► 3.8% (5)**

*Expected annual average for the 2010-2020 period.

2010
PRODUCT SPACE ▶

○ PRODUCTS EXPORTED WITH RCA > 1

● PRODUCTS NOT EXPORTED WITH RCA > 1

NODE SIZE IS PROPORTIONAL TO WORLD TRADE

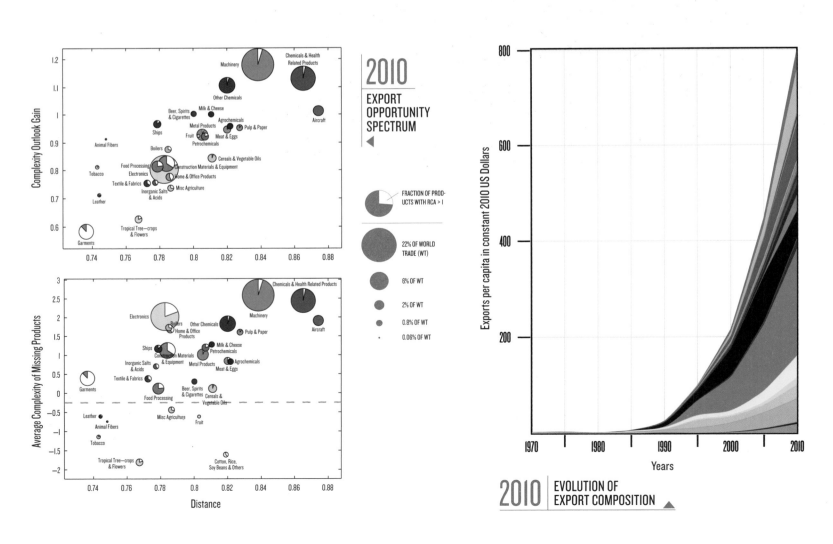

2010
EXPORT OPPORTUNITY SPECTRUM ◀

⬤ FRACTION OF PRODUCTS WITH RCA > 1

⬤ 22% OF WORLD TRADE (WT)

⬤ 6% OF WT

⬤ 2% OF WT

• 0.8% OF WT

· 0.06% OF WT

2010 | EVOLUTION OF EXPORT COMPOSITION ▲

POPULATION ▸ 87 M / (13)
TOTAL EXPORTS ▸ USD 70 B / (38)

GDP ▸ USD 106 B / (57)
GDPᴘᴄ ▸ USD 1,224 / (106)

EXPORTS PER CAPITA ▸ USD 804 / (79)
EXPORTS AS SHARE OF GDP ▸ 66 % (7)

* Data are from 2010. Numbers indicate:
Value (World Ranking among 128 countries)
Region: East Asia and Pacific.

ELECTRONICS · MACHINERY · AIRCRAFT · BOILERS · SHIPS · METAL PRODUCTS · CONSTR. MATL. & EQPT. · HOME & OFFICE · PULP & PAPER · CHEMICALS & HEALTH · AGROCHEMICALS · OTHER CHEMICALS · INOR. SALTS & ACIDS · PETROCHEMICALS · LEATHER · MILK & CHEESE · ANIMAL FIBERS · MEAT & EGGS · FISH & SEAFOOD · TROPICAL AGRIC. · CEREALS & VEG. OILS · COTTON/RICE/SOY & OTHERS · TOBACCO · FRUIT · MISC. AGRICULTURE · NOT CLASSIFIED · TEXTILE & FABRICS · GARMENTS · FOOD PROCESSING · BEER/SPIRITS & CIGS. · PRECIOUS STONES · COAL · OIL · MINING

2010 EXPORT TREEMAP ▼ TOTAL: $ 69,896,078,034

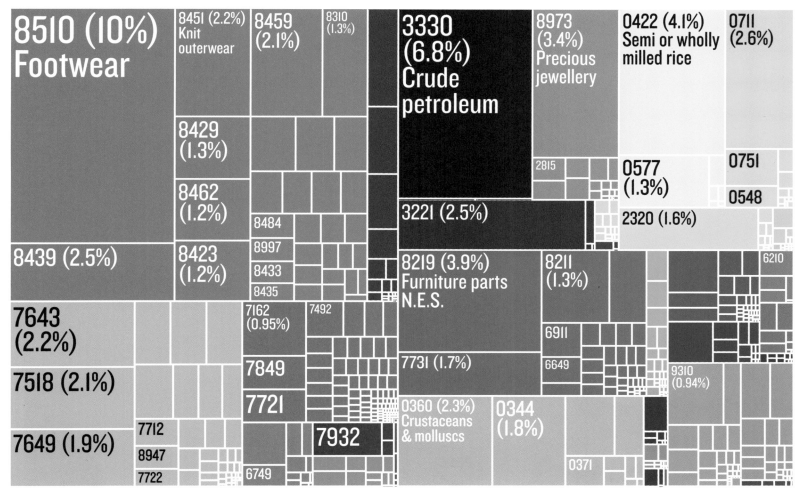

* Numbers indicate SITC-4 Rev 2 codes which can be found in the Appendix. Percentages next to the product codes indicate proportion of the product in the exports of the country. Treemap headers show the total trade of the country.

2010 EXPORT DESTINATIONS ▼ TOTAL: $ 69,896,078,034

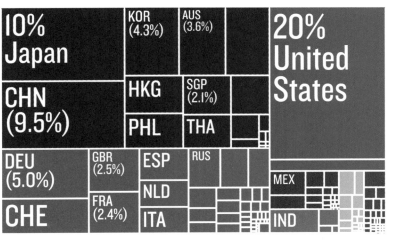

2010 IMPORT SOURCES ▼ TOTAL: $ 72,249,594,822

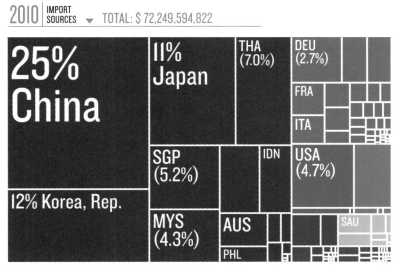

EAST ASIA & PACIFIC · EUROPE & CENTRAL ASIA · LATIN AMERICA & CARIBBEAN · MIDDLE EAST & NORTH AFRICA · NORTH AMERICA · SOUTH ASIA · SUB-SAHARAN AFRICA

YEMEN

ECONOMIC COMPLEXITY INDEX [2010] ▸ -1.535 (121) | COMPLEXITY OUTLOOK INDEX [2010] ▸ -1.185 (127) | EXPECTED GDPᴘᴄ GROWTH * ▸ 0.5% (105)

*Expected annual average for the 2010-2020 period.

2010 PRODUCT SPACE ▸

○ PRODUCTS EXPORTED WITH RCA > 1

○ PRODUCTS NOT EXPORTED WITH RCA > 1

NODE SIZE IS PROPORTIONAL TO WORLD TRADE

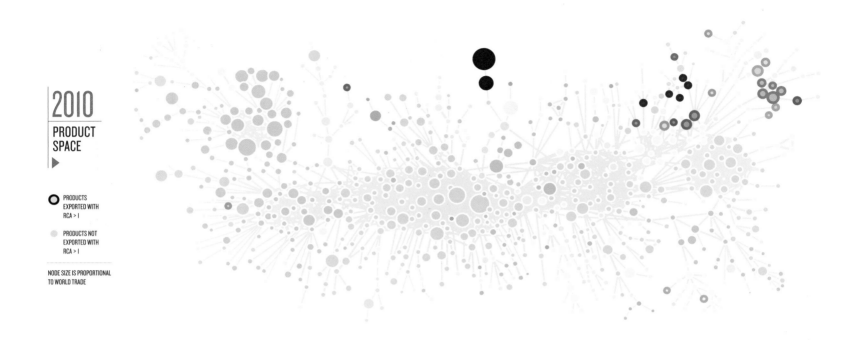

2010 EXPORT OPPORTUNITY SPECTRUM ◂

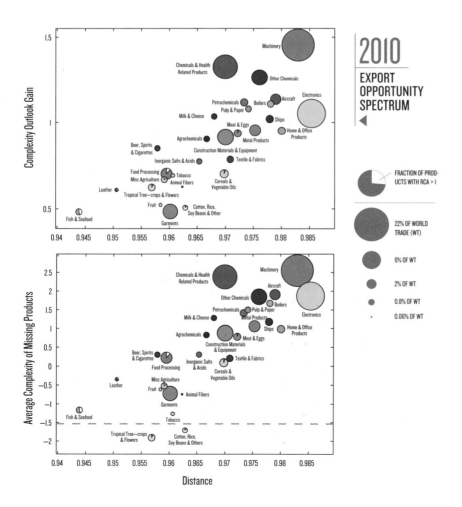

◓ FRACTION OF PRODUCTS WITH RCA > 1

● 22% OF WORLD TRADE (WT)

● 6% OF WT

● 2% OF WT

● 0.8% OF WT

· 0.06% OF WT

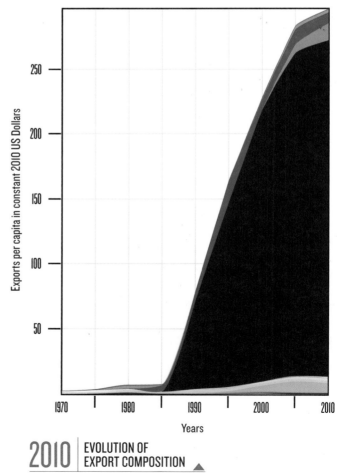

2010 EVOLUTION OF EXPORT COMPOSITION ▲

POPULATION ▸ 24 M / (43)	GDP ▸ USD 31 B / (85)	EXPORTS PER CAPITA ▸ USD 298 / (105)
TOTAL EXPORTS ▸ USD 7.2 B / (83)	GDPᴘᴄ ▸ USD 1,291 / (103)	EXPORTS AS SHARE OF GDP ▸ 23 % / (71)

* Data are from 2010. Numbers indicate:
Value (World Ranking among 128 countries)
Region: Middle East and North Africa.

ELECTRONICS · MACHINERY · AIRCRAFT · BOILERS · SHIPS · METAL PRODUCTS · CONSTR. MATL. & EQPT. · HOME & OFFICE · PULP & PAPER · CHEMICALS & HEALTH · AGROCHEMICALS · OTHER CHEMICALS · INGR. SALTS & ACIDS · PETROCHEMICALS · LEATHER · MILK & CHEESE · ANIMAL FIBERS · MEAT & EGGS · FISH & SEAFOOD · TROPICAL AGRIC. · CEREALS & VEG. OILS · COTTON/RICE/SOY & OTHERS · TOBACCO · FRUIT · MISC. AGRICULTURE · NOT CLASSIFIED · TEXTILE & FABRICS · GARMENTS · FOOD PROCESSING · BEER/SPIRITS & CIGS. · PRECIOUS STONES · COAL · OIL · MINING

2010 | EXPORT TREEMAP ▾ TOTAL: $ 7,158,061,965

3330 (72%) Crude petroleum

3413 (15%) liquified hydrocarbons

0341 (1.1%)

0350

3345 (2.3%)

5839

0741

0579

0545

* Numbers indicate SITC-4 Rev 2 codes which can be found in the Appendix. Percentages next to the product codes indicate proportion of the product in the exports of the country. Treemap headers show the total trade of the country.

2010 | EXPORT DESTINATIONS ▾ TOTAL: $ 7,158,061,965

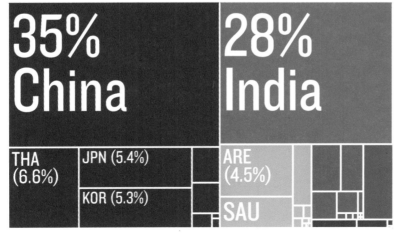

35% China
28% India
THA (6.6%)
JPN (5.4%)
KOR (5.3%)
ARE (4.5%)
SAU

2010 | IMPORT SOURCES ▾ TOTAL: $ 6,754,662,367

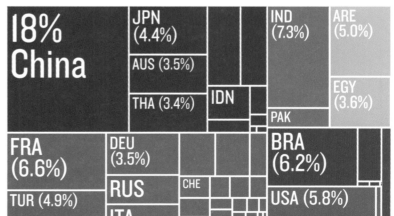

18% China
JPN (4.4%)
AUS (3.5%)
THA (3.4%)
IDN
IND (7.3%)
ARE (5.0%)
EGY (3.6%)
PAK
FRA (6.6%)
DEU (3.5%)
CHE
BRA (6.2%)
TUR (4.9%)
RUS
ITA
USA (5.8%)

EAST ASIA & PACIFIC · EUROPE & CENTRAL ASIA · LATIN AMERICA & CARIBBEAN · MIDDLE EAST & NORTH AFRICA · NORTH AMERICA · SOUTH ASIA · SUB-SAHARAN AFRICA

ZAMBIA

ECONOMIC COMPLEXITY INDEX [2010] ▸ -0.676 (93)   **COMPLEXITY OUTLOOK INDEX [2010]** ▸ -0.927 (101)   **EXPECTED GDPᴘᴄ GROWTH *** ▸ 1.9% (64)

*Expected annual average for the 2010-2020 period.

2010 PRODUCT SPACE ▸

- ● PRODUCTS EXPORTED WITH RCA > 1
- ○ PRODUCTS NOT EXPORTED WITH RCA > 1

NODE SIZE IS PROPORTIONAL TO WORLD TRADE

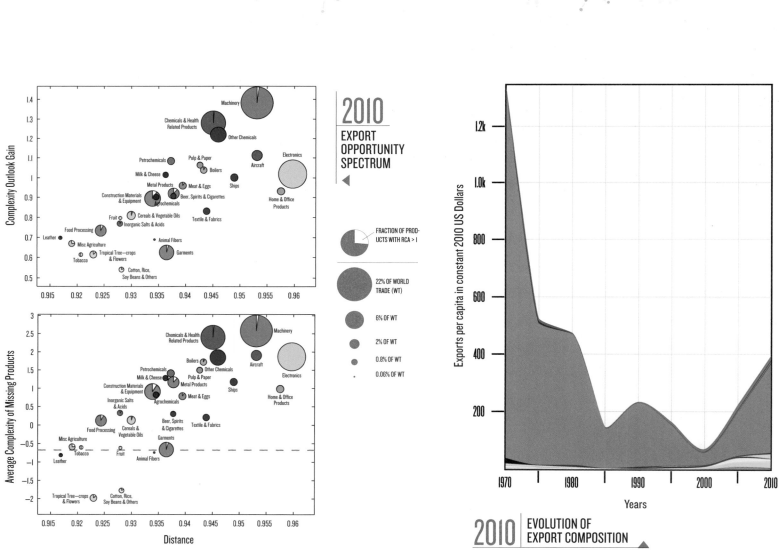

2010 EXPORT OPPORTUNITY SPECTRUM ◂

- FRACTION OF PRODUCTS WITH RCA > 1
- 22% OF WORLD TRADE (WT)
- 6% OF WT
- 2% OF WT
- 0.8% OF WT
- 0.06% OF WT

2010 | EVOLUTION OF EXPORT COMPOSITION ▸

POPULATION ▸ 13 M / (61)	GDP ▸ USD 16 B / (101)	EXPORTS PER CAPITA ▸ USD 397 / (99)
TOTAL EXPORTS ▸ USD 5.1 B / (91)	GDPᴘᴄ ▸ USD 1,253 / (104)	EXPORTS AS SHARE OF GDP ▸ 32 % (49)

* Data are from 2010. Numbers indicate:
Value (World Ranking among 128 countries)
Region: Sub-Saharan Africa.

ELECTRONICS · MACHINERY · AIRCRAFT · BOILERS · SHIPS · METAL PRODUCTS · CONSTR. MATL. & EQPT. · HOME & OFFICE · PULP & PAPER · CHEMICALS & HEALTH · AGROCHEMICALS · OTHER CHEMICALS · INOR. SALTS & ACIDS · PETROCHEMICALS · LEATHER · MILK & CHEESE · ANIMAL FIBERS · MEAT & EGGS · FISH & SEAFOOD · TROPICAL AGRIC. · CEREALS & VEG. OILS · COTTON/RICE/SOY & OTHERS · TOBACCO · FRUIT · MISC. AGRICULTURE · NOT CLASSIFIED · TEXTILE & FABRICS · GARMENTS · FOOD PROCESSING · BEER/SPIRITS & CIGS. · PRECIOUS STONES · COAL · OIL · MINING

2010 | EXPORT TREEMAP ▾ · TOTAL: $ 5,131,623,194

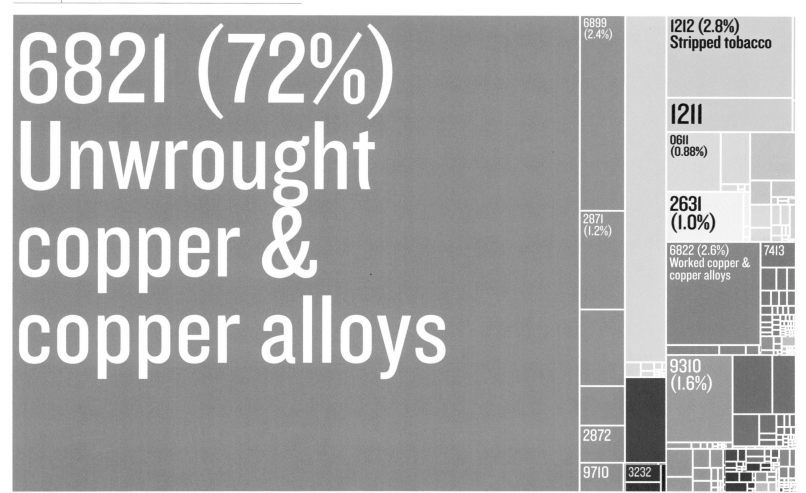

6821 (72%) Unwrought copper & copper alloys

6899 (2.4%)
2871 (1.2%)
2872
9710
3232
1212 (2.8%) Stripped tobacco
1211
0611 (0.88%)
2631 (1.0%)
6822 (2.6%) Worked copper & copper alloys
7413
9310 (1.6%)

* Numbers indicate SITC-4 Rev 2 codes which can be found in the Appendix. Percentages next to the product codes indicate proportion of the product in the exports of the country. Treemap headers show the total trade of the country.

2010 | EXPORT DESTINATIONS ▾ · TOTAL: $ 5,131,623,194

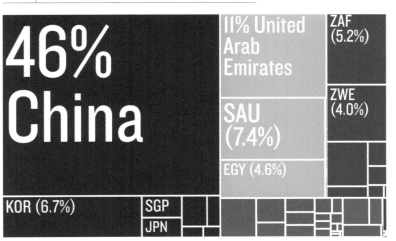

46% China
11% United Arab Emirates
ZAF (5.2%)
ZWE (4.0%)
SAU (7.4%)
EGY (4.6%)
KOR (6.7%)
SGP
JPN

2010 | IMPORT SOURCES ▾ · TOTAL: $ 4,836,831,269

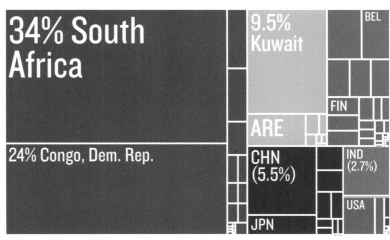

34% South Africa
24% Congo, Dem. Rep.
9.5% Kuwait
BEL
FIN
ARE
CHN (5.5%)
IND (2.7%)
JPN
USA

EAST ASIA & PACIFIC · EUROPE & CENTRAL ASIA · LATIN AMERICA & CARIBBEAN · MIDDLE EAST & NORTH AFRICA · NORTH AMERICA · SOUTH ASIA · SUB-SAHARAN AFRICA

ZIMBABWE

ECONOMIC COMPLEXITY INDEX [2010] ▶ -0.608 (89) | **COMPLEXITY OUTLOOK INDEX [2010]** ▶ -0.59 (79) | **EXPECTED GDPᴘᴄ GROWTH** * ▶ 3.0% (24)

*Expected annual average for the 2010-2020 period.

2010
PRODUCT SPACE
▶

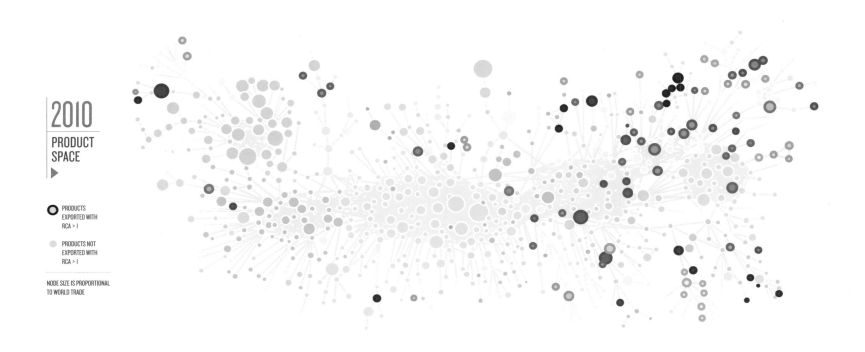

○ PRODUCTS EXPORTED WITH RCA > 1

○ PRODUCTS NOT EXPORTED WITH RCA > 1

NODE SIZE IS PROPORTIONAL TO WORLD TRADE

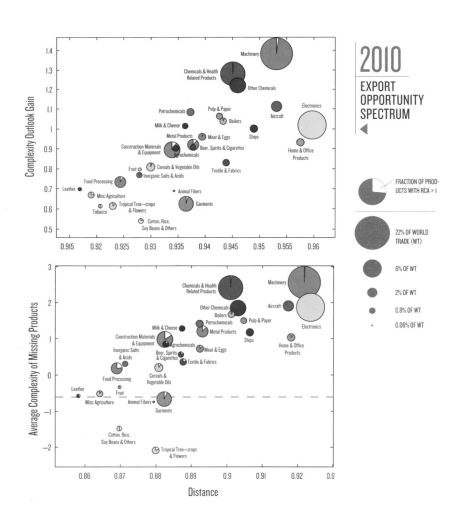

2010
EXPORT OPPORTUNITY SPECTRUM
◀

◔ FRACTION OF PRODUCTS WITH RCA > 1

● 22% OF WORLD TRADE (WT)

● 6% OF WT

● 2% OF WT

● 0.8% OF WT

· 0.06% OF WT

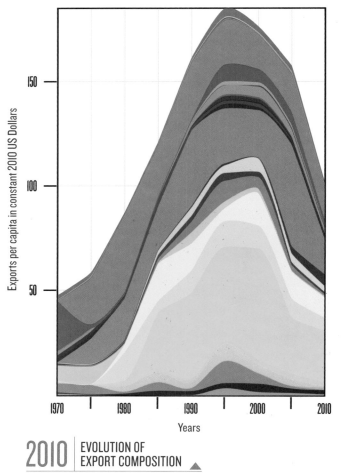

2010 | EVOLUTION OF EXPORT COMPOSITION ▲

* Data are from 2010. Numbers indicate:
Value (World Ranking among 128 countries)
Region: Sub-Saharan Africa.

POPULATION ▸ 13 M / (62)
TOTAL EXPORTS ▸ USD 1.3 B / (120)

GDP ▸ USD 7.5 B / (118)
GDPᴘᴄ ▸ USD 595 / (120)

EXPORTS PER CAPITA ▸ USD 101 / (121)
EXPORTS AS SHARE OF GDP ▸ 17 % (92)

ELECTRONICS · MACHINERY · AIRCRAFT · BOILERS · SHIPS · METAL PRODUCTS · CONSTR. MATL. & EQPT. · HOME & OFFICE · PULP & PAPER · CHEMICALS & HEALTH · AGROCHEMICALS · OTHER CHEMICALS · INOR. SALTS & ACIDS · PETROCHEMICALS · LEATHER · MILK & CHEESE · ANIMAL FIBERS · MEAT & EGGS · FISH & SEAFOOD · TROPICAL AGRIC. · CEREALS & VEG. OILS · COTTON/RICE/SOY & OTHERS · TOBACCO · FRUIT · MISC. AGRICULTURE · NOT CLASSIFIED · TEXTILE & FABRICS · GARMENTS · FOOD PROCESSING · BEER/SPIRITS & CIGS. · PRECIOUS STONES · COAL · OIL · MINING

2010 EXPORT TREEMAP ▾ TOTAL: $ 1,267,893,549

1212 (20%) Stripped tobacco

1223 (1.7%)

1211 (1.3%)

1213 (0.59%)

1222

0571 (1.6%)

2631 (8.0%) Raw cotton

0741 (0.94%)   2223
0577

0611 (4.0%) Raw sugars

2927 (1.6%) Cut flowers

6716 (15%) Ferro alloys

7211
7758

2119 (1.2%)

0360 (0.94%)

8219

6513 (0.55%)   6521

6831 (6.6%) Unwrought nickel & nickel alloys

2879 (4.1%)

6821 (2.5%) Unwrought copper & copper alloys

6612 (1.5%)

6672 (5.5%) Unmounted diamonds

2872   9710

2871

2731 (1.5%)

2789 (0.69%)

2785

8931
0579

5322

*Numbers indicate SITC-4 Rev 2 codes which can be found in the Appendix. Percentages next to the product codes indicate proportion of the product in the exports of the country. Treemap headers show the total trade of the country.

2010 EXPORT DESTINATIONS ▾ TOTAL: $ 1,267,893,549

ITA (6.4%)

NLD (5.8%)

DEU (3.0%)

GBR (3.0%)

LUX

PRT

ROU

RUS

BEL

14% South Africa

ZMB (5.2%)

18% China

JPN (3.8%)

IDN

HKG

ARE (3.7%)

EGY

USA (4.3%)

2010 IMPORT SOURCES ▾ TOTAL: $ 8,199,333,720

50% South Africa

GBR (2.8%)

ITA

BEL

CHE

CHN (5.8%)

USA (8.5%)

ARE (5.2%)

KWT (3.4%)

EAST ASIA & PACIFIC · EUROPE & CENTRAL ASIA · LATIN AMERICA & CARIBBEAN · MIDDLE EAST & NORTH AFRICA · NORTH AMERICA · SOUTH ASIA · SUB-SAHARAN AFRICA

PRODUCT CODES

▶

SITC4 CODE	PRODUCT
0011	Live bovines
0012	Live sheep & goat
0013	Live swine
0014	Live poultry
0015	Live equine
0111	Bovine meat
0112	Sheep & goat meat
0113	Swine meat
0114	Poultry meat
0115	Equine meat
0116	Bovine & equine entrails
0118	Other animal meats
0121	Other animal entrails
0129	Dried, salted or smoked meat & entrails
0141	Meat & fish extract & juices
0142	Sausages
0149	Other prepared or preserved meat & entrails
0223	Fresh milk & cream
0224	Preserved, concentrated or sweetened milk & cream
0230	Butter
0240	Cheese & curd
0251	Fresh, dried or preserved bird eggs in shell
0252	Fresh dried or preserved bird eggs not in shell
0341	Fresh or chilled fish, excluding fillets
0342	Frozen fish, excluding fillets
0343	Fresh or chilled fish fillets
0344	Frozen fish fillets
0350	Salted, dried or smoked fish
0360	Fresh, chilled, frozen or salted crustaceans & molluscs
0371	Fish N.E.S.
0372	Prepared crustaceans & molluscs
0411	Unmilled durum wheat
0412	Other wheat & meslin, unmilled
0421	Unprepared rice in the husk or husked
0422	Semi or wholly milled rice
0430	Unmilled barley
0440	Unmilled maize
0451	Unmilled rye
0452	Unmilled oats
0459	Unmilled buckwheat, millet & other cereals N.E.S.
0460	Wheat or meslin meal or flour
0470	Meals & flour from cereals other than wheat
0481	Work or prepared cereal grains N.E.S.
0482	Roasted & unroasted malt, including flour

SITC4 CODE	PRODUCT
0483	Pasta
0484	Bakery
0488	Malt extract & cereal preparations containing less than 50% cocoa
0541	Fresh or chilled potatoes, excluding sweet potatoes
0542	Dried or shelled legumes
0544	Fresh or chilled tomatoes
0545	Other fresh or chilled vegetables
0546	Frozen or temporarily preserved vegatables
0548	Fresh & dried vegetables, roots & tubers N.E.S.
0561	Dried or evaporated vegetables, excluding leguminous
0564	Meals & flours from potatoes, fruits & vegetables
0565	Prepared or preserved vegetables
0571	Fresh or dried oranges & m&arines
0572	Fresh or dried citrus N.E.S
0573	Fresh or dried banana & plantains
0574	Fresh apples
0575	Grapes & raisins
0576	Figs
0577	Edible nuts
0579	Fresh or dried fruit N.E.S.
0582	Fruit peels & plant parts preserved by sugar
0583	Jams, jellies & marmalades
0585	Fruit or vegetable juices
0586	Temporarily preserved fruit
0589	Prepared or preserved fruit
0611	Raw sugar beet & cane
0612	Refined sugar
0615	Molasses
0616	Honey
0619	Sugar syrups, caramel & artificial honey
0620	Sugar confectionary (not chocolate)
0711	Green & roasted coffee & coffee substitutes
0712	Coffee extracts, essences or concentrates
0721	Raw & roasted cocoa beans
0722	Unsweetened cocoa powder
0723	Cocoa butter & paste
0730	Chocolate
0741	Tea
0742	Mate
0751	Pepper
0752	Spices other than pepper
0811	Green or dry hay
0812	Bran, sharps & other cereal residues

SITC4 CODE	PRODUCT
0813	Oilcake
0814	Meat and fish flour, not for humans
0819	Animal feed and food waste
0913	Pig and poultry lard and fat
0914	Margarine
0980	Edible products N.E.S.
1110	Non-alcoholic beverages N.E.S.
1121	Wine
1122	Fermented beverages
1123	Beer
1124	Alcoholic beverages
1211	Unstripped tobacco
1212	Wholly or partly stripped tobacco
1213	Tobacco refuse
1221	Cigars
1222	Cigarretes
1223	Tobbacco, extract, essences & manufactures
2111	Raw bovine & equine hides
2112	Raw calf skins
2114	Raw goat skins
2116	Raw sheep skin without wool
2117	Raw sheep skin with wool
2119	Hides and skins N.E.S.
2120	Raw furs
2221	Green groundnuts
2222	Soya beans
2223	Cotton seeds
2224	Sunflower seeds
2225	Sesame seeds
2226	Rape & colza seeds
2231	Copra
2232	Palm nuts & kernels
2234	Linseed
2235	Castor oil seeds
2238	Oil seeds & fruits N.E.S.
2239	Meals and flours from oil seeds
2320	Natural rubber, latex & gums
2331	Synthetic rubber & latex
2332	Reclaimed & scrap rubber
2440	Raw cork
2450	Fuel wood & charcoal
2460	Pulpwood
2471	Sawlogs & veneer logs of coniferous
2472	Sawlogs & veneer logs of non-coniferous

SITC4 CODE	PRODUCT
2479	Pitprops, poles, piling, post and other wood in the rough
2481	Railway or tramway sleepers
2482	Worked wood of coniferous
2483	Worked wood of non-coniferous
2511	Waste paper and paperboard
2512	Mechanical wood pulp
2516	Chemical wood pulp, dissolving grades
2517	Chemical wood pulp, soda or sulphate
2518	Chemical wood pulp, sulphite
2519	Other cellulosic pulps
2613	Raw Silk
2614	Worm cocoons and waste from silk
2631	Raw cotton
2632	Cotton linters
2633	Cotton waste
2634	Cotton
2640	Raw processed jute and other fibres
2651	Flax & ramie
2652	True Hemp
2654	Agave fibers
2655	Manila hemp
2659	Vegetable textile fibres N.E.S.
2665	No carded discontinuous synthetic fibres
2666	Continuous synthetic fibres
2667	Carded discontinuous synthetic fibres
2671	Regenerated fibre
2672	Waste of man-made fibres
2681	Sheep or lambs greasy wool
2682	Degreased sheep or lambs wool
2683	Fine animal hair
2685	Coarse animal hair
2686	Animal hair waste N.E.S.
2687	Carded animal hair
2690	Rags
2711	Crude fertilizer
2712	Natural sodium nitrate
2713	Natural calcium phosphates & aluminium
2714	Crude natural potassium salts
2731	Building stone
2732	Gypsum, plasters, limestone flux & calcareous stone
2733	Non metal-bearing sands
2734	Stones
2741	Other Sulphurs
2742	Unroasted iron pyrites

SITC4 CODE	PRODUCT
2771	Industrial diamonds
2772	Other natural abrasives
2782	Clay & refractory minerals, N.E.S.
2783	Sodium chloride
2784	Asbestos
2785	Quartz metal family
2786	Metal waste
2789	Crude minerals N.E.S.
2814	Roasted iron pyrites
2815	Not agglomerated iron ore
2816	Agglomerated iron ore
2820	Iron & steel waste
2860	Uranium & thorium
2871	Copper
2872	Nickel
2873	Aluminium ore
2874	Lead ore
2875	Zinc
2876	Tin
2877	Manganese
2879	Other non-ferrous base metals
2881	Ash
2882	Other non-ferrous base metals
2890	Ores and precious metals
2911	Bones, horns, corals & ivory
2919	Animal origin materials
2922	Natural gums, resins, lacs & balsams
2923	Vegetable plaiting materials
2924	Flora in pharmacy
2925	Planting seeds & spores
2926	Live plants
2927	Flora
2929	Vegetable origin materials
3221	Anthracite
3222	Other coal
3223	Lignite
3224	Peat
3231	Solid fuels
3232	Coke & semi-coke of coal
3330	Crude petroleum
3345	Lubricating petroleum oils N.E.S.
3351	Petroleum jelly & mineral waxes
3352	Mineral tars
3353	Mineral tar pitch

SITC4 CODE	PRODUCT
3354	Petroleum bitumen N.E.S.
3413	liquified hydrocarbons
3414	petroleum gases
3415	Coal & water gases
3510	Electric current
4111	Fat & oils of marine animals
4113	Animal oils N.E.S.
4232	Soya bean oil
4233	Cotton seed oil
4234	Peanut oil
4235	Olive oil
4236	Sunflower seed oil
4239	Other soft vegetable oils
4241	Linseed oil
4242	Palm oil
4243	Coconut oil
4244	Palm kernel oil
4245	Castor oil
4249	Vegetable oils N.E.S.
4311	Processed oils
4312	Hydrogenated oils
4313	Fatty & oil acids
4314	Waxes
5111	Acyclic hydrocarbons
5112	Cyclic hydrocarbons
5113	Halogenated derivatives of hydrocarbons
5114	Non halogenated hydrocarbons derivatives
5121	Acyclic alcohols & derivatives
5122	Cyclic alcohols & derivatives
5123	Phenols, phenol-alcohols & derivatives
5137	Monocarboxylic acids & derivatives
5138	Polycarboxylic acids & derivatives
5139	Oxygen-function acids & derivatives
5145	Amine-function compounds
5146	Oxygen-function amino-compounds
5147	Amide-function compounds, excluding urea
5148	Other nitrogen-function compounds
5154	Organo-sulphur compounds
5155	Other organo-inorganic compounds
5156	Heterocyclic compound; nucleic acids
5157	Sulphonamides, sultones & sultams
5161	Ethers, epoxides, acetals
5162	Aldehyde, ketone & quinone-function compounds.
5163	Inorganic esters & derivatives

SITC4 CODE	PRODUCT
5169	Organic chemicals
5221	Chemical elements
5222	Non-metals inorganic acids & oxygen compounds
5223	Halogen & non-metal sulphur compounds
5224	Metallic oxides of zinc, iron, lead, chromium etc
5225	Inorganic bases & metallic oxides, hydroxides & peroxides
5231	Inorganic acids metallic salts & peroxysalts
5232	Inorganic acids metallic salts & peroxysalts
5233	Compounds of precious metals
5239	Inorganic chemical products
5241	Radioactive chemical elements
5249	Other radioactive materials
5311	Synthetic organic dyes
5312	Synthetic organic luminophores
5322	Tanning extracts
5323	Synthetic tanning substances
5331	Other colouring matter
5332	Printing inks
5334	Varnishes & lacquers
5335	Glazes, driers, putty
5411	Provitamins & vitamins
5413	Antibiotics
5414	Vegetable alkaloids & derivatives
5415	Bulk hormones
5416	Glycosides & vaccines
5417	Medicaments
5419	Not medicaments pharmaceutical goods
5513	Essential oils
5514	Odoriferous substances
5530	Perfumery & cosmetics
5541	Soaps
5542	Organic surface-active agents N.E.S.
5543	Polishes & creams
5621	Nitrogenous fertilizers
5622	Phosphatic fertilizers
5623	Potassic fertilizers
5629	Fertilizers
5721	Prepared explosives
5722	Initiating devices
5723	Pyrotechnic articles
5821	Phenoplasts
5822	Aminoplasts
5823	Polyesters
5824	Polyamides

SITC4 CODE	PRODUCT
5825	Polyurethanes
5826	Epoxide resins
5827	Silicones
5829	Other condensation products
5831	Polyethylene
5832	Polypropylene
5833	Polystyrene
5834	Polyvinyl chloride
5835	Copolymers of vinyl chloride & vinyl acetate
5836	Acrylic & methaacrylic polymers & copolymers
5837	Polyvinyl acetate
5838	Polymerization/copolymerization ion exchangers
5839	Other polymerization & copolymarization products
5841	Regenerated cellulose
5842	Cellulose nitrates
5843	Cellulose acetates
5849	Derivates of cellulose
5851	Derivatives of natural rubber
5852	Artificial plastic materials
5911	Insecticides
5912	Fungicides
5913	Herbicides
5914	Disinfectants
5921	Starches
5922	Glues
5981	Woods & resin chemical products
5982	Anti-knock & anti-corrosive preparation
5983	Organic chemical products
5989	Chemical products
6112	Leather sheets or rolls
6113	Calf leather
6114	Bovine & equine leather
6115	Sheep & lamb leather
6116	Leather of other hides or skins
6118	Dressed or finished leather
6121	Leather articles used in machinery
6122	Saddlery & harness
6123	Non-metal & non-abestos footwear material
6129	Other articles of leather
6130	Tanned or dressed furskins
6210	Materials of rubber
6251	Tires & pneumatic for cars
6252	Tires & pneumatic for buses
6253	Tires & pneumatic for aircraft

SITC4 CODE	PRODUCT
6254	Tires & pneumatic for bikes
6259	Other tires articles
6281	Rubber for hygienic & pharmaceutical articles
6282	Transmission & conveyor belts
6289	Other articles of rubber
6330	Cork manufactures
6341	Wood sawn lengthwise up to 5 mm in thickness
6342	Sheets of plywood
6343	Improved wood & reconstituted wood
6344	Wood-based panels
6349	Simply shaped wood N.E.S.
6351	Wood boxes
6352	Coopers products
6353	Builders` carpentry & joinery
6354	Decorative manufactures of wood
6359	Manufactured of wood N.E.S.
6411	Newsprint
6412	Printing & writing paper in rolls or seets
6413	Rolls/sheets of kraft paper
6415	Paper & paperboad in rolls or sheets
6416	Fibre building board of wood
6417	Rolls/sheets of creped paper
6418	Rolls/sheets of coated paper
6419	Converted paper N.E.S.
6421	Paper packing containers
6422	Correspondence stationary
6423	Books & registers
6424	Cut to size paper N.E.S.
6428	Articles of paper pulp N.E.S.
6511	Silk yarn & spun from noil and waste
6512	Wool yarn or animal hair
6513	Cotton yarn
6514	Yarn not for retail (>=85% synthetic fibres)
6515	Yarn for retail (>=85% synthetic fibres)
6516	Yarn (<85% synthetic fibres)
6517	Yarn of regenerated fibres not for retail
6518	Yarn of regenerated fibres
6519	Yarn of textile fibres
6521	Unbleached cotton woven fabrics
6522	Finished cotton woven fabrics
6531	Continuous synthetic woven fabrics
6532	>=85% discontinuous synthetic woven fabrics
6534	<85% discontinuous synthetic woven fabrics
6535	"Continuous regenerated woven fabrics"

SITC4 CODE	PRODUCT
6536	>=85% continuous regenerated woven fabrics
6538	<85% continuous regenerated woven fabrics
6539	Man-made pile & chenille woven fabrics
6541	Silk woven fabrics
6542	>=85% wool woven fabrics
6543	Wool woven fabrics N.E.S.
6544	Flar/ramie woven fabrics
6545	Jute woven fabrics
6546	Glass fibre fabrics
6549	Woven fabrics N.E.S.
6551	Knitted synthetic fibres
6552	Non synthetic knitted fibres
6553	Elastic knitted fibres
6560	Tulle, lace, ribbons & similar
6571	Not coated articles of felt N.E.S.
6572	Not coated bonded fibre fabrics
6573	Coated textile fabrics N.E.S.
6574	Elastic fabrics and trimming
6575	Ropes & cables
6576	Hats & hoods
6577	Wadding, wicks & textiles fabrics
6579	Special products of textile
6581	Bags & sacks for packing
6582	Textile camping goods
6583	Travelling rugs & blankets
6584	Linens & furnishing textile articles
6589	Other textile articles N.E.S.
6591	Linoleum
6592	Knotted carpets
6593	Kelem, schumacks & karamanie
6594	Wool carpets
6595	Man-made carpets N.E.S.
6596	Other materials carpets N.E.S.
6597	Plaited products
6611	Lime
6612	Cement
6613	Building & monumental stone
6618	Asbestos/fibre cements
6623	Refractory bricks
6624	Non-refractory ceramic bricks
6631	Polishing stones
6632	Abrasive powder
6633	Non ceramic mineral materials N.E.S.
6635	Mineral wool N.E.S.

SITC4 CODE	PRODUCT
6637	Refractory goods N.E.S.
6638	Asbestos manufactures
6639	Ceramic materials articles N.E.S.
6641	Nonoptical balls, rods or tubes of glass
6642	Optical glass
6643	Unworked drawn or blown gladd
6644	Unworked surface-ground cast glass
6645	Unworked cast glass
6646	Pressed or moulded glass
6647	Safety glass
6648	Mirrors
6649	Glass N.E.S.
6651	Glass bottles
6652	Glassware
6658	Glass articles N.E.S.
6664	Porcelain
6665	Pottery
6666	Ceramic & porcelain ornaments N.E.S.
6671	Not mounted pearls
6672	Not mounted diamonds
6673	Not mounted precious stones
6674	Synthetic precious stones
6712	Pig & cast iron
6713	Iron & steel powders
6716	Ferro-alloys
6724	Iron/steel bars
6725	Iron/steel billets
6727	Iron/steel coils
6731	Iron/steel wire rod
6732	Iron/steel rods
6733	Iron/steel shapes
6744	Iron/steel >=4.75mm tick sheets
6745	Iron/steel 3 - 4.75mm tick sheets
6746	Iron/steel <3mm tick sheets
6747	Steel tinned sheets
6749	Other worked iron/steel sheets
6760	Iron/steel rail construction materials
6770	Not insulated iron/steel wire
6781	Iron pipes
6782	Seamless tubes, pipes of iron or steel
6783	Other iron or steel tubes & pipes
6785	Iron or steel tubes, pipes, & fittings
6793	Iron/steel rough forging & stampings
6794	Iron/steel rough castings

SITC4 CODE	PRODUCT
6811	Unwrought silver
6812	Unwrought metals of platinum
6821	Unwrought copper & copper alloys
6822	Worked copper & copper alloys
6831	Unwrought nickel & nickel alloys
6832	Worked nickel & nickel alloys
6841	Unwrought aluminium & aluminium alloys
6842	Worked aluminium & aluminium alloys
6851	Unwrought lead & alloys
6852	Worked lead & alloys
6861	Unwrought zinc & alloys
6863	Worked zinc & alloys
6871	Unwrought tin & alloys
6872	Worked tin & alloys
6880	Depleted uranium & waste N.E.S.
6891	Waste of unwrought tungsten and related metals
6899	Waste of unwrought cermets & base metals
6911	Iron/steel structures
6912	Aluminium structures
6921	>300lt capacity metal tanks
6924	Metal cask for packing goods
6931	Wires, cables & ropes
6932	Barbed wire
6935	Gauze & netting
6940	Nails, nuts & bolts
6951	Farming and forestry hand tools
6953	Other handtools
6954	Interchangeable hand and machine tools
6960	Cutlery
6973	Domestic non-electric stoves
6974	Base metal domestic articles N.E.S.
6975	Base metal indoors sanitary ware N.E.S.
6978	Base metal household appliances N.E.S.
6991	Base metal locksmiths wares N.E.S.
6992	Metal chains
6993	Pins and needles
6994	Metal springs
6996	Miscellaneous articles of base metal
6997	Articles of iron or steel N.E.S.
6998	Metal articles N.E.S.
6999	Other base metal manufactures N.E.S.
7111	Super-heated water boiler
7112	Condensers
7119	Parts of boilers N.E.S.

SITC4 CODE	PRODUCT
7126	Steam power units
7129	Parts of steam power units N.E.S.
7131	Internal combustion engines for aircraft
7132	Internal combustion engines for motor vehicles
7133	Internal combustion piston engines for ships & boats
7138	Internal combustion piston engines N.E.S.
7139	Piston engines parts N.E.S.
7144	Reaction engines
7148	Gas turbines N.E.S.
7149	Parts of gas & reaction engines
7161	DC motors & generators
7162	AC electric motors & generators
7163	Rotary converters
7169	Parts of rotating electric plants N.E.S.
7187	Nuclear reactors
7188	Engines & motors
7211	Machinery for soil preparation
7212	Harvesting & threshing machines
7213	Diary machinery
7219	Agricultural machinery, appliances, & parts
7223	Track-laying tractors
7224	Wheeled tractors
7233	Road rollers
7234	Construction & mining machinery
7239	Bulldozers, angledozers & levellers parts N.E.S.
7243	Sewing machines & parts N.E.S.
7244	Textile machinery
7245	Weaving, knitting & yarn preparing machines
7246	Auxiliary weaving machinery
7247	Cleaning & cutting textile machinery N.E.S.
7248	Tanning leather machinery N.E.S.
7251	Cellulose pulp making machines
7252	Paper making machines
7259	Parts of paper making machines
7263	Type-setting machines
7264	Printing presses
7267	Other printing machines
7268	Bookbinding machines
7269	Parts of printing press machines
7271	Grain milling machinery
7272	Food processing machinery & parts N.E.S.
7281	Specialized industry machinery tools & parts N.E.S
7283	Mineral working machinery & parts N.E.S.
7284	Specialized industry machinery & parts N.E.S

SITC4 CODE	PRODUCT
7361	Metal cutting machine-tools
7362	Metal forming machine-tools
7367	Working metal & metal carbides machines N.E.S.
7368	Dividing heads for machine-tools
7369	Metalworking machine-tools parts
7371	Metal foundry equipment & parts N.E.S.
7372	Rolling mills
7373	Welding, brazing & cutting machines & appliances N.E.S.
7411	Gas generators & parts
7412	Furnace burners, mechanical stokers & parts
7413	Furnaces, ovens & parts N.E.S.
7414	Non-domestic refrigerators & parts N.E.S.
7415	Air conditioning machines
7416	Heating & cooling equipment N.E.S.
7421	Reciprocating pumps
7422	Centrifugal pumps
7423	Rotary pumps
7428	Other pumps for liquids & liquid elevators
7429	Pumps & liquid elevators parts N.E.S.
7431	Air pumps, vacuum pumps & compressors
7432	Parts of pumps and compressors
7434	Fans & parts N.E.S.
7435	Centrifuges
7436	Liquid & gas filters & purifiers
7439	Centrifuges machinery parts N.E.S.
7441	Work trucks
7442	Lifting & loading machinery
7449	Centrifugal pumps parts N.E.S.
7451	Non-electric powertools
7452	Non-electrical machines parts N.E.S.
7491	Roller bearings
7492	Valves
7493	Mechanical tools for building
7499	Non-electric parts of machinery N.E.S.
7511	Typewriters & cheque-writing machines
7512	Calculating & ticketing machines
7518	Office machines N.E.S.
7521	Analogue data processing machines
7522	Digital data processing machines
7523	CPUs
7525	Control & peripheral hardware
7528	Data processing equipment N.E.S.
7591	Parts of type writters
7599	Parts of cash registers & calculating machines

SITC4 CODE	PRODUCT
7611	Color T.V.
7612	Black & White T.V.
7621	Vehicles radio receivers
7622	Portable radio receivers
7628	Other radio receivers
7631	Electric record players
7638	Video & sound recorders N.E.S.
7641	Telephone lines
7642	Microphone, amplifiers & loudspeakers
7643	Television & radio transmitters
7648	Telecom equipment N.E.S.
7649	Parts of telecom & sound recording equipment
7711	Electrical transformers
7712	Parts of electric power machinery N.E.S.
7721	Switchboards, relays & fuses
7722	Printed circuits & parts N.E.S.
7723	Electrical resistors
7731	Electric wire
7732	Electrical insulators
7741	Electro-medical equipment
7742	X-ray apparatus
7751	Laundry equipment
7752	Refrigerators & freezers
7753	Dishwashers
7754	Shavers & hair clippers
7757	Electro-mechanical home appliances N.E.S.
7758	Electro-thermal home appliances N.E.S.
7761	T.V. tubes & cathode rays
7762	Electronic valves & tubes
7763	Diodes & transistors
7764	Electronic microcircuits
7768	Parts N.E.S. of electronic circuits
7781	Batteries
7782	Incandescent & fluorescent bulbs
7783	Auto parts
7784	Powertools & parts
7788	Other electrical machinery & equipment N.E.S.
7810	Cars
7821	Trucks & vans
7822	Special purpose trucks & vans
7831	Public transportation vehicles
7832	Tractors for semi-trailers
7841	Chassis fitted with engines
7842	Vehicle bodies

SITC4 CODE	PRODUCT
7849	Other vehicles parts
7851	Motorcycles
7852	Bicycles
7853	Wheelchairs
7861	Containers for transportation
7868	Not mechanically propelled vehicles N.E.S.
7911	Electric trains
7912	Rail tenders
7913	Mechanically propelled railway
7914	Not mechanically propelled railway for passengers
7915	Not mechanically propelled railway for freight
7919	Railway track & vehicle parts N.E.S.
7921	Helicopters
7922	Aircrafts of less than 2 tons
7923	Aircrafts of between 2 and 15 tons
7924	Aircrafts of more than 15 tons
7928	Aircraft equipment N.E.S.
7929	Aircraft equipment parts N.E.S.
7931	Warships
7932	Ships & boats
7933	Ships & boats for breaking up
7938	Special floating structures
8121	Parts of not electrical heating equipment N.E.S.
8122	Ceramic fixtures
8124	Lighting fixture & lamp parts N.E.S.
8211	Chairs & seats
8212	Medical & dental furniture
8219	Furniture parts N.E.S.
8310	Luggage & handbags
8421	Men's coats
8422	Men's suits
8423	Men's trousers
8424	Men's jackets
8429	Other men outerwear
8431	Women's coats & jackets
8432	Women's suits
8433	Dresses
8434	Skirts
8435	Blouses
8439	Other women outerwear
8441	Men's undershirt
8442	Men's underwear
8443	Women's underwear
8451	Knitted jerseys, pullovers & cardigans

SITC4 CODE	PRODUCT
8452	Knitted women's suits & dresses
8459	Other knitted outerwear
8461	Under-garments of wool or fine animal hair
8462	Knitted undergarments of cotton
8463	Knitted undergarments of synthetic fibers
8464	Under-garments of other fibres
8465	Corsets
8471	Clothing accessories of textile fabrics
8472	Knitted clothing accessories of textile fabrics
8481	Clothing accessories from leather
8482	Clothing accessories from rubber
8483	Fur clothing (not headgear)
8484	Headgear
8510	Footwear
8710	Optical instruments
8720	Medical instruments N.E.S.
8731	Gas, liquid & electric meters
8732	Non-electrical counting devices
8741	Non-electrical navigating devices, compasses
8742	Drawing & mathematical calculating instruments
8743	Gas, liquid & electric control instruments
8744	Nonmechanical or electrical instruments for physical analysis
8745	Scientific instruments N.E.S.
8748	Electrical measuring & controlling instruments N.E.S.
8749	Parts & accessories for meters & counters
8811	Photo cameras & parts
8812	Movie cameras, projectors & parts
8813	Photo & movie equipment
8821	Photographic chemicals
8822	Photographic film, plates & paper
8830	Cinematographic film (developed)
8841	Lenses
8842	Spectacles
8851	Watches
8852	Clocks
8921	Printed books & maps
8922	Newspapers & journals
8924	Postcards & stickers
8928	Printed matter N.E.S.
8931	Closable plastic packing
8932	Plastic sanitary & toilet articles
8933	Plastic ornaments
8935	Plastic lamps
8939	Miscellaneous articles of plastic

SITC4 CODE	PRODUCT
8941	Strollers & parts
8942	Toys
8946	Non-military arms
8947	Sporting goods
8951	Metal office products
8952	Pens & pencils
8959	Other office supplies
8960	Works of art
8972	Imitation jewellery
8973	Precious jewellery
8974	Other articles of precious metals N.E.S.
8981	Pianos & string instruments
8982	Musical instruments N.E.S.
8983	Sound recording tapes & discs
8989	Musical instrument parts
8991	Carving & molding tools
8993	Candles & matches
8994	Umbrellas & canes
8996	Orthopaedic appliances
8997	Basketwork, wickerwork, brooms & paint rollers
8998	Small-wares & toilet articles
8999	Manufactures N.E.S.
9410	Live animals, N.E.S. (zoo animals, pets, insects, etc)
9510	Armoured fighting vehicles
9610	Coin, non-gold
9710	Gold, non-monetary

GLOSSARY

COMPLEXITY OUTLOOK GAIN is a characteristic of a country–product pair. It measures how much the *Complexity Outlook Index* of a country will change if the country develops the capacity to export the product in question with comparative advantage.

COMPLEXITY OUTLOOK INDEX (COI) is a characteristic of a country. It measures how well a country is positioned in the product space by calculating the distance of the country to the products it is currently not exporting with comparative advantage, weighted by the complexity value of each product. This number is higher for countries that are closer to more products and to products that are more complex.

DISTANCE is a characteristic of a country-product pair. It measures how "far" a product is from a country's current productive capabilities. It is calculated by adding the products in which the country does not have comparative advantage, weighted by their proximity to the product in question.

DIVERSITY $(k_{c,0})$ is a country characteristic. It is the number of products that a country exports with comparative advantage.

ECONOMIC COMPLEXITY INDEX (ECI) is a country characteristic. It is a measure of how diversified and complex a country's export basket is. It is calculated as the mathematical limit—or eigenvector—of a measure based on how many products a country exports and how many other exporters each product has.

PEOPLEBYTE is more than one *personbyte*. It needs to be embedded in an organization or network.

PERSONBYTE is the maximum amount of productive knowledge that an average person can hold.

PRODUCT COMMUNITY is a product characteristic. A product belongs to a community if it is closer to the other members of the community than it is to products outside of the community.

PRODUCT COMPLEXITY INDEX (PCI) is a product characteristic. It is a measure of how complex a product is. It is calculated as the mathematical limit of a measure based on how many countries export the product and how diversified those exporters are.

PROXIMITY is a characteristic of a pair of products. It measures the minimum probability that a country exports product 1 given that it exports product 2 or vice versa.

REVEALED COMPARATIVE ADVANTAGE (RCA) is a characteristic of a country-product pair. It is calculated as the ratio of the share of a product in a country's export basket to the share of that product in world trade. A country has RCA greater than 1 in a certain product if that product represents a larger share of its exports than of world exports.

UBIQUITY $(k_{p,0})$ is a product characteristic. It measures how many countries export a given product with comparative advantage.

REFERENCES & FURTHER READING

▶

SECTION 1: WHAT DO WE MEAN BY ECONOMIC COMPLEXITY?

· Nonaka, I. & Takeuchi, H. "The Knowledge-Creating Company: How Japanese Companies Create the Dynamics of innovation," Oxford University Press (1991).
· Read, L.E. "I, pencil. My family tree as told to Leonard E. Read," The Foundation for Economic Education (2006).
· Polanyi, M. "The Tacit Dimension," Doubleday & Co (1966).
· Arrow, K. "The economic implications of learning by doing," *Review of Economic Studies* **29**(3), 155-73 (1962).

SECTION 2: HOW DO WE MEASURE ECONOMIC COMPLEXITY?

· Hidalgo, C.A. & Hausmann, R. "The Building Blocks of Economic Complexity," *Proceedings of the National Academy of Sciences* **106**, 10570-10575 (2009).
· Hidalgo, C.A. "The Dynamics of Economic Complexity and the Product Space over a 42 year period," CID Working Paper No 189, Kennedy School of Government, Harvard University (2009).
· Hausmann, R. & Hidalgo, C.A. "The network structure of economic output" *Journal of Economic Growth* **16,** 309-342 (2011).

REFERENCES

· Balassa, B., "The Purchasing Power Parity Doctrine - A Reappraisal," *Journal of Political Economy* **72**, 584-596 (1964).
· Feenstra, R.; Lipsey, R.; Deng, H.; Ma, A. & Mo, H. "World Trade Flows: 1962-2000" NBER working paper 11040. National Bureau of Economic Research, Cambridge MA (2005).
· United Nations Commodity Trade Statistics Database (http://comtrade.un.org/db/), accessed in August 2011.

SECTION 4: HOW IS COMPLEXITY DIFFERENT FROM OTHER APPROACHES?

REFERENCES

· The World Economic Forum, "The global competitiveness report," (various years).
· Barro, R. & Lee, J-W. "A New Data Set of Educational Attainment in the World, 1950-2010," NBER Working Paper No. 1590 (2010).
· Kaufmann, D. & Kraay, A. "Governance Indicators: Where Are We, Where Should We Be Going?" Policy Research Working Paper 4370. Washington, DC: World Bank (2008).
· Hanushek, E.A. & Woessmann, L. "The Role of Cognitive Skills in Economic Development," *Journal of Economic Literature* **46**(3), 607-668 (2008).
· Aghion, P., Howitt, P., and Mayer-Foulkes, D. "The Effect of Financial Development on Convergence: Theory and Evidence," *The Quarterly Journal of Economics,* **120**(1). 173-222 (2005).
· Arcand, J.L. Berkes, E. and Panizza, U. "Too Much Finance?," IMF Working Paper WP/12/61 (2012).
· Barro, R. J. and Sala-i-Martin, X. "Economic Growth," The MIT Press, Cambridge, MA, 2nd edition (2004).
· Beck, T., Levine, R., and Loayza, N. "Finance and the Sources of Growth," *Journal of Financial Economics,* **58**(1–2): 261–300 (2000).
· Demirgüç-Kunt, A. and Levine, R., editors "Financial Structure and Economic Growth: A Cross-Country Comparison of Banks, Markets and Development," MIT Press (2001).
· *Easterly,* W. "National Policies and Economic Growth: A Reappraisal," Handbook of Economic Growth, Philippe Aghion & Steven *Durlauf (editors)* (2005).

· King, R. G. and Levine, R. "Finance and Growth: Schumpeter might be right," *Quarterly Journal of Economics* **108**(3): 717–37 (1993).
· Levine, R. "Finance and Growth: Theory, Mechanisms and Evidence," in Aghion, P. and Durlauf, S.N. (*editors*.). Handbook of Economic Growth. Elsevier (2005).
· Trew, A. "Finance and Growth: A Critical Survey," *Economic Record* **82**: 481–490 (2006).

SECTION 5: HOW DOES ECONOMIC COMPLEXITY EVOLVE?

· Hausmann, R. & Rodrik, D. "Economic development as self-discovery," *Journal of Development Economics* **72**(2), 603-633 (2003).
· Hausmann, R. & Klinger, B. "Structural Transformation and Patterns of Comparative Advantage in the Product Space," CID Working Paper No 128. Kennedy School of Government, Harvard University (2006).
· Hausmann, R.; Hwang, J. & Rodrik, D. "What you export matters," *Journal of Economic Growth* **12**(1), 1-25 (2007).
· Hidalgo, C. A.; Klinger, B.; Barabási, A. & Hausmann, R. "The Product Space Conditions the Development of Nations," *Science* **317**, 482-487 (2007).
· Hausmann, R. & Klinger, B. "South Africa's export predicament," *The Economics of Transition* **16**(4), 609-637 (2008).
· European Bank for Reconstruction and Development "Trade, pro-duct mix and Growth," Transition Report, Chapter 4 (2008).
· Hausmann, R. & Klinger, B. "Policies for Achieving Structural Transformation in the Caribbean," Private Sector Development Discussion Paper 2. Washington, D.C.: IDB (2010).
· Hausmann, R., Klinger, B. & Lopez-Calix, J. "Export Diversification in Algeria" in Lopez-Calix, J.; Walkenhorst, P. & Diop, N. (editors). Trade Competitiveness of the Middle East and North Africa, World Bank, Washington DC (2010).
· United Nations Economic and Social Commission for Asia and the Pacific (ESCAP) "Building the productive capacity of the least developed countries," In Economic and Social Survey of Asia and the Pacific 2011, Chapter 4 (2011).
· Hidalgo, C.A. "Discovering Southern and East Africa's Industrial Opportunities," German Marshall Fund Economic Policy Series (2011).
· Hidalgo, C.A. "Thinking Outside the Cube," CA Hidalgo *Physicsworld* **21**(12), 34-37 (2008).
· Hidalgo, C.A. & Hausmann, R. "A Network View of Economic Development," *Developing Alternatives* **12**(1), 5-10 (2008).

PRODUCT CLASSIFICATIONS AND COMMUNITY DISCOVERY ALGORITHMS

· Leamer, E. E. "Sources of Comparative Advantage: Theory and Evidence," The MIT Press, Cambridge, MA (1984).
· Lall, S. "The technological structure and performance of developing country manufactured exports, 1985-1998," Queen Elizabeth House Working Paper #44, University of Oxford (2000).
· Rosvall, M. & Bergstrom, C. "Maps of random walks on complex networks reveal community structure," *Proceedings of the National Academy of Sciences* **105**, 1118, (2008).
· Coscia, M.; Giannotti, F. & Pedreschi, D. "A classification for community discovery methods in complex networks," *Statistical Analysis and Data Mining* **4**(5), 512–546, (2011).

COLOPHON

▶

PAPER: 120gsm Thai Pro New woodfree paper.
COLORS: 5/5. **TYPOGRAPHY:** Knockout by Hoefler & Frere-Jones
and Caecilia LT by Peter Matthias Noordzii.